8 SAINT☆YOUNG MEN

C O N T E N T S

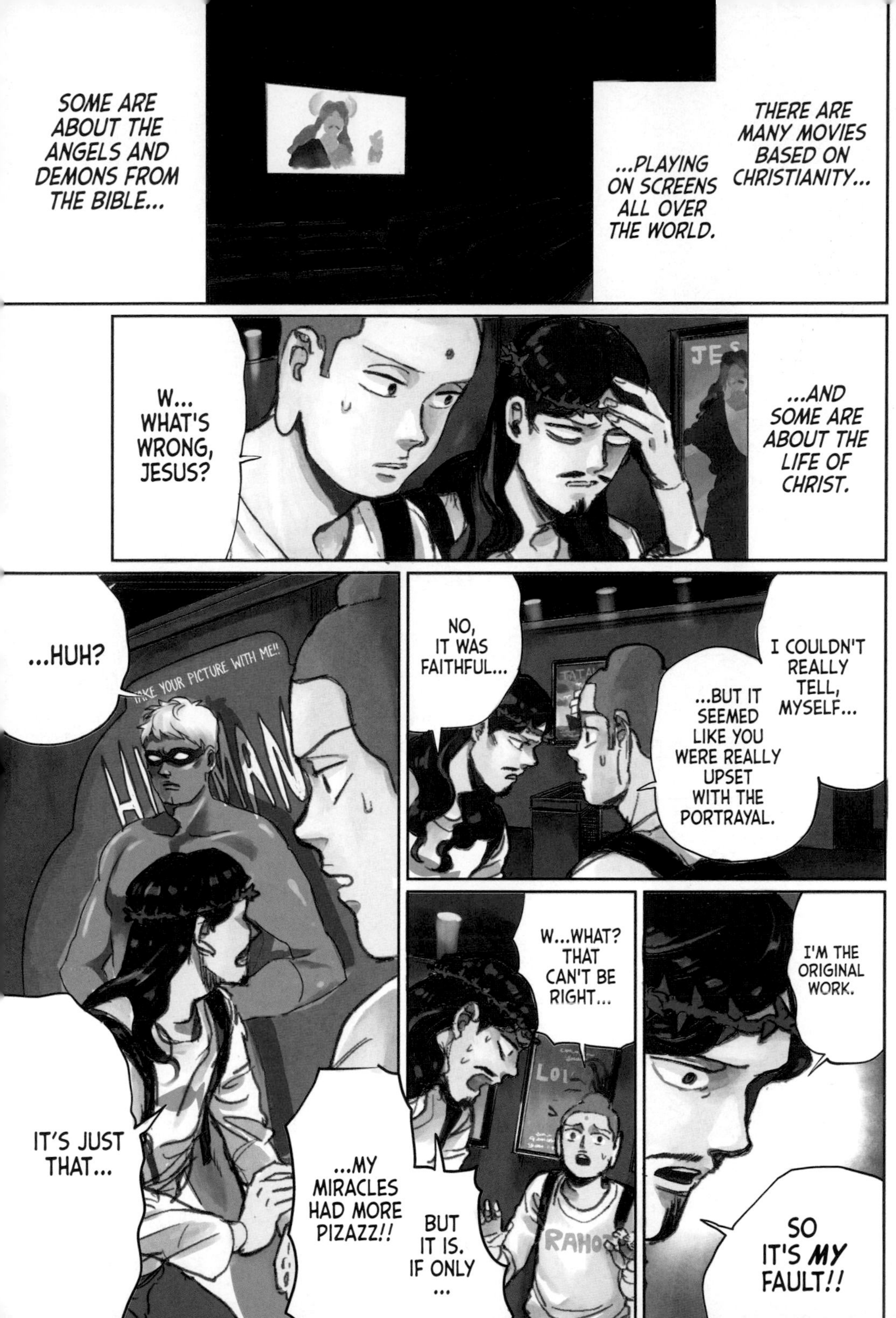
THERE ARE MANY MOVIES BASED ON CHRISTIANITY...
...PLAYING ON SCREENS ALL OVER THE WORLD.
SOME ARE ABOUT THE ANGELS AND DEMONS FROM THE BIBLE...
...AND SOME ARE ABOUT THE LIFE OF CHRIST.
W... WHAT'S WRONG, JESUS?
I COULDN'T REALLY TELL, MYSELF...
...BUT IT SEEMED LIKE YOU WERE REALLY UPSET WITH THE PORTRAYAL.
NO, IT WAS FAITHFUL...
I'M THE ORIGINAL WORK.
SO IT'S *MY* FAULT!!
W...WHAT? THAT CAN'T BE RIGHT...
BUT IT IS. IF ONLY ...
...HUH?
TAKE YOUR PICTURE WITH ME!!
IT'S JUST THAT...
...MY MIRACLES HAD MORE PIZAZZ!!

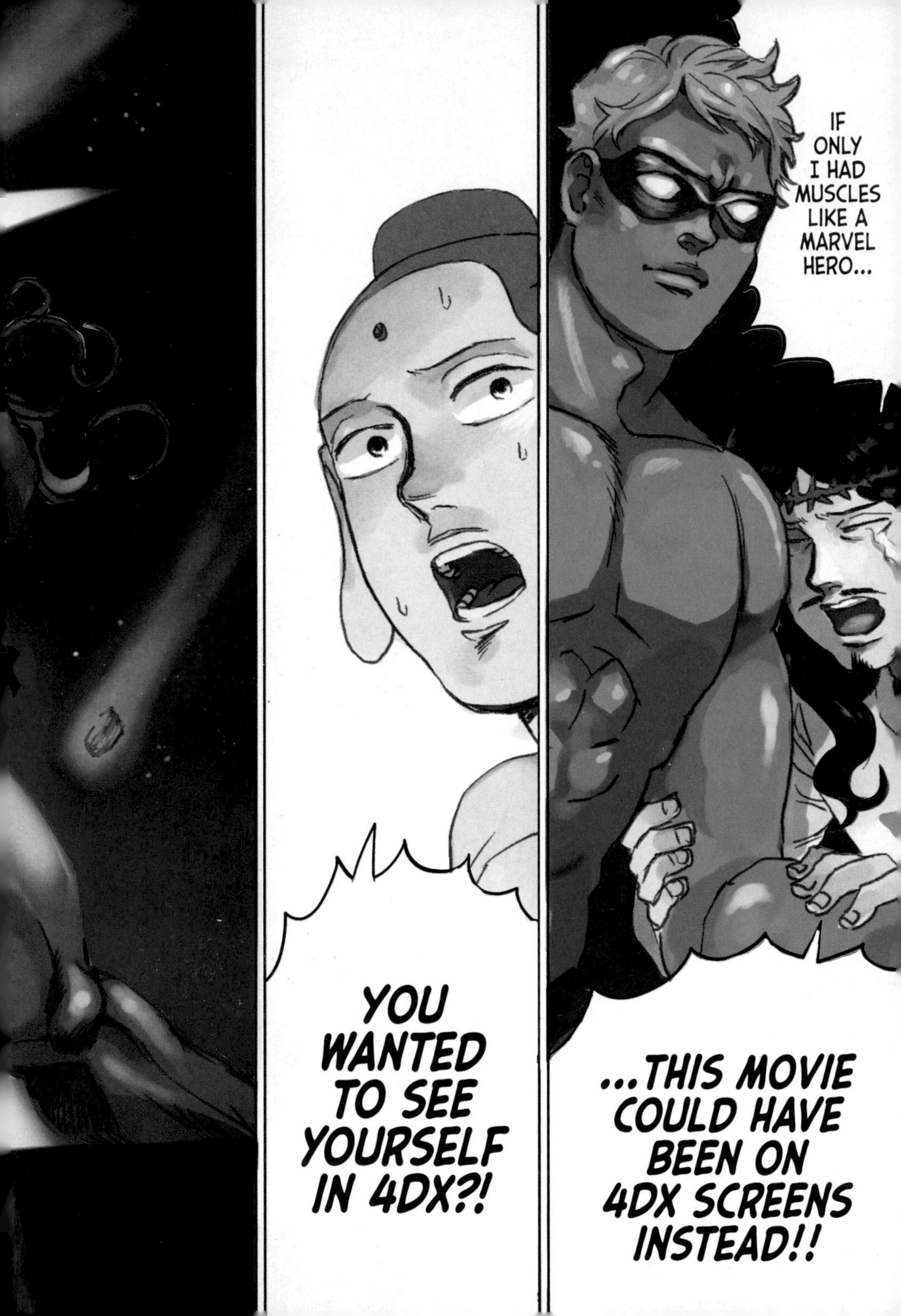
IF ONLY I HAD MUSCLES LIKE A MARVEL HERO...
...THIS MOVIE COULD HAVE BEEN ON 4DX SCREENS INSTEAD!!
YOU WANTED TO SEE YOURSELF IN 4DX?!

SAINT YOUNG MEN

Chapter 104

Saint Muscle Men?!

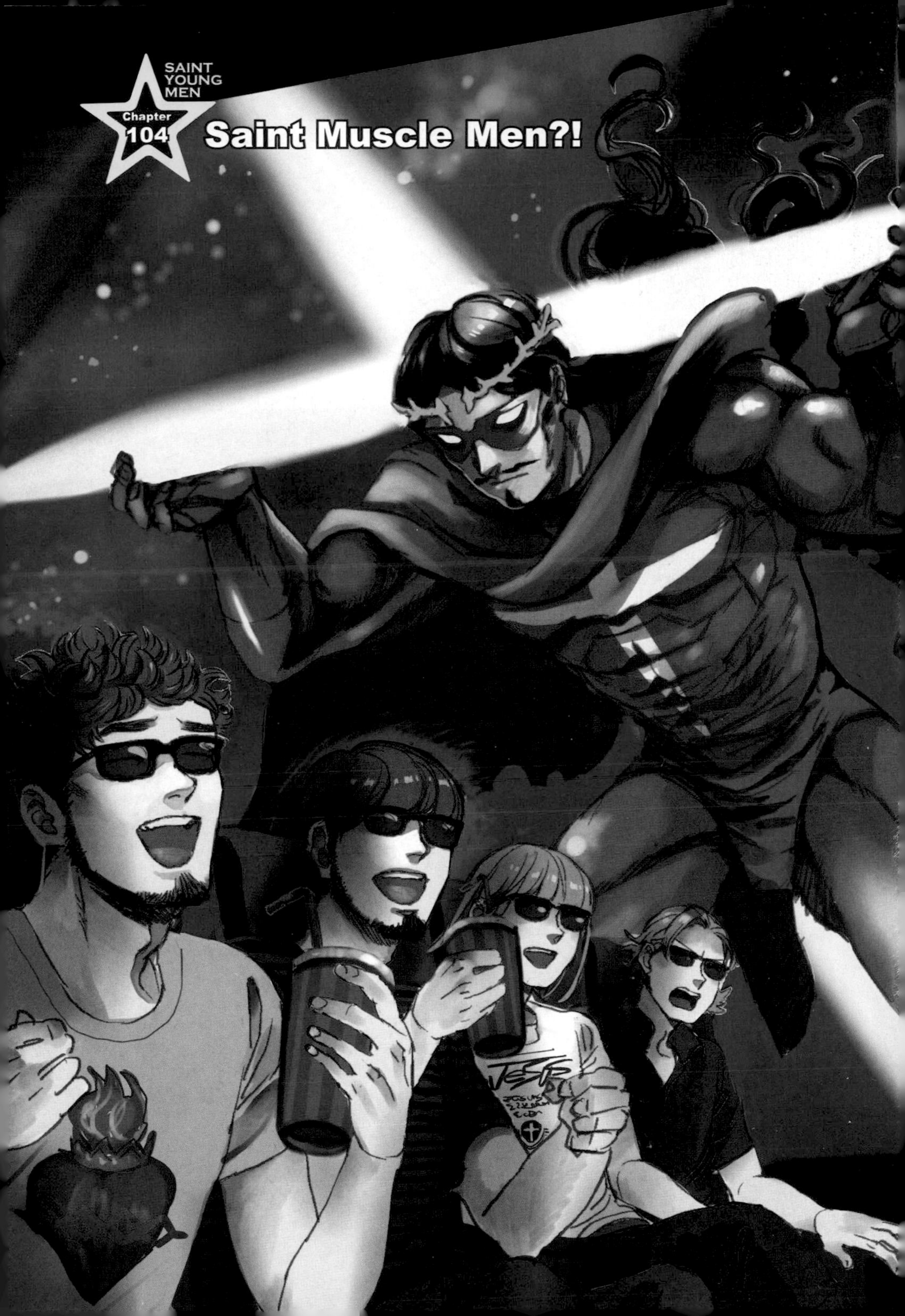

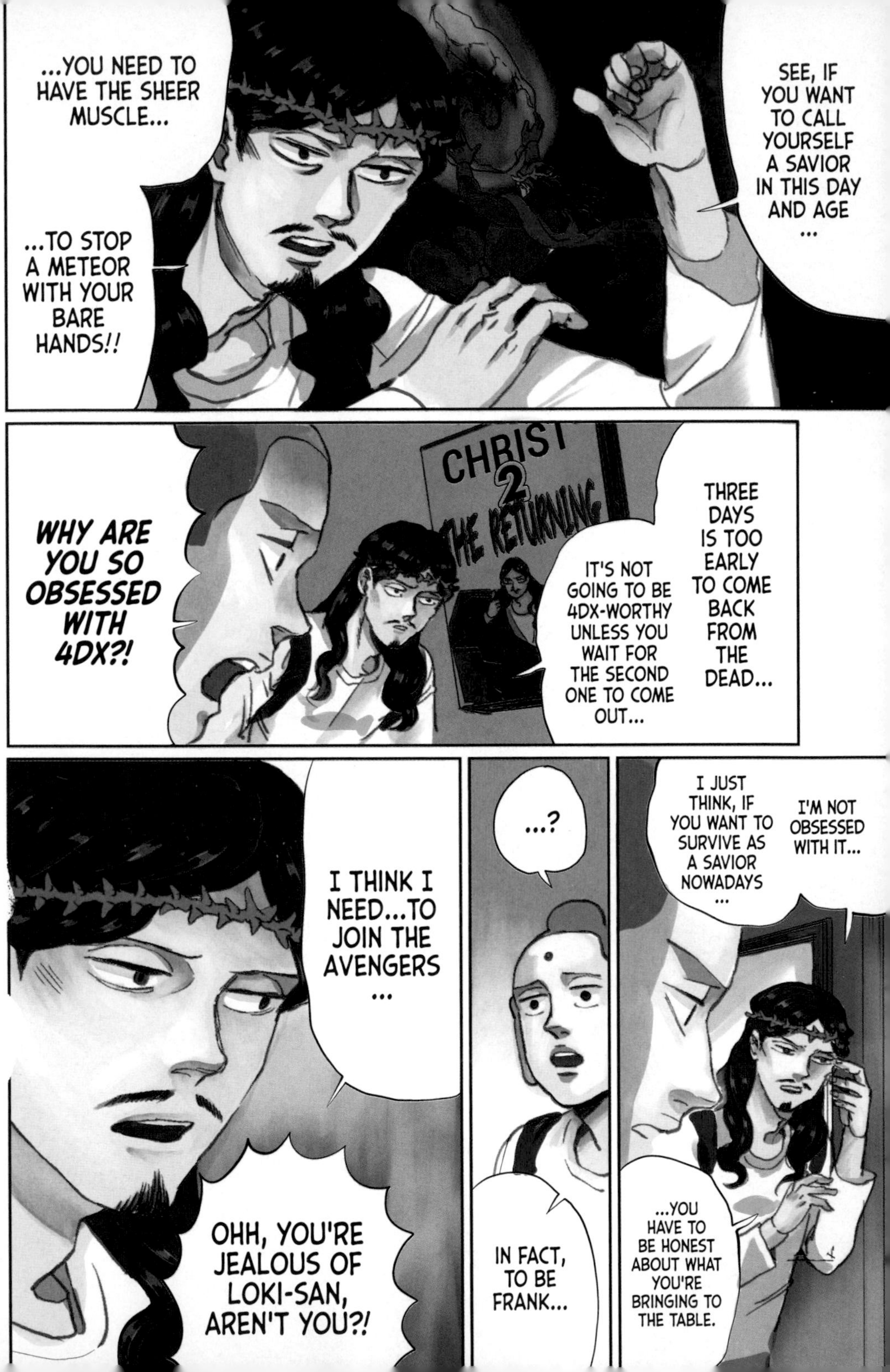
SEE, IF YOU WANT TO CALL YOURSELF A SAVIOR IN THIS DAY AND AGE ...
...YOU NEED TO HAVE THE SHEER MUSCLE...
...TO STOP A METEOR WITH YOUR BARE HANDS!!
THREE DAYS IS TOO EARLY TO COME BACK FROM THE DEAD...
IT'S NOT GOING TO BE 4DX-WORTHY UNLESS YOU WAIT FOR THE SECOND ONE TO COME OUT...
CHRIST 2 THE RETURNING
WHY ARE YOU SO OBSESSED WITH 4DX?!
I'M NOT OBSESSED WITH IT...
I JUST THINK, IF YOU WANT TO SURVIVE AS A SAVIOR NOWADAYS ...
...YOU HAVE TO BE HONEST ABOUT WHAT YOU'RE BRINGING TO THE TABLE.
...?
IN FACT, TO BE FRANK...
I THINK I NEED...TO JOIN THE AVENGERS ...
OHH, YOU'RE JEALOUS OF LOKI-SAN, AREN'T YOU?!

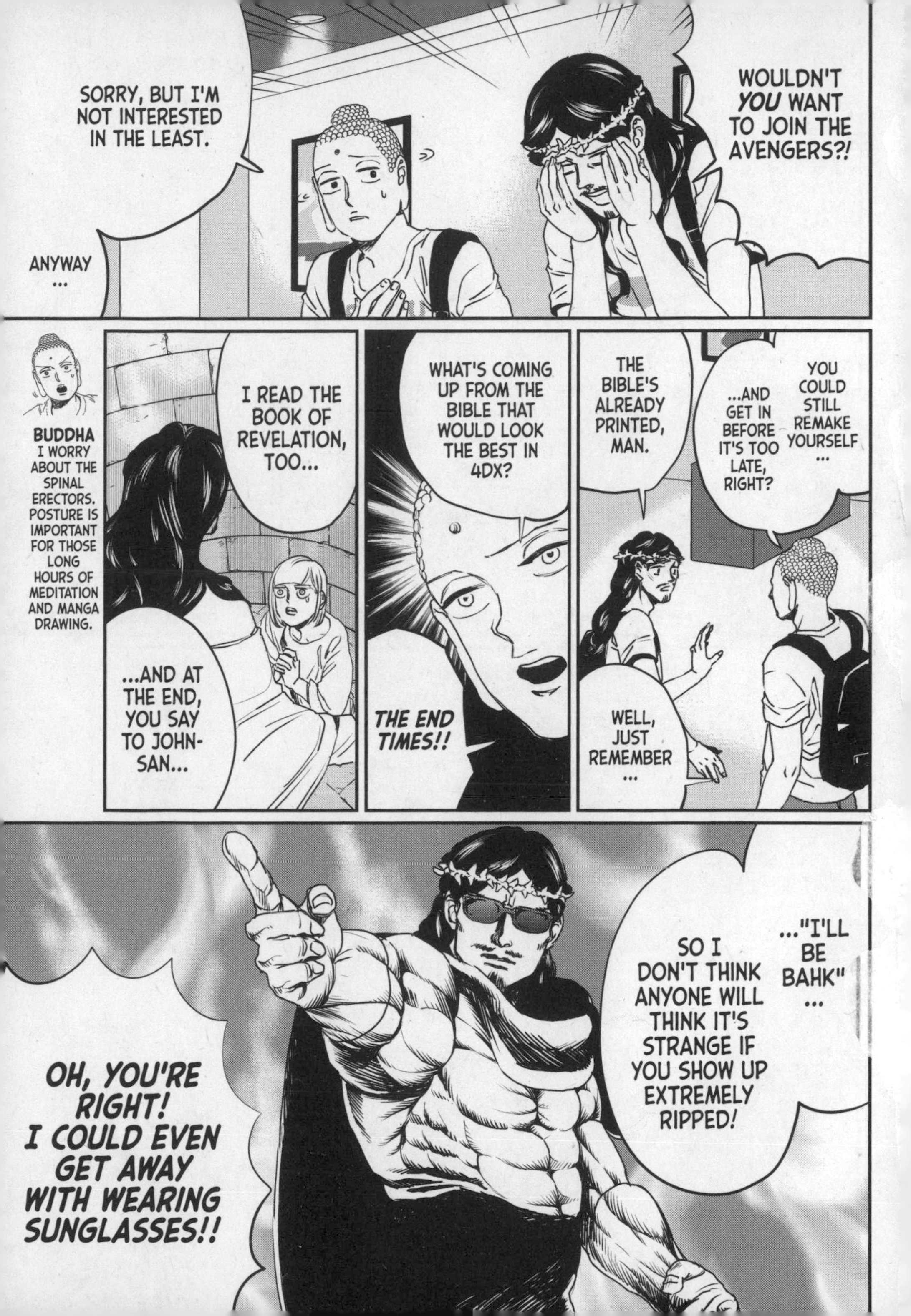
WOULDN'T *YOU* WANT TO JOIN THE AVENGERS?!
SORRY, BUT I'M NOT INTERESTED IN THE LEAST.
ANYWAY ...
YOU COULD STILL REMAKE YOURSELF ...
...AND GET IN BEFORE IT'S TOO LATE, RIGHT?
THE BIBLE'S ALREADY PRINTED, MAN.
WELL, JUST REMEMBER ...
WHAT'S COMING UP FROM THE BIBLE THAT WOULD LOOK THE BEST IN 4DX?
THE END TIMES!!
I READ THE BOOK OF REVELATION, TOO...
...AND AT THE END, YOU SAY TO JOHN-SAN...
BUDDHA I WORRY ABOUT THE SPINAL ERECTORS. POSTURE IS IMPORTANT FOR THOSE LONG HOURS OF MEDITATION AND MANGA DRAWING.
..."I'LL BE BAHK" ...
SO I DON'T THINK ANYONE WILL THINK IT'S STRANGE IF YOU SHOW UP EXTREMELY RIPPED!
OH, YOU'RE RIGHT! I COULD EVEN GET AWAY WITH WEARING SUNGLASSES!!

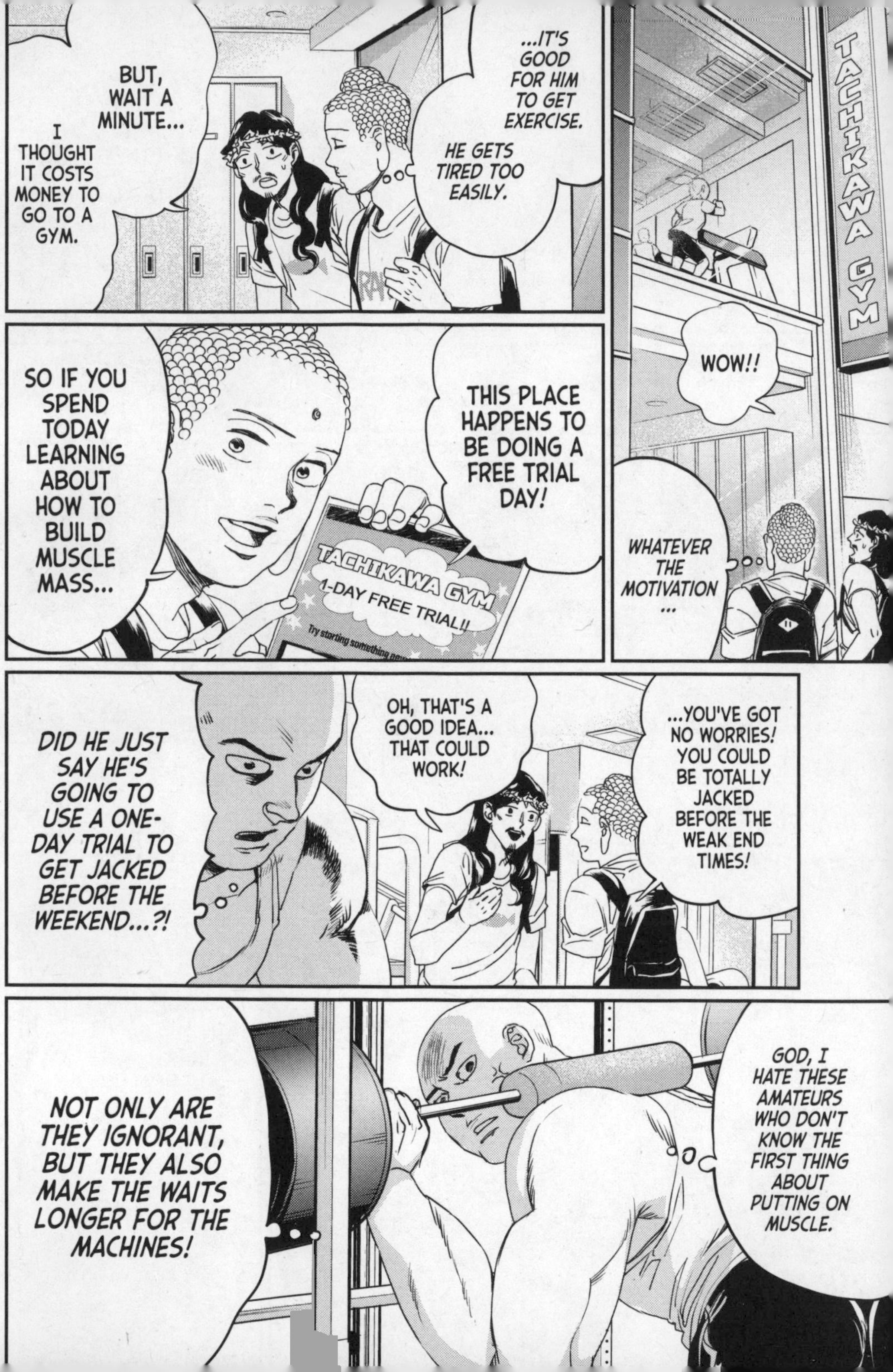
TACHIKAWA GYM
WOW!!
WHATEVER THE MOTIVATION ...
...IT'S GOOD FOR HIM TO GET EXERCISE.
HE GETS TIRED TOO EASILY.
BUT, WAIT A MINUTE...
I THOUGHT IT COSTS MONEY TO GO TO A GYM.
THIS PLACE HAPPENS TO BE DOING A FREE TRIAL DAY!
SO IF YOU SPEND TODAY LEARNING ABOUT HOW TO BUILD MUSCLE MASS...
TACHIKAWA GYM
1-DAY FREE TRIAL!!
Try starting something
...YOU'VE GOT NO WORRIES! YOU COULD BE TOTALLY JACKED BEFORE THE WEAK END TIMES!
OH, THAT'S A GOOD IDEA... THAT COULD WORK!
DID HE JUST SAY HE'S GOING TO USE A ONE-DAY TRIAL TO GET JACKED BEFORE THE WEEKEND...?!
GOD, I HATE THESE AMATEURS WHO DON'T KNOW THE FIRST THING ABOUT PUTTING ON MUSCLE.
NOT ONLY ARE THEY IGNORANT, BUT THEY ALSO MAKE THE WAITS LONGER FOR THE MACHINES!

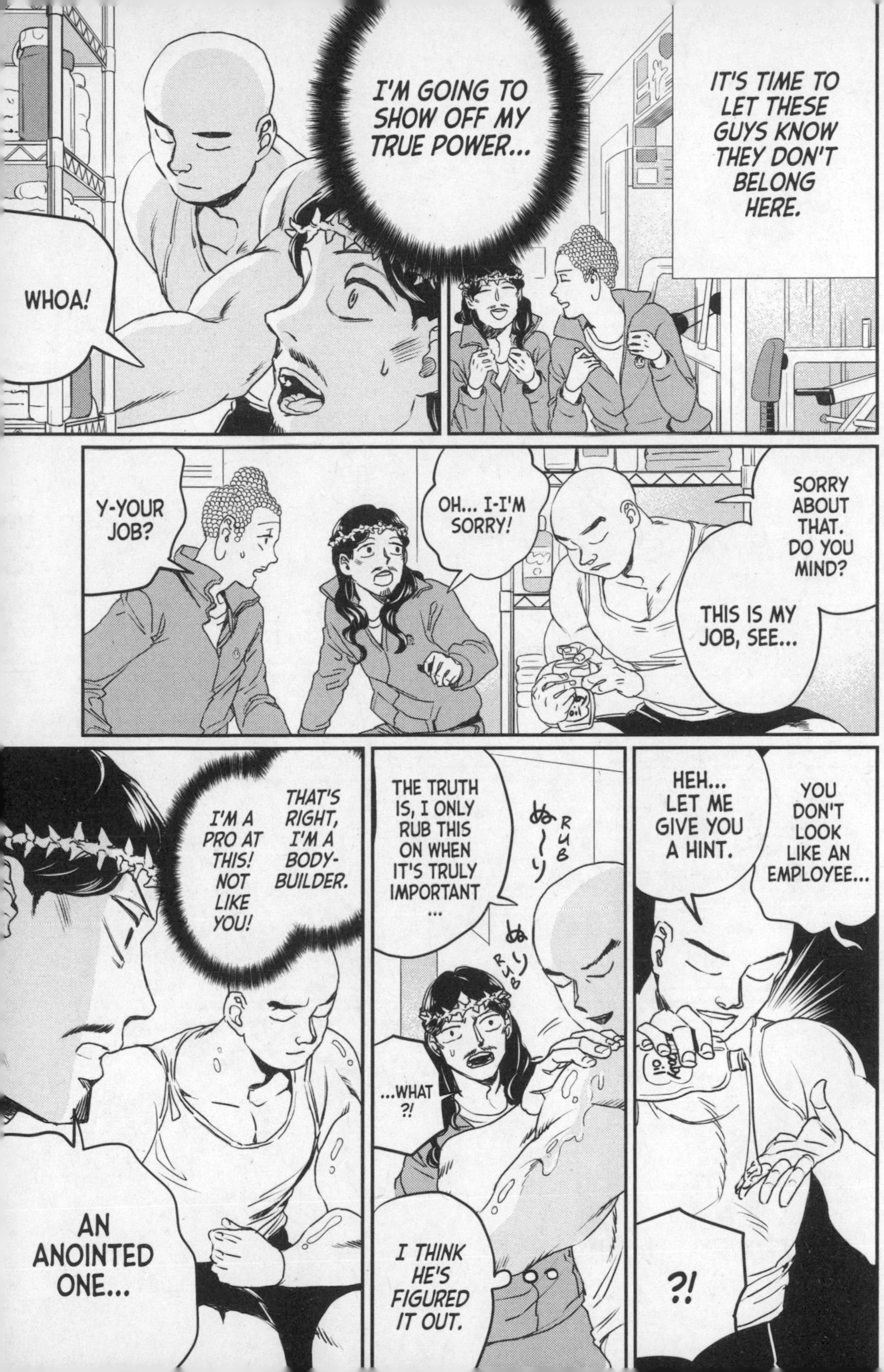
IT'S TIME TO LET THESE GUYS KNOW THEY DON'T BELONG HERE.
I'M GOING TO SHOW OFF MY TRUE POWER...
WHOA!
SORRY ABOUT THAT. DO YOU MIND?
THIS IS MY JOB, SEE...
OH... I-I'M SORRY!
Y-YOUR JOB?
YOU DON'T LOOK LIKE AN EMPLOYEE...
HEH... LET ME GIVE YOU A HINT.
?!
THE TRUTH IS, I ONLY RUB THIS ON WHEN IT'S TRULY IMPORTANT...
ぬ～り RUB
ぬり RUB
...WHAT?!
I THINK HE'S FIGURED IT OUT.
THAT'S RIGHT, I'M A BODY-BUILDER.
I'M A PRO AT THIS! NOT LIKE YOU!
AN ANOINTED ONE...

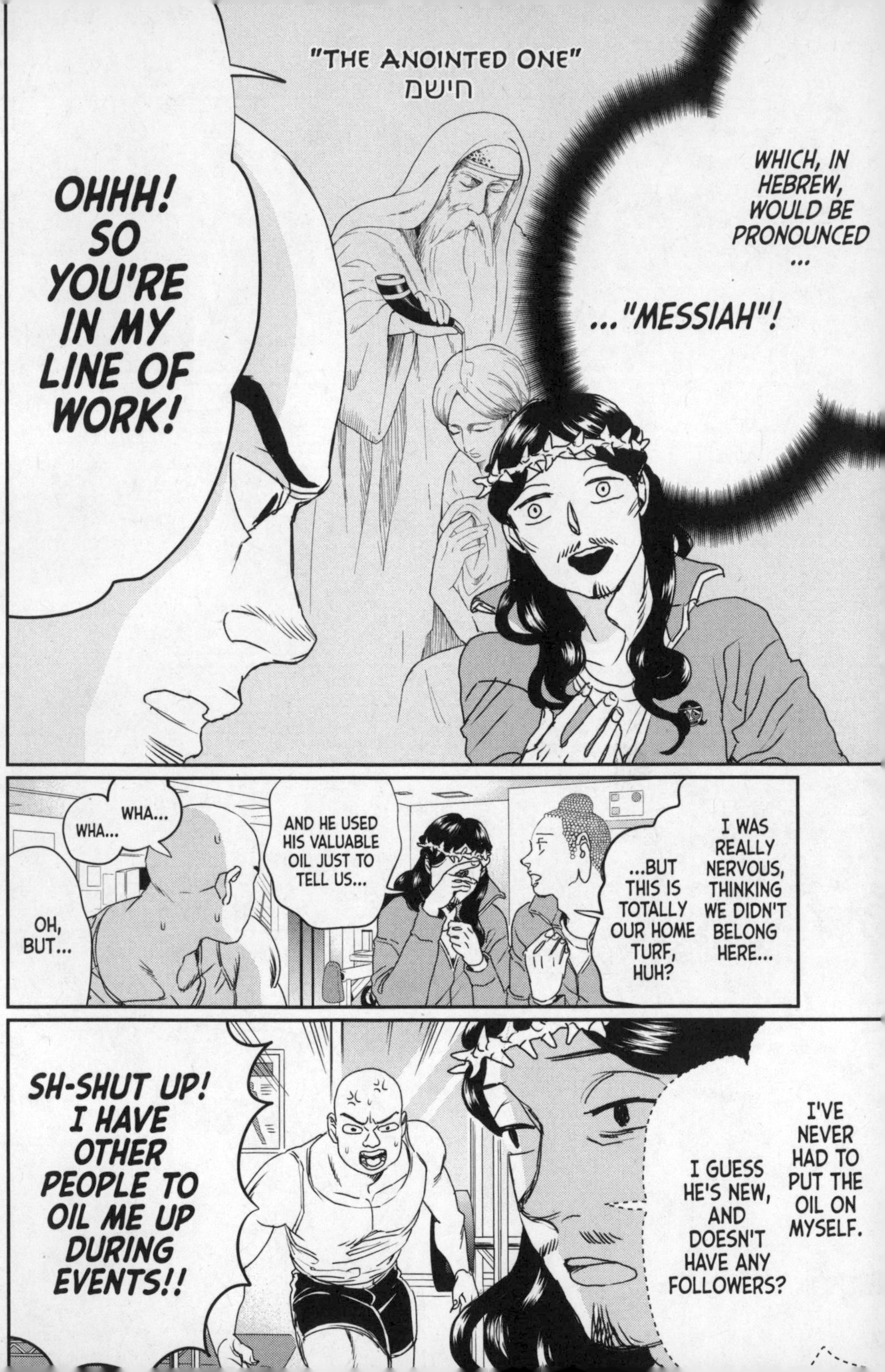
"THE ANOINTED ONE"
משיח
WHICH, IN HEBREW, WOULD BE PRONOUNCED ...
..."MESSIAH"!
OHHH! SO YOU'RE IN MY LINE OF WORK!
I WAS REALLY NERVOUS, THINKING WE DIDN'T BELONG HERE...
...BUT THIS IS TOTALLY OUR HOME TURF, HUH?
AND HE USED HIS VALUABLE OIL JUST TO TELL US...
WHA... WHA...
OH, BUT...
I'VE NEVER HAD TO PUT THE OIL ON MYSELF.
I GUESS HE'S NEW, AND DOESN'T HAVE ANY FOLLOWERS?
SH-SHUT UP! I HAVE OTHER PEOPLE TO OIL ME UP DURING EVENTS!!

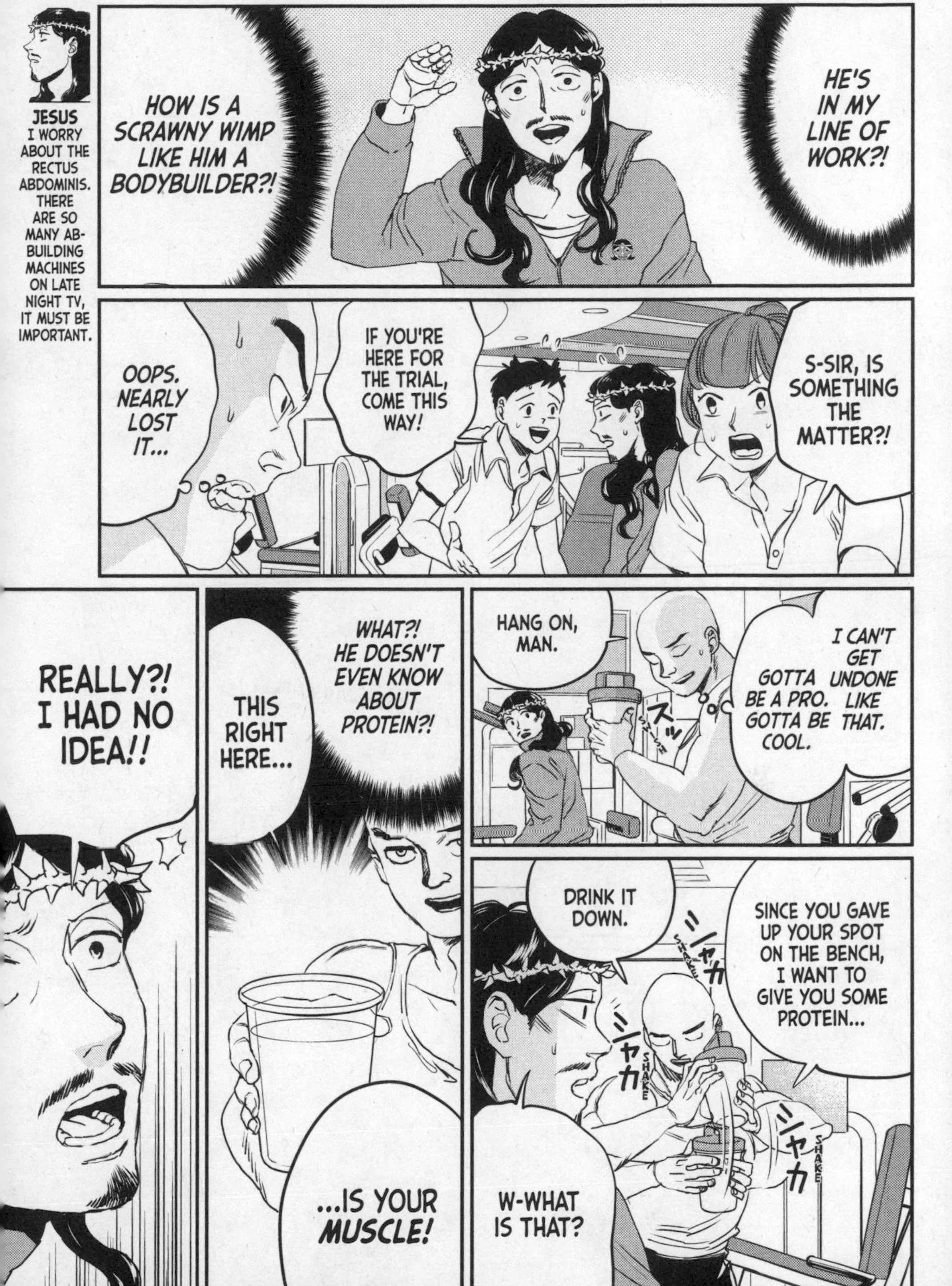
JESUS
I WORRY ABOUT THE RECTUS ABDOMINIS. THERE ARE SO MANY AB-BUILDING MACHINES ON LATE NIGHT TV, IT MUST BE IMPORTANT.
HE'S IN MY LINE OF WORK?!
HOW IS A SCRAWNY WIMP LIKE HIM A BODYBUILDER?!
S-SIR, IS SOMETHING THE MATTER?!
IF YOU'RE HERE FOR THE TRIAL, COME THIS WAY!
OOPS. NEARLY LOST IT...
I CAN'T GET UNDONE LIKE THAT.
GOTTA BE A PRO. GOTTA BE COOL.
ズッ
HANG ON, MAN.
SINCE YOU GAVE UP YOUR SPOT ON THE BENCH, I WANT TO GIVE YOU SOME PROTEIN...
DRINK IT DOWN.
シャカ SHAKE
シャカ SHAKE
シャカ SHAKE
W-WHAT IS THAT?
WHAT?! HE DOESN'T EVEN KNOW ABOUT PROTEIN?!
THIS RIGHT HERE...
...IS YOUR MUSCLE!
REALLY?! I HAD NO IDEA!!

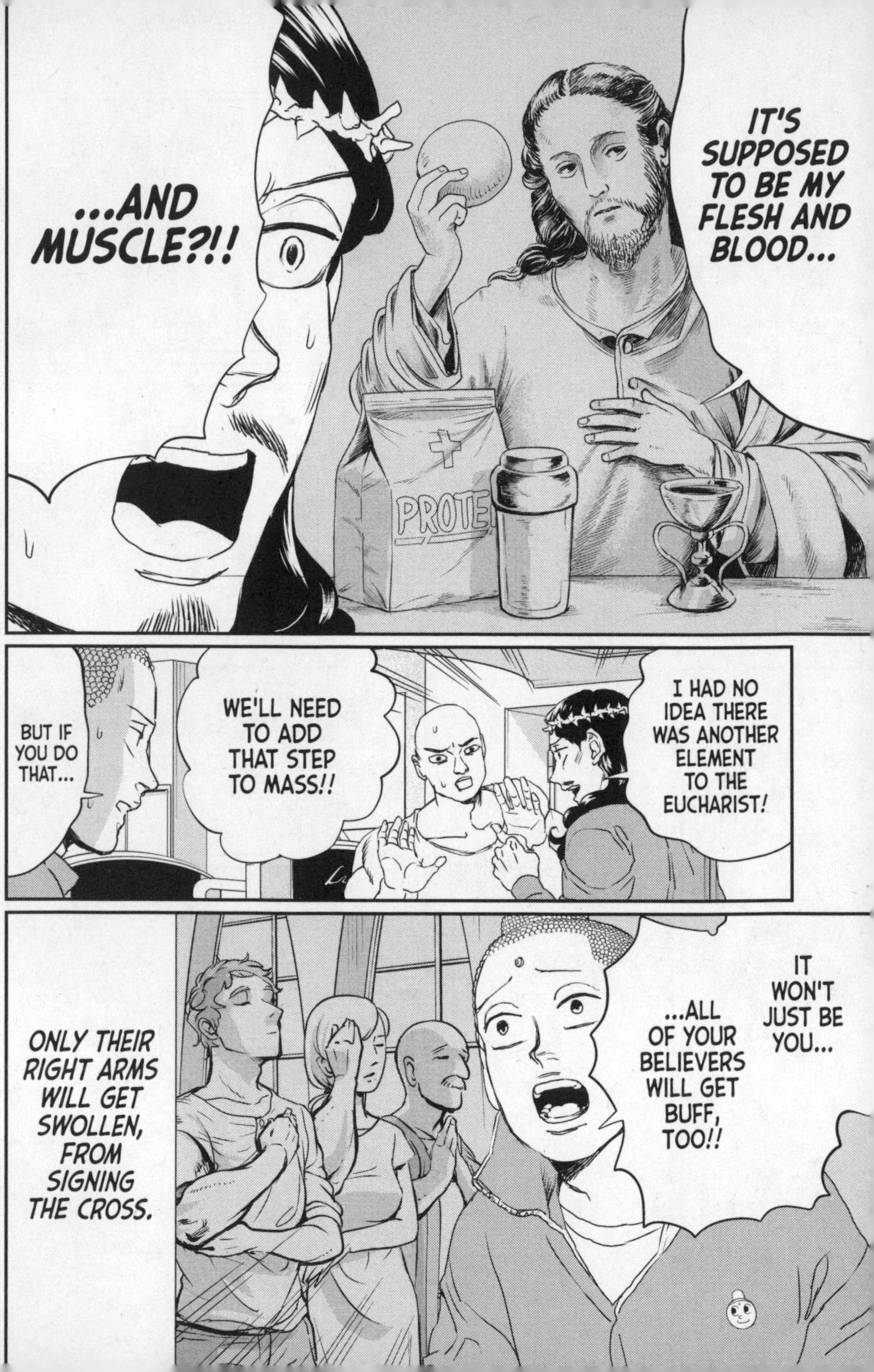
IT'S SUPPOSED TO BE MY FLESH AND BLOOD...
...AND MUSCLE?!!
PROTE
I HAD NO IDEA THERE WAS ANOTHER ELEMENT TO THE EUCHARIST!
WE'LL NEED TO ADD THAT STEP TO MASS!!
BUT IF YOU DO THAT...
IT WON'T JUST BE YOU...
...ALL OF YOUR BELIEVERS WILL GET BUFF, TOO!!
ONLY THEIR RIGHT ARMS WILL GET SWOLLEN, FROM SIGNING THE CROSS.

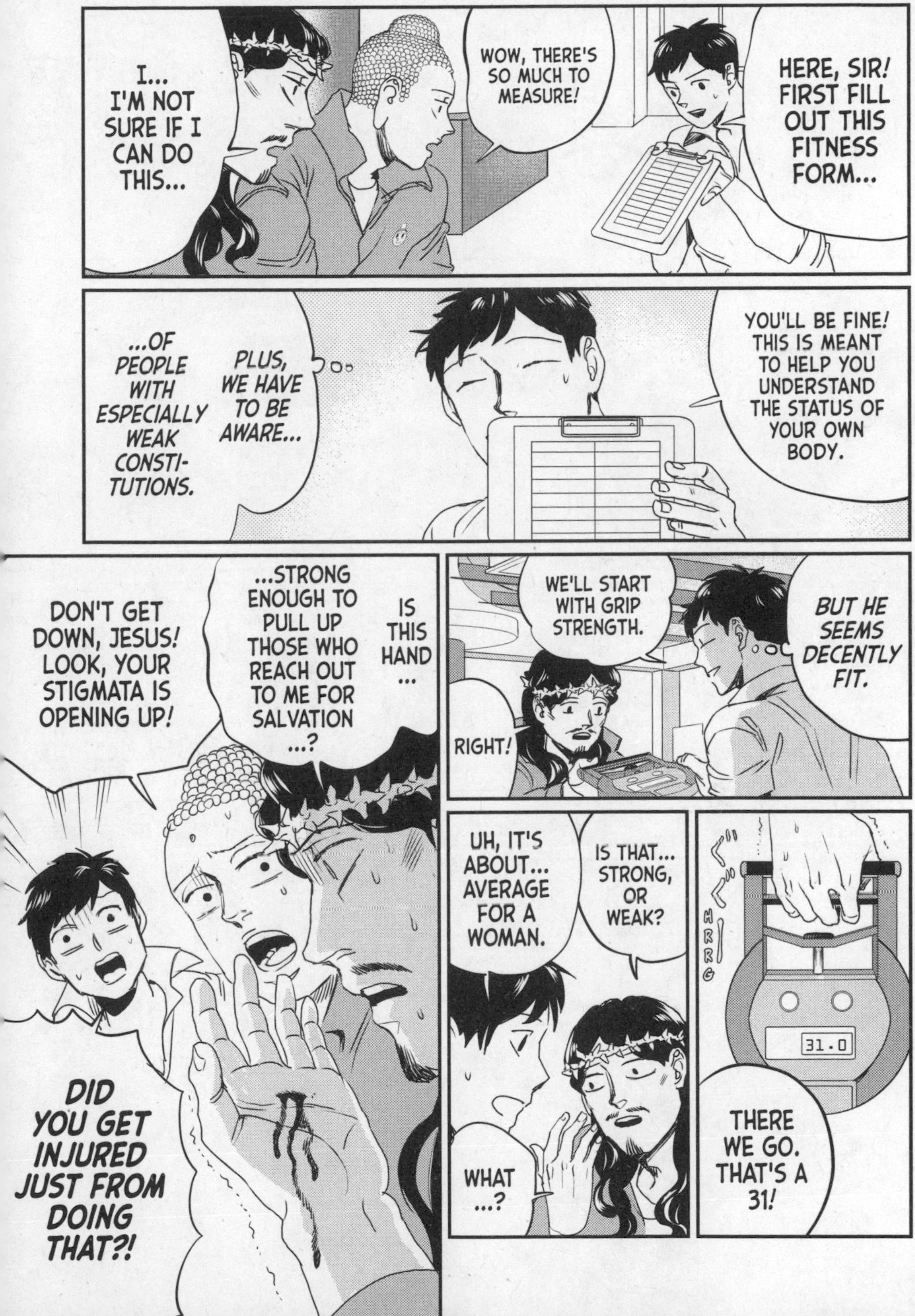
HERE, SIR! FIRST FILL OUT THIS FITNESS FORM...
WOW, THERE'S SO MUCH TO MEASURE!
I... I'M NOT SURE IF I CAN DO THIS...
YOU'LL BE FINE! THIS IS MEANT TO HELP YOU UNDERSTAND THE STATUS OF YOUR OWN BODY.
PLUS, WE HAVE TO BE AWARE...
...OF PEOPLE WITH ESPECIALLY WEAK CONSTI-TUTIONS.
BUT HE SEEMS DECENTLY FIT.
WE'LL START WITH GRIP STRENGTH.
RIGHT!
HRRG
31.0
THERE WE GO. THAT'S A 31!
IS THAT... STRONG, OR WEAK?
UH, IT'S ABOUT... AVERAGE FOR A WOMAN.
WHAT ...?
IS THIS HAND ...
...STRONG ENOUGH TO PULL UP THOSE WHO REACH OUT TO ME FOR SALVATION ...?
DON'T GET DOWN, JESUS! LOOK, YOUR STIGMATA IS OPENING UP!
DID YOU GET INJURED JUST FROM DOING THAT?!

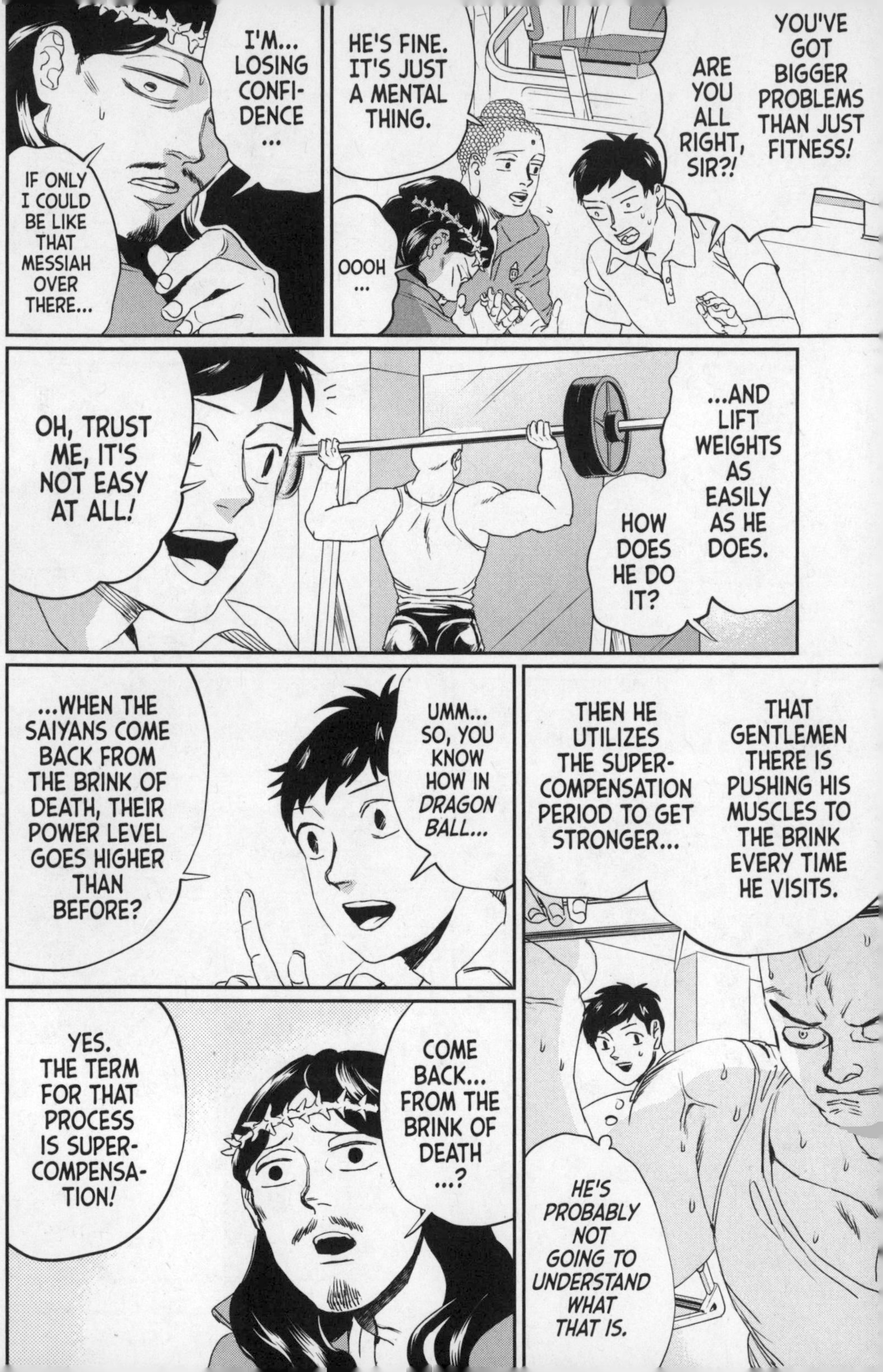
YOU'VE GOT BIGGER PROBLEMS THAN JUST FITNESS!
ARE YOU ALL RIGHT, SIR?!
HE'S FINE. IT'S JUST A MENTAL THING.
OOOH ...
I'M... LOSING CONFI-DENCE ...
IF ONLY I COULD BE LIKE THAT MESSIAH OVER THERE...
...AND LIFT WEIGHTS AS EASILY AS HE DOES.
HOW DOES HE DO IT?
OH, TRUST ME, IT'S NOT EASY AT ALL!
THAT GENTLEMEN THERE IS PUSHING HIS MUSCLES TO THE BRINK EVERY TIME HE VISITS.
THEN HE UTILIZES THE SUPER-COMPENSATION PERIOD TO GET STRONGER...
UMM... SO, YOU KNOW HOW IN *DRAGON BALL*...
...WHEN THE SAIYANS COME BACK FROM THE BRINK OF DEATH, THEIR POWER LEVEL GOES HIGHER THAN BEFORE?
HE'S PROBABLY NOT GOING TO UNDERSTAND WHAT THAT IS.
COME BACK... FROM THE BRINK OF DEATH ...?
YES. THE TERM FOR THAT PROCESS IS SUPER-COMPENSA-TION!

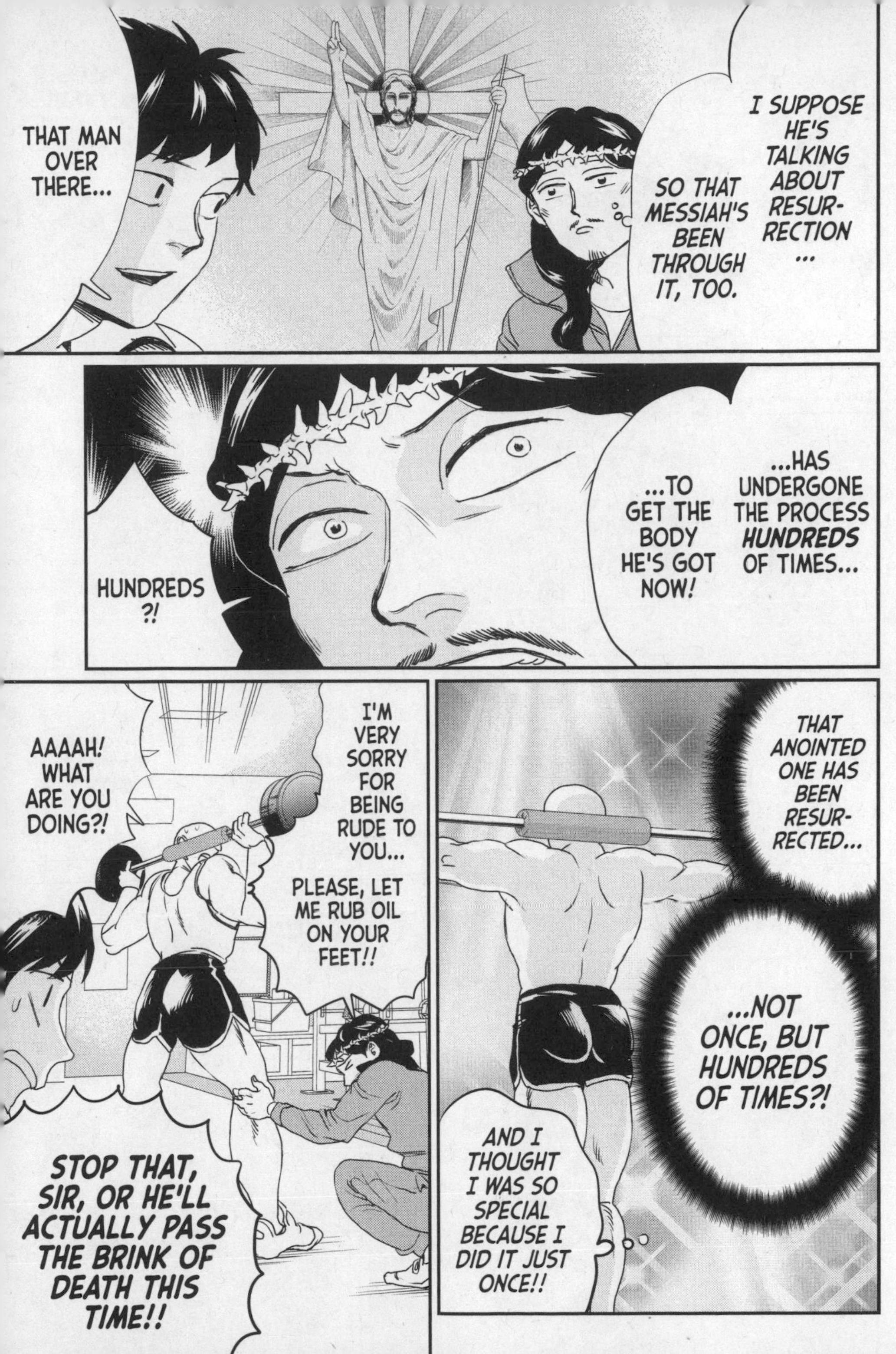
I SUPPOSE HE'S TALKING ABOUT RESURRECTION...
SO THAT MESSIAH'S BEEN THROUGH IT, TOO.
THAT MAN OVER THERE...
...HAS UNDERGONE THE PROCESS HUNDREDS OF TIMES...
...TO GET THE BODY HE'S GOT NOW!
HUNDREDS?!
THAT ANOINTED ONE HAS BEEN RESURRECTED...
...NOT ONCE, BUT HUNDREDS OF TIMES?!
AND I THOUGHT I WAS SO SPECIAL BECAUSE I DID IT JUST ONCE!!
I'M VERY SORRY FOR BEING RUDE TO YOU...
PLEASE, LET ME RUB OIL ON YOUR FEET!!
AAAAH! WHAT ARE YOU DOING?!
STOP THAT, SIR, OR HE'LL ACTUALLY PASS THE BRINK OF DEATH THIS TIME!!

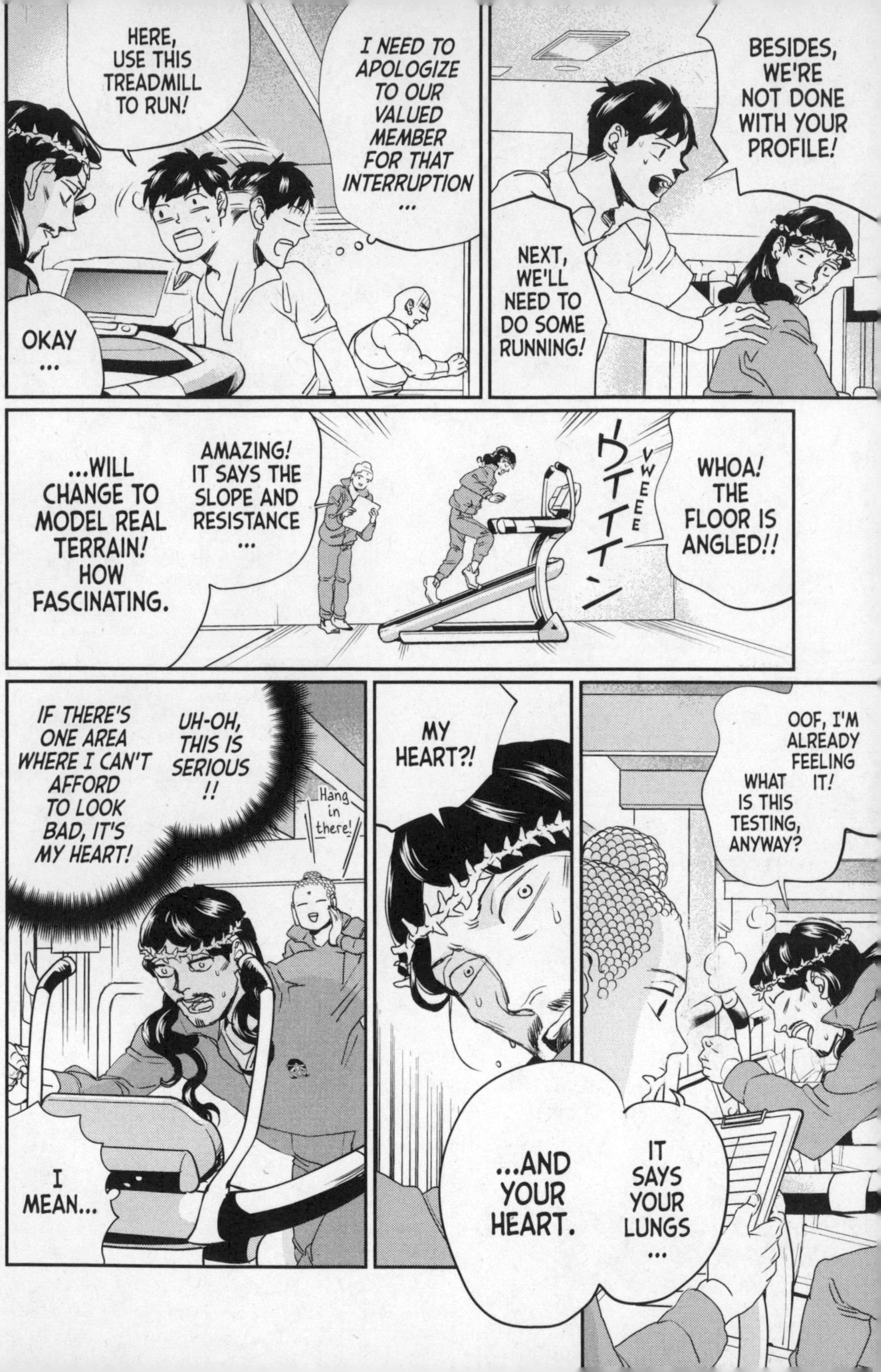
BESIDES, WE'RE NOT DONE WITH YOUR PROFILE!
NEXT, WE'LL NEED TO DO SOME RUNNING!
I NEED TO APOLOGIZE TO OUR VALUED MEMBER FOR THAT INTERRUPTION ...
HERE, USE THIS TREADMILL TO RUN!
OKAY ...
WHOA! THE FLOOR IS ANGLED!!
VWEEE
AMAZING! IT SAYS THE SLOPE AND RESISTANCE ...
...WILL CHANGE TO MODEL REAL TERRAIN! HOW FASCINATING.
OOF, I'M ALREADY FEELING IT!
WHAT IS THIS TESTING, ANYWAY?
IT SAYS YOUR LUNGS ...
...AND YOUR HEART.
MY HEART?!
UH-OH, THIS IS SERIOUS !!
IF THERE'S ONE AREA WHERE I CAN'T AFFORD TO LOOK BAD, IT'S MY HEART!
Hang in there!
I MEAN...

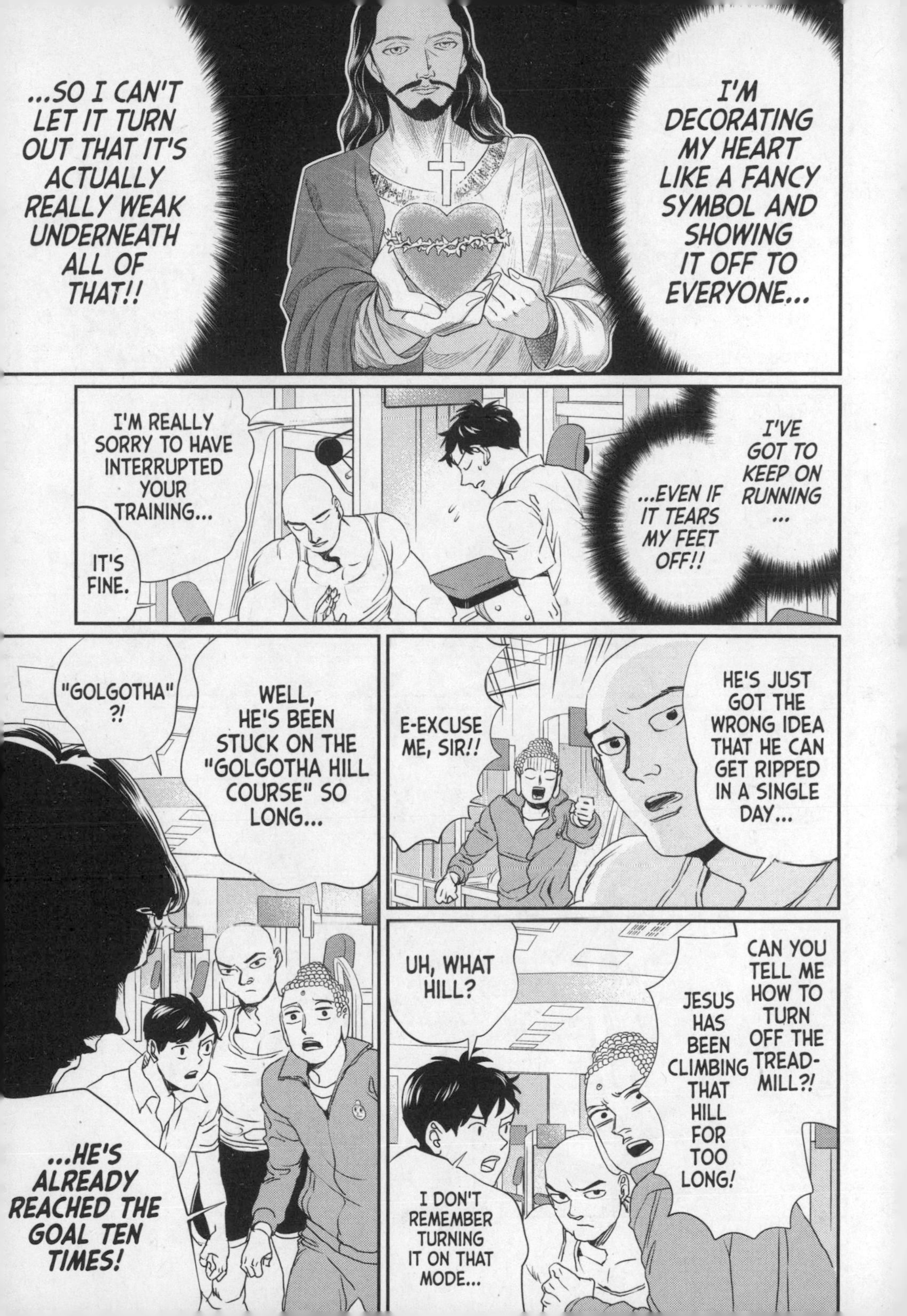
I'M DECORATING MY HEART LIKE A FANCY SYMBOL AND SHOWING IT OFF TO EVERYONE...
...SO I CAN'T LET IT TURN OUT THAT IT'S ACTUALLY REALLY WEAK UNDERNEATH ALL OF THAT!!
I'VE GOT TO KEEP ON RUNNING...
...EVEN IF IT TEARS MY FEET OFF!!
I'M REALLY SORRY TO HAVE INTERRUPTED YOUR TRAINING...
IT'S FINE.
HE'S JUST GOT THE WRONG IDEA THAT HE CAN GET RIPPED IN A SINGLE DAY...
E-EXCUSE ME, SIR!!
CAN YOU TELL ME HOW TO TURN OFF THE TREAD-MILL?!
JESUS HAS BEEN CLIMBING THAT HILL FOR TOO LONG!
UH, WHAT HILL?
I DON'T REMEMBER TURNING IT ON THAT MODE...
WELL, HE'S BEEN STUCK ON THE "GOLGOTHA HILL COURSE" SO LONG...
"GOLGOTHA"?!
...HE'S ALREADY REACHED THE GOAL TEN TIMES!

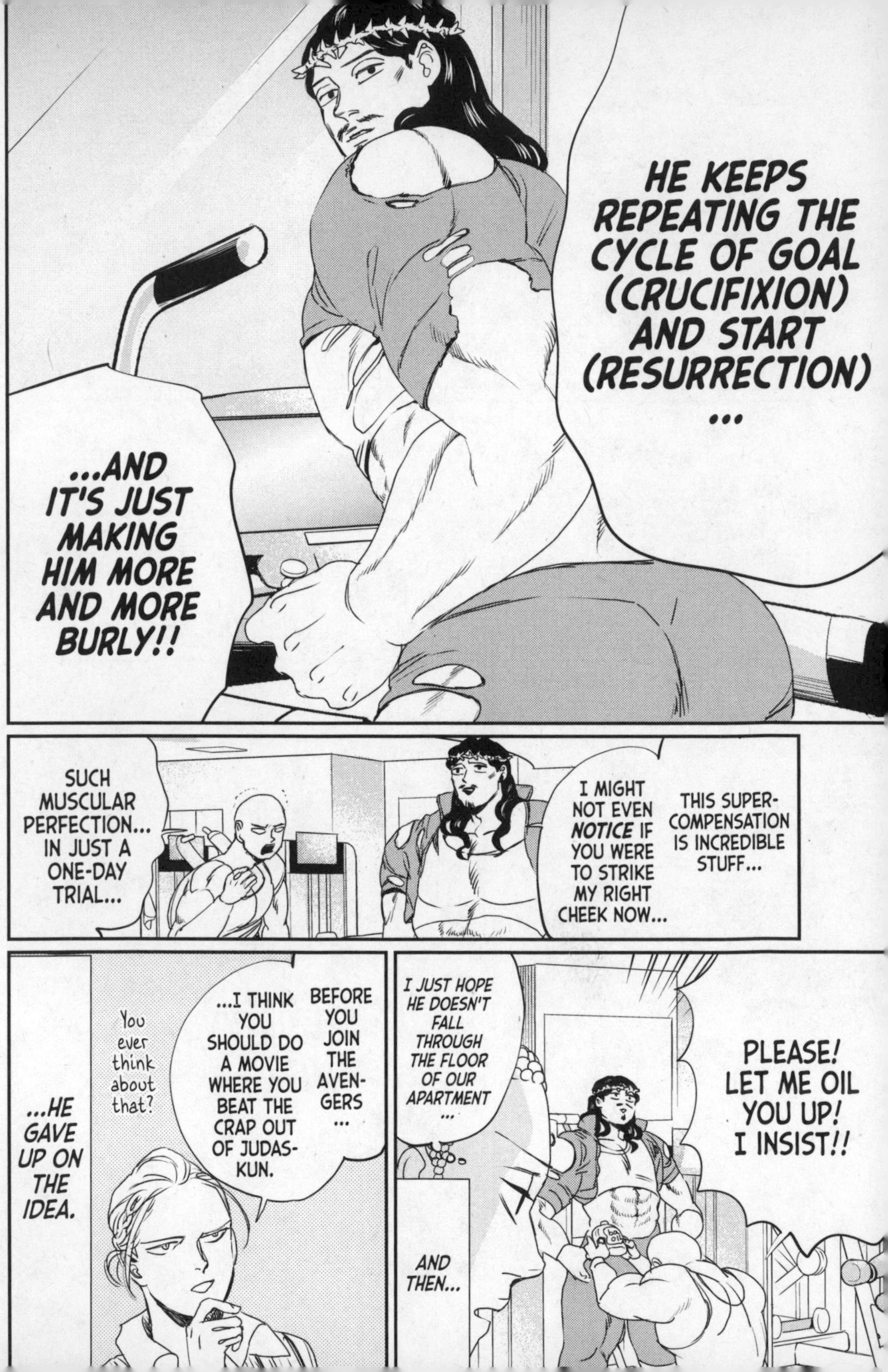
HE KEEPS REPEATING THE CYCLE OF GOAL (CRUCIFIXION) AND START (RESURRECTION)...
...AND IT'S JUST MAKING HIM MORE AND MORE BURLY!!
THIS SUPER-COMPENSATION IS INCREDIBLE STUFF...
I MIGHT NOT EVEN NOTICE IF YOU WERE TO STRIKE MY RIGHT CHEEK NOW...
SUCH MUSCULAR PERFECTION... IN JUST A ONE-DAY TRIAL...
PLEASE! LET ME OIL YOU UP! I INSIST!!
I JUST HOPE HE DOESN'T FALL THROUGH THE FLOOR OF OUR APARTMENT...
AND THEN...
BEFORE YOU JOIN THE AVEN-GERS...
...I THINK YOU SHOULD DO A MOVIE WHERE YOU BEAT THE CRAP OUT OF JUDAS-KUN.
You ever think about that?
...HE GAVE UP ON THE IDEA.

The resurrected
Christ vs. the rebuilt
Mecha-Judas!!

And this
has to
come
first...

MARVEL BIBLICAL
UNIVERSE

I want
to see it!
But
still—!

CHAPTER 104 TRANSLATION NOTES

Eucharist, page 10
A Christian ritual, also known as Communion or the Lord's Supper, in which members of the church receive bread (usually an unleavened wafer) and wine, symbolizing Christ's body and blood. This practice stems from the actions of Jesus at the Last Supper, when he gave his disciples bread and wine and told them, "This is my body which is for you. Do this in remembrance of me."

Mass, page 10
The term for the liturgical church service in the Catholic Church and Eastern Orthodox Church.

Golgotha, page 16
The site at which Jesus was crucified. According to the Gospels, it was located just outside of Jerusalem's walls, although the exact location is disputed.

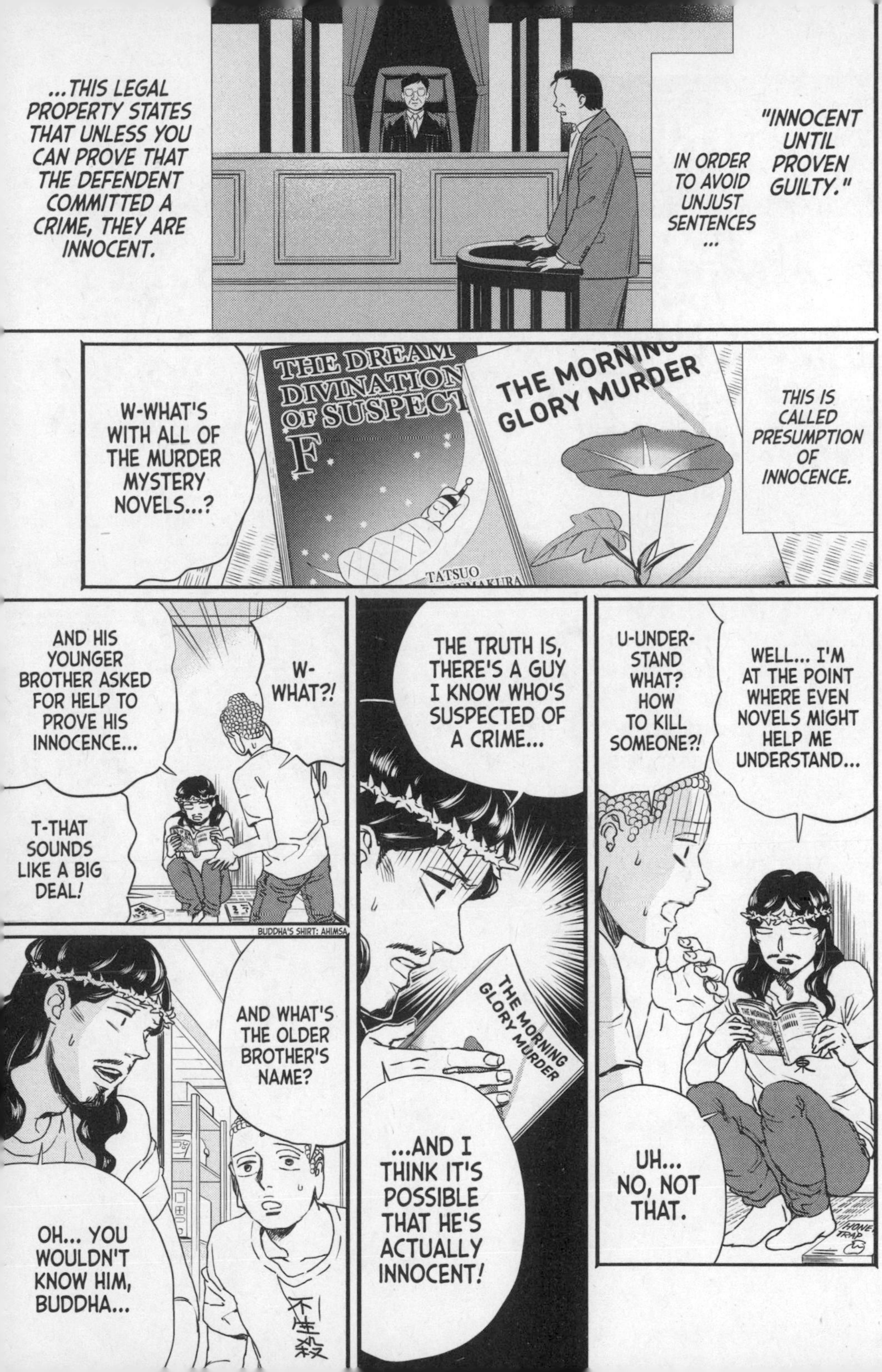
"INNOCENT UNTIL PROVEN GUILTY."
IN ORDER TO AVOID UNJUST SENTENCES ...
...THIS LEGAL PROPERTY STATES THAT UNLESS YOU CAN PROVE THAT THE DEFENDENT COMMITTED A CRIME, THEY ARE INNOCENT.
THIS IS CALLED PRESUMPTION OF INNOCENCE.
THE MORNING GLORY MURDER
THE DREAM DIVINATION OF SUSPECT F
TATSUO
W-WHAT'S WITH ALL OF THE MURDER MYSTERY NOVELS...?
WELL... I'M AT THE POINT WHERE EVEN NOVELS MIGHT HELP ME UNDERSTAND...
U-UNDER-STAND WHAT? HOW TO KILL SOMEONE?!
UH... NO, NOT THAT.
THE TRUTH IS, THERE'S A GUY I KNOW WHO'S SUSPECTED OF A CRIME...
THE MORNING GLORY MURDER
...AND I THINK IT'S POSSIBLE THAT HE'S ACTUALLY INNOCENT!
W- WHAT?!
AND HIS YOUNGER BROTHER ASKED FOR HELP TO PROVE HIS INNOCENCE...
T-THAT SOUNDS LIKE A BIG DEAL!
BUDDHA'S SHIRT: AHIMSA
AND WHAT'S THE OLDER BROTHER'S NAME?
OH... YOU WOULDN'T KNOW HIM, BUDDHA...

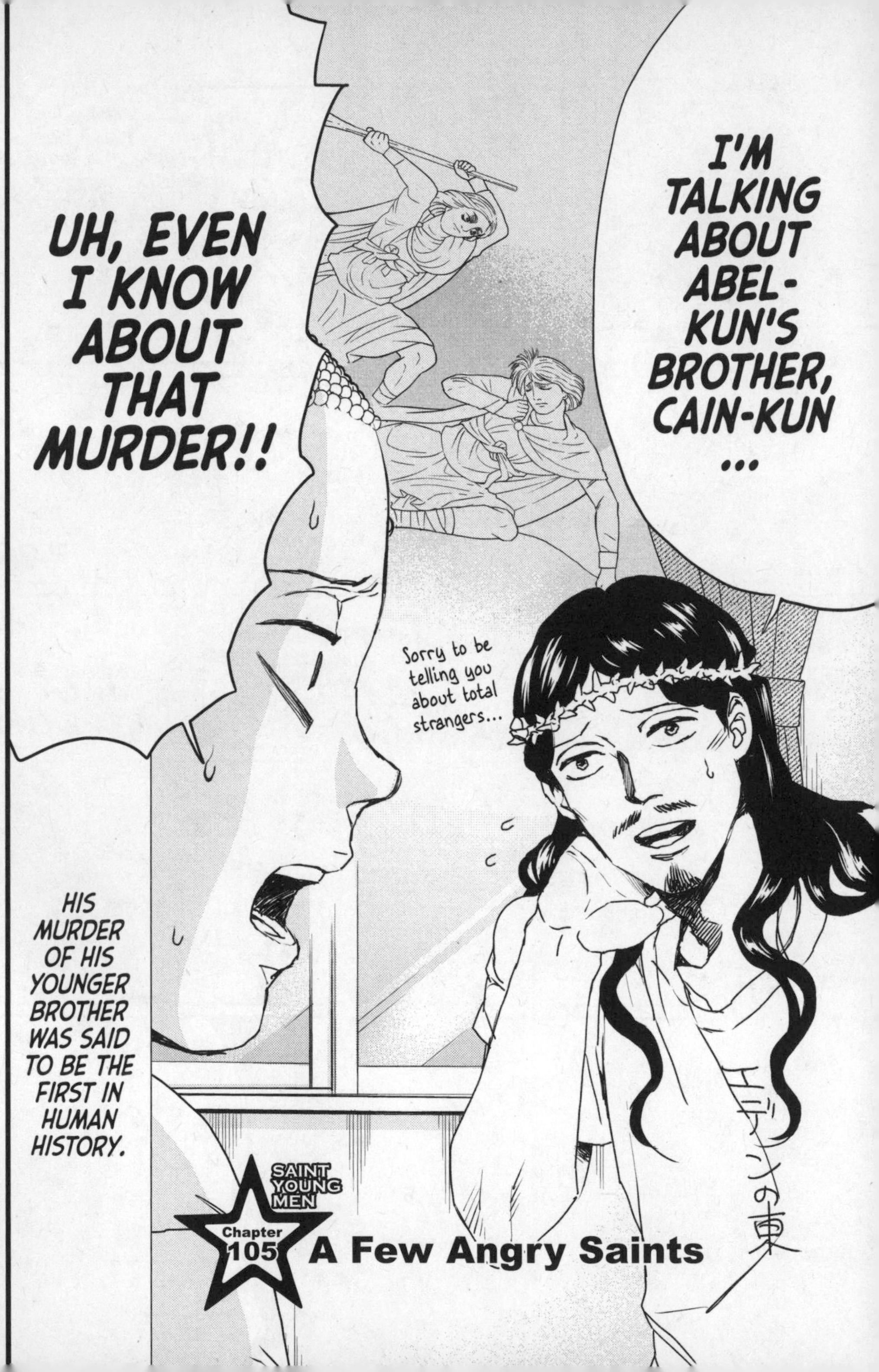
I'M TALKING ABOUT ABEL-KUN'S BROTHER, CAIN-KUN ...
UH, EVEN I KNOW ABOUT THAT MURDER!!
Sorry to be telling you about total strangers...
HIS MURDER OF HIS YOUNGER BROTHER WAS SAID TO BE THE FIRST IN HUMAN HISTORY.
エデンの東
SAINT YOUNG MEN
Chapter 105
A Few Angry Saints

JESUS'S SHIRT: EAST OF EDEN

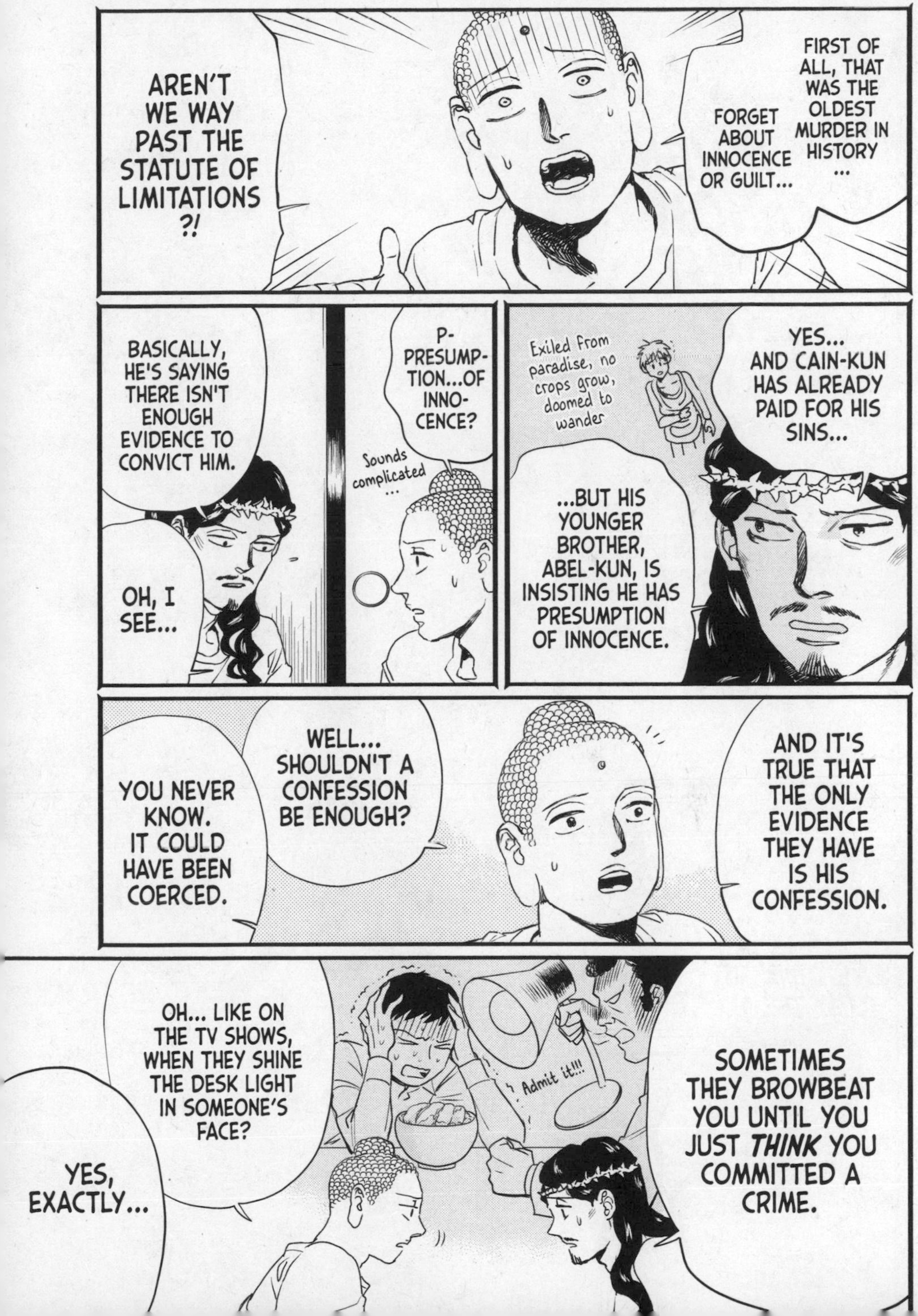
FIRST OF ALL, THAT WAS THE OLDEST MURDER IN HISTORY ...
FORGET ABOUT INNOCENCE OR GUILT...
AREN'T WE WAY PAST THE STATUTE OF LIMITATIONS ?!
YES... AND CAIN-KUN HAS ALREADY PAID FOR HIS SINS...
Exiled from paradise, no crops grow, doomed to wander
...BUT HIS YOUNGER BROTHER, ABEL-KUN, IS INSISTING HE HAS PRESUMPTION OF INNOCENCE.
P-PRESUMPTION...OF INNO-CENCE?
Sounds complicated ...
BASICALLY, HE'S SAYING THERE ISN'T ENOUGH EVIDENCE TO CONVICT HIM.
OH, I SEE...
AND IT'S TRUE THAT THE ONLY EVIDENCE THEY HAVE IS HIS CONFESSION.
WELL... SHOULDN'T A CONFESSION BE ENOUGH?
YOU NEVER KNOW. IT COULD HAVE BEEN COERCED.
SOMETIMES THEY BROWBEAT YOU UNTIL YOU JUST *THINK* YOU COMMITTED A CRIME.
Admit it!!!
OH... LIKE ON THE TV SHOWS, WHEN THEY SHINE THE DESK LIGHT IN SOMEONE'S FACE?
YES, EXACTLY...

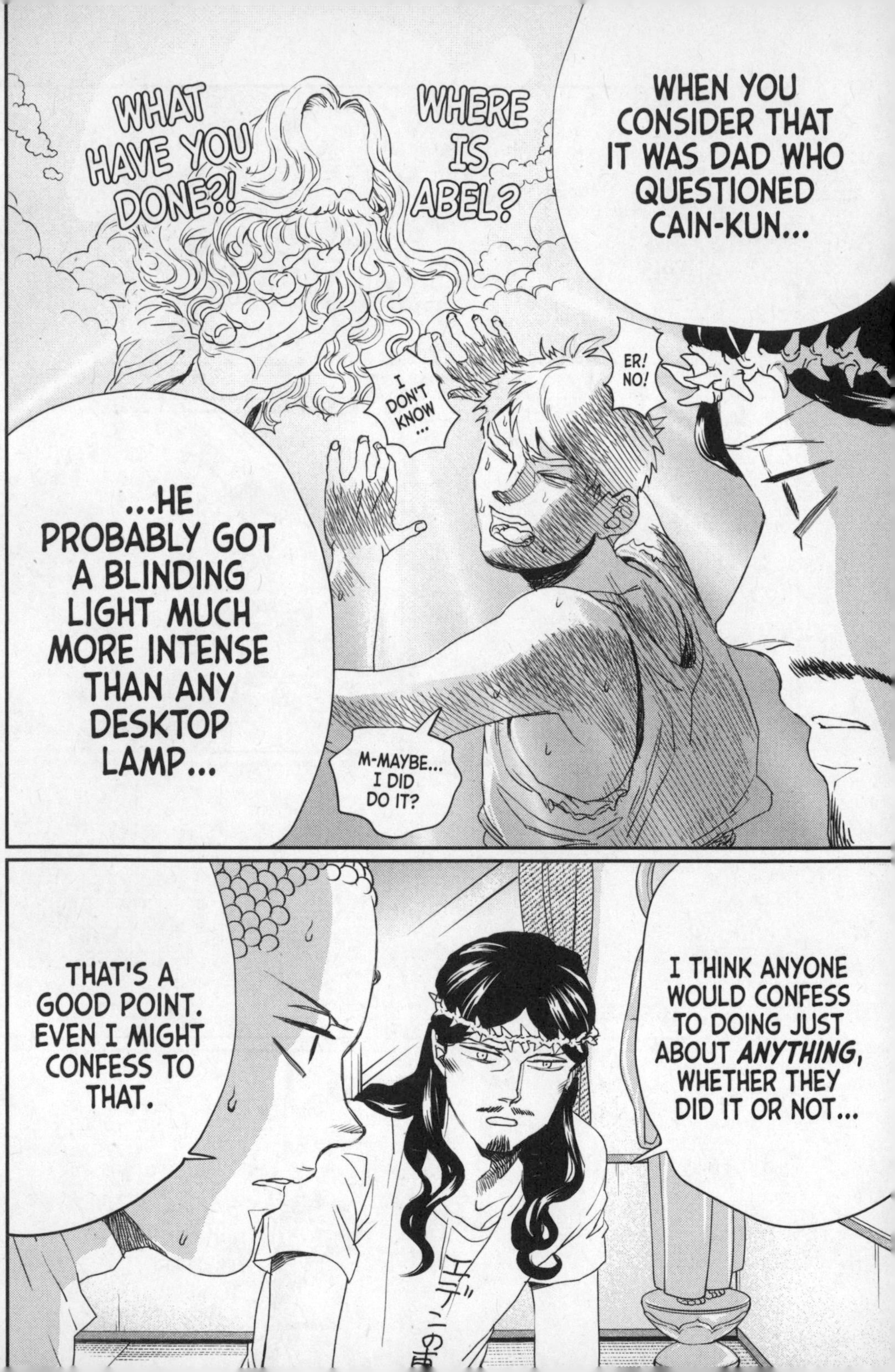
WHEN YOU CONSIDER THAT IT WAS DAD WHO QUESTIONED CAIN-KUN...
WHERE IS ABEL?
WHAT HAVE YOU DONE?!
ER! NO!
I DON'T KNOW...
...HE PROBABLY GOT A BLINDING LIGHT MUCH MORE INTENSE THAN ANY DESKTOP LAMP...
M-MAYBE... I DID DO IT?
I THINK ANYONE WOULD CONFESS TO DOING JUST ABOUT *ANYTHING*, WHETHER THEY DID IT OR NOT...
THAT'S A GOOD POINT. EVEN I MIGHT CONFESS TO THAT.

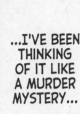

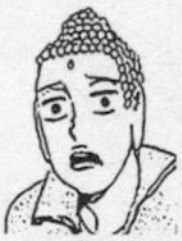

BUDDHA
MY FAVORITE DETECTIVE IS KOGORO AKECHI. HE PLAYS IT COOL WHEN WORKING WITH YOUNG KOBAYASHI, BUT I LIKE HOW BUMBLING HE SEEMS IN D. HILL.

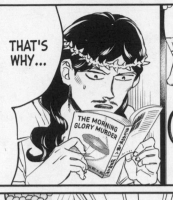

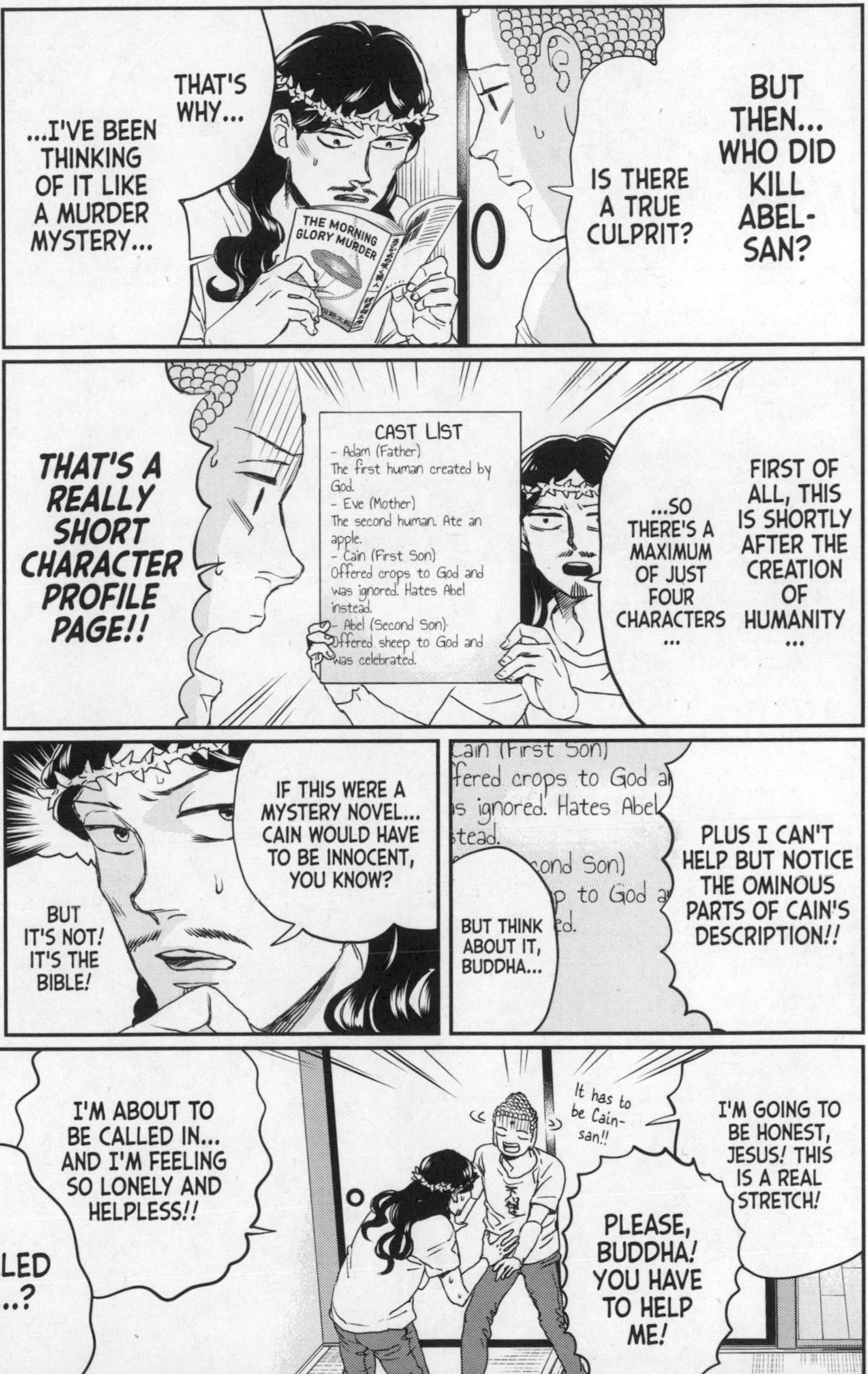

BUT THEN... WHO DID KILL ABEL-SAN?
IS THERE A TRUE CULPRIT?
THAT'S WHY...
...I'VE BEEN THINKING OF IT LIKE A MURDER MYSTERY...
THE MORNING GLORY MURDER
FIRST OF ALL, THIS IS SHORTLY AFTER THE CREATION OF HUMANITY...
...SO THERE'S A MAXIMUM OF JUST FOUR CHARACTERS...
CAST LIST
- Adam (Father)
The first human created by God.
- Eve (Mother)
The second human. Ate an apple.
- Cain (First Son)
Offered crops to God and was ignored. Hates Abel instead.
- Abel (Second Son)
Offered sheep to God and was celebrated.
THAT'S A REALLY SHORT CHARACTER PROFILE PAGE!!
PLUS I CAN'T HELP BUT NOTICE THE OMINOUS PARTS OF CAIN'S DESCRIPTION!!
BUT THINK ABOUT IT, BUDDHA...
IF THIS WERE A MYSTERY NOVEL... CAIN WOULD HAVE TO BE INNOCENT, YOU KNOW?
BUT IT'S NOT! IT'S THE BIBLE!
I'M GOING TO BE HONEST, JESUS! THIS IS A REAL STRETCH!
It has to be Cain-san!!
PLEASE, BUDDHA! YOU HAVE TO HELP ME!
I'M ABOUT TO BE CALLED IN... AND I'M FEELING SO LONELY AND HELPLESS!!
CALLED IN...?

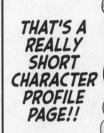

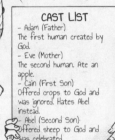

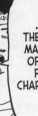

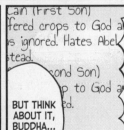

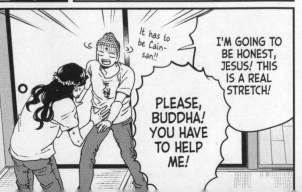

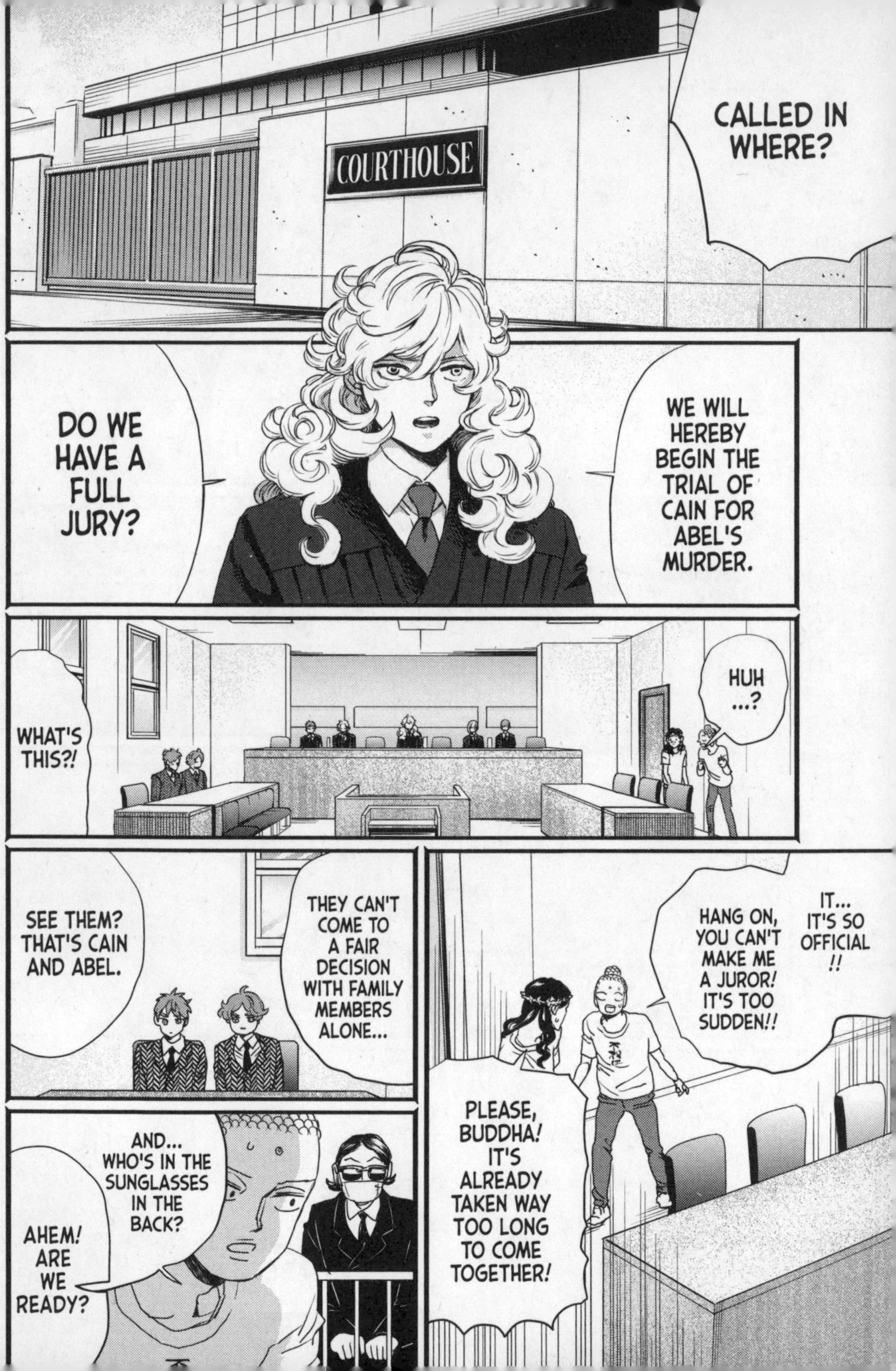
CALLED IN WHERE?
COURTHOUSE
...
WE WILL HEREBY BEGIN THE TRIAL OF CAIN FOR ABEL'S MURDER.
DO WE HAVE A FULL JURY?
HUH ...?
WHAT'S THIS?!
IT... IT'S SO OFFICIAL!!
HANG ON, YOU CAN'T MAKE ME A JUROR! IT'S TOO SUDDEN!!
PLEASE, BUDDHA! IT'S ALREADY TAKEN WAY TOO LONG TO COME TOGETHER!
THEY CAN'T COME TO A FAIR DECISION WITH FAMILY MEMBERS ALONE...
SEE THEM? THAT'S CAIN AND ABEL.
AND... WHO'S IN THE SUNGLASSES IN THE BACK?
AHEM! ARE WE READY?

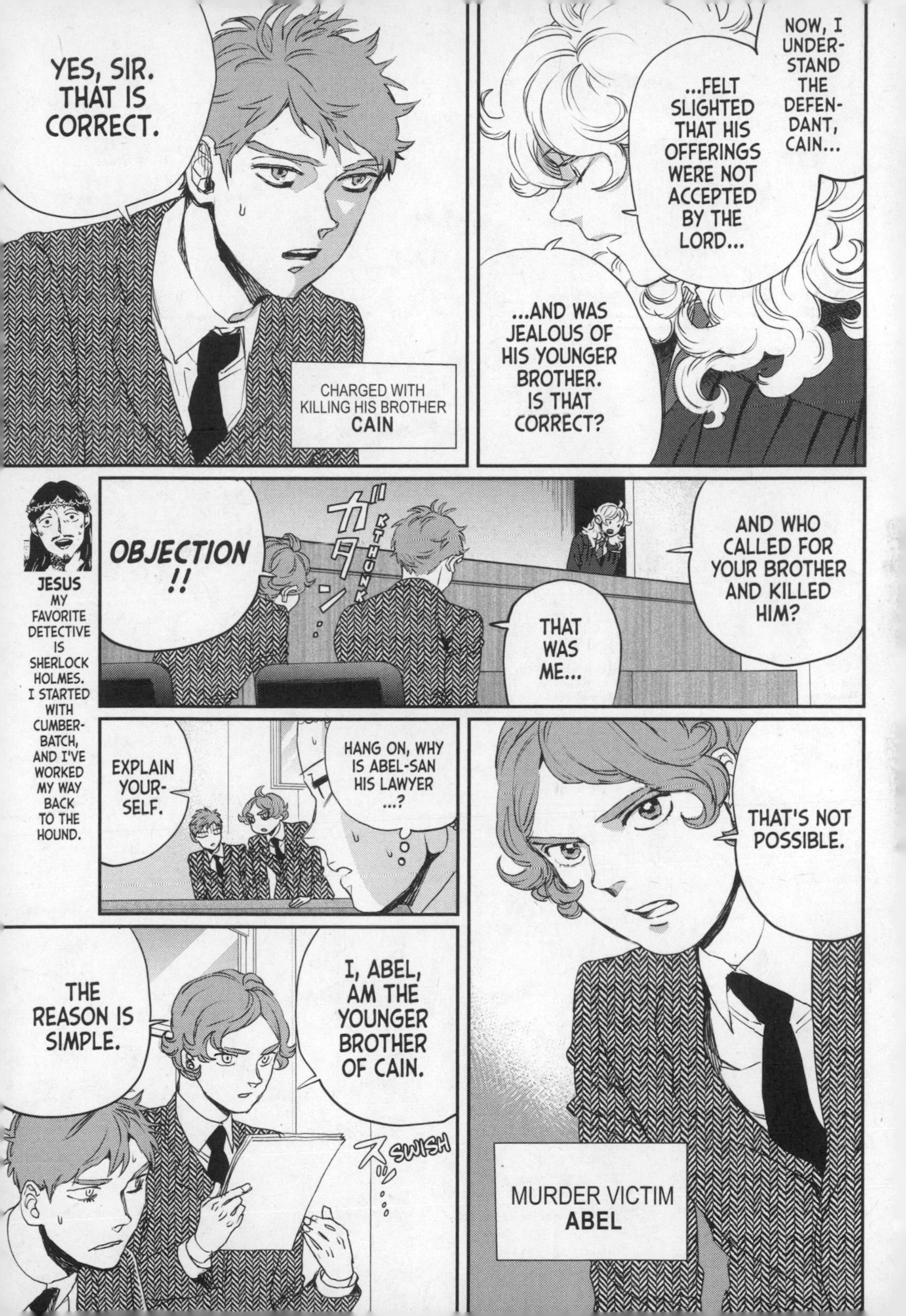
NOW, I UNDERSTAND THE DEFENDANT, CAIN...
...FELT SLIGHTED THAT HIS OFFERINGS WERE NOT ACCEPTED BY THE LORD...
...AND WAS JEALOUS OF HIS YOUNGER BROTHER. IS THAT CORRECT?
YES, SIR. THAT IS CORRECT.
CHARGED WITH KILLING HIS BROTHER
CAIN
AND WHO CALLED FOR YOUR BROTHER AND KILLED HIM?
THAT WAS ME...
KTHUNK
OBJECTION!!
JESUS
MY FAVORITE DETECTIVE IS SHERLOCK HOLMES. I STARTED WITH CUMBER-BATCH, AND I'VE WORKED MY WAY BACK TO THE HOUND.
THAT'S NOT POSSIBLE.
MURDER VICTIM
ABEL
HANG ON, WHY IS ABEL-SAN HIS LAWYER ...?
EXPLAIN YOUR-SELF.
I, ABEL, AM THE YOUNGER BROTHER OF CAIN.
THE REASON IS SIMPLE.
SWISH

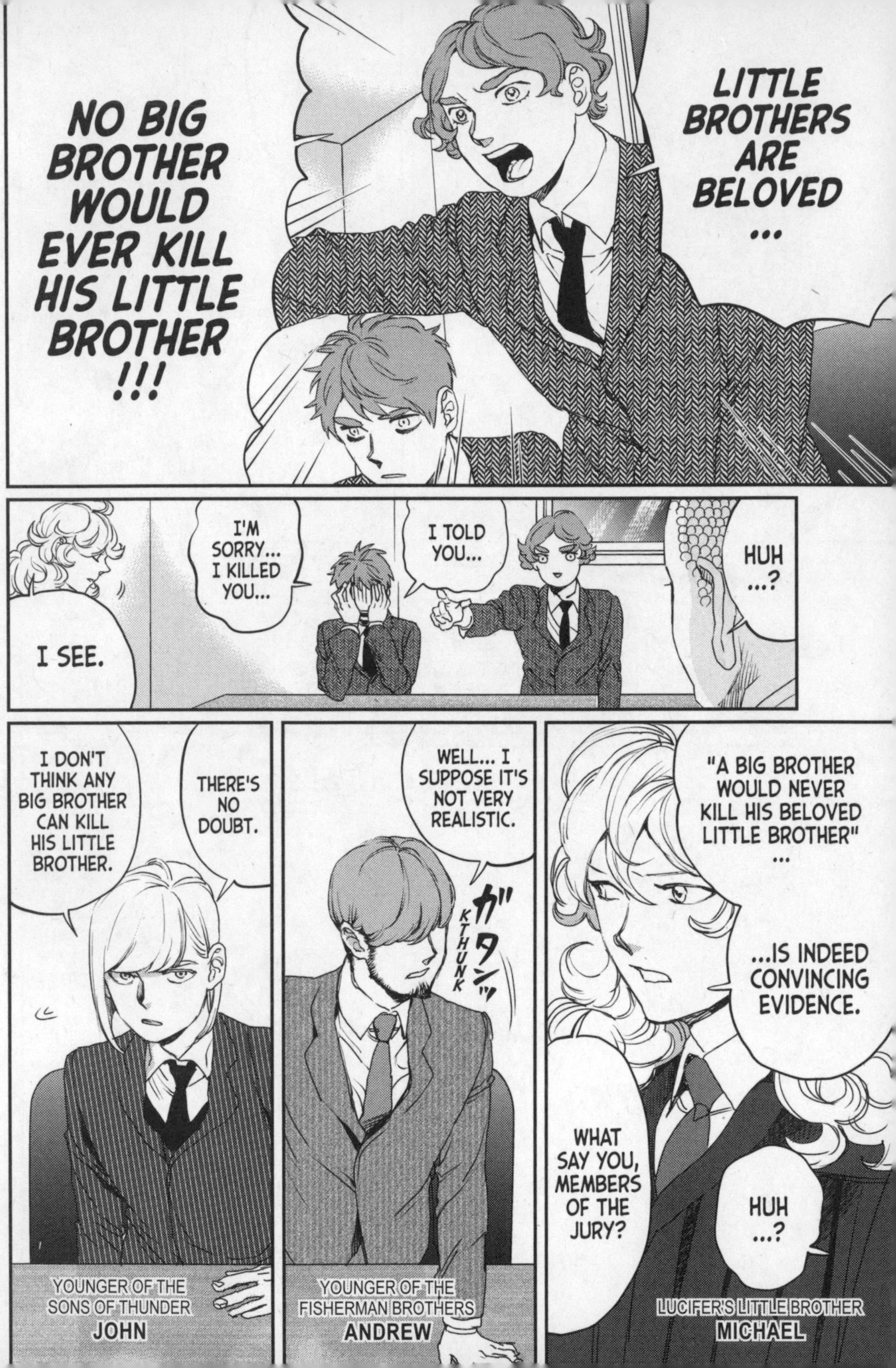

LITTLE BROTHERS ARE BELOVED ...
NO BIG BROTHER WOULD EVER KILL HIS LITTLE BROTHER !!!
HUH ...?
I TOLD YOU...
I'M SORRY... I KILLED YOU...
I SEE.
"A BIG BROTHER WOULD NEVER KILL HIS BELOVED LITTLE BROTHER" ...
...IS INDEED CONVINCING EVIDENCE.
WHAT SAY YOU, MEMBERS OF THE JURY?
HUH ...?
LUCIFER'S LITTLE BROTHER
MICHAEL
WELL... I SUPPOSE IT'S NOT VERY REALISTIC.
KTHUNK
YOUNGER OF THE FISHERMAN BROTHERS
ANDREW
THERE'S NO DOUBT.
I DON'T THINK ANY BIG BROTHER CAN KILL HIS LITTLE BROTHER.
YOUNGER OF THE SONS OF THUNDER
JOHN

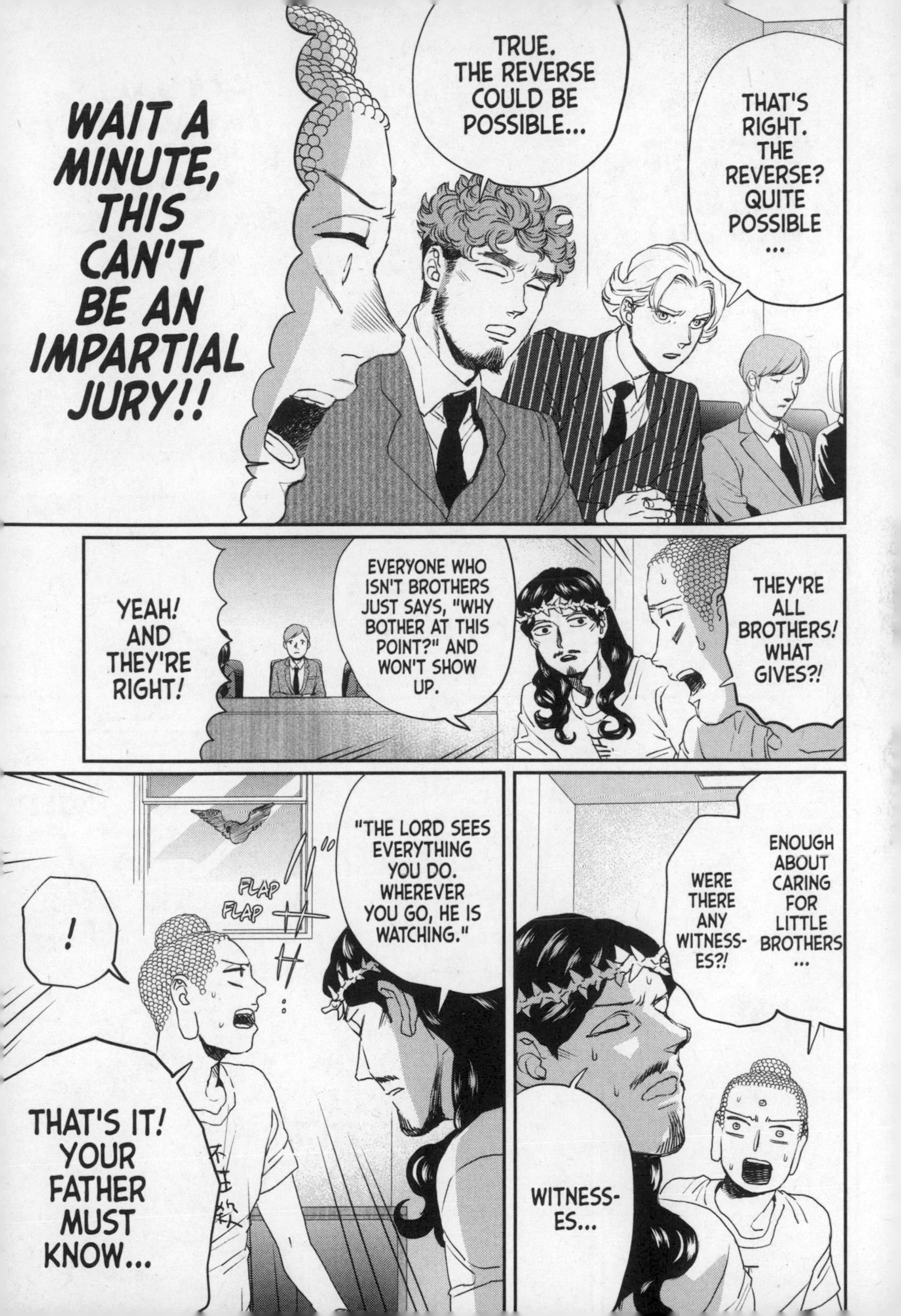
THAT'S RIGHT. THE REVERSE? QUITE POSSIBLE ...
TRUE. THE REVERSE COULD BE POSSIBLE...
WAIT A MINUTE, THIS CAN'T BE AN IMPARTIAL JURY!!
THEY'RE ALL BROTHERS! WHAT GIVES?!
EVERYONE WHO ISN'T BROTHERS JUST SAYS, "WHY BOTHER AT THIS POINT?" AND WON'T SHOW UP.
YEAH! AND THEY'RE RIGHT!
ENOUGH ABOUT CARING FOR LITTLE BROTHERS ...
WERE THERE ANY WITNESS-ES?!
WITNESS-ES...
"THE LORD SEES EVERYTHING YOU DO. WHEREVER YOU GO, HE IS WATCHING."
FLAP FLAP
!
THAT'S IT! YOUR FATHER MUST KNOW...

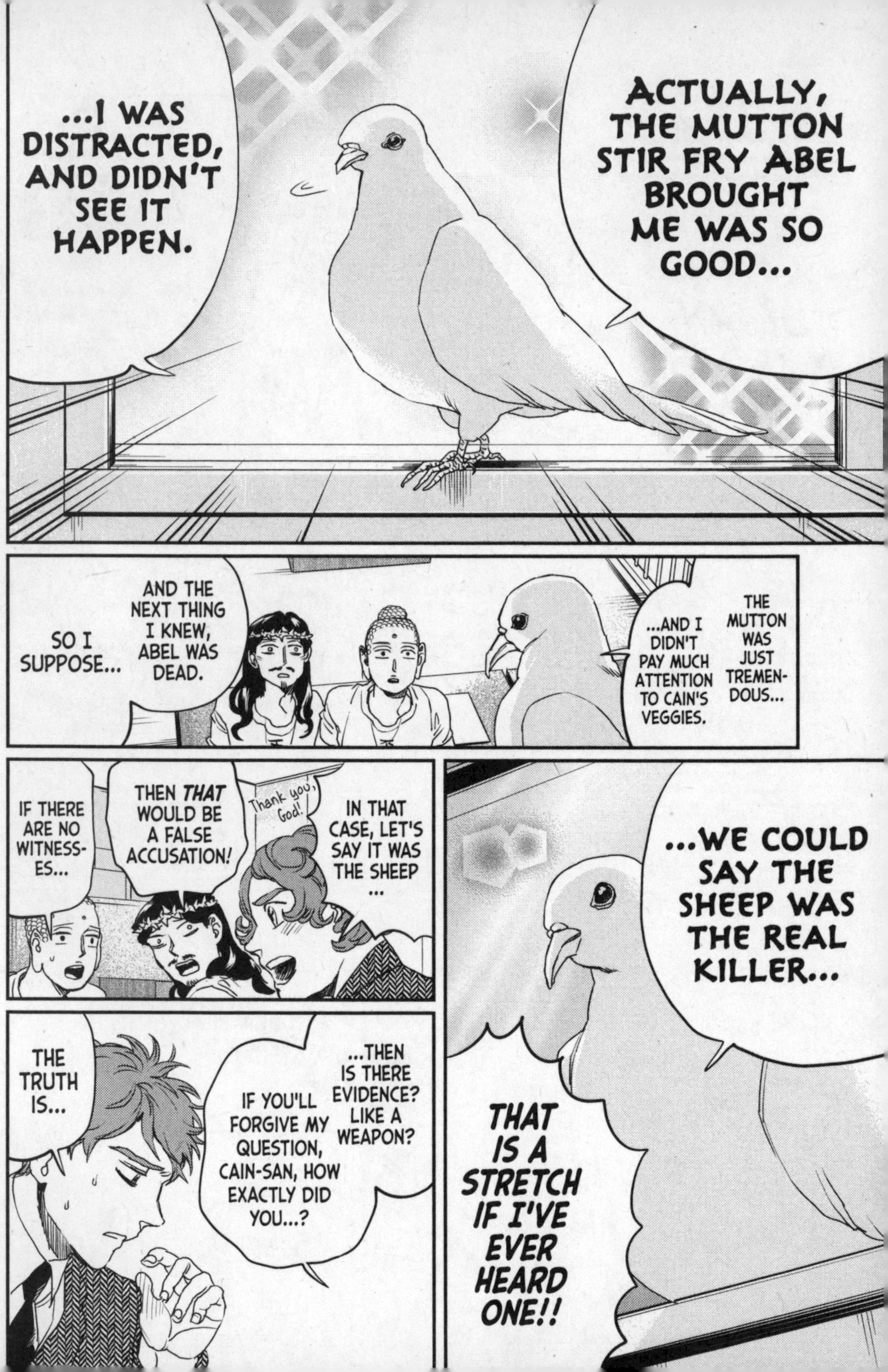
ACTUALLY, THE MUTTON STIR FRY ABEL BROUGHT ME WAS SO GOOD...
...I WAS DISTRACTED, AND DIDN'T SEE IT HAPPEN.
THE MUTTON WAS JUST TREMENDOUS...
...AND I DIDN'T PAY MUCH ATTENTION TO CAIN'S VEGGIES.
AND THE NEXT THING I KNEW, ABEL WAS DEAD.
SO I SUPPOSE...
...WE COULD SAY THE SHEEP WAS THE REAL KILLER...
THAT IS A STRETCH IF I'VE EVER HEARD ONE!!
IN THAT CASE, LET'S SAY IT WAS THE SHEEP ...
Thank you, God!
THEN *THAT* WOULD BE A FALSE ACCUSATION!
IF THERE ARE NO WITNESSES...
...THEN IS THERE EVIDENCE? LIKE A WEAPON?
IF YOU'LL FORGIVE MY QUESTION, CAIN-SAN, HOW EXACTLY DID YOU...?
THE TRUTH IS...

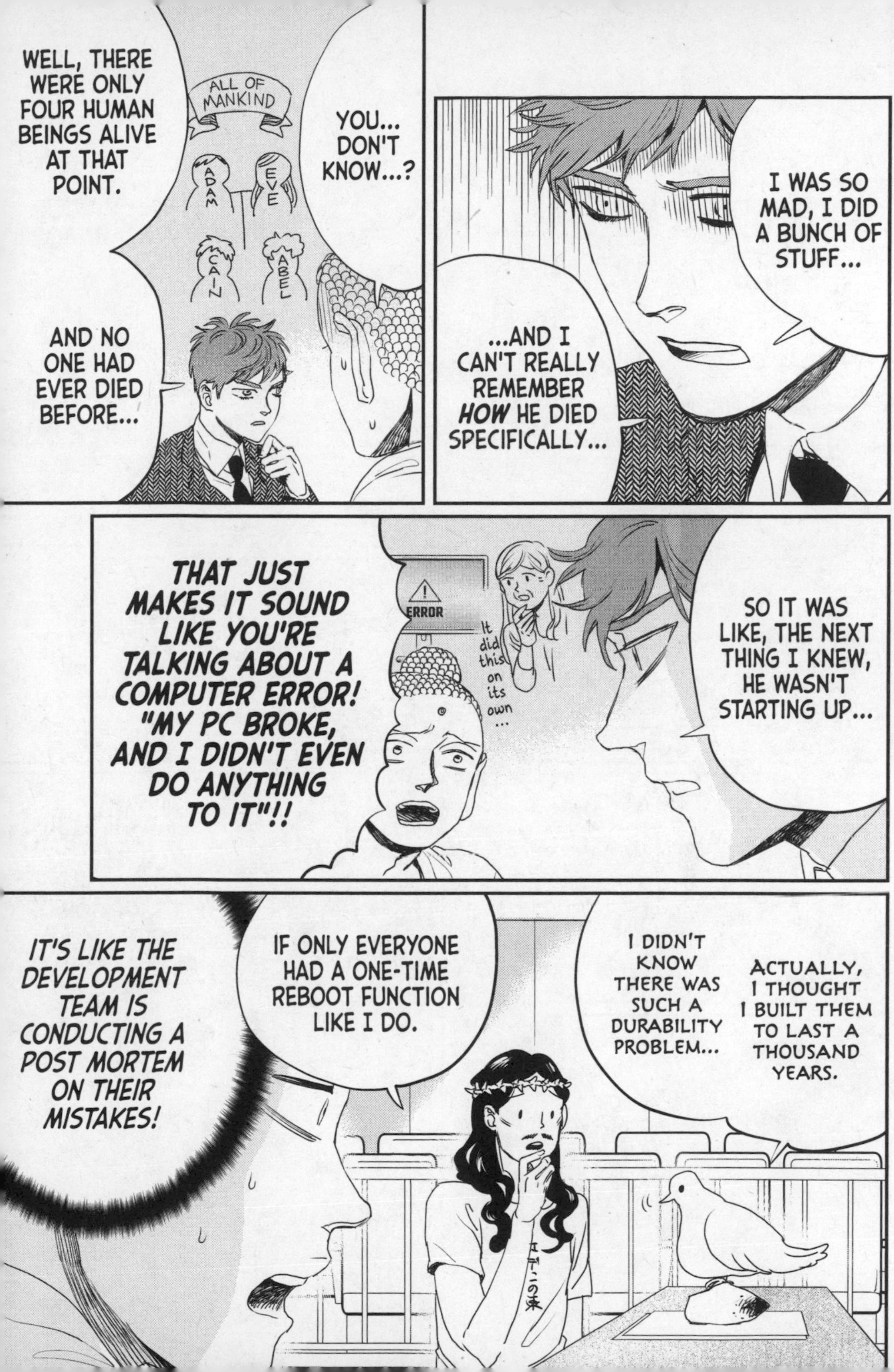
I WAS SO MAD, I DID A BUNCH OF STUFF...
...AND I CAN'T REALLY REMEMBER *HOW* HE DIED SPECIFICALLY...
YOU... DON'T KNOW...?
WELL, THERE WERE ONLY FOUR HUMAN BEINGS ALIVE AT THAT POINT.
ALL OF MANKIND
ADAM
EVE
CAIN
ABEL
AND NO ONE HAD EVER DIED BEFORE...
SO IT WAS LIKE, THE NEXT THING I KNEW, HE WASN'T STARTING UP...
ERROR
It did this on its own...
THAT JUST MAKES IT SOUND LIKE YOU'RE TALKING ABOUT A COMPUTER ERROR! "MY PC BROKE, AND I DIDN'T EVEN DO ANYTHING TO IT"!!
ACTUALLY, I THOUGHT I BUILT THEM TO LAST A THOUSAND YEARS.
I DIDN'T KNOW THERE WAS SUCH A DURABILITY PROBLEM...
IF ONLY EVERYONE HAD A ONE-TIME REBOOT FUNCTION LIKE I DO.
IT'S LIKE THE DEVELOPMENT TEAM IS CONDUCTING A POST MORTEM ON THEIR MISTAKES!

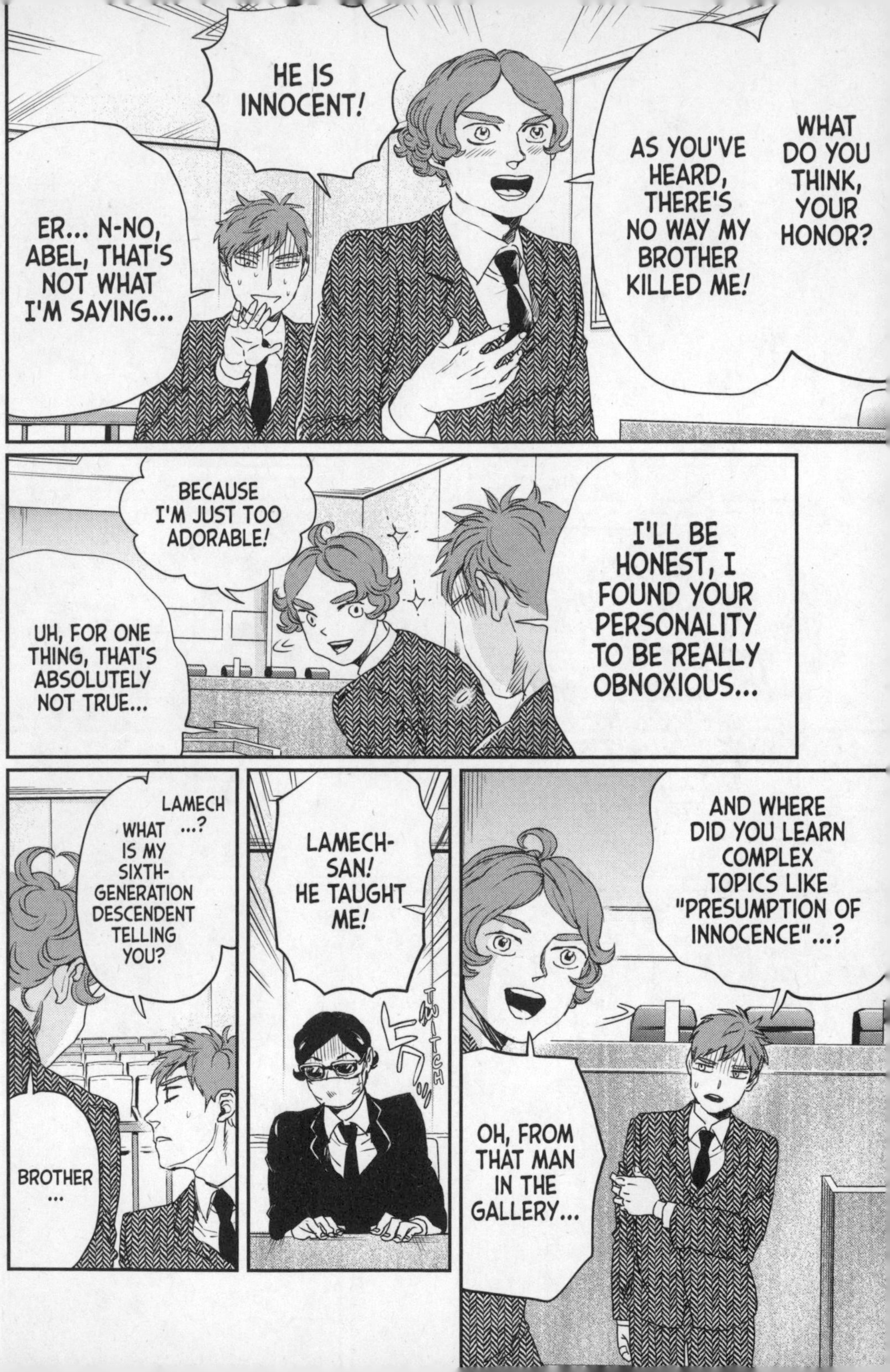
AS YOU'VE HEARD, THERE'S NO WAY MY BROTHER KILLED ME!
WHAT DO YOU THINK, YOUR HONOR?
HE IS INNOCENT!
ER... N-NO, ABEL, THAT'S NOT WHAT I'M SAYING...
I'LL BE HONEST, I FOUND YOUR PERSONALITY TO BE REALLY OBNOXIOUS...
BECAUSE I'M JUST TOO ADORABLE!
UH, FOR ONE THING, THAT'S ABSOLUTELY NOT TRUE...
AND WHERE DID YOU LEARN COMPLEX TOPICS LIKE "PRESUMPTION OF INNOCENCE"...?
OH, FROM THAT MAN IN THE GALLERY...
LAMECH-SAN! HE TAUGHT ME!
TWITCH
LAMECH ...?
WHAT IS MY SIXTH-GENERATION DESCENDENT TELLING YOU?
BROTHER ...

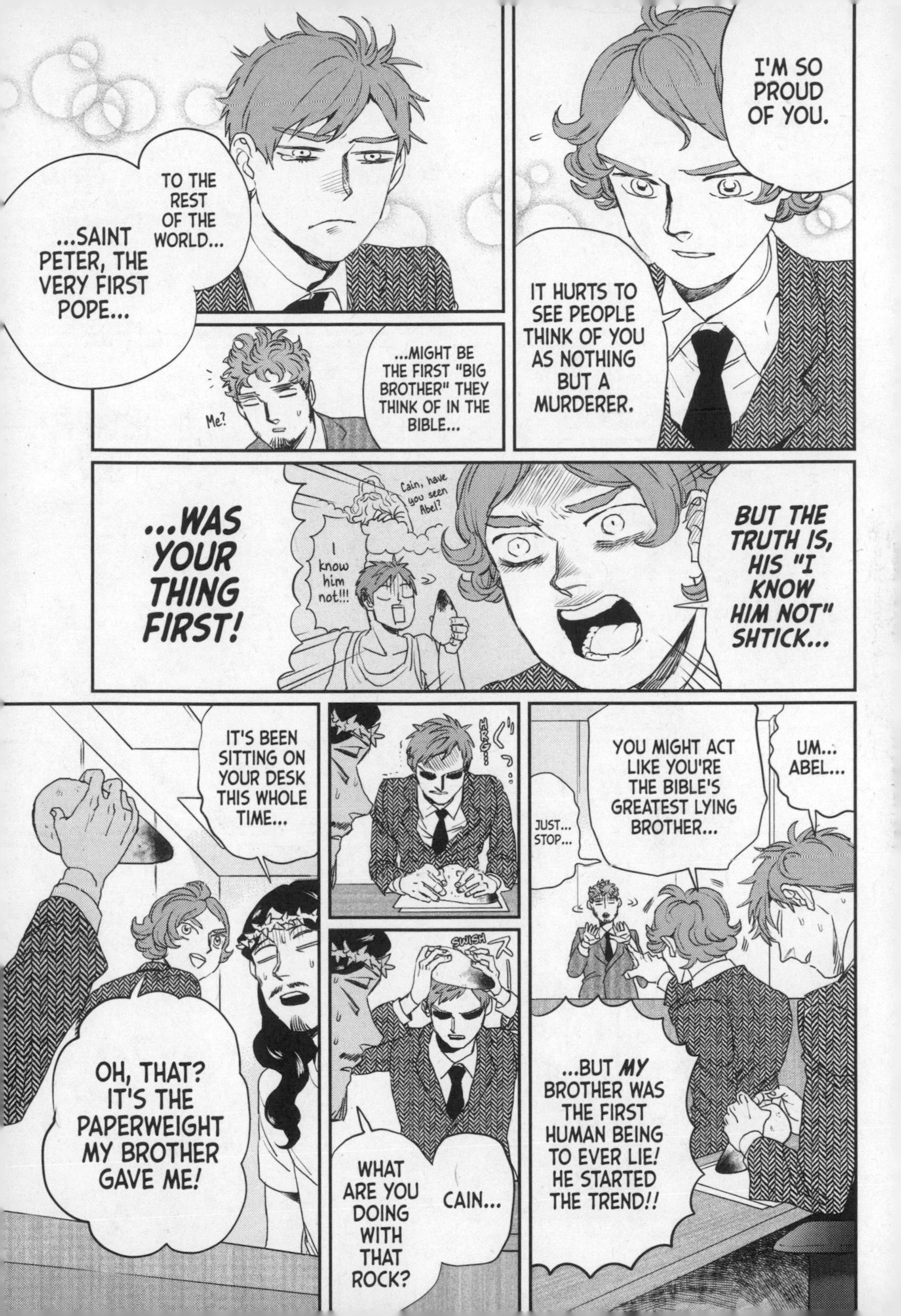
I'M SO PROUD OF YOU.
IT HURTS TO SEE PEOPLE THINK OF YOU AS NOTHING BUT A MURDERER.
TO THE REST OF THE WORLD...
...SAINT PETER, THE VERY FIRST POPE...
...MIGHT BE THE FIRST "BIG BROTHER" THEY THINK OF IN THE BIBLE...
Me?
BUT THE TRUTH IS, HIS "I KNOW HIM NOT" SHTICK...
Cain, have you seen Abel?
I know him not!!!
...WAS YOUR THING FIRST!
UM... ABEL...
YOU MIGHT ACT LIKE YOU'RE THE BIBLE'S GREATEST LYING BROTHER...
JUST... STOP...
...BUT *MY* BROTHER WAS THE FIRST HUMAN BEING TO EVER LIE! HE STARTED THE TREND!!
HRG...
SWISH
CAIN...
WHAT ARE YOU DOING WITH THAT ROCK?
IT'S BEEN SITTING ON YOUR DESK THIS WHOLE TIME...
OH, THAT? IT'S THE PAPERWEIGHT MY BROTHER GAVE ME!

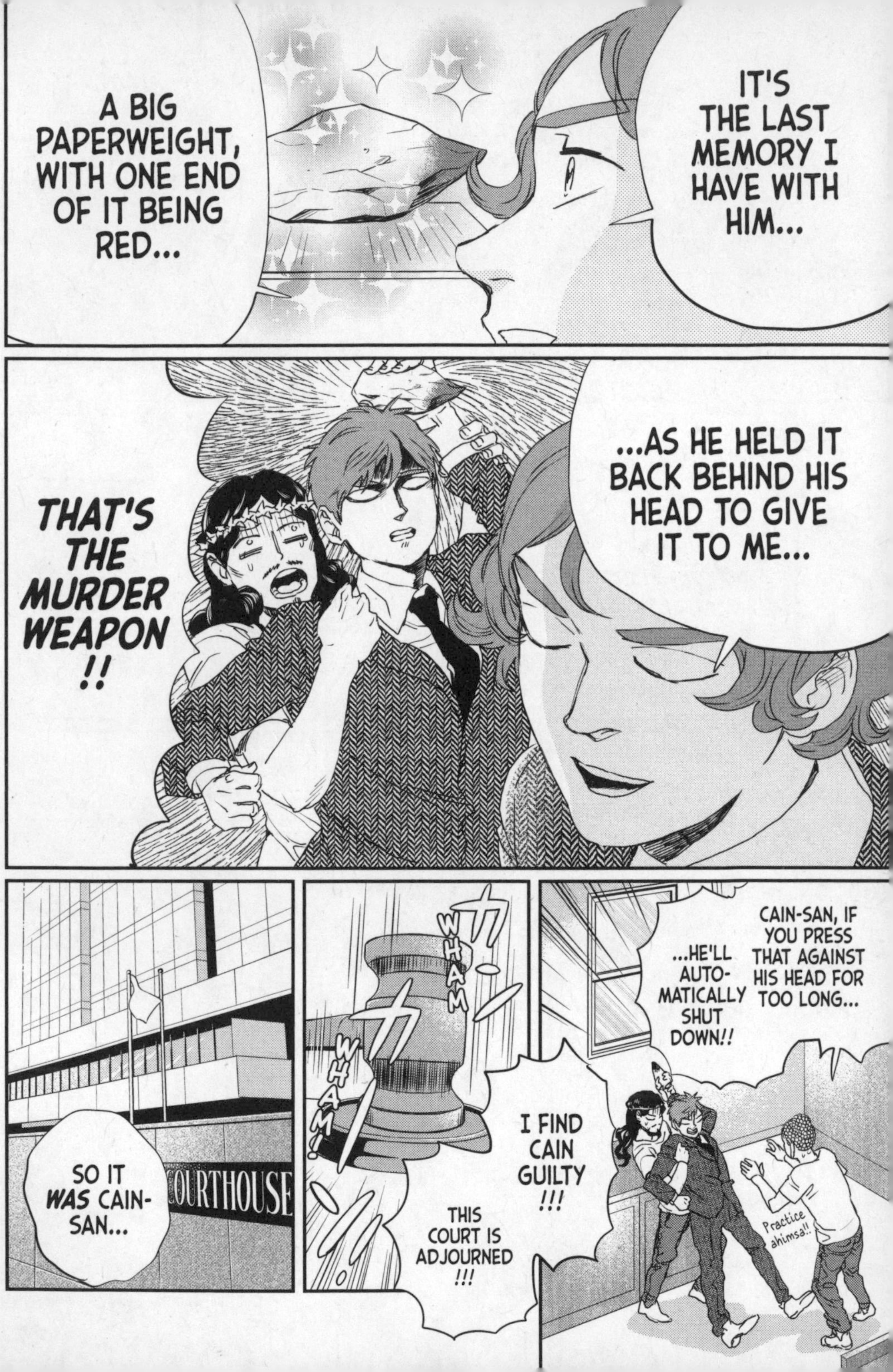
IT'S THE LAST MEMORY I HAVE WITH HIM...
A BIG PAPERWEIGHT, WITH ONE END OF IT BEING RED...
...AS HE HELD IT BACK BEHIND HIS HEAD TO GIVE IT TO ME...
THAT'S THE MURDER WEAPON!!
CAIN-SAN, IF YOU PRESS THAT AGAINST HIS HEAD FOR TOO LONG...
...HE'LL AUTO-MATICALLY SHUT DOWN!!
Practice ahimsa!!
WHAM
WHAM
I FIND CAIN GUILTY!!!
THIS COURT IS ADJOURNED!!!
COURTHOUSE
SO IT WAS CAIN-SAN...

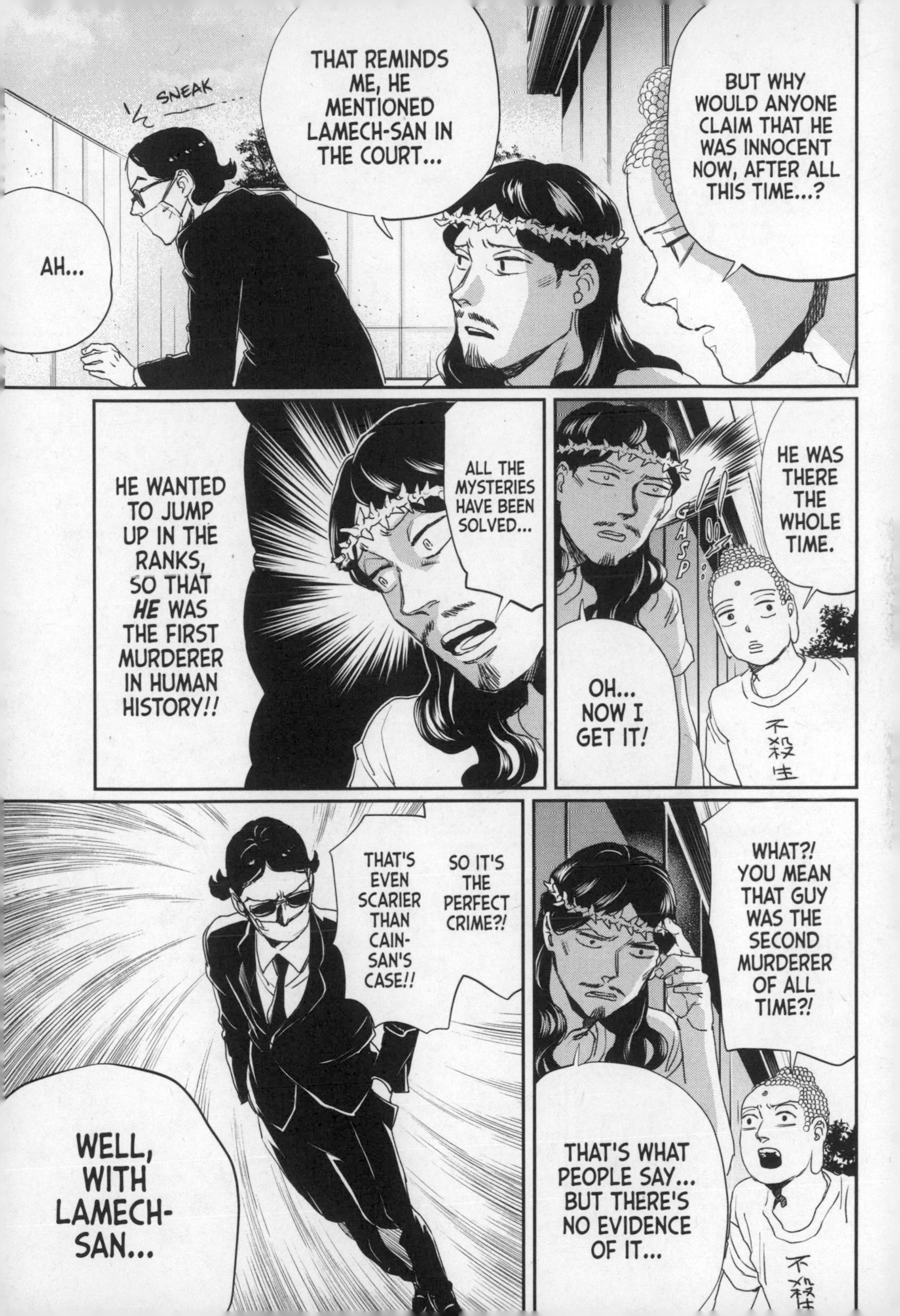
BUT WHY WOULD ANYONE CLAIM THAT HE WAS INNOCENT NOW, AFTER ALL THIS TIME...?
THAT REMINDS ME, HE MENTIONED LAMECH-SAN IN THE COURT...
SNEAK
AH...
HE WAS THERE THE WHOLE TIME.
GASP
OH... NOW I GET IT!
不殺生
ALL THE MYSTERIES HAVE BEEN SOLVED...
HE WANTED TO JUMP UP IN THE RANKS, SO THAT *HE* WAS THE FIRST MURDERER IN HUMAN HISTORY!!
WHAT?! YOU MEAN THAT GUY WAS THE SECOND MURDERER OF ALL TIME?!
THAT'S WHAT PEOPLE SAY... BUT THERE'S NO EVIDENCE OF IT...
SO IT'S THE PERFECT CRIME?!
THAT'S EVEN SCARIER THAN CAIN-SAN'S CASE!!
WELL, WITH LAMECH-SAN...

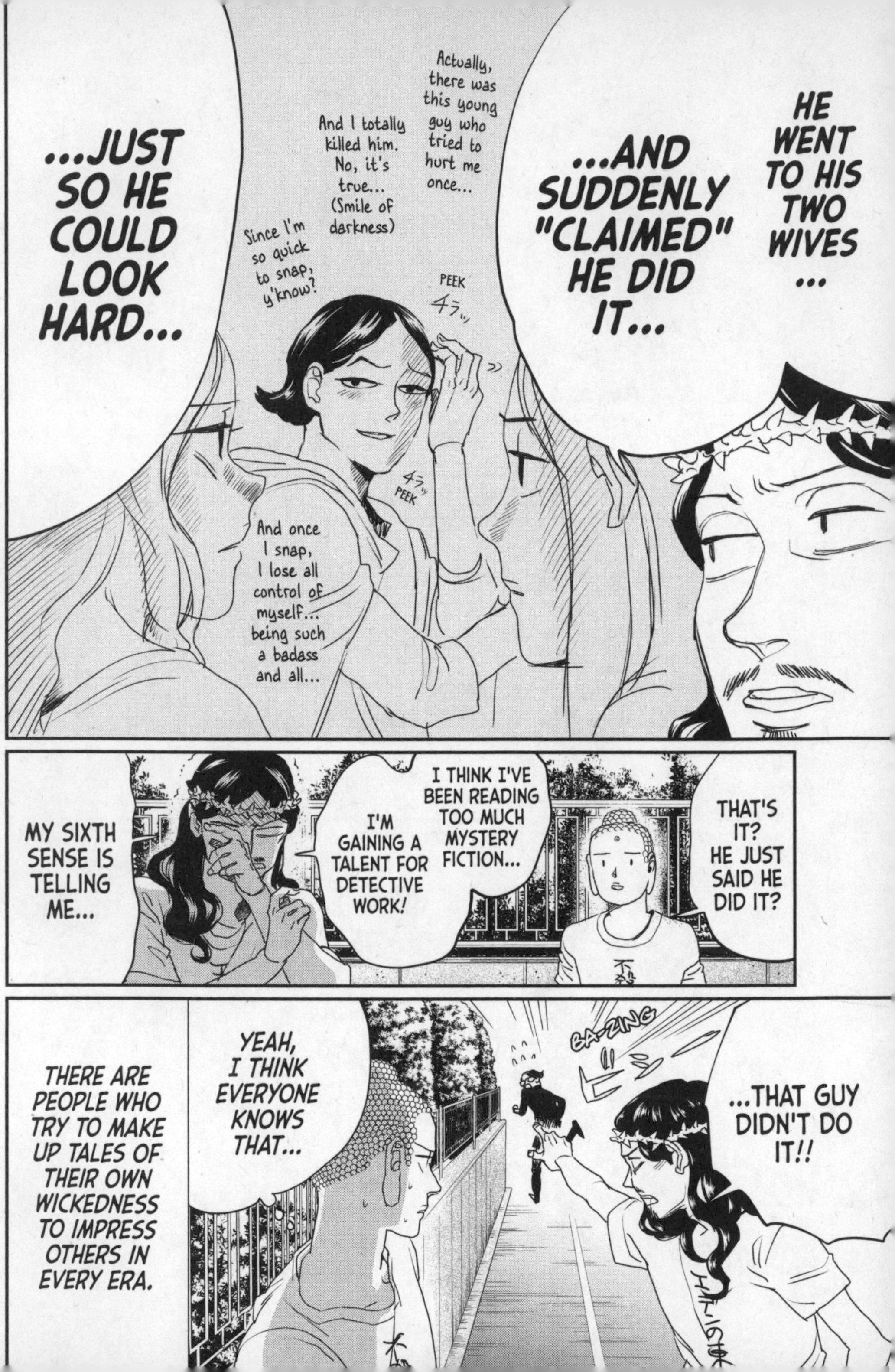
HE WENT TO HIS TWO WIVES...
...AND SUDDENLY "CLAIMED" HE DID IT...
Actually, there was this young guy who tried to hurt me once...
And I totally killed him. No, it's true... (Smile of darkness)
Since I'm so quick to snap, y'know?
PEEK
...JUST SO HE COULD LOOK HARD...
PEEK
And once I snap, I lose all control of myself... being such a badass and all...
THAT'S IT? HE JUST SAID HE DID IT?
I THINK I'VE BEEN READING TOO MUCH MYSTERY FICTION...
I'M GAINING A TALENT FOR DETECTIVE WORK!
MY SIXTH SENSE IS TELLING ME...
...THAT GUY DIDN'T DO IT!!
BA-ZING
YEAH, I THINK EVERYONE KNOWS THAT...
THERE ARE PEOPLE WHO TRY TO MAKE UP TALES OF THEIR OWN WICKEDNESS TO IMPRESS OTHERS IN EVERY ERA.

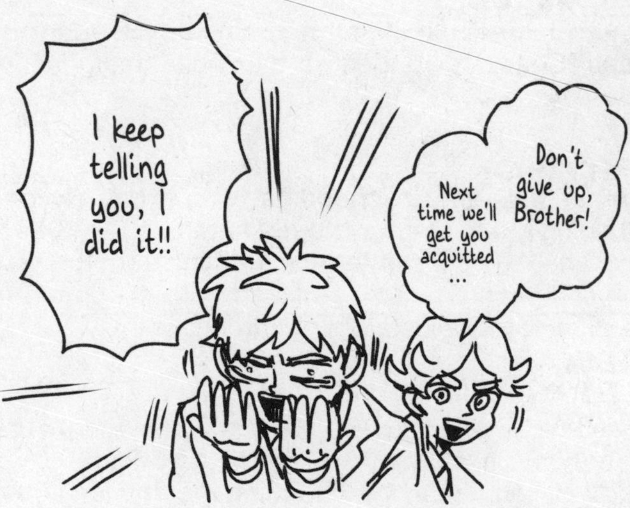
Don't give up, Brother!
Next time we'll get you acquitted ...
I keep telling you, I did it!!

CHAPTER 105 TRANSLATION NOTES

East of Eden, page 20
The place where Cain is said to have been banished by God after killing Abel.

Kogoro Akechi, page 23
The famous detective character created by Edogawa Rampo, inspired by Sherlock Holmes. Like Holmes, Akechi appears in many stories, the first of which (in 1925) was titled "The Case of the Murder on D. Hill."

Sherlock Hound, page 25
A mid-1980s steampunk-styled take on Sherlock Holmes in which all of the characters are dogs. The animated series was produced jointly between Japanese and Italian companies, and Hayao Miyazaki directed some of the episodes.

Sons of Thunder, page 26
Jesus gave the brothers James and John the nickname "Boanerges," which is taken to mean "Sons of Thunder," due to their impetuous personalities.

A thousand years, page 29
Many early figures in the Bible are described as living extremely long lives, with the oldest being Methuselah, who died at the age of 969. There are various explanations offered for this, ranging from more literal (i.e. the burden of sin shortening humanity's lifespan as the generations passed) to mistranslation or miscalculation of numbers.

Lamech, page 30
A sixth-generation descendent of Cain. He was the first person in the Bible mentioned to have multiple wives. In Genesis 4:23-24 he says to his two wives, "I have killed a man for wounding me, a young man for injuring me. If Cain is avenged seven times, then Lamech seventy-seven times."

Ahimsa, page 34
A term from Sanskrit meaning non-violence.

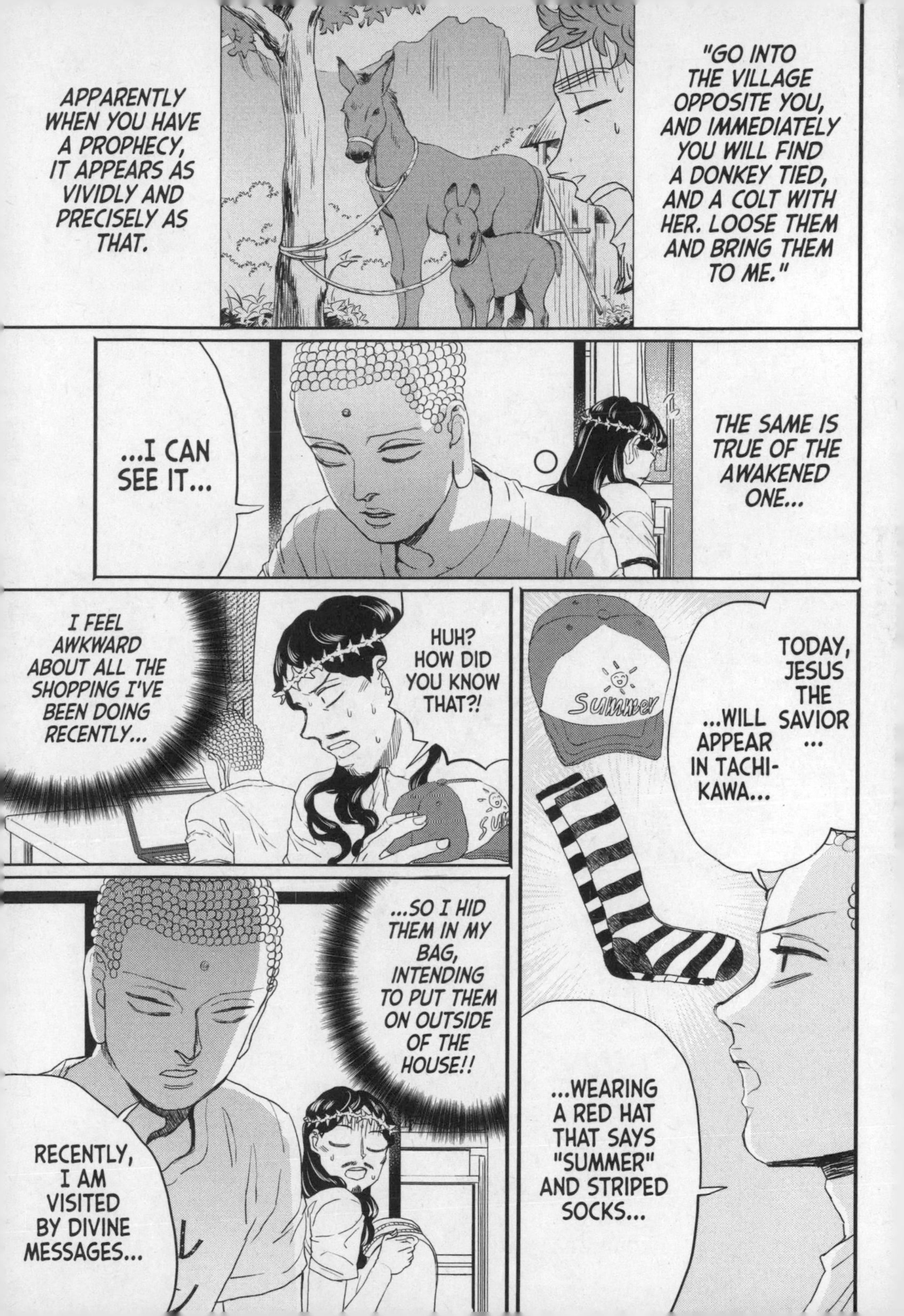
"GO INTO THE VILLAGE OPPOSITE YOU, AND IMMEDIATELY YOU WILL FIND A DONKEY TIED, AND A COLT WITH HER. LOOSE THEM AND BRING THEM TO ME."
APPARENTLY WHEN YOU HAVE A PROPHECY, IT APPEARS AS VIVIDLY AND PRECISELY AS THAT.
THE SAME IS TRUE OF THE AWAKENED ONE...
...I CAN SEE IT...
TODAY, JESUS THE SAVIOR ...
...WILL APPEAR IN TACHIKAWA...
Summer
...WEARING A RED HAT THAT SAYS "SUMMER" AND STRIPED SOCKS...
HUH? HOW DID YOU KNOW THAT?!
I FEEL AWKWARD ABOUT ALL THE SHOPPING I'VE BEEN DOING RECENTLY...
...SO I HID THEM IN MY BAG, INTENDING TO PUT THEM ON OUTSIDE OF THE HOUSE!!
RECENTLY, I AM VISITED BY DIVINE MESSAGES...

THE TRACES OF ONLINE SHOPPING CAN LINGER FOR A WHILE.

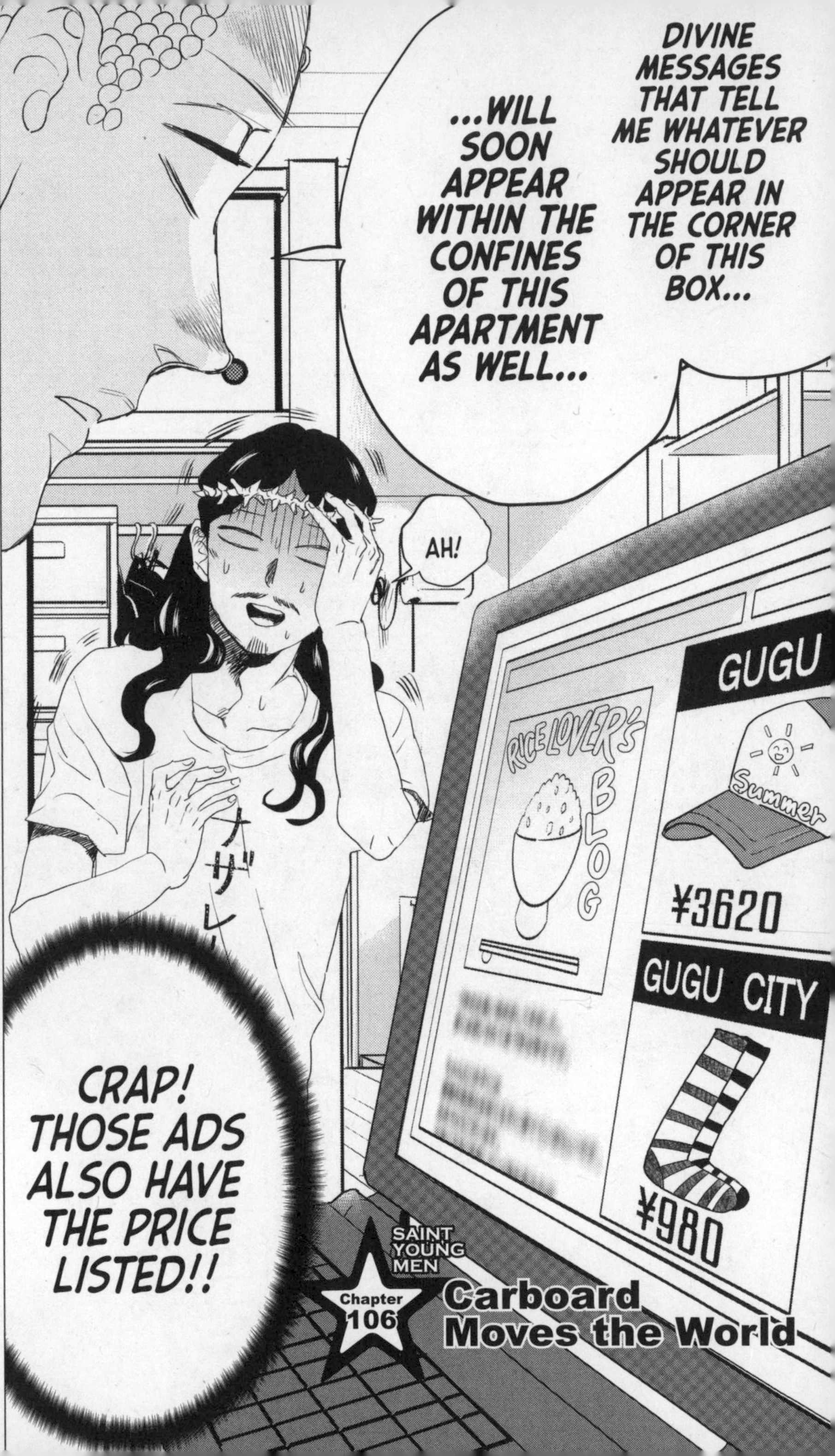
DIVINE MESSAGES THAT TELL ME WHATEVER SHOULD APPEAR IN THE CORNER OF THIS BOX...
...WILL SOON APPEAR WITHIN THE CONFINES OF THIS APARTMENT AS WELL...
AH!
GUGU
Summer
¥3620
RICE LOVER'S BLOG
GUGU CITY
¥980
ナザレ
CRAP! THOSE ADS ALSO HAVE THE PRICE LISTED!!
SAINT YOUNG MEN
Chapter 106
Carboard Moves the World

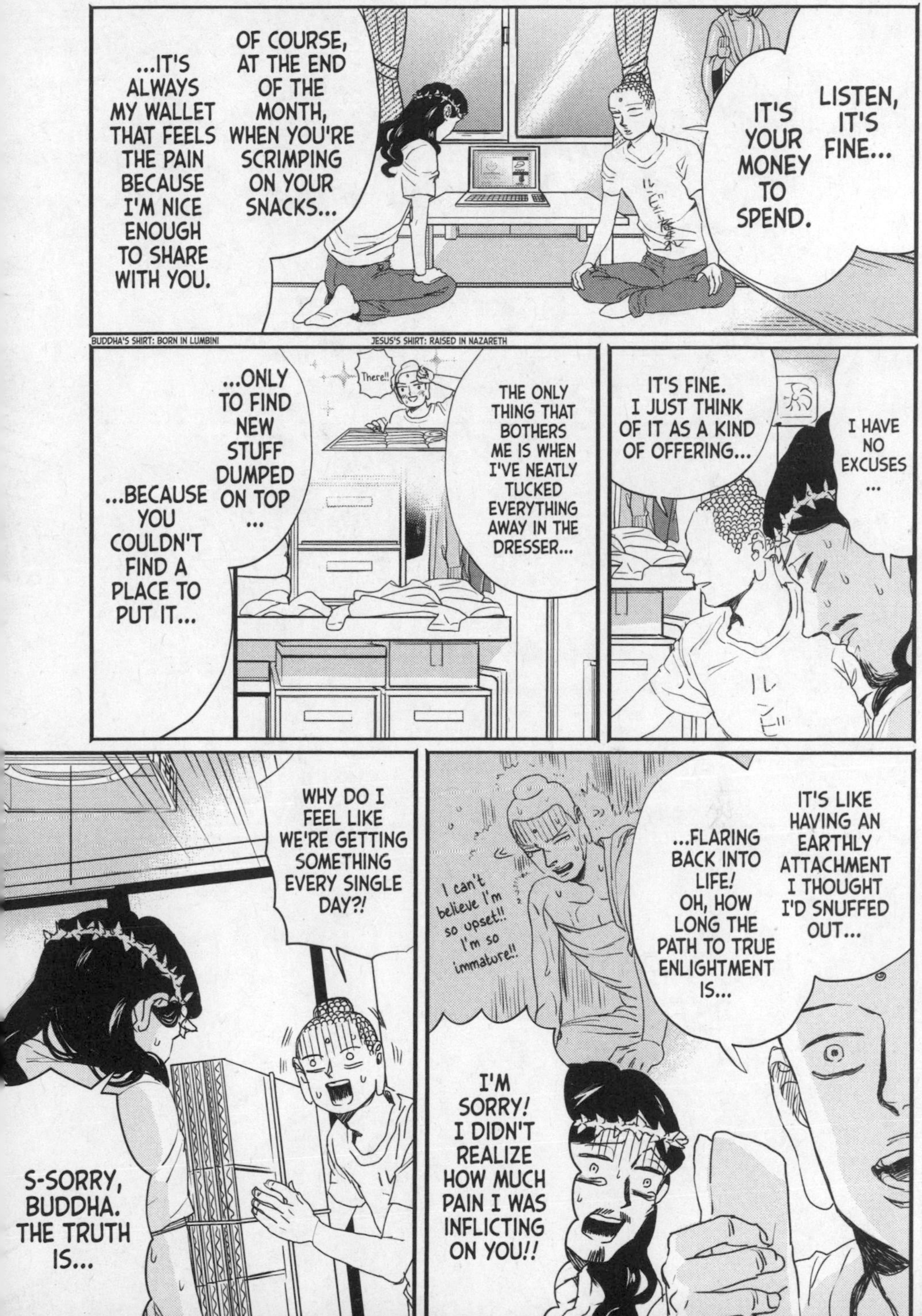
LISTEN, IT'S FINE...
IT'S YOUR MONEY TO SPEND.
OF COURSE, AT THE END OF THE MONTH, WHEN YOU'RE SCRIMPING ON YOUR SNACKS...
...IT'S ALWAYS MY WALLET THAT FEELS THE PAIN BECAUSE I'M NICE ENOUGH TO SHARE WITH YOU.
BUDDHA'S SHIRT: BORN IN LUMBINI
JESUS'S SHIRT: RAISED IN NAZARETH
I HAVE NO EXCUSES...
IT'S FINE. I JUST THINK OF IT AS A KIND OF OFFERING...
THE ONLY THING THAT BOTHERS ME IS WHEN I'VE NEATLY TUCKED EVERYTHING AWAY IN THE DRESSER...
There!!
...ONLY TO FIND NEW STUFF DUMPED ON TOP...
...BECAUSE YOU COULDN'T FIND A PLACE TO PUT IT...
IT'S LIKE HAVING AN EARTHLY ATTACHMENT I THOUGHT I'D SNUFFED OUT...
...FLARING BACK INTO LIFE! OH, HOW LONG THE PATH TO TRUE ENLIGHTMENT IS...
I can't believe I'm so upset!! I'm so immature!!
I'M SORRY! I DIDN'T REALIZE HOW MUCH PAIN I WAS INFLICTING ON YOU!!
WHY DO I FEEL LIKE WE'RE GETTING SOMETHING EVERY SINGLE DAY?!
S-SORRY, BUDDHA. THE TRUTH IS...

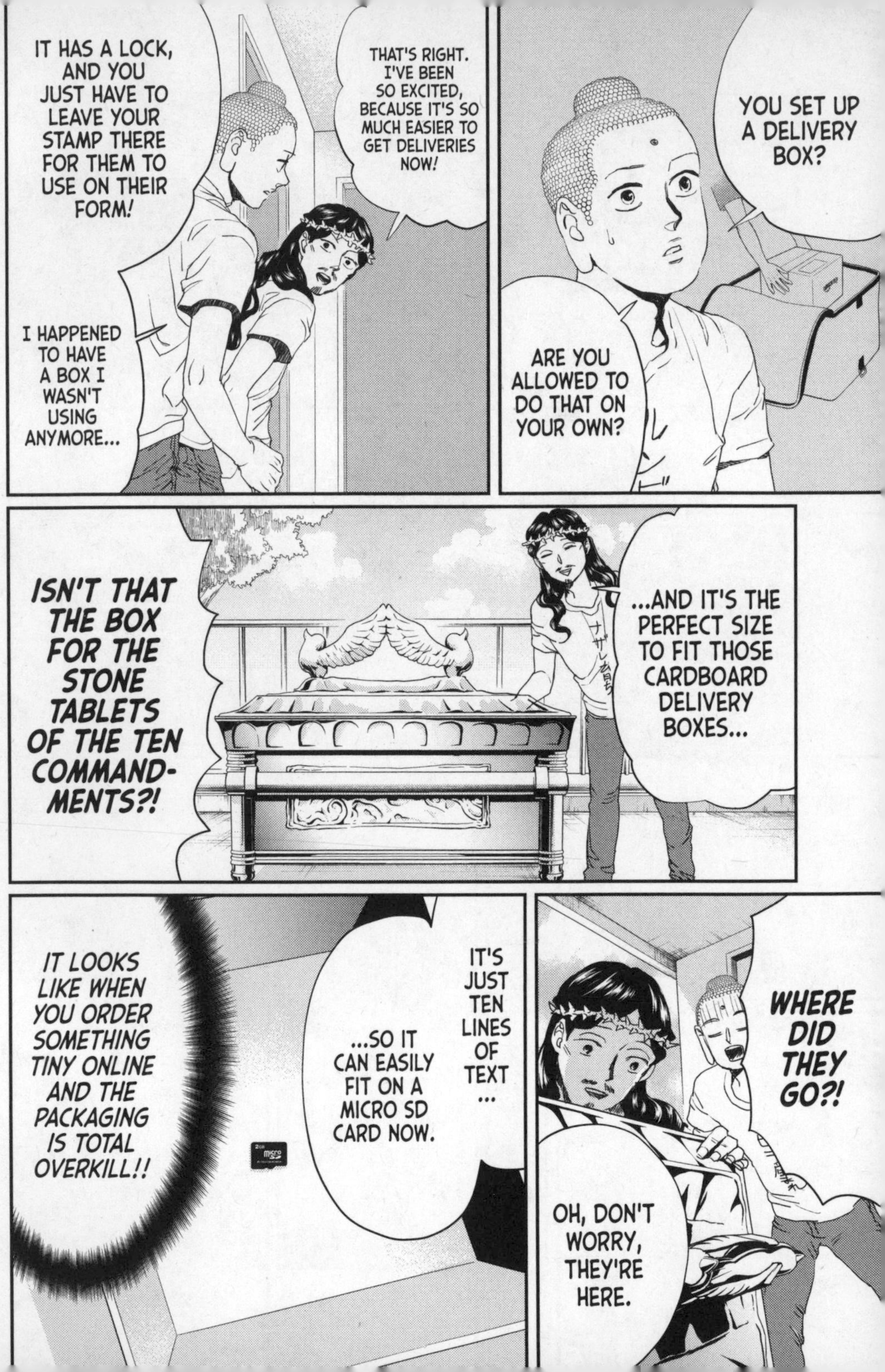
YOU SET UP A DELIVERY BOX?
ARE YOU ALLOWED TO DO THAT ON YOUR OWN?
THAT'S RIGHT. I'VE BEEN SO EXCITED, BECAUSE IT'S SO MUCH EASIER TO GET DELIVERIES NOW!
IT HAS A LOCK, AND YOU JUST HAVE TO LEAVE YOUR STAMP THERE FOR THEM TO USE ON THEIR FORM!
I HAPPENED TO HAVE A BOX I WASN'T USING ANYMORE...
...AND IT'S THE PERFECT SIZE TO FIT THOSE CARDBOARD DELIVERY BOXES...
ISN'T THAT THE BOX FOR THE STONE TABLETS OF THE TEN COMMAND-MENTS?!
WHERE DID THEY GO?!
OH, DON'T WORRY, THEY'RE HERE.
IT'S JUST TEN LINES OF TEXT...
...SO IT CAN EASILY FIT ON A MICRO SD CARD NOW.
IT LOOKS LIKE WHEN YOU ORDER SOMETHING TINY ONLINE AND THE PACKAGING IS TOTAL OVERKILL!!

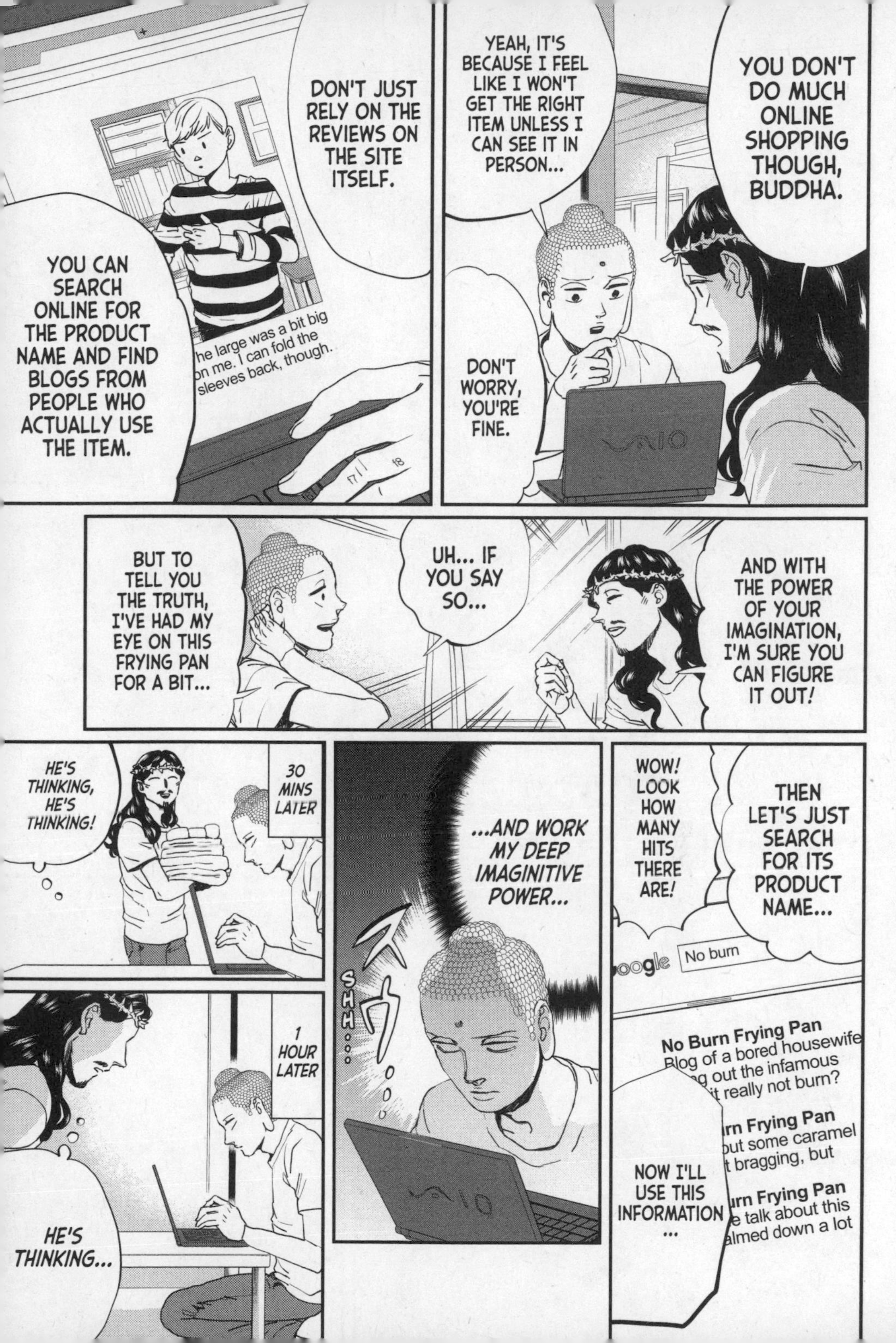
YOU DON'T DO MUCH ONLINE SHOPPING THOUGH, BUDDHA.
YEAH, IT'S BECAUSE I FEEL LIKE I WON'T GET THE RIGHT ITEM UNLESS I CAN SEE IT IN PERSON...
DON'T WORRY, YOU'RE FINE.
DON'T JUST RELY ON THE REVIEWS ON THE SITE ITSELF.
YOU CAN SEARCH ONLINE FOR THE PRODUCT NAME AND FIND BLOGS FROM PEOPLE WHO ACTUALLY USE THE ITEM.
he large was a bit big
on me. I can fold the
sleeves back, though.
AND WITH THE POWER OF YOUR IMAGINATION, I'M SURE YOU CAN FIGURE IT OUT!
UH... IF YOU SAY SO...
BUT TO TELL YOU THE TRUTH, I'VE HAD MY EYE ON THIS FRYING PAN FOR A BIT...
THEN LET'S JUST SEARCH FOR ITS PRODUCT NAME...
WOW! LOOK HOW MANY HITS THERE ARE!
oogle
No burn
No Burn Frying Pan
Blog of a bored housewife
rn Frying Pan
rn Frying Pan
NOW I'LL USE THIS INFORMATION ...
...AND WORK MY DEEP IMAGINITIVE POWER...
SHH...
30 MINS LATER
HE'S THINKING, HE'S THINKING!
1 HOUR LATER
HE'S THINKING...

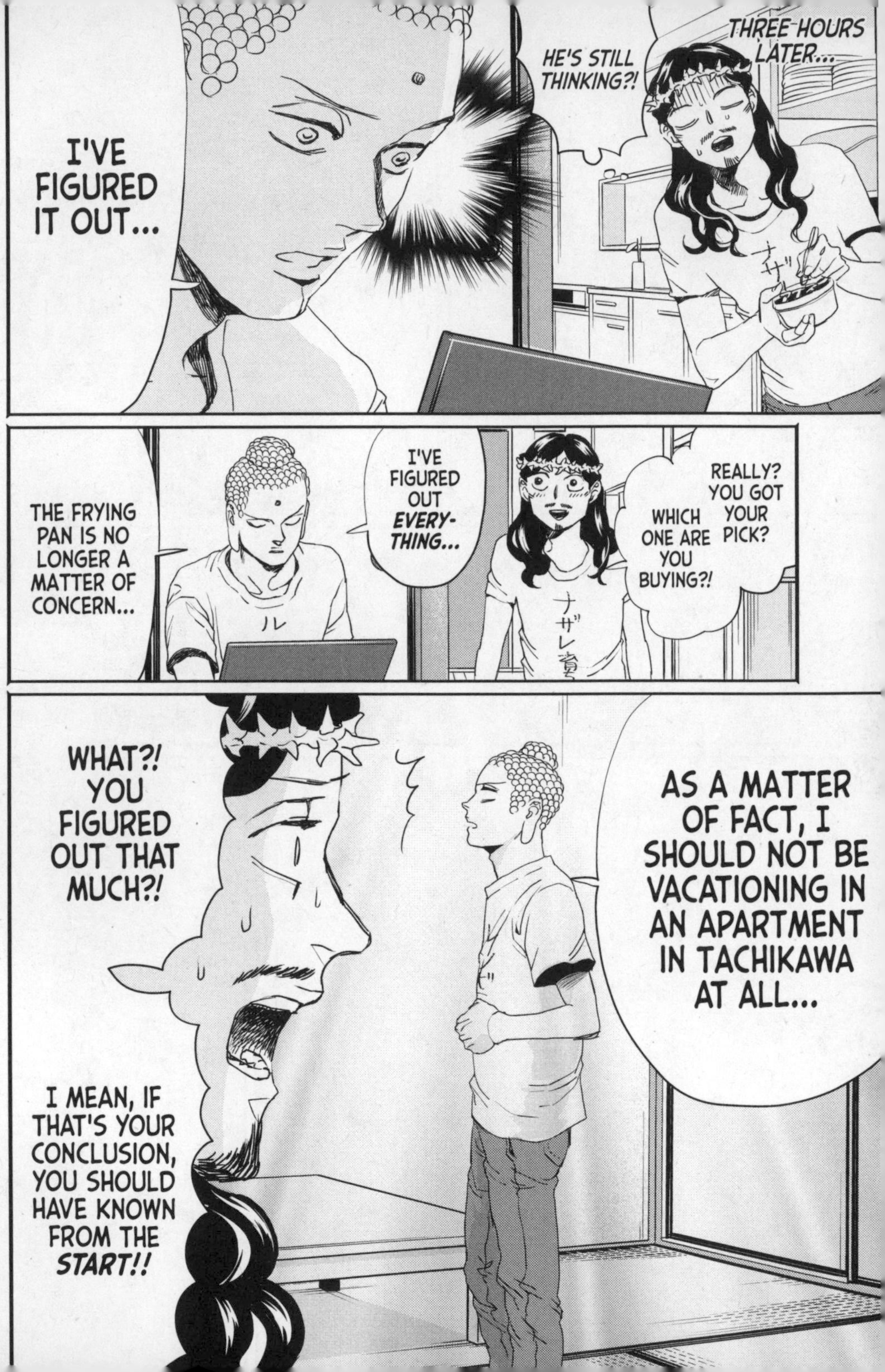
THREE HOURS LATER...
HE'S STILL THINKING?!
I'VE FIGURED IT OUT...
REALLY? YOU GOT YOUR PICK?
WHICH ONE ARE YOU BUYING?!
I'VE FIGURED OUT *EVERYTHING...*
THE FRYING PAN IS NO LONGER A MATTER OF CONCERN...
AS A MATTER OF FACT, I SHOULD NOT BE VACATIONING IN AN APARTMENT IN TACHIKAWA AT ALL...
WHAT?! YOU FIGURED OUT THAT MUCH?!
I MEAN, IF THAT'S YOUR CONCLUSION, YOU SHOULD HAVE KNOWN FROM THE *START!!*

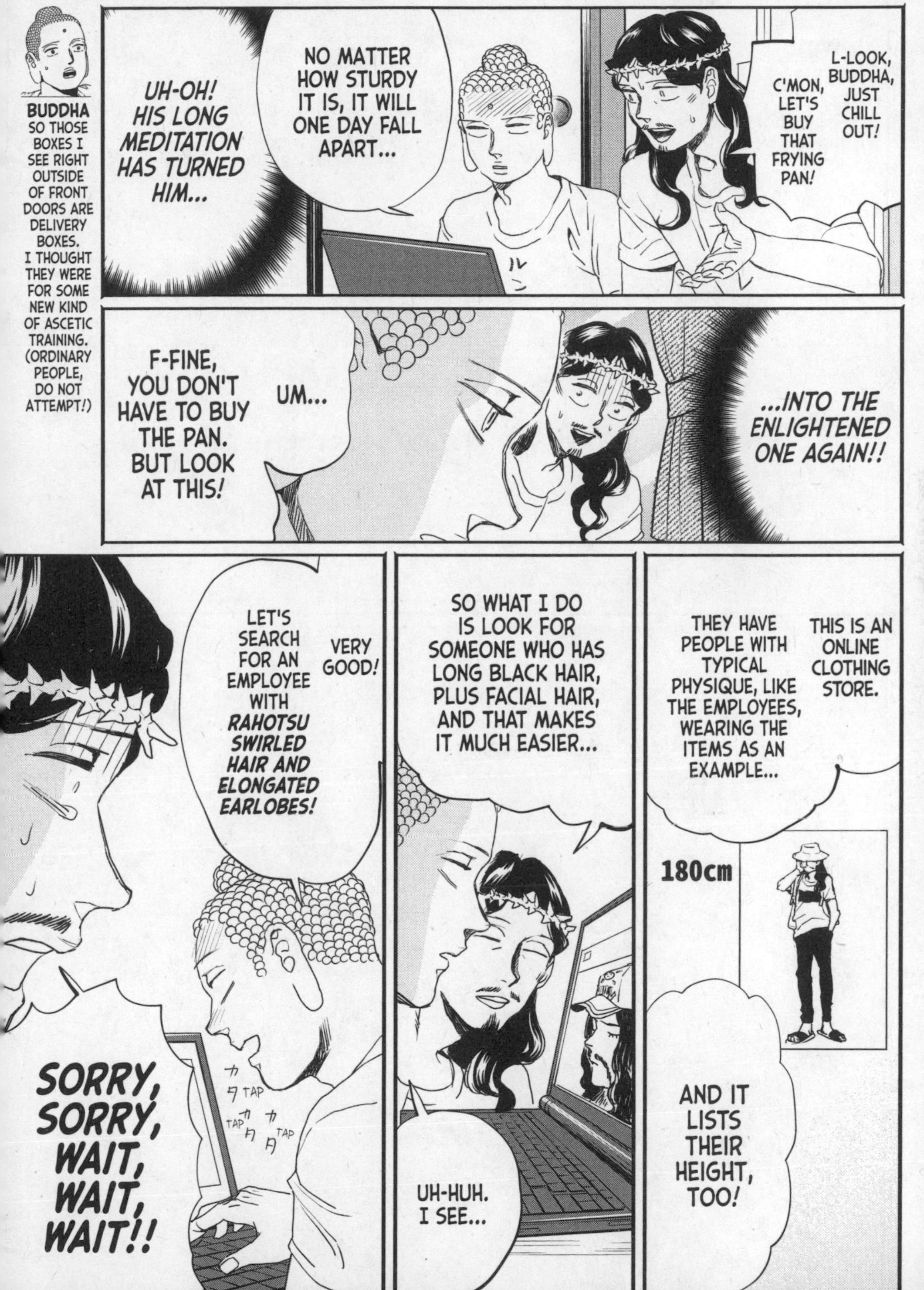
L-LOOK, BUDDHA, JUST CHILL OUT!
C'MON, LET'S BUY THAT FRYING PAN!
NO MATTER HOW STURDY IT IS, IT WILL ONE DAY FALL APART...
UH-OH! HIS LONG MEDITATION HAS TURNED HIM...
...INTO THE ENLIGHTENED ONE AGAIN!!
UM...
F-FINE, YOU DON'T HAVE TO BUY THE PAN. BUT LOOK AT THIS!
BUDDHA SO THOSE BOXES I SEE RIGHT OUTSIDE OF FRONT DOORS ARE DELIVERY BOXES. I THOUGHT THEY WERE FOR SOME NEW KIND OF ASCETIC TRAINING. (ORDINARY PEOPLE, DO NOT ATTEMPT!)
THIS IS AN ONLINE CLOTHING STORE.
THEY HAVE PEOPLE WITH TYPICAL PHYSIQUE, LIKE THE EMPLOYEES, WEARING THE ITEMS AS AN EXAMPLE...
180cm
AND IT LISTS THEIR HEIGHT, TOO!
SO WHAT I DO IS LOOK FOR SOMEONE WHO HAS LONG BLACK HAIR, PLUS FACIAL HAIR, AND THAT MAKES IT MUCH EASIER...
UH-HUH. I SEE...
VERY GOOD!
LET'S SEARCH FOR AN EMPLOYEE WITH RAHOTSU SWIRLED HAIR AND ELONGATED EARLOBES!
カタ TAP カタ TAP カタ TAP
SORRY, SORRY, WAIT, WAIT, WAIT!!

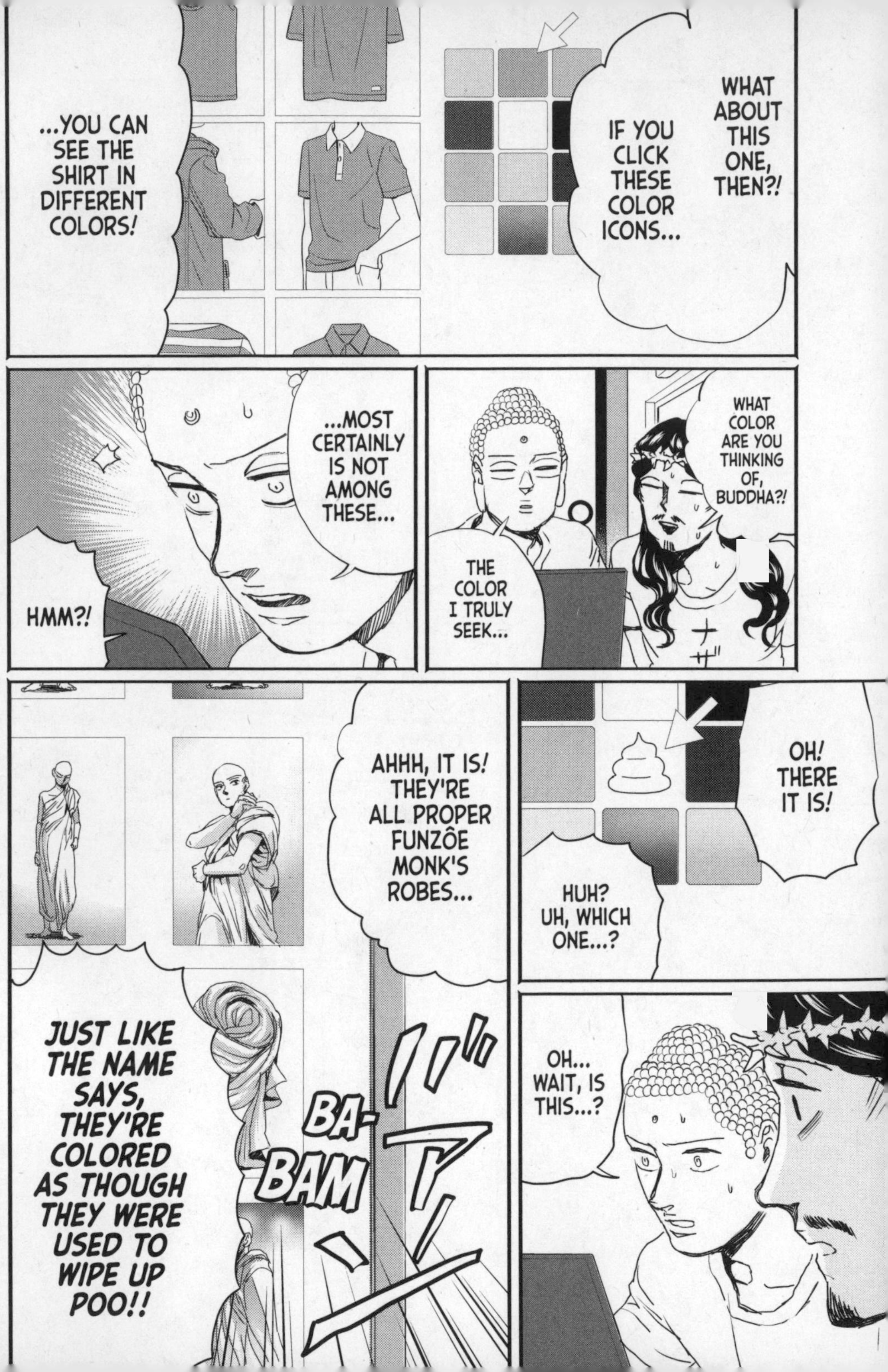
WHAT ABOUT THIS ONE, THEN?!
IF YOU CLICK THESE COLOR ICONS...
...YOU CAN SEE THE SHIRT IN DIFFERENT COLORS!
WHAT COLOR ARE YOU THINKING OF, BUDDHA?!
ナザ
THE COLOR I TRULY SEEK...
...MOST CERTAINLY IS NOT AMONG THESE...
HMM?!
OH! THERE IT IS!
HUH? UH, WHICH ONE...?
OH... WAIT, IS THIS...?
AHHH, IT IS! THEY'RE ALL PROPER FUNZÔE MONK'S ROBES...
JUST LIKE THE NAME SAYS, THEY'RE COLORED AS THOUGH THEY WERE USED TO WIPE UP POO!!
BA-BAM

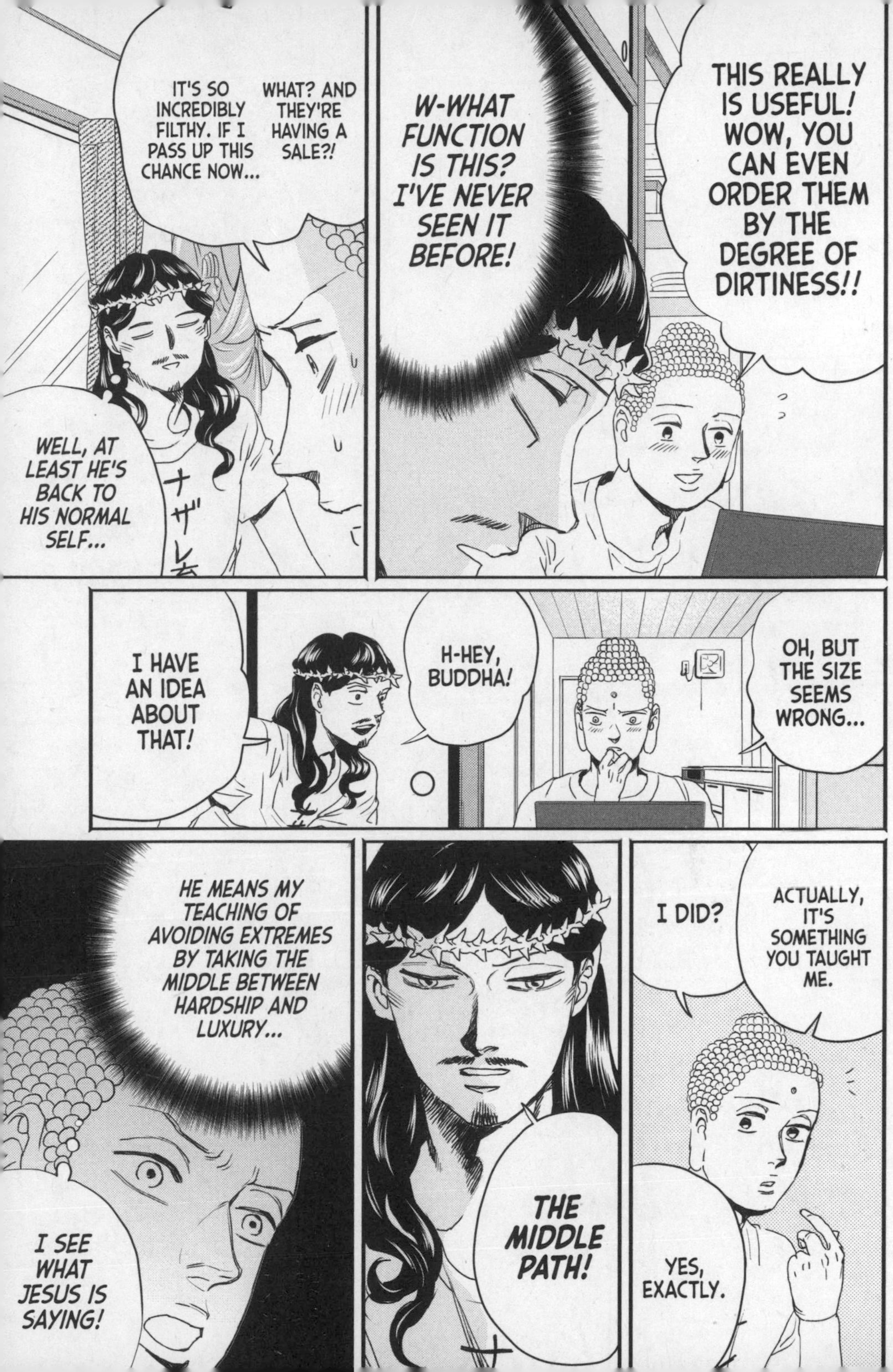
THIS REALLY IS USEFUL! WOW, YOU CAN EVEN ORDER THEM BY THE DEGREE OF DIRTINESS!!
W-WHAT FUNCTION IS THIS? I'VE NEVER SEEN IT BEFORE!
WHAT? AND THEY'RE HAVING A SALE?!
IT'S SO INCREDIBLY FILTHY. IF I PASS UP THIS CHANCE NOW...
WELL, AT LEAST HE'S BACK TO HIS NORMAL SELF...
OH, BUT THE SIZE SEEMS WRONG...
H-HEY, BUDDHA!
I HAVE AN IDEA ABOUT THAT!
ACTUALLY, IT'S SOMETHING YOU TAUGHT ME.
I DID?
YES, EXACTLY.
THE MIDDLE PATH!
HE MEANS MY TEACHING OF AVOIDING EXTREMES BY TAKING THE MIDDLE BETWEEN HARDSHIP AND LUXURY...
I SEE WHAT JESUS IS SAYING!

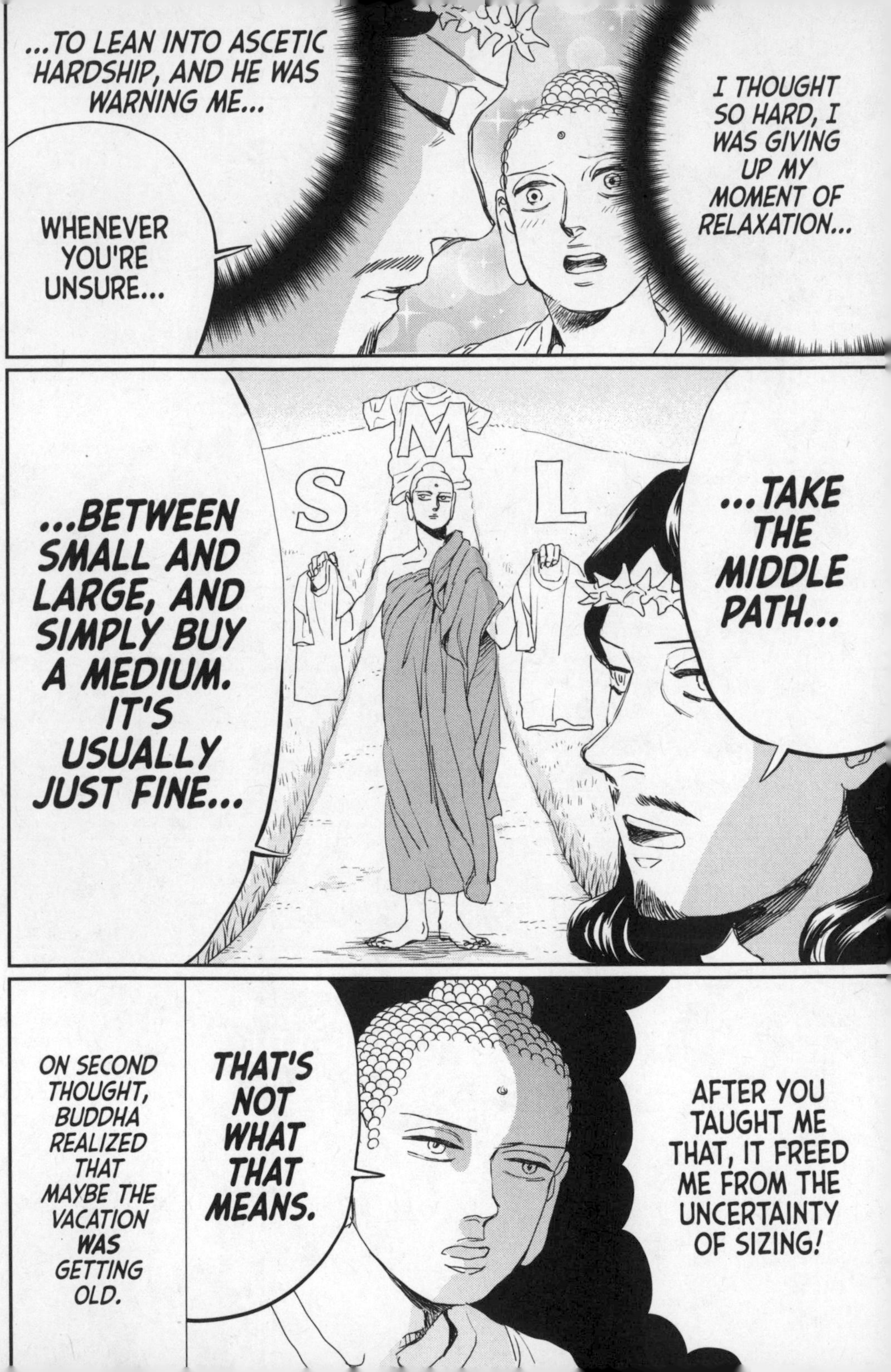
I THOUGHT SO HARD, I WAS GIVING UP MY MOMENT OF RELAXATION...
...TO LEAN INTO ASCETIC HARDSHIP, AND HE WAS WARNING ME...
WHENEVER YOU'RE UNSURE...
...TAKE THE MIDDLE PATH...
M
L
S
...BETWEEN SMALL AND LARGE, AND SIMPLY BUY A MEDIUM. IT'S USUALLY JUST FINE...
AFTER YOU TAUGHT ME THAT, IT FREED ME FROM THE UNCERTAINTY OF SIZING!
THAT'S NOT WHAT THAT MEANS.
ON SECOND THOUGHT, BUDDHA REALIZED THAT MAYBE THE VACATION WAS GETTING OLD.

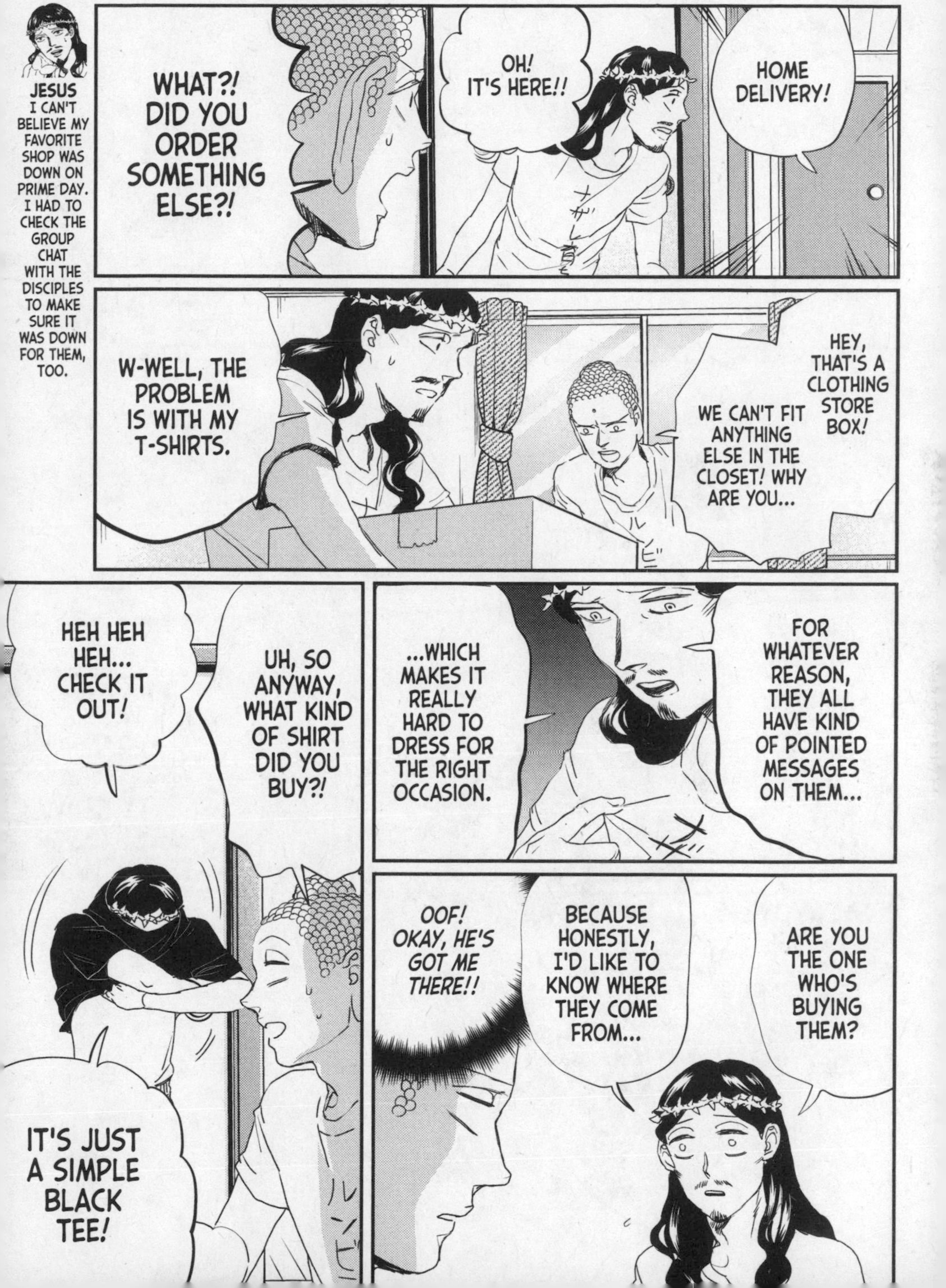
JESUS
I CAN'T BELIEVE MY FAVORITE SHOP WAS DOWN ON PRIME DAY. I HAD TO CHECK THE GROUP CHAT WITH THE DISCIPLES TO MAKE SURE IT WAS DOWN FOR THEM, TOO.
HOME DELIVERY!
OH! IT'S HERE!!
WHAT?! DID YOU ORDER SOMETHING ELSE?!
HEY, THAT'S A CLOTHING STORE BOX!
WE CAN'T FIT ANYTHING ELSE IN THE CLOSET! WHY ARE YOU...
W-WELL, THE PROBLEM IS WITH MY T-SHIRTS.
FOR WHATEVER REASON, THEY ALL HAVE KIND OF POINTED MESSAGES ON THEM...
...WHICH MAKES IT REALLY HARD TO DRESS FOR THE RIGHT OCCASION.
ARE YOU THE ONE WHO'S BUYING THEM?
BECAUSE HONESTLY, I'D LIKE TO KNOW WHERE THEY COME FROM...
OOF! OKAY, HE'S GOT ME THERE!!
UH, SO ANYWAY, WHAT KIND OF SHIRT DID YOU BUY?!
HEH HEH HEH... CHECK IT OUT!
IT'S JUST A SIMPLE BLACK TEE!

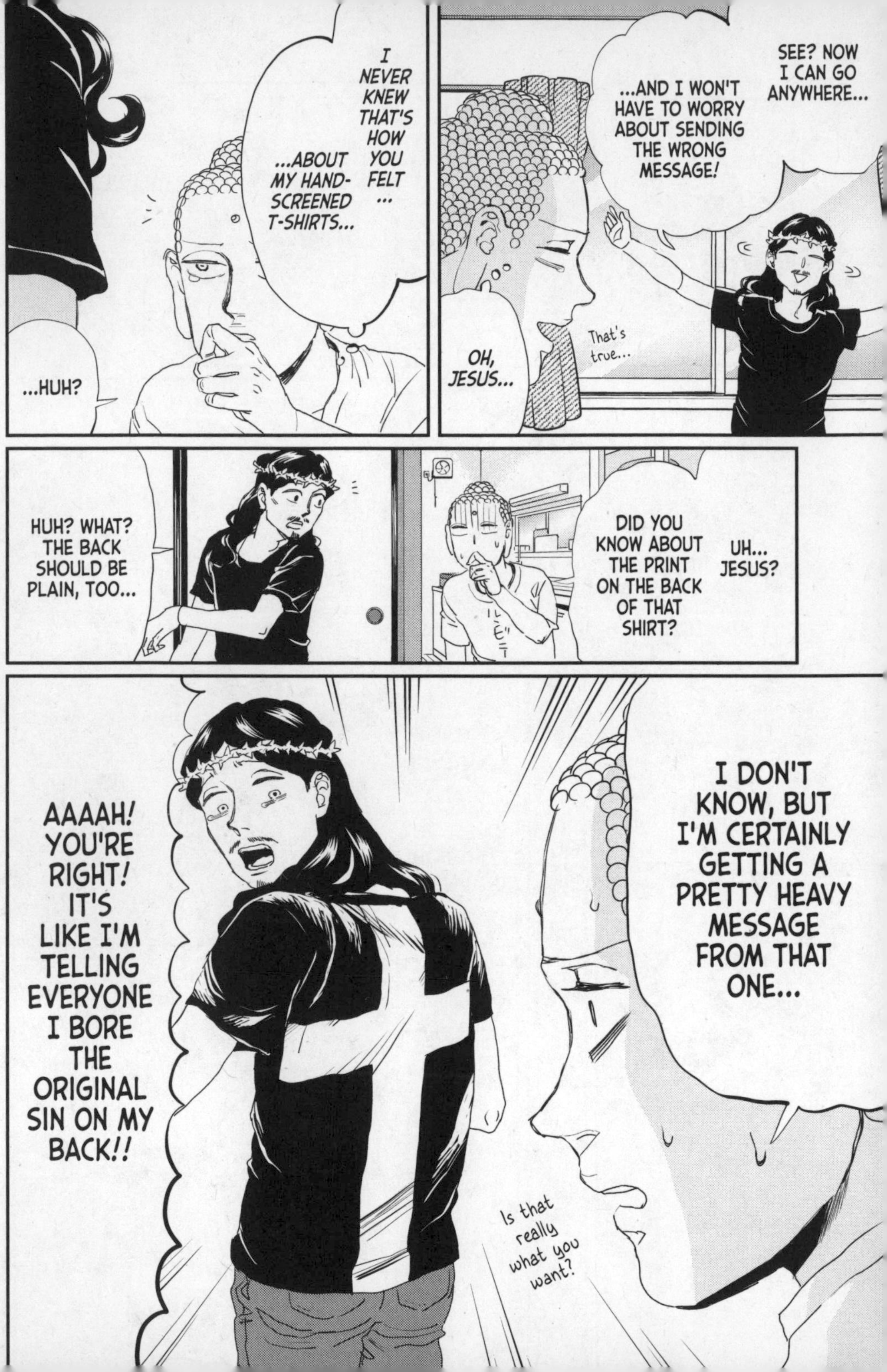
SEE? NOW I CAN GO ANYWHERE...
...AND I WON'T HAVE TO WORRY ABOUT SENDING THE WRONG MESSAGE!
That's true...
OH, JESUS...
I NEVER KNEW THAT'S HOW YOU FELT ...
...ABOUT MY HAND-SCREENED T-SHIRTS...
...HUH?
UH... JESUS?
DID YOU KNOW ABOUT THE PRINT ON THE BACK OF THAT SHIRT?
HUH? WHAT? THE BACK SHOULD BE PLAIN, TOO...
I DON'T KNOW, BUT I'M CERTAINLY GETTING A PRETTY HEAVY MESSAGE FROM THAT ONE...
AAAAH! YOU'RE RIGHT! IT'S LIKE I'M TELLING EVERYONE I BORE THE ORIGINAL SIN ON MY BACK!!
Is that really what you want?

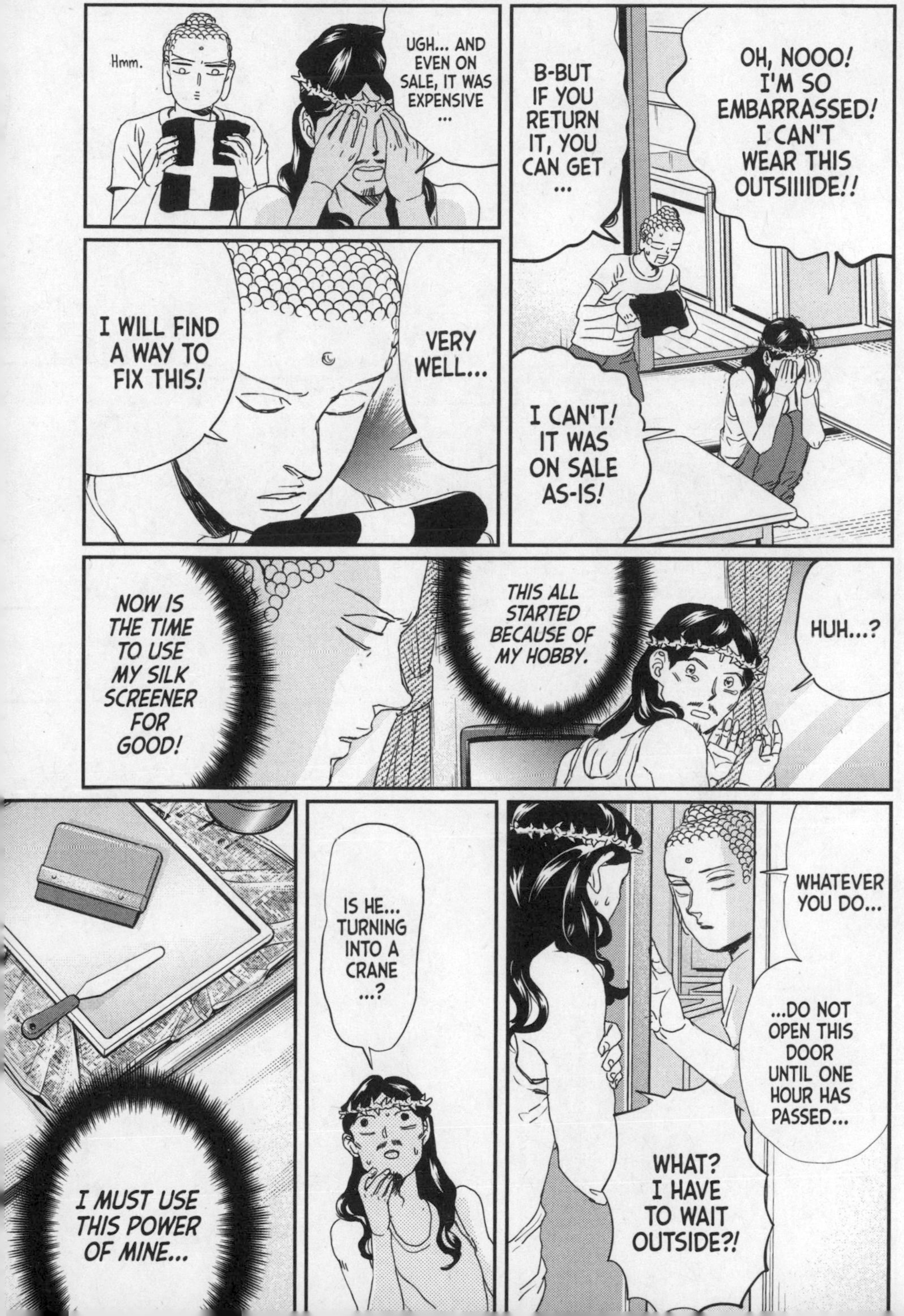
OH, NOOO! I'M SO EMBARRASSED! I CAN'T WEAR THIS OUTSIIIIDE!!
B-BUT IF YOU RETURN IT, YOU CAN GET ...
I CAN'T! IT WAS ON SALE AS-IS!
UGH... AND EVEN ON SALE, IT WAS EXPENSIVE ...
Hmm.
VERY WELL...
I WILL FIND A WAY TO FIX THIS!
HUH...?
THIS ALL STARTED BECAUSE OF MY HOBBY.
NOW IS THE TIME TO USE MY SILK SCREENER FOR GOOD!
WHATEVER YOU DO...
...DO NOT OPEN THIS DOOR UNTIL ONE HOUR HAS PASSED...
WHAT? I HAVE TO WAIT OUTSIDE?!
IS HE... TURNING INTO A CRANE ...?
I MUST USE THIS POWER OF MINE...

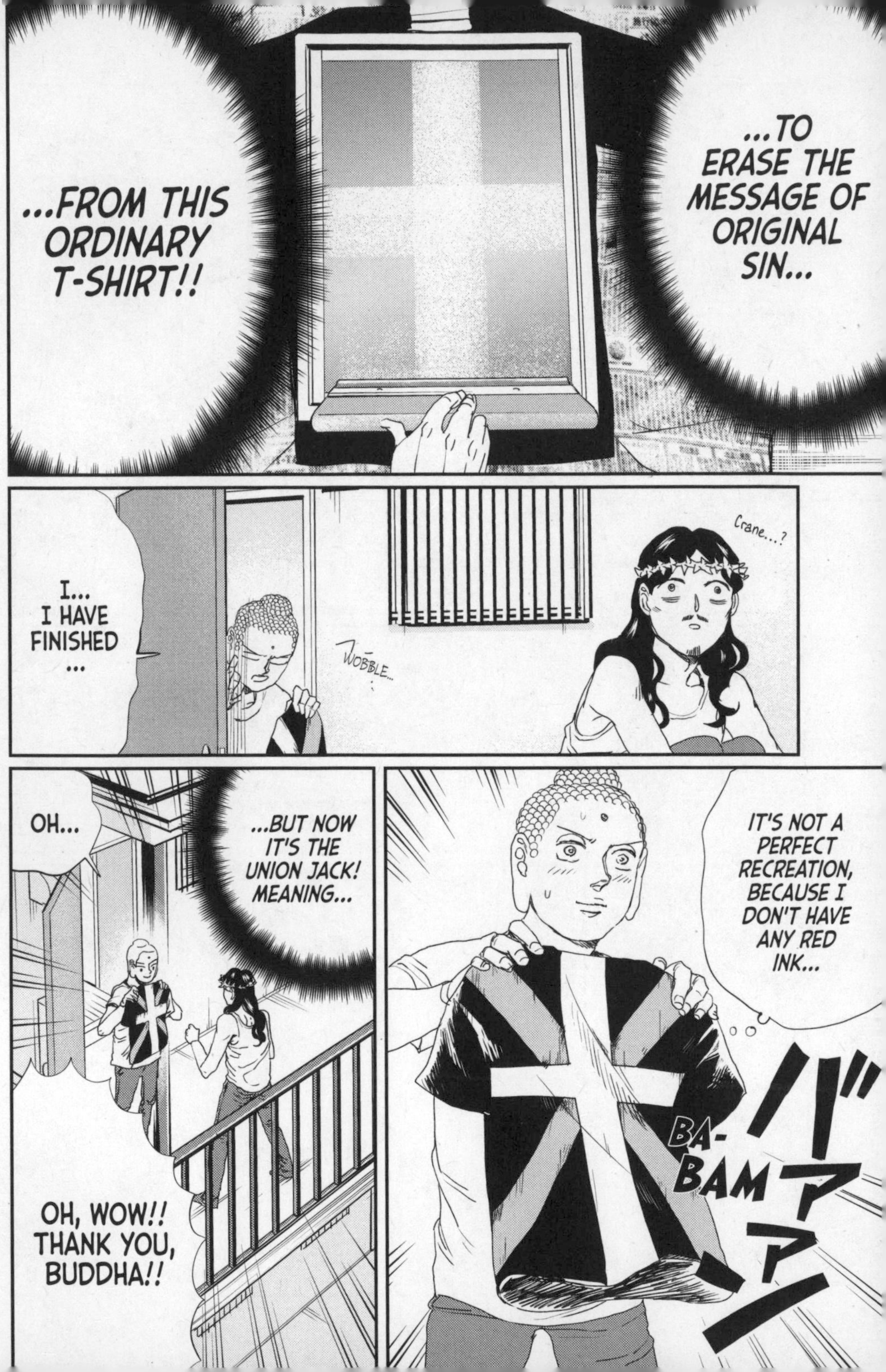
...TO ERASE THE MESSAGE OF ORIGINAL SIN...
...FROM THIS ORDINARY T-SHIRT!!
Crane...?
I... I HAVE FINISHED...
WOBBLE...
IT'S NOT A PERFECT RECREATION, BECAUSE I DON'T HAVE ANY RED INK...
バアアー
BA-BAM
...BUT NOW IT'S THE UNION JACK! MEANING...
OH...
OH, WOW!! THANK YOU, BUDDHA!!

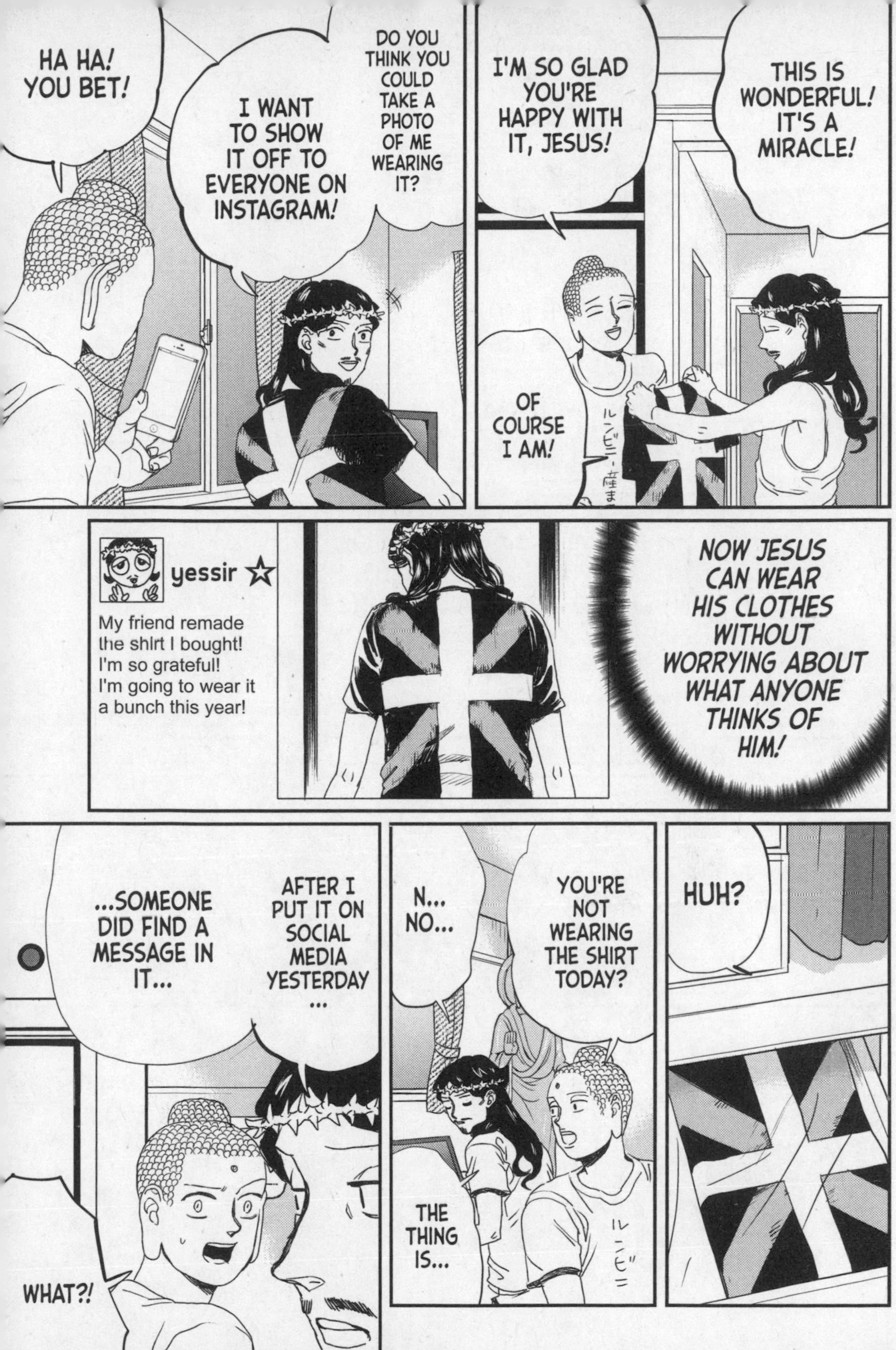
THIS IS WONDERFUL! IT'S A MIRACLE!
I'M SO GLAD YOU'RE HAPPY WITH IT, JESUS!
OF COURSE I AM!
DO YOU THINK YOU COULD TAKE A PHOTO OF ME WEARING IT?
I WANT TO SHOW IT OFF TO EVERYONE ON INSTAGRAM!
HA HA! YOU BET!
NOW JESUS CAN WEAR HIS CLOTHES WITHOUT WORRYING ABOUT WHAT ANYONE THINKS OF HIM!
yessir ☆
My friend remade the shirt I bought! I'm so grateful! I'm going to wear it a bunch this year!
HUH?
YOU'RE NOT WEARING THE SHIRT TODAY?
N... NO...
ルンビニ
THE THING IS...
AFTER I PUT IT ON SOCIAL MEDIA YESTERDAY ...
...SOMEONE DID FIND A MESSAGE IN IT...
WHAT?!

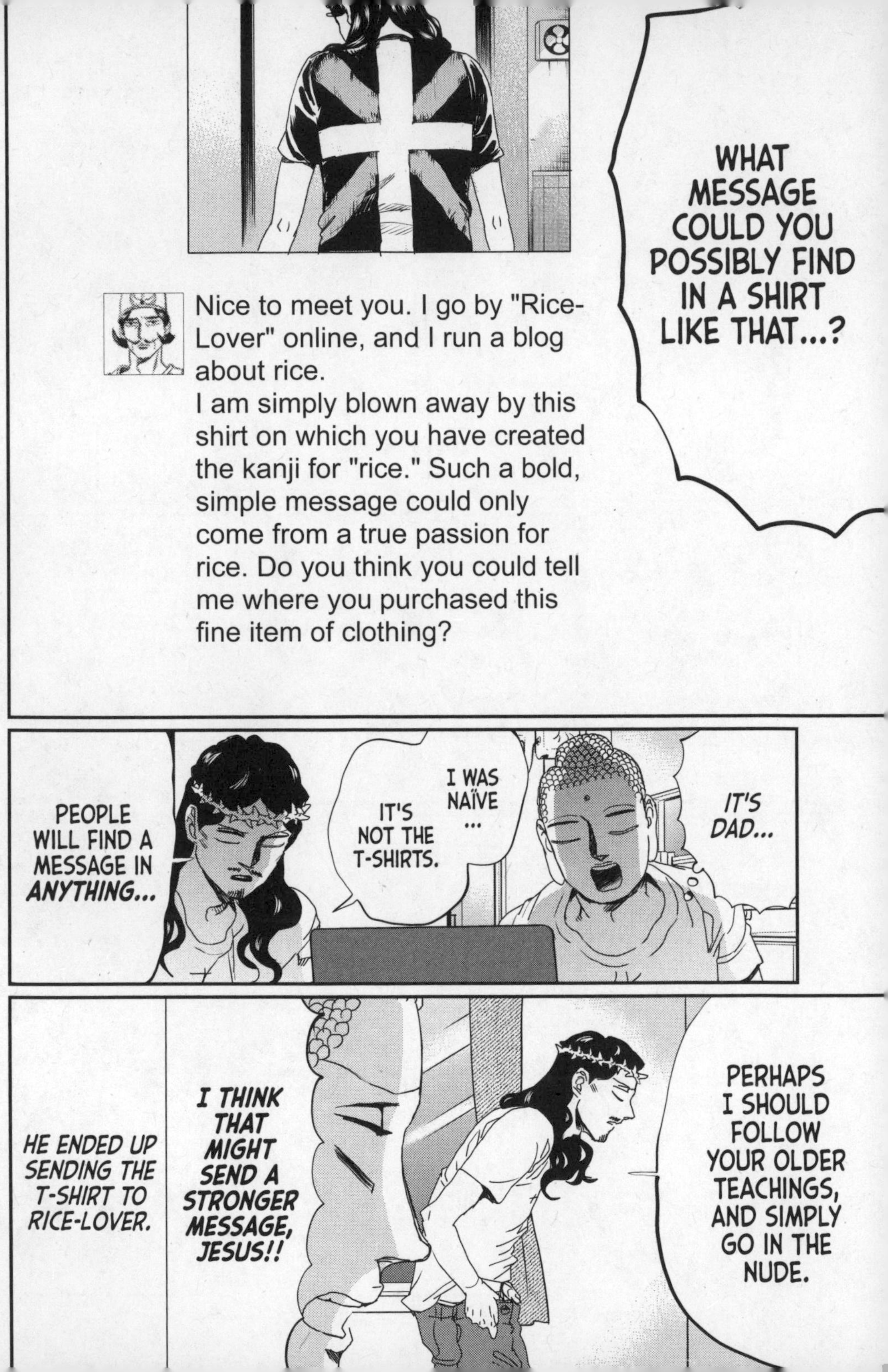
WHAT MESSAGE COULD YOU POSSIBLY FIND IN A SHIRT LIKE THAT...?
Nice to meet you. I go by "Rice-Lover" online, and I run a blog about rice.
I am simply blown away by this shirt on which you have created the kanji for "rice." Such a bold, simple message could only come from a true passion for rice. Do you think you could tell me where you purchased this fine item of clothing?
IT'S DAD...
I WAS NAÏVE ...
IT'S NOT THE T-SHIRTS.
PEOPLE WILL FIND A MESSAGE IN ANYTHING...
PERHAPS I SHOULD FOLLOW YOUR OLDER TEACHINGS, AND SIMPLY GO IN THE NUDE.
I THINK THAT MIGHT SEND A STRONGER MESSAGE, JESUS!!
HE ENDED UP SENDING THE T-SHIRT TO RICE-LOVER.

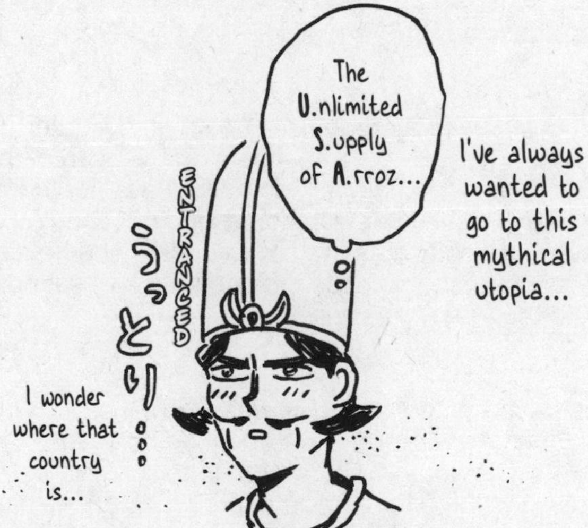
The U.nlimited S.upply of A.rroz...
I've always wanted to go to this mythical utopia...
ENTRANCED
うっとり...
I wonder where that country is...

SAINT ☆ YOUNG MEN

CHAPTER 106 TRANSLATION NOTES

Donkey prophecy, page 37
A reference to the story of Jesus's triumphal entry into Jerusalem. The Gospels each describe instructions that Jesus gives the disciples regarding a donkey and its child that will be found outside of a village. This donkey is the creature he will ride into Jerusalem.

Lumbini & Nazareth, page 39
As the shirts say, these are important locations in the lives of Gautama Buddha and Jesus Christ. Lumbini is a place in present-day Nepal, close to the border with India, where Siddhartha Gautama is said to have been born. Nazareth is famously the place where Jesus grew up, and he is often styled "Jesus of Nazareth" in the New Testament for that reason.

Funzôe, page 44
One of the Japanese terms for the *kesa* or *kasaya*, the humble brown-colored robes of Buddhist monks. When entering the priesthood, monks give up their worldly possessions, and were classically robed in discarded cloth scraps, the clothes of the deceased left at a morgue, or cloth that had no use but to wipe up filth. For this reason, one of the terms for these robes in Japanese is *funzôe*, meaning "excrement-cleaning robes."

Crane, page 49
A classic Japanese folktale. A man saves a crane from death, and is later visited by a beautiful woman who claims she is his wife, in one version of the tale. The woman often claims she must go into her room and he is not to look inside, until she eventually emerges days later with some kind of riches (rice, or fine cloth). One day, the man's curiosity gets the better of him, and he looks inside before she is done. He discovers that it was the crane he had saved, who flies away, having returned the favor.

USA, page 53
In Japanese, the kanji used to describe the United States of America (as opposed to saying the phonetic *A-me-ri-ka*) is pronounced *beikoku*, which means "country of rice." This is not a literal reference to rice, but a holdover from an older form of using kanji to represent foreign countries based on pronunciation. Buddha's father, who died two thousand years before the USA was founded, would of course be curious about what this magical "rice country" is like.

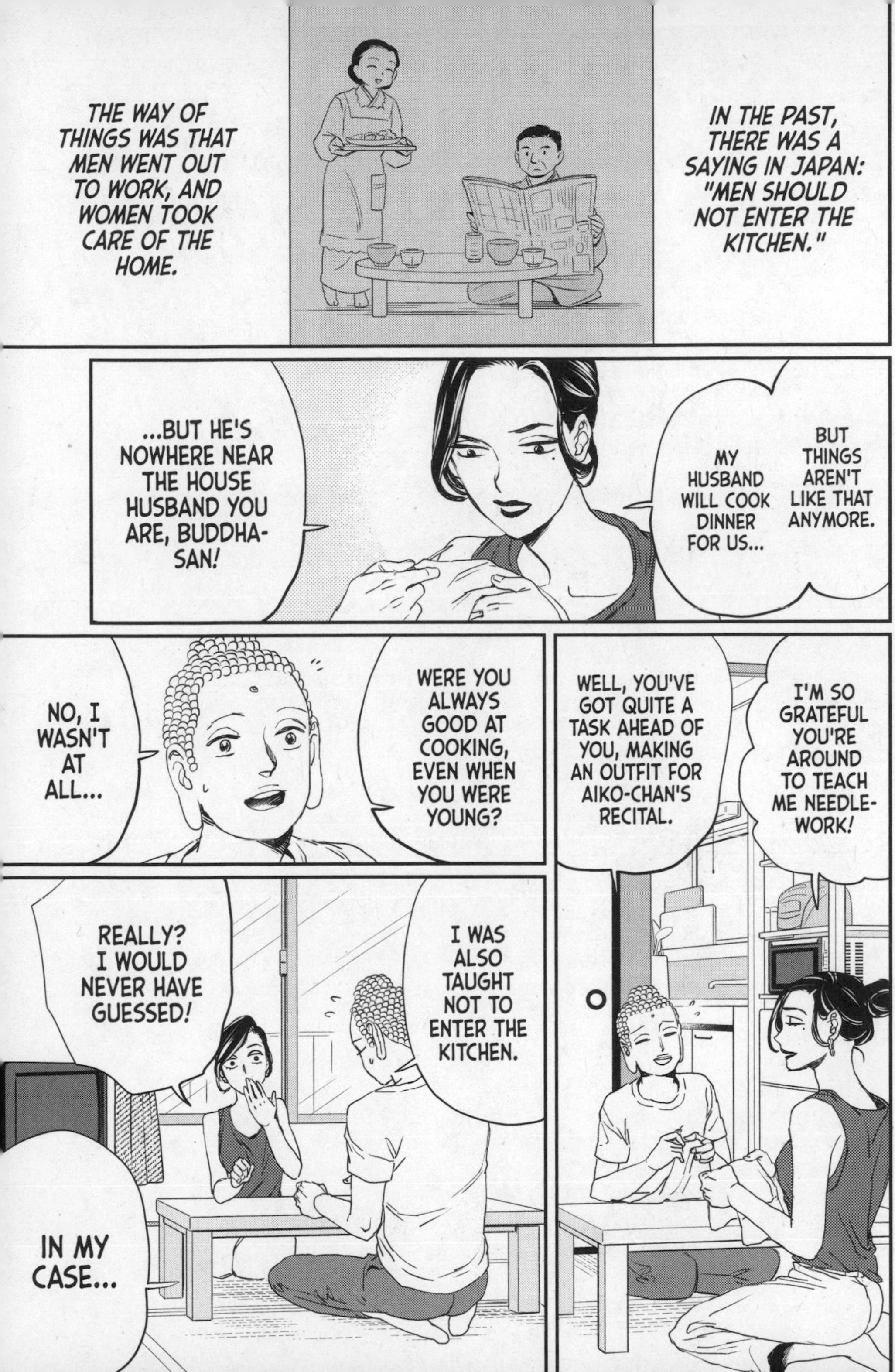
IN THE PAST, THERE WAS A SAYING IN JAPAN: "MEN SHOULD NOT ENTER THE KITCHEN."
THE WAY OF THINGS WAS THAT MEN WENT OUT TO WORK, AND WOMEN TOOK CARE OF THE HOME.
BUT THINGS AREN'T LIKE THAT ANYMORE.
MY HUSBAND WILL COOK DINNER FOR US...
...BUT HE'S NOWHERE NEAR THE HOUSE HUSBAND YOU ARE, BUDDHA-SAN!
I'M SO GRATEFUL YOU'RE AROUND TO TEACH ME NEEDLE-WORK!
WELL, YOU'VE GOT QUITE A TASK AHEAD OF YOU, MAKING AN OUTFIT FOR AIKO-CHAN'S RECITAL.
WERE YOU ALWAYS GOOD AT COOKING, EVEN WHEN YOU WERE YOUNG?
NO, I WASN'T AT ALL...
I WAS ALSO TAUGHT NOT TO ENTER THE KITCHEN.
REALLY? I WOULD NEVER HAVE GUESSED!
IN MY CASE...

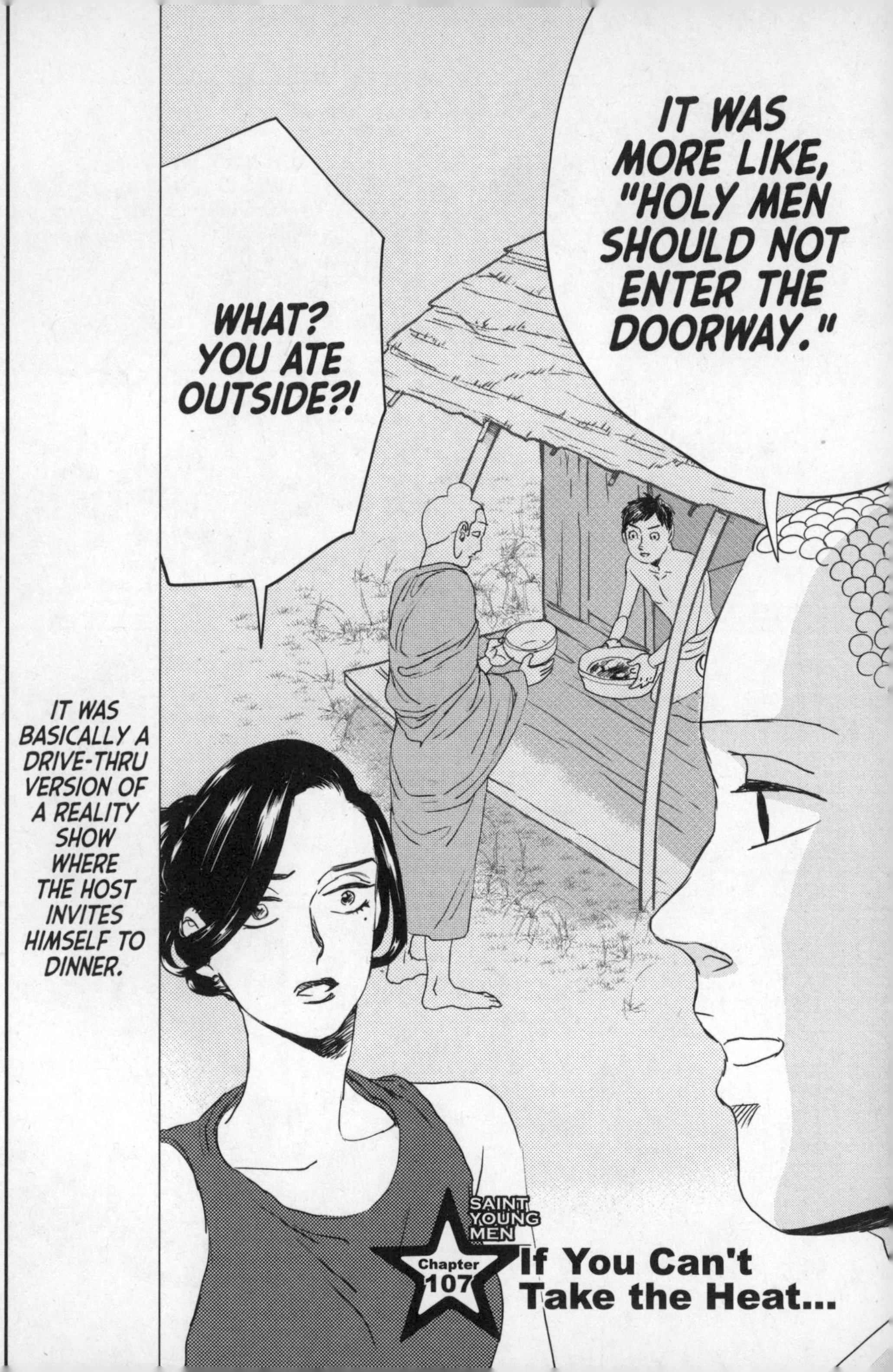
IT WAS MORE LIKE, "HOLY MEN SHOULD NOT ENTER THE DOORWAY."
WHAT? YOU ATE OUTSIDE?!
IT WAS BASICALLY A DRIVE-THRU VERSION OF A REALITY SHOW WHERE THE HOST INVITES HIMSELF TO DINNER.
SAINT YOUNG MEN
Chapter 107
If You Can't Take the Heat...

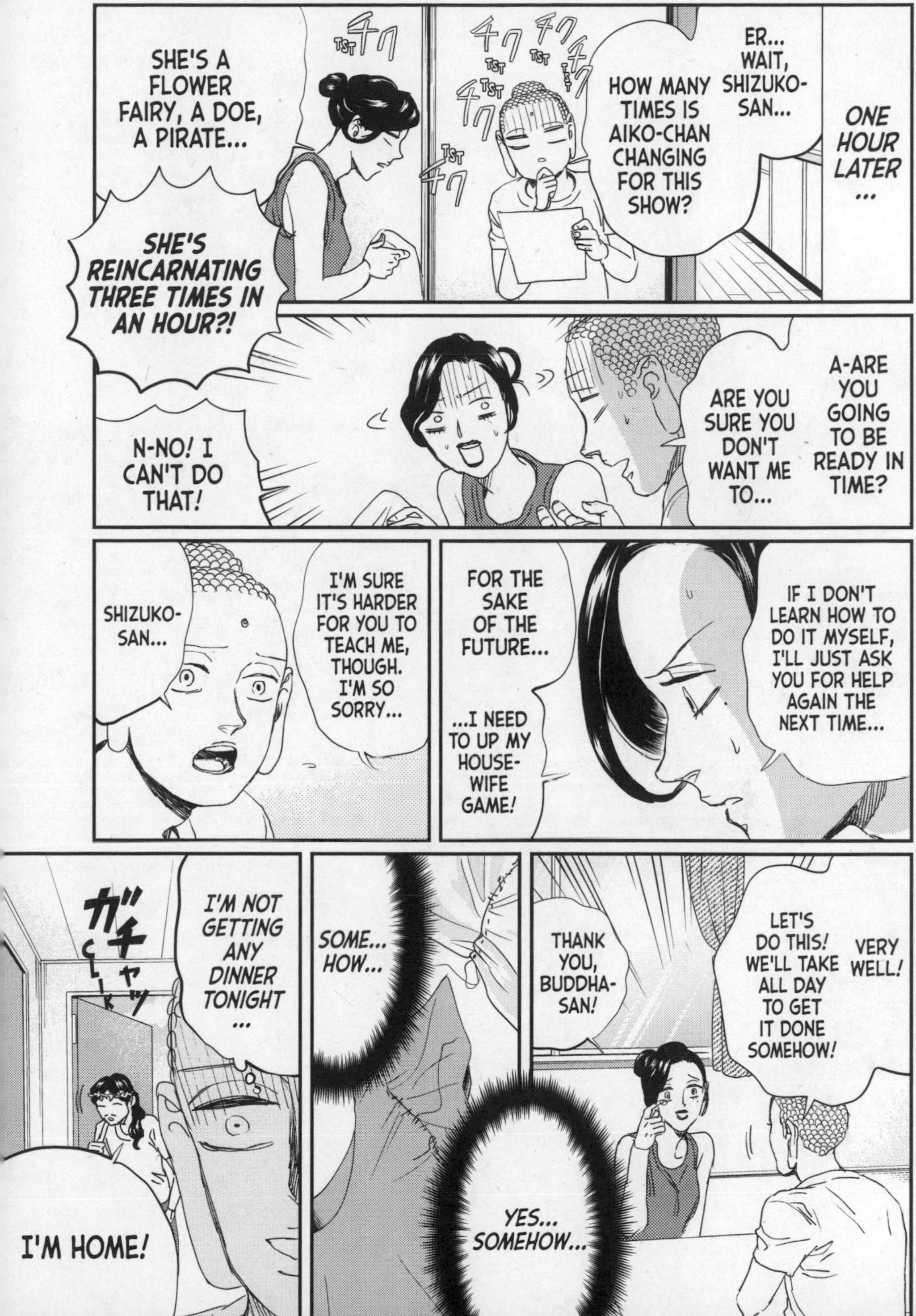
ONE HOUR LATER...
ER... WAIT, SHIZUKO-SAN...
HOW MANY TIMES IS AIKO-CHAN CHANGING FOR THIS SHOW?
TST TST TST TST TST TST
SHE'S A FLOWER FAIRY, A DOE, A PIRATE...
SHE'S REINCARNATING THREE TIMES IN AN HOUR?!
A-ARE YOU GOING TO BE READY IN TIME?
ARE YOU SURE YOU DON'T WANT ME TO...
N-NO! I CAN'T DO THAT!
IF I DON'T LEARN HOW TO DO IT MYSELF, I'LL JUST ASK YOU FOR HELP AGAIN THE NEXT TIME...
FOR THE SAKE OF THE FUTURE...
...I NEED TO UP MY HOUSE-WIFE GAME!
I'M SURE IT'S HARDER FOR YOU TO TEACH ME, THOUGH. I'M SO SORRY...
SHIZUKO-SAN...
VERY WELL!
LET'S DO THIS! WE'LL TAKE ALL DAY TO GET IT DONE SOMEHOW!
THANK YOU, BUDDHA-SAN!
SOME... HOW...
YES... SOMEHOW...
I'M NOT GETTING ANY DINNER TONIGHT...
CLICK
I'M HOME!

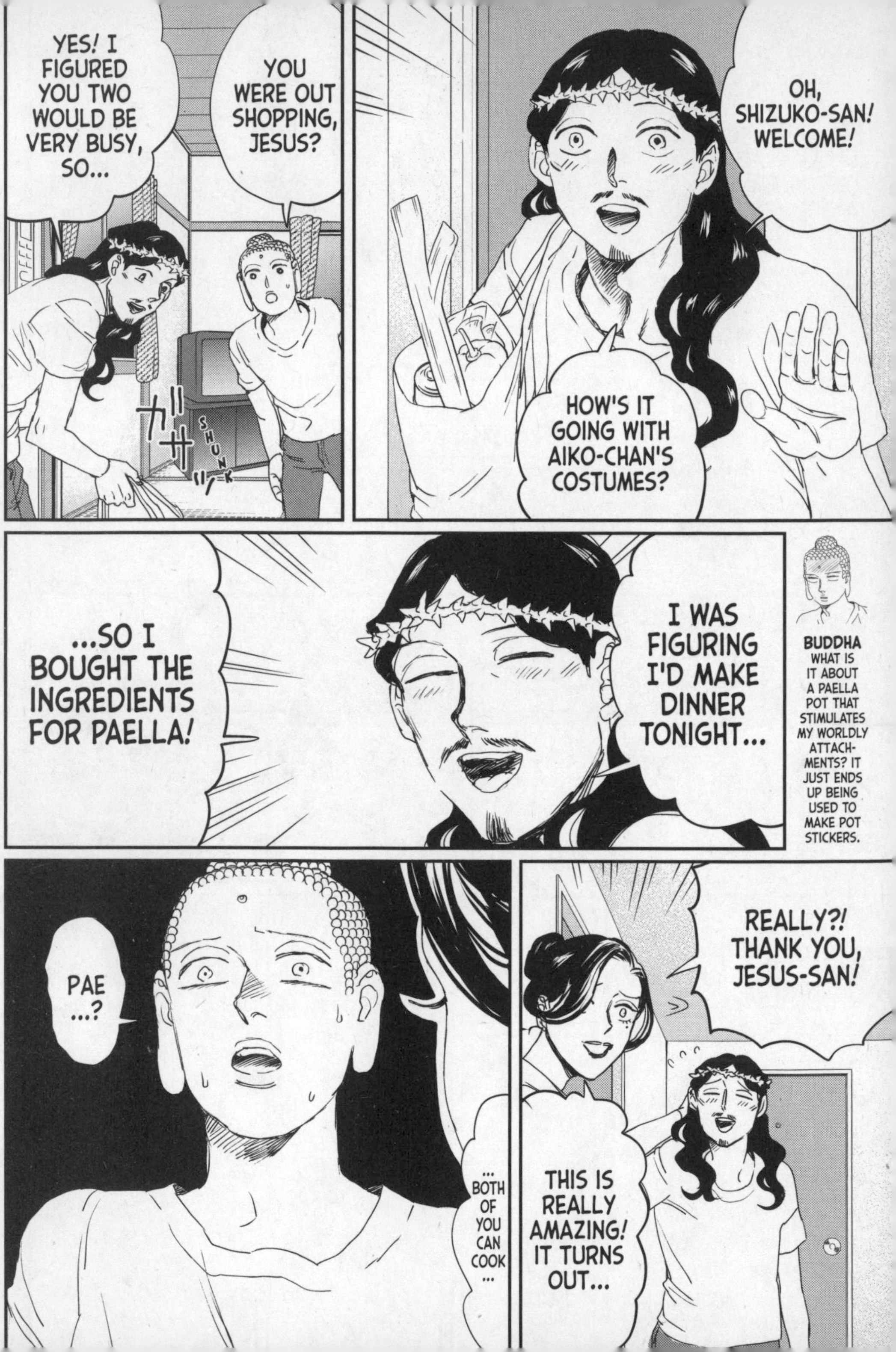
OH, SHIZUKO-SAN! WELCOME!
HOW'S IT GOING WITH AIKO-CHAN'S COSTUMES?
YOU WERE OUT SHOPPING, JESUS?
YES! I FIGURED YOU TWO WOULD BE VERY BUSY, SO...
SHUNK
BUDDHA WHAT IS IT ABOUT A PAELLA POT THAT STIMULATES MY WORLDLY ATTACHMENTS? IT JUST ENDS UP BEING USED TO MAKE POT STICKERS.
I WAS FIGURING I'D MAKE DINNER TONIGHT...
...SO I BOUGHT THE INGREDIENTS FOR PAELLA!
REALLY?! THANK YOU, JESUS-SAN!
THIS IS REALLY AMAZING! IT TURNS OUT...
...BOTH OF YOU CAN COOK...
PAE ...?

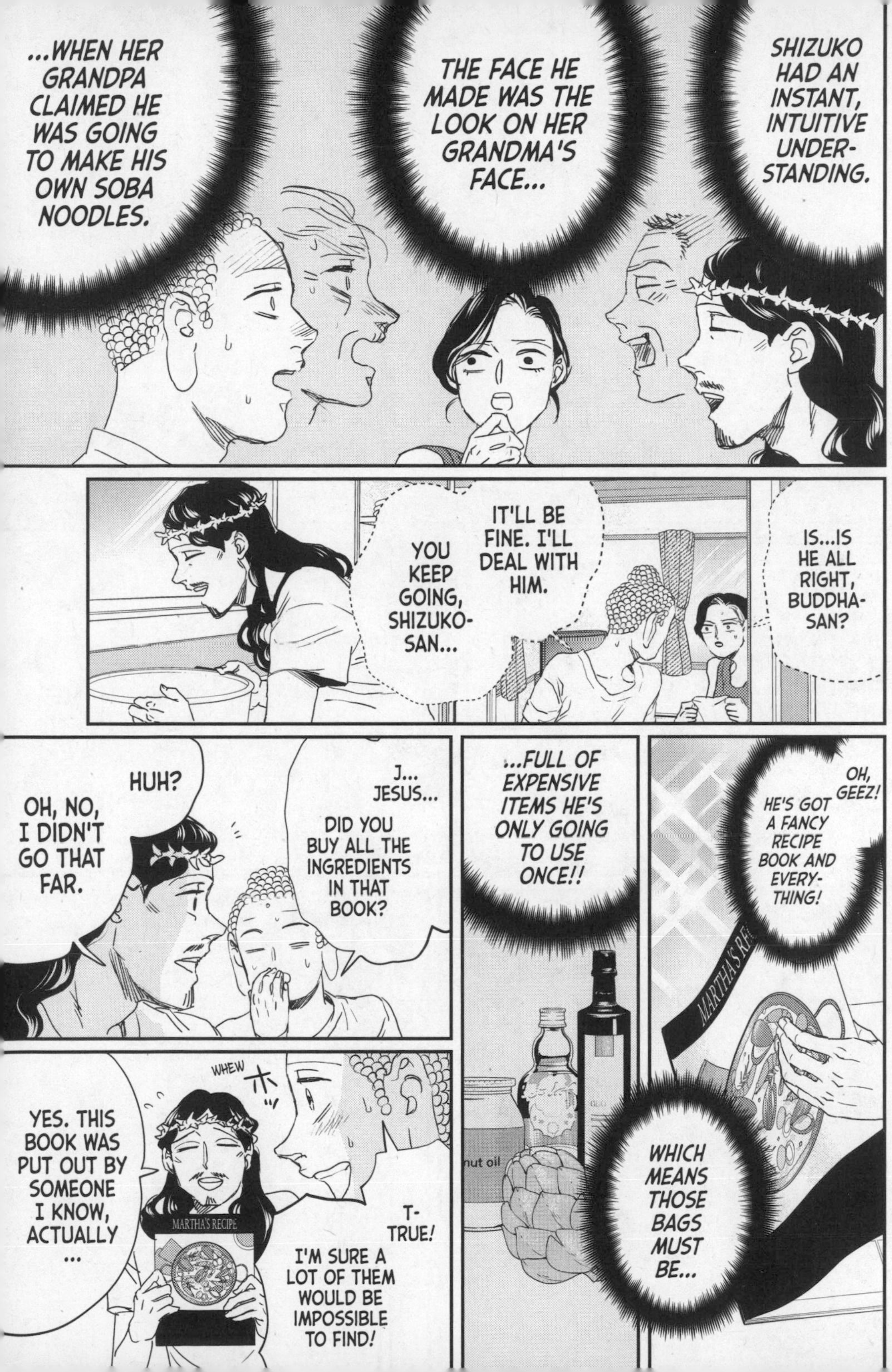
SHIZUKO HAD AN INSTANT, INTUITIVE UNDER-STANDING.
THE FACE HE MADE WAS THE LOOK ON HER GRANDMA'S FACE...
...WHEN HER GRANDPA CLAIMED HE WAS GOING TO MAKE HIS OWN SOBA NOODLES.
IS...IS HE ALL RIGHT, BUDDHA-SAN?
IT'LL BE FINE. I'LL DEAL WITH HIM.
YOU KEEP GOING, SHIZUKO-SAN...
OH, GEEZ!
HE'S GOT A FANCY RECIPE BOOK AND EVERY-THING!
WHICH MEANS THOSE BAGS MUST BE...
...FULL OF EXPENSIVE ITEMS HE'S ONLY GOING TO USE ONCE!!
nut oil
J... JESUS...
DID YOU BUY ALL THE INGREDIENTS IN THAT BOOK?
HUH?
OH, NO, I DIDN'T GO THAT FAR.
WHEW ホッ
YES. THIS BOOK WAS PUT OUT BY SOMEONE I KNOW, ACTUALLY ...
MARTHA'S RECIPE
T-TRUE!
I'M SURE A LOT OF THEM WOULD BE IMPOSSIBLE TO FIND!

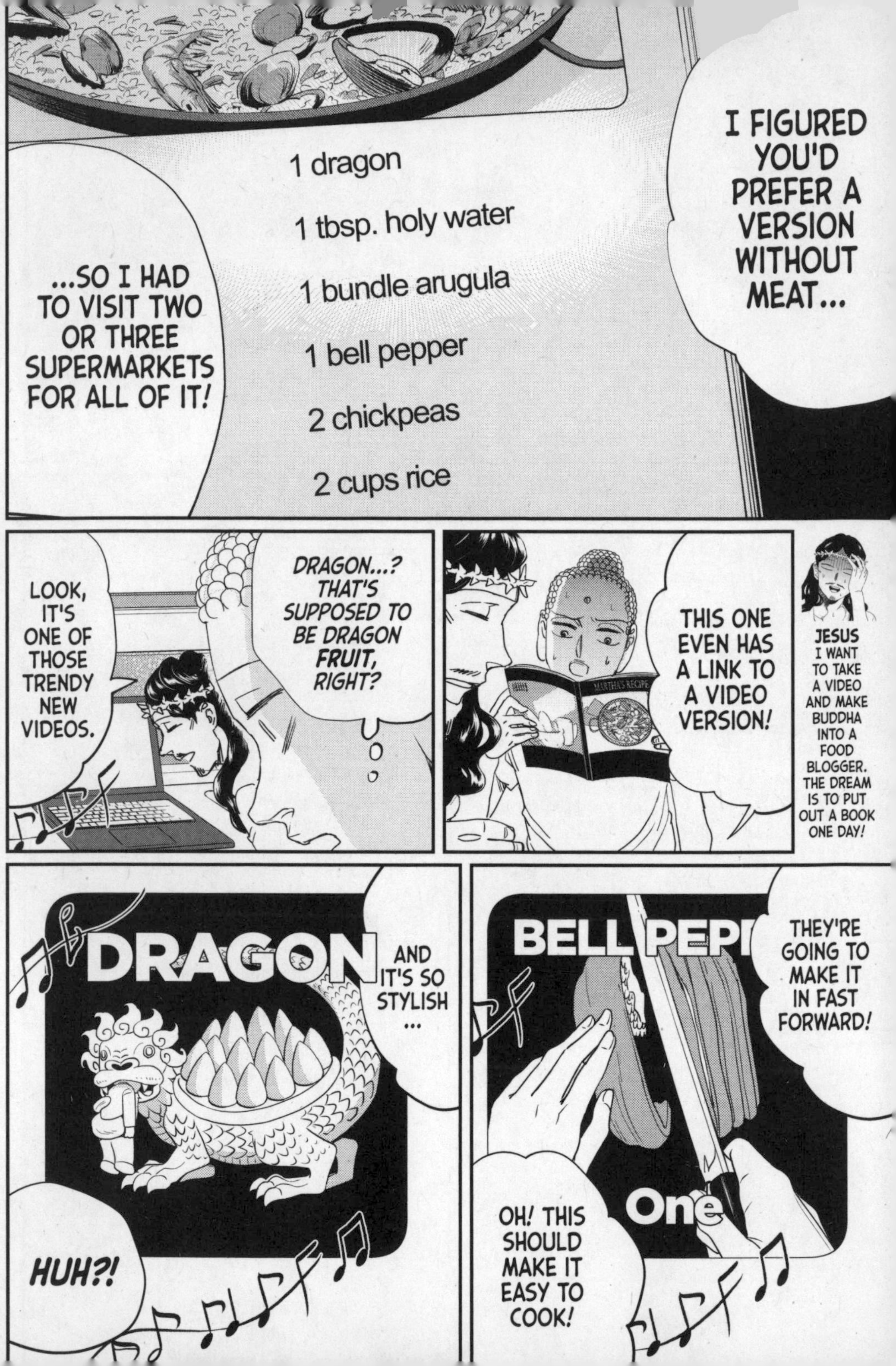
I FIGURED YOU'D PREFER A VERSION WITHOUT MEAT...
1 dragon
1 tbsp. holy water
1 bundle arugula
1 bell pepper
2 chickpeas
2 cups rice
...SO I HAD TO VISIT TWO OR THREE SUPERMARKETS FOR ALL OF IT!
JESUS I WANT TO TAKE A VIDEO AND MAKE BUDDHA INTO A FOOD BLOGGER. THE DREAM IS TO PUT OUT A BOOK ONE DAY!
THIS ONE EVEN HAS A LINK TO A VIDEO VERSION!
MARTHA'S RECIPE
DRAGON...? THAT'S SUPPOSED TO BE DRAGON FRUIT, RIGHT?
LOOK, IT'S ONE OF THOSE TRENDY NEW VIDEOS.
BELL PEPP
THEY'RE GOING TO MAKE IT IN FAST FORWARD!
One
OH! THIS SHOULD MAKE IT EASY TO COOK!
DRAGON
AND IT'S SO STYLISH ...
HUH?!

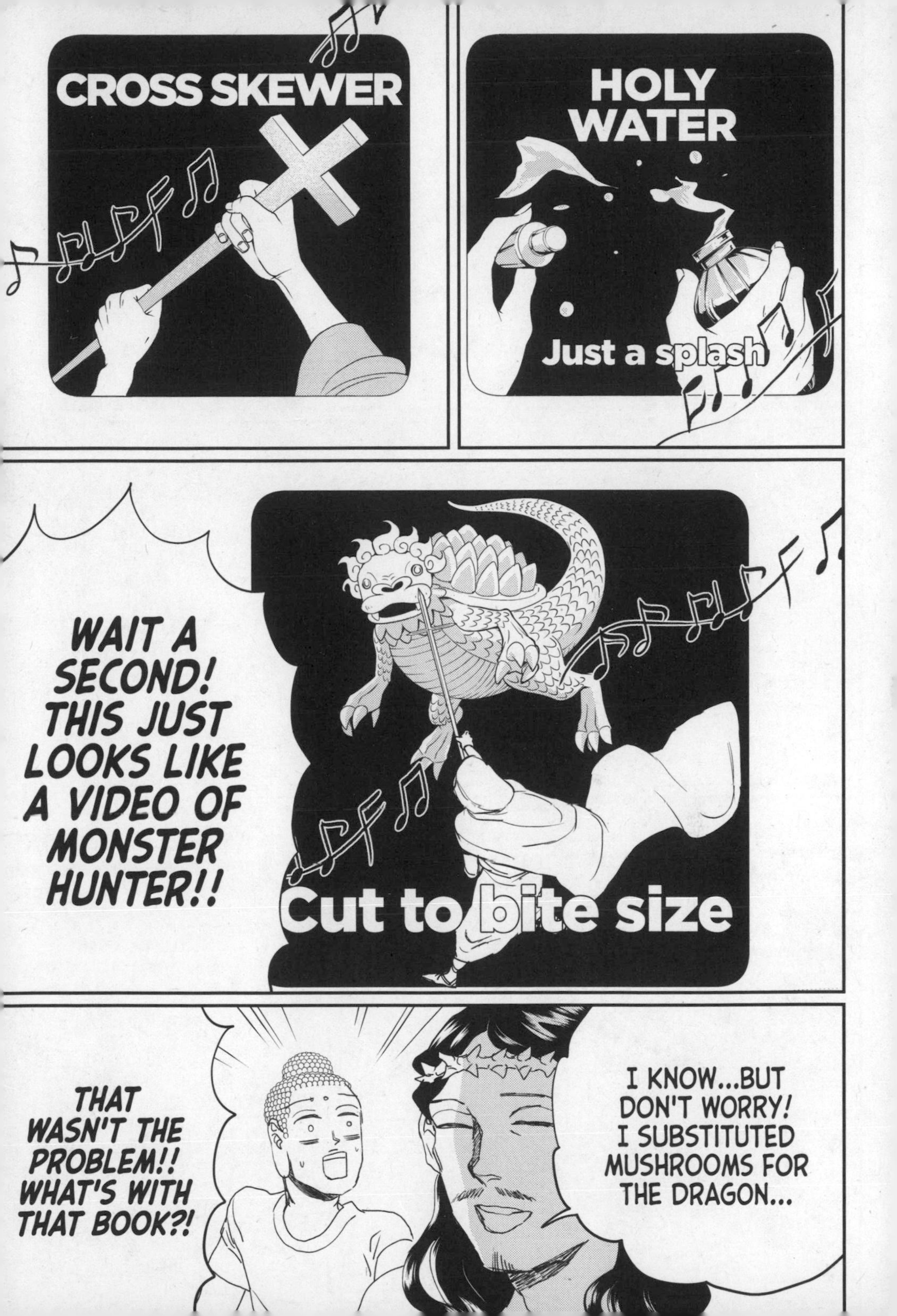
HOLY WATER
Just a splash
CROSS SKEWER
Cut to bite size
WAIT A SECOND! THIS JUST LOOKS LIKE A VIDEO OF MONSTER HUNTER!!
I KNOW...BUT DON'T WORRY! I SUBSTITUTED MUSHROOMS FOR THE DRAGON...
THAT WASN'T THE PROBLEM!! WHAT'S WITH THAT BOOK?!

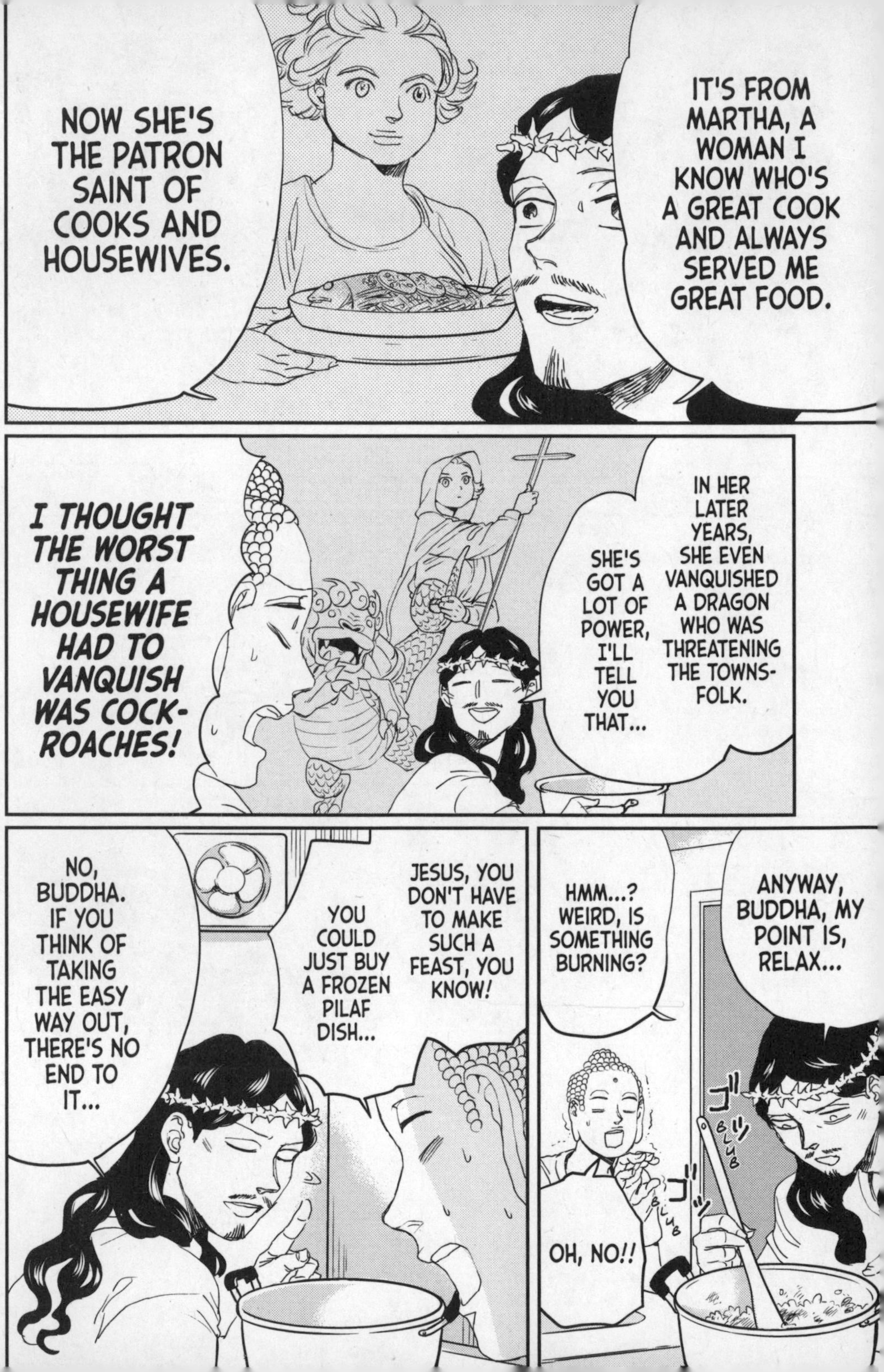
IT'S FROM MARTHA, A WOMAN I KNOW WHO'S A GREAT COOK AND ALWAYS SERVED ME GREAT FOOD.
NOW SHE'S THE PATRON SAINT OF COOKS AND HOUSEWIVES.
IN HER LATER YEARS, SHE EVEN VANQUISHED A DRAGON WHO WAS THREATENING THE TOWNS-FOLK.
SHE'S GOT A LOT OF POWER, I'LL TELL YOU THAT...
I THOUGHT THE WORST THING A HOUSEWIFE HAD TO VANQUISH WAS COCK-ROACHES!
ANYWAY, BUDDHA, MY POINT IS, RELAX...
HMM...? WEIRD, IS SOMETHING BURNING?
BLUB
BLUB
OH, NO!!
JESUS, YOU DON'T HAVE TO MAKE SUCH A FEAST, YOU KNOW!
YOU COULD JUST BUY A FROZEN PILAF DISH...
NO, BUDDHA. IF YOU THINK OF TAKING THE EASY WAY OUT, THERE'S NO END TO IT...

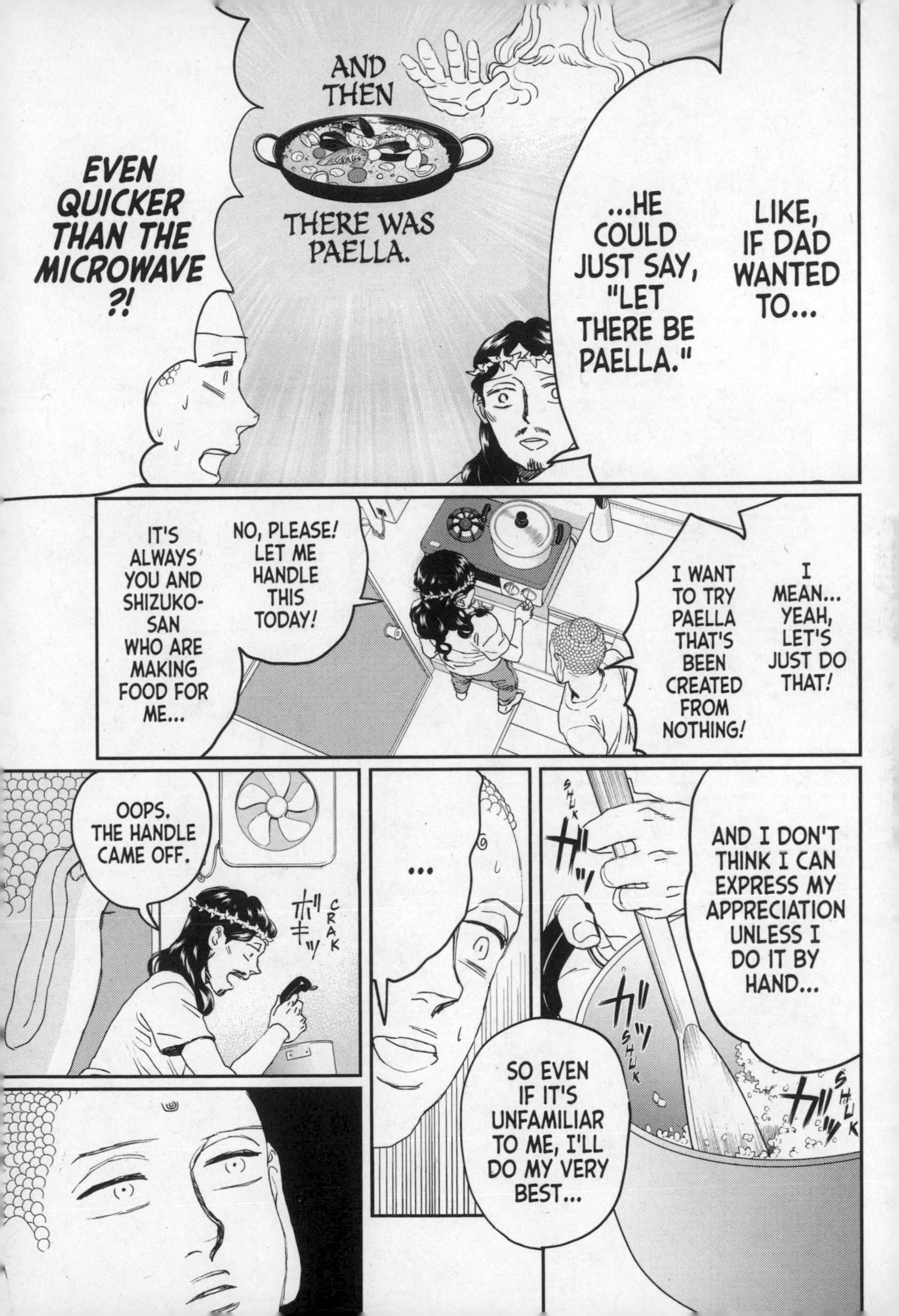
LIKE, IF DAD WANTED TO...
...HE COULD JUST SAY, "LET THERE BE PAELLA."
AND THEN
THERE WAS PAELLA.
EVEN QUICKER THAN THE MICROWAVE ?!
I MEAN... YEAH, LET'S JUST DO THAT!
I WANT TO TRY PAELLA THAT'S BEEN CREATED FROM NOTHING!
NO, PLEASE! LET ME HANDLE THIS TODAY!
IT'S ALWAYS YOU AND SHIZUKO-SAN WHO ARE MAKING FOOD FOR ME...
SHUK
AND I DON'T THINK I CAN EXPRESS MY APPRECIATION UNLESS I DO IT BY HAND...
SHUK
SHUK
SO EVEN IF IT'S UNFAMILIAR TO ME, I'LL DO MY VERY BEST...
...
OOPS. THE HANDLE CAME OFF.
CRAK

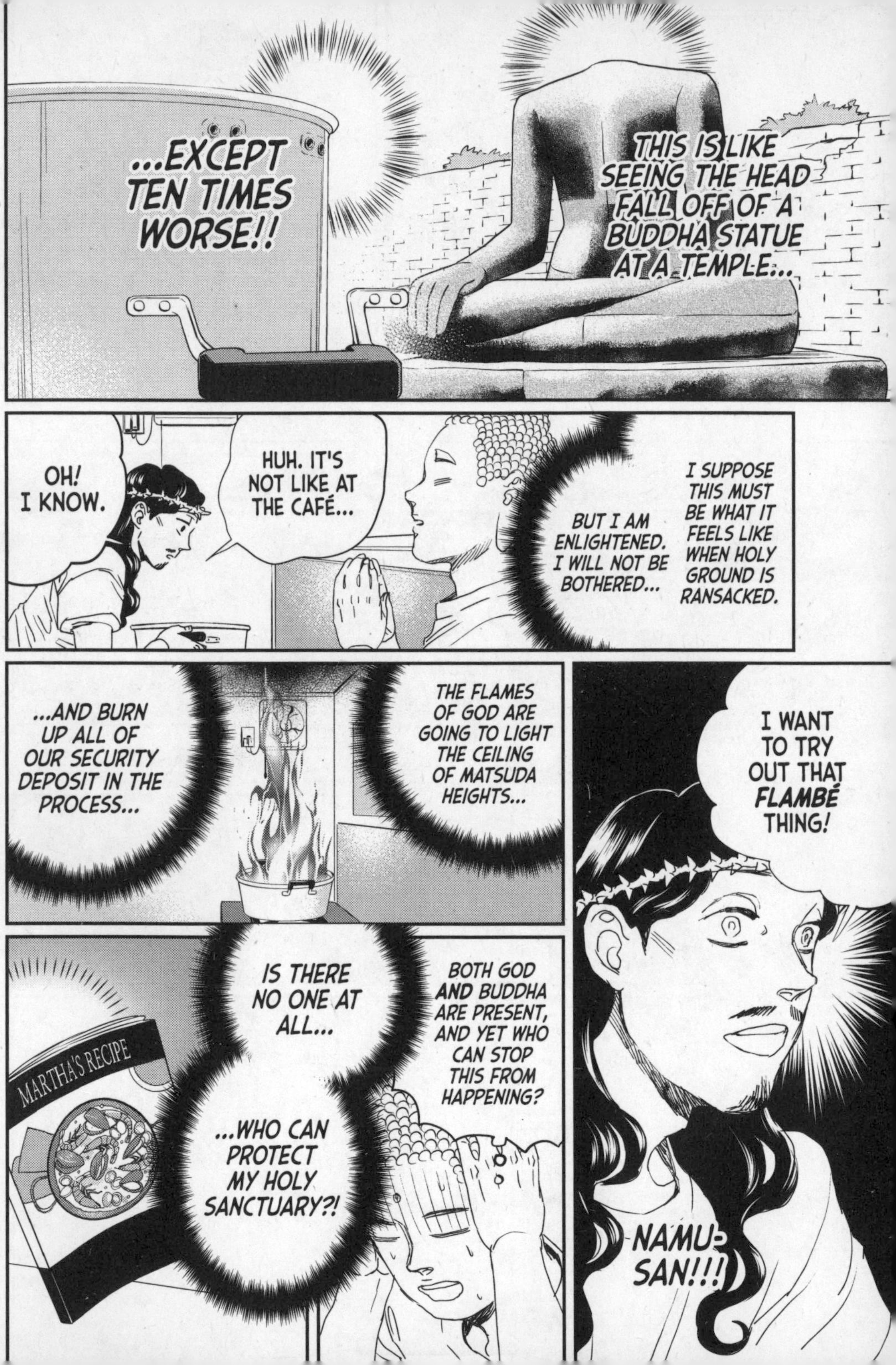
THIS IS LIKE SEEING THE HEAD FALL OFF OF A BUDDHA STATUE AT A TEMPLE...
...EXCEPT TEN TIMES WORSE!!
I SUPPOSE THIS MUST BE WHAT IT FEELS LIKE WHEN HOLY GROUND IS RANSACKED.
BUT I AM ENLIGHTENED. I WILL NOT BE BOTHERED...
HUH. IT'S NOT LIKE AT THE CAFÉ...
OH! I KNOW.
I WANT TO TRY OUT THAT FLAMBÉ THING!
NAMU-SAN!!!
THE FLAMES OF GOD ARE GOING TO LIGHT THE CEILING OF MATSUDA HEIGHTS...
...AND BURN UP ALL OF OUR SECURITY DEPOSIT IN THE PROCESS...
BOTH GOD AND BUDDHA ARE PRESENT, AND YET WHO CAN STOP THIS FROM HAPPENING?
IS THERE NO ONE AT ALL...
...WHO CAN PROTECT MY HOLY SANCTUARY?!
MARTHA'S RECIPE

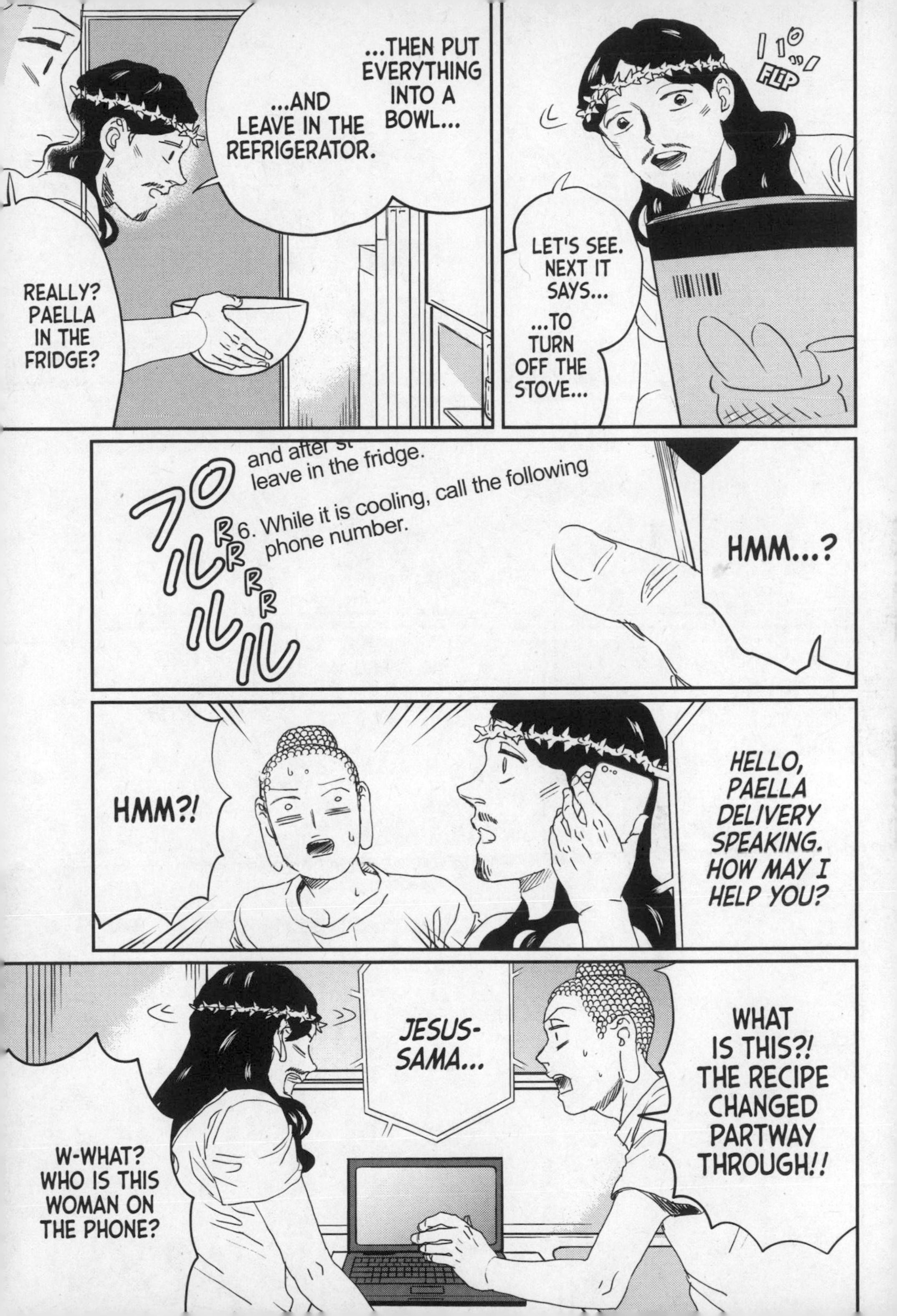
FLIP
LET'S SEE. NEXT IT SAYS...
...TO TURN OFF THE STOVE...
...THEN PUT EVERYTHING INTO A BOWL...
...AND LEAVE IN THE REFRIGERATOR.
REALLY? PAELLA IN THE FRIDGE?
HMM...?
leave in the fridge.
6. While it is cooling, call the following phone number.
HELLO, PAELLA DELIVERY SPEAKING. HOW MAY I HELP YOU?
HMM?!
WHAT IS THIS?! THE RECIPE CHANGED PARTWAY THROUGH!!
JESUS-SAMA...
W-WHAT? WHO IS THIS WOMAN ON THE PHONE?

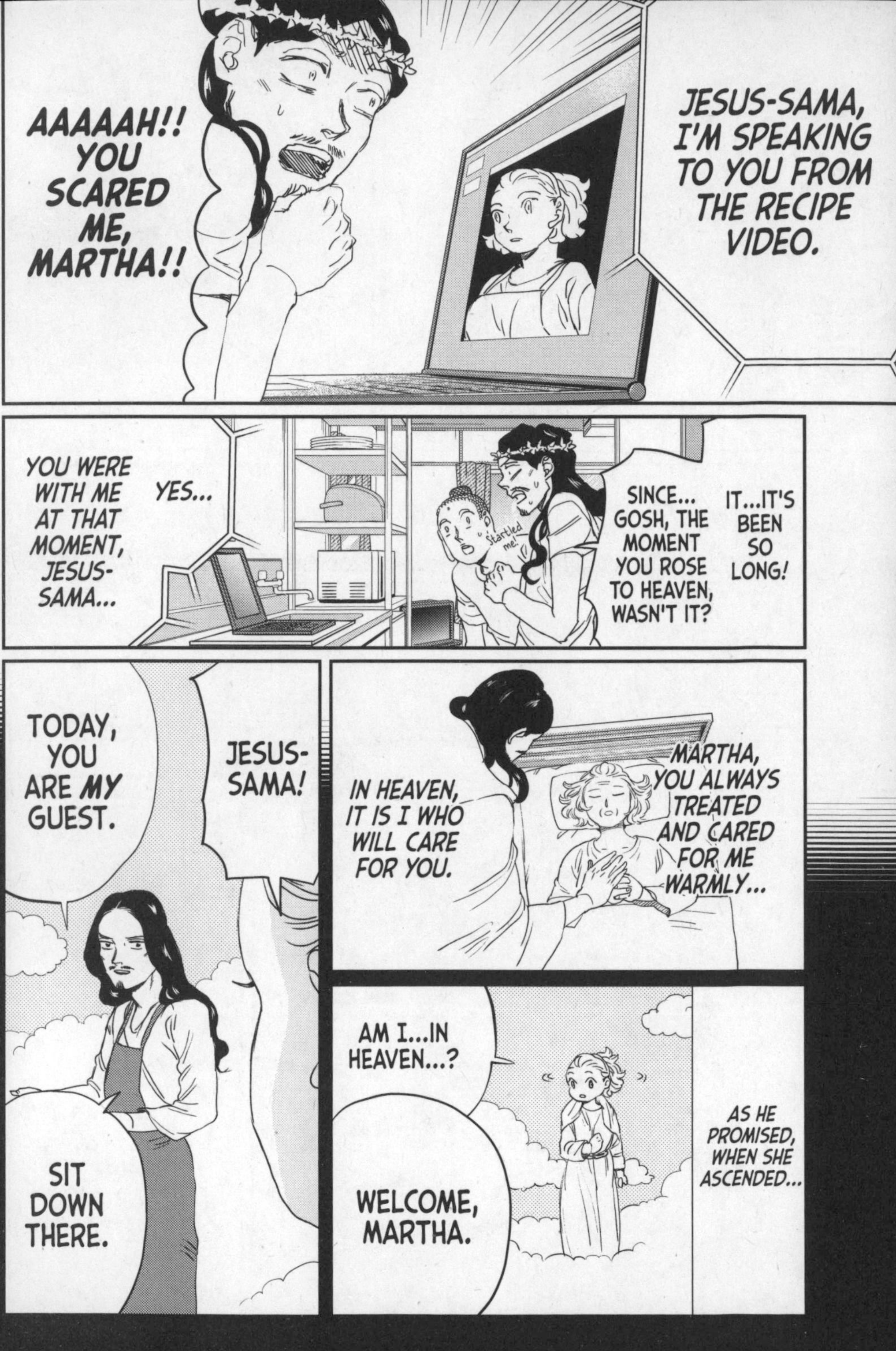
JESUS-SAMA, I'M SPEAKING TO YOU FROM THE RECIPE VIDEO.
AAAAAH!! YOU SCARED ME, MARTHA!!
IT...IT'S BEEN SO LONG!
SINCE... GOSH, THE MOMENT YOU ROSE TO HEAVEN, WASN'T IT?
Startled me!
YES...
YOU WERE WITH ME AT THAT MOMENT, JESUS-SAMA...
MARTHA, YOU ALWAYS TREATED AND CARED FOR ME WARMLY...
IN HEAVEN, IT IS I WHO WILL CARE FOR YOU.
AS HE PROMISED, WHEN SHE ASCENDED...
AM I...IN HEAVEN...?
WELCOME, MARTHA.
JESUS-SAMA!
TODAY, YOU ARE MY GUEST.
SIT DOWN THERE.

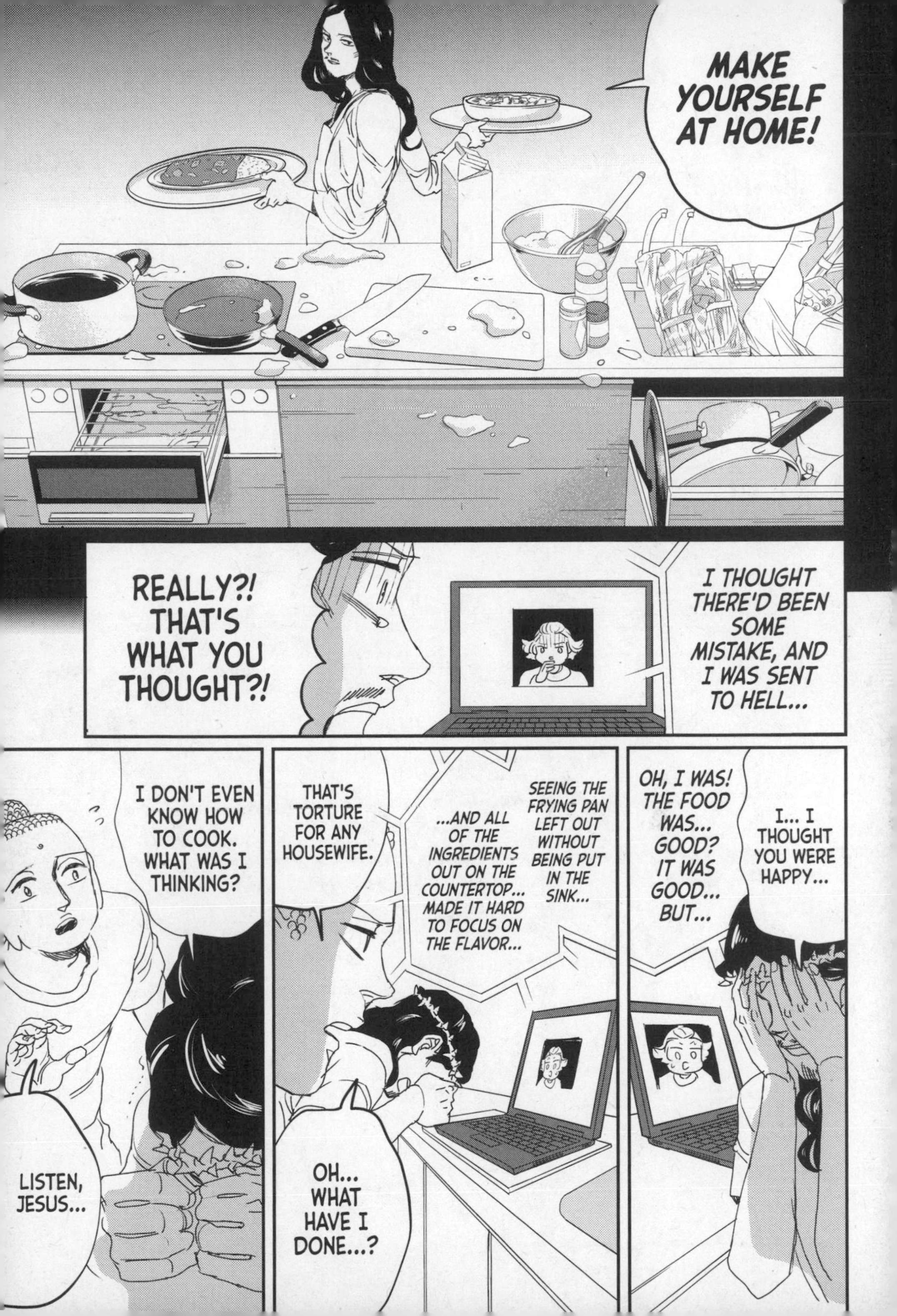
MAKE YOURSELF AT HOME!
I THOUGHT THERE'D BEEN SOME MISTAKE, AND I WAS SENT TO HELL...
REALLY?! THAT'S WHAT YOU THOUGHT?!
I... I THOUGHT YOU WERE HAPPY...
OH, I WAS! THE FOOD WAS... GOOD? IT WAS GOOD... BUT...
SEEING THE FRYING PAN LEFT OUT WITHOUT BEING PUT IN THE SINK...
...AND ALL OF THE INGREDIENTS OUT ON THE COUNTERTOP... MADE IT HARD TO FOCUS ON THE FLAVOR...
THAT'S TORTURE FOR ANY HOUSEWIFE.
OH... WHAT HAVE I DONE...?
I DON'T EVEN KNOW HOW TO COOK. WHAT WAS I THINKING?
LISTEN, JESUS...

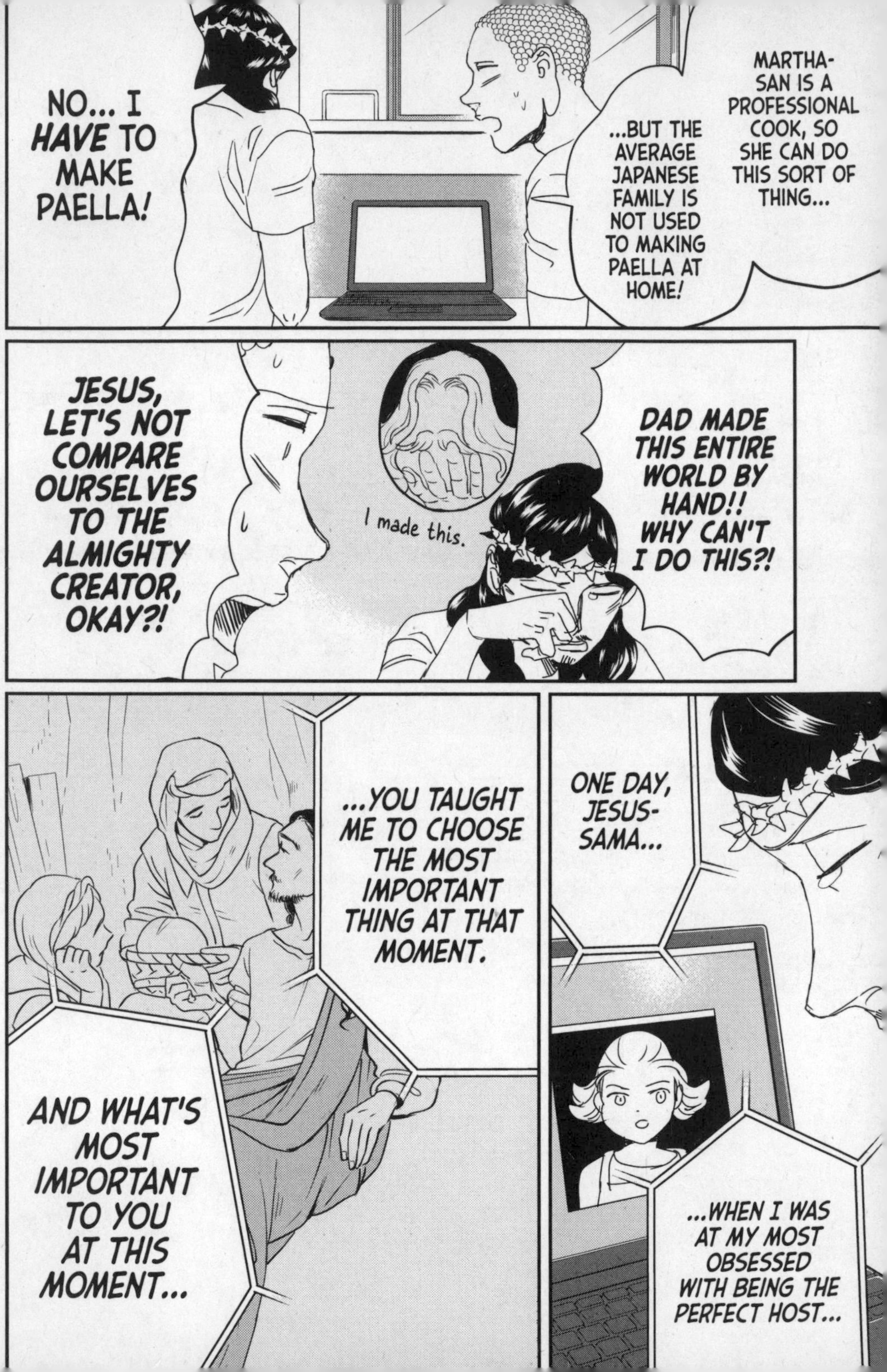
MARTHA-SAN IS A PROFESSIONAL COOK, SO SHE CAN DO THIS SORT OF THING...
...BUT THE AVERAGE JAPANESE FAMILY IS NOT USED TO MAKING PAELLA AT HOME!
NO... I *HAVE* TO MAKE PAELLA!
DAD MADE THIS ENTIRE WORLD BY HAND!! WHY CAN'T I DO THIS?!
I made this.
JESUS, LET'S NOT COMPARE OURSELVES TO THE ALMIGHTY CREATOR, OKAY?!
ONE DAY, JESUS-SAMA...
...WHEN I WAS AT MY MOST OBSESSED WITH BEING THE PERFECT HOST...
...YOU TAUGHT ME TO CHOOSE THE MOST IMPORTANT THING AT THAT MOMENT.
AND WHAT'S MOST IMPORTANT TO YOU AT THIS MOMENT...

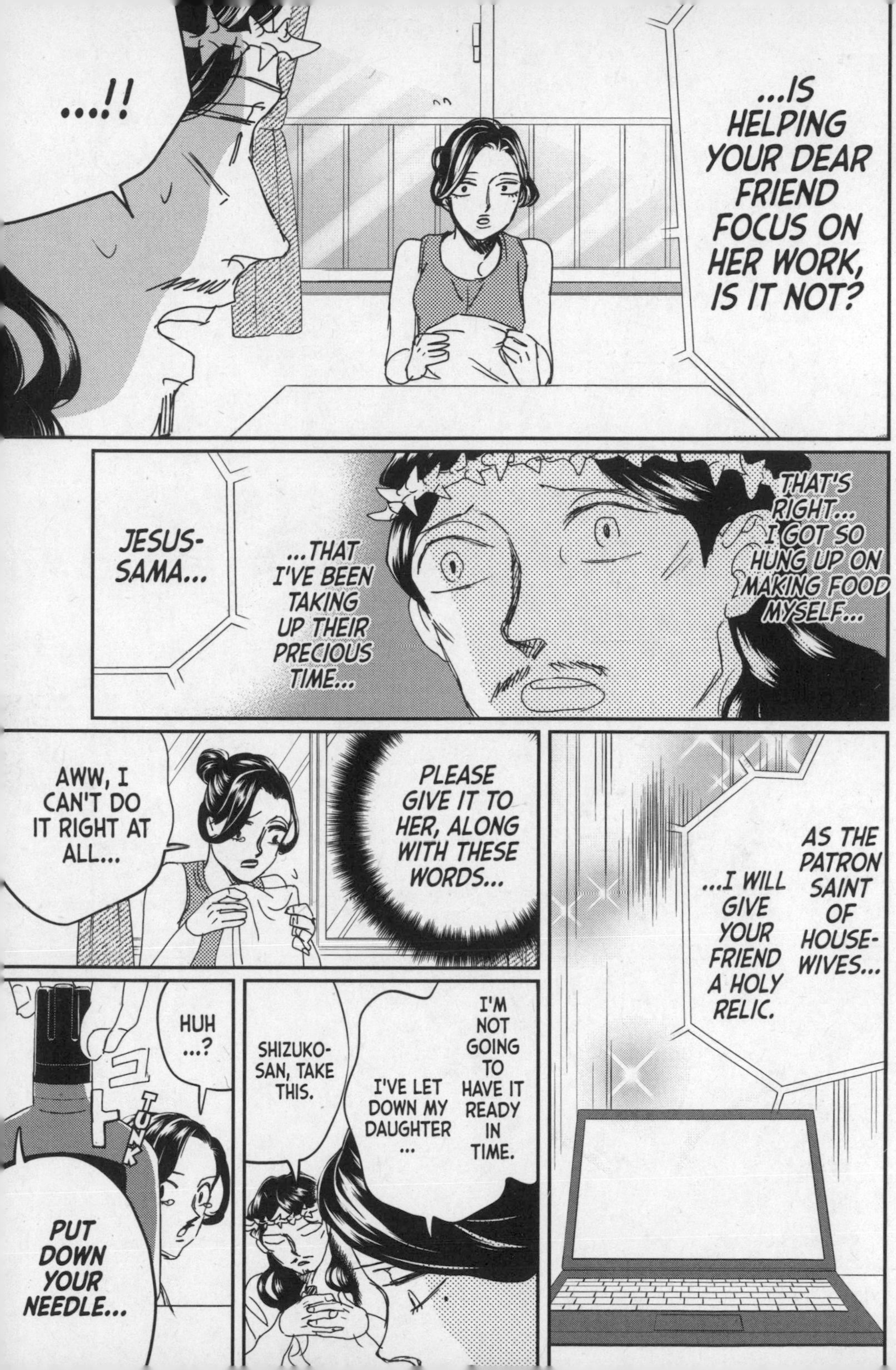
...IS HELPING YOUR DEAR FRIEND FOCUS ON HER WORK, IS IT NOT?
...!!
THAT'S RIGHT... I GOT SO HUNG UP ON MAKING FOOD MYSELF...
...THAT I'VE BEEN TAKING UP THEIR PRECIOUS TIME...
JESUS-SAMA...
AS THE PATRON SAINT OF HOUSE-WIVES...
...I WILL GIVE YOUR FRIEND A HOLY RELIC.
PLEASE GIVE IT TO HER, ALONG WITH THESE WORDS...
AWW, I CAN'T DO IT RIGHT AT ALL...
I'M NOT GOING TO HAVE IT READY IN TIME.
I'VE LET DOWN MY DAUGHTER ...
SHIZUKO-SAN, TAKE THIS.
HUH ...?
TUNK
PUT DOWN YOUR NEEDLE...

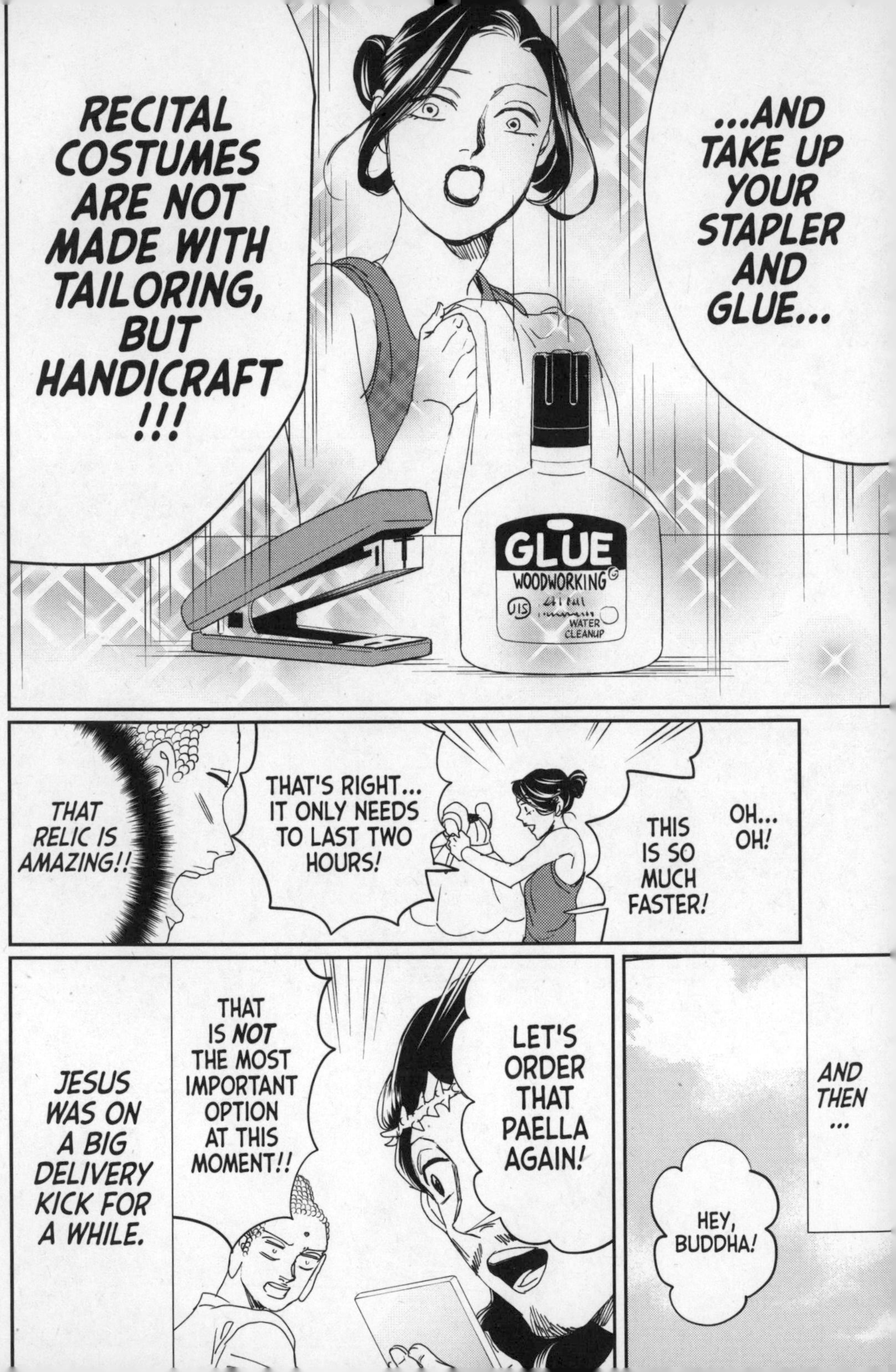
...AND TAKE UP YOUR STAPLER AND GLUE...
RECITAL COSTUMES ARE NOT MADE WITH TAILORING, BUT HANDICRAFT!!!
GLUE
WOODWORKING
WATER CLEANUP
OH... OH!
THIS IS SO MUCH FASTER!
THAT'S RIGHT... IT ONLY NEEDS TO LAST TWO HOURS!
THAT RELIC IS AMAZING!!
AND THEN...
HEY, BUDDHA!
LET'S ORDER THAT PAELLA AGAIN!
THAT IS *NOT* THE MOST IMPORTANT OPTION AT THIS MOMENT!!
JESUS WAS ON A BIG DELIVERY KICK FOR A WHILE.

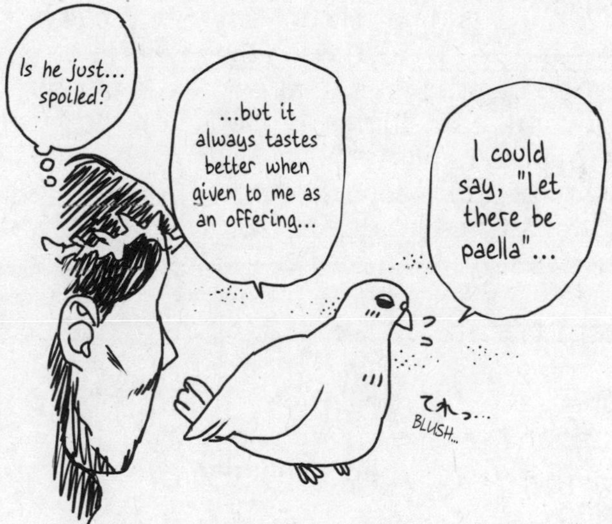
I could say, "Let there be paella"...
てれっ...
BLUSH...
...but it always tastes better when given to me as an offering...
Is he just... spoiled?

CHAPTER 107 TRANSLATION NOTES

Reality show, page 56

The narration here is referencing a long-running show called *Totsugeki! Tonari no Bangohan* (Charge! Dinner Next Door) in which the host, Yonesuke, intrudes upon an unsuspecting family's dinner, showing what the ordinary Japanese family is eating on a regular basis. The Buddha's teachings, of course, call for monks to carry about a begging bowl to receive the gift of food from lay people (who will themselves receive good karma for their generosity).

Martha, Page 62

A woman named Martha of Bethany. In the Gospel of Luke, Jesus visits the home of Martha and her sister Mary. Martha is busying herself with serving and being host, while Mary listens to Jesus speak. When Martha frets about her chores, Jesus advises her to not be upset about so many things, but focus on the most important thing at that moment. As a saint, she is typically the patron of housewives and domestic servants. A legend from the Middle Ages held that Martha made her way to France, where she tamed or defeated a dragon-like beast called the Tarasque.

Namusan, Page 64

Namusan is an abbreviation of *namusanpô*, which literally means, "I take refuge in the Three Jewels," the Buddha, Dharma (teachings), and Sangha (the spiritual community). In modern Japanese, it is a phrase used when something goes unexpectedly wrong or is shocking.

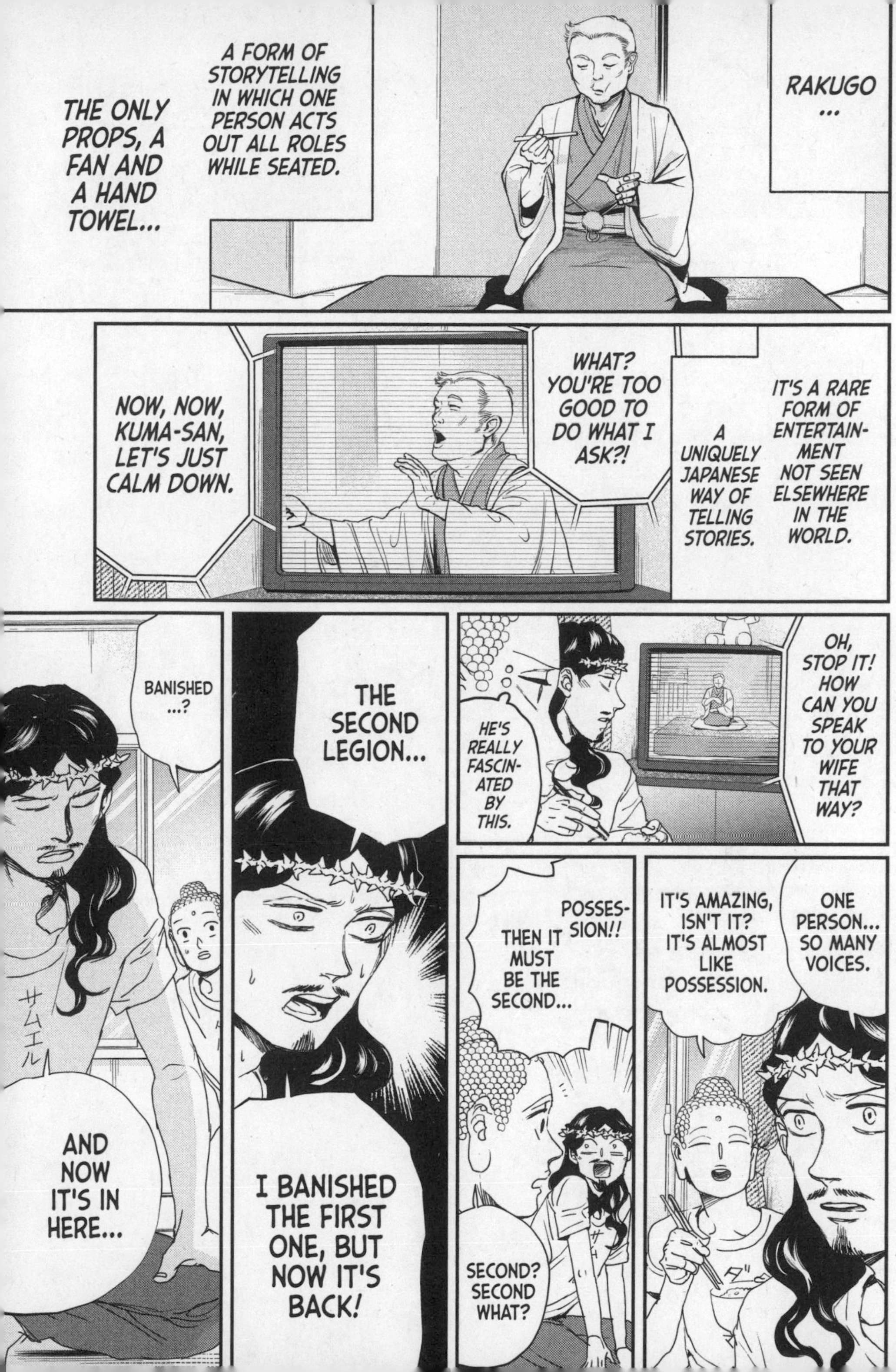
RAKUGO ...
A FORM OF STORYTELLING IN WHICH ONE PERSON ACTS OUT ALL ROLES WHILE SEATED.
THE ONLY PROPS, A FAN AND A HAND TOWEL...
IT'S A RARE FORM OF ENTERTAIN-MENT NOT SEEN ELSEWHERE IN THE WORLD.
A UNIQUELY JAPANESE WAY OF TELLING STORIES.
WHAT? YOU'RE TOO GOOD TO DO WHAT I ASK?!
NOW, NOW, KUMA-SAN, LET'S JUST CALM DOWN.
OH, STOP IT! HOW CAN YOU SPEAK TO YOUR WIFE THAT WAY?
HE'S REALLY FASCIN-ATED BY THIS.
ONE PERSON... SO MANY VOICES.
IT'S AMAZING, ISN'T IT? IT'S ALMOST LIKE POSSESSION.
POSSES-SION!!
THEN IT MUST BE THE SECOND...
SECOND? SECOND WHAT?
THE SECOND LEGION...
I BANISHED THE FIRST ONE, BUT NOW IT'S BACK!
BANISHED ...?
サムエル
AND NOW IT'S IN HERE...

JESUS'S SHIRT: SAMUEL

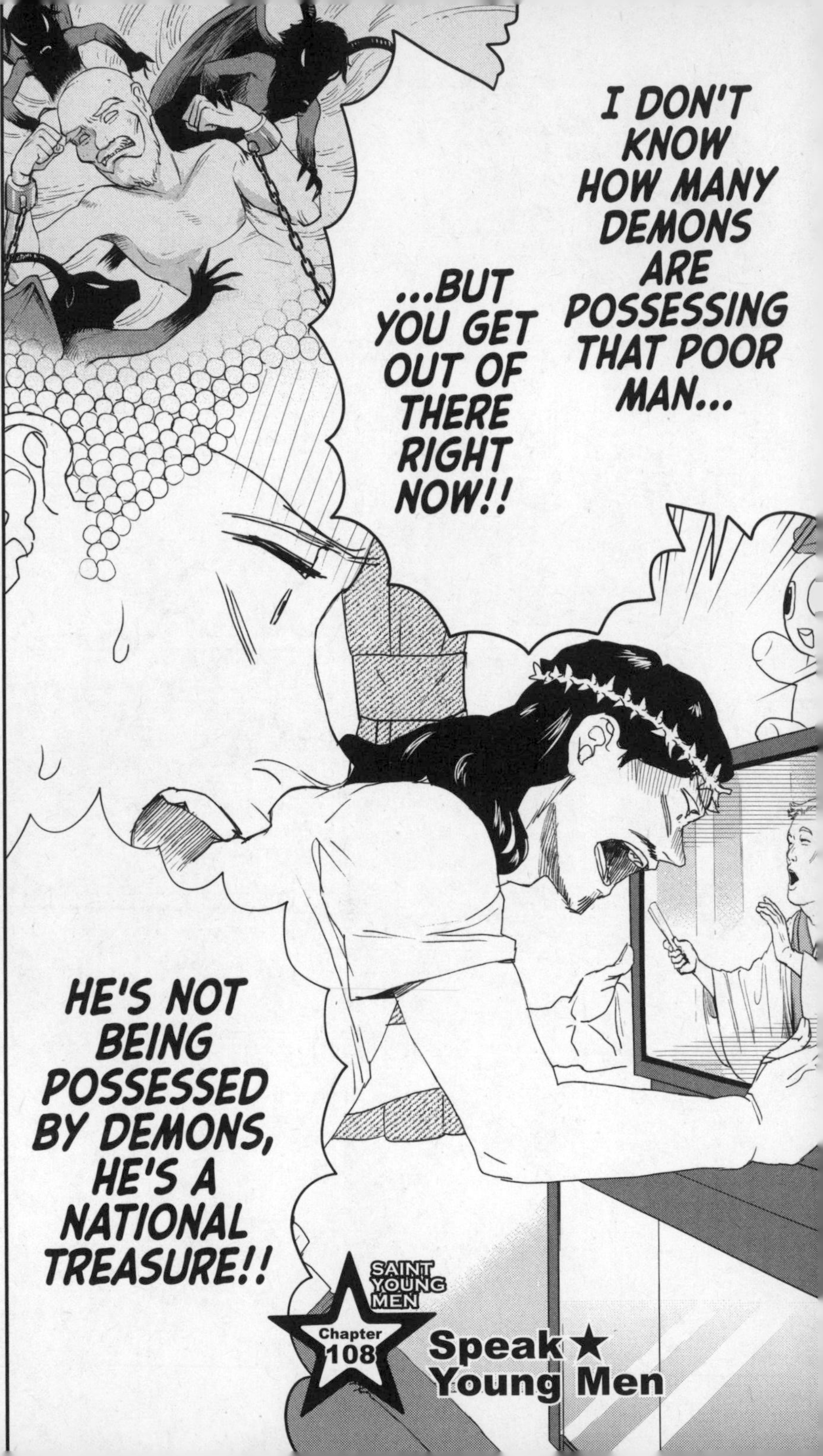

I DON'T KNOW HOW MANY DEMONS ARE POSSESSING THAT POOR MAN...
...BUT YOU GET OUT OF THERE RIGHT NOW!!
HE'S NOT BEING POSSESSED BY DEMONS, HE'S A NATIONAL TREASURE!!
SAINT YOUNG MEN
Chapter 108
Speak ★ Young Men

THEY SAY THOSE POSSESSED BY LEGION APPEAR TO HAVE MULTIPLE PERSON-ALITIES.

BUDDHA
I CAN SIT IN THE LOTUS POSITION INDEFINITELY, BUT I COULDN'T KNEEL THAT LONG. IS THERE A SECRET TO THE CUSHION?

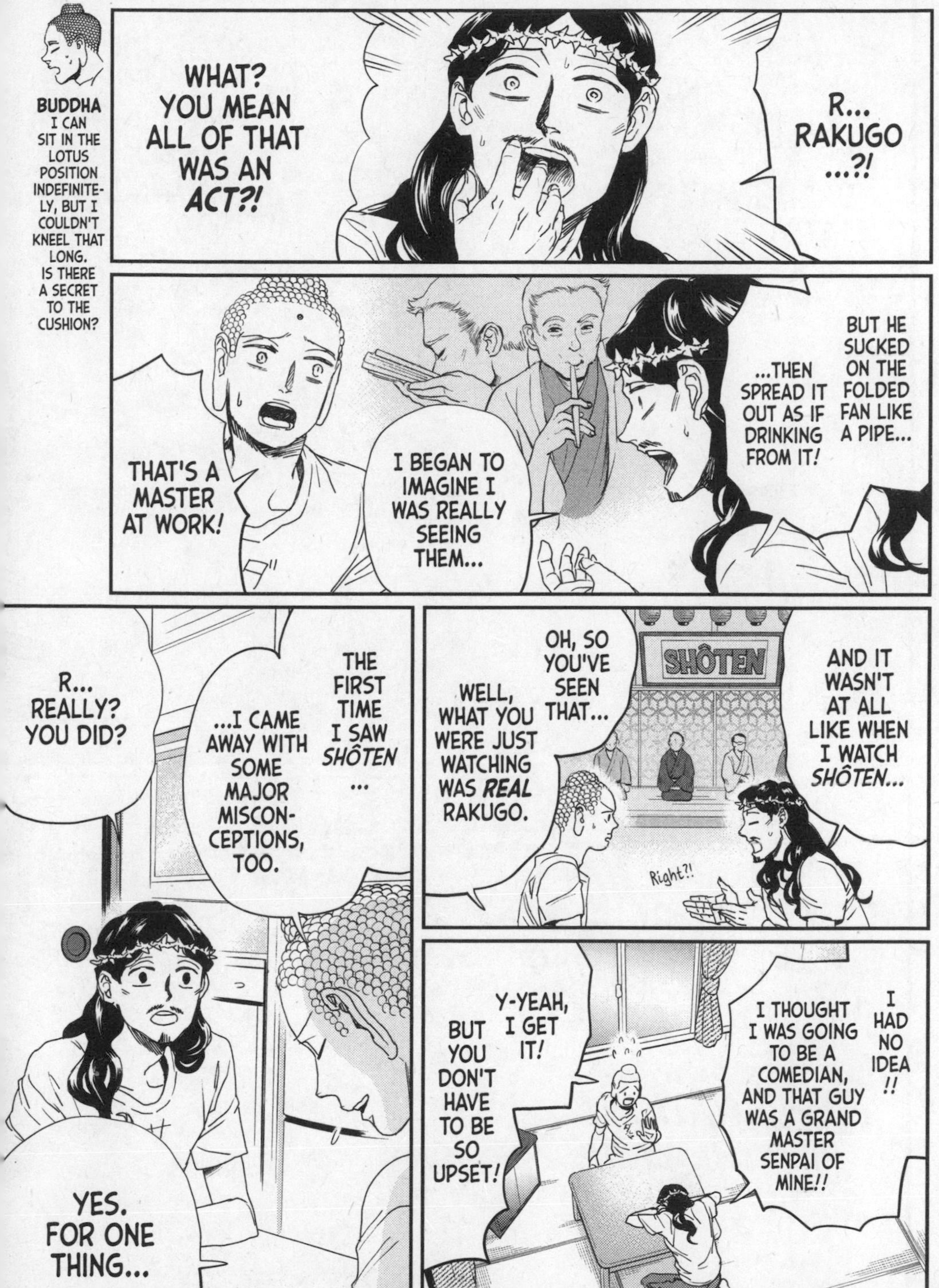
R... RAKUGO ...?!
WHAT? YOU MEAN ALL OF THAT WAS AN *ACT?!*
BUT HE SUCKED ON THE FOLDED FAN LIKE A PIPE...
...THEN SPREAD IT OUT AS IF DRINKING FROM IT!
I BEGAN TO IMAGINE I WAS REALLY SEEING THEM...
THAT'S A MASTER AT WORK!
AND IT WASN'T AT ALL LIKE WHEN I WATCH *SHÔTEN*...
SHÔTEN
Right?!
OH, SO YOU'VE SEEN THAT...
WELL, WHAT YOU WERE JUST WATCHING WAS *REAL* RAKUGO.
I HAD NO IDEA!!
I THOUGHT I WAS GOING TO BE A COMEDIAN, AND THAT GUY WAS A GRAND MASTER SENPAI OF MINE!!
Y-YEAH, I GET IT!
BUT YOU DON'T HAVE TO BE SO UPSET!
THE FIRST TIME I SAW *SHÔTEN* ...
...I CAME AWAY WITH SOME MAJOR MISCONCEPTIONS, TOO.
R... REALLY? YOU DID?
YES. FOR ONE THING...

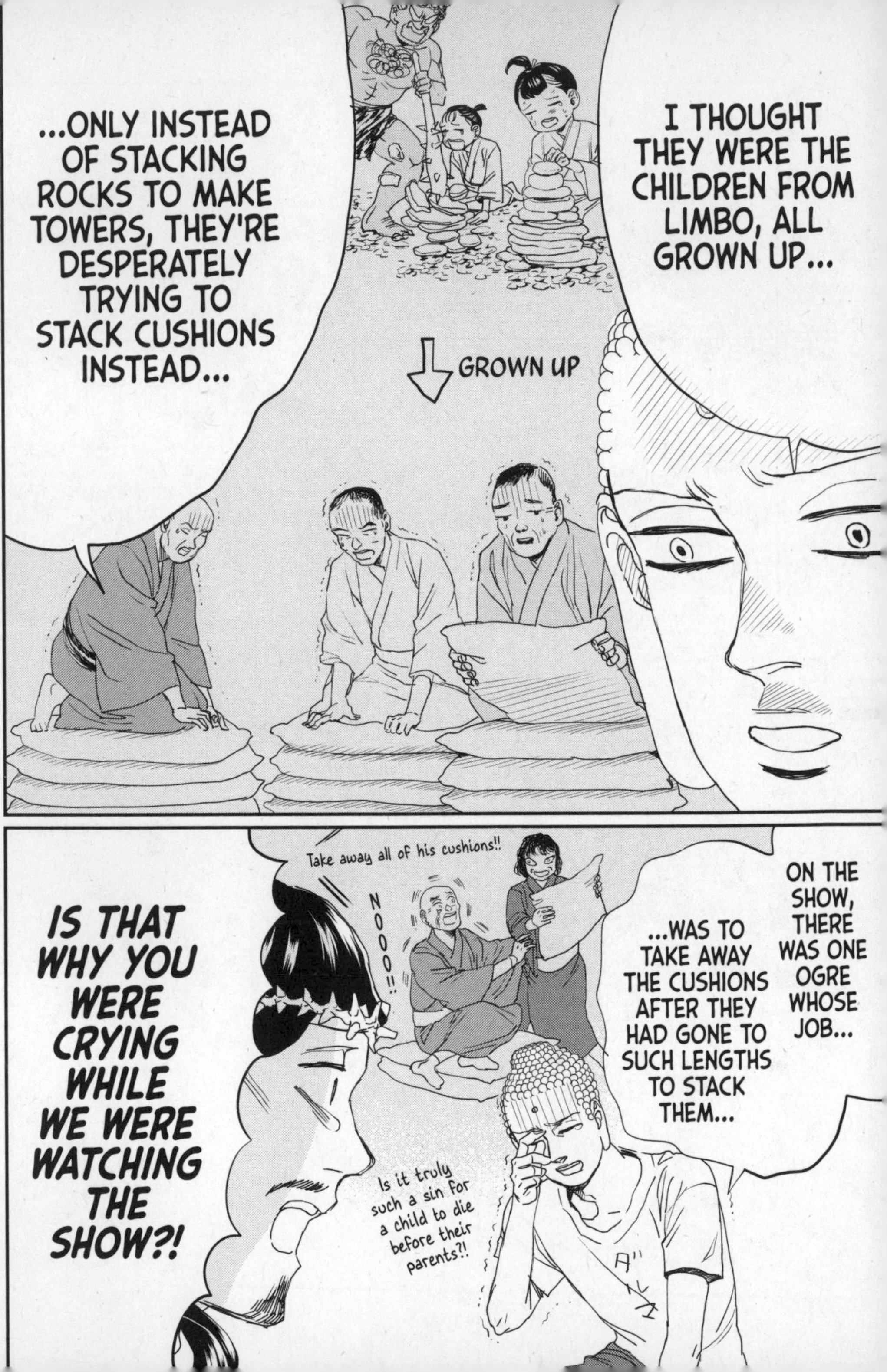
I THOUGHT THEY WERE THE CHILDREN FROM LIMBO, ALL GROWN UP...
...ONLY INSTEAD OF STACKING ROCKS TO MAKE TOWERS, THEY'RE DESPERATELY TRYING TO STACK CUSHIONS INSTEAD...
GROWN UP
ON THE SHOW, THERE WAS ONE OGRE WHOSE JOB...
...WAS TO TAKE AWAY THE CUSHIONS AFTER THEY HAD GONE TO SUCH LENGTHS TO STACK THEM...
Take away all of his cushions!!
NOOO!!
Is it truly such a sin for a child to die before their parents?!
IS THAT WHY YOU WERE CRYING WHILE WE WERE WATCHING THE SHOW?!

BUDDHA'S SHIRT: DARUMA

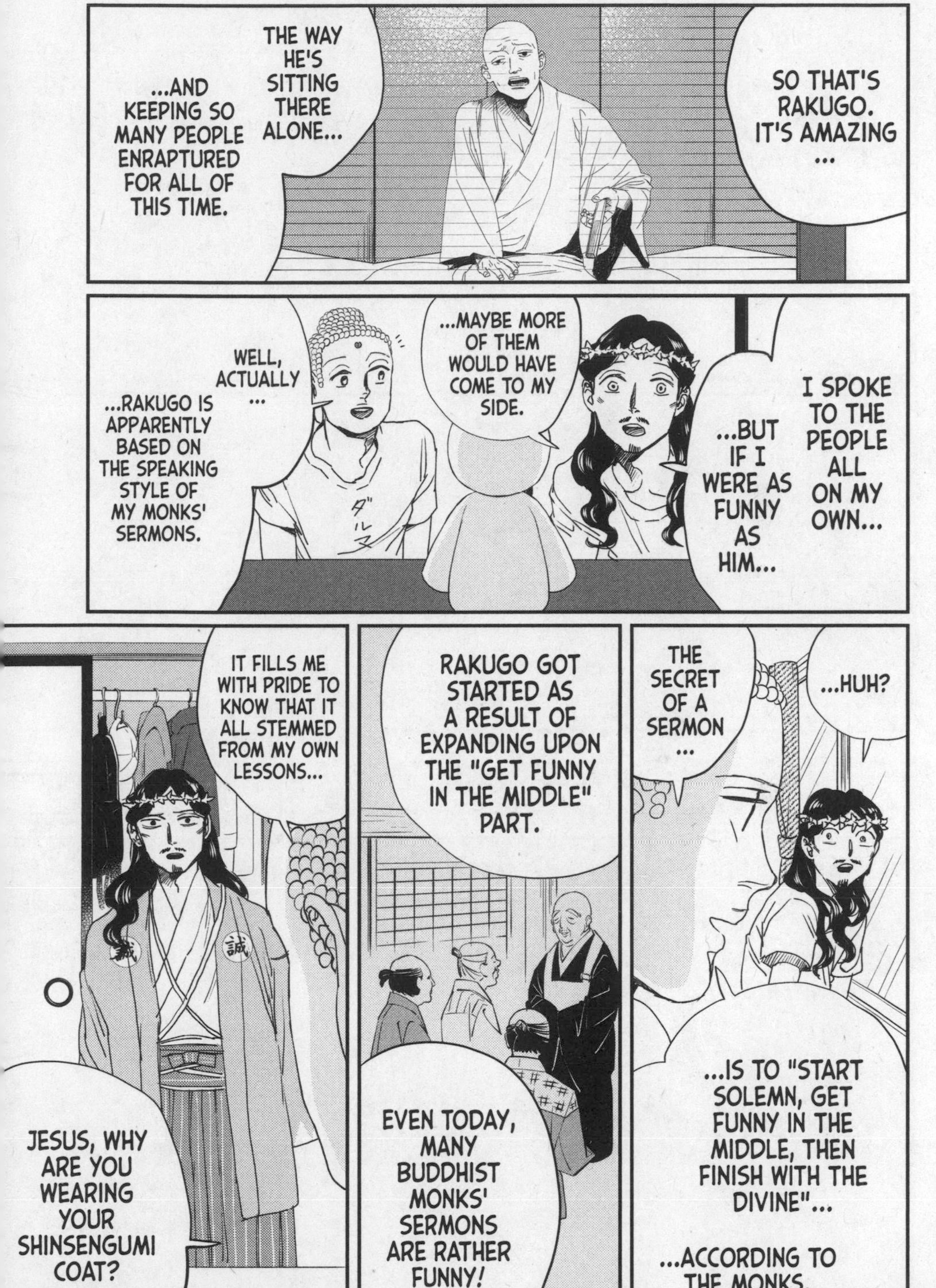
SO THAT'S RAKUGO. IT'S AMAZING ...
THE WAY HE'S SITTING THERE ALONE...
...AND KEEPING SO MANY PEOPLE ENRAPTURED FOR ALL OF THIS TIME.
I SPOKE TO THE PEOPLE ALL ON MY OWN...
...BUT IF I WERE AS FUNNY AS HIM...
...MAYBE MORE OF THEM WOULD HAVE COME TO MY SIDE.
WELL, ACTUALLY ...
ダルマ
...RAKUGO IS APPARENTLY BASED ON THE SPEAKING STYLE OF MY MONKS' SERMONS.
...HUH?
THE SECRET OF A SERMON ...
...IS TO "START SOLEMN, GET FUNNY IN THE MIDDLE, THEN FINISH WITH THE DIVINE"...
...ACCORDING TO THE MONKS.
RAKUGO GOT STARTED AS A RESULT OF EXPANDING UPON THE "GET FUNNY IN THE MIDDLE" PART.
EVEN TODAY, MANY BUDDHIST MONKS' SERMONS ARE RATHER FUNNY!
IT FILLS ME WITH PRIDE TO KNOW THAT IT ALL STEMMED FROM MY OWN LESSONS...
誠
JESUS, WHY ARE YOU WEARING YOUR SHINSENGUMI COAT?

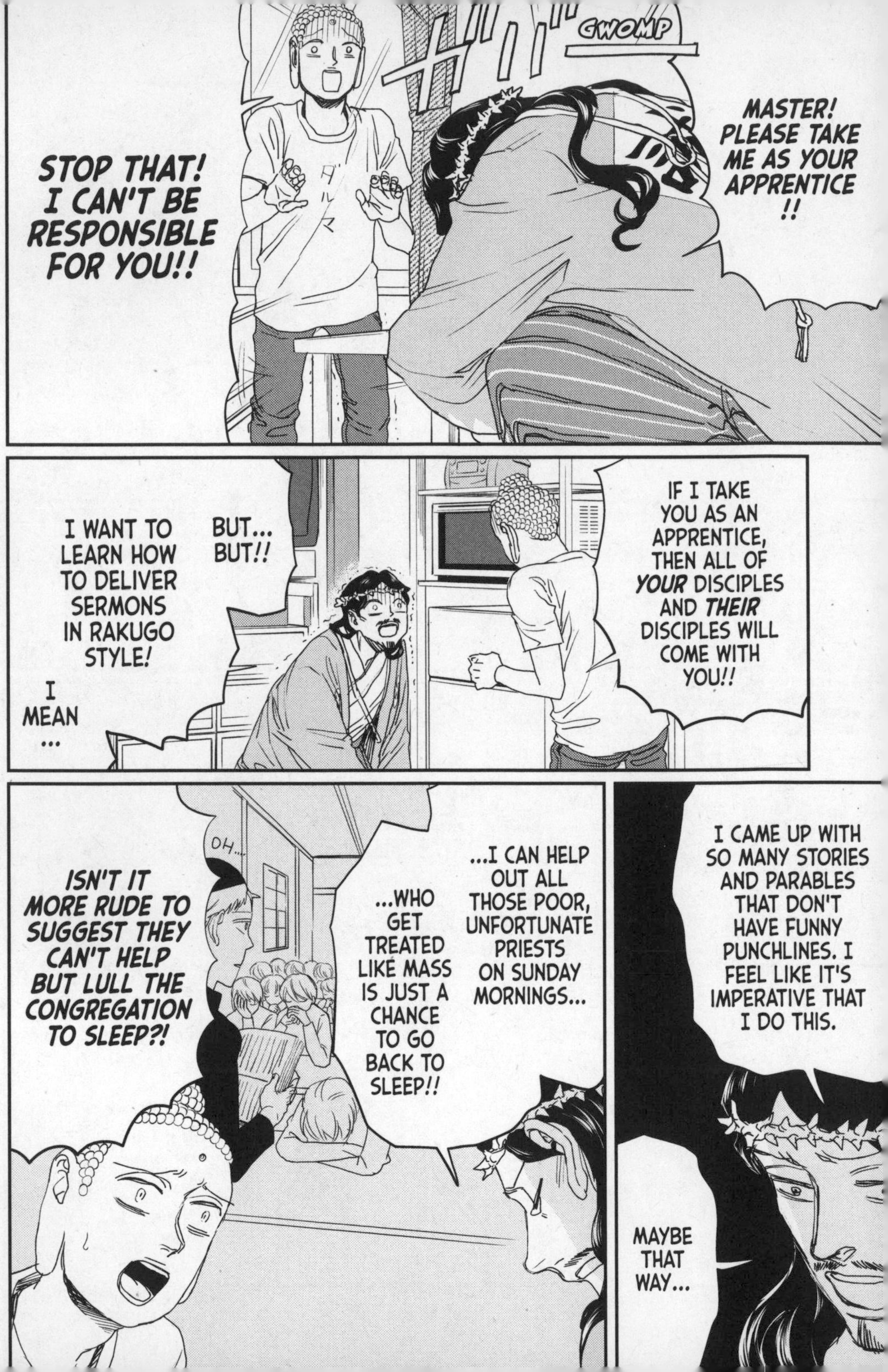
GWOMP
MASTER! PLEASE TAKE ME AS YOUR APPRENTICE!!
STOP THAT! I CAN'T BE RESPONSIBLE FOR YOU!!
IF I TAKE YOU AS AN APPRENTICE, THEN ALL OF *YOUR* DISCIPLES AND *THEIR* DISCIPLES WILL COME WITH YOU!!
BUT... BUT!!
I WANT TO LEARN HOW TO DELIVER SERMONS IN RAKUGO STYLE!
I MEAN...
I CAME UP WITH SO MANY STORIES AND PARABLES THAT DON'T HAVE FUNNY PUNCHLINES. I FEEL LIKE IT'S IMPERATIVE THAT I DO THIS.
MAYBE THAT WAY...
...I CAN HELP OUT ALL THOSE POOR, UNFORTUNATE PRIESTS ON SUNDAY MORNINGS...
...WHO GET TREATED LIKE MASS IS JUST A CHANCE TO GO BACK TO SLEEP!!
OH...
ISN'T IT MORE RUDE TO SUGGEST THEY CAN'T HELP BUT LULL THE CONGREGATION TO SLEEP?!

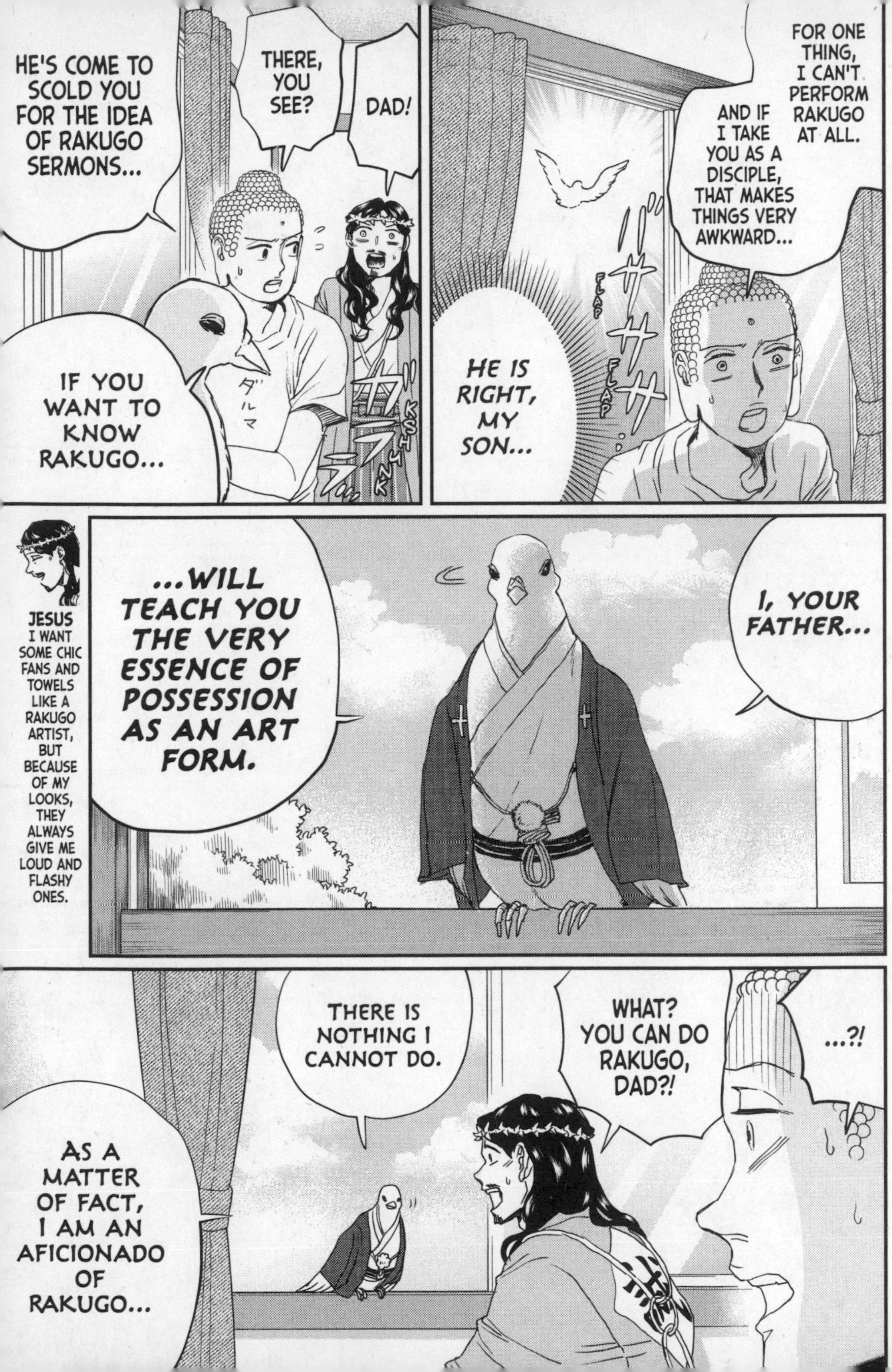
FOR ONE THING, I CAN'T PERFORM RAKUGO AT ALL.
AND IF I TAKE YOU AS A DISCIPLE, THAT MAKES THINGS VERY AWKWARD...
FLAP
FLAP
HE IS RIGHT, MY SON...
DAD!
THERE, YOU SEE?
HE'S COME TO SCOLD YOU FOR THE IDEA OF RAKUGO SERMONS...
ダルマ
KSHUNK
IF YOU WANT TO KNOW RAKUGO...
I, YOUR FATHER...
...WILL TEACH YOU THE VERY ESSENCE OF POSSESSION AS AN ART FORM.
JESUS
I WANT SOME CHIC FANS AND TOWELS LIKE A RAKUGO ARTIST, BUT BECAUSE OF MY LOOKS, THEY ALWAYS GIVE ME LOUD AND FLASHY ONES.
...?!
WHAT? YOU CAN DO RAKUGO, DAD?!
THERE IS NOTHING I CANNOT DO.
AS A MATTER OF FACT, I AM AN AFICIONADO OF RAKUGO...

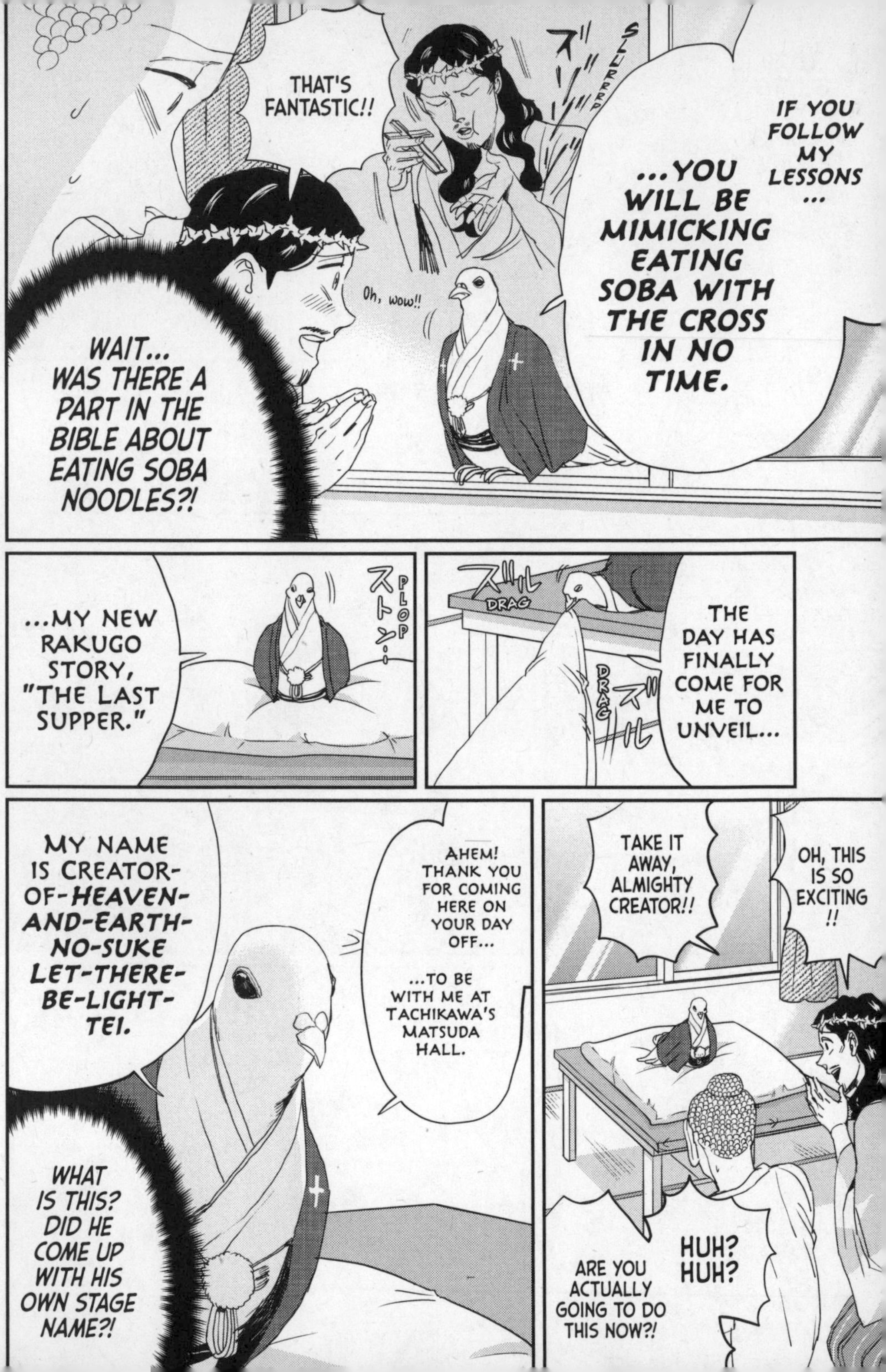
IF YOU FOLLOW MY LESSONS...
...YOU WILL BE MIMICKING EATING SOBA WITH THE CROSS IN NO TIME.
SLURRRP
THAT'S FANTASTIC!!
Oh, wow!!
WAIT... WAS THERE A PART IN THE BIBLE ABOUT EATING SOBA NOODLES?!
THE DAY HAS FINALLY COME FOR ME TO UNVEIL...
DRAG
DRAG
PLOP
...MY NEW RAKUGO STORY, "THE LAST SUPPER."
OH, THIS IS SO EXCITING!!
TAKE IT AWAY, ALMIGHTY CREATOR!!
HUH? HUH?
ARE YOU ACTUALLY GOING TO DO THIS NOW?!
AHEM! THANK YOU FOR COMING HERE ON YOUR DAY OFF...
...TO BE WITH ME AT TACHIKAWA'S MATSUDA HALL.
MY NAME IS CREATOR-OF-HEAVEN-AND-EARTH-NO-SUKE LET-THERE-BE-LIGHT-TEI.
WHAT IS THIS? DID HE COME UP WITH HIS OWN STAGE NAME?!

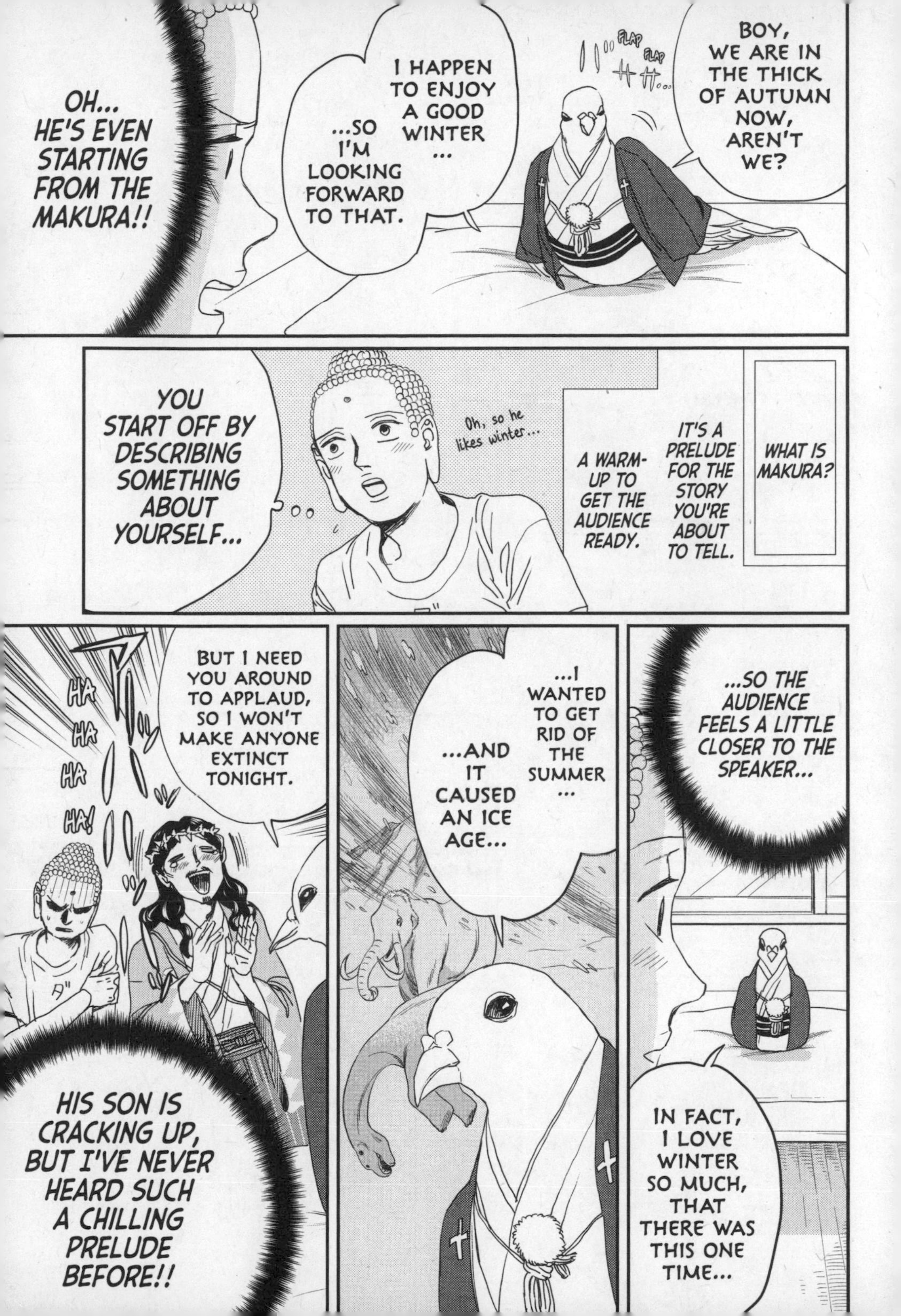
FLAP FLAP
BOY, WE ARE IN THE THICK OF AUTUMN NOW, AREN'T WE?
I HAPPEN TO ENJOY A GOOD WINTER ...
...SO I'M LOOKING FORWARD TO THAT.
OH... HE'S EVEN STARTING FROM THE MAKURA!!
WHAT IS MAKURA?
IT'S A PRELUDE FOR THE STORY YOU'RE ABOUT TO TELL.
A WARM-UP TO GET THE AUDIENCE READY.
Oh, so he likes winter...
YOU START OFF BY DESCRIBING SOMETHING ABOUT YOURSELF...
...SO THE AUDIENCE FEELS A LITTLE CLOSER TO THE SPEAKER...
IN FACT, I LOVE WINTER SO MUCH, THAT THERE WAS THIS ONE TIME...
...I WANTED TO GET RID OF THE SUMMER ...
...AND IT CAUSED AN ICE AGE...
BUT I NEED YOU AROUND TO APPLAUD, SO I WON'T MAKE ANYONE EXTINCT TONIGHT.
HA HA HA HA!
HIS SON IS CRACKING UP, BUT I'VE NEVER HEARD SUCH A CHILLING PRELUDE BEFORE!!

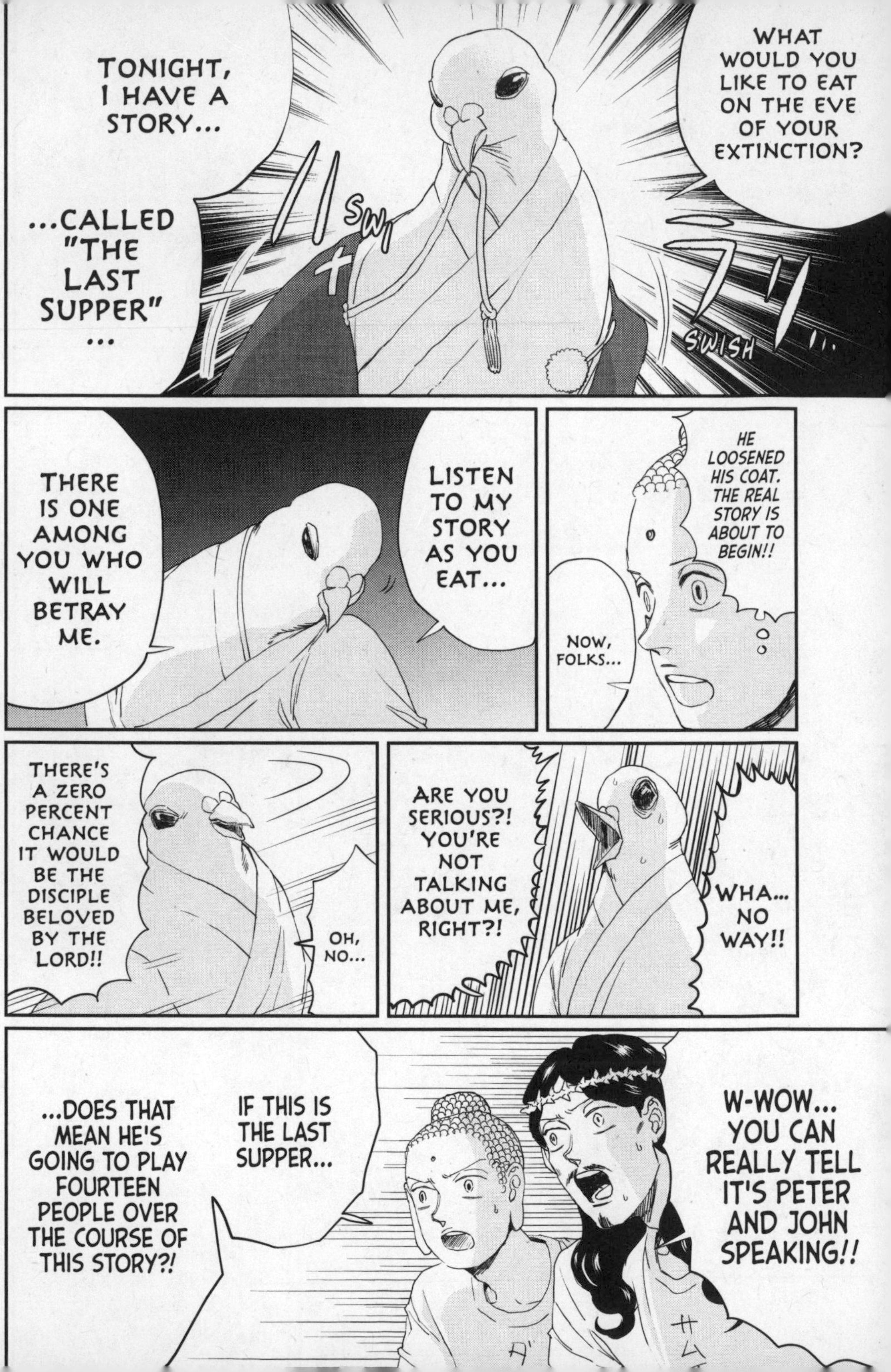
WHAT WOULD YOU LIKE TO EAT ON THE EVE OF YOUR EXTINCTION?
SWISH
TONIGHT, I HAVE A STORY...
SWI
...CALLED "THE LAST SUPPER"...
HE LOOSENED HIS COAT. THE REAL STORY IS ABOUT TO BEGIN!!
NOW, FOLKS...
LISTEN TO MY STORY AS YOU EAT...
THERE IS ONE AMONG YOU WHO WILL BETRAY ME.
WHA... NO WAY!!
ARE YOU SERIOUS?! YOU'RE NOT TALKING ABOUT ME, RIGHT?!
OH, NO...
THERE'S A ZERO PERCENT CHANCE IT WOULD BE THE DISCIPLE BELOVED BY THE LORD!!
W-WOW... YOU CAN REALLY TELL IT'S PETER AND JOHN SPEAKING!!
IF THIS IS THE LAST SUPPER...
...DOES THAT MEAN HE'S GOING TO PLAY FOURTEEN PEOPLE OVER THE COURSE OF THIS STORY?!

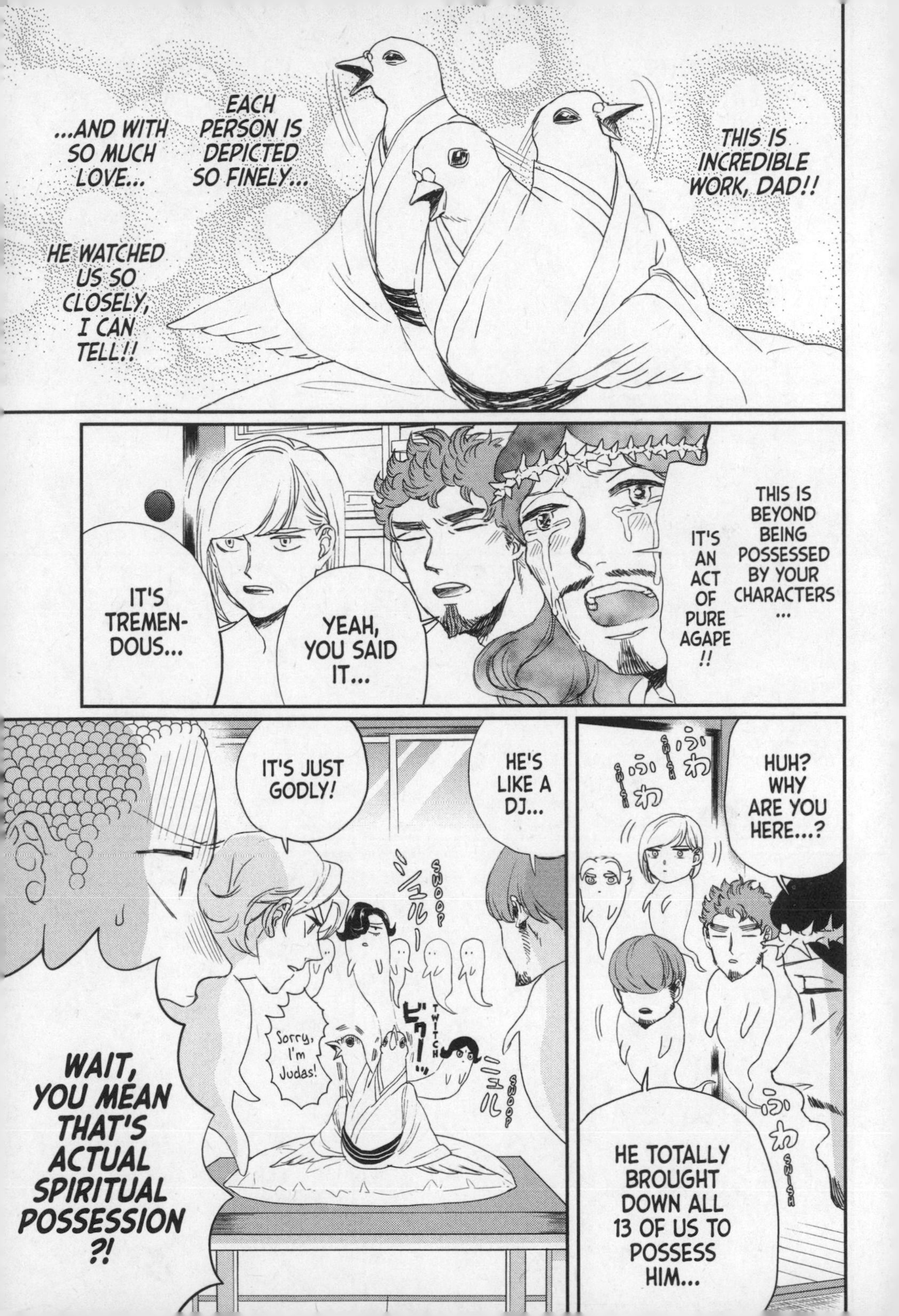
THIS IS INCREDIBLE WORK, DAD!!
EACH PERSON IS DEPICTED SO FINELY...
...AND WITH SO MUCH LOVE...
HE WATCHED US SO CLOSELY, I CAN TELL!!
THIS IS BEYOND BEING POSSESSED BY YOUR CHARACTERS ...
IT'S AN ACT OF PURE AGAPE !!
YEAH, YOU SAID IT...
IT'S TREMENDOUS...
ふわ SWISH
ふわ SWISH
HUH? WHY ARE YOU HERE...?
ふわ SWISH
HE TOTALLY BROUGHT DOWN ALL 13 OF US TO POSSESS HIM...
HE'S LIKE A DJ...
IT'S JUST GODLY!
シュルー SWOOP
ビクー!! TWITCH
ニュル SWOOP
Sorry, I'm Judas!
WAIT, YOU MEAN THAT'S ACTUAL SPIRITUAL POSSESSION ?!

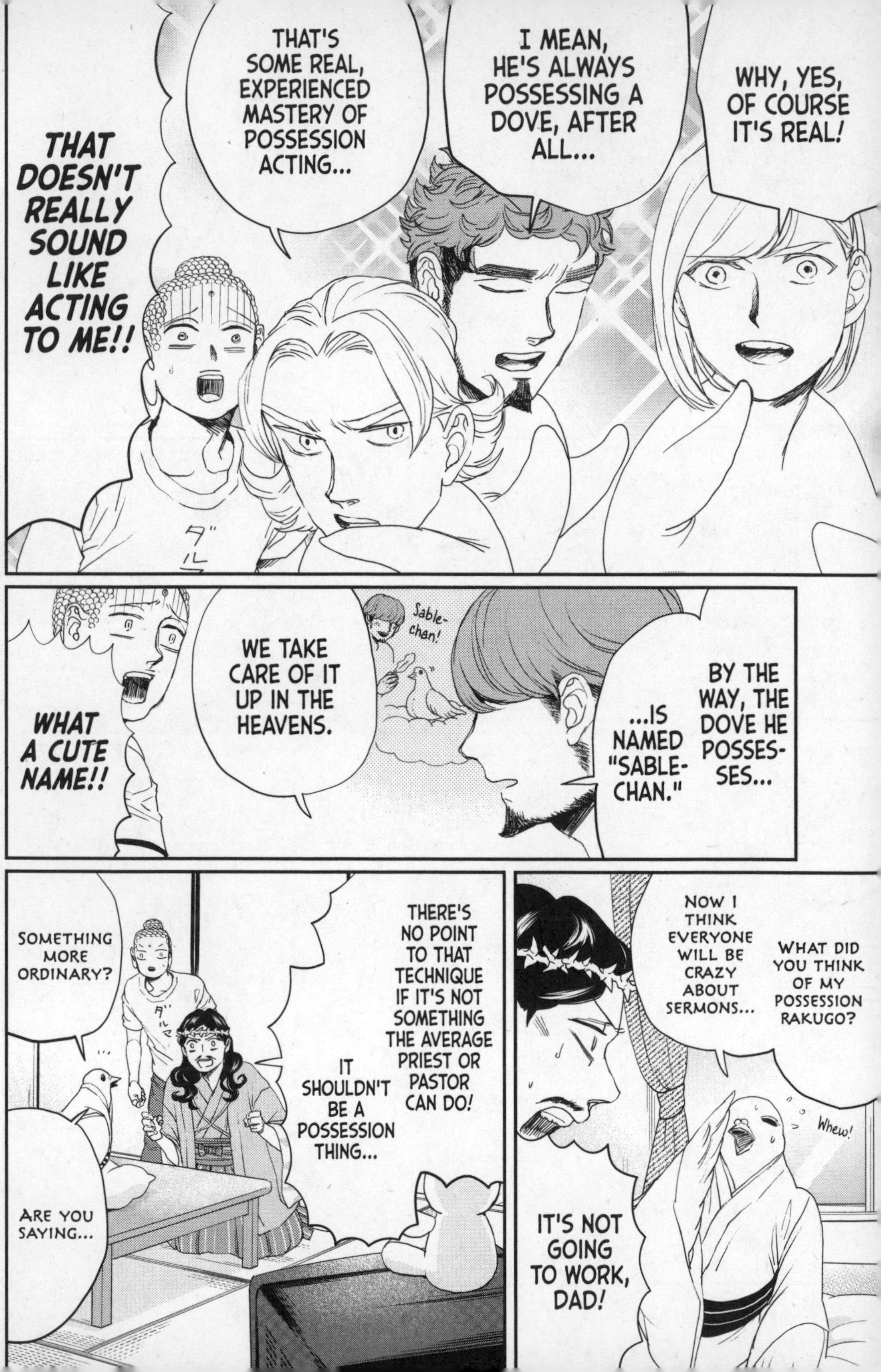
WHY, YES, OF COURSE IT'S REAL!
I MEAN, HE'S ALWAYS POSSESSING A DOVE, AFTER ALL...
THAT'S SOME REAL, EXPERIENCED MASTERY OF POSSESSION ACTING...
THAT DOESN'T REALLY SOUND LIKE ACTING TO ME!!
BY THE WAY, THE DOVE HE POSSESSES...
...IS NAMED "SABLE-CHAN."
Sable-chan!
WE TAKE CARE OF IT UP IN THE HEAVENS.
WHAT A CUTE NAME!!
WHAT DID YOU THINK OF MY POSSESSION RAKUGO?
NOW I THINK EVERYONE WILL BE CRAZY ABOUT SERMONS...
Whew!
IT'S NOT GOING TO WORK, DAD!
THERE'S NO POINT TO THAT TECHNIQUE IF IT'S NOT SOMETHING THE AVERAGE PRIEST OR PASTOR CAN DO!
IT SHOULDN'T BE A POSSESSION THING...
ARE YOU SAYING...
SOMETHING MORE ORDINARY?

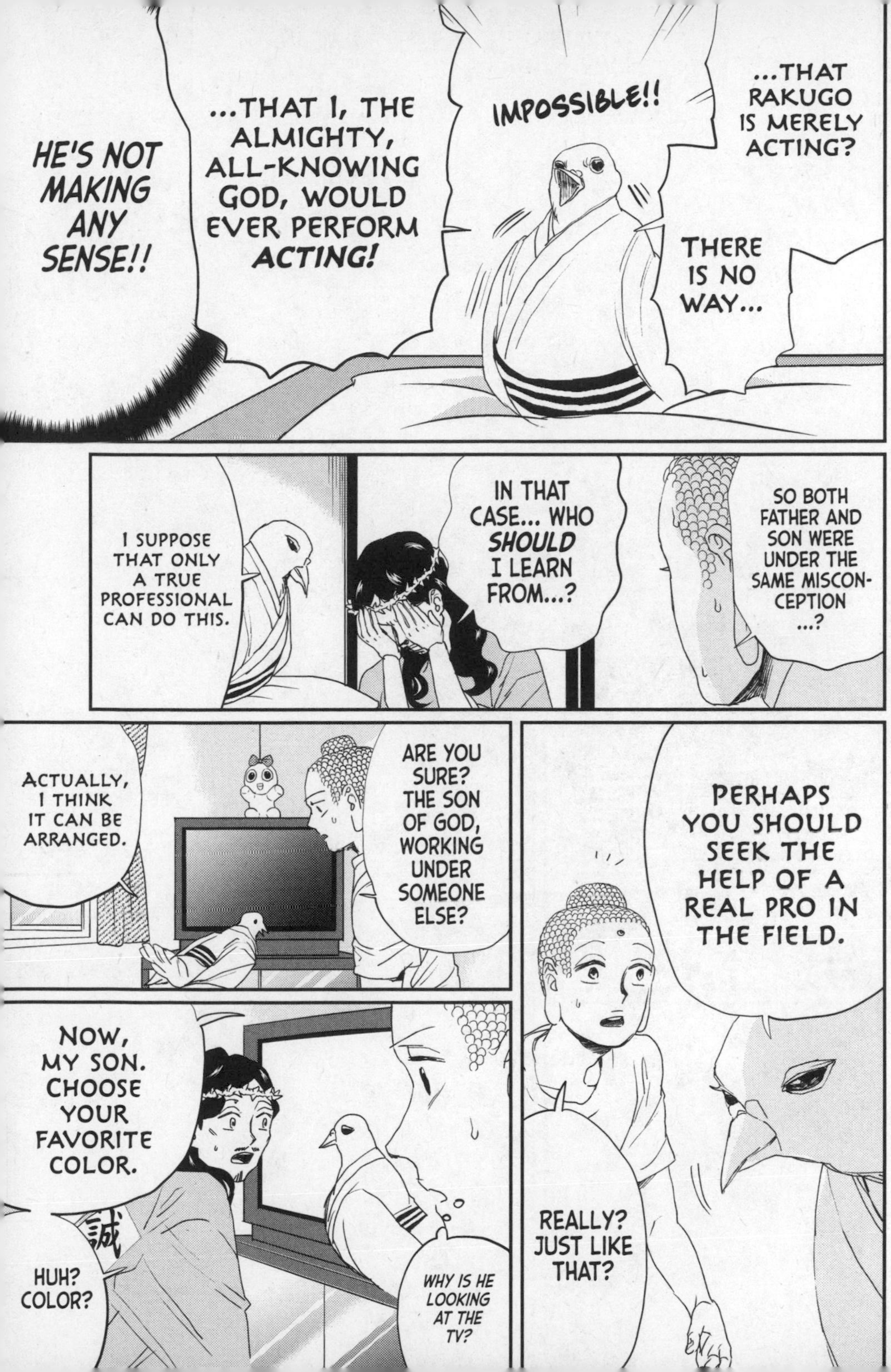
...THAT RAKUGO IS MERELY ACTING?
THERE IS NO WAY...
IMPOSSIBLE!!
...THAT I, THE ALMIGHTY, ALL-KNOWING GOD, WOULD EVER PERFORM ACTING!
HE'S NOT MAKING ANY SENSE!!
SO BOTH FATHER AND SON WERE UNDER THE SAME MISCONCEPTION ...?
IN THAT CASE... WHO SHOULD I LEARN FROM...?
I SUPPOSE THAT ONLY A TRUE PROFESSIONAL CAN DO THIS.
PERHAPS YOU SHOULD SEEK THE HELP OF A REAL PRO IN THE FIELD.
REALLY? JUST LIKE THAT?
ARE YOU SURE? THE SON OF GOD, WORKING UNDER SOMEONE ELSE?
ACTUALLY, I THINK IT CAN BE ARRANGED.
WHY IS HE LOOKING AT THE TV?
NOW, MY SON. CHOOSE YOUR FAVORITE COLOR.
誠
HUH? COLOR?

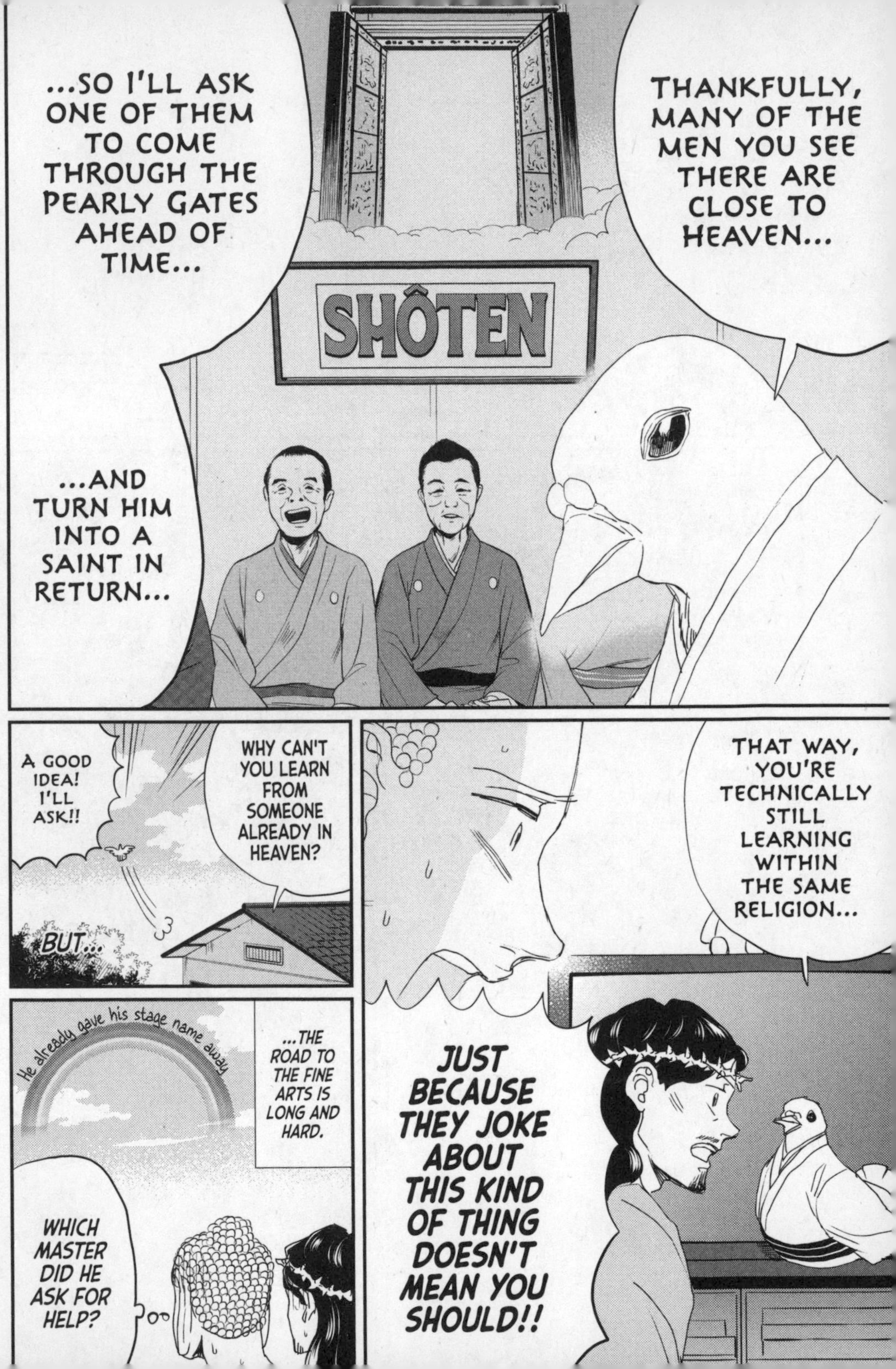
THANKFULLY, MANY OF THE MEN YOU SEE THERE ARE CLOSE TO HEAVEN...
...SO I'LL ASK ONE OF THEM TO COME THROUGH THE PEARLY GATES AHEAD OF TIME...
SHÔTEN
...AND TURN HIM INTO A SAINT IN RETURN...
THAT WAY, YOU'RE TECHNICALLY STILL LEARNING WITHIN THE SAME RELIGION...
WHY CAN'T YOU LEARN FROM SOMEONE ALREADY IN HEAVEN?
A GOOD IDEA! I'LL ASK!!
BUT...
JUST BECAUSE THEY JOKE ABOUT THIS KIND OF THING DOESN'T MEAN YOU SHOULD!!
...THE ROAD TO THE FINE ARTS IS LONG AND HARD.
He already gave his stage name away
WHICH MASTER DID HE ASK FOR HELP?

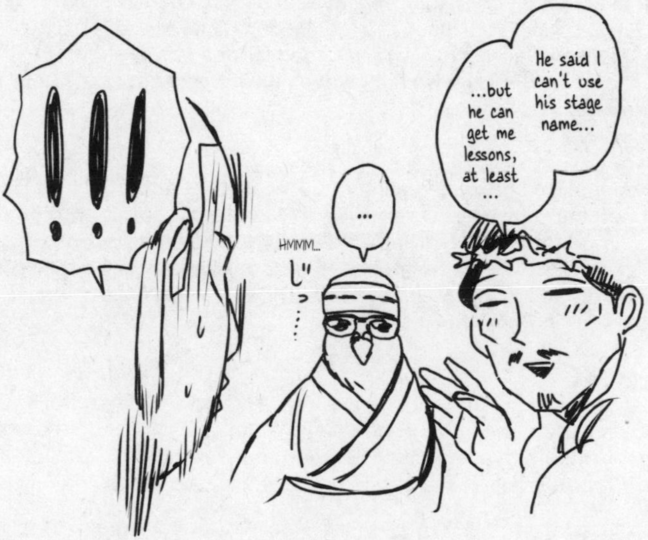

He said I can't use his stage name...
...but he can get me lessons, at least ...
...
HMMM...
じっ……
!!!

SAINT☆YOUNG MEN

CHAPTER 108 TRANSLATION NOTES

Legion, page 74
The name of a group of demons who possessed a man in an account that appears in Mark, Luke, and Matthew. According to Mark, when asked for his name, the possessed man replied, "My name is Legion; for we are many." Jesus then exorcises the demons from him. The name "Legion" has been reused many names in pop culture since then.

Shôten, page 75
An extremely long-running (since 1966) comedy program based on the storytelling art of rakugo and featuring prominent rakugo practitioners, each one wearing a different colored kimono. The show's structure involves a host who poses questions to the panel members, each of whom has a chance to offer answers to make the audience and host laugh. Rakugo-ka typically sit in formal kneeling position on a large *zabuton* cushion, and in *Shôten*, the participants can either receive or lose their cushions depending on the quality of their answers. While the format differs from traditional rakugo, the focus on fast-paced wordplay and wittiness makes use of a rakugo-ka's natural skill.

Limbo, page 76
The Sanzu is the Japanese name for the river that separates the living world from the realm of the dead. There is a Japan-specific belief dating back to the Japanese Middle Ages that an area of Sanzu's riverbank (called *Sai no Kawara*) is a Limbo for dead children, where they must stack rocks from the riverside into towers. However, their cruel ogre tormenters continually knock down the stacks of stones.

Shinsengumi, page 77
A police force assembled by the Tokugawa Shogunate to maintain order in the late Edo period (1860s) at a time when imperial loyalists seeking to restore the emperor to power were ascendant. After the shogunate was overthrown, creating the Empire of Japan, the Shinsengumi were quickly forgotten, but interest in the doomed group was rekindled after WWII with romanticized depictions of their downfall. In *Saint Young Men*, Jesus bought a souvenir Shinsengumi uniform back in Volume 1.

Rakugo names, page 80
Rakugo performers typically apprentice under older masters and receive their stage name in that manner, in many cases as a direct lineage--in other words, handing down the same name through generations of performers. God's name, which was translated into an English form here, was originally Hikariaritei Tentochitsukurinosuke.

Deceased master, page 88
This chapter caused a bit of a stir upon its publication, because the joke at the end about "calling up a master a bit early" was an ill-concealed reference to the longtime host of *Shôten*, Utamaru Katsura, who had recently retired from the program after 50 years due to his health. Within six months of the chapter's initial release (just a month or two after it was collected into paperback form in Japan) Katsura passed away at the age of 81.

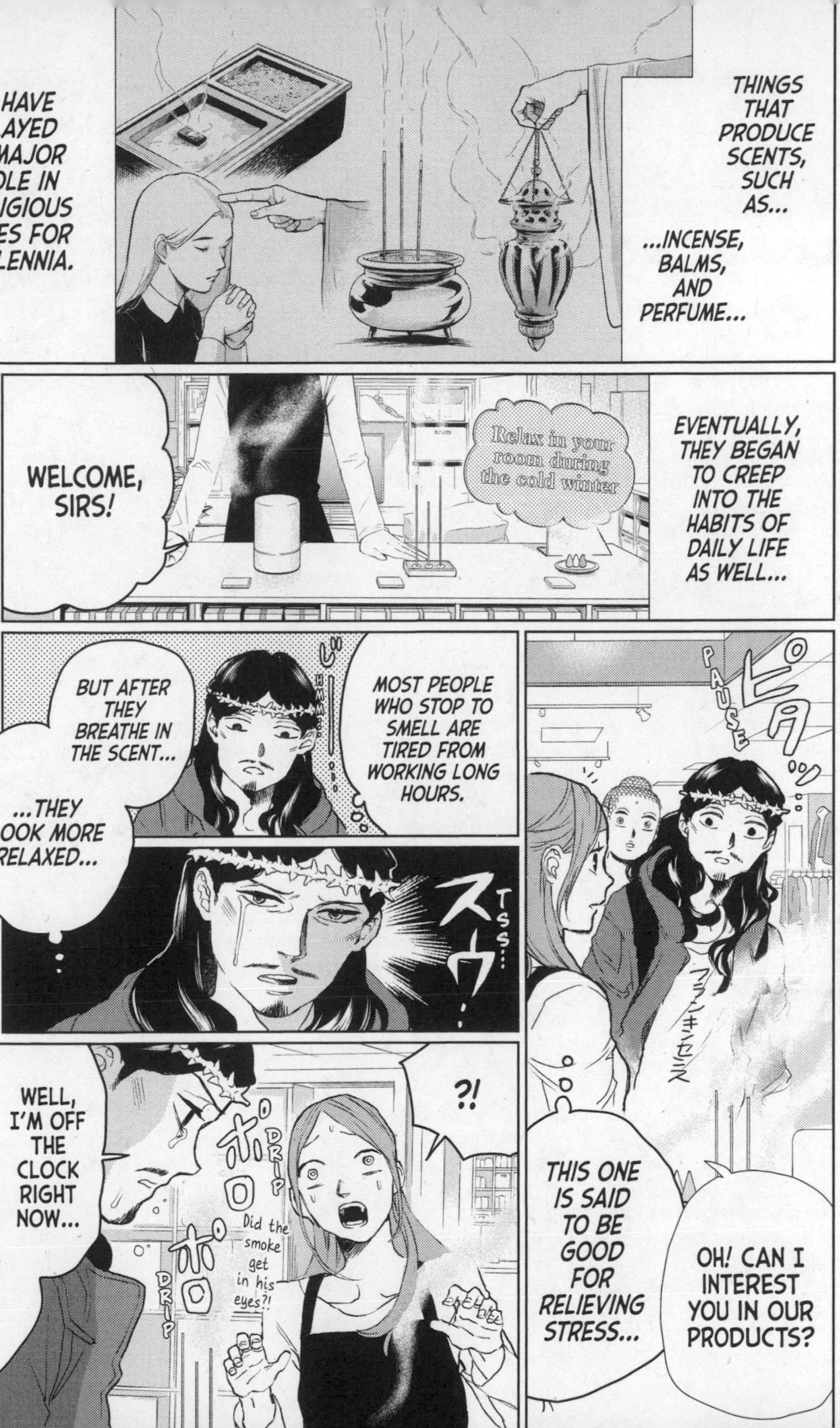
THINGS THAT PRODUCE SCENTS, SUCH AS...
...INCENSE, BALMS, AND PERFUME...
...HAVE PLAYED A MAJOR ROLE IN RELIGIOUS RITES FOR MILLENNIA.
EVENTUALLY, THEY BEGAN TO CREEP INTO THE HABITS OF DAILY LIFE AS WELL...
Relax in your room during the cold winter
WELCOME, SIRS!
ピタ
PAUSE
フランキンセンス
MOST PEOPLE WHO STOP TO SMELL ARE TIRED FROM WORKING LONG HOURS.
じー
HMM...
BUT AFTER THEY BREATHE IN THE SCENT...
...THEY LOOK MORE RELAXED...
スゥ
TSS...
OH! CAN I INTEREST YOU IN OUR PRODUCTS?
THIS ONE IS SAID TO BE GOOD FOR RELIEVING STRESS...
?!
Did the smoke get in his eyes?!
ポロ
DRIP
ポロ
DRIP
WELL, I'M OFF THE CLOCK RIGHT NOW...
...BUT I CAN MAKE AN EXCEPTION.

JESUS'S SHIRT: FRANKINCENSE

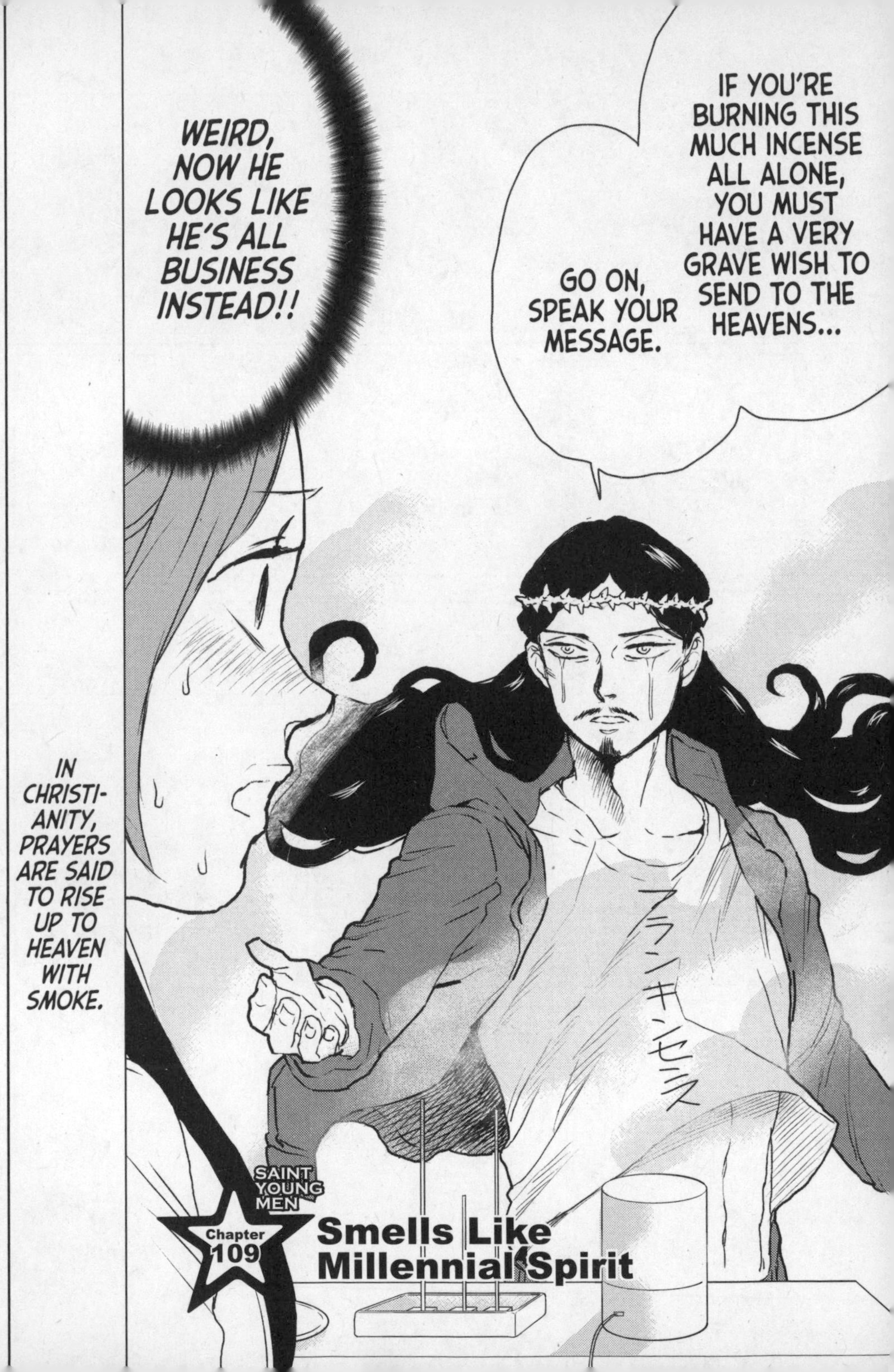
IF YOU'RE BURNING THIS MUCH INCENSE ALL ALONE, YOU MUST HAVE A VERY GRAVE WISH TO SEND TO THE HEAVENS...
GO ON, SPEAK YOUR MESSAGE.
WEIRD, NOW HE LOOKS LIKE HE'S ALL BUSINESS INSTEAD!!
フランキンセンス
SAINT YOUNG MEN
Chapter 109
Smells Like Millennial Spirit
IN CHRISTIANITY, PRAYERS ARE SAID TO RISE UP TO HEAVEN WITH SMOKE.

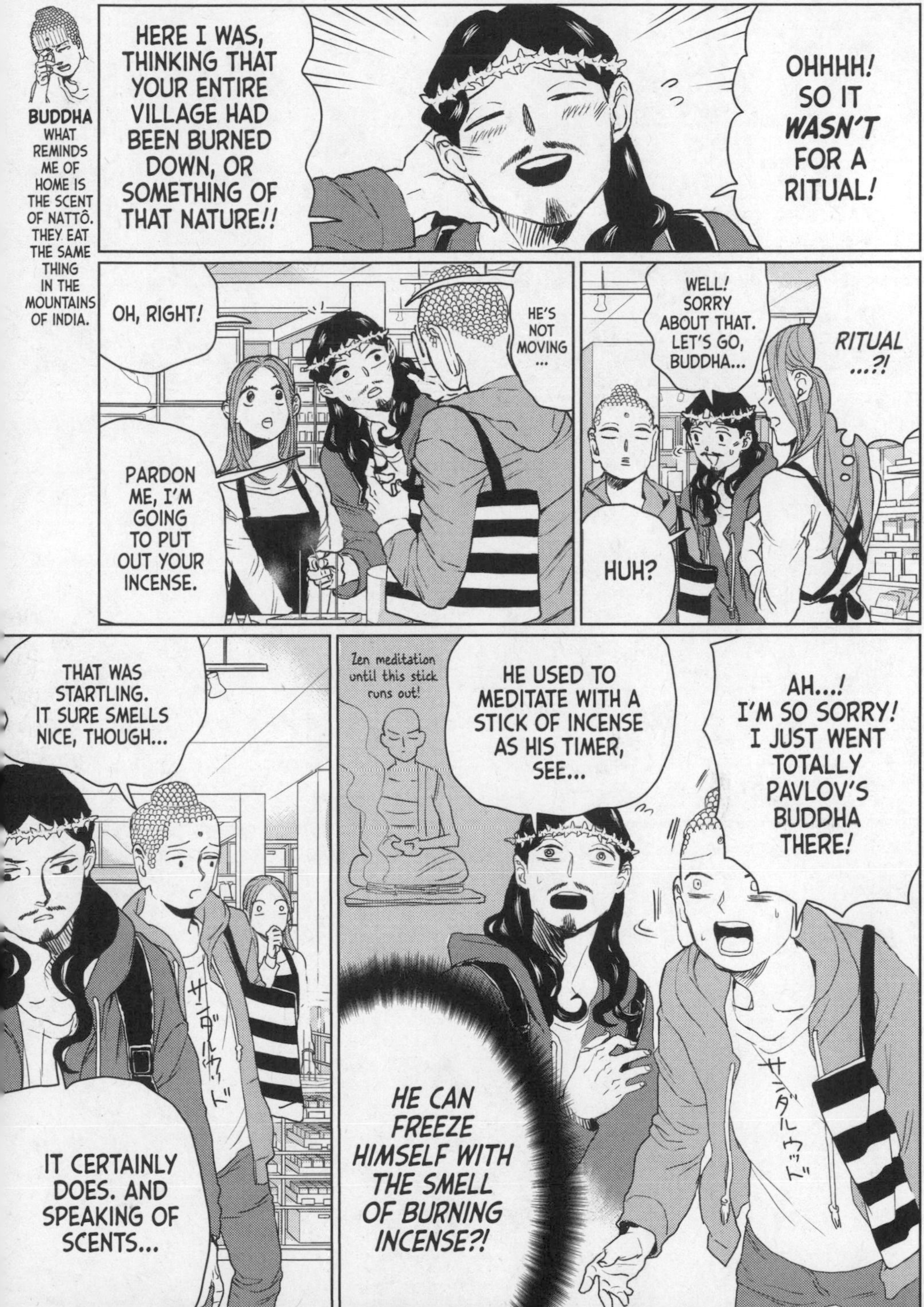

OHHHH! SO IT *WASN'T* FOR A RITUAL!
HERE I WAS, THINKING THAT YOUR ENTIRE VILLAGE HAD BEEN BURNED DOWN, OR SOMETHING OF THAT NATURE!!
RITUAL ...?!
WELL! SORRY ABOUT THAT. LET'S GO, BUDDHA...
HUH?
HE'S NOT MOVING ...
OH, RIGHT!
PARDON ME, I'M GOING TO PUT OUT YOUR INCENSE.
AH...! I'M SO SORRY! I JUST WENT TOTALLY PAVLOV'S BUDDHA THERE!
HE USED TO MEDITATE WITH A STICK OF INCENSE AS HIS TIMER, SEE...
Zen meditation until this stick runs out!
HE CAN FREEZE HIMSELF WITH THE SMELL OF BURNING INCENSE?!
サンダルウッド
THAT WAS STARTLING. IT SURE SMELLS NICE, THOUGH...
IT CERTAINLY DOES. AND SPEAKING OF SCENTS...
サンダルウッド

BUDDHA
WHAT REMINDS ME OF HOME IS THE SCENT OF NATTÔ. THEY EAT THE SAME THING IN THE MOUNTAINS OF INDIA.

BUDDHA'S SHIRT: SANDALWOOD

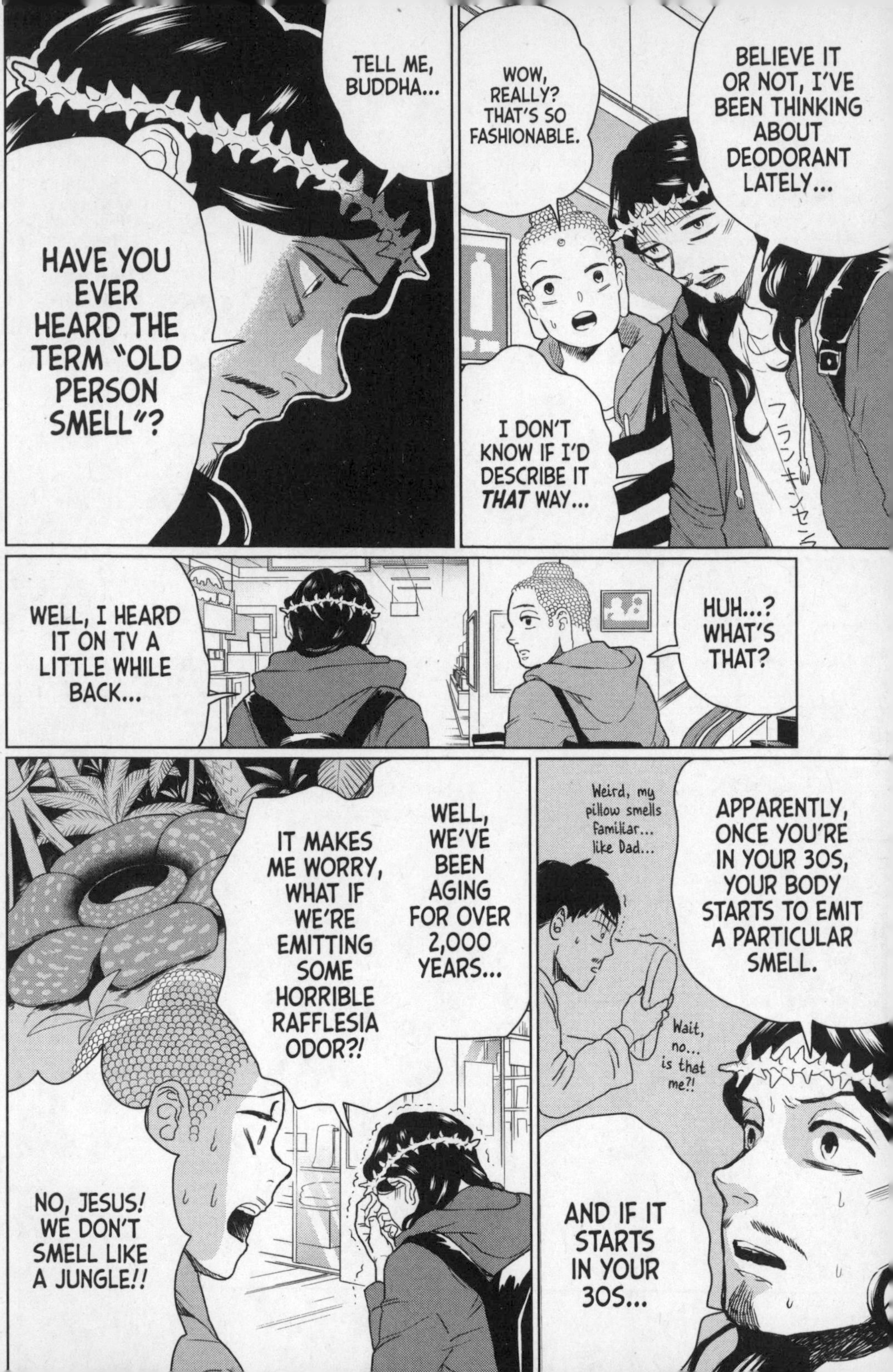
BELIEVE IT OR NOT, I'VE BEEN THINKING ABOUT DEODORANT LATELY...
WOW, REALLY? THAT'S SO FASHIONABLE.
I DON'T KNOW IF I'D DESCRIBE IT *THAT* WAY...
フランキンセ
TELL ME, BUDDHA...
HAVE YOU EVER HEARD THE TERM "OLD PERSON SMELL"?
HUH...? WHAT'S THAT?
WELL, I HEARD IT ON TV A LITTLE WHILE BACK...
APPARENTLY, ONCE YOU'RE IN YOUR 30S, YOUR BODY STARTS TO EMIT A PARTICULAR SMELL.
Weird, my pillow smells familiar... like Dad...
Wait, no... is that me?!
AND IF IT STARTS IN YOUR 30S...
WELL, WE'VE BEEN AGING FOR OVER 2,000 YEARS...
IT MAKES ME WORRY, WHAT IF WE'RE EMITTING SOME HORRIBLE RAFFLESIA ODOR?!
NO, JESUS! WE DON'T SMELL LIKE A JUNGLE!!

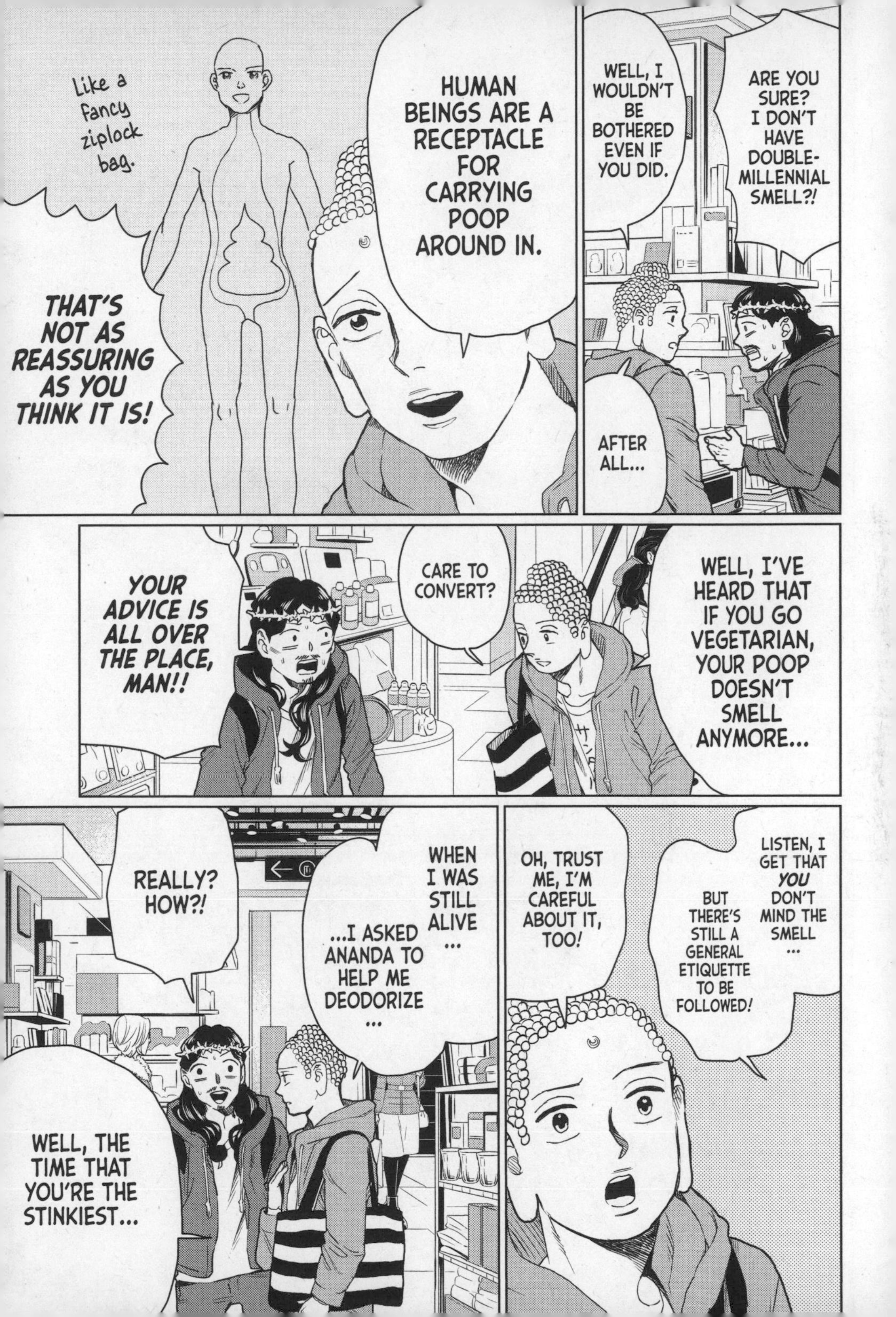

ARE YOU SURE? I DON'T HAVE DOUBLE-MILLENNIAL SMELL?!
WELL, I WOULDN'T BE BOTHERED EVEN IF YOU DID.
AFTER ALL...
HUMAN BEINGS ARE A RECEPTACLE FOR CARRYING POOP AROUND IN.
Like a fancy ziplock bag.
THAT'S NOT AS REASSURING AS YOU THINK IT IS!
WELL, I'VE HEARD THAT IF YOU GO VEGETARIAN, YOUR POOP DOESN'T SMELL ANYMORE...
CARE TO CONVERT?
YOUR ADVICE IS ALL OVER THE PLACE, MAN!!
LISTEN, I GET THAT *YOU* DON'T MIND THE SMELL...
BUT THERE'S STILL A GENERAL ETIQUETTE TO BE FOLLOWED!
OH, TRUST ME, I'M CAREFUL ABOUT IT, TOO!
WHEN I WAS STILL ALIVE...
...I ASKED ANANDA TO HELP ME DEODORIZE...
REALLY? HOW?!
WELL, THE TIME THAT YOU'RE THE STINKIEST...

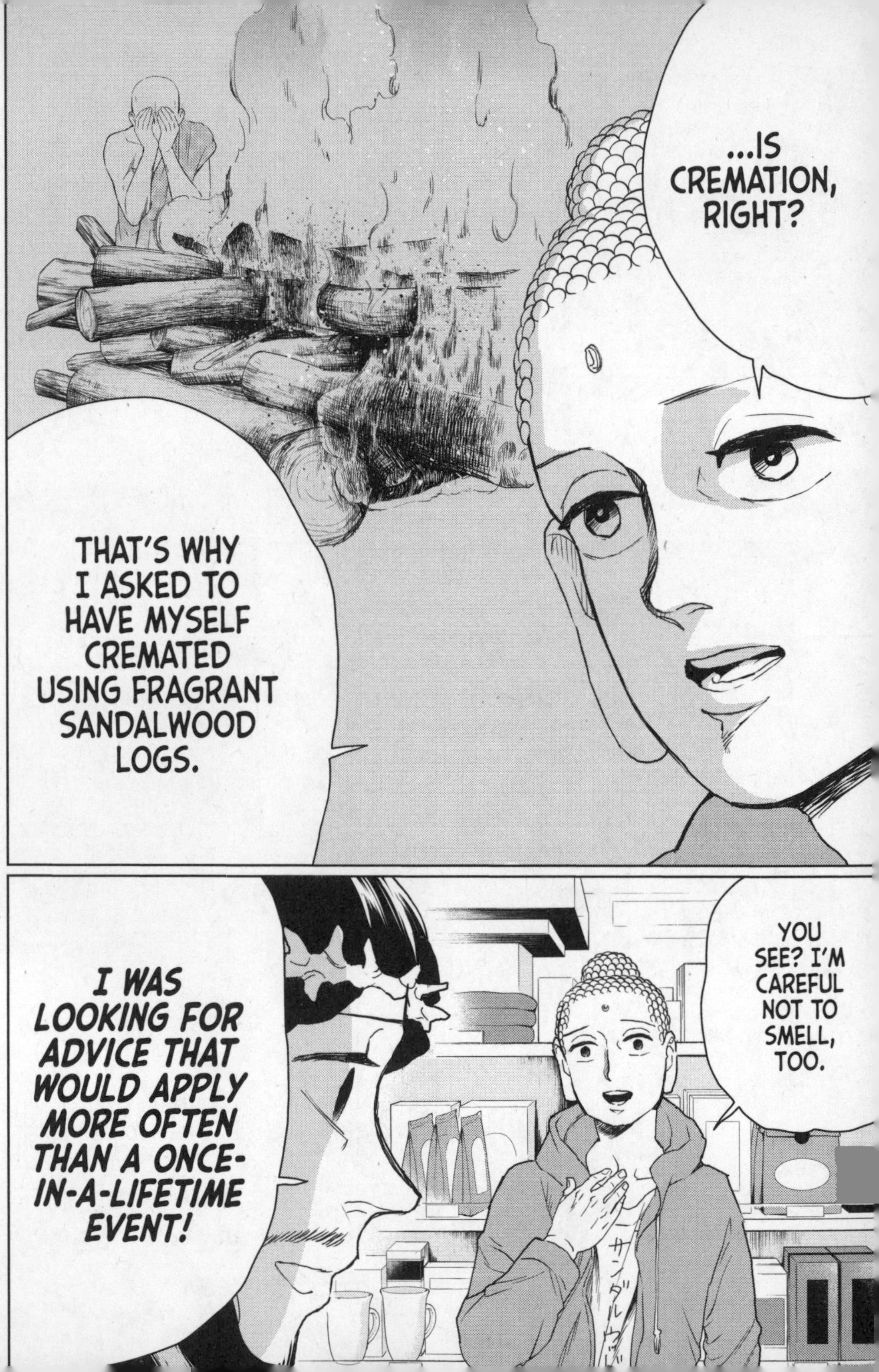
...IS CREMATION, RIGHT?
THAT'S WHY I ASKED TO HAVE MYSELF CREMATED USING FRAGRANT SANDALWOOD LOGS.
YOU SEE? I'M CAREFUL NOT TO SMELL, TOO.
I WAS LOOKING FOR ADVICE THAT WOULD APPLY MORE OFTEN THAN A ONCE-IN-A-LIFETIME EVENT!

JESUS
WHAT REMINDS ME OF HOME IS THE SMELL OF THE FISH MARKET. SURPRISED? ANCHOVY FLAVOR WAS HUGE BACK HOME.

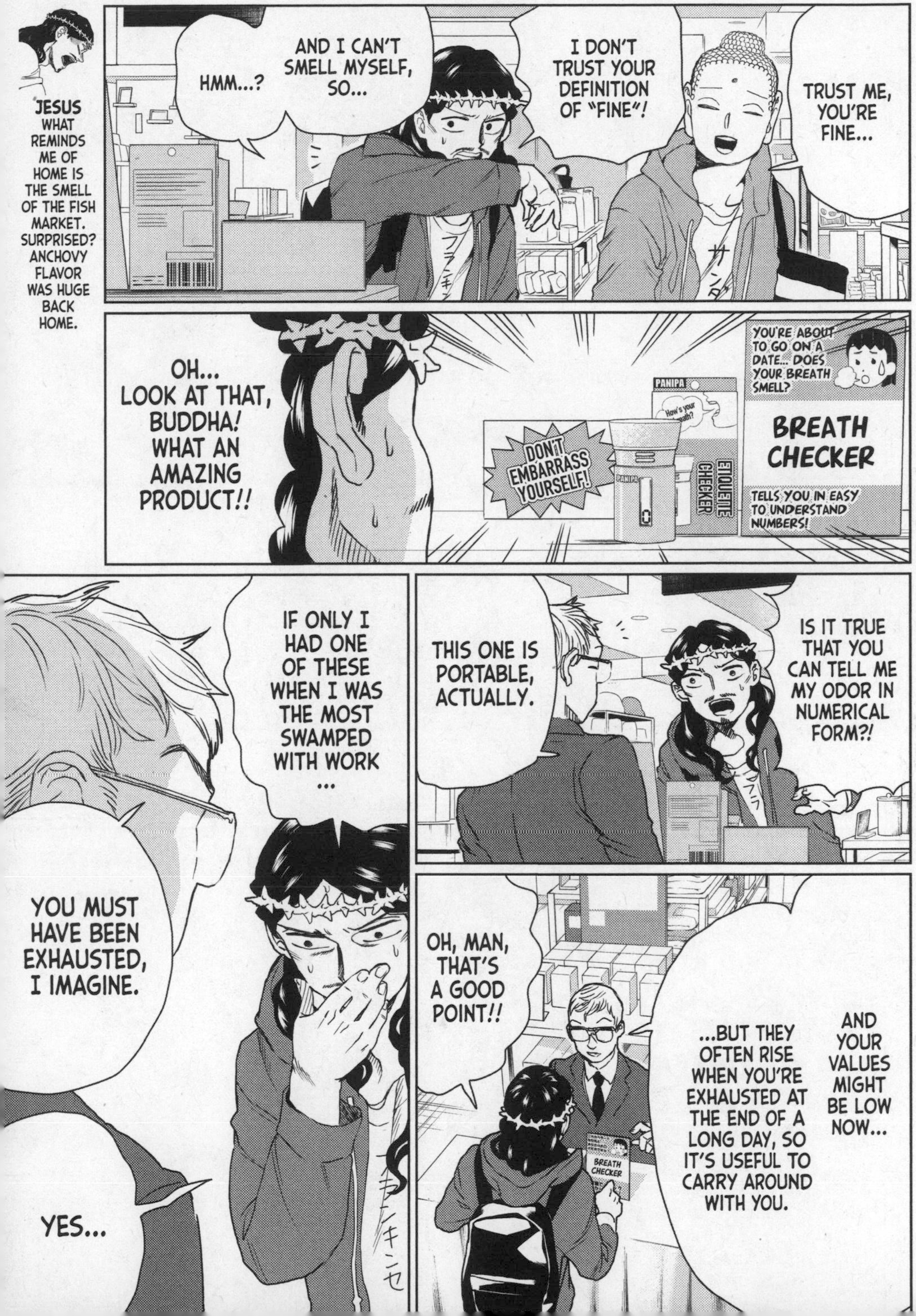

TRUST ME, YOU'RE FINE...
I DON'T TRUST YOUR DEFINITION OF "FINE"!
AND I CAN'T SMELL MYSELF, SO...
HMM...?
YOU'RE ABOUT TO GO ON A DATE... DOES YOUR BREATH SMELL?
BREATH CHECKER
TELLS YOU IN EASY TO UNDERSTAND NUMBERS!
PANIPA
ETIQUETTE CHECKER
DON'T EMBARRASS YOURSELF!
OH... LOOK AT THAT, BUDDHA! WHAT AN AMAZING PRODUCT!!
IS IT TRUE THAT YOU CAN TELL ME MY ODOR IN NUMERICAL FORM?!
THIS ONE IS PORTABLE, ACTUALLY.
AND YOUR VALUES MIGHT BE LOW NOW...
...BUT THEY OFTEN RISE WHEN YOU'RE EXHAUSTED AT THE END OF A LONG DAY, SO IT'S USEFUL TO CARRY AROUND WITH YOU.
OH, MAN, THAT'S A GOOD POINT!!
BREATH CHECKER
IF ONLY I HAD ONE OF THESE WHEN I WAS THE MOST SWAMPED WITH WORK ...
YOU MUST HAVE BEEN EXHAUSTED, I IMAGINE.
YES...

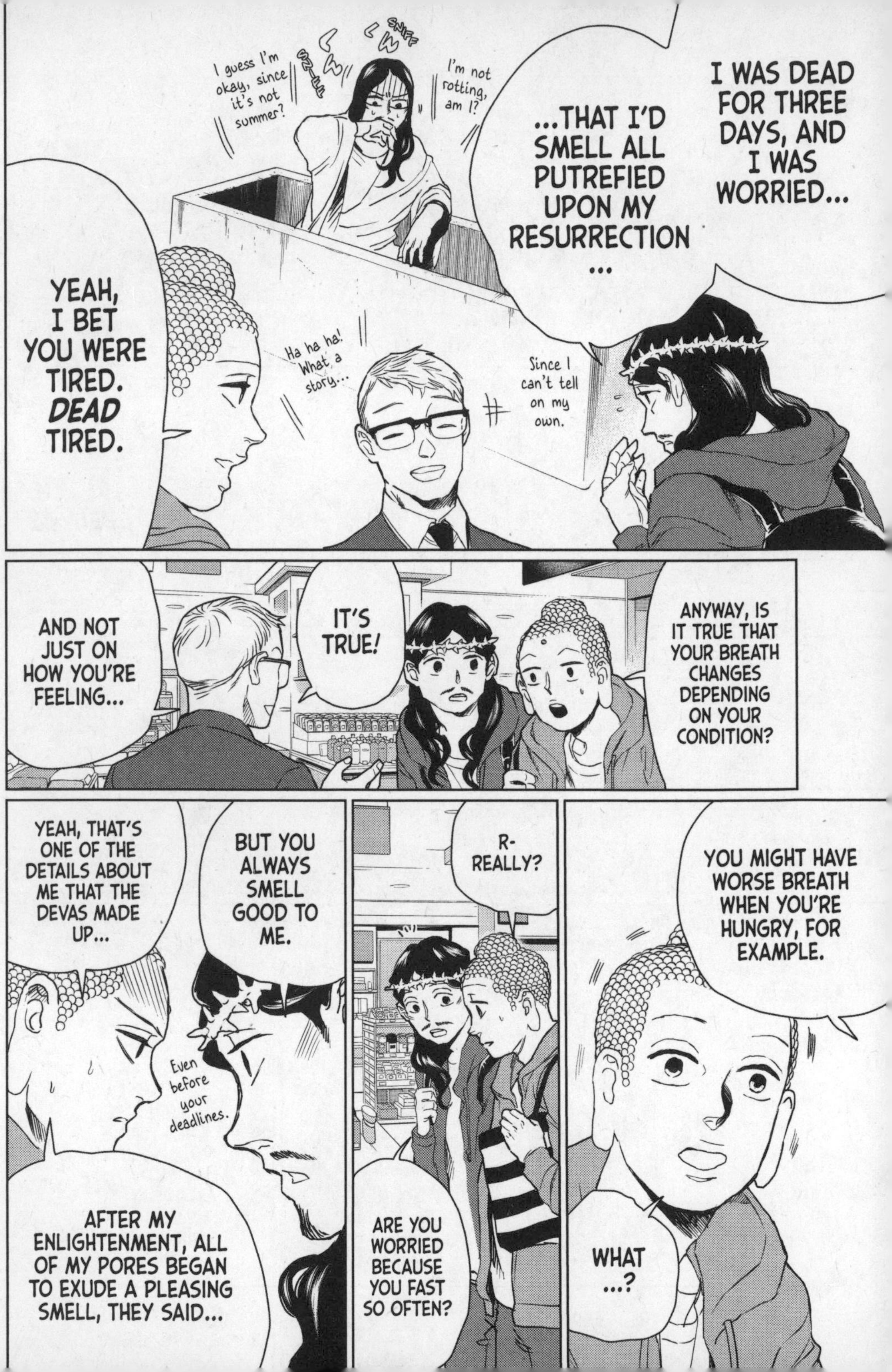
I WAS DEAD FOR THREE DAYS, AND I WAS WORRIED...
...THAT I'D SMELL ALL PUTREFIED UPON MY RESURRECTION ...
I'm not rotting, am I?
SNIFF
SNIFF
I guess I'm okay, since it's not summer?
Since I can't tell on my own.
Ha ha ha! What a story...
YEAH, I BET YOU WERE TIRED. *DEAD* TIRED.
ANYWAY, IS IT TRUE THAT YOUR BREATH CHANGES DEPENDING ON YOUR CONDITION?
IT'S TRUE!
AND NOT JUST ON HOW YOU'RE FEELING...
YOU MIGHT HAVE WORSE BREATH WHEN YOU'RE HUNGRY, FOR EXAMPLE.
WHAT ...?
R- REALLY?
ARE YOU WORRIED BECAUSE YOU FAST SO OFTEN?
BUT YOU ALWAYS SMELL GOOD TO ME.
YEAH, THAT'S ONE OF THE DETAILS ABOUT ME THAT THE DEVAS MADE UP...
Even before your deadlines.
AFTER MY ENLIGHTENMENT, ALL OF MY PORES BEGAN TO EXUDE A PLEASING SMELL, THEY SAID...

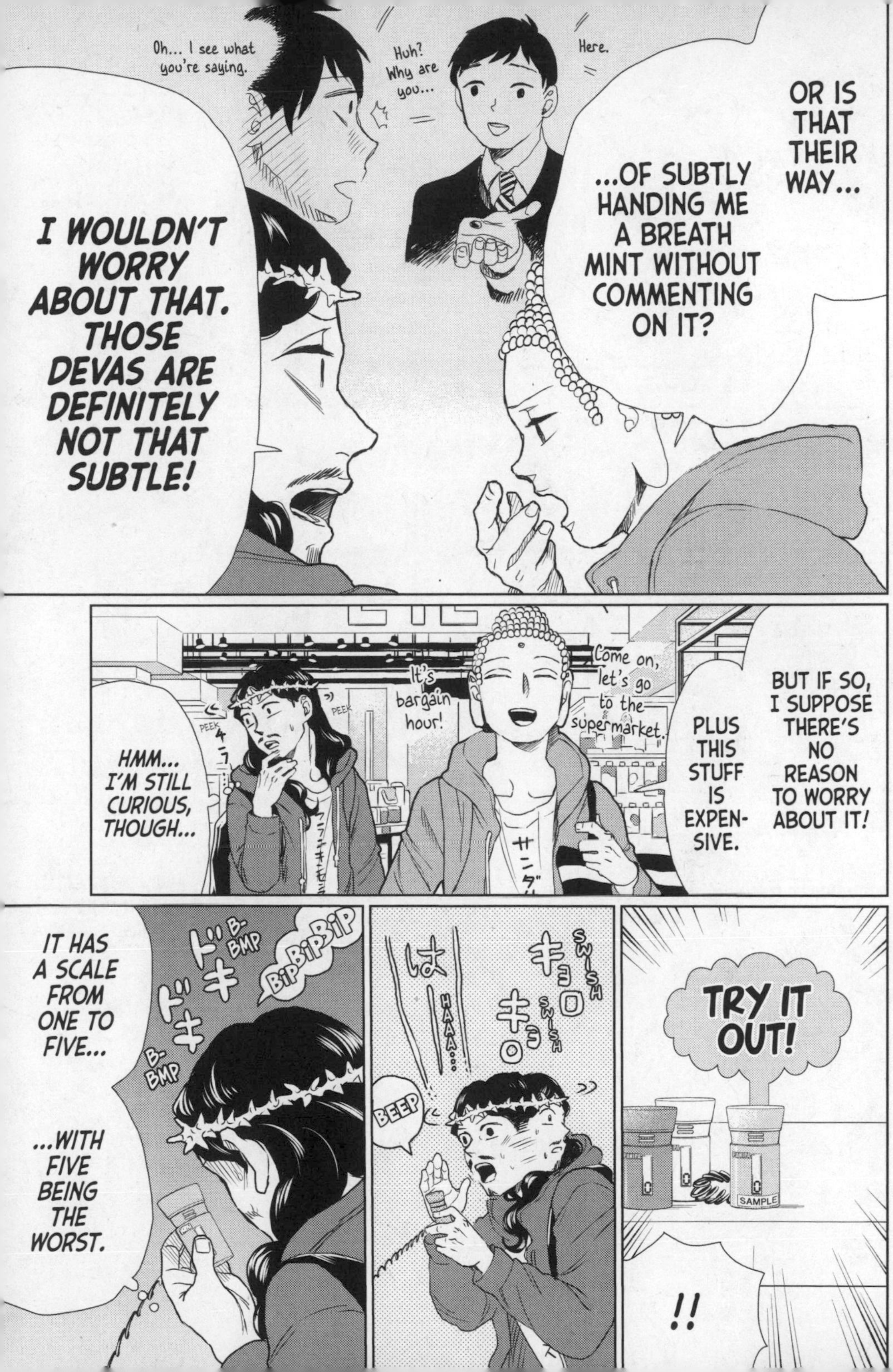
OR IS THAT THEIR WAY...
...OF SUBTLY HANDING ME A BREATH MINT WITHOUT COMMENTING ON IT?
Here.
Huh? Why are you...
Oh... I see what you're saying.
I WOULDN'T WORRY ABOUT THAT. THOSE DEVAS ARE DEFINITELY NOT THAT SUBTLE!
BUT IF SO, I SUPPOSE THERE'S NO REASON TO WORRY ABOUT IT!
PLUS THIS STUFF IS EXPENSIVE.
Come on, let's go to the supermarket.
It's bargain hour!
PEEK
PEEK
HMM... I'M STILL CURIOUS, THOUGH...
TRY IT OUT!
SAMPLE
!!
SWISH
SWISH
HAAA...
BEEP
B-BMP
BiP BiP BiP
B-BMP
IT HAS A SCALE FROM ONE TO FIVE...
...WITH FIVE BEING THE WORST.

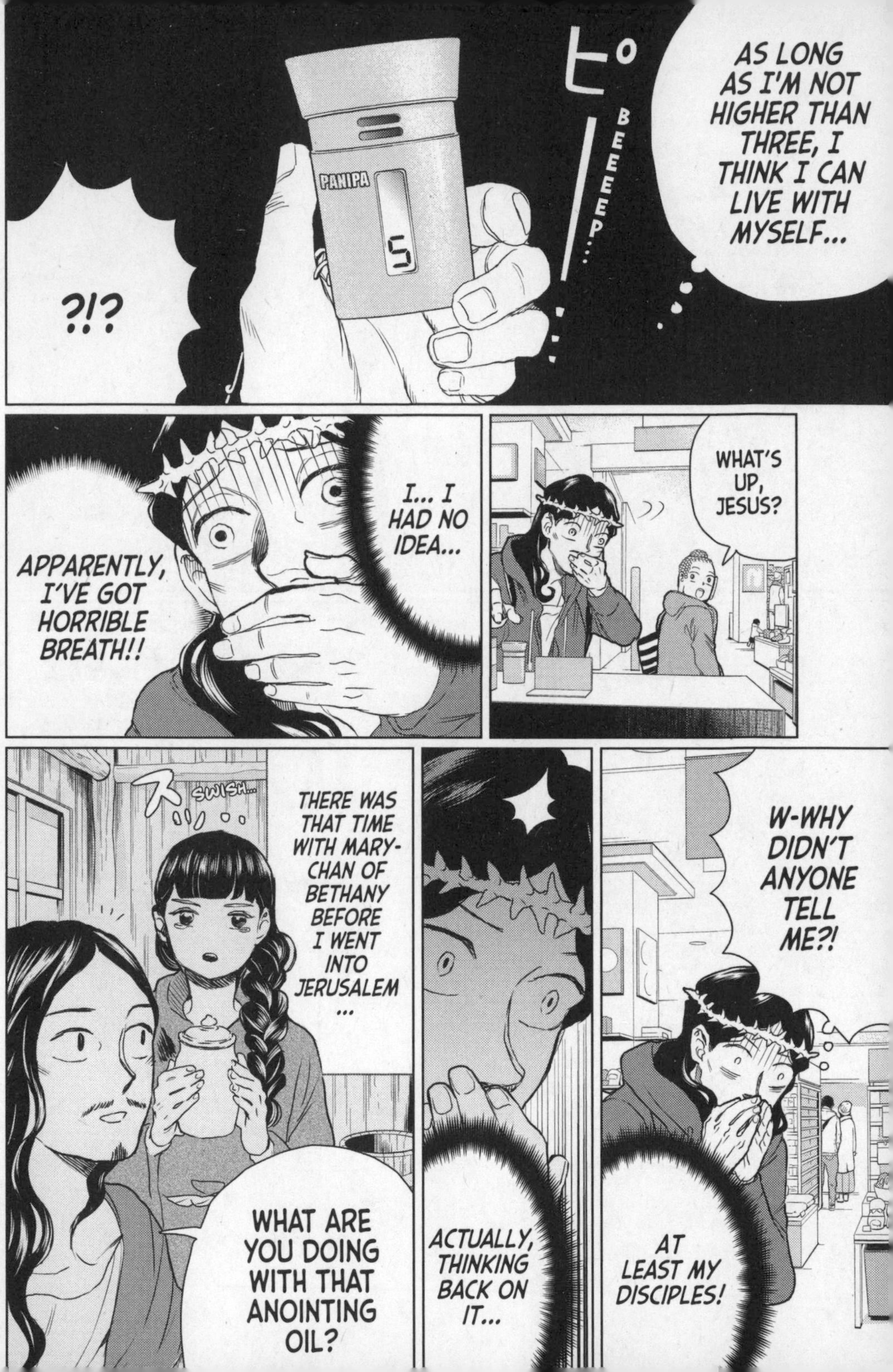
AS LONG AS I'M NOT HIGHER THAN THREE, I THINK I CAN LIVE WITH MYSELF...
BEEEEEP...
PANIPA
5
?!?
WHAT'S UP, JESUS?
I... I HAD NO IDEA...
APPARENTLY, I'VE GOT HORRIBLE BREATH!!
W-WHY DIDN'T ANYONE TELL ME?!
AT LEAST MY DISCIPLES!
ACTUALLY, THINKING BACK ON IT...
THERE WAS THAT TIME WITH MARY-CHAN OF BETHANY BEFORE I WENT INTO JERUSALEM ...
SWISH...
WHAT ARE YOU DOING WITH THAT ANOINTING OIL?

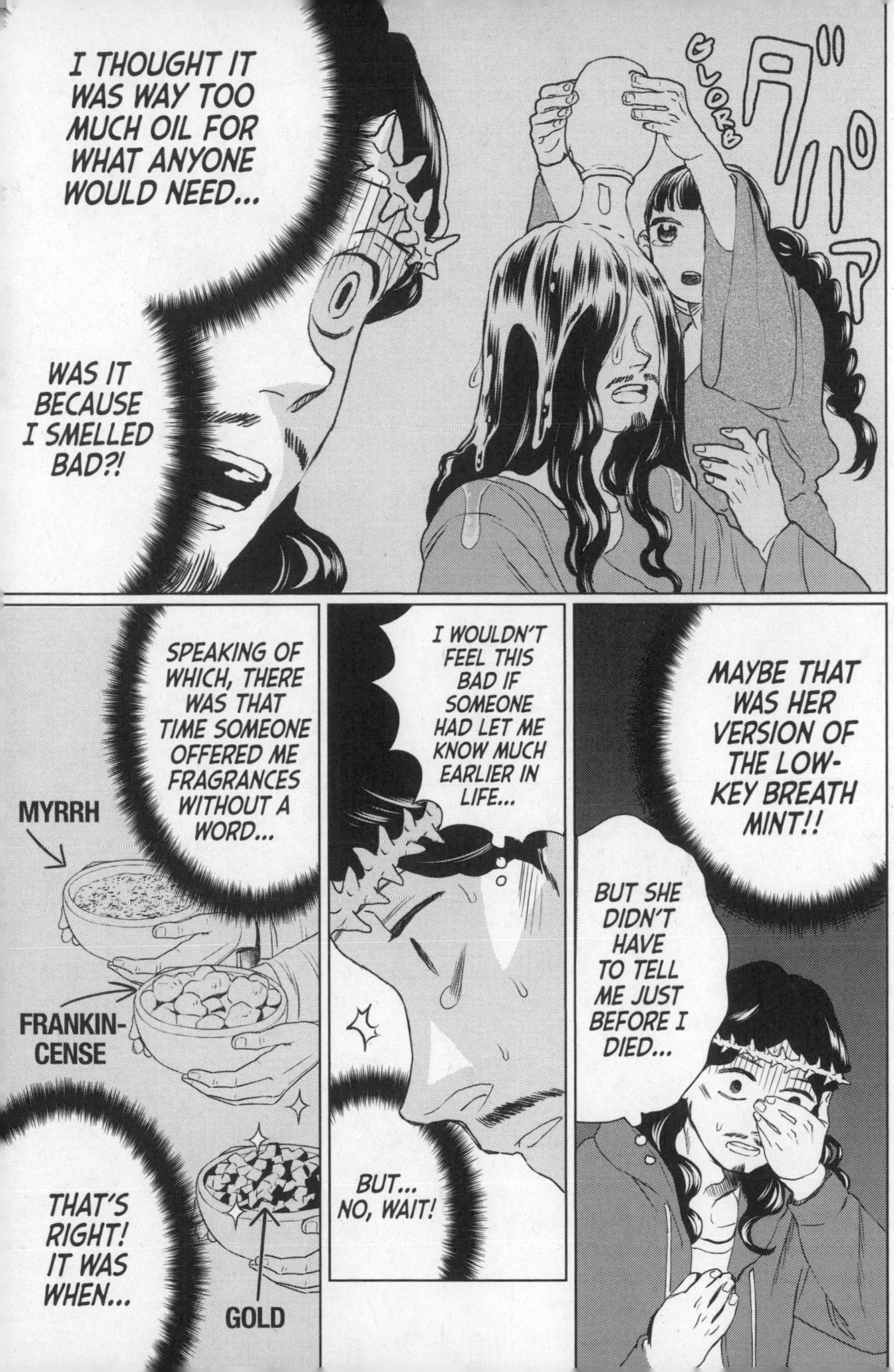
GLORB
I THOUGHT IT WAS WAY TOO MUCH OIL FOR WHAT ANYONE WOULD NEED...
WAS IT BECAUSE I SMELLED BAD?!
MAYBE THAT WAS HER VERSION OF THE LOW-KEY BREATH MINT!!
BUT SHE DIDN'T HAVE TO TELL ME JUST BEFORE I DIED...
I WOULDN'T FEEL THIS BAD IF SOMEONE HAD LET ME KNOW MUCH EARLIER IN LIFE...
BUT... NO, WAIT!
SPEAKING OF WHICH, THERE WAS THAT TIME SOMEONE OFFERED ME FRAGRANCES WITHOUT A WORD...
MYRRH
FRANKIN-CENSE
GOLD
THAT'S RIGHT! IT WAS WHEN...

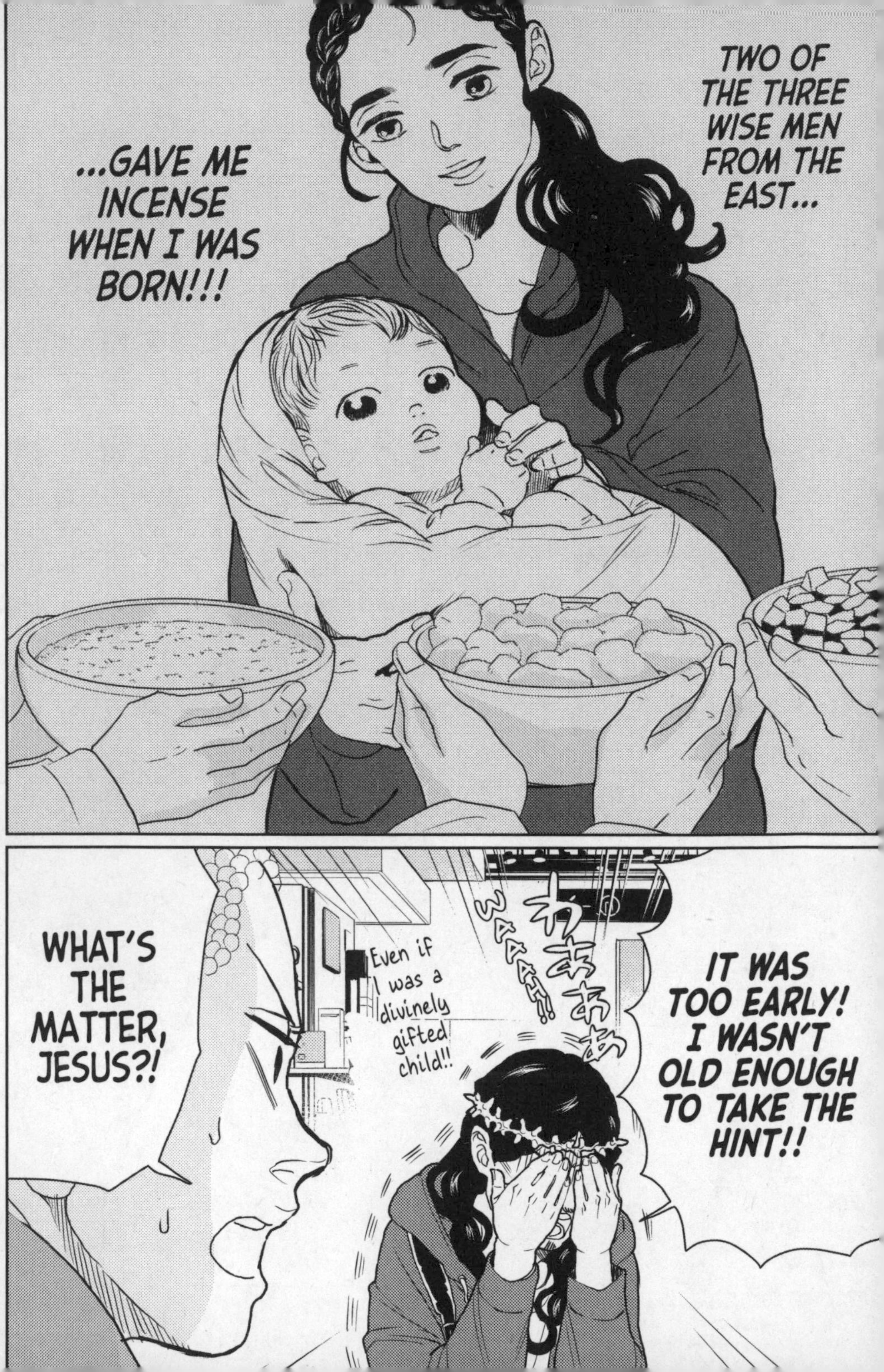
TWO OF THE THREE WISE MEN FROM THE EAST...
...GAVE ME INCENSE WHEN I WAS BORN!!!
IT WAS TOO EARLY! I WASN'T OLD ENOUGH TO TAKE THE HINT!!
わあああ
WAAAH!!
Even if I was a divinely gifted child!!
WHAT'S THE MATTER, JESUS?!

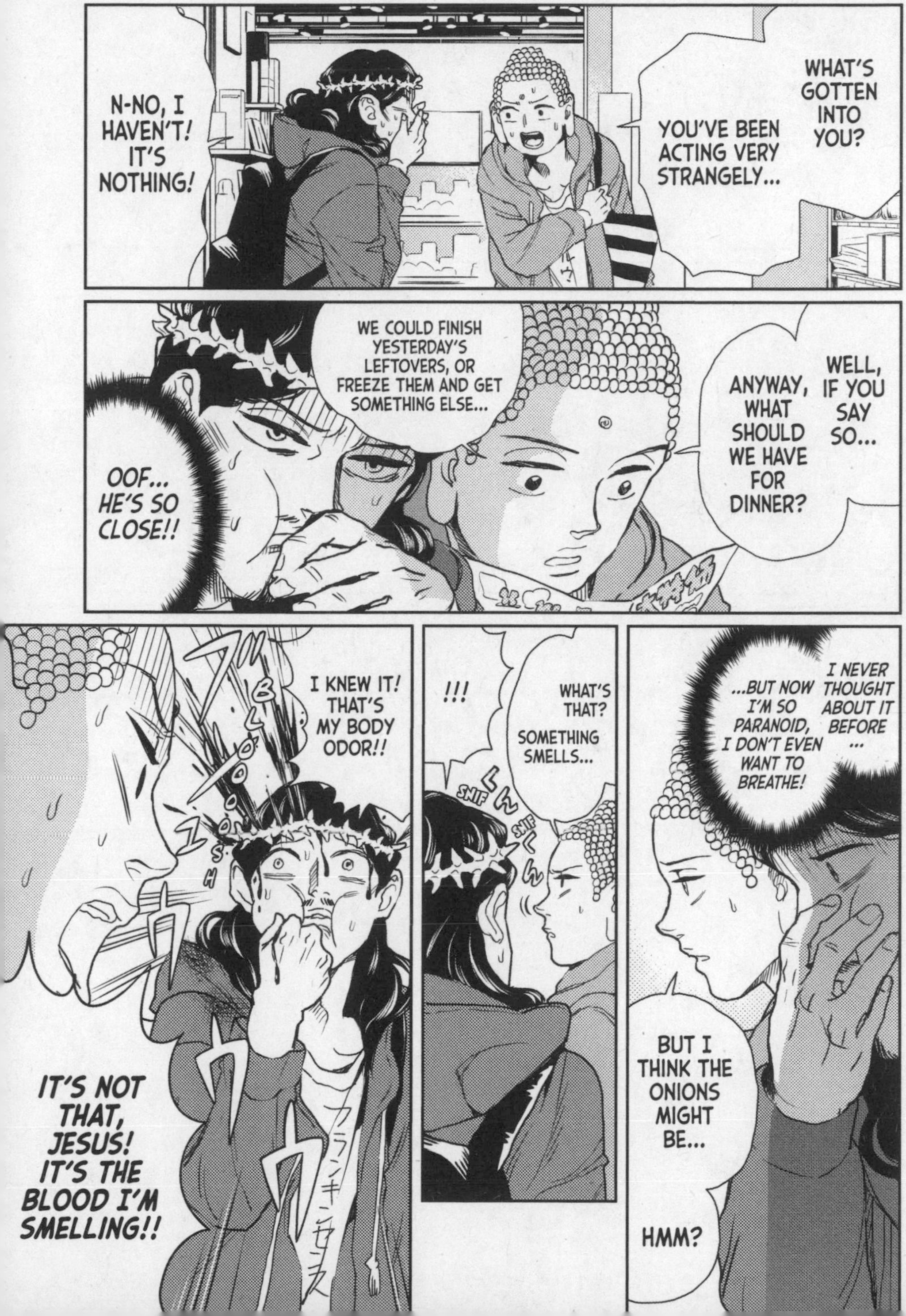
WHAT'S GOTTEN INTO YOU?
YOU'VE BEEN ACTING VERY STRANGELY...
N-NO, I HAVEN'T! IT'S NOTHING!
WELL, IF YOU SAY SO...
ANYWAY, WHAT SHOULD WE HAVE FOR DINNER?
WE COULD FINISH YESTERDAY'S LEFTOVERS, OR FREEZE THEM AND GET SOMETHING ELSE...
OOF... HE'S SO CLOSE!!
I NEVER THOUGHT ABOUT IT BEFORE ...
...BUT NOW I'M SO PARANOID, I DON'T EVEN WANT TO BREATHE!
BUT I THINK THE ONIONS MIGHT BE...
HMM?
WHAT'S THAT?
SOMETHING SMELLS...
SNIF
SNIF
!!!
I KNEW IT! THAT'S MY BODY ODOR!!
IT'S NOT THAT, JESUS! IT'S THE BLOOD I'M SMELLING!!
フランキンセンス

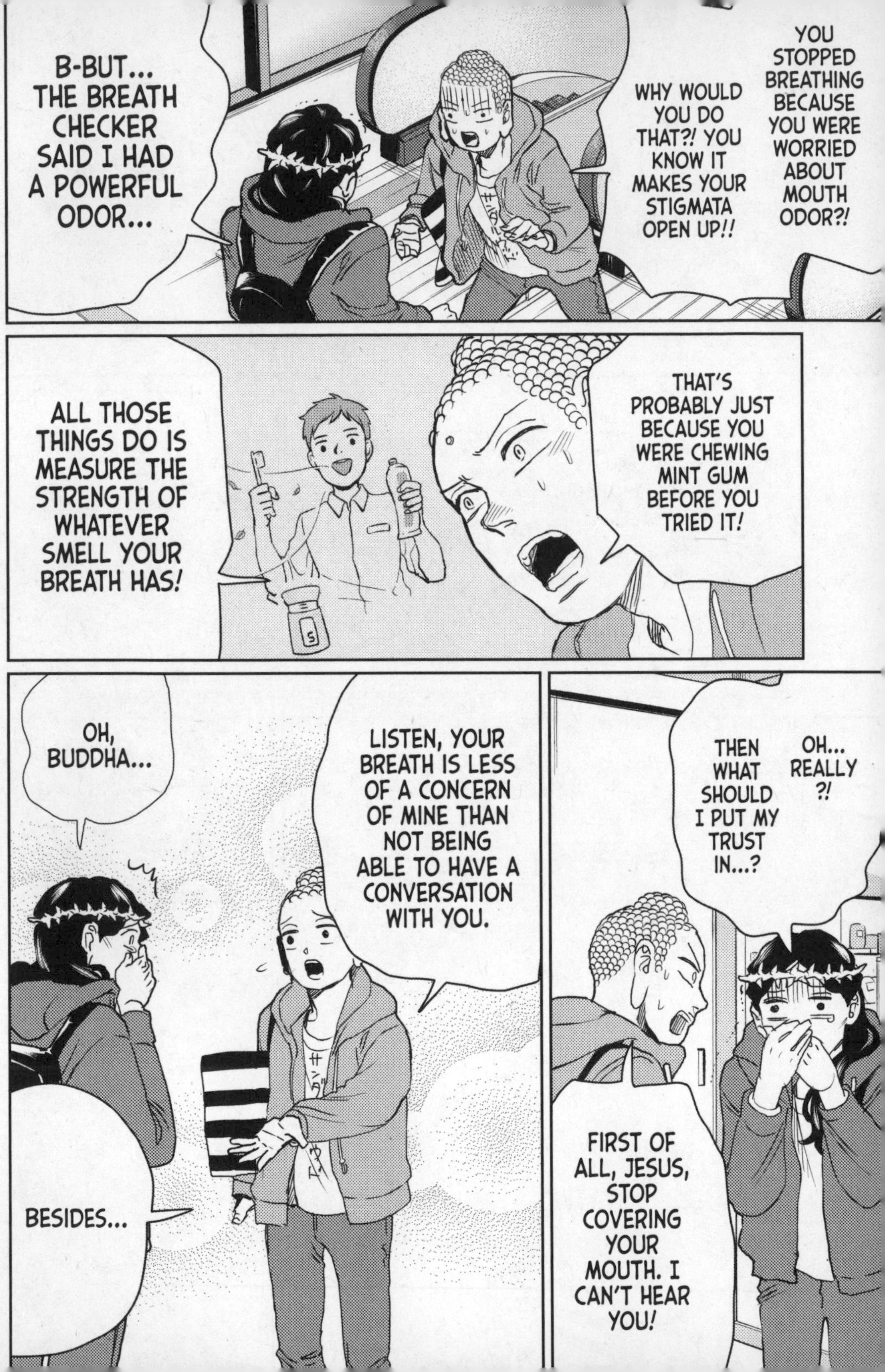
YOU STOPPED BREATHING BECAUSE YOU WERE WORRIED ABOUT MOUTH ODOR?!
WHY WOULD YOU DO THAT?! YOU KNOW IT MAKES YOUR STIGMATA OPEN UP!!
B-BUT... THE BREATH CHECKER SAID I HAD A POWERFUL ODOR...
THAT'S PROBABLY JUST BECAUSE YOU WERE CHEWING MINT GUM BEFORE YOU TRIED IT!
ALL THOSE THINGS DO IS MEASURE THE STRENGTH OF WHATEVER SMELL YOUR BREATH HAS!
OH... REALLY?!
THEN WHAT SHOULD I PUT MY TRUST IN...?
FIRST OF ALL, JESUS, STOP COVERING YOUR MOUTH. I CAN'T HEAR YOU!
LISTEN, YOUR BREATH IS LESS OF A CONCERN OF MINE THAN NOT BEING ABLE TO HAVE A CONVERSATION WITH YOU.
OH, BUDDHA...
BESIDES...

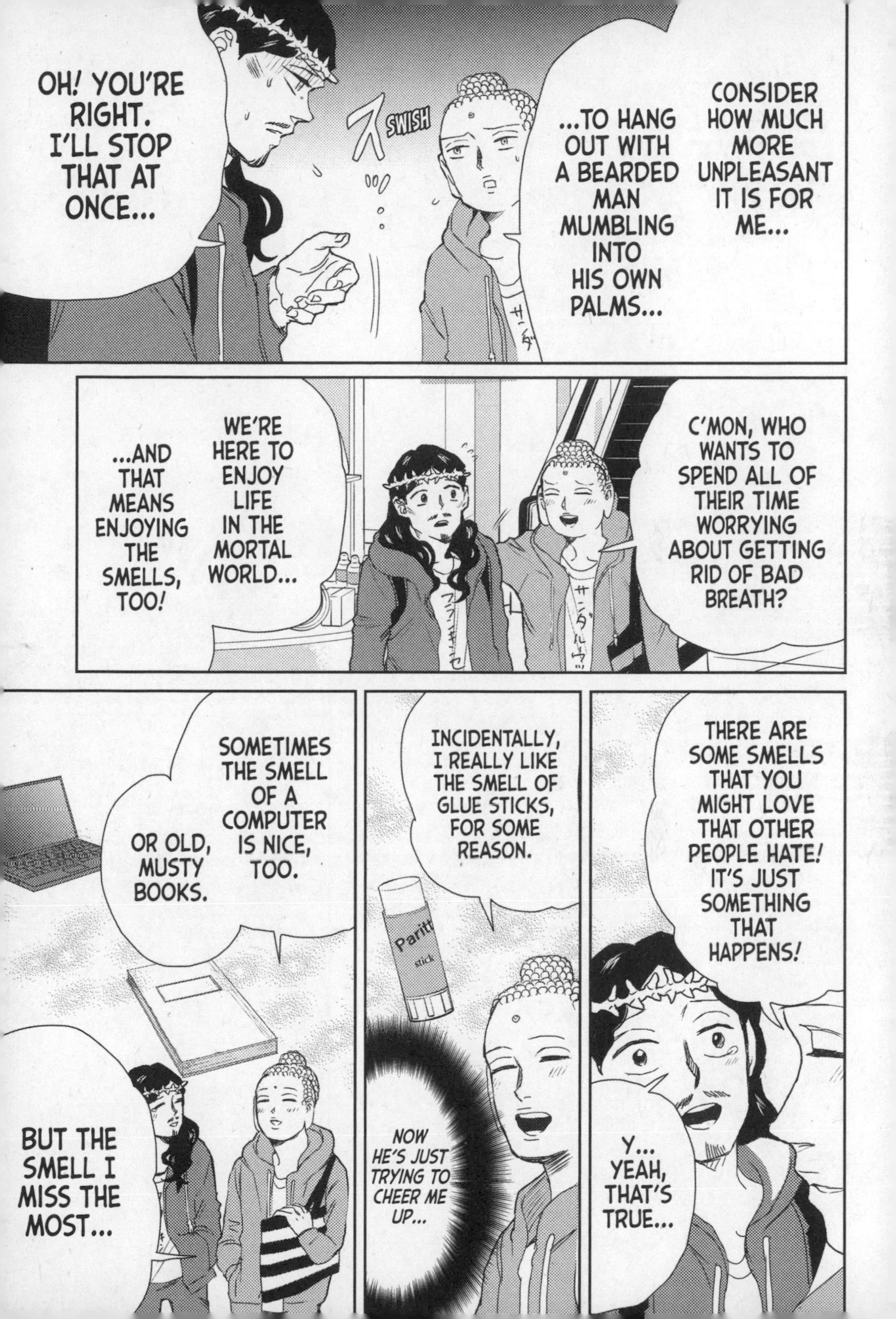
CONSIDER HOW MUCH MORE UNPLEASANT IT IS FOR ME...
...TO HANG OUT WITH A BEARDED MAN MUMBLING INTO HIS OWN PALMS...
SWISH
OH! YOU'RE RIGHT. I'LL STOP THAT AT ONCE...
C'MON, WHO WANTS TO SPEND ALL OF THEIR TIME WORRYING ABOUT GETTING RID OF BAD BREATH?
WE'RE HERE TO ENJOY LIFE IN THE MORTAL WORLD...
...AND THAT MEANS ENJOYING THE SMELLS, TOO!
THERE ARE SOME SMELLS THAT YOU MIGHT LOVE THAT OTHER PEOPLE HATE! IT'S JUST SOMETHING THAT HAPPENS!
Y... YEAH, THAT'S TRUE...
INCIDENTALLY, I REALLY LIKE THE SMELL OF GLUE STICKS, FOR SOME REASON.
NOW HE'S JUST TRYING TO CHEER ME UP...
SOMETIMES THE SMELL OF A COMPUTER IS NICE, TOO.
OR OLD, MUSTY BOOKS.
BUT THE SMELL I MISS THE MOST...

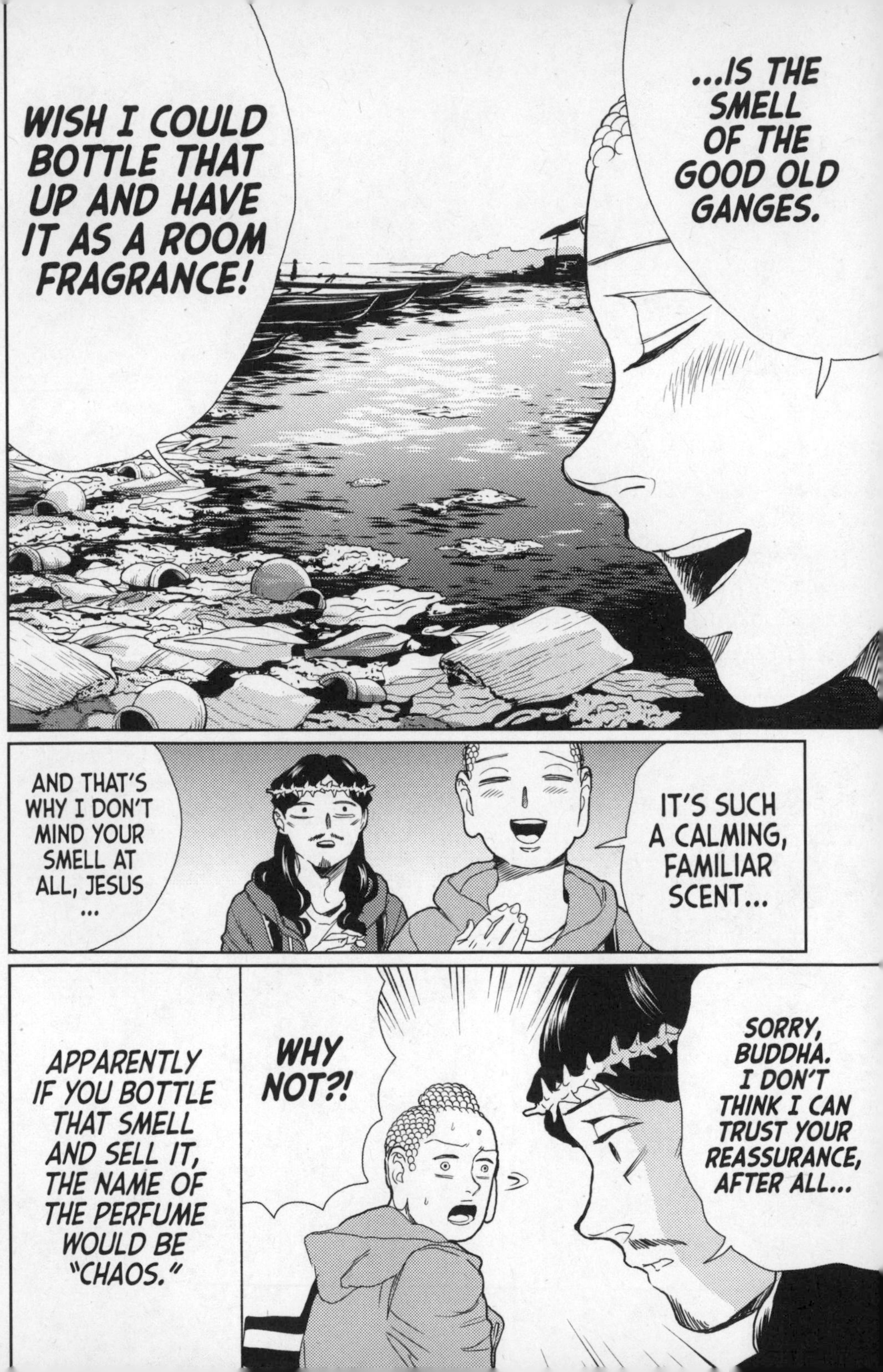
...IS THE SMELL OF THE GOOD OLD GANGES.
WISH I COULD BOTTLE THAT UP AND HAVE IT AS A ROOM FRAGRANCE!
IT'S SUCH A CALMING, FAMILIAR SCENT...
AND THAT'S WHY I DON'T MIND YOUR SMELL AT ALL, JESUS ...
SORRY, BUDDHA. I DON'T THINK I CAN TRUST YOUR REASSURANCE, AFTER ALL...
WHY NOT?!
APPARENTLY IF YOU BOTTLE THAT SMELL AND SELL IT, THE NAME OF THE PERFUME WOULD BE "CHAOS."

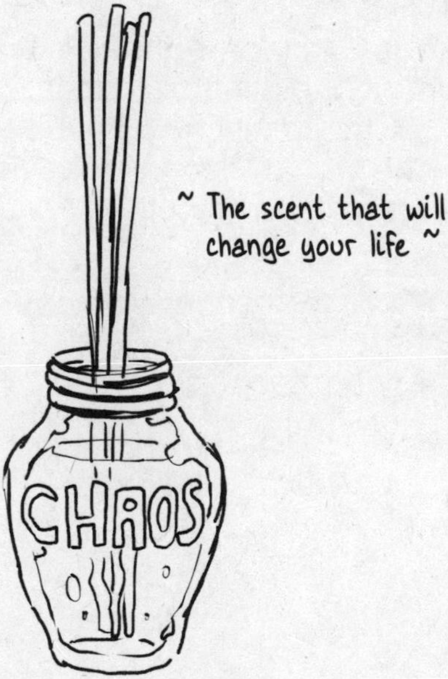
~ The scent that will
change your life ~
CHAOS

SAINT ☆ YOUNG MEN

CHAPTER 109 TRANSLATION NOTES

Frankincense, page 89

A resin used in incense and perfumes that has been cultivated from Boswellia trees for thousands of years. Frankincense, along with gold and another aromatic resin named myrrh, was a gift brought by the three Magi (Wise Men) from the East to the baby Jesus upon his birth in the manger.

Sandalwood, page 91

A highly prized and expensive kind of wood that produces a fragrant oil used in incense. Sandalwood is used as a scent during Buddhist meditation.

Mary of Bethany, page 98

The sister of Martha and Lazarus. Mary of Bethany is known for pouring an extravagant amount of anointing oil onto Jesus's feet. Judas protested, thinking that so much oil could have been sold to give them more money (which he would then take, being a thief). it is one of the events leading up to Judas's betrayal of Jesus.

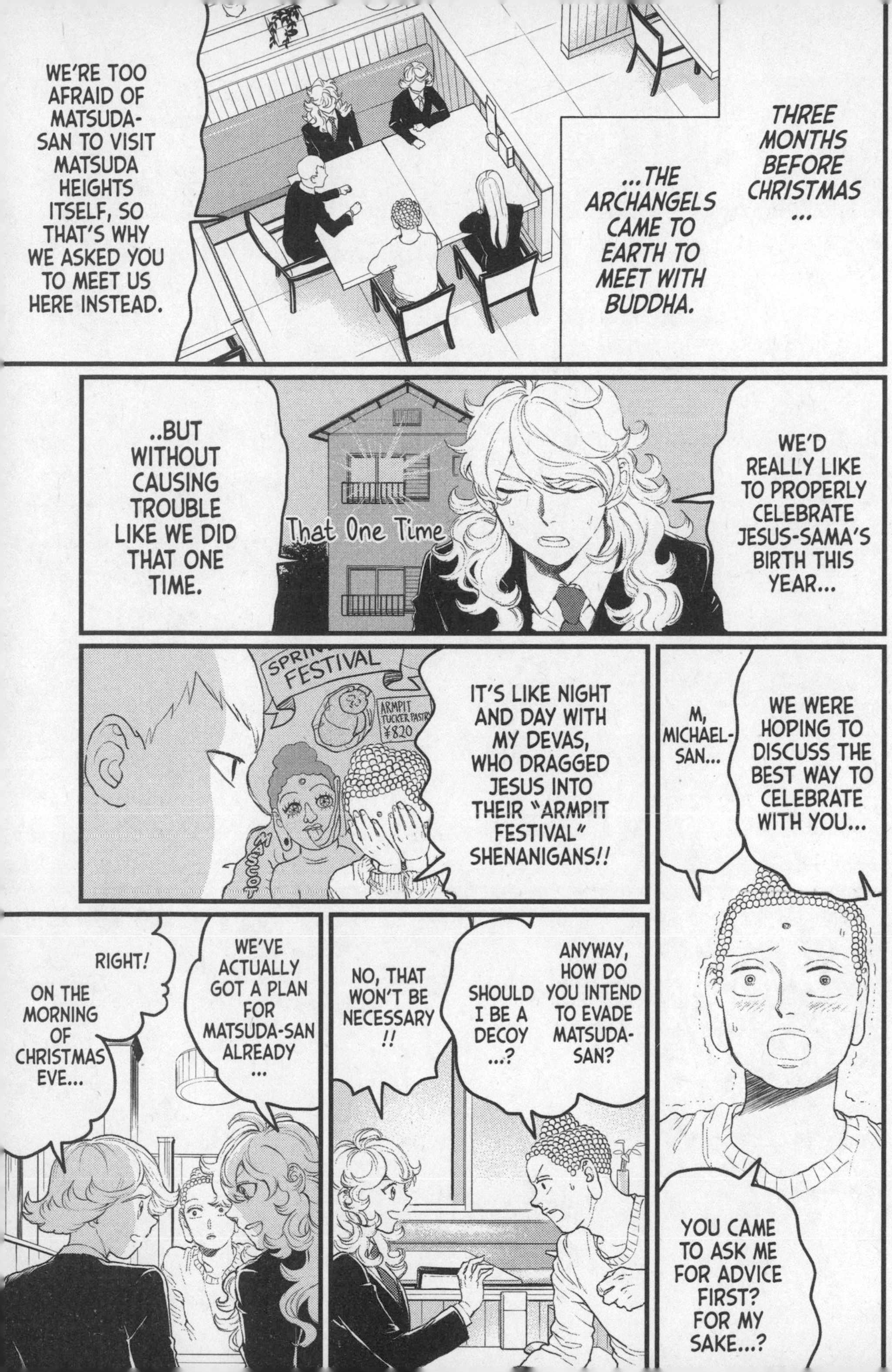
THREE MONTHS BEFORE CHRISTMAS...
...THE ARCHANGELS CAME TO EARTH TO MEET WITH BUDDHA.
WE'RE TOO AFRAID OF MATSUDA-SAN TO VISIT MATSUDA HEIGHTS ITSELF, SO THAT'S WHY WE ASKED YOU TO MEET US HERE INSTEAD.
WE'D REALLY LIKE TO PROPERLY CELEBRATE JESUS-SAMA'S BIRTH THIS YEAR...
..BUT WITHOUT CAUSING TROUBLE LIKE WE DID THAT ONE TIME.
That One Time
WE WERE HOPING TO DISCUSS THE BEST WAY TO CELEBRATE WITH YOU...
M, MICHAEL-SAN...
YOU CAME TO ASK ME FOR ADVICE FIRST? FOR MY SAKE...?
IT'S LIKE NIGHT AND DAY WITH MY DEVAS, WHO DRAGGED JESUS INTO THEIR "ARMPIT FESTIVAL" SHENANIGANS!!
FESTIVAL
ARMPIT
¥820
ANYWAY, HOW DO YOU INTEND TO EVADE MATSUDA-SAN?
SHOULD I BE A DECOY ...?
NO, THAT WON'T BE NECESSARY !!
WE'VE ACTUALLY GOT A PLAN FOR MATSUDA-SAN ALREADY ...
RIGHT!
ON THE MORNING OF CHRISTMAS EVE...

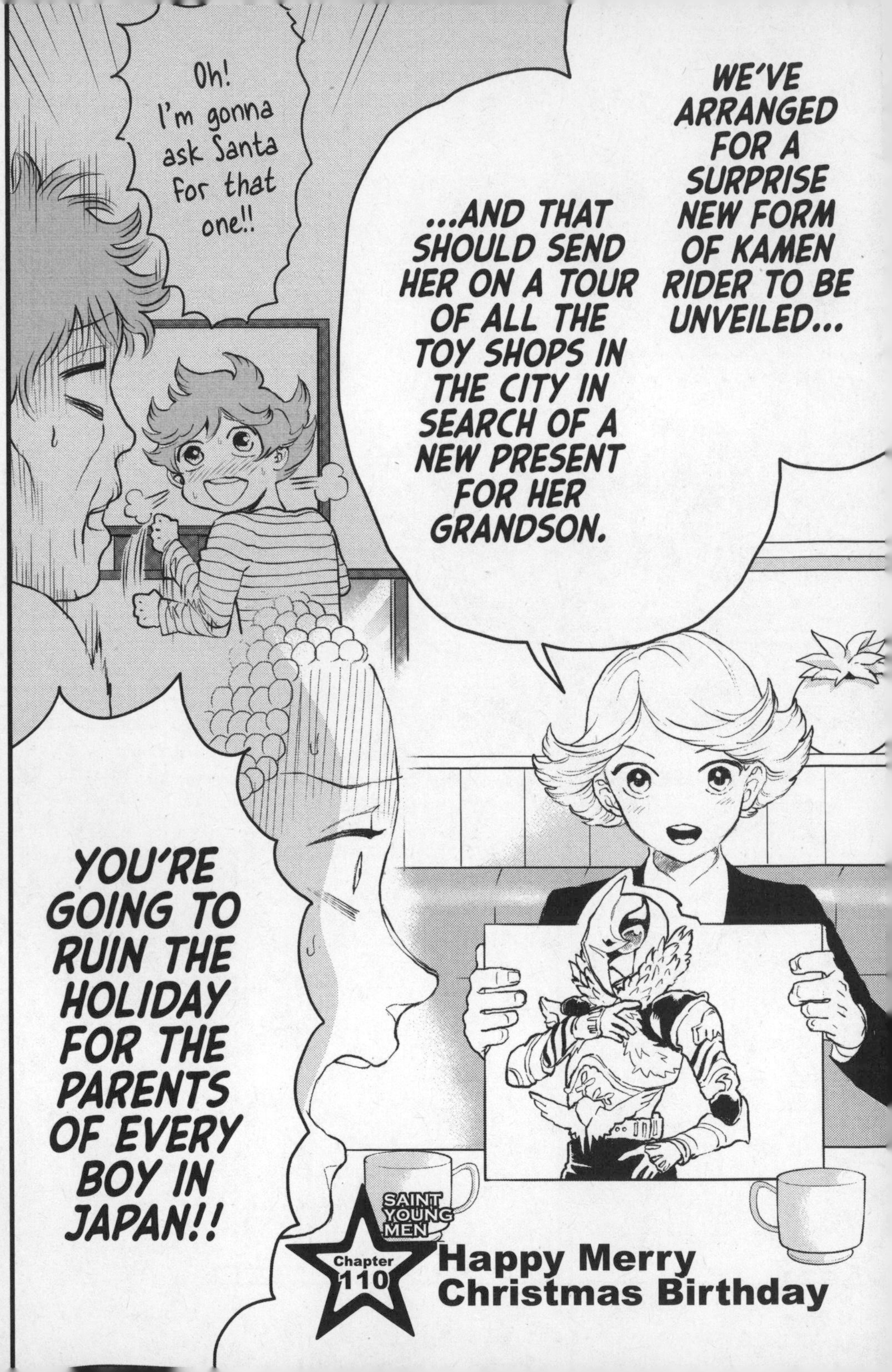
WE'VE ARRANGED FOR A SURPRISE NEW FORM OF KAMEN RIDER TO BE UNVEILED...
...AND THAT SHOULD SEND HER ON A TOUR OF ALL THE TOY SHOPS IN THE CITY IN SEARCH OF A NEW PRESENT FOR HER GRANDSON.
Oh! I'm gonna ask Santa for that one!!
YOU'RE GOING TO RUIN THE HOLIDAY FOR THE PARENTS OF EVERY BOY IN JAPAN!!
SAINT YOUNG MEN
Chapter 110
Happy Merry Christmas Birthday

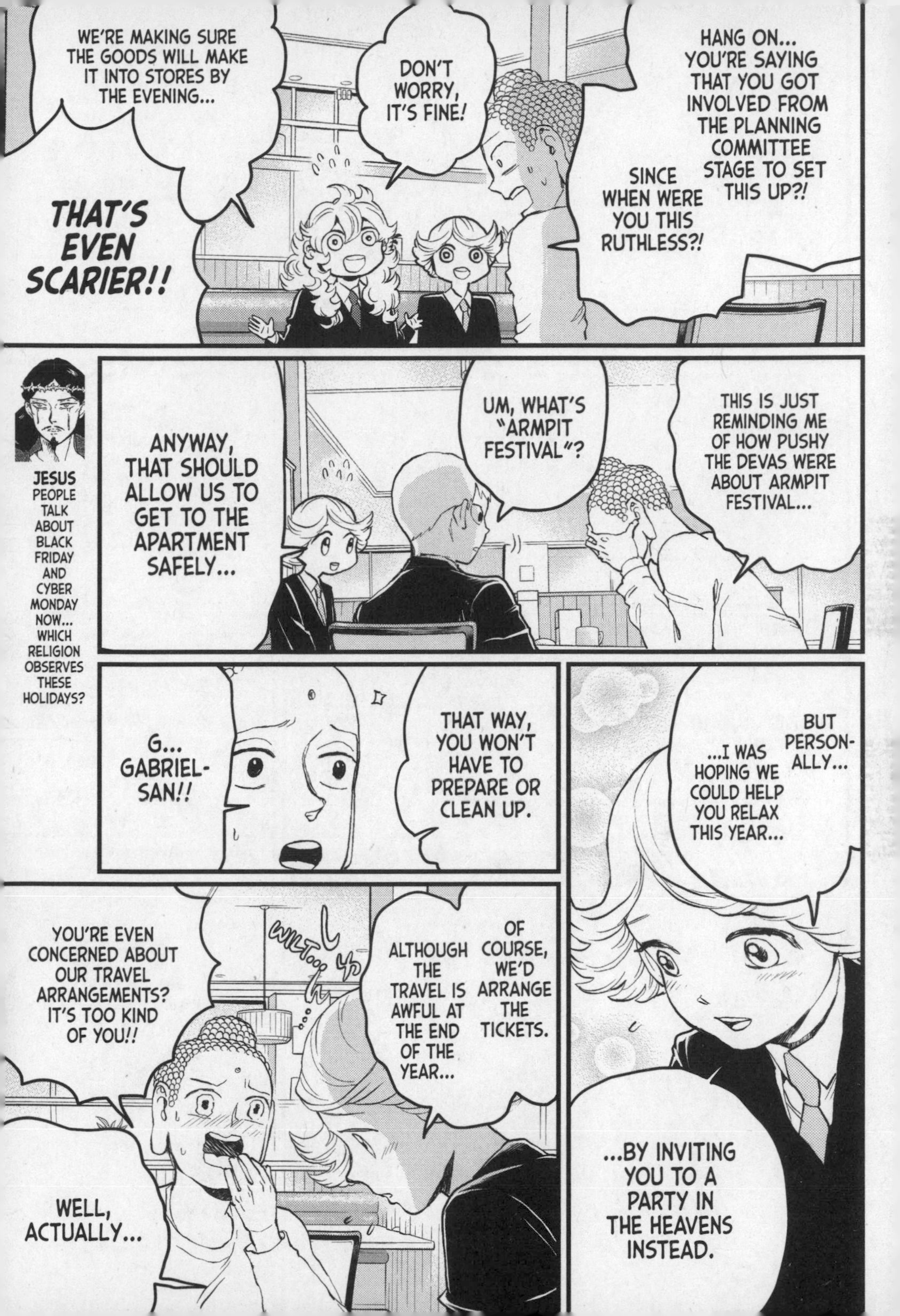
HANG ON... YOU'RE SAYING THAT YOU GOT INVOLVED FROM THE PLANNING COMMITTEE STAGE TO SET THIS UP?!
SINCE WHEN WERE YOU THIS RUTHLESS?!
DON'T WORRY, IT'S FINE!
WE'RE MAKING SURE THE GOODS WILL MAKE IT INTO STORES BY THE EVENING...
THAT'S EVEN SCARIER!!
THIS IS JUST REMINDING ME OF HOW PUSHY THE DEVAS WERE ABOUT ARMPIT FESTIVAL...
UM, WHAT'S "ARMPIT FESTIVAL"?
ANYWAY, THAT SHOULD ALLOW US TO GET TO THE APARTMENT SAFELY...
JESUS
PEOPLE TALK ABOUT BLACK FRIDAY AND CYBER MONDAY NOW... WHICH RELIGION OBSERVES THESE HOLIDAYS?
BUT PERSON-ALLY...
...I WAS HOPING WE COULD HELP YOU RELAX THIS YEAR...
...BY INVITING YOU TO A PARTY IN THE HEAVENS INSTEAD.
THAT WAY, YOU WON'T HAVE TO PREPARE OR CLEAN UP.
G... GABRIEL-SAN!!
OF COURSE, WE'D ARRANGE THE TICKETS.
ALTHOUGH THE TRAVEL IS AWFUL AT THE END OF THE YEAR...
WILT...
YOU'RE EVEN CONCERNED ABOUT OUR TRAVEL ARRANGEMENTS? IT'S TOO KIND OF YOU!!
WELL, ACTUALLY...

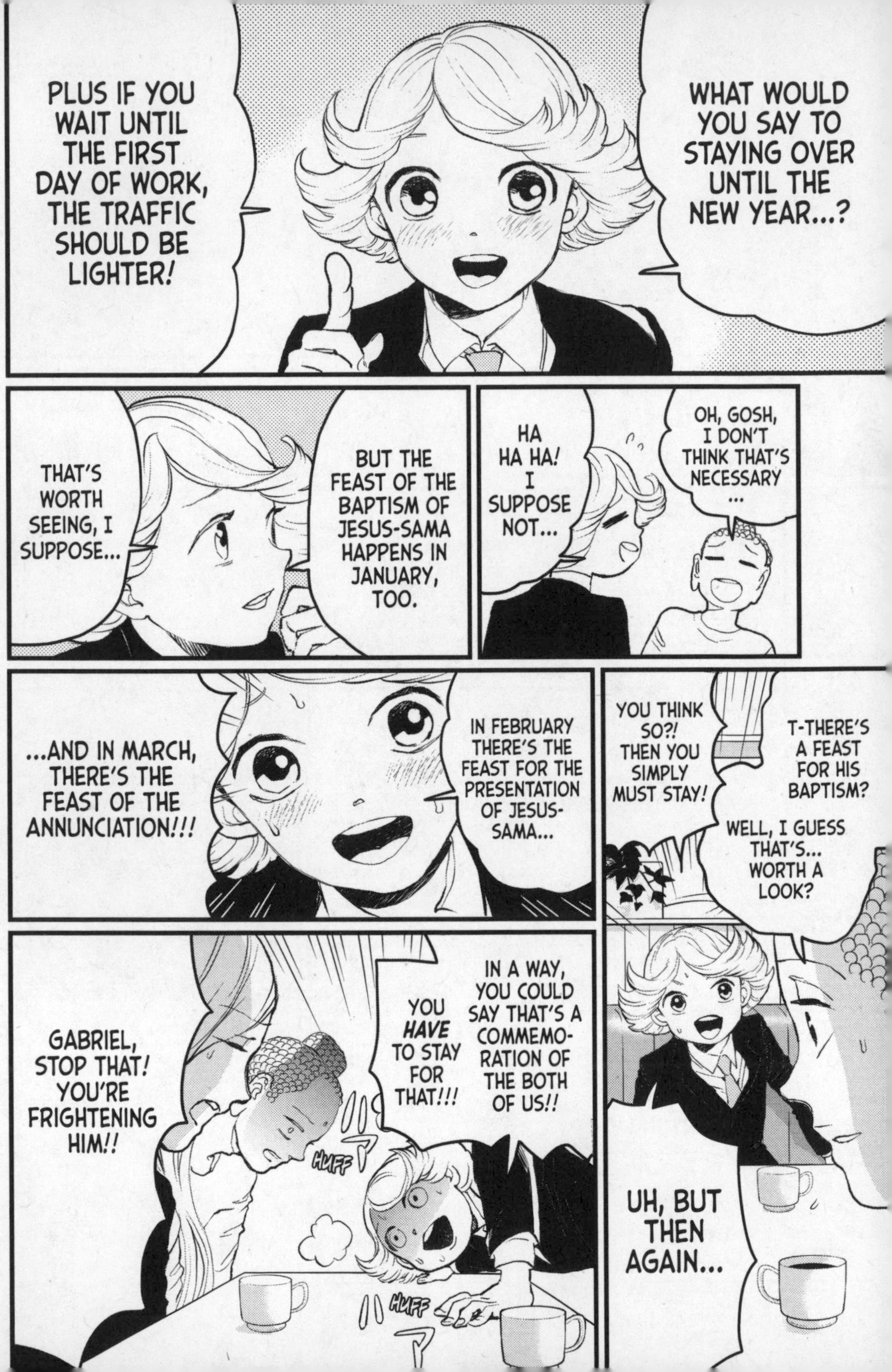
WHAT WOULD YOU SAY TO STAYING OVER UNTIL THE NEW YEAR...?
PLUS IF YOU WAIT UNTIL THE FIRST DAY OF WORK, THE TRAFFIC SHOULD BE LIGHTER!
OH, GOSH, I DON'T THINK THAT'S NECESSARY ...
HA HA HA! I SUPPOSE NOT...
BUT THE FEAST OF THE BAPTISM OF JESUS-SAMA HAPPENS IN JANUARY, TOO.
THAT'S WORTH SEEING, I SUPPOSE...
T-THERE'S A FEAST FOR HIS BAPTISM?
YOU THINK SO?! THEN YOU SIMPLY MUST STAY!
WELL, I GUESS THAT'S... WORTH A LOOK?
UH, BUT THEN AGAIN...
IN FEBRUARY THERE'S THE FEAST FOR THE PRESENTATION OF JESUS-SAMA...
...AND IN MARCH, THERE'S THE FEAST OF THE ANNUNCIATION!!!
IN A WAY, YOU COULD SAY THAT'S A COMMEMO-RATION OF THE BOTH OF US!!
YOU *HAVE* TO STAY FOR THAT!!!
GABRIEL, STOP THAT! YOU'RE FRIGHTENING HIM!!
HUFF
HUFF

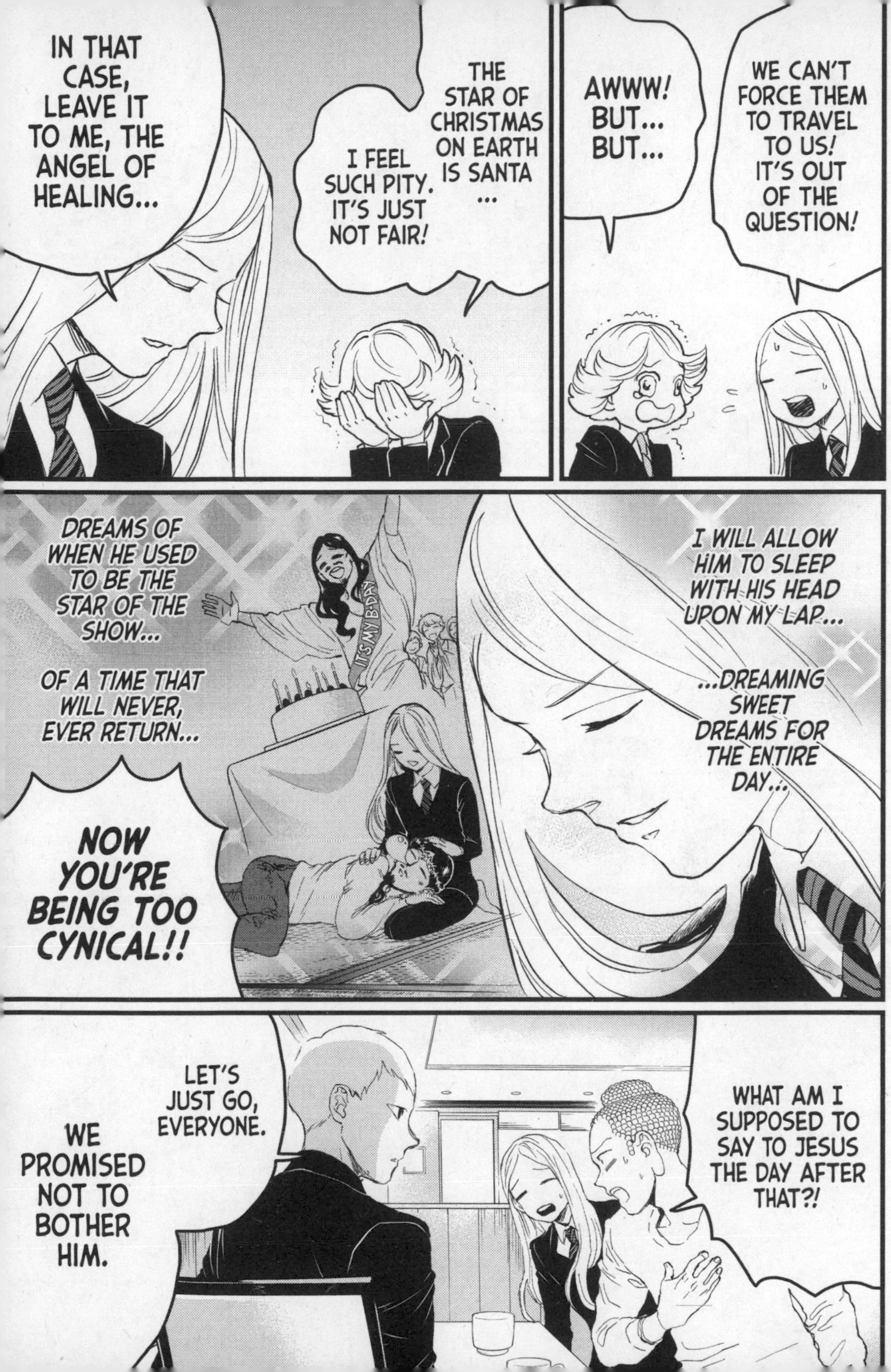
WE CAN'T FORCE THEM TO TRAVEL TO US! IT'S OUT OF THE QUESTION!
AWWW! BUT... BUT...
THE STAR OF CHRISTMAS ON EARTH IS SANTA ...
I FEEL SUCH PITY. IT'S JUST NOT FAIR!
IN THAT CASE, LEAVE IT TO ME, THE ANGEL OF HEALING...
I WILL ALLOW HIM TO SLEEP WITH HIS HEAD UPON MY LAP...
...DREAMING SWEET DREAMS FOR THE ENTIRE DAY...
DREAMS OF WHEN HE USED TO BE THE STAR OF THE SHOW...
OF A TIME THAT WILL NEVER, EVER RETURN...
IT'S MY B-DAY
NOW YOU'RE BEING TOO CYNICAL!!
WHAT AM I SUPPOSED TO SAY TO JESUS THE DAY AFTER THAT?!
LET'S JUST GO, EVERYONE.
WE PROMISED NOT TO BOTHER HIM.

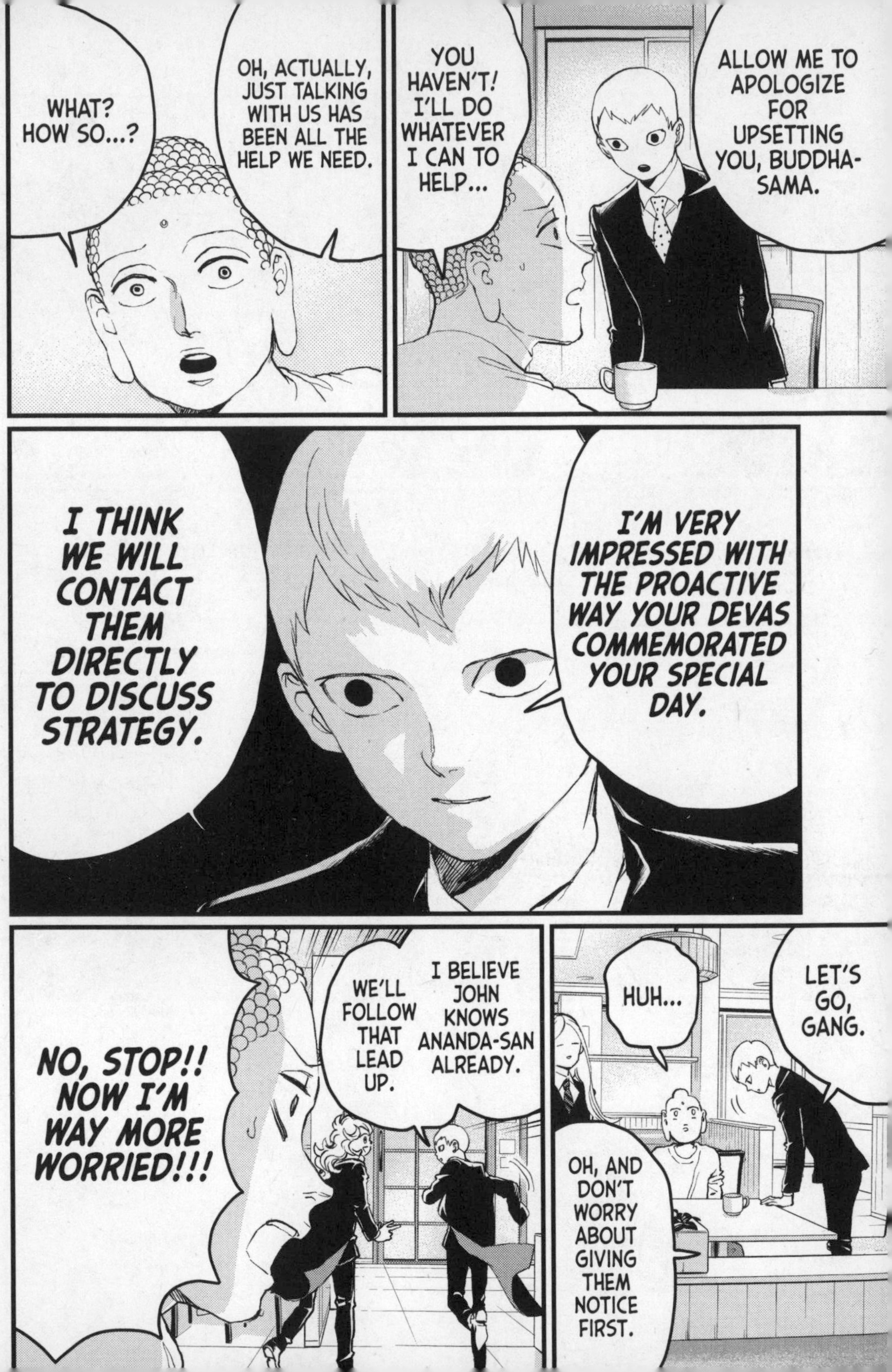
ALLOW ME TO APOLOGIZE FOR UPSETTING YOU, BUDDHA-SAMA.
YOU HAVEN'T! I'LL DO WHATEVER I CAN TO HELP...
OH, ACTUALLY, JUST TALKING WITH US HAS BEEN ALL THE HELP WE NEED.
WHAT? HOW SO...?
I'M VERY IMPRESSED WITH THE PROACTIVE WAY YOUR DEVAS COMMEMORATED YOUR SPECIAL DAY.
I THINK WE WILL CONTACT THEM DIRECTLY TO DISCUSS STRATEGY.
LET'S GO, GANG.
HUH...
OH, AND DON'T WORRY ABOUT GIVING THEM NOTICE FIRST.
I BELIEVE JOHN KNOWS ANANDA-SAN ALREADY.
WE'LL FOLLOW THAT LEAD UP.
NO, STOP!! NOW I'M WAY MORE WORRIED!!!

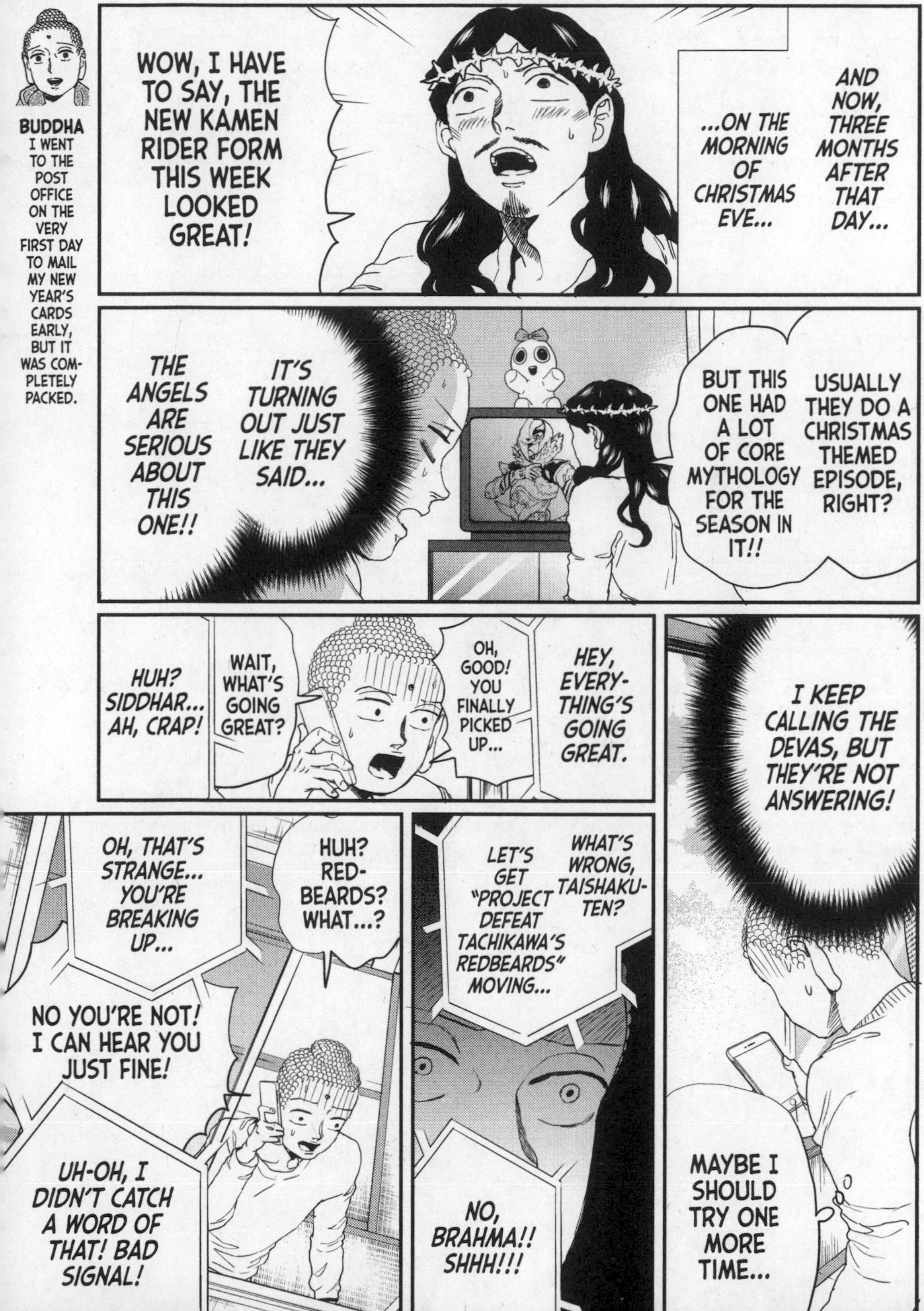
AND NOW, THREE MONTHS AFTER THAT DAY...
...ON THE MORNING OF CHRISTMAS EVE...
WOW, I HAVE TO SAY, THE NEW KAMEN RIDER FORM THIS WEEK LOOKED GREAT!
USUALLY THEY DO A CHRISTMAS THEMED EPISODE, RIGHT?
BUT THIS ONE HAD A LOT OF CORE MYTHOLOGY FOR THE SEASON IN IT!!
IT'S TURNING OUT JUST LIKE THEY SAID...
THE ANGELS ARE SERIOUS ABOUT THIS ONE!!
I KEEP CALLING THE DEVAS, BUT THEY'RE NOT ANSWERING!
MAYBE I SHOULD TRY ONE MORE TIME...
HEY, EVERYTHING'S GOING GREAT.
OH, GOOD! YOU FINALLY PICKED UP...
WAIT, WHAT'S GOING GREAT?
HUH? SIDDHAR... AH, CRAP!
WHAT'S WRONG, TAISHAKUTEN?
LET'S GET "PROJECT DEFEAT TACHIKAWA'S REDBEARDS" MOVING...
NO, BRAHMA!! SHHH!!!
HUH? REDBEARDS? WHAT...?
OH, THAT'S STRANGE... YOU'RE BREAKING UP...
NO YOU'RE NOT! I CAN HEAR YOU JUST FINE!
UH-OH, I DIDN'T CATCH A WORD OF THAT! BAD SIGNAL!
BUDDHA
I WENT TO THE POST OFFICE ON THE VERY FIRST DAY TO MAIL MY NEW YEAR'S CARDS EARLY, BUT IT WAS COMPLETELY PACKED.

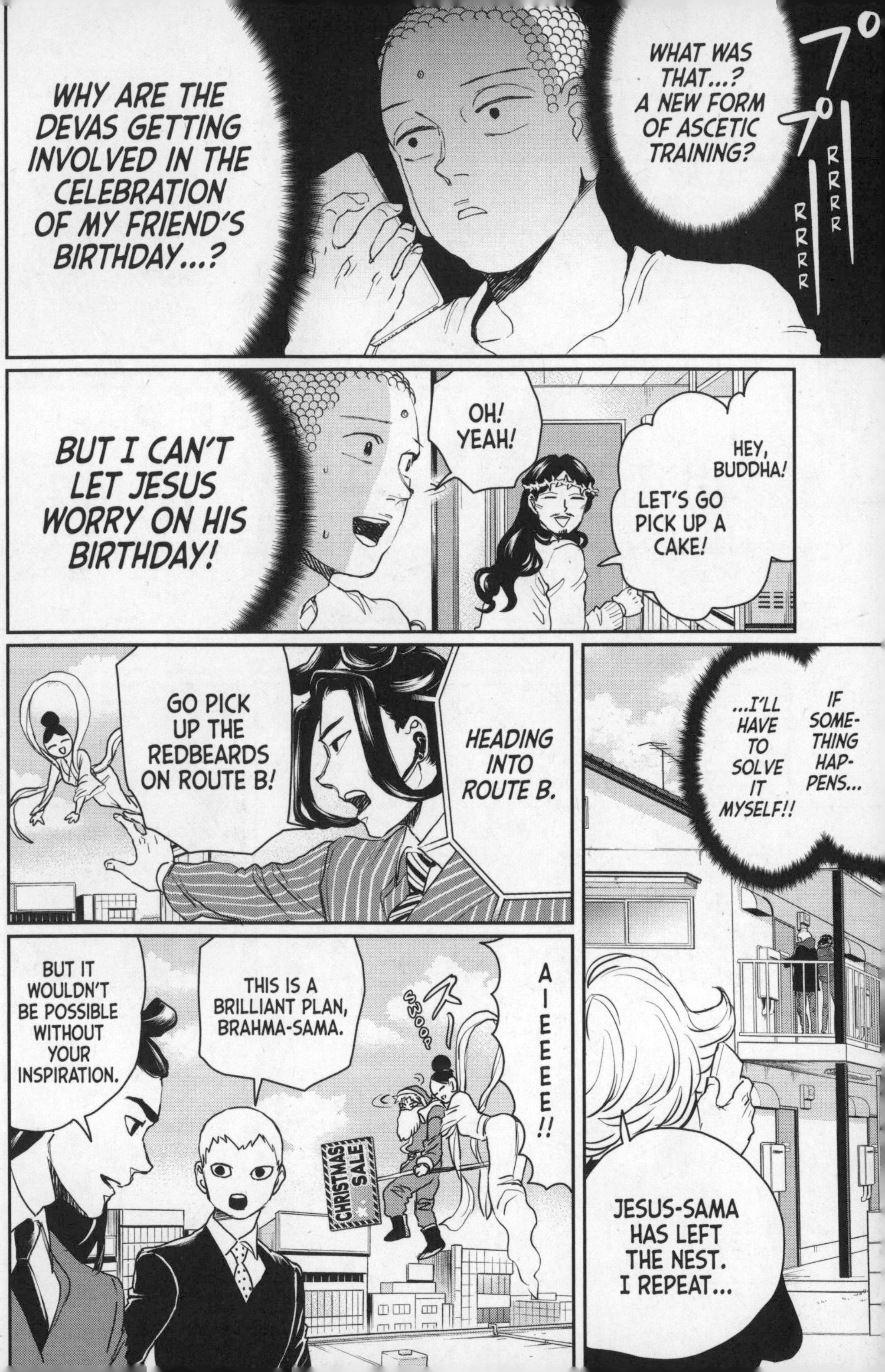
RRRR RRRR
WHAT WAS THAT...? A NEW FORM OF ASCETIC TRAINING?
WHY ARE THE DEVAS GETTING INVOLVED IN THE CELEBRATION OF MY FRIEND'S BIRTHDAY...?
HEY, BUDDHA!
LET'S GO PICK UP A CAKE!
OH! YEAH!
BUT I CAN'T LET JESUS WORRY ON HIS BIRTHDAY!
IF SOME-THING HAP-PENS...
...I'LL HAVE TO SOLVE IT MYSELF!!
JESUS-SAMA HAS LEFT THE NEST. I REPEAT...
HEADING INTO ROUTE B.
GO PICK UP THE REDBEARDS ON ROUTE B!
AIEEEEE!!
SWOOP
CHRISTMAS SALE
THIS IS A BRILLIANT PLAN, BRAHMA-SAMA.
BUT IT WOULDN'T BE POSSIBLE WITHOUT YOUR INSPIRATION.

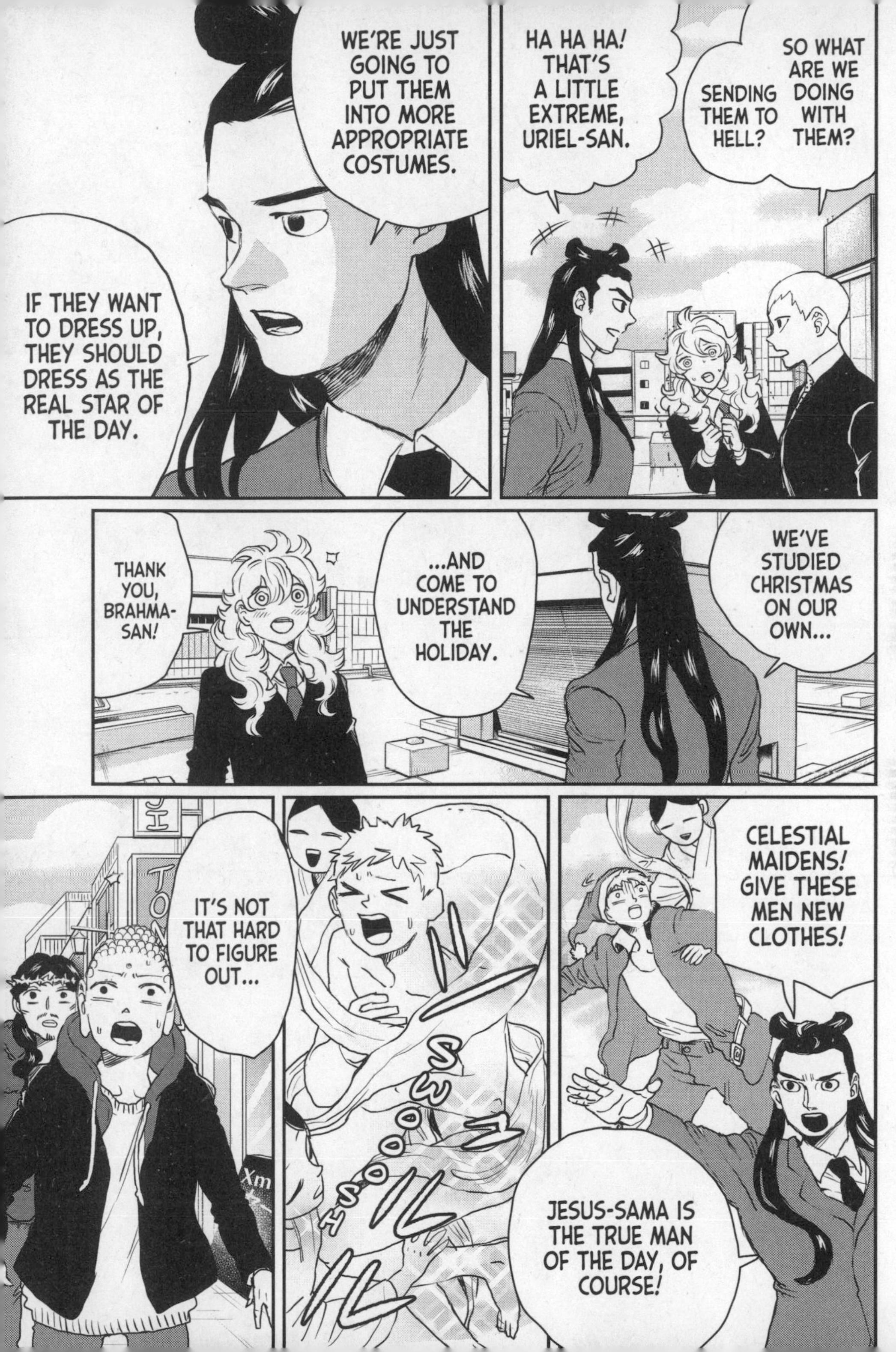
SO WHAT ARE WE DOING WITH THEM?
SENDING THEM TO HELL?
HA HA HA! THAT'S A LITTLE EXTREME, URIEL-SAN.
WE'RE JUST GOING TO PUT THEM INTO MORE APPROPRIATE COSTUMES.
IF THEY WANT TO DRESS UP, THEY SHOULD DRESS AS THE REAL STAR OF THE DAY.
WE'VE STUDIED CHRISTMAS ON OUR OWN...
...AND COME TO UNDERSTAND THE HOLIDAY.
THANK YOU, BRAHMA-SAN!
CELESTIAL MAIDENS! GIVE THESE MEN NEW CLOTHES!
JESUS-SAMA IS THE TRUE MAN OF THE DAY, OF COURSE!
SWOOSH
WHOOSH
IT'S NOT THAT HARD TO FIGURE OUT...

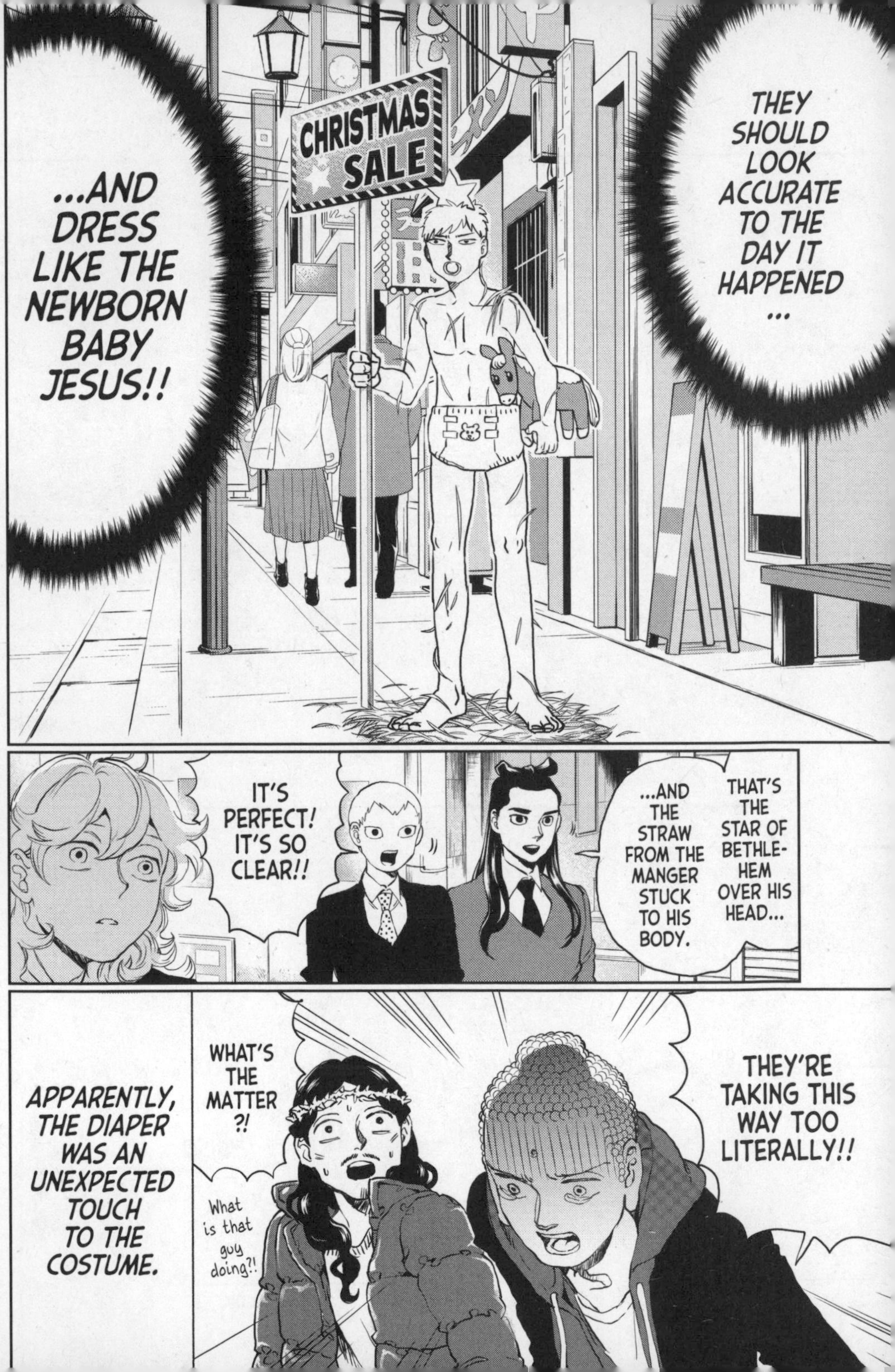
THEY SHOULD LOOK ACCURATE TO THE DAY IT HAPPENED ...
CHRISTMAS SALE
...AND DRESS LIKE THE NEWBORN BABY JESUS!!
THAT'S THE STAR OF BETHLE-HEM OVER HIS HEAD...
...AND THE STRAW FROM THE MANGER STUCK TO HIS BODY.
IT'S PERFECT! IT'S SO CLEAR!!
THEY'RE TAKING THIS WAY TOO LITERALLY!!
WHAT'S THE MATTER ?!
What is that guy doing?!
APPARENTLY, THE DIAPER WAS AN UNEXPECTED TOUCH TO THE COSTUME.

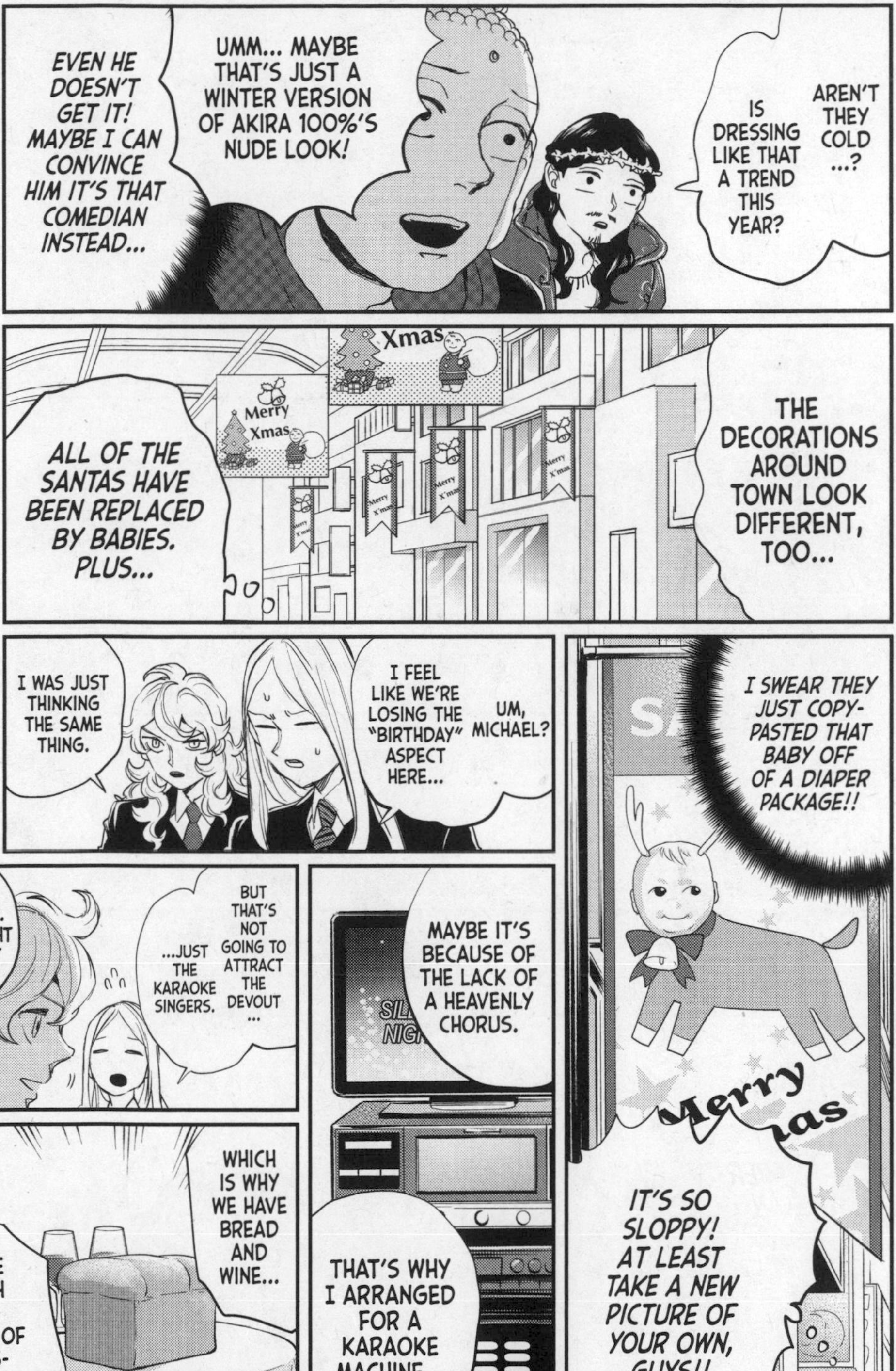
AREN'T THEY COLD ...?
IS DRESSING LIKE THAT A TREND THIS YEAR?
UMM... MAYBE THAT'S JUST A WINTER VERSION OF AKIRA 100%'S NUDE LOOK!
EVEN HE DOESN'T GET IT! MAYBE I CAN CONVINCE HIM IT'S THAT COMEDIAN INSTEAD...
Xmas
THE DECORATIONS AROUND TOWN LOOK DIFFERENT, TOO...
Merry X'mas
Merry Xmas
ALL OF THE SANTAS HAVE BEEN REPLACED BY BABIES. PLUS...
I SWEAR THEY JUST COPY-PASTED THAT BABY OFF OF A DIAPER PACKAGE!!
IT'S SO SLOPPY! AT LEAST TAKE A NEW PICTURE OF YOUR OWN, GUYS!!
UM, MICHAEL?
I FEEL LIKE WE'RE LOSING THE "BIRTHDAY" ASPECT HERE...
I WAS JUST THINKING THE SAME THING.
MAYBE IT'S BECAUSE OF THE LACK OF A HEAVENLY CHORUS.
THAT'S WHY I ARRANGED FOR A KARAOKE MACHINE...
BUT THAT'S NOT GOING TO ATTRACT THE DEVOUT ...
...JUST THE KARAOKE SINGERS.
EXACTLY. I THOUGHT OF THAT TOO...
WHICH IS WHY WE HAVE BREAD AND WINE...
...THE FLESH AND BLOOD OF JESUS-SAMA!

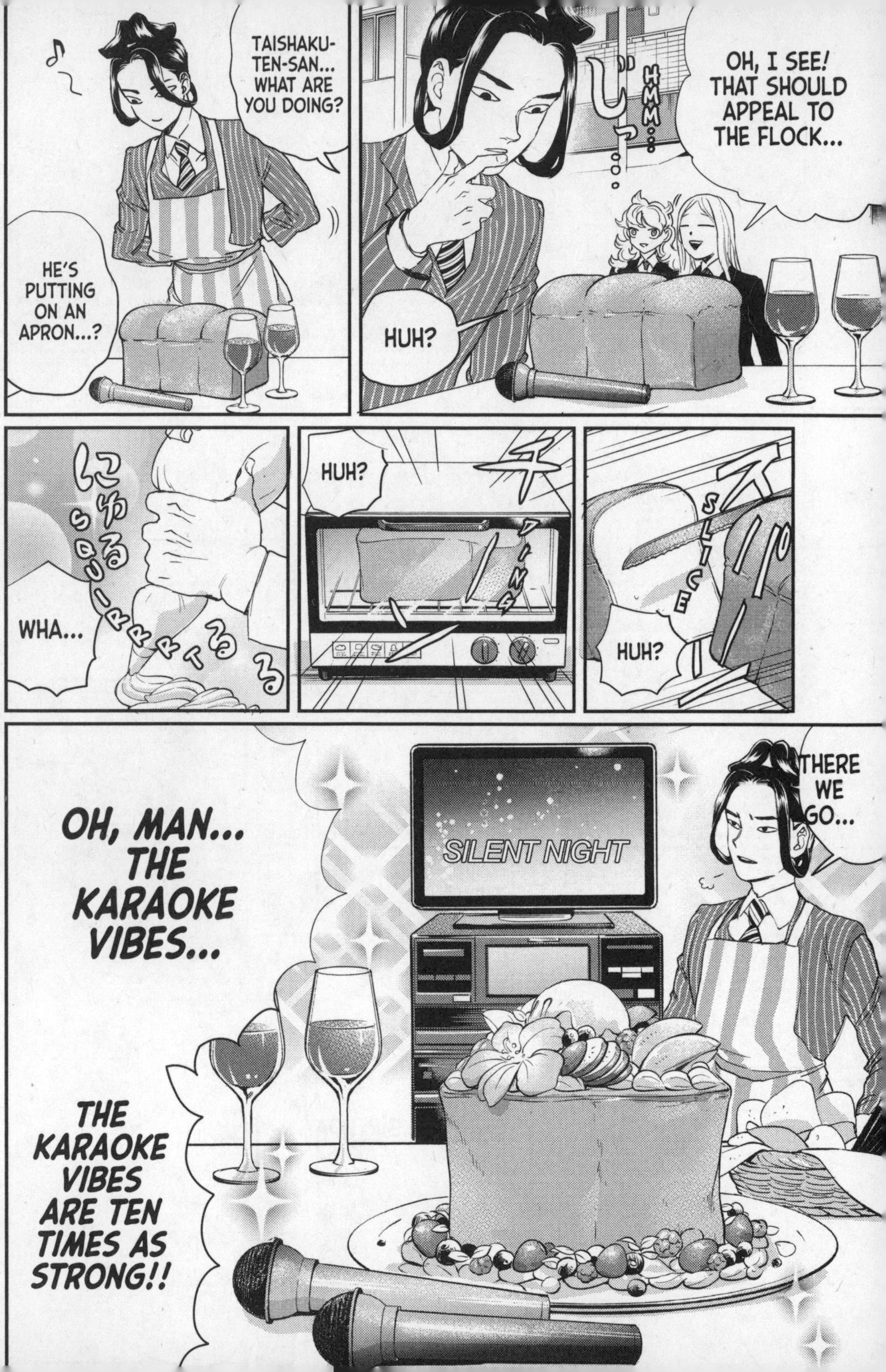
OH, I SEE! THAT SHOULD APPEAL TO THE FLOCK...
HMM...
HUH?
TAISHAKU-TEN-SAN... WHAT ARE YOU DOING?
HE'S PUTTING ON AN APRON...?
SLICE
HUH?
HUH?
DING
SQUIRRRT
WHA...
THERE WE GO...
SILENT NIGHT
OH, MAN... THE KARAOKE VIBES...
THE KARAOKE VIBES ARE TEN TIMES AS STRONG!!

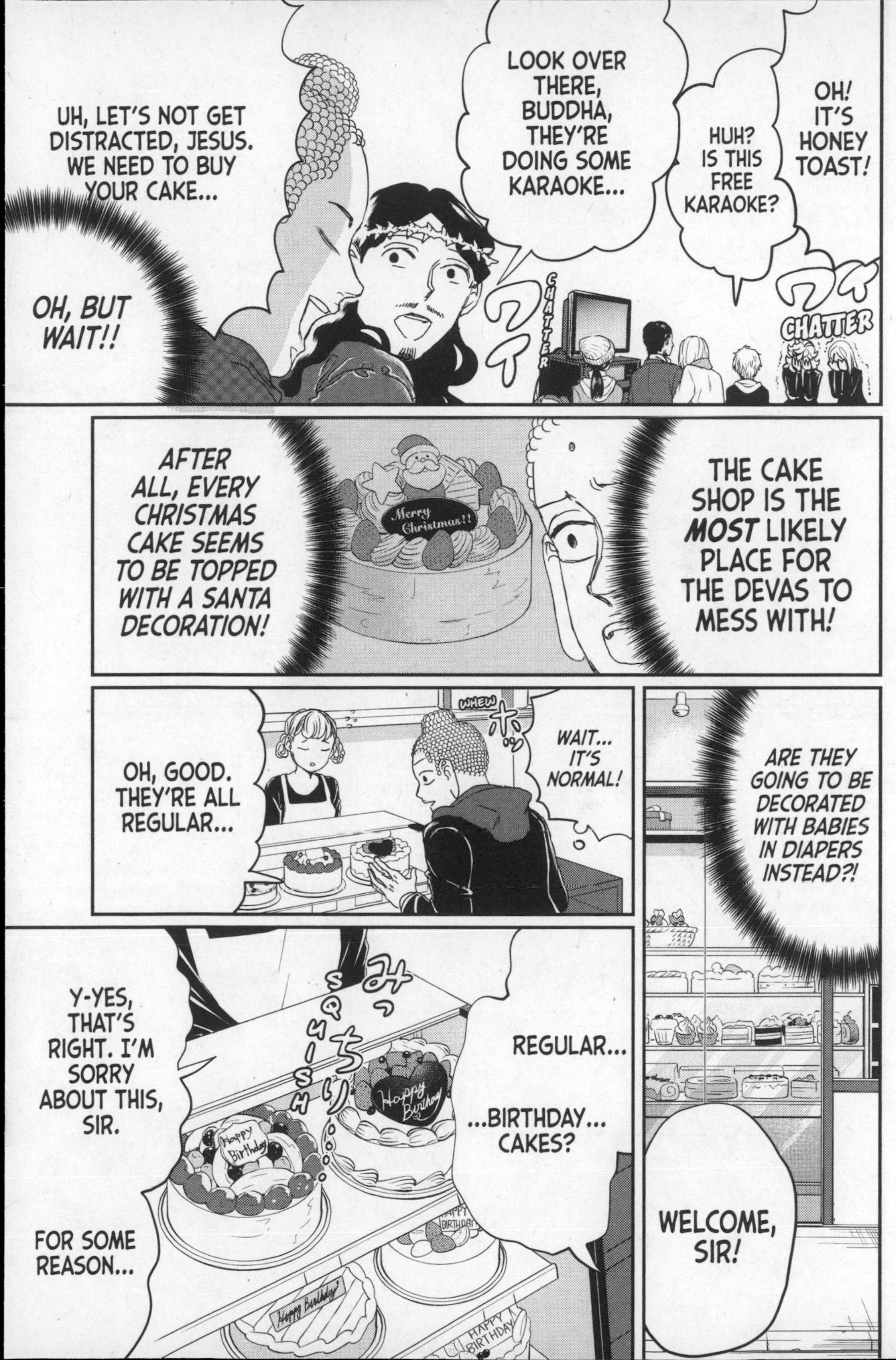

OH! IT'S HONEY TOAST!
HUH? IS THIS FREE KARAOKE?
CHATTER
LOOK OVER THERE, BUDDHA, THEY'RE DOING SOME KARAOKE...
CHATTER
UH, LET'S NOT GET DISTRACTED, JESUS. WE NEED TO BUY YOUR CAKE...
OH, BUT WAIT!!
THE CAKE SHOP IS THE *MOST* LIKELY PLACE FOR THE DEVAS TO MESS WITH!
Merry Christmas!!
AFTER ALL, EVERY CHRISTMAS CAKE SEEMS TO BE TOPPED WITH A SANTA DECORATION!
ARE THEY GOING TO BE DECORATED WITH BABIES IN DIAPERS INSTEAD?!
WELCOME, SIR!
WHEW
WAIT... IT'S NORMAL!
OH, GOOD. THEY'RE ALL REGULAR...
REGULAR...
...BIRTHDAY... CAKES?
SQUISH
Happy Birthday
Happy Birthday
Y-YES, THAT'S RIGHT. I'M SORRY ABOUT THIS, SIR.
HAPPY BIRTHDAY
Happy Birthday
HAPPY BIRTHDAY
FOR SOME REASON...

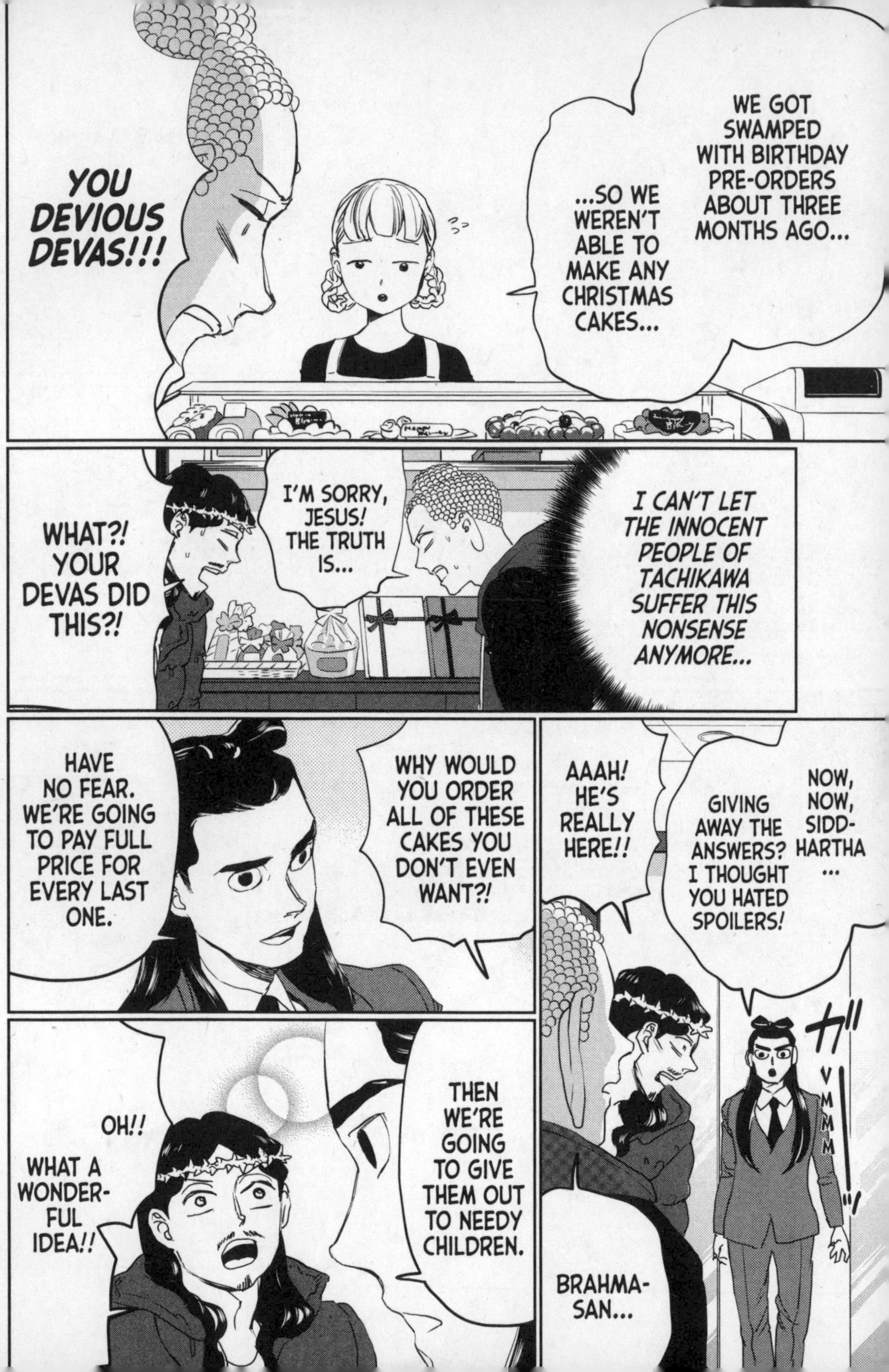
WE GOT SWAMPED WITH BIRTHDAY PRE-ORDERS ABOUT THREE MONTHS AGO...
...SO WE WEREN'T ABLE TO MAKE ANY CHRISTMAS CAKES...
YOU DEVIOUS DEVAS!!!
I CAN'T LET THE INNOCENT PEOPLE OF TACHIKAWA SUFFER THIS NONSENSE ANYMORE...
I'M SORRY, JESUS! THE TRUTH IS...
WHAT?! YOUR DEVAS DID THIS?!
NOW, NOW, SIDD-HARTHA...
GIVING AWAY THE ANSWERS? I THOUGHT YOU HATED SPOILERS!
ガッ
VMMM
AAAH! HE'S REALLY HERE!!
BRAHMA-SAN...
WHY WOULD YOU ORDER ALL OF THESE CAKES YOU DON'T EVEN WANT?!
HAVE NO FEAR. WE'RE GOING TO PAY FULL PRICE FOR EVERY LAST ONE.
THEN WE'RE GOING TO GIVE THEM OUT TO NEEDY CHILDREN.
OH!! WHAT A WONDERFUL IDEA!!

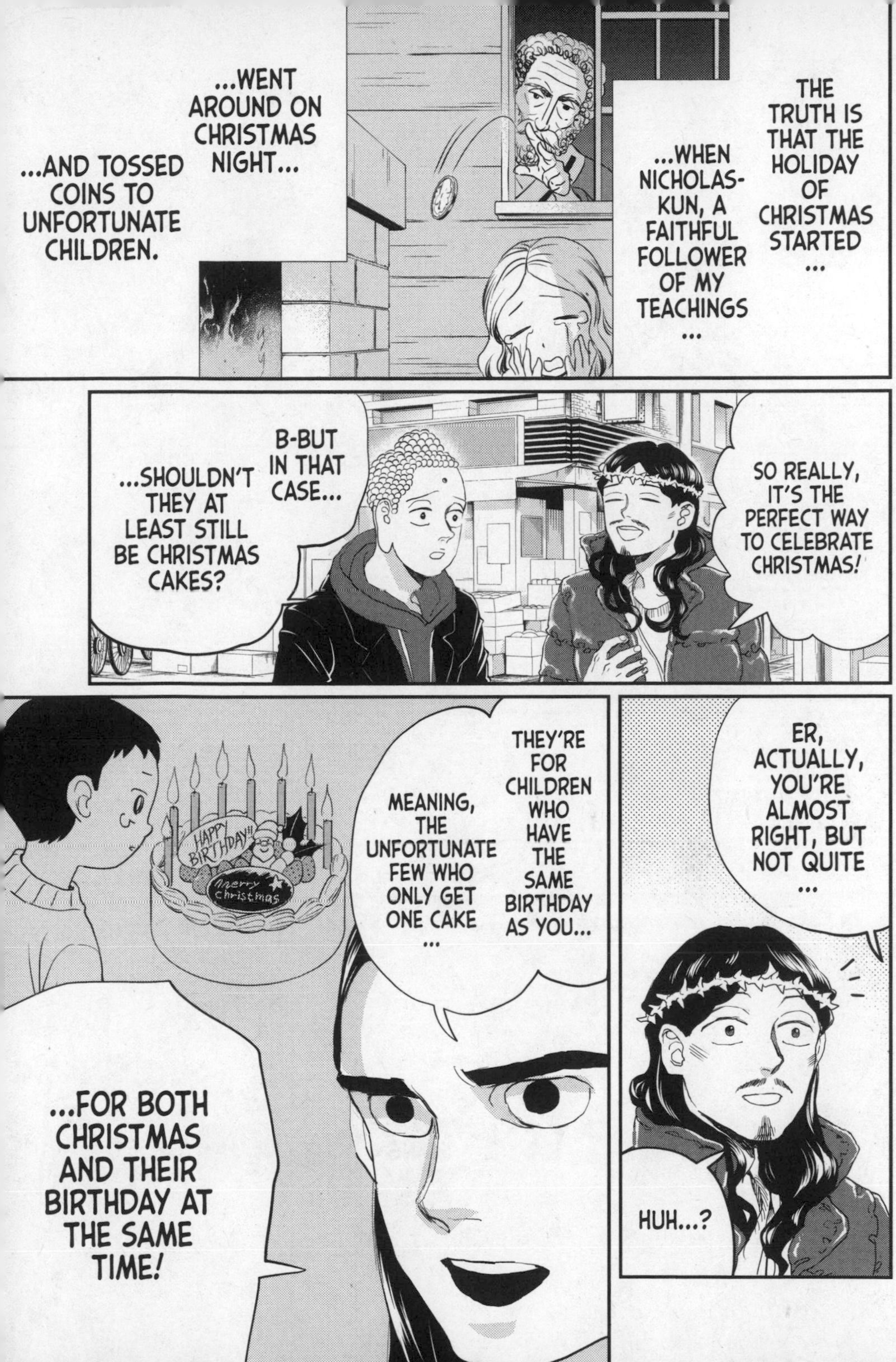
THE TRUTH IS THAT THE HOLIDAY OF CHRISTMAS STARTED...
...WHEN NICHOLAS-KUN, A FAITHFUL FOLLOWER OF MY TEACHINGS...
...WENT AROUND ON CHRISTMAS NIGHT...
...AND TOSSED COINS TO UNFORTUNATE CHILDREN.
SO REALLY, IT'S THE PERFECT WAY TO CELEBRATE CHRISTMAS!
B-BUT IN THAT CASE...
...SHOULDN'T THEY AT LEAST STILL BE CHRISTMAS CAKES?
ER, ACTUALLY, YOU'RE ALMOST RIGHT, BUT NOT QUITE...
HUH...?
THEY'RE FOR CHILDREN WHO HAVE THE SAME BIRTHDAY AS YOU...
MEANING, THE UNFORTUNATE FEW WHO ONLY GET ONE CAKE...
HAPPY BIRTHDAY!!
Merry Christmas
...FOR BOTH CHRISTMAS AND THEIR BIRTHDAY AT THE SAME TIME!

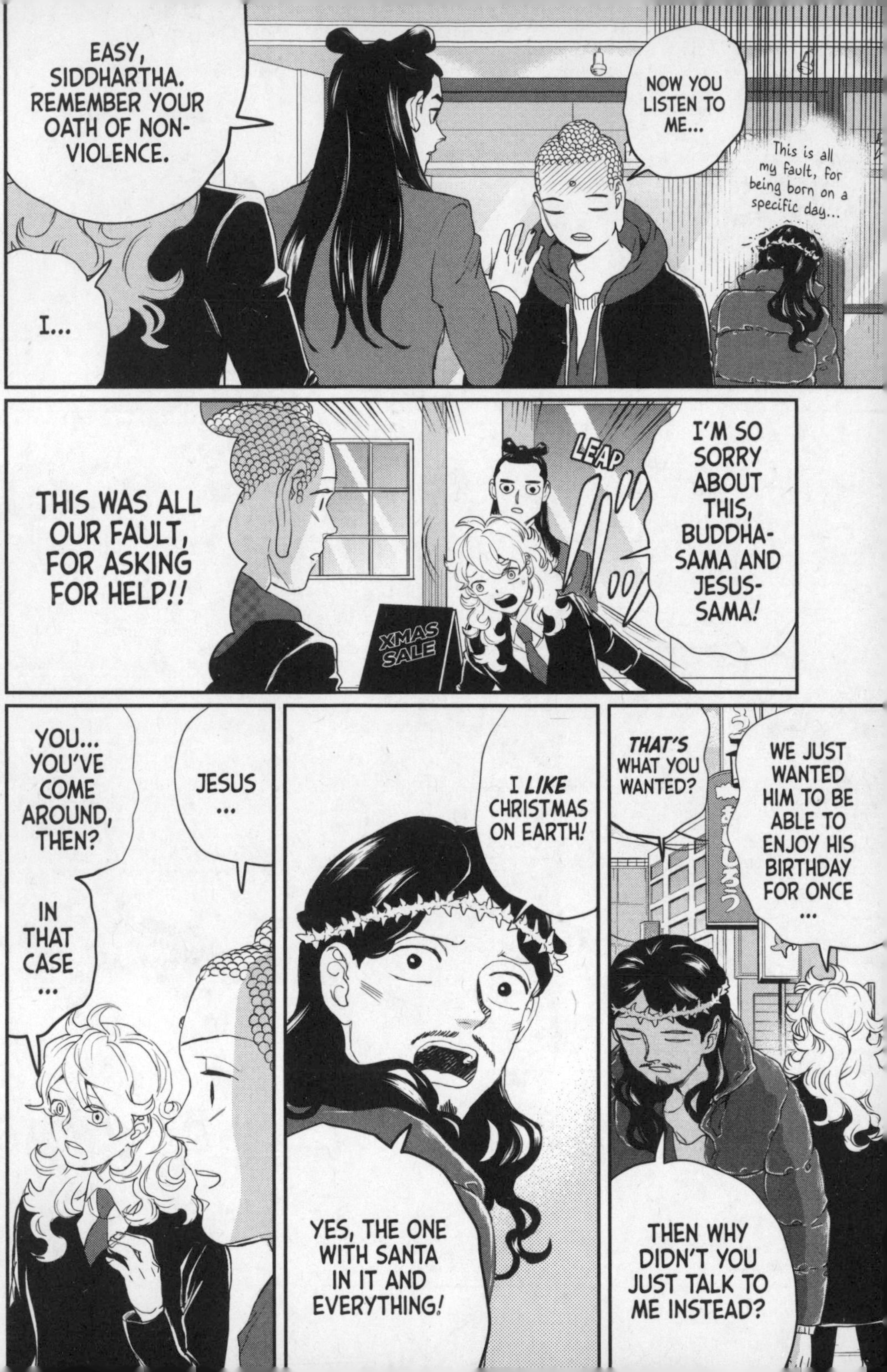
NOW YOU LISTEN TO ME...
This is all my fault, for being born on a specific day...
EASY, SIDDHARTHA. REMEMBER YOUR OATH OF NON-VIOLENCE.
I...
LEAP
I'M SO SORRY ABOUT THIS, BUDDHA-SAMA AND JESUS-SAMA!
THIS WAS ALL OUR FAULT, FOR ASKING FOR HELP!!
XMAS SALE
WE JUST WANTED HIM TO BE ABLE TO ENJOY HIS BIRTHDAY FOR ONCE ...
THAT'S WHAT YOU WANTED?
THEN WHY DIDN'T YOU JUST TALK TO ME INSTEAD?
I *LIKE* CHRISTMAS ON EARTH!
YES, THE ONE WITH SANTA IN IT AND EVERYTHING!
JESUS ...
YOU... YOU'VE COME AROUND, THEN?
IN THAT CASE ...

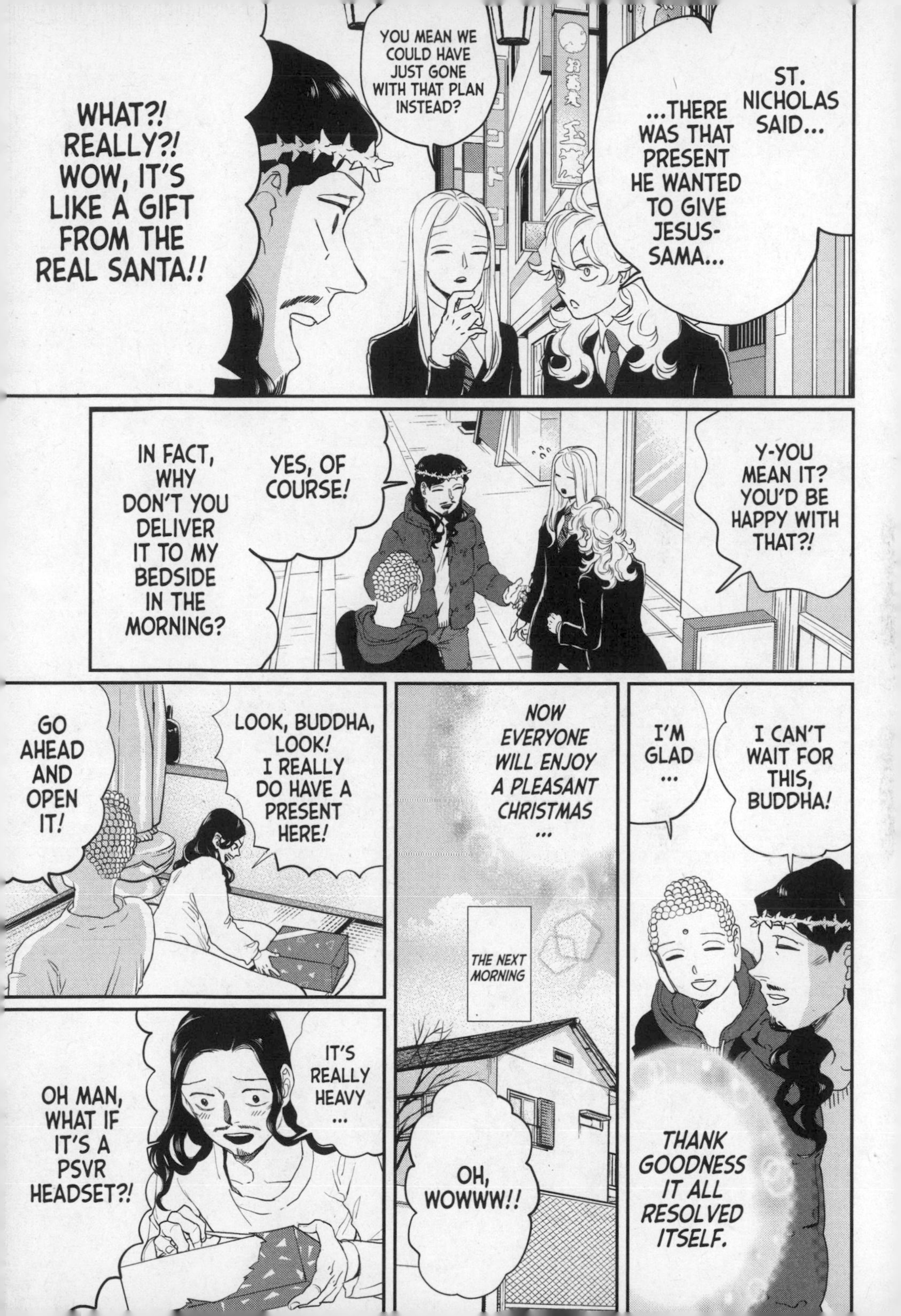
ST. NICHOLAS SAID...
...THERE WAS THAT PRESENT HE WANTED TO GIVE JESUS-SAMA...
YOU MEAN WE COULD HAVE JUST GONE WITH THAT PLAN INSTEAD?
WHAT?! REALLY?! WOW, IT'S LIKE A GIFT FROM THE REAL SANTA!!
Y-YOU MEAN IT? YOU'D BE HAPPY WITH THAT?!
YES, OF COURSE!
IN FACT, WHY DON'T YOU DELIVER IT TO MY BEDSIDE IN THE MORNING?
I CAN'T WAIT FOR THIS, BUDDHA!
I'M GLAD ...
THANK GOODNESS IT ALL RESOLVED ITSELF.
NOW EVERYONE WILL ENJOY A PLEASANT CHRISTMAS ...
THE NEXT MORNING
OH, WOWWW!!
LOOK, BUDDHA, LOOK! I REALLY DO HAVE A PRESENT HERE!
GO AHEAD AND OPEN IT!
IT'S REALLY HEAVY ...
OH MAN, WHAT IF IT'S A PSVR HEADSET?!

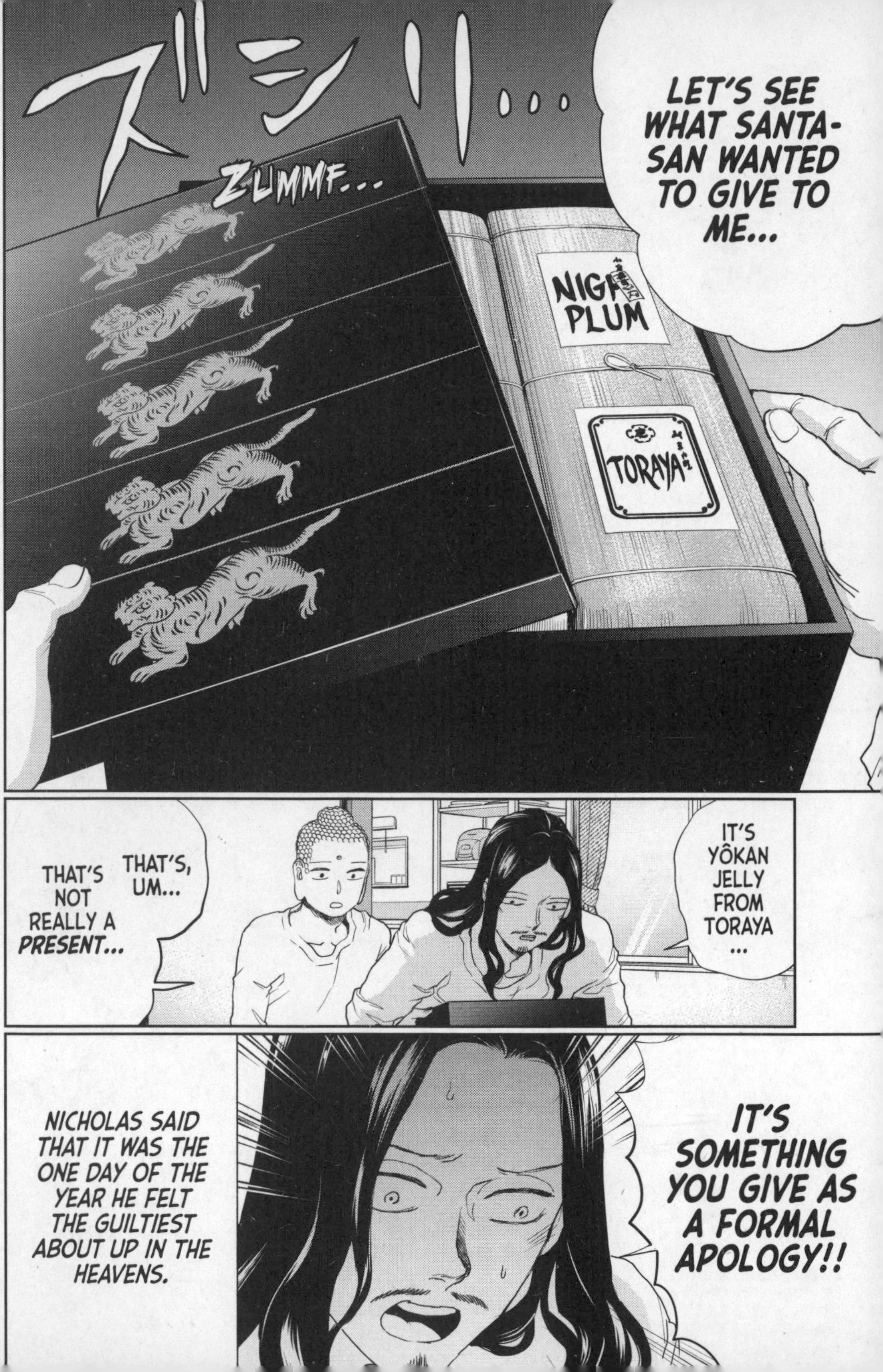
LET'S SEE WHAT SANTA-SAN WANTED TO GIVE TO ME...
ズシリ...
ZUMMF...
NIGA PLUM
TORAYA
IT'S YÔKAN JELLY FROM TORAYA ...
THAT'S, UM...
THAT'S NOT REALLY A PRESENT...
IT'S SOMETHING YOU GIVE AS A FORMAL APOLOGY!!
NICHOLAS SAID THAT IT WAS THE ONE DAY OF THE YEAR HE FELT THE GUILTIEST ABOUT UP IN THE HEAVENS.

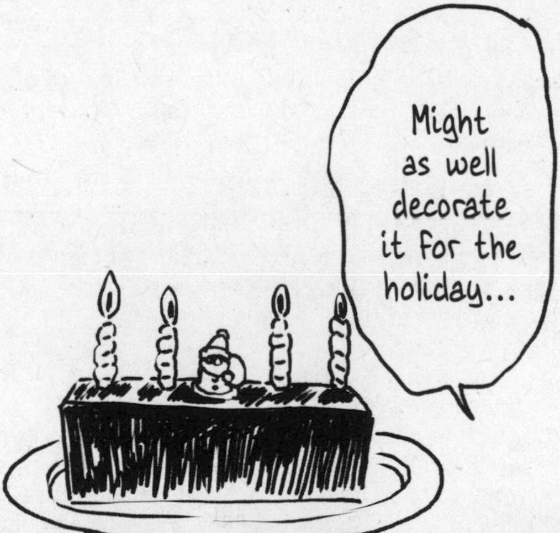
Might as well decorate it for the holiday...

SAINT ☆ YOUNG MEN

CHAPTER 110 TRANSLATION NOTES

Kamen Rider, page 108
A long-running tokusatsu live action TV franchise, which translates to "Masked Rider." Virtually every year sees the unveiling of a different Kamen Rider series, featuring an insect-styled superhero who rides a motorcycle and fights against villains.

Christian feasts, page 110
The Christian feast day for the baptism of Jesus is also called Theophany, and falls on January 6th. In the Eastern Orthodox Church, it is observed on Epiphany, January 19th. The Feast of the Presentation of Jesus Christ, also known as Candlemas, commemorates the occasion of the presentation of the infant Jesus to the temple, a Jewish rite of the time. This holiday falls on February 2nd. Lastly, the Feast of the Annunciation celebrates the event in which Mary's conception of Jesus was confirmed in a visit by the archangel Gabriel. it is observed on March 25th.

Akira 100%, page 117
A newer comedian who gained infamy for his stage antics of appearing wearing only a bowtie, and holding a tray that he uses to conceal his groin with plenty of careful acrobatics. His most famous routine involves playing a police detective named Marugoshi Deka, or "Detective Buff."

Honey toast, page 118
A trendy dessert often sold at karaoke parlors in Tokyo, honey toast is a loaf of buttered, honeyed bread browned in the oven, then garnished with fruits, syrup, and whipped or ice cream.

Nicholas, page 121
Saint Nicholas was a figure of the early Christian church, and the patron saint of fisherman, merchants and children. His reputation for giving gifts clandestinely was the root of northern European traditions that evolved in North America into the modern image of Santa Claus.

Yôkan, page 124
A traditional dessert made of an (red bean paste) solidified with agar and sugar. it's presented in neat little cubes (or larger blocks) that can be easily picked up and eaten with a toothpick. The Toraya brand is some of the most prestigious and expensive that is available, thanks in part to its imposing packaging. The "Night Plum" branding seen here is the traditional azuki bean flavor (there are others such as matcha and brown sugar) and is named for its color similarity to plum blossoms in the night.

SAINT☆YOUNG MEN

SAINT☆YOUNG MEN

SAINT☆YOUNG MEN

SAINT☆YOUNG MEN

SAINT☆YOUNG MEN

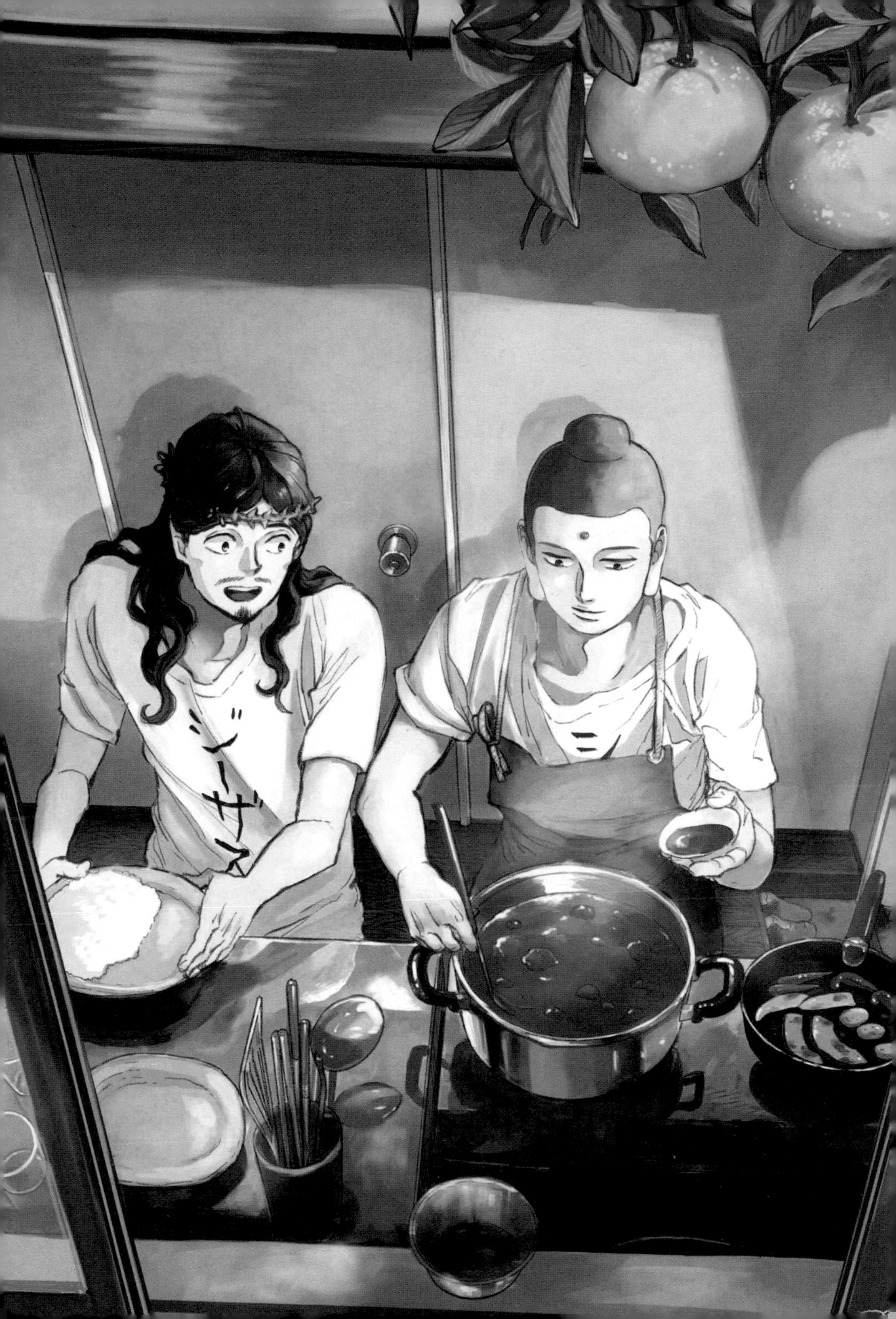
ジーザス

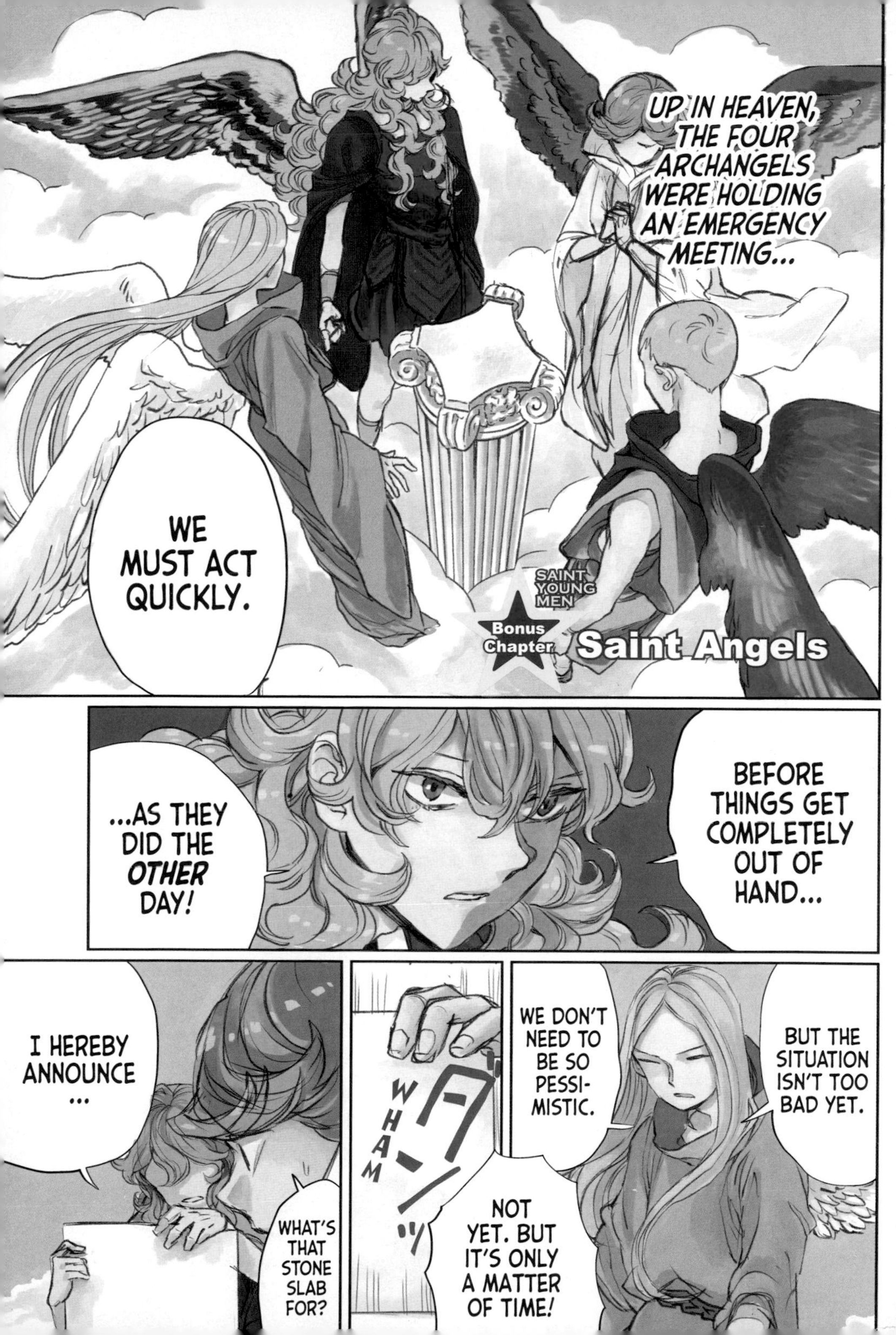
UP IN HEAVEN, THE FOUR ARCHANGELS WERE HOLDING AN EMERGENCY MEETING...
SAINT YOUNG MEN
Bonus Chapter
Saint Angels
WE MUST ACT QUICKLY.
BEFORE THINGS GET COMPLETELY OUT OF HAND...
...AS THEY DID THE *OTHER* DAY!
BUT THE SITUATION ISN'T TOO BAD YET.
WE DON'T NEED TO BE SO PESSI-MISTIC.
NOT YET. BUT IT'S ONLY A MATTER OF TIME!
WHAM
I HEREBY ANNOUNCE ...
WHAT'S THAT STONE SLAB FOR?

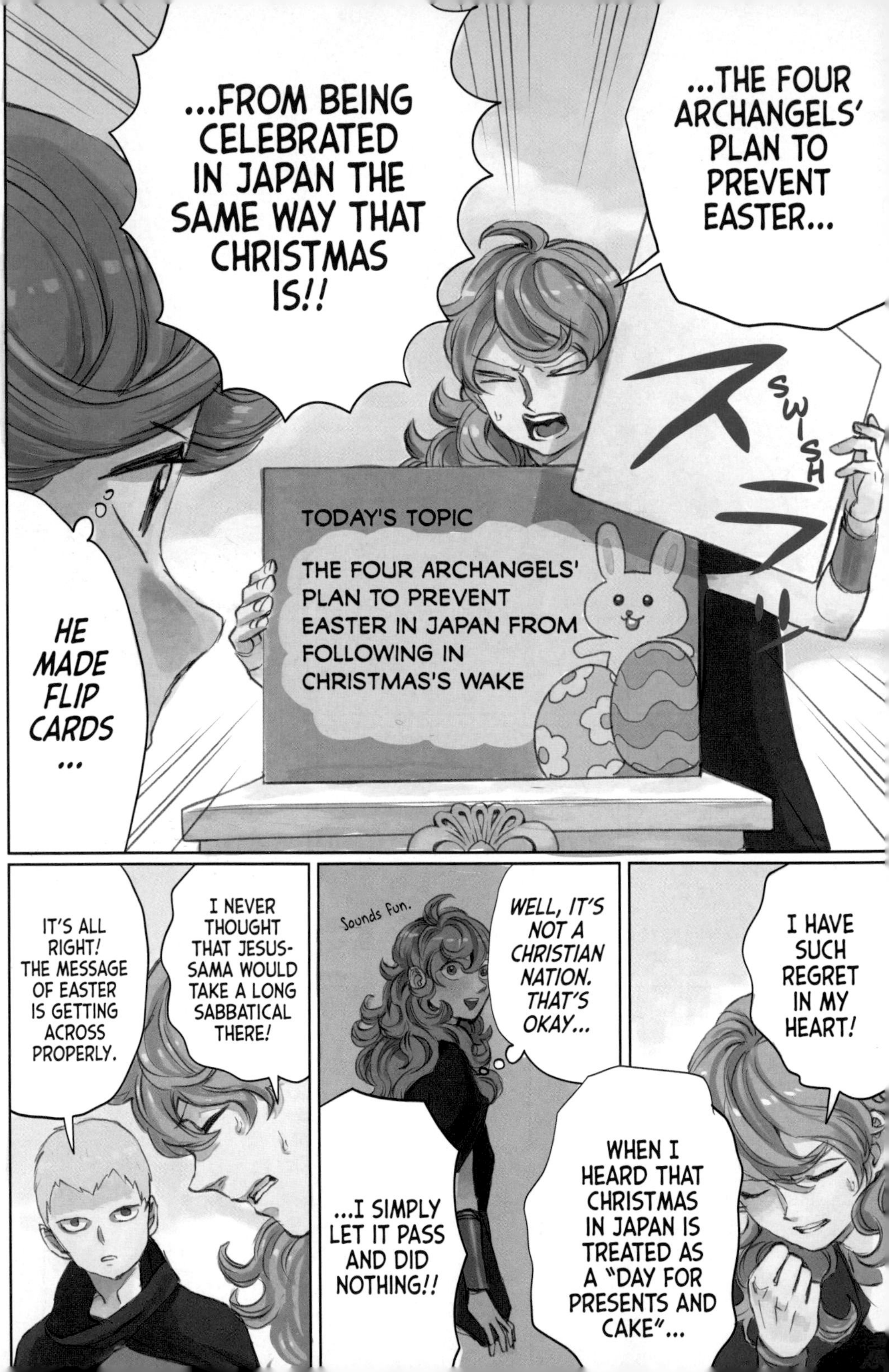
...THE FOUR ARCHANGELS' PLAN TO PREVENT EASTER...
...FROM BEING CELEBRATED IN JAPAN THE SAME WAY THAT CHRISTMAS IS!!
SWISH
TODAY'S TOPIC
THE FOUR ARCHANGELS' PLAN TO PREVENT EASTER IN JAPAN FROM FOLLOWING IN CHRISTMAS'S WAKE
HE MADE FLIP CARDS...
I HAVE SUCH REGRET IN MY HEART!
WHEN I HEARD THAT CHRISTMAS IN JAPAN IS TREATED AS A "DAY FOR PRESENTS AND CAKE"...
WELL, IT'S NOT A CHRISTIAN NATION. THAT'S OKAY...
...I SIMPLY LET IT PASS AND DID NOTHING!!
Sounds fun.
I NEVER THOUGHT THAT JESUS-SAMA WOULD TAKE A LONG SABBATICAL THERE!
IT'S ALL RIGHT! THE MESSAGE OF EASTER IS GETTING ACROSS PROPERLY.

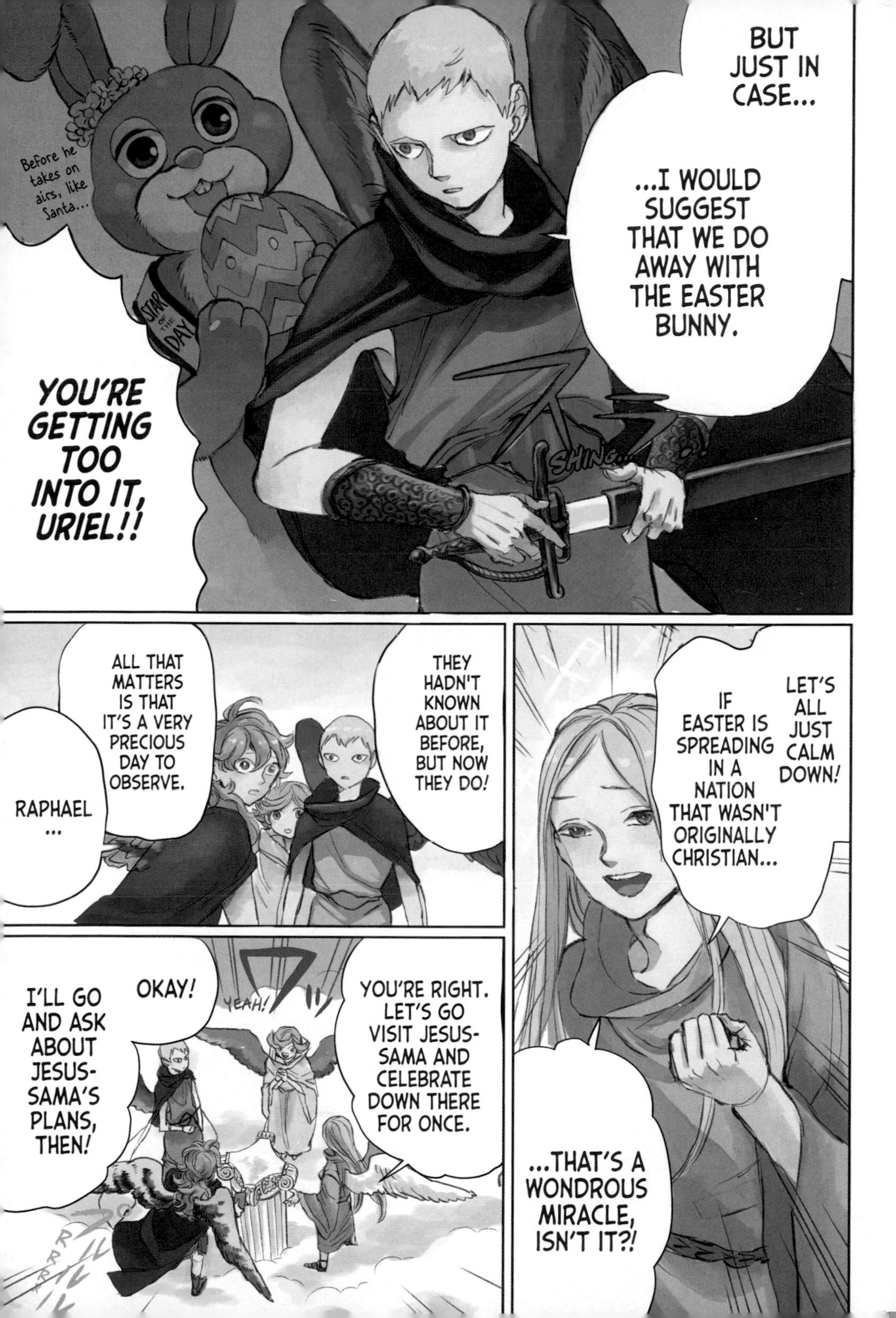
BUT JUST IN CASE...
...I WOULD SUGGEST THAT WE DO AWAY WITH THE EASTER BUNNY.
SHING...
STAR OF THE DAY
Before he takes on airs, like Santa...
YOU'RE GETTING TOO INTO IT, URIEL!!
LET'S ALL JUST CALM DOWN!
IF EASTER IS SPREADING IN A NATION THAT WASN'T ORIGINALLY CHRISTIAN...
...THAT'S A WONDROUS MIRACLE, ISN'T IT?!
THEY HADN'T KNOWN ABOUT IT BEFORE, BUT NOW THEY DO!
ALL THAT MATTERS IS THAT IT'S A VERY PRECIOUS DAY TO OBSERVE.
RAPHAEL...
YOU'RE RIGHT. LET'S GO VISIT JESUS-SAMA AND CELEBRATE DOWN THERE FOR ONCE.
YEAH!
OKAY!
I'LL GO AND ASK ABOUT JESUS-SAMA'S PLANS, THEN!

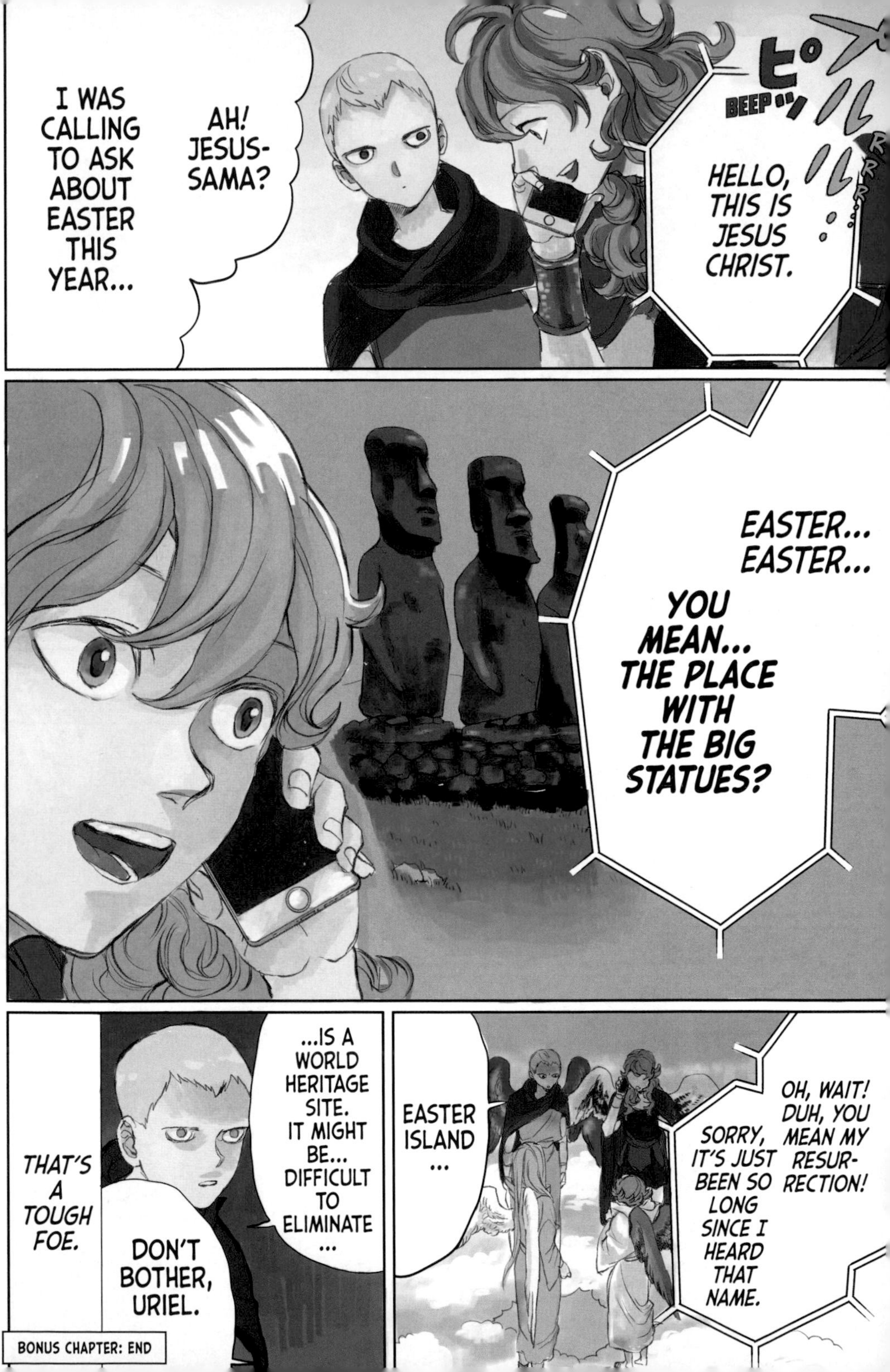
BEEP
HELLO, THIS IS JESUS CHRIST.
AH! JESUS-SAMA?
I WAS CALLING TO ASK ABOUT EASTER THIS YEAR...
EASTER... EASTER...
YOU MEAN... THE PLACE WITH THE BIG STATUES?
OH, WAIT! DUH, YOU MEAN MY RESUR-RECTION!
SORRY, IT'S JUST BEEN SO LONG SINCE I HEARD THAT NAME.
EASTER ISLAND ...
...IS A WORLD HERITAGE SITE. IT MIGHT BE... DIFFICULT TO ELIMINATE ...
THAT'S A TOUGH FOE.
DON'T BOTHER, URIEL.

BONUS CHAPTER: END

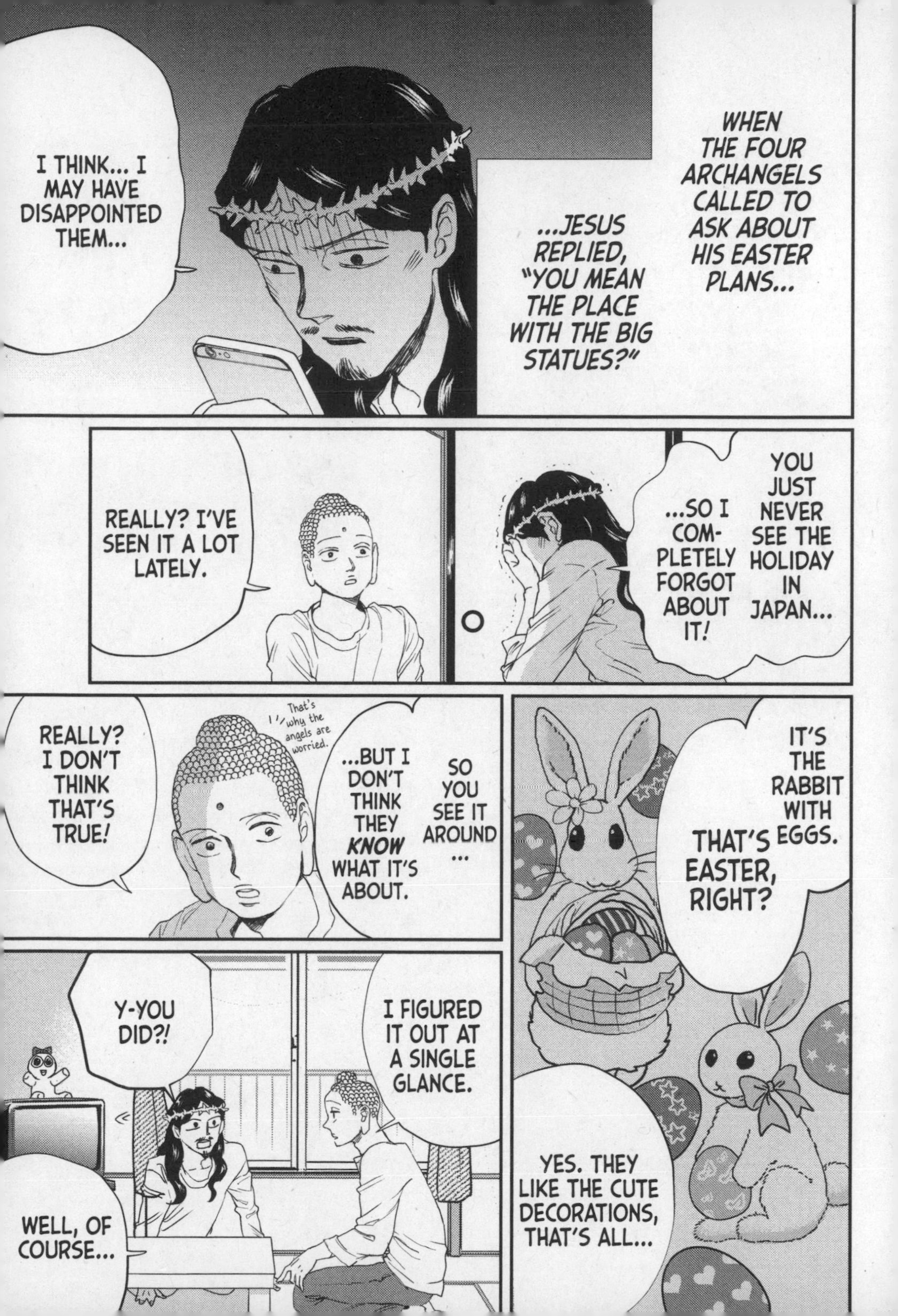
WHEN THE FOUR ARCHANGELS CALLED TO ASK ABOUT HIS EASTER PLANS...
...JESUS REPLIED, "YOU MEAN THE PLACE WITH THE BIG STATUES?"
I THINK... I MAY HAVE DISAPPOINTED THEM...
YOU JUST NEVER SEE THE HOLIDAY IN JAPAN...
...SO I COM-PLETELY FORGOT ABOUT IT!
REALLY? I'VE SEEN IT A LOT LATELY.
IT'S THE RABBIT WITH EGGS.
THAT'S EASTER, RIGHT?
YES. THEY LIKE THE CUTE DECORATIONS, THAT'S ALL...
SO YOU SEE IT AROUND...
...BUT I DON'T THINK THEY *KNOW* WHAT IT'S ABOUT.
That's why the angels are worried.
REALLY? I DON'T THINK THAT'S TRUE!
I FIGURED IT OUT AT A SINGLE GLANCE.
Y-YOU DID?!
WELL, OF COURSE...

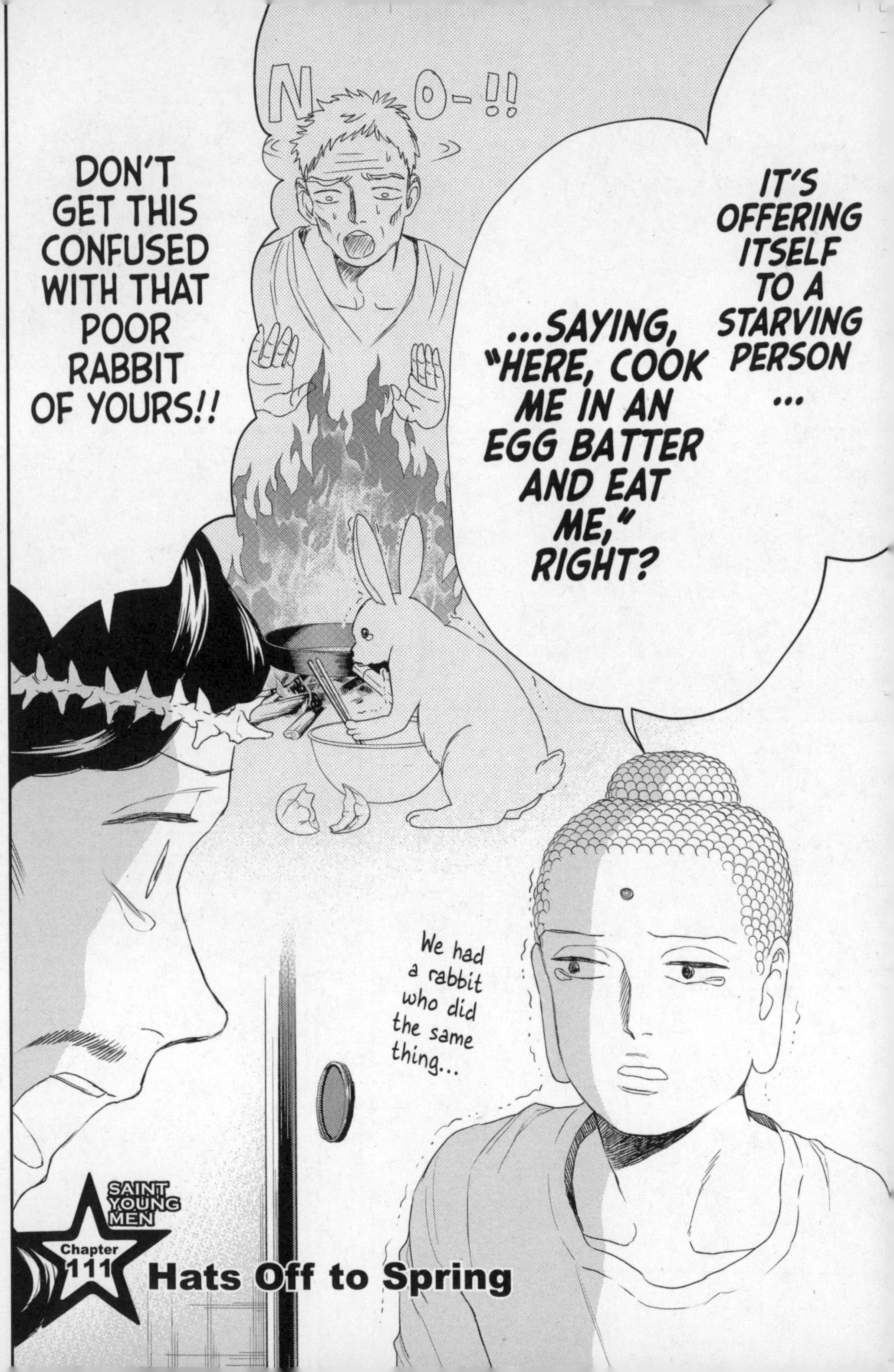
IT'S OFFERING ITSELF TO A STARVING PERSON ...
...SAYING, "HERE, COOK ME IN AN EGG BATTER AND EAT ME," RIGHT?
NO-!!
DON'T GET THIS CONFUSED WITH THAT POOR RABBIT OF YOURS!!
We had a rabbit who did the same thing...
SAINT YOUNG MEN
Chapter 111
Hats Off to Spring

BUDDHA
THE RABBIT ON THE MOON IS SUPPOSED TO BE THE ONE WHO GAVE ITS OWN BODY FOR FOOD. THE STARVING OLD MAN WAS TAISHAKU-TEN, BUT I'M GUESSING HE WASN'T WEARING ARMANI AT THE TIME.

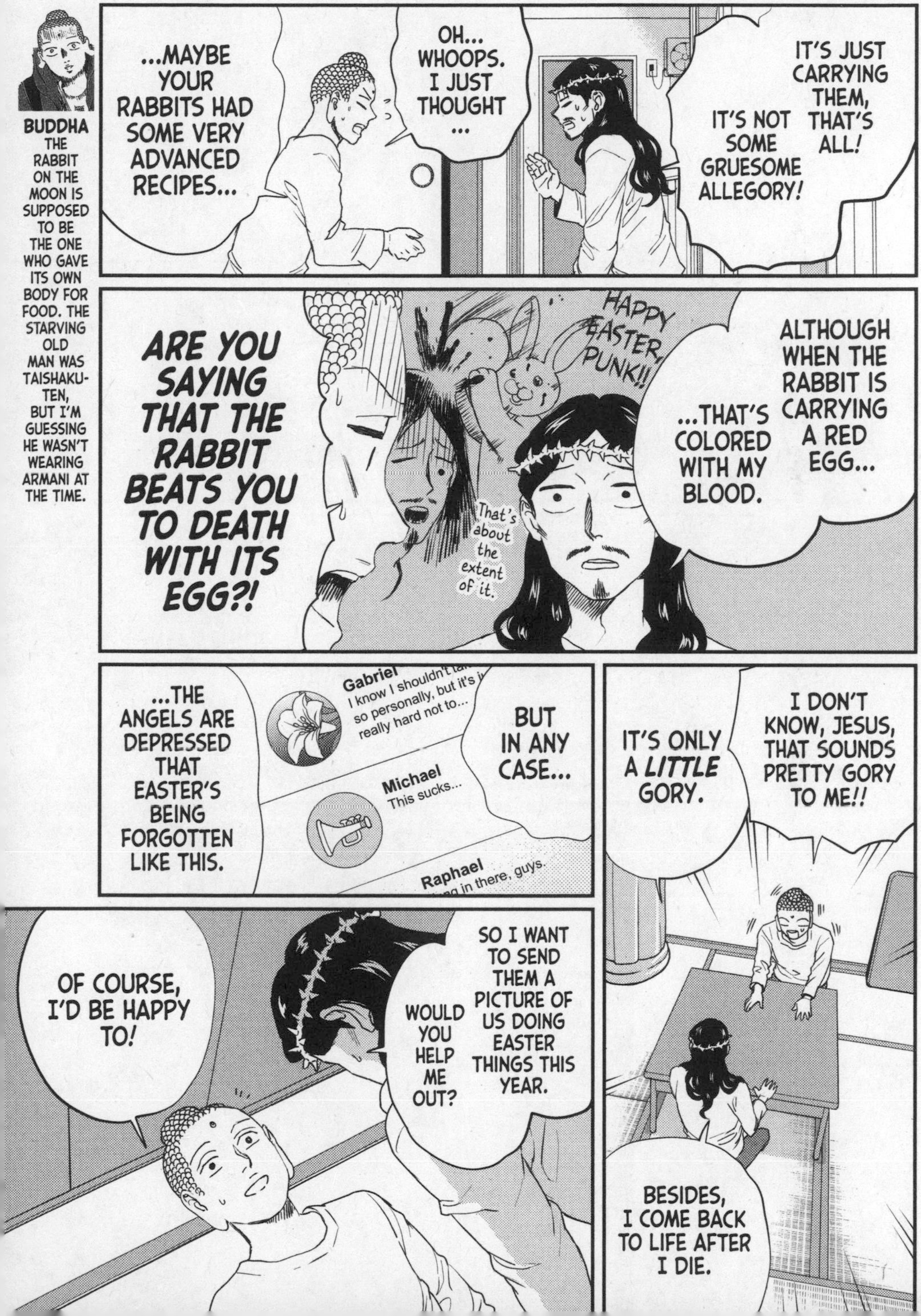
IT'S JUST CARRYING THEM, THAT'S ALL!
IT'S NOT SOME GRUESOME ALLEGORY!
OH... WHOOPS. I JUST THOUGHT ...
...MAYBE YOUR RABBITS HAD SOME VERY ADVANCED RECIPES...
ALTHOUGH WHEN THE RABBIT IS CARRYING A RED EGG...
...THAT'S COLORED WITH MY BLOOD.
HAPPY EASTER, PUNK!!
That's about the extent of it.
ARE YOU SAYING THAT THE RABBIT BEATS YOU TO DEATH WITH ITS EGG?!
I DON'T KNOW, JESUS, THAT SOUNDS PRETTY GORY TO ME!!
IT'S ONLY A *LITTLE* GORY.
BESIDES, I COME BACK TO LIFE AFTER I DIE.
BUT IN ANY CASE...
Gabriel
so personally, but it's
really hard not to...
Michael
This sucks...
Raphael
in there, guys.
...THE ANGELS ARE DEPRESSED THAT EASTER'S BEING FORGOTTEN LIKE THIS.
SO I WANT TO SEND THEM A PICTURE OF US DOING EASTER THINGS THIS YEAR.
WOULD YOU HELP ME OUT?
OF COURSE, I'D BE HAPPY TO!

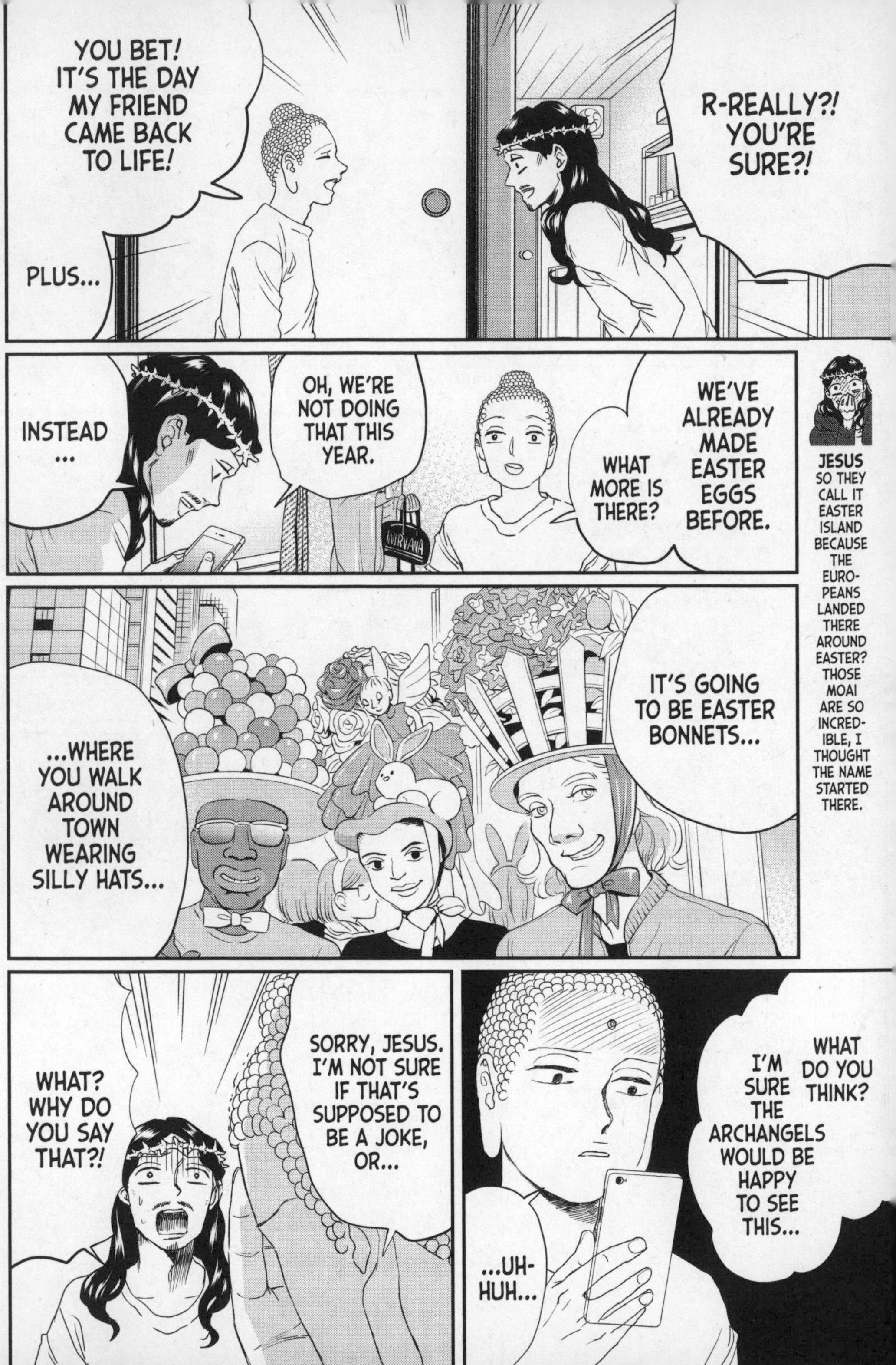
R-REALLY?! YOU'RE SURE?!
YOU BET! IT'S THE DAY MY FRIEND CAME BACK TO LIFE!
PLUS...
WE'VE ALREADY MADE EASTER EGGS BEFORE.
WHAT MORE IS THERE?
OH, WE'RE NOT DOING THAT THIS YEAR.
INSTEAD...
NIRVANA
IT'S GOING TO BE EASTER BONNETS...
...WHERE YOU WALK AROUND TOWN WEARING SILLY HATS...
WHAT DO YOU THINK?
I'M SURE THE ARCHANGELS WOULD BE HAPPY TO SEE THIS...
...UH-HUH...
SORRY, JESUS. I'M NOT SURE IF THAT'S SUPPOSED TO BE A JOKE, OR...
WHAT? WHY DO YOU SAY THAT?!
JESUS
SO THEY CALL IT EASTER ISLAND BECAUSE THE EUROPEANS LANDED THERE AROUND EASTER? THOSE MOAI ARE SO INCREDIBLE, I THOUGHT THE NAME STARTED THERE.

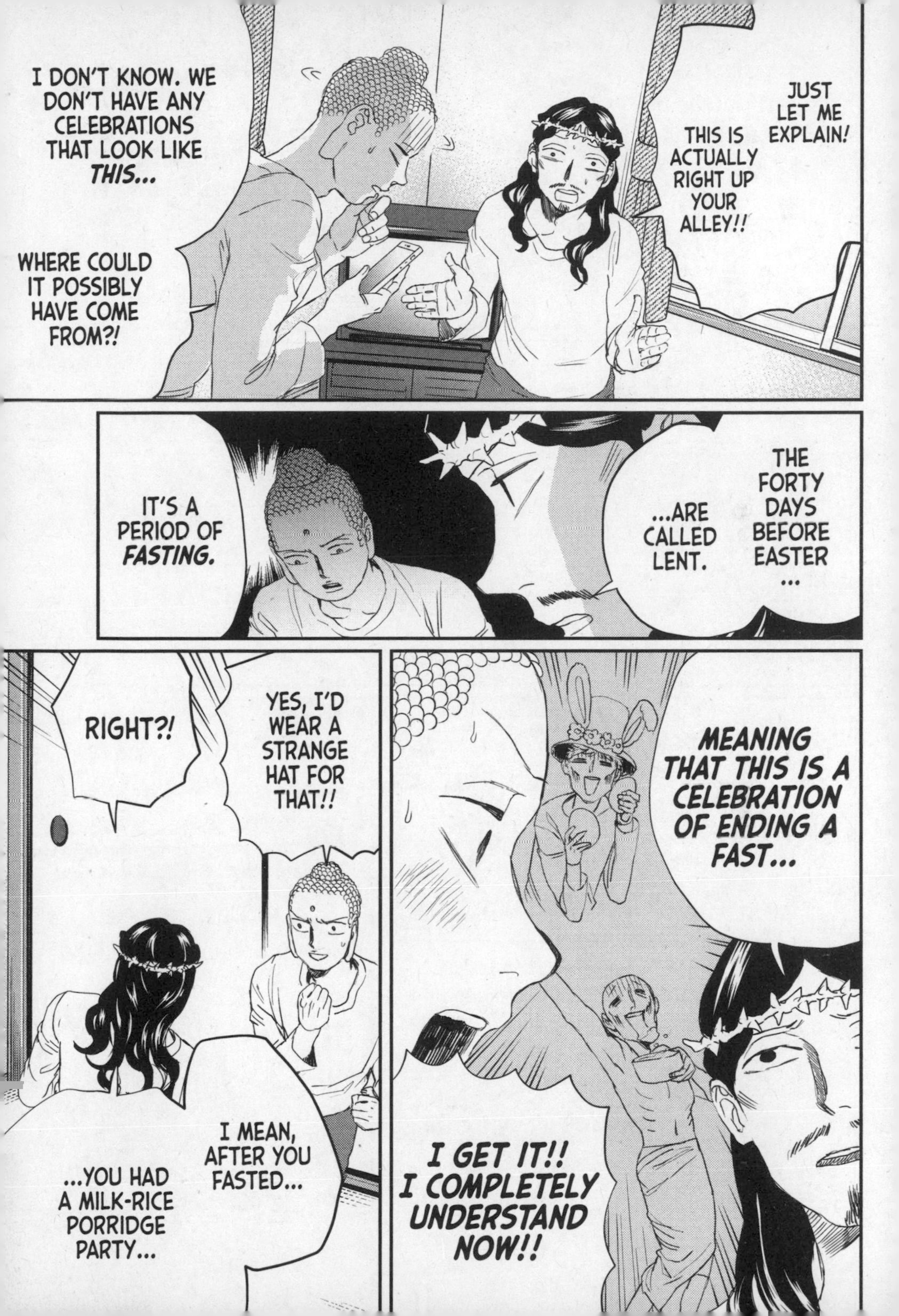
JUST LET ME EXPLAIN!
THIS IS ACTUALLY RIGHT UP YOUR ALLEY!!
I DON'T KNOW. WE DON'T HAVE ANY CELEBRATIONS THAT LOOK LIKE *THIS...*
WHERE COULD IT POSSIBLY HAVE COME FROM?!
THE FORTY DAYS BEFORE EASTER ...
...ARE CALLED LENT.
IT'S A PERIOD OF *FASTING.*
MEANING THAT THIS IS A CELEBRATION OF ENDING A FAST...
I GET IT!! I COMPLETELY UNDERSTAND NOW!!
YES, I'D WEAR A STRANGE HAT FOR THAT!!
RIGHT?!
I MEAN, AFTER YOU FASTED...
...YOU HAD A MILK-RICE PORRIDGE PARTY...

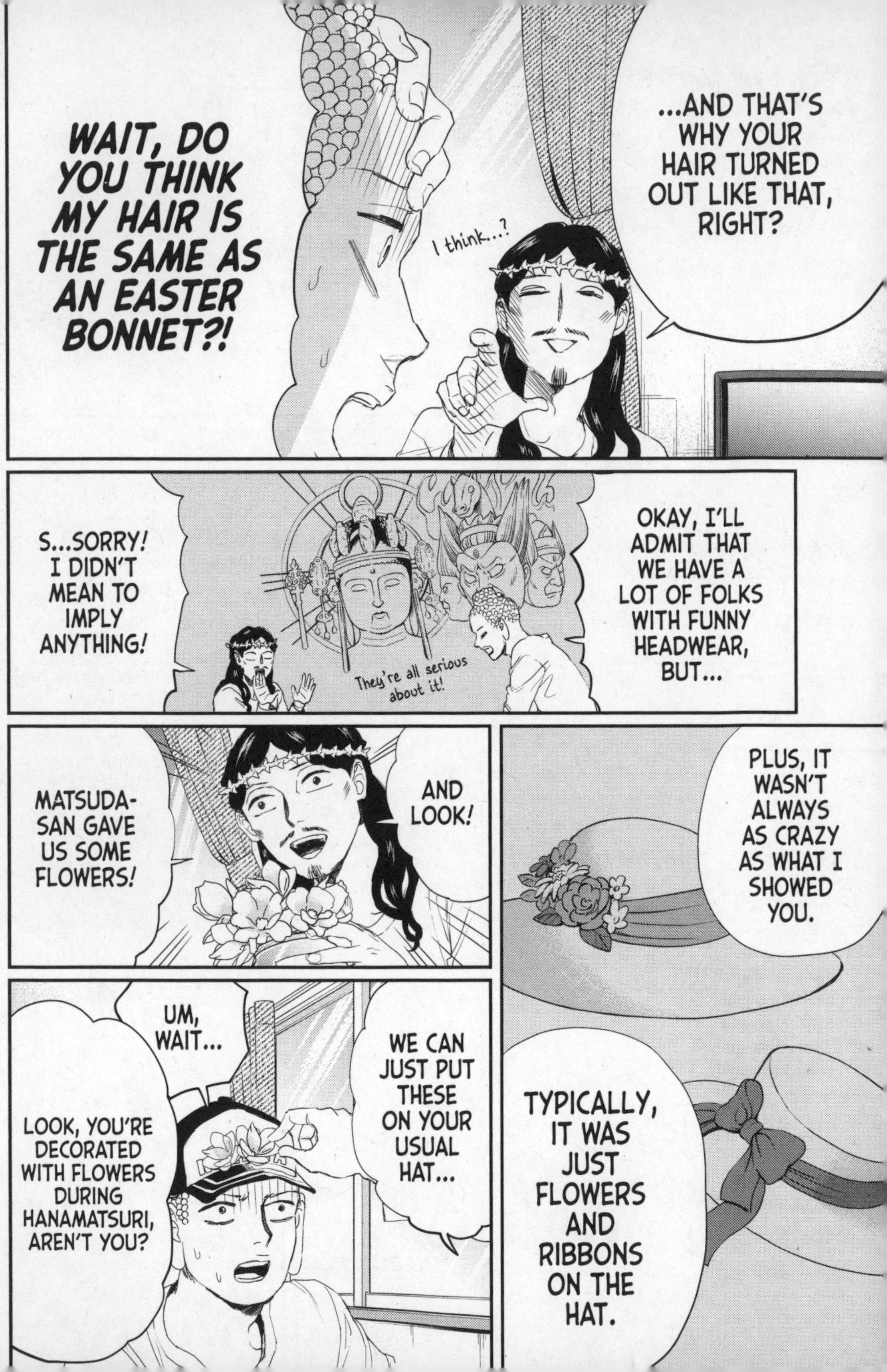
...AND THAT'S WHY YOUR HAIR TURNED OUT LIKE THAT, RIGHT?
I think...?
WAIT, DO YOU THINK MY HAIR IS THE SAME AS AN EASTER BONNET?!
OKAY, I'LL ADMIT THAT WE HAVE A LOT OF FOLKS WITH FUNNY HEADWEAR, BUT...
They're all serious about it!
S...SORRY! I DIDN'T MEAN TO IMPLY ANYTHING!
PLUS, IT WASN'T ALWAYS AS CRAZY AS WHAT I SHOWED YOU.
TYPICALLY, IT WAS JUST FLOWERS AND RIBBONS ON THE HAT.
AND LOOK!
MATSUDA-SAN GAVE US SOME FLOWERS!
WE CAN JUST PUT THESE ON YOUR USUAL HAT...
UM, WAIT...
LOOK, YOU'RE DECORATED WITH FLOWERS DURING HANAMATSURI, AREN'T YOU?

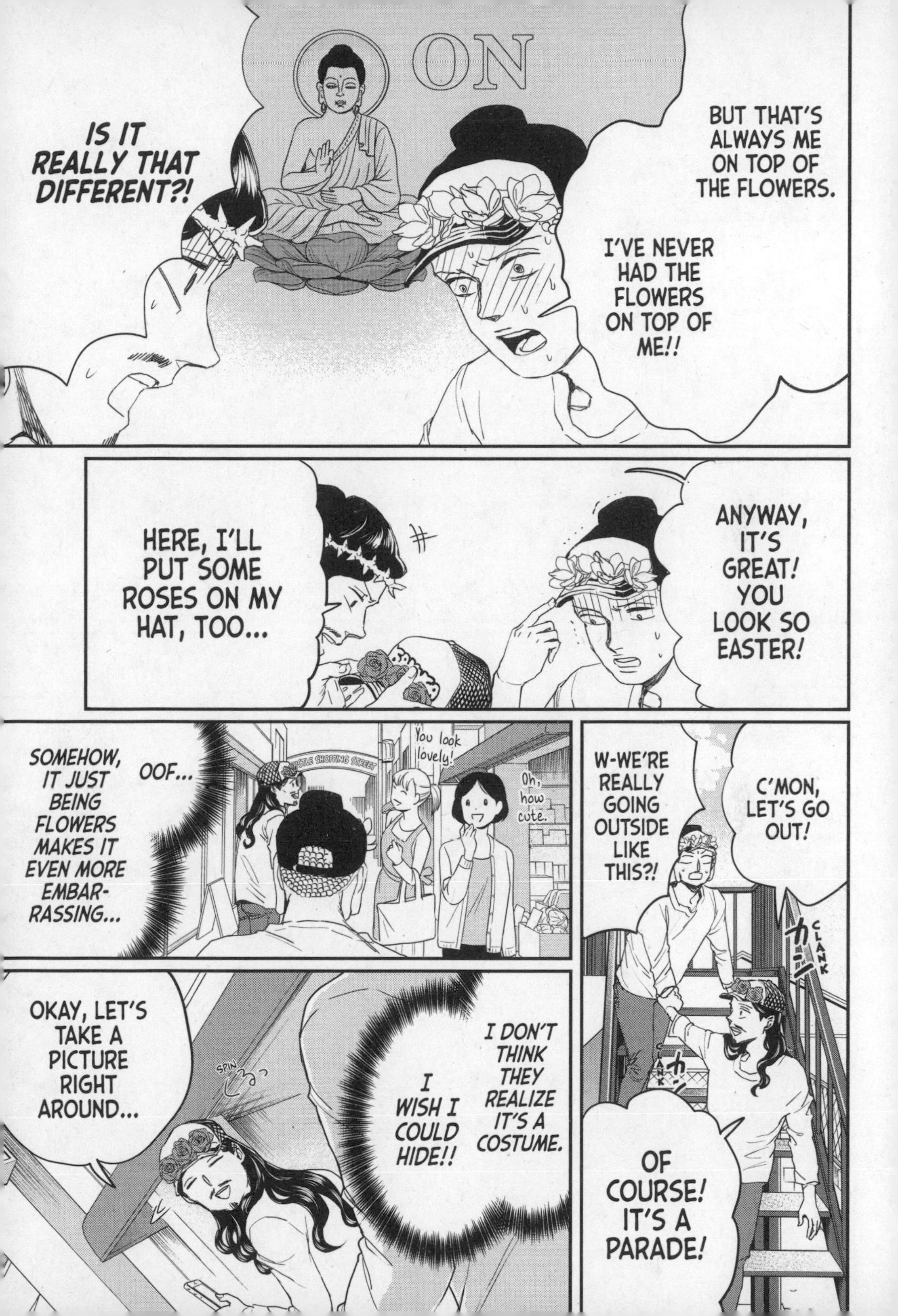
ON
BUT THAT'S ALWAYS ME ON TOP OF THE FLOWERS.
I'VE NEVER HAD THE FLOWERS ON TOP OF ME!!
IS IT REALLY THAT DIFFERENT?!
ANYWAY, IT'S GREAT! YOU LOOK SO EASTER!
HERE, I'LL PUT SOME ROSES ON MY HAT, TOO...
C'MON, LET'S GO OUT!
W-WE'RE REALLY GOING OUTSIDE LIKE THIS?!
CLANK
CLANK
OF COURSE! IT'S A PARADE!
You look lovely!
Oh, how cute.
OOF...
SOMEHOW, IT JUST BEING FLOWERS MAKES IT EVEN MORE EMBARRASSING...
I DON'T THINK THEY REALIZE IT'S A COSTUME.
I WISH I COULD HIDE!!
SPIN
OKAY, LET'S TAKE A PICTURE RIGHT AROUND...

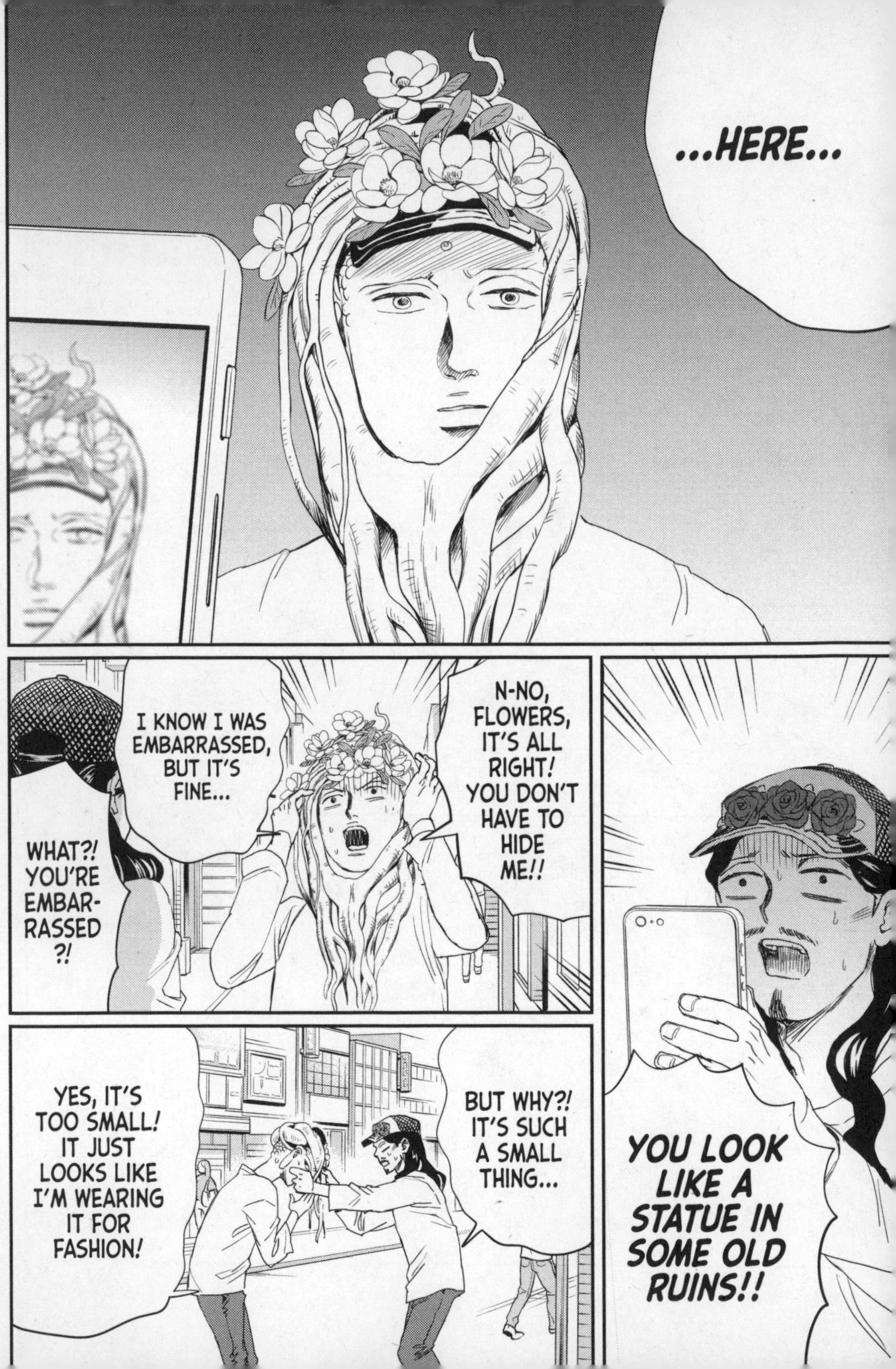
...HERE...
YOU LOOK LIKE A STATUE IN SOME OLD RUINS!!
N-NO, FLOWERS, IT'S ALL RIGHT! YOU DON'T HAVE TO HIDE ME!!
I KNOW I WAS EMBARRASSED, BUT IT'S FINE...
WHAT?! YOU'RE EMBAR-RASSED?!
BUT WHY?! IT'S SUCH A SMALL THING...
YES, IT'S TOO SMALL! IT JUST LOOKS LIKE I'M WEARING IT FOR FASHION!

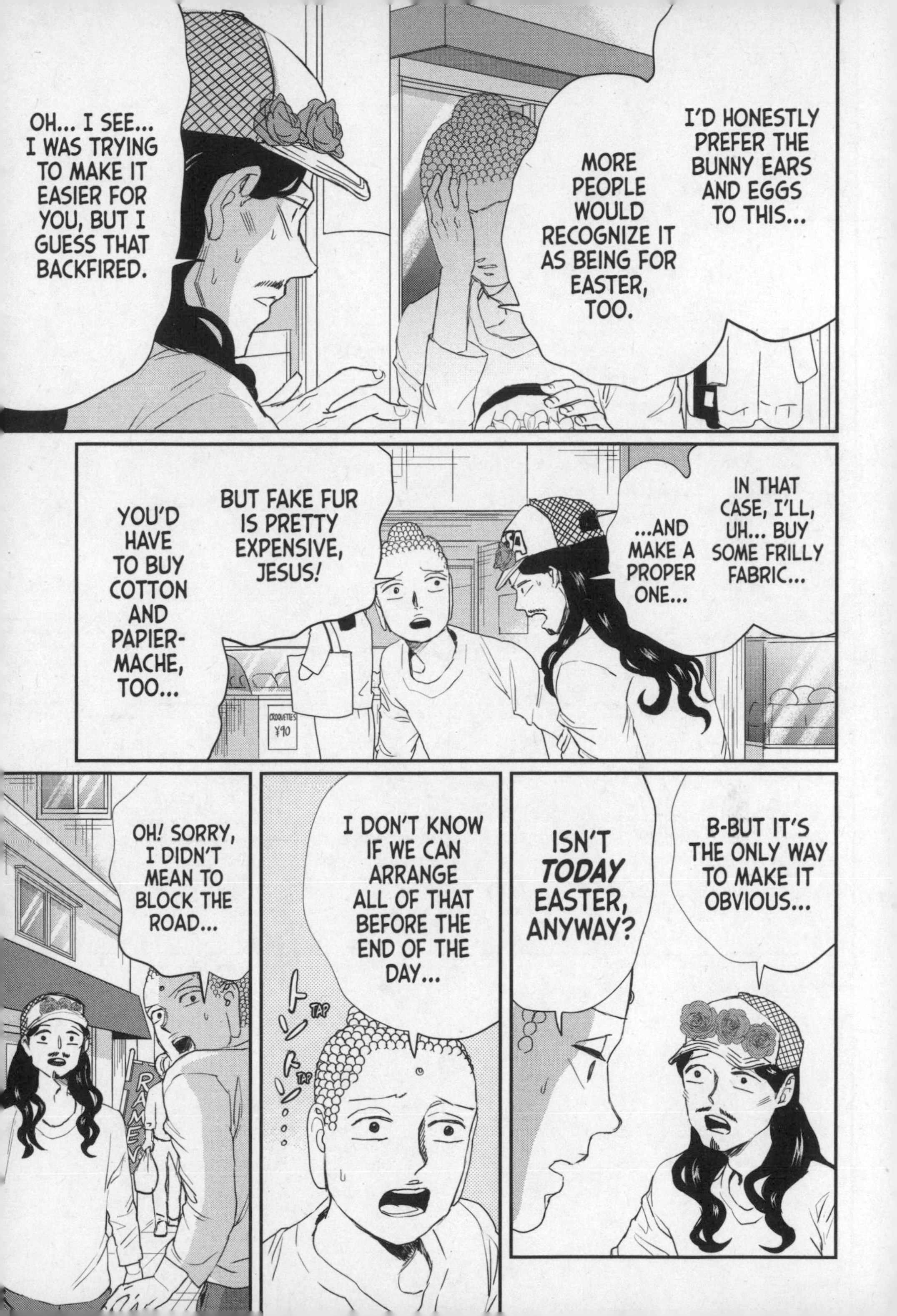
I'D HONESTLY PREFER THE BUNNY EARS AND EGGS TO THIS...
MORE PEOPLE WOULD RECOGNIZE IT AS BEING FOR EASTER, TOO.
OH... I SEE... I WAS TRYING TO MAKE IT EASIER FOR YOU, BUT I GUESS THAT BACKFIRED.
IN THAT CASE, I'LL, UH... BUY SOME FRILLY FABRIC...
...AND MAKE A PROPER ONE...
BUT FAKE FUR IS PRETTY EXPENSIVE, JESUS!
YOU'D HAVE TO BUY COTTON AND PAPIER-MACHE, TOO...
CROQUETTES ¥90
B-BUT IT'S THE ONLY WAY TO MAKE IT OBVIOUS...
ISN'T *TODAY* EASTER, ANYWAY?
I DON'T KNOW IF WE CAN ARRANGE ALL OF THAT BEFORE THE END OF THE DAY...
TAP
TAP
OH! SORRY, I DIDN'T MEAN TO BLOCK THE ROAD...

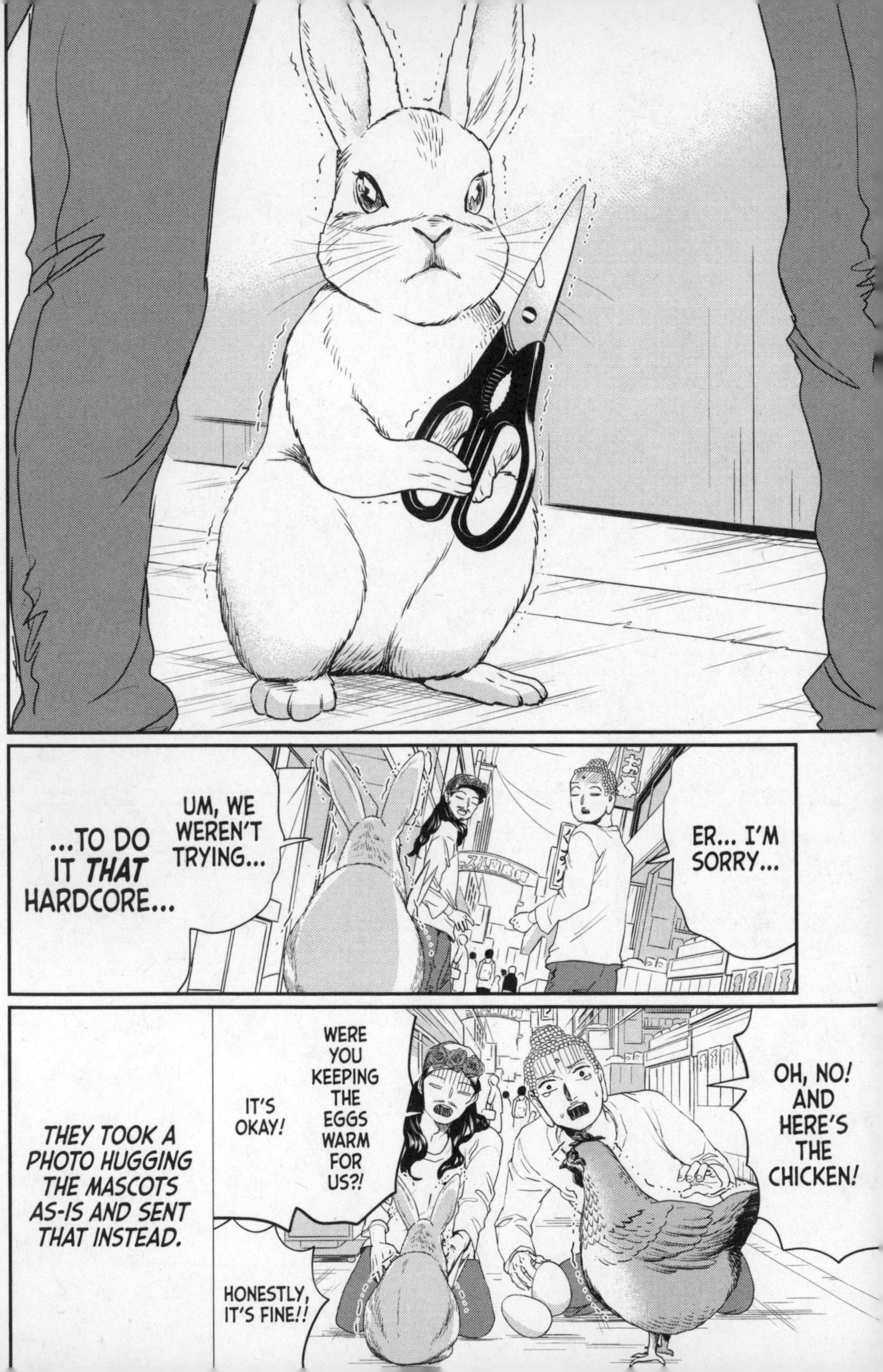
ER... I'M SORRY...
UM, WE WEREN'T TRYING...
...TO DO IT *THAT* HARDCORE...
OH, NO! AND HERE'S THE CHICKEN!
WERE YOU KEEPING THE EGGS WARM FOR US?!
IT'S OKAY!
HONESTLY, IT'S FINE!!
THEY TOOK A PHOTO HUGGING THE MASCOTS AS-IS AND SENT THAT INSTEAD.

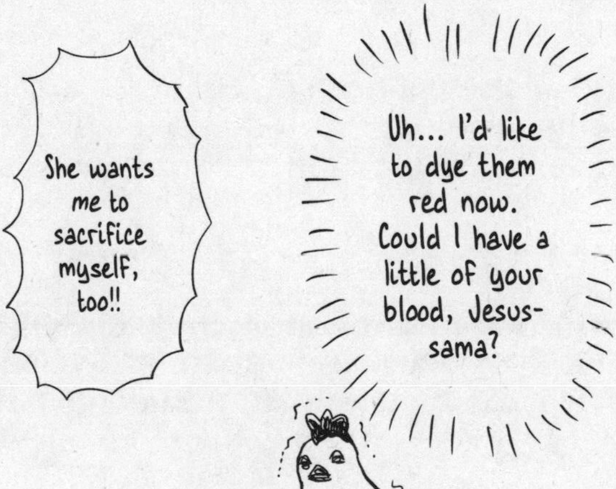
Uh… I'd like to dye them red now. Could I have a little of your blood, Jesus-sama?
She wants me to sacrifice myself, too!!

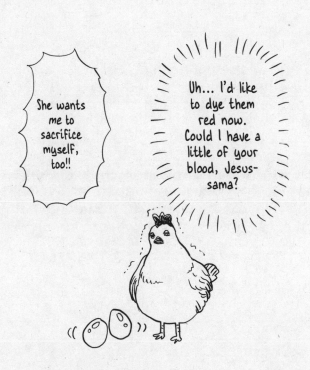

SAINT ☆ YOUNG MEN

CHAPTER 111 TRANSLATION NOTES

Rabbit, page 142

A famous story found in the Jataka tales, a collection of writings about the Buddha's human and animal lives. In the story, several animals attempt to help a starving old man by using their tools and cunning to bring food to him, and thus earn good karma. But the rabbit, having only grass to offer, instead sacrifices itself to the fire. The old man is secretly Taishakuten (Sakra) in disguise, and to reward its sacrifice, he places the rabbit on the face of the moon.

Lent, page 145

The observance of the period between Ash Wednesday and Easter Sunday, a forty-day stretch in which believers are encouraged to fast or otherwise deprive themselves of certain luxuries, meat in particular. This is meant to mirror Jesus's forty days in the desert.

Hanamatsuri, page 146

The celebration of Buddha's Birthday (April 8th) is known as "Hanamatsuri" or the "Flower Festival" in Japan. It's typically observed by pouring sweet tea over miniature Buddha statues in little shrines that have been decorated with colorful flowers.

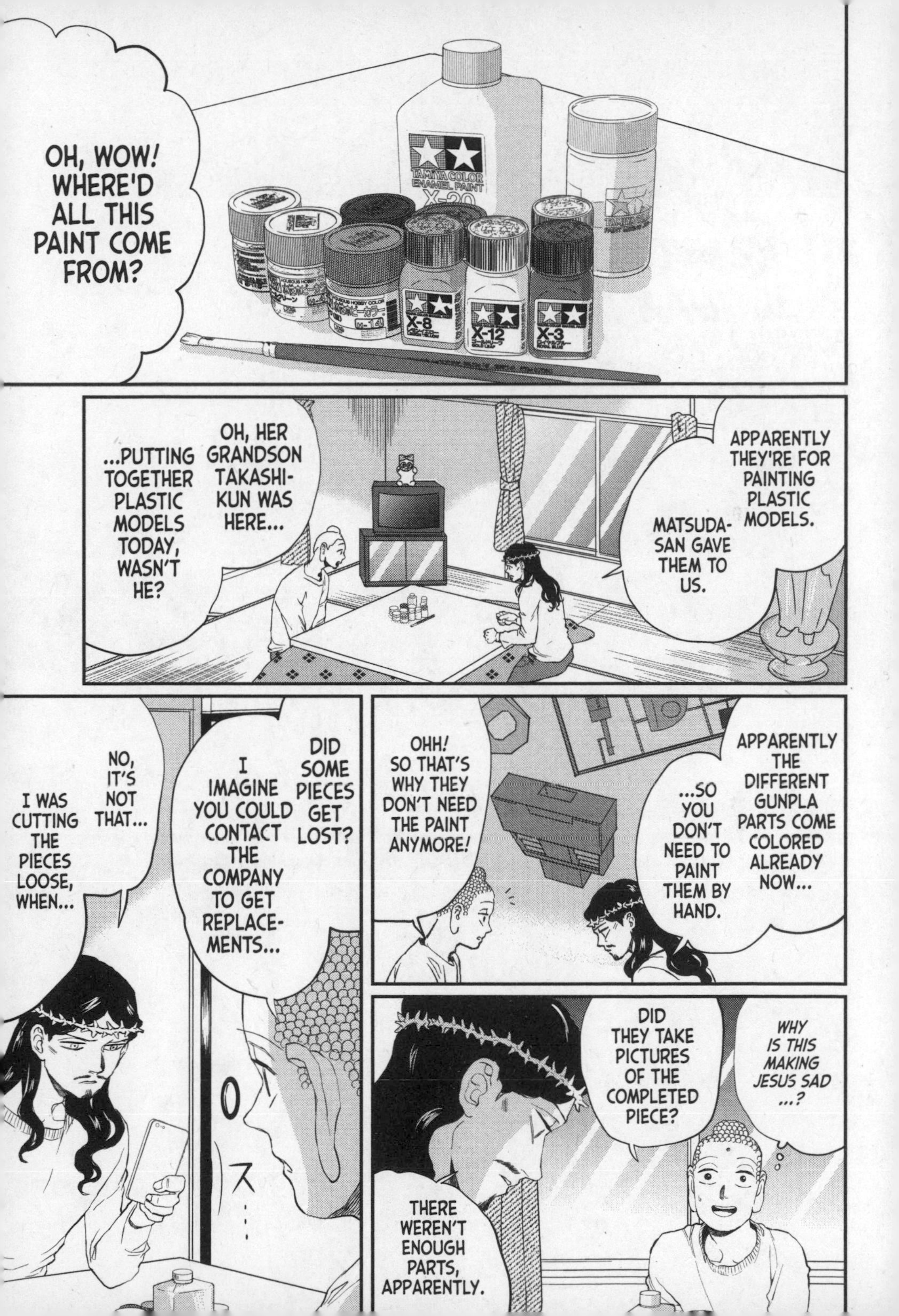
OH, WOW! WHERE'D ALL THIS PAINT COME FROM?
TAMIYA COLOR ENAMEL PAINT X-20
X-8
X-12
X-3
APPARENTLY THEY'RE FOR PAINTING PLASTIC MODELS.
MATSUDA-SAN GAVE THEM TO US.
OH, HER GRANDSON TAKASHI-KUN WAS HERE...
...PUTTING TOGETHER PLASTIC MODELS TODAY, WASN'T HE?
APPARENTLY THE DIFFERENT GUNPLA PARTS COME COLORED ALREADY NOW...
...SO YOU DON'T NEED TO PAINT THEM BY HAND.
OHH! SO THAT'S WHY THEY DON'T NEED THE PAINT ANYMORE!
WHY IS THIS MAKING JESUS SAD ...?
DID THEY TAKE PICTURES OF THE COMPLETED PIECE?
THERE WEREN'T ENOUGH PARTS, APPARENTLY.
DID SOME PIECES GET LOST?
I IMAGINE YOU COULD CONTACT THE COMPANY TO GET REPLACE-MENTS...
NO, IT'S NOT THAT...
I WAS CUTTING THE PIECES LOOSE, WHEN...
ス...

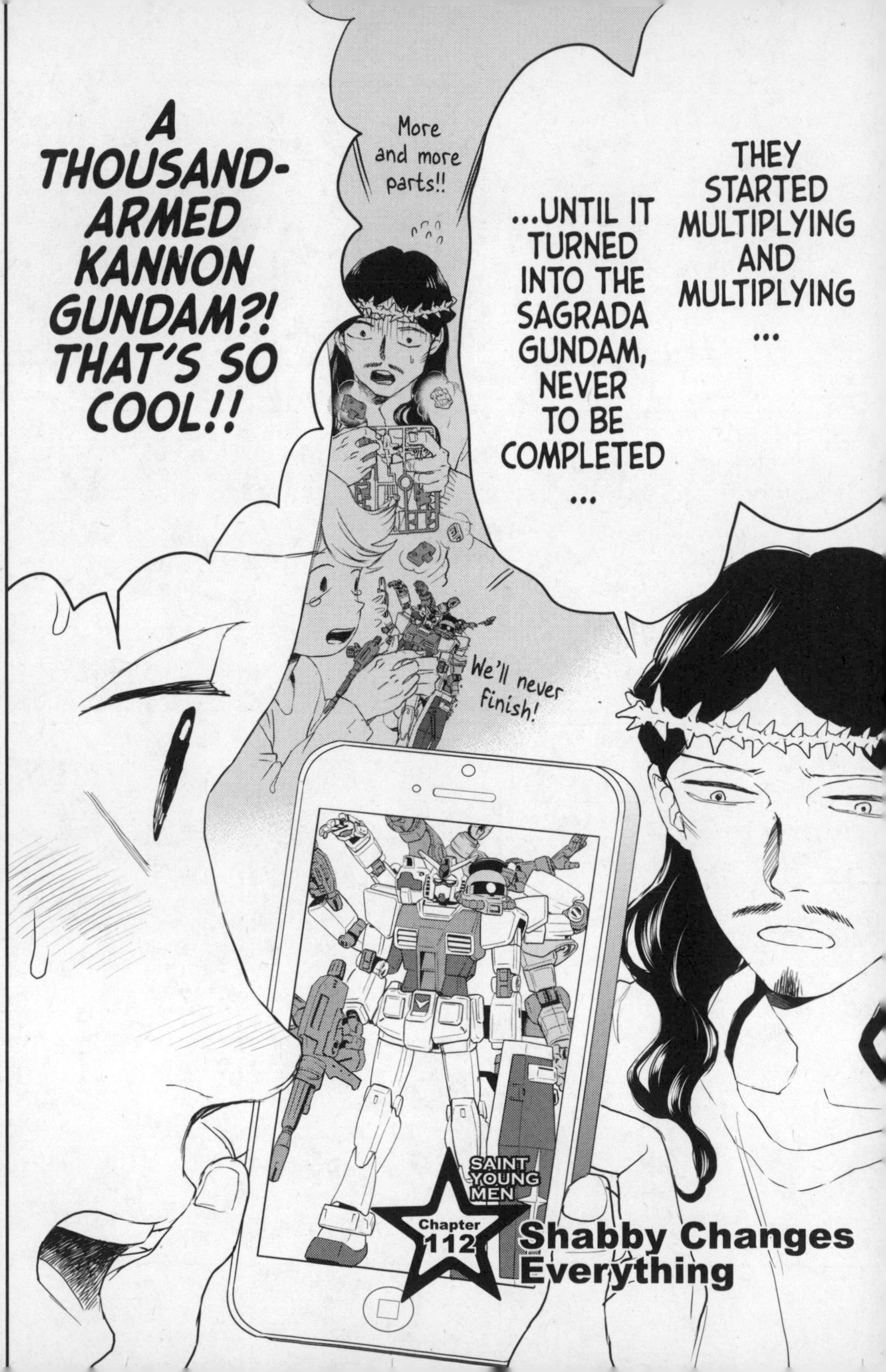
THEY STARTED MULTIPLYING AND MULTIPLYING...
...UNTIL IT TURNED INTO THE SAGRADA GUNDAM, NEVER TO BE COMPLETED...
More and more parts!!
We'll never finish!
A THOUSAND-ARMED KANNON GUNDAM?! THAT'S SO COOL!!
SAINT YOUNG MEN
Chapter 112
Shabby Changes Everything

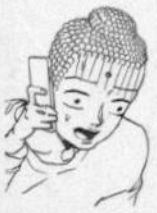

BUDDHA
YELLOW IS OUR RELIGION'S FAVORITE COLOR? THAT'S THE TOUGHEST PAINT TO USE ON PLASTIC MODELS. YOU NEED TO PRIME IT FOR A SMOOTH COAT.

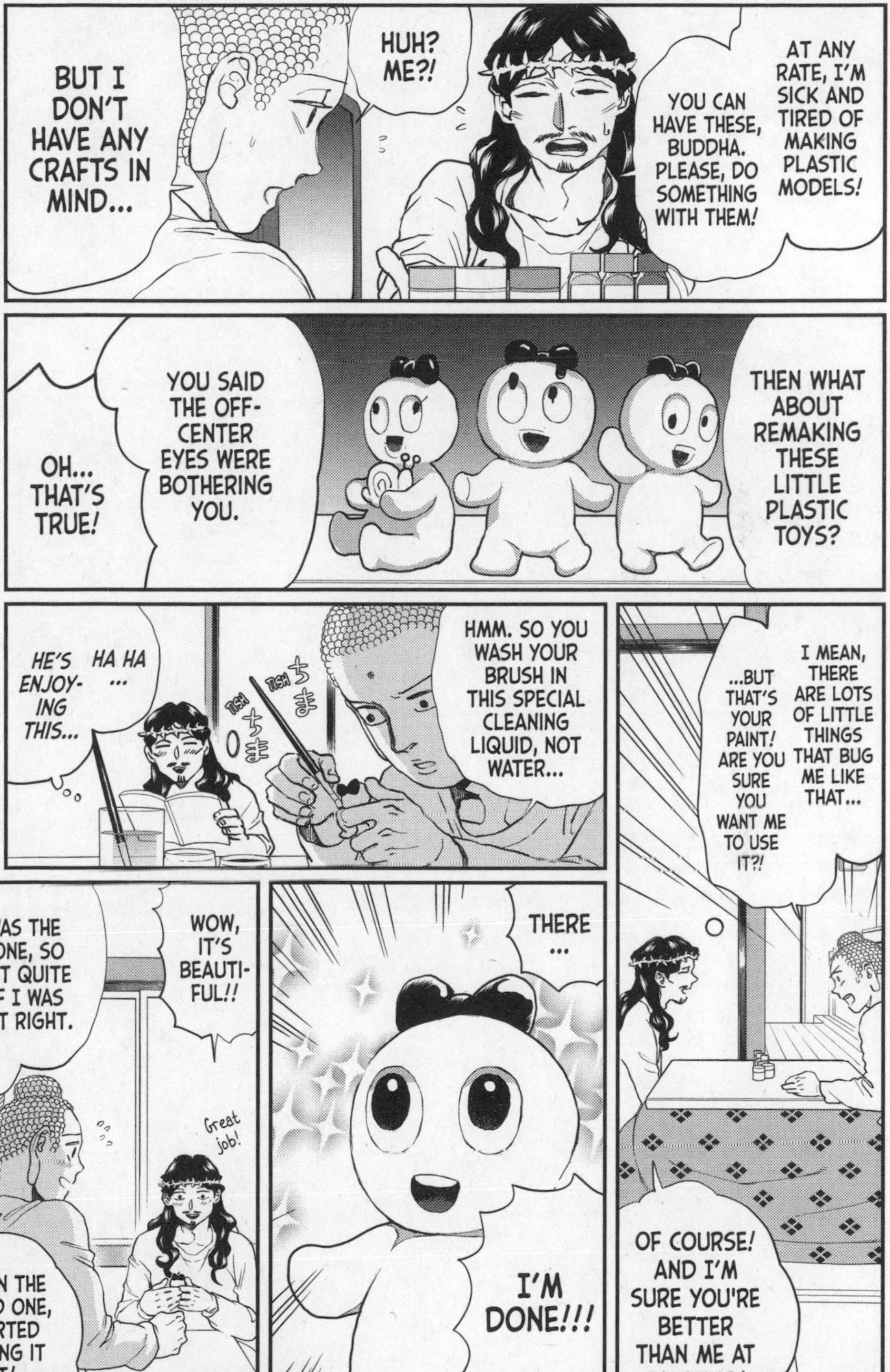

AT ANY RATE, I'M SICK AND TIRED OF MAKING PLASTIC MODELS!
YOU CAN HAVE THESE, BUDDHA. PLEASE, DO SOMETHING WITH THEM!
HUH? ME?!
BUT I DON'T HAVE ANY CRAFTS IN MIND...
THEN WHAT ABOUT REMAKING THESE LITTLE PLASTIC TOYS?
YOU SAID THE OFF-CENTER EYES WERE BOTHERING YOU.
OH... THAT'S TRUE!
I MEAN, THERE ARE LOTS OF LITTLE THINGS THAT BUG ME LIKE THAT...
...BUT THAT'S YOUR PAINT! ARE YOU SURE YOU WANT ME TO USE IT?!
OF COURSE! AND I'M SURE YOU'RE BETTER THAN ME AT PAINTING!
HMM. SO YOU WASH YOUR BRUSH IN THIS SPECIAL CLEANING LIQUID, NOT WATER...
TISH ちま
TISH ちま
HA HA ...
HE'S ENJOYING THIS...
THERE ...
I'M DONE!!!
WOW, IT'S BEAUTIFUL!!
THIS WAS THE FIRST ONE, SO I WASN'T QUITE SURE IF I WAS DOING IT RIGHT.
Great job!
BUT ON THE SECOND ONE, I STARTED FIGURING IT OUT!

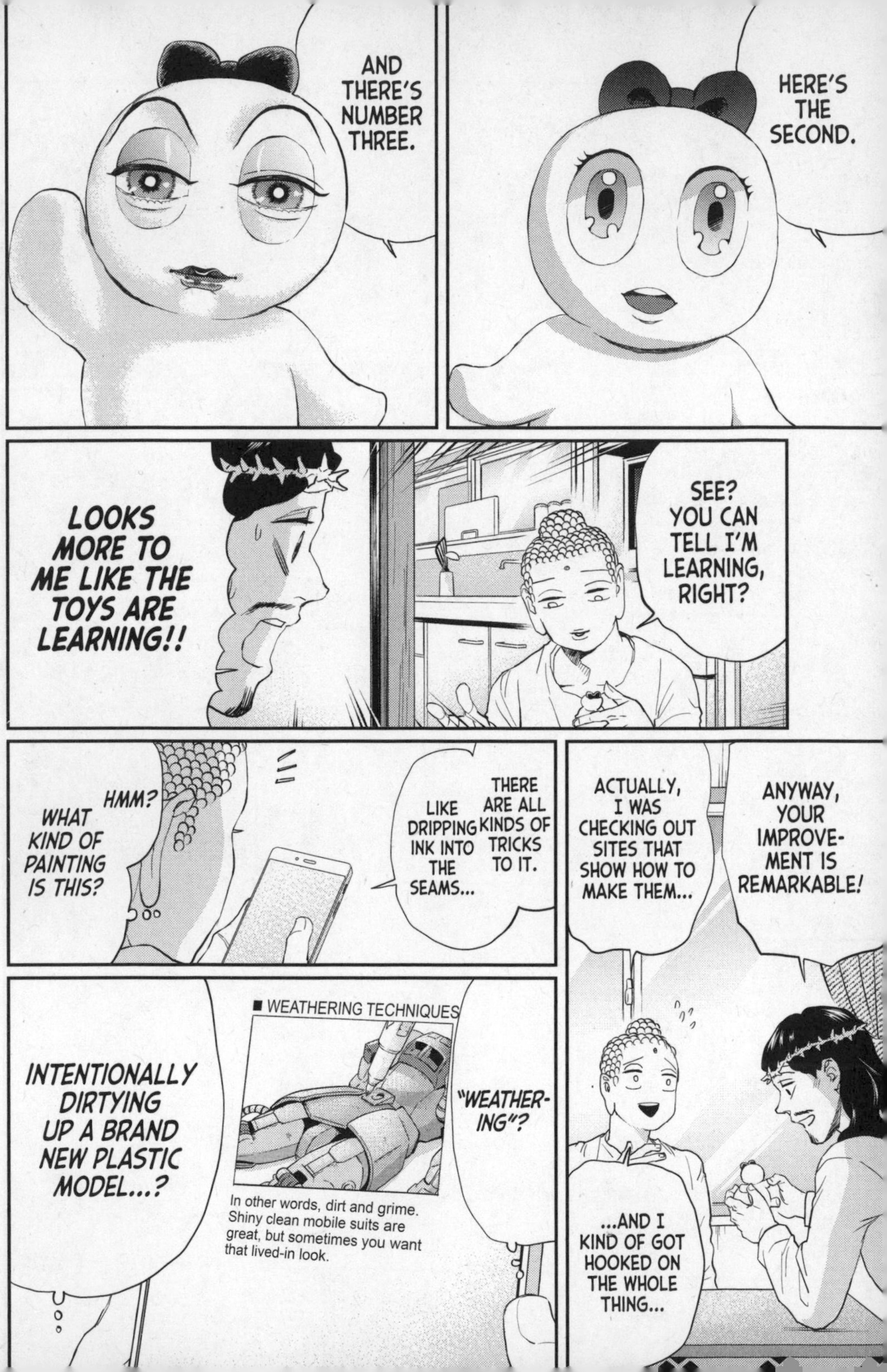
HERE'S THE SECOND.
AND THERE'S NUMBER THREE.
SEE? YOU CAN TELL I'M LEARNING, RIGHT?
LOOKS MORE TO ME LIKE THE TOYS ARE LEARNING!!
ANYWAY, YOUR IMPROVE-MENT IS REMARKABLE!
ACTUALLY, I WAS CHECKING OUT SITES THAT SHOW HOW TO MAKE THEM...
...AND I KIND OF GOT HOOKED ON THE WHOLE THING...
THERE ARE ALL KINDS OF TRICKS TO IT.
LIKE DRIPPING INK INTO THE SEAMS...
HMM?
WHAT KIND OF PAINTING IS THIS?
"WEATHER-ING"?
■ WEATHERING TECHNIQUES
In other words, dirt and grime. Shiny clean mobile suits are great, but sometimes you want that lived-in look.
INTENTIONALLY DIRTYING UP A BRAND NEW PLASTIC MODEL...?

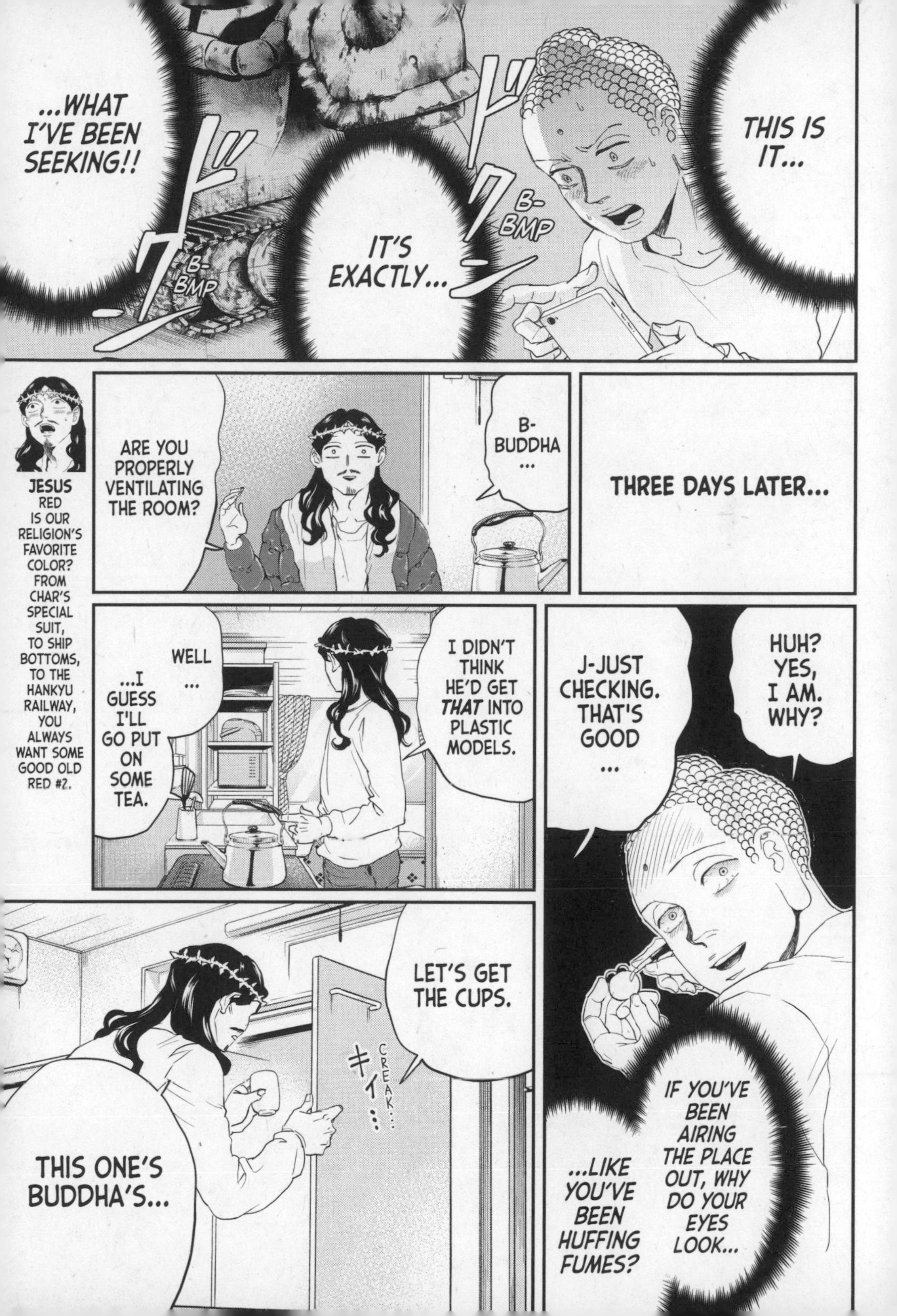
THIS IS IT...
B-BMP
IT'S EXACTLY...
B-BMP
...WHAT I'VE BEEN SEEKING!!
THREE DAYS LATER...
B-BUDDHA ...
ARE YOU PROPERLY VENTILATING THE ROOM?
JESUS
RED IS OUR RELIGION'S FAVORITE COLOR? FROM CHAR'S SPECIAL SUIT, TO SHIP BOTTOMS, TO THE HANKYU RAILWAY, YOU ALWAYS WANT SOME GOOD OLD RED #2.
HUH? YES, I AM. WHY?
J-JUST CHECKING. THAT'S GOOD ...
IF YOU'VE BEEN AIRING THE PLACE OUT, WHY DO YOUR EYES LOOK...
...LIKE YOU'VE BEEN HUFFING FUMES?
I DIDN'T THINK HE'D GET *THAT* INTO PLASTIC MODELS.
WELL ...
...I GUESS I'LL GO PUT ON SOME TEA.
LET'S GET THE CUPS.
CREAK...
THIS ONE'S BUDDHA'S...

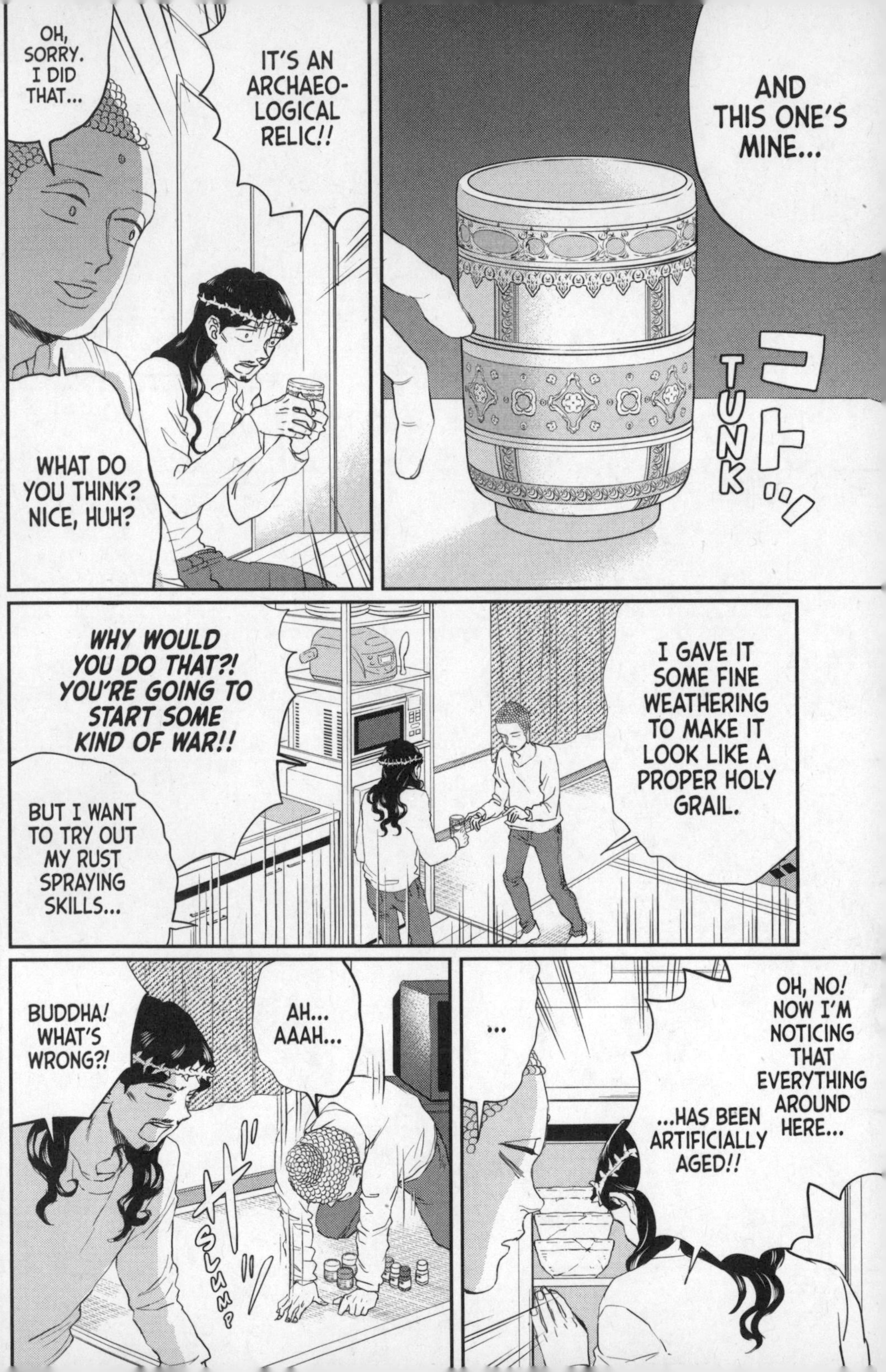
AND THIS ONE'S MINE...
TUNK
IT'S AN ARCHAEO-LOGICAL RELIC!!
OH, SORRY. I DID THAT...
WHAT DO YOU THINK? NICE, HUH?
I GAVE IT SOME FINE WEATHERING TO MAKE IT LOOK LIKE A PROPER HOLY GRAIL.
WHY WOULD YOU DO THAT?! YOU'RE GOING TO START SOME KIND OF WAR!!
BUT I WANT TO TRY OUT MY RUST SPRAYING SKILLS...
OH, NO! NOW I'M NOTICING THAT EVERYTHING AROUND HERE...
...HAS BEEN ARTIFICIALLY AGED!!
...
AH... AAAH...
BUDDHA! WHAT'S WRONG?!
SLUMP

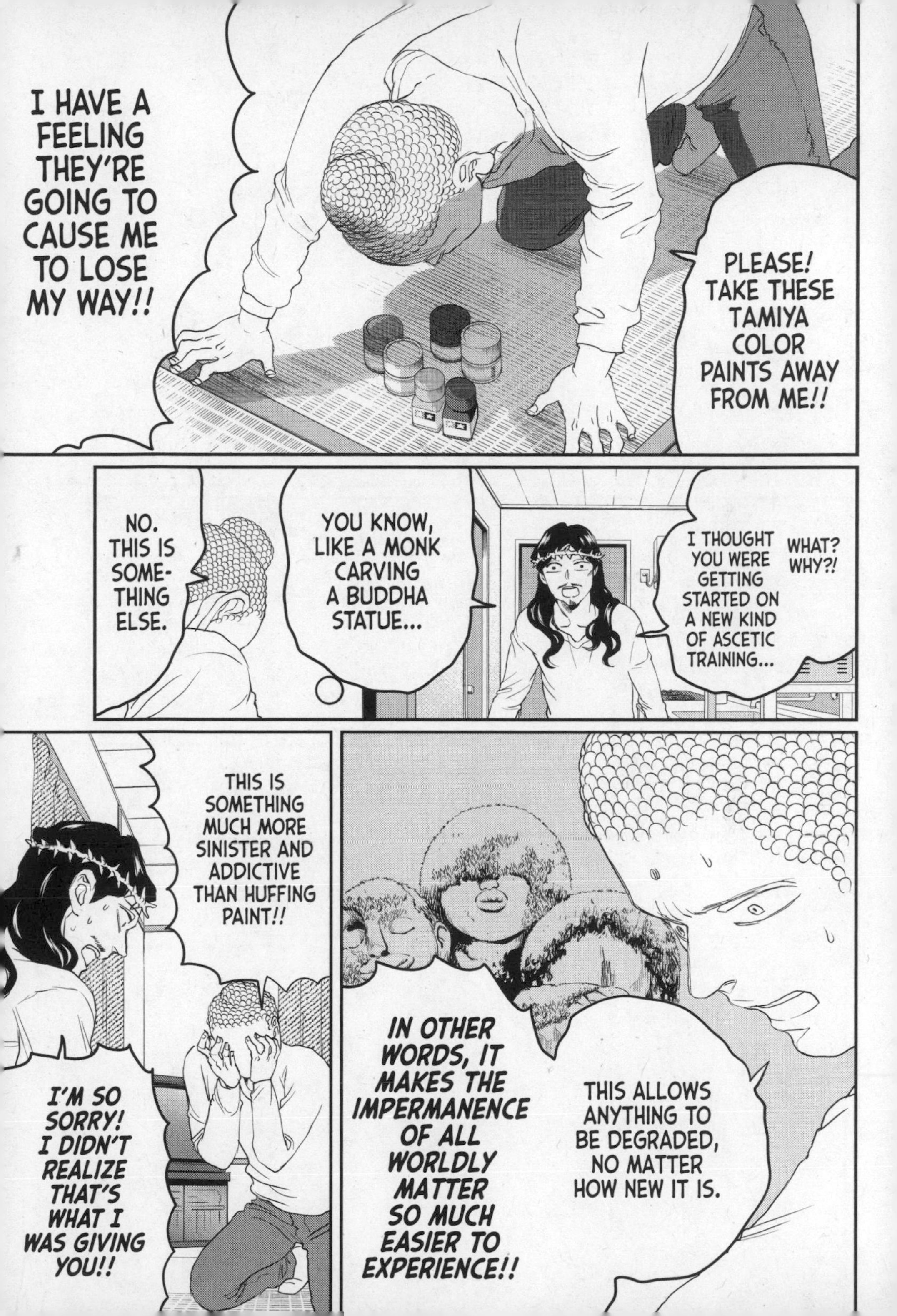
PLEASE! TAKE THESE TAMIYA COLOR PAINTS AWAY FROM ME!!
I HAVE A FEELING THEY'RE GOING TO CAUSE ME TO LOSE MY WAY!!
WHAT? WHY?!
I THOUGHT YOU WERE GETTING STARTED ON A NEW KIND OF ASCETIC TRAINING...
YOU KNOW, LIKE A MONK CARVING A BUDDHA STATUE...
NO. THIS IS SOME-THING ELSE.
THIS ALLOWS ANYTHING TO BE DEGRADED, NO MATTER HOW NEW IT IS.
IN OTHER WORDS, IT MAKES THE IMPERMANENCE OF ALL WORLDLY MATTER SO MUCH EASIER TO EXPERIENCE!!
THIS IS SOMETHING MUCH MORE SINISTER AND ADDICTIVE THAN HUFFING PAINT!!
I'M SO SORRY! I DIDN'T REALIZE THAT'S WHAT I WAS GIVING YOU!!

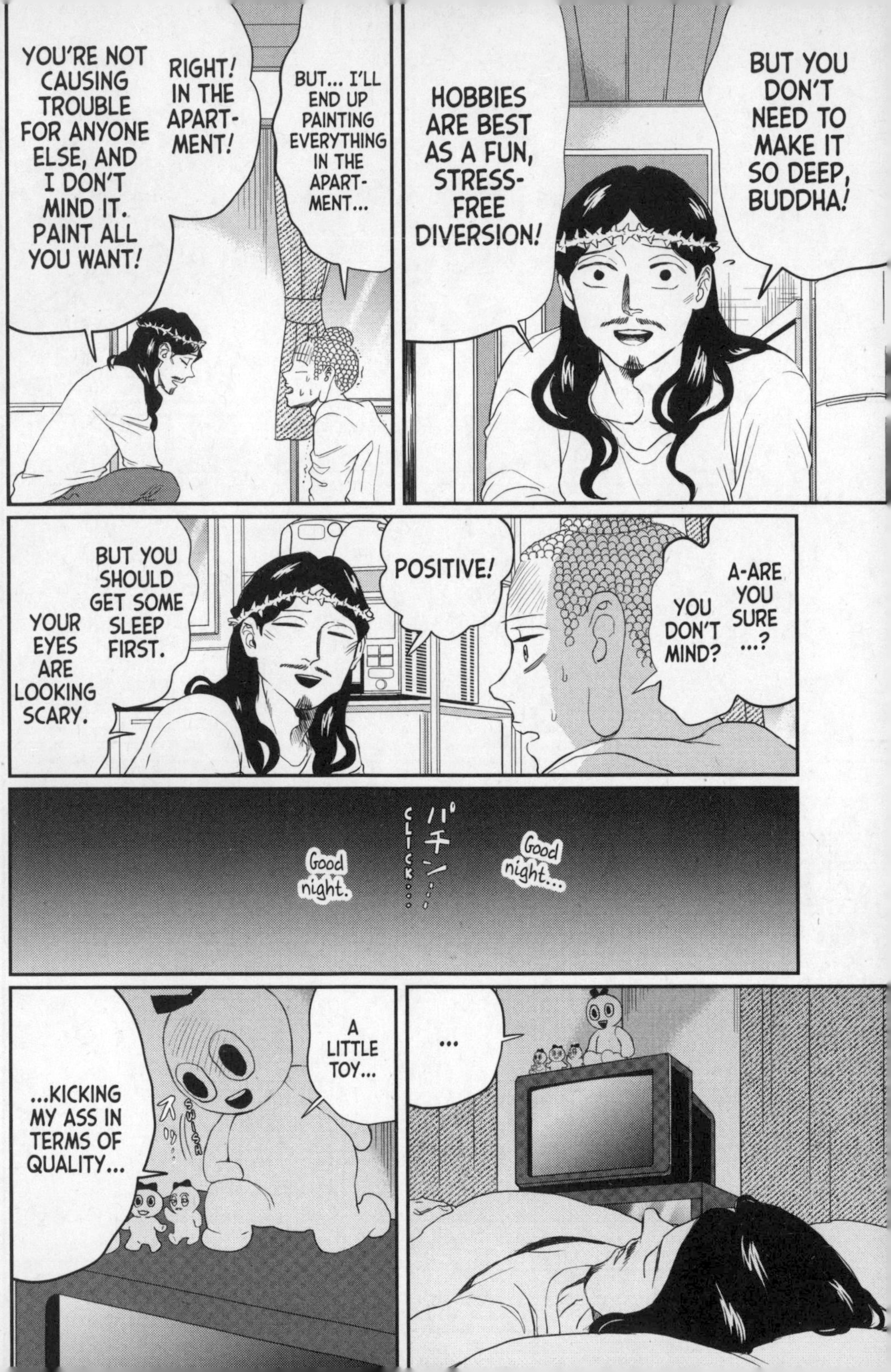
BUT YOU DON'T NEED TO MAKE IT SO DEEP, BUDDHA!
HOBBIES ARE BEST AS A FUN, STRESS-FREE DIVERSION!
BUT... I'LL END UP PAINTING EVERYTHING IN THE APARTMENT...
RIGHT! IN THE APARTMENT!
YOU'RE NOT CAUSING TROUBLE FOR ANYONE ELSE, AND I DON'T MIND IT. PAINT ALL YOU WANT!
A-ARE YOU SURE ...?
YOU DON'T MIND?
POSITIVE!
BUT YOU SHOULD GET SOME SLEEP FIRST.
YOUR EYES ARE LOOKING SCARY.
Good night...
パチン
CLICK...
Good night.
...
A LITTLE TOY...
...KICKING MY ASS IN TERMS OF QUALITY...
ス
SWISH

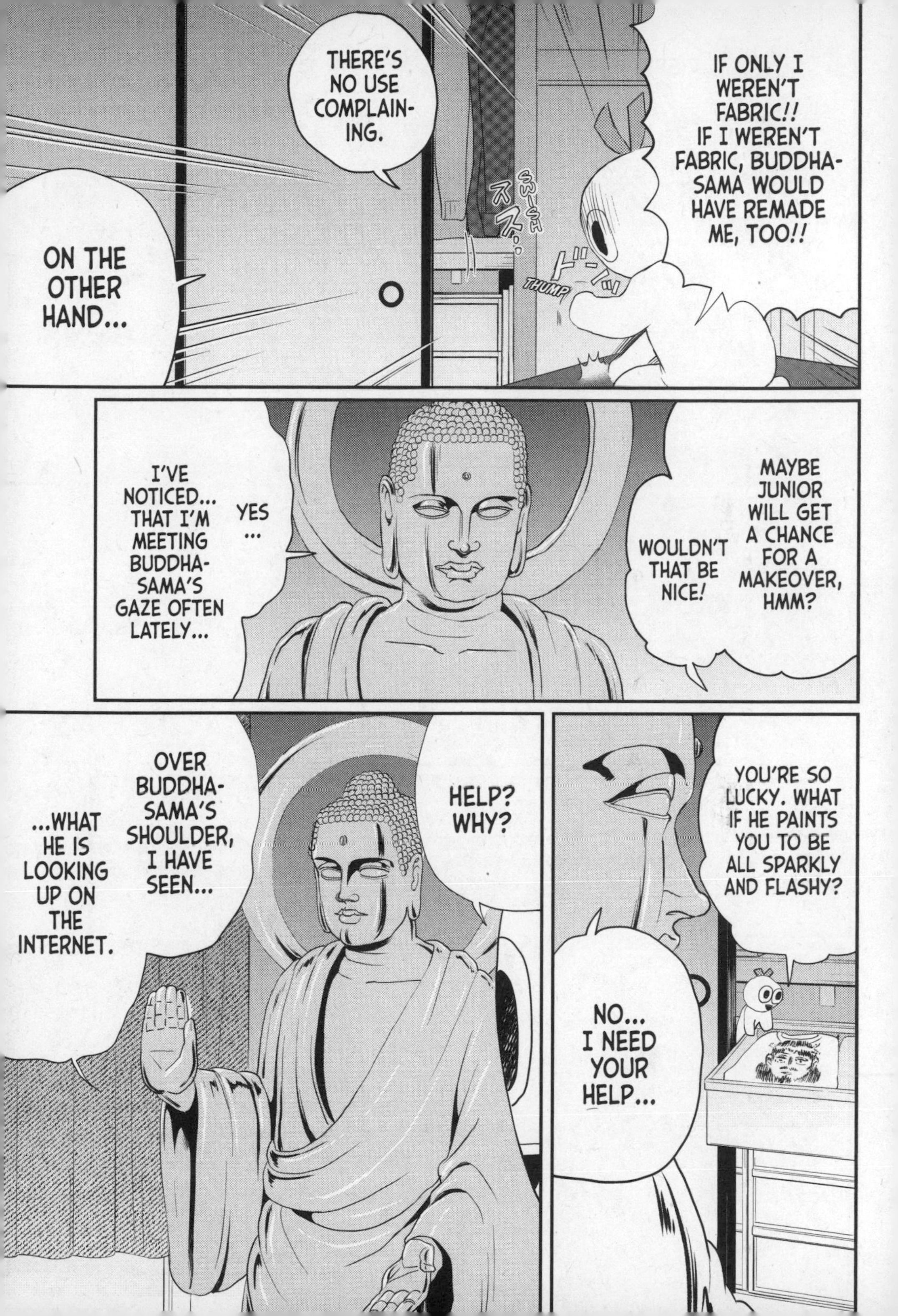
IF ONLY I WEREN'T FABRIC!! IF I WEREN'T FABRIC, BUDDHA-SAMA WOULD HAVE REMADE ME, TOO!!
THUMP
THERE'S NO USE COMPLAINING.
SWISH
ON THE OTHER HAND...
MAYBE JUNIOR WILL GET A CHANCE FOR A MAKEOVER, HMM?
WOULDN'T THAT BE NICE!
YES...
I'VE NOTICED... THAT I'M MEETING BUDDHA-SAMA'S GAZE OFTEN LATELY...
YOU'RE SO LUCKY. WHAT IF HE PAINTS YOU TO BE ALL SPARKLY AND FLASHY?
NO... I NEED YOUR HELP...
HELP? WHY?
OVER BUDDHA-SAMA'S SHOULDER, I HAVE SEEN...
...WHAT HE IS LOOKING UP ON THE INTERNET.

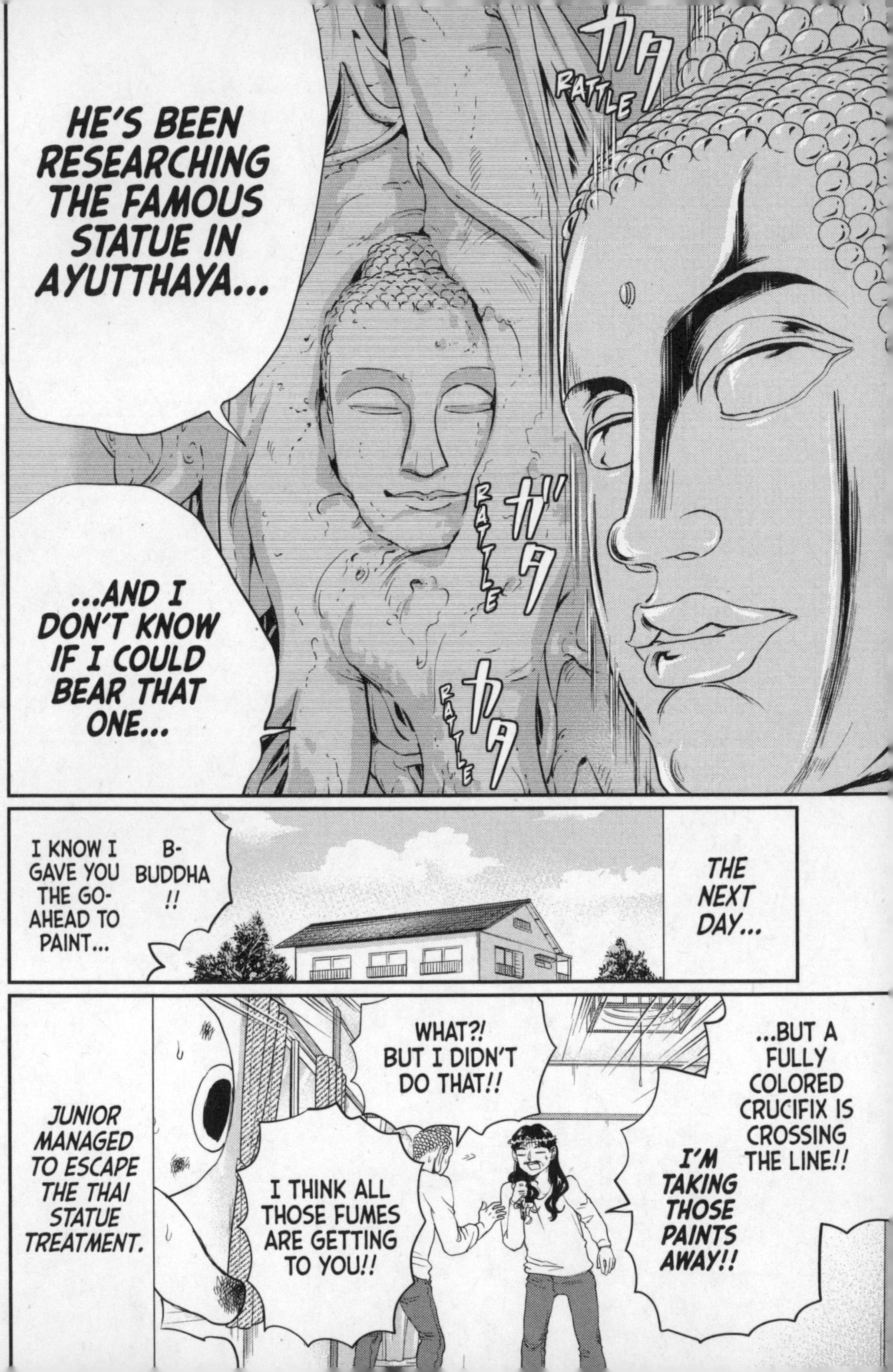
カタ
RATTLE
HE'S BEEN RESEARCHING THE FAMOUS STATUE IN AYUTTHAYA...
ガタ
RATTLE
...AND I DON'T KNOW IF I COULD BEAR THAT ONE...
カタ
RATTLE
THE NEXT DAY...
B- BUDDHA !!
I KNOW I GAVE YOU THE GO-AHEAD TO PAINT...
...BUT A FULLY COLORED CRUCIFIX IS CROSSING THE LINE!!
I'M TAKING THOSE PAINTS AWAY!!
WHAT?! BUT I DIDN'T DO THAT!!
I THINK ALL THOSE FUMES ARE GETTING TO YOU!!
JUNIOR MANAGED TO ESCAPE THE THAI STATUE TREATMENT.

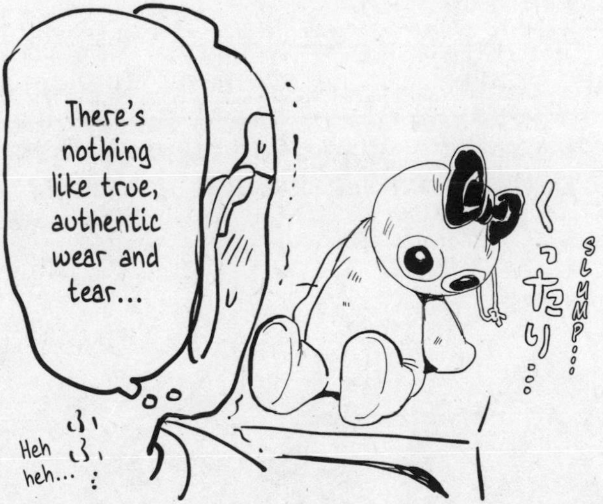

There's nothing like true, authentic wear and tear...
くったり…
SLUMP...
ふふ
Heh heh...

SAINT✩YOUNG MEN

CHAPTER 112 TRANSLATION NOTES

Gunpla, page 153
Short for "Gundam plastic model," these kits are a major pillar of the *Mobile Suit Gundam* franchise's popularity. While fully assembled figures are available, of course, the experience of gluing together and (sometimes) painting small plastic pieces has been a popular pastime nearly as long as the series has existed.

Red items, page 157
Char Aznable is an antagonist from the original *Mobile Suit Gundam* series who appears in several other entries of the series, and remains one of its most iconic characters. He famously uses a red-colored mobile suit that is "three times as fast." The Hankyu Railway line in the western Japan area around Osaka is known for its maroon-red cars.

Ayutthaya, page 162
A city in central Thailand that is known for its many temples built in the 14th and 15th centuries AD. At one of the temples, named Wat Mahathat, is a striking stone Buddha head that is enveloped in huge tree roots. The original cause of the head being stuck in the roots is unknown, as is the time when it was first placed there.

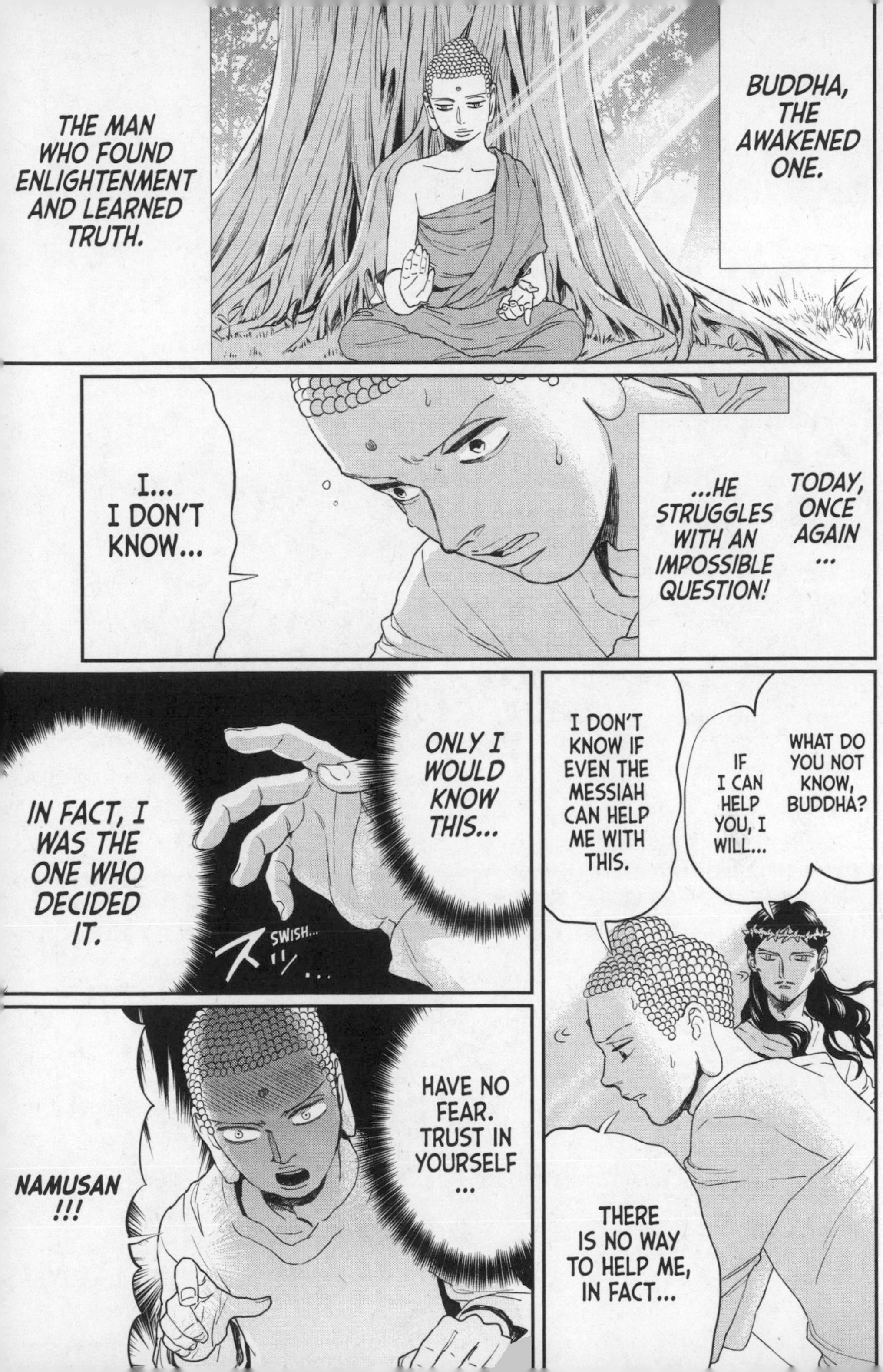
BUDDHA, THE AWAKENED ONE.
THE MAN WHO FOUND ENLIGHTENMENT AND LEARNED TRUTH.
TODAY, ONCE AGAIN ...
...HE STRUGGLES WITH AN IMPOSSIBLE QUESTION!
I... I DON'T KNOW...
WHAT DO YOU NOT KNOW, BUDDHA?
IF I CAN HELP YOU, I WILL...
I DON'T KNOW IF EVEN THE MESSIAH CAN HELP ME WITH THIS.
THERE IS NO WAY TO HELP ME, IN FACT...
ONLY I WOULD KNOW THIS...
IN FACT, I WAS THE ONE WHO DECIDED IT.
SWISH...
HAVE NO FEAR. TRUST IN YOURSELF ...
NAMUSAN !!!

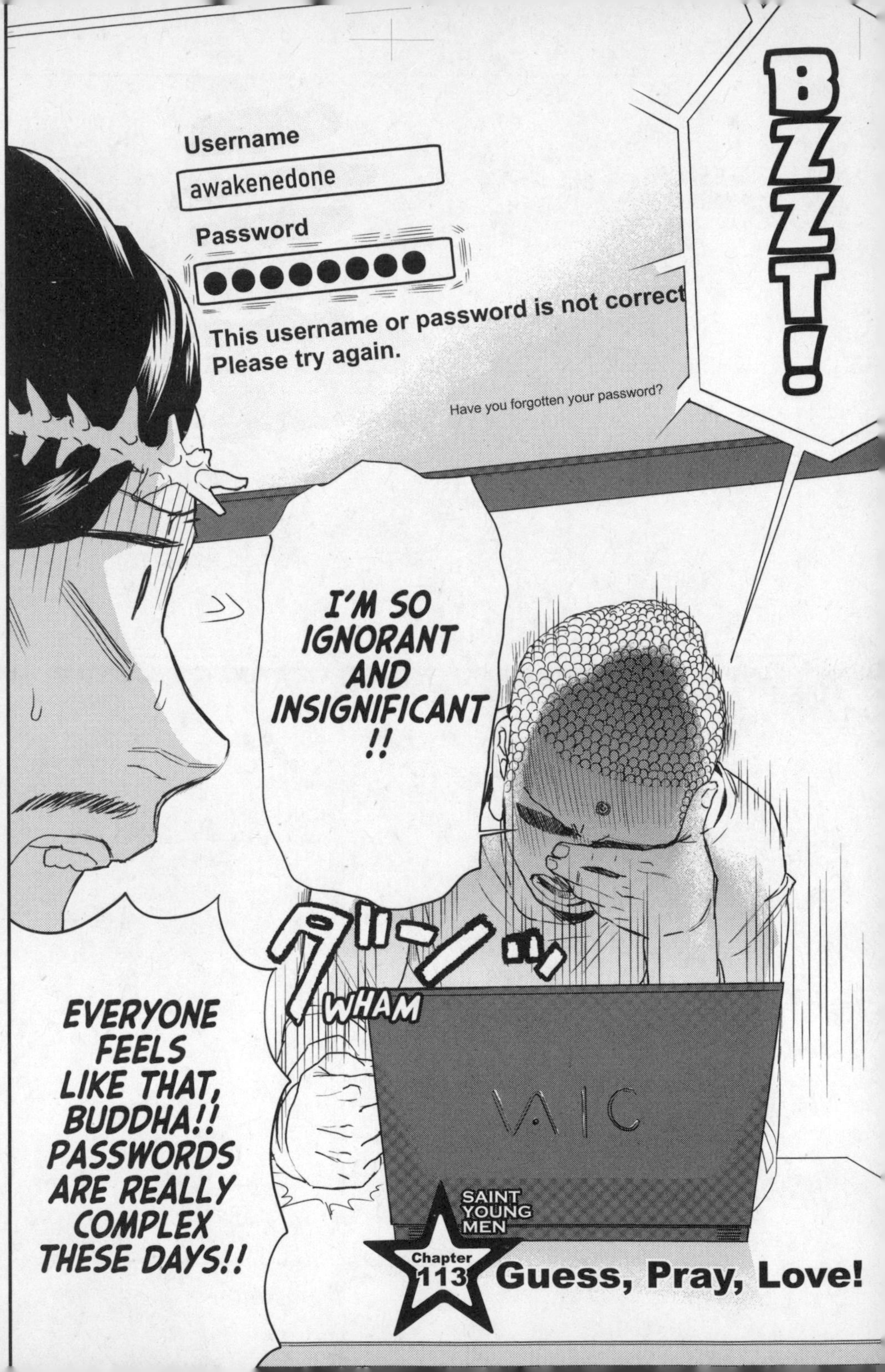
BZZT!
Username
awakenedone
Password
This username or password is not correct
Please try again.
Have you forgotten your password?
I'M SO IGNORANT AND INSIGNIFICANT !!
WHAM
EVERYONE FEELS LIKE THAT, BUDDHA!! PASSWORDS ARE REALLY COMPLEX THESE DAYS!!
SAINT YOUNG MEN
Chapter 113 Guess, Pray, Love!

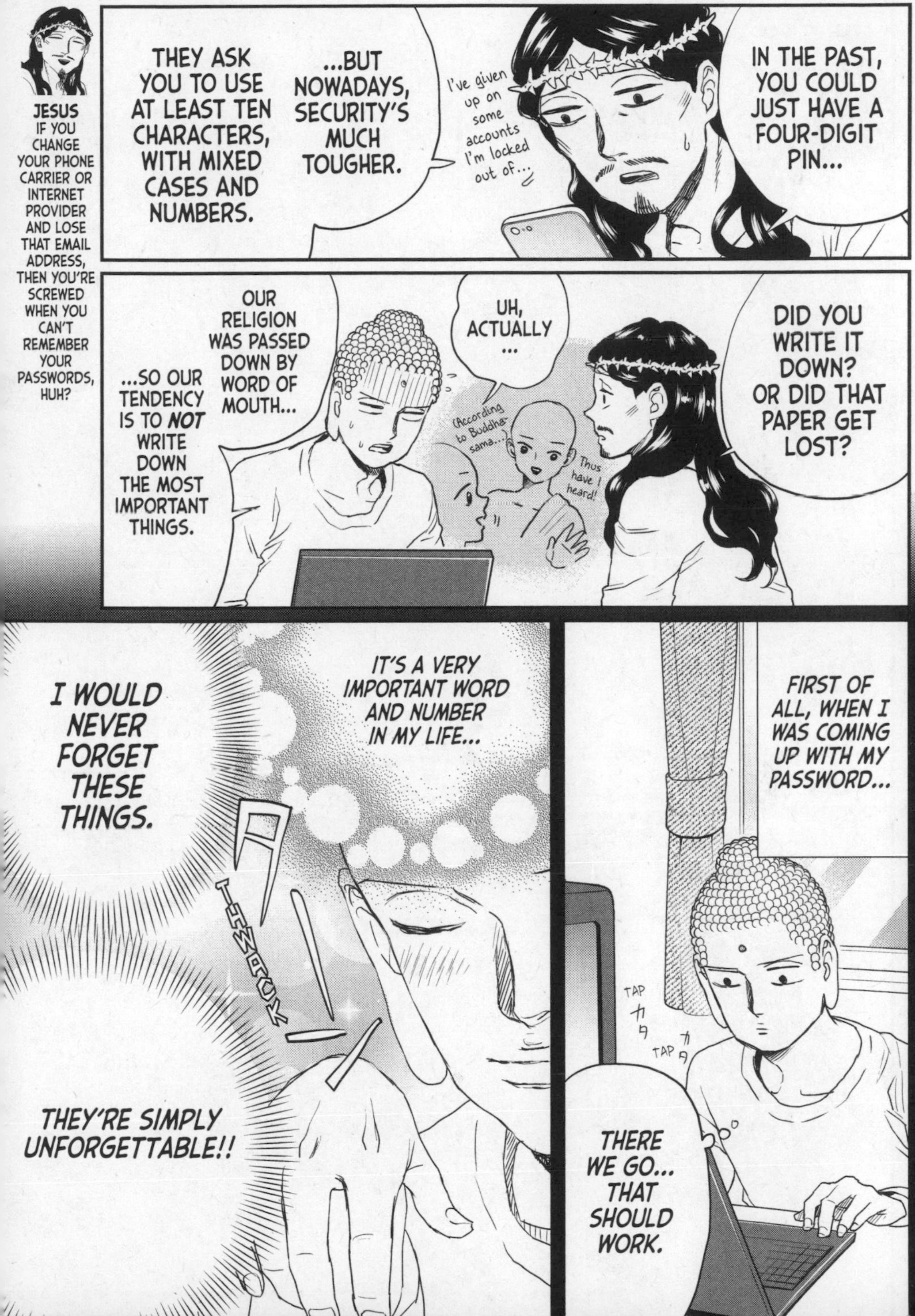
JESUS
IF YOU CHANGE YOUR PHONE CARRIER OR INTERNET PROVIDER AND LOSE THAT EMAIL ADDRESS, THEN YOU'RE SCREWED WHEN YOU CAN'T REMEMBER YOUR PASSWORDS, HUH?
IN THE PAST, YOU COULD JUST HAVE A FOUR-DIGIT PIN...
I've given up on some accounts I'm locked out of...
...BUT NOWADAYS, SECURITY'S MUCH TOUGHER.
THEY ASK YOU TO USE AT LEAST TEN CHARACTERS, WITH MIXED CASES AND NUMBERS.
DID YOU WRITE IT DOWN? OR DID THAT PAPER GET LOST?
UH, ACTUALLY ...
(According to Buddha-sama...)
Thus have I heard!
OUR RELIGION WAS PASSED DOWN BY WORD OF MOUTH...
...SO OUR TENDENCY IS TO *NOT* WRITE DOWN THE MOST IMPORTANT THINGS.
FIRST OF ALL, WHEN I WAS COMING UP WITH MY PASSWORD...
TAP
TAP
THERE WE GO... THAT SHOULD WORK.
IT'S A VERY IMPORTANT WORD AND NUMBER IN MY LIFE...
I WOULD NEVER FORGET THESE THINGS.
THWACK
THEY'RE SIMPLY UNFORGETTABLE!!

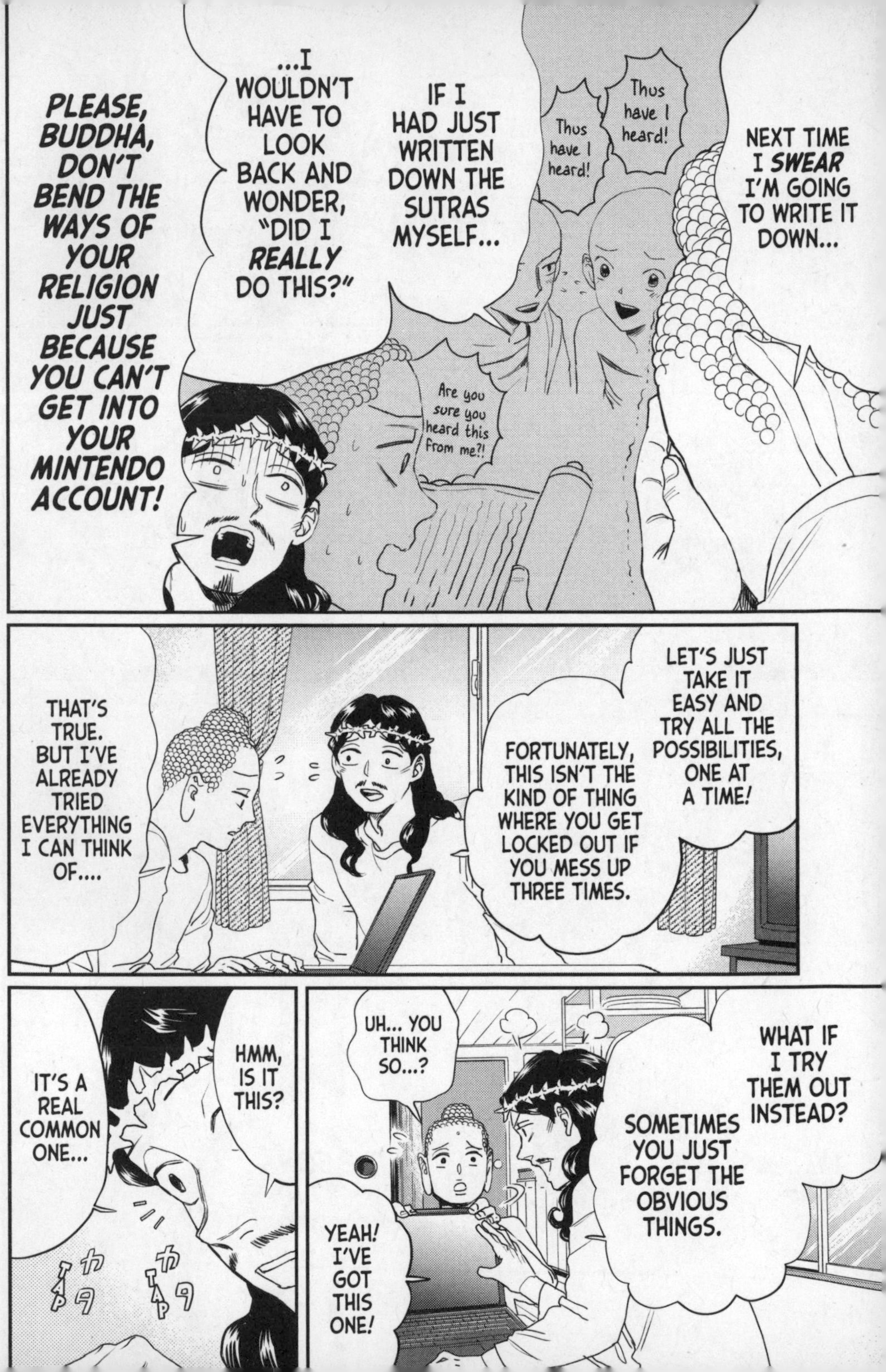
NEXT TIME I *SWEAR* I'M GOING TO WRITE IT DOWN...
Thus have I heard!
Thus have I heard!
IF I HAD JUST WRITTEN DOWN THE SUTRAS MYSELF...
...I WOULDN'T HAVE TO LOOK BACK AND WONDER, "DID I *REALLY* DO THIS?"
Are you sure you heard this from me?!
PLEASE, BUDDHA, DON'T BEND THE WAYS OF YOUR RELIGION JUST BECAUSE YOU CAN'T GET INTO YOUR MINTENDO ACCOUNT!
LET'S JUST TAKE IT EASY AND TRY ALL THE POSSIBILITIES, ONE AT A TIME!
FORTUNATELY, THIS ISN'T THE KIND OF THING WHERE YOU GET LOCKED OUT IF YOU MESS UP THREE TIMES.
THAT'S TRUE. BUT I'VE ALREADY TRIED EVERYTHING I CAN THINK OF....
WHAT IF I TRY THEM OUT INSTEAD?
SOMETIMES YOU JUST FORGET THE OBVIOUS THINGS.
UH... YOU THINK SO...?
YEAH! I'VE GOT THIS ONE!
HMM, IS IT THIS?
IT'S A REAL COMMON ONE...
TAP
TAP

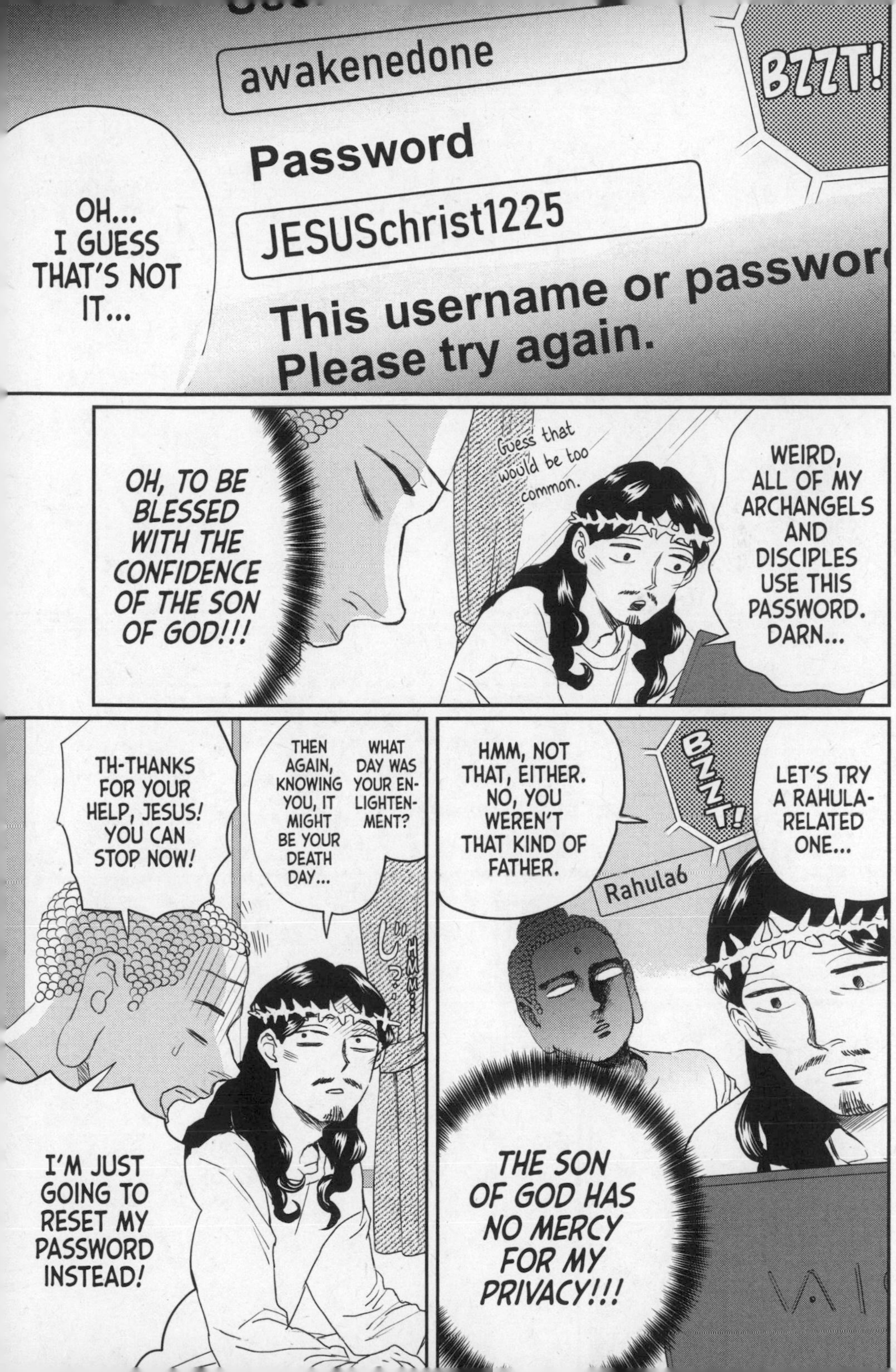
BZZT!
awakenedone
Password
JESUSchrist1225
This username or passwor
Please try again.
OH... I GUESS THAT'S NOT IT...
WEIRD, ALL OF MY ARCHANGELS AND DISCIPLES USE THIS PASSWORD. DARN...
Guess that would be too common.
OH, TO BE BLESSED WITH THE CONFIDENCE OF THE SON OF GOD!!!
LET'S TRY A RAHULA-RELATED ONE...
BZZT!
Rahula6
HMM, NOT THAT, EITHER. NO, YOU WEREN'T THAT KIND OF FATHER.
THE SON OF GOD HAS NO MERCY FOR MY PRIVACY!!!
WHAT DAY WAS YOUR EN-LIGHTEN-MENT?
THEN AGAIN, KNOWING YOU, IT MIGHT BE YOUR DEATH DAY...
HMM...
TH-THANKS FOR YOUR HELP, JESUS! YOU CAN STOP NOW!
I'M JUST GOING TO RESET MY PASSWORD INSTEAD!

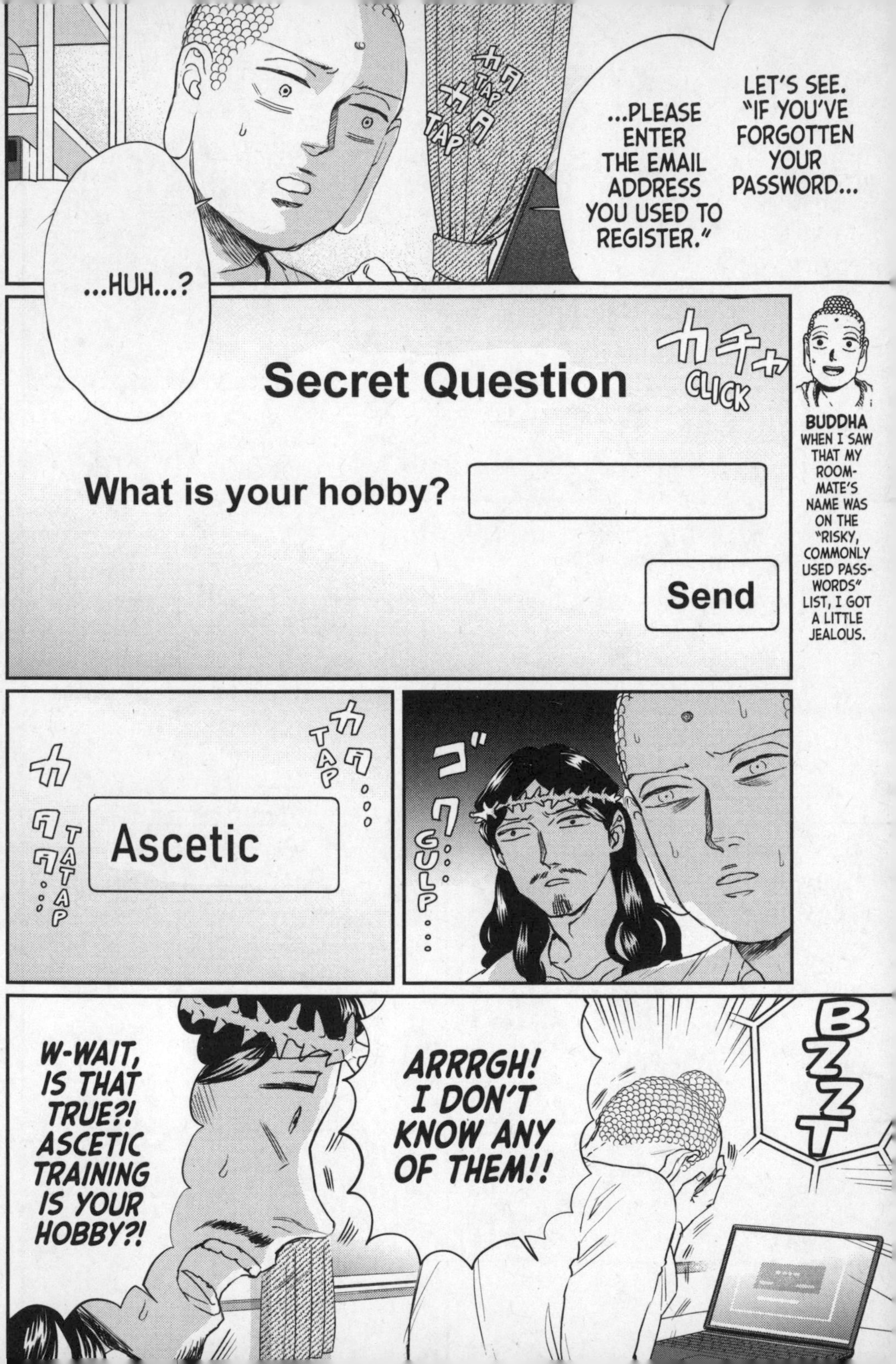

LET'S SEE. "IF YOU'VE FORGOTTEN YOUR PASSWORD...
...PLEASE ENTER THE EMAIL ADDRESS YOU USED TO REGISTER."
カタ TAP カタ TAP
...HUH...?
BUDDHA
WHEN I SAW THAT MY ROOM-MATE'S NAME WAS ON THE "RISKY, COMMONLY USED PASS-WORDS" LIST, I GOT A LITTLE JEALOUS.
カチャ CLICK
Secret Question
What is your hobby?
Send
ゴク GULP...
カタ TAP...
カタ TATAP...
Ascetic
BZZT
ARRRGH! I DON'T KNOW ANY OF THEM!!
W-WAIT, IS THAT TRUE?! ASCETIC TRAINING IS YOUR HOBBY?!

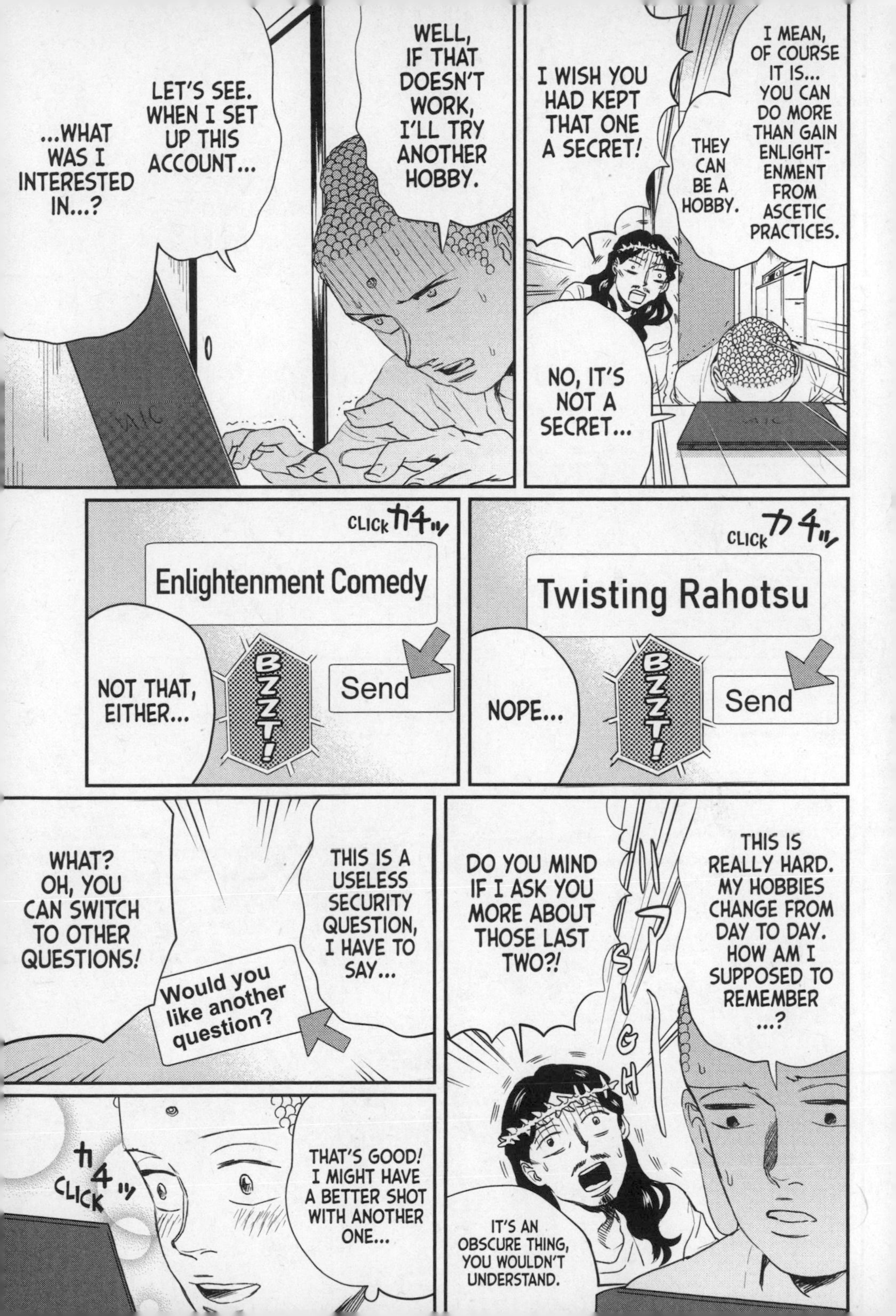
I MEAN, OF COURSE IT IS... YOU CAN DO MORE THAN GAIN ENLIGHTENMENT FROM ASCETIC PRACTICES.
THEY CAN BE A HOBBY.
I WISH YOU HAD KEPT THAT ONE A SECRET!
NO, IT'S NOT A SECRET...
WELL, IF THAT DOESN'T WORK, I'LL TRY ANOTHER HOBBY.
LET'S SEE. WHEN I SET UP THIS ACCOUNT...
...WHAT WAS I INTERESTED IN...?
CLICK カチッ
Twisting Rahotsu
Send
BZZT!
NOPE...
CLICK カチッ
Enlightenment Comedy
Send
BZZT!
NOT THAT, EITHER...
THIS IS REALLY HARD. MY HOBBIES CHANGE FROM DAY TO DAY. HOW AM I SUPPOSED TO REMEMBER ...?
DO YOU MIND IF I ASK YOU MORE ABOUT THOSE LAST TWO?!
SIGH
IT'S AN OBSCURE THING, YOU WOULDN'T UNDERSTAND.
THIS IS A USELESS SECURITY QUESTION, I HAVE TO SAY...
WHAT? OH, YOU CAN SWITCH TO OTHER QUESTIONS!
Would you like another question?
THAT'S GOOD! I MIGHT HAVE A BETTER SHOT WITH ANOTHER ONE...
カチッ CLICK

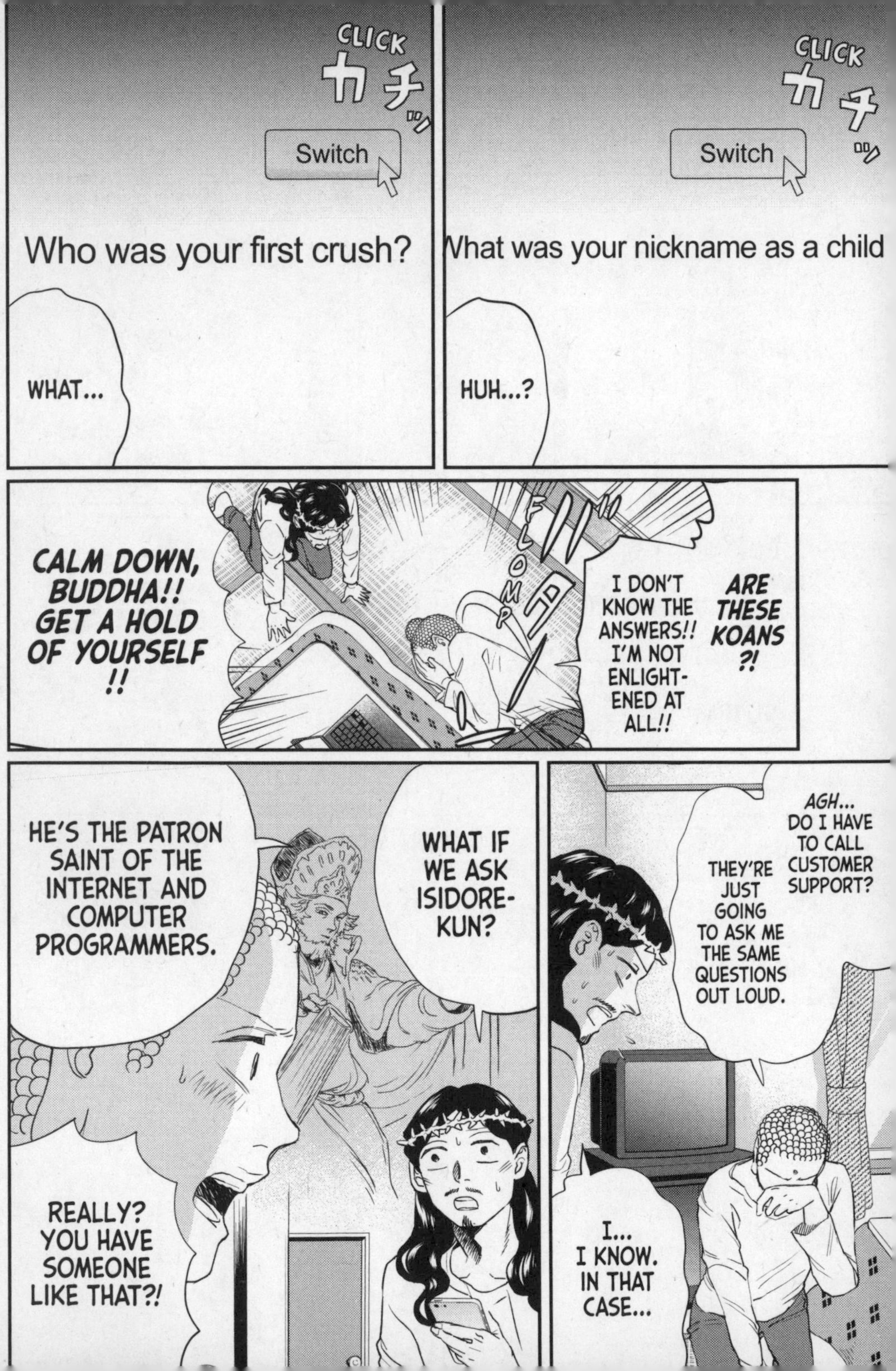
CLICK
カチッ
Switch
What was your nickname as a child
HUH...?
CLICK
カチッ
Switch
Who was your first crush?
WHAT...
ARE THESE KOANS?!
I DON'T KNOW THE ANSWERS!! I'M NOT ENLIGHTENED AT ALL!!
FLOMP
CALM DOWN, BUDDHA!! GET A HOLD OF YOURSELF!!
AGH... DO I HAVE TO CALL CUSTOMER SUPPORT?
THEY'RE JUST GOING TO ASK ME THE SAME QUESTIONS OUT LOUD.
I... I KNOW. IN THAT CASE...
WHAT IF WE ASK ISIDORE-KUN?
HE'S THE PATRON SAINT OF THE INTERNET AND COMPUTER PROGRAMMERS.
REALLY? YOU HAVE SOMEONE LIKE THAT?!

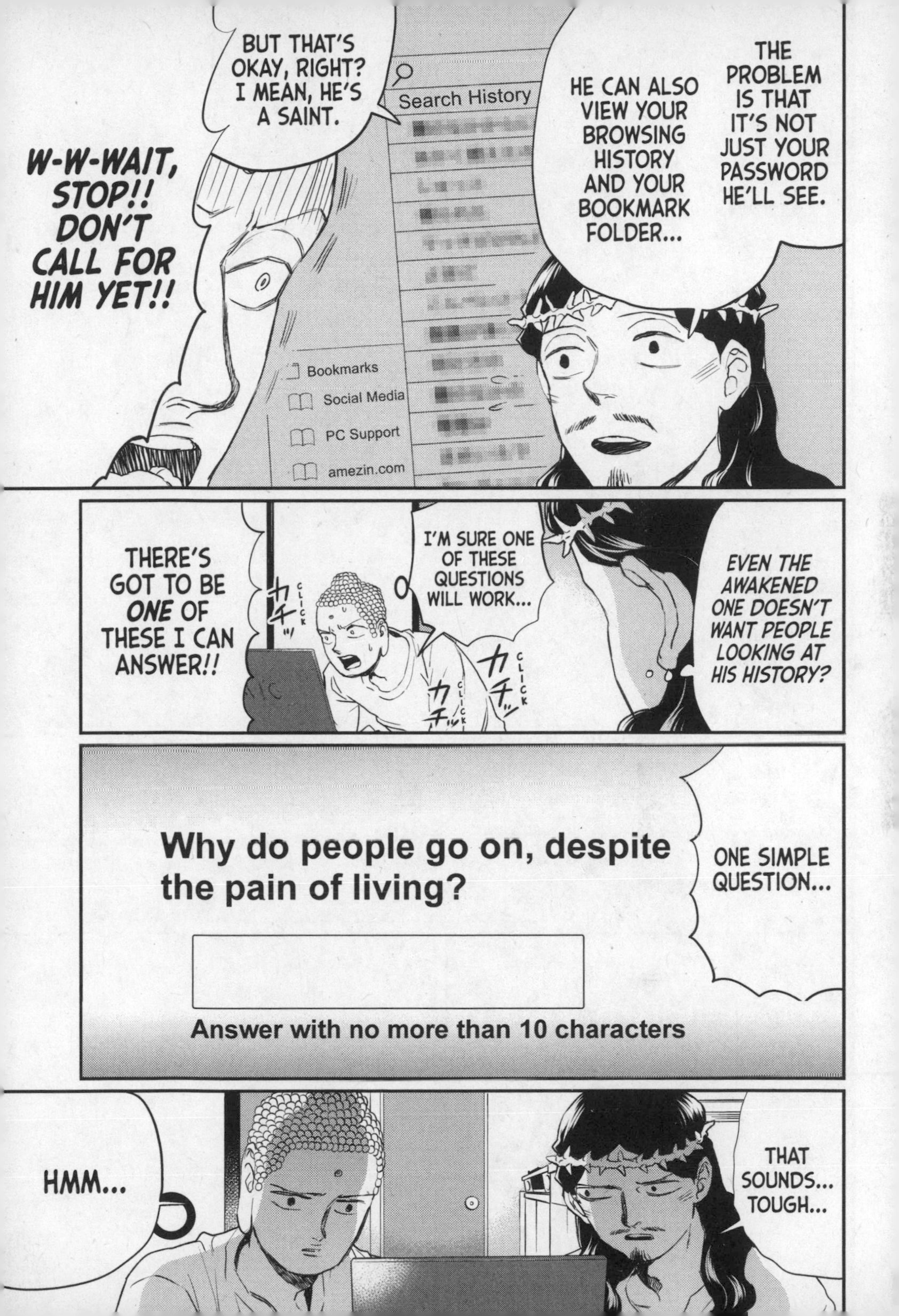
THE PROBLEM IS THAT IT'S NOT JUST YOUR PASSWORD HE'LL SEE.
HE CAN ALSO VIEW YOUR BROWSING HISTORY AND YOUR BOOKMARK FOLDER...
Search History
Bookmarks
Social Media
PC Support
amezin.com
BUT THAT'S OKAY, RIGHT? I MEAN, HE'S A SAINT.
W-W-WAIT, STOP!! DON'T CALL FOR HIM YET!!
EVEN THE AWAKENED ONE DOESN'T WANT PEOPLE LOOKING AT HIS HISTORY?
カチッ CLICK
I'M SURE ONE OF THESE QUESTIONS WILL WORK...
カチッ CLICK
カチッ CLICK
THERE'S GOT TO BE ONE OF THESE I CAN ANSWER!!
ONE SIMPLE QUESTION...
Why do people go on, despite the pain of living?
Answer with no more than 10 characters
THAT SOUNDS... TOUGH...
HMM...

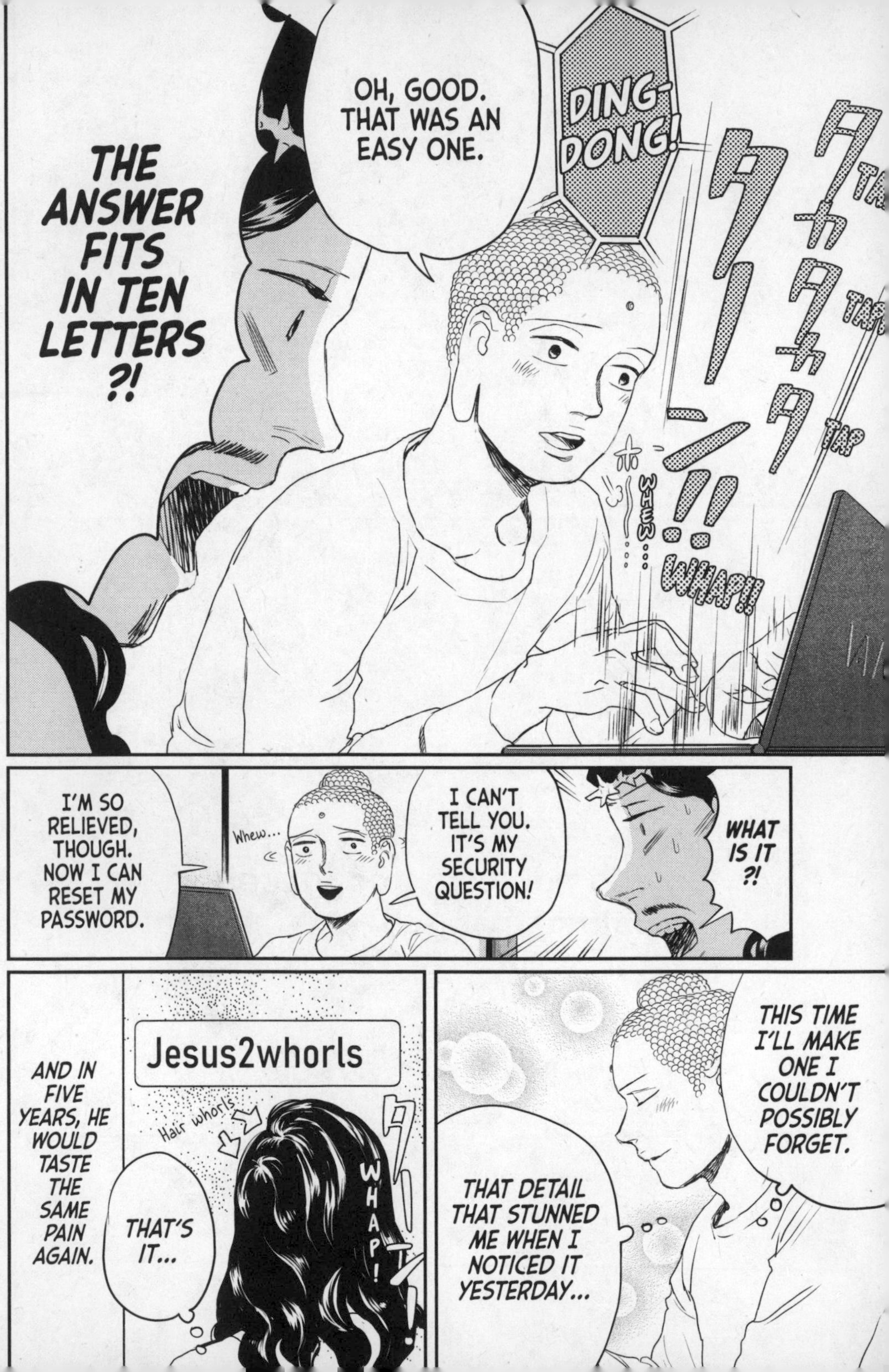
TAP
TAP
TAP
DING-DONG!
OH, GOOD. THAT WAS AN EASY ONE.
WHEW...
WHAP!!
THE ANSWER FITS IN TEN LETTERS?!
WHAT IS IT?!
I CAN'T TELL YOU. IT'S MY SECURITY QUESTION!
Whew...
I'M SO RELIEVED, THOUGH. NOW I CAN RESET MY PASSWORD.
THIS TIME I'LL MAKE ONE I COULDN'T POSSIBLY FORGET.
THAT DETAIL THAT STUNNED ME WHEN I NOTICED IT YESTERDAY...
Jesus2whorls
WHAP!
Hair whorls
THAT'S IT...
AND IN FIVE YEARS, HE WOULD TASTE THE SAME PAIN AGAIN.

Jesus's Security Question

How many rahotsu does Buddha have on his head?
Send
Did you count them?!

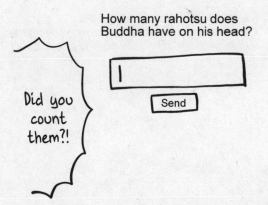

SAINT ☆ YOUNG MEN

CHAPTER 113 TRANSLATION NOTES

Thus have I heard, page 31
The phrase that begins the introduction to any Buddhist discourse. It is said to have been first used by Ananda, the Buddha's primary disciple, in reference to what the Buddha said, and became the standard prelude to any lesson.

St. Isidore, page 36
St. Isidore of Seville was a Spanish scholar from the 6th and 7th century venerated for his influence on culture and education in the Middle Ages. Today, he is unofficially considered a patron saint of the internet and computers.

Rahotsu, page 39
The Japanese word for the rounded swirls of hair on Buddha's head.

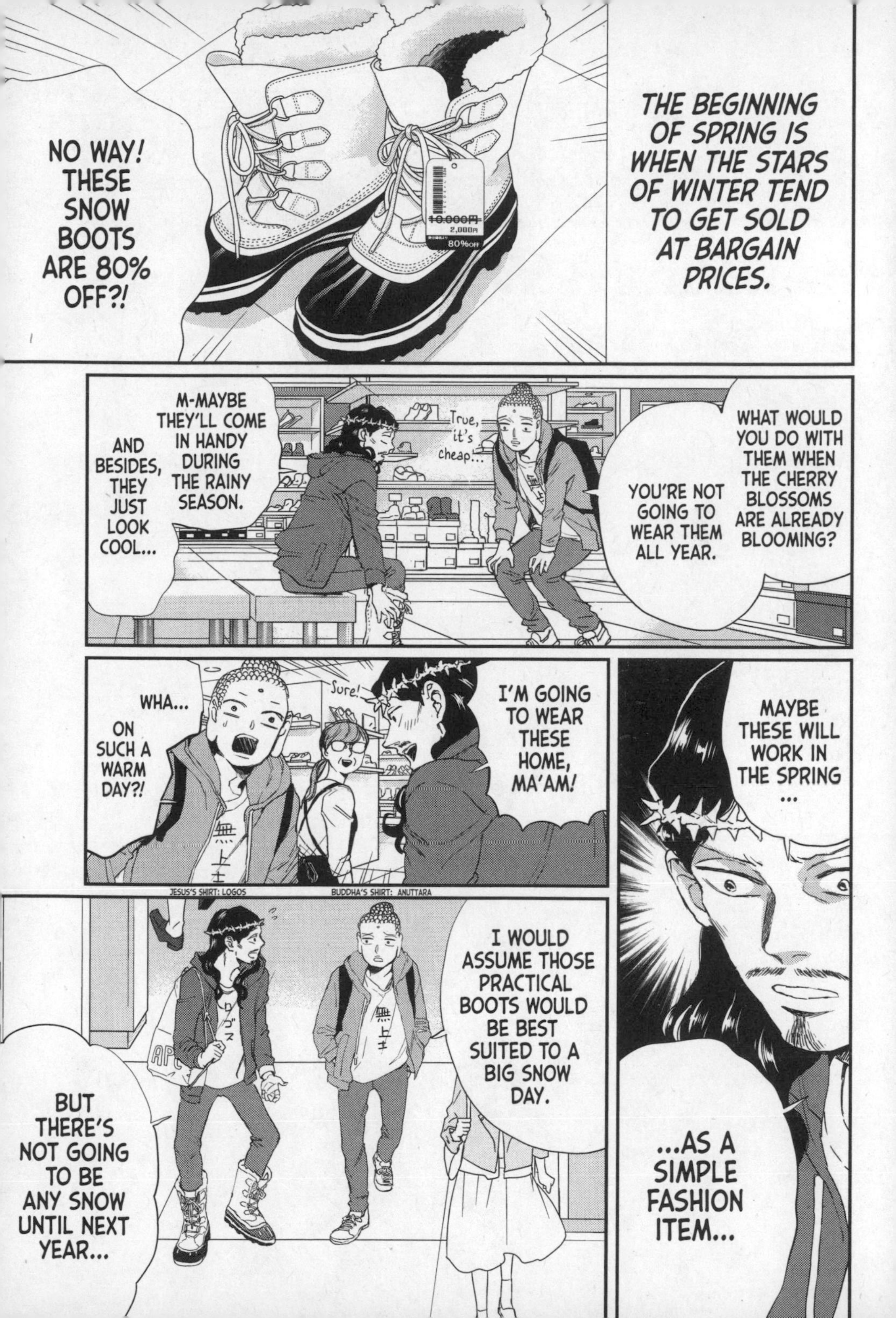
THE BEGINNING OF SPRING IS WHEN THE STARS OF WINTER TEND TO GET SOLD AT BARGAIN PRICES.
10,000円
2,000円
80%OFF
NO WAY! THESE SNOW BOOTS ARE 80% OFF?!
WHAT WOULD YOU DO WITH THEM WHEN THE CHERRY BLOSSOMS ARE ALREADY BLOOMING?
YOU'RE NOT GOING TO WEAR THEM ALL YEAR.
True, it's cheap...
M-MAYBE THEY'LL COME IN HANDY DURING THE RAINY SEASON.
AND BESIDES, THEY JUST LOOK COOL...
MAYBE THESE WILL WORK IN THE SPRING ...
...AS A SIMPLE FASHION ITEM...
I'M GOING TO WEAR THESE HOME, MA'AM!
Sure!
WHA...
ON SUCH A WARM DAY?!
JESUS'S SHIRT: LOGOS
BUDDHA'S SHIRT: ANUTTARA
I WOULD ASSUME THOSE PRACTICAL BOOTS WOULD BE BEST SUITED TO A BIG SNOW DAY.
BUT THERE'S NOT GOING TO BE ANY SNOW UNTIL NEXT YEAR...

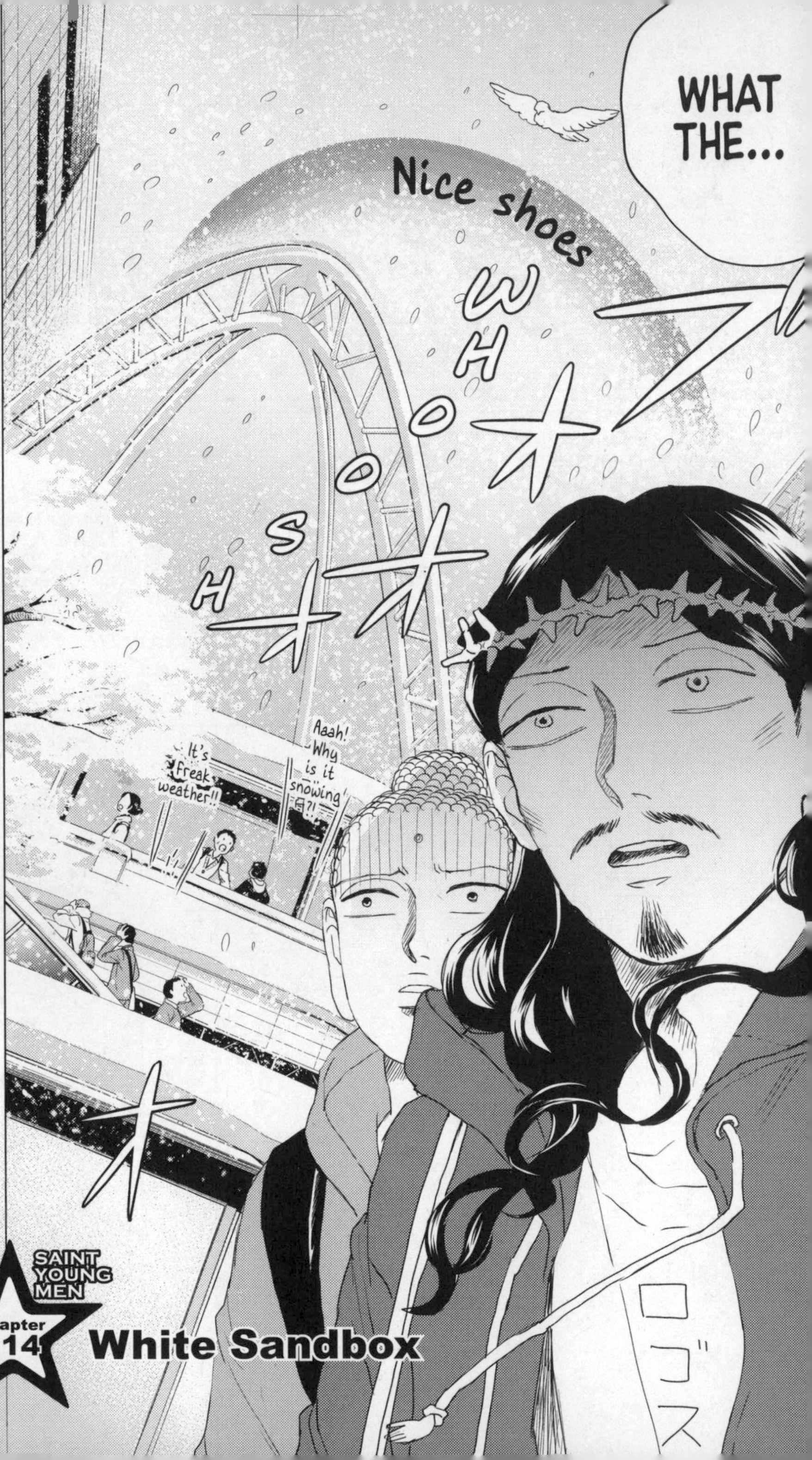
WHAT THE...
Nice shoes
WHOOSH
Aaah! Why is it snowing?!
It's freak weather!!
ロゴス

IT WAS ALL THE SON OF GOD'S FAULT.

SAINT YOUNG MEN

Chapter 114

White Sandbox

JESUS
NO ONE'S ASSOCIATED WITH BREAD MORE THAN ME, RIGHT? BUT IN THE EARLY SPRING, PEOPLE ARE MORE EXCITED ABOUT THE "BREAD FESTIVAL" THAN THE BREAD OF CHRIST.

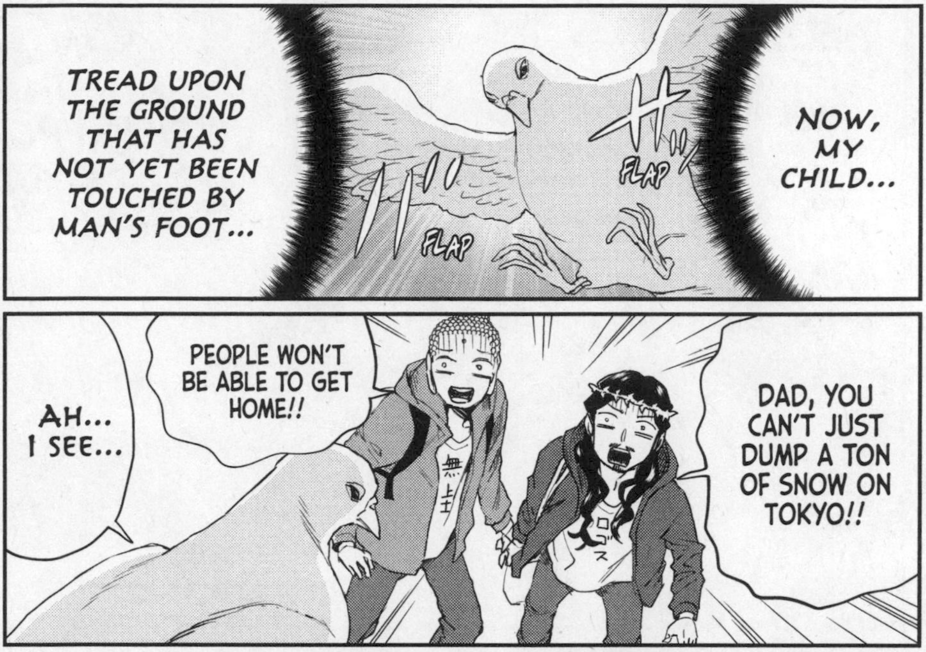
NOW, MY CHILD...
TREAD UPON THE GROUND THAT HAS NOT YET BEEN TOUCHED BY MAN'S FOOT...
FLAP
FLAP
DAD, YOU CAN'T JUST DUMP A TON OF SNOW ON TOKYO!!
PEOPLE WON'T BE ABLE TO GET HOME!!
AH... I SEE...

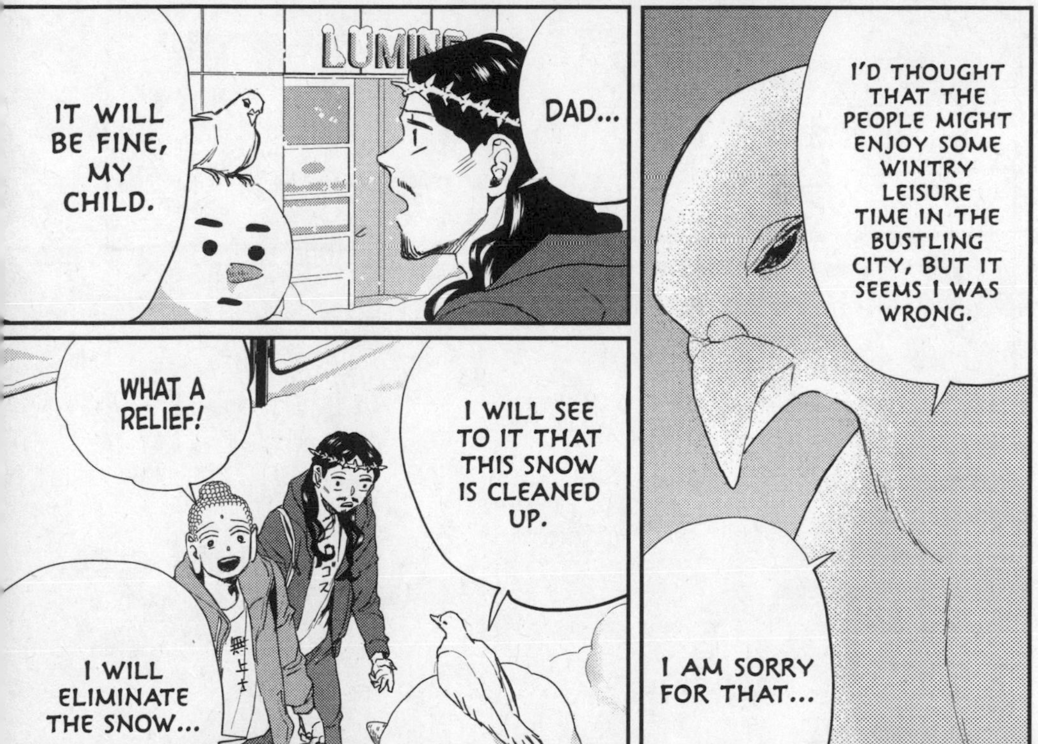
I'D THOUGHT THAT THE PEOPLE MIGHT ENJOY SOME WINTRY LEISURE TIME IN THE BUSTLING CITY, BUT IT SEEMS I WAS WRONG.
I AM SORRY FOR THAT...
DAD...
LUMIN
IT WILL BE FINE, MY CHILD.
I WILL ELIMINATE THE SNOW...
I WILL SEE TO IT THAT THIS SNOW IS CLEANED UP.
WHAT A RELIEF!

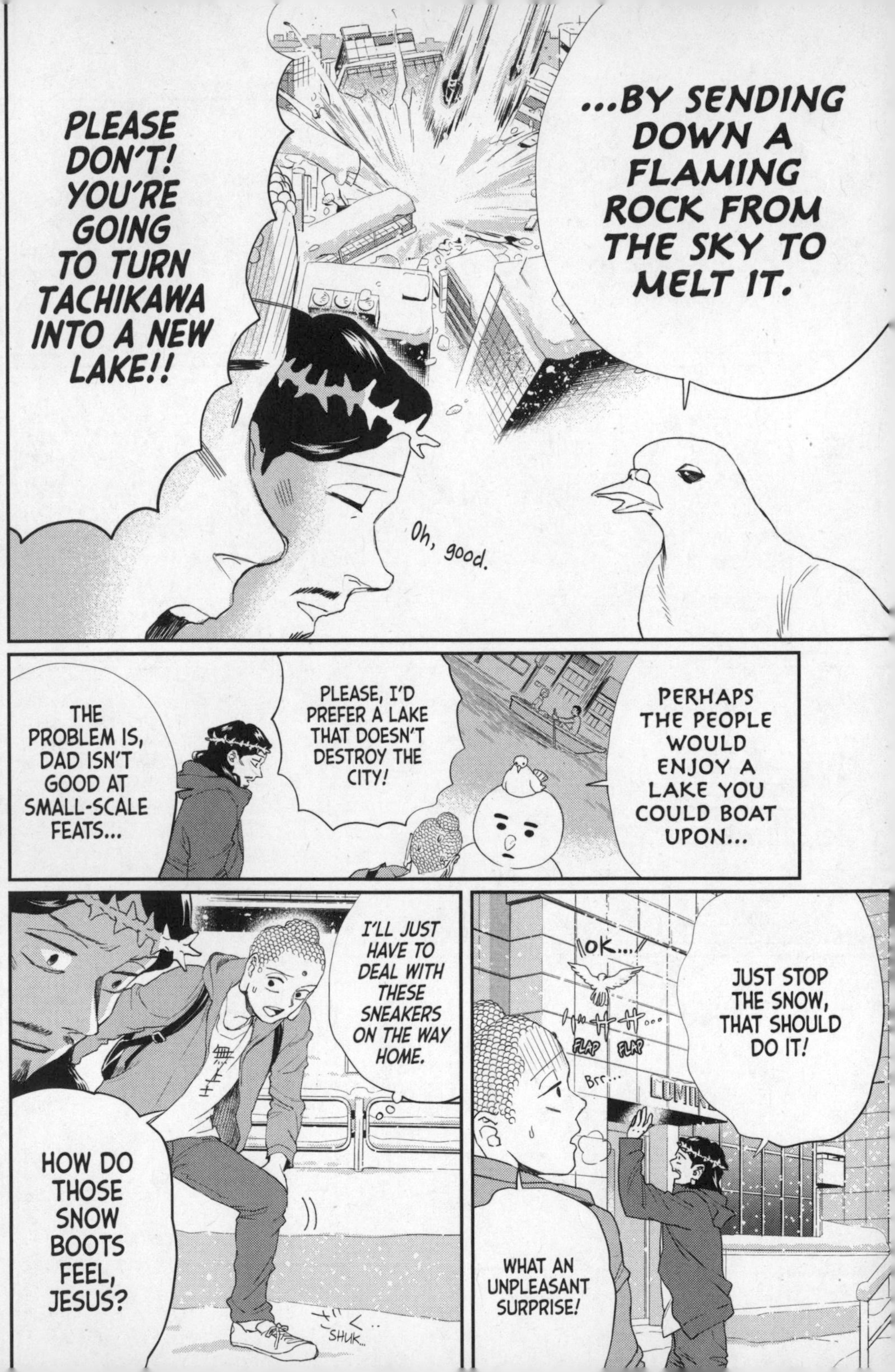
...BY SENDING DOWN A FLAMING ROCK FROM THE SKY TO MELT IT.
PLEASE DON'T! YOU'RE GOING TO TURN TACHIKAWA INTO A NEW LAKE!!
Oh, good.
PERHAPS THE PEOPLE WOULD ENJOY A LAKE YOU COULD BOAT UPON...
PLEASE, I'D PREFER A LAKE THAT DOESN'T DESTROY THE CITY!
THE PROBLEM IS, DAD ISN'T GOOD AT SMALL-SCALE FEATS...
JUST STOP THE SNOW, THAT SHOULD DO IT!
OK...
FLAP FLAP
Brr...
WHAT AN UNPLEASANT SURPRISE!
I'LL JUST HAVE TO DEAL WITH THESE SNEAKERS ON THE WAY HOME.
HOW DO THOSE SNOW BOOTS FEEL, JESUS?
SHUK...

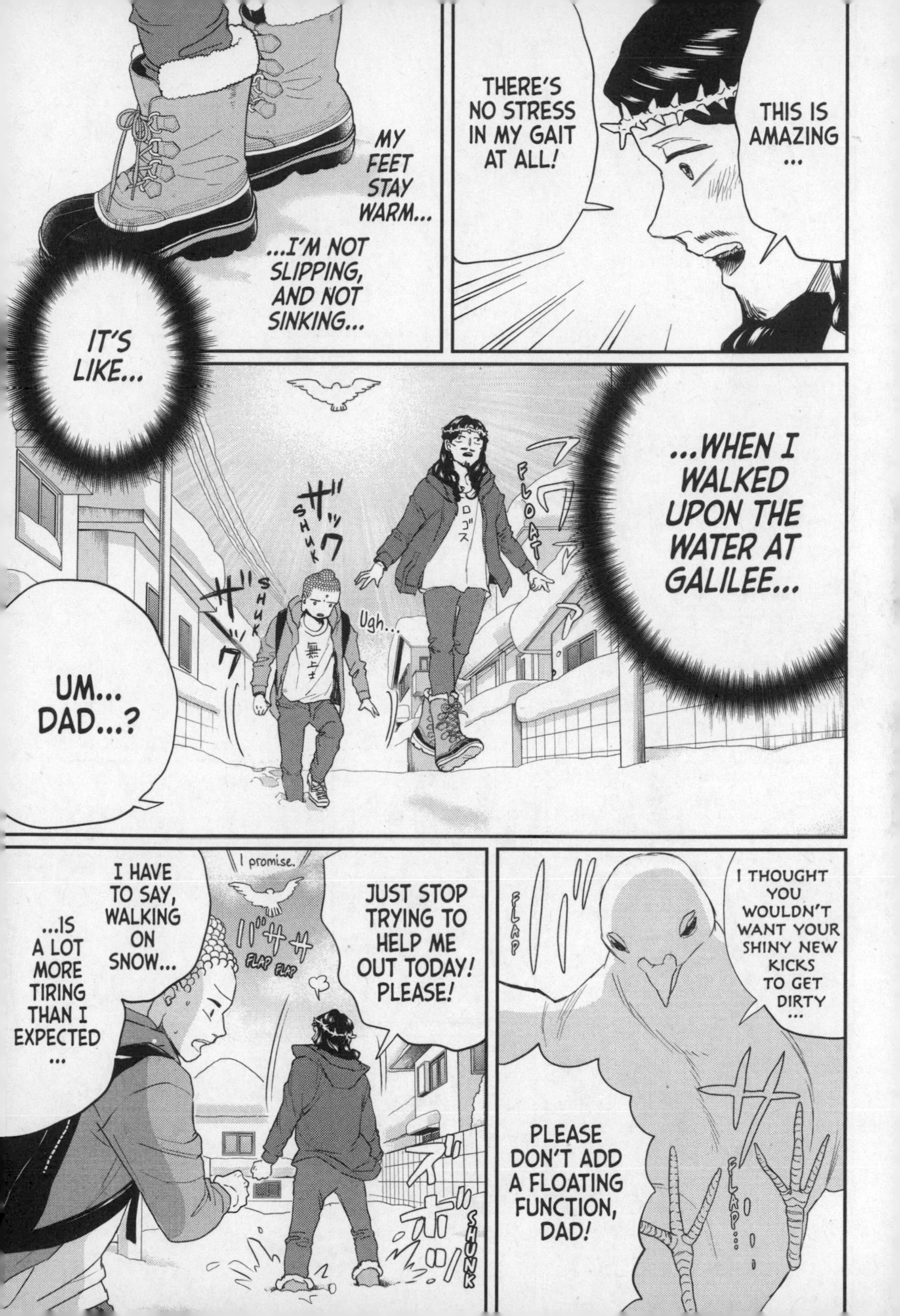
THIS IS AMAZING...
THERE'S NO STRESS IN MY GAIT AT ALL!
MY FEET STAY WARM...
...I'M NOT SLIPPING, AND NOT SINKING...
IT'S LIKE...
...WHEN I WALKED UPON THE WATER AT GALILEE...
FLOAT
SHUK
SHUK
Ugh...
UM... DAD...?
I THOUGHT YOU WOULDN'T WANT YOUR SHINY NEW KICKS TO GET DIRTY...
FLAP
PLEASE DON'T ADD A FLOATING FUNCTION, DAD!
FLAP...
JUST STOP TRYING TO HELP ME OUT TODAY! PLEASE!
I promise.
FLAP FLAP
I HAVE TO SAY, WALKING ON SNOW...
...IS A LOT MORE TIRING THAN I EXPECTED...
SHUNK

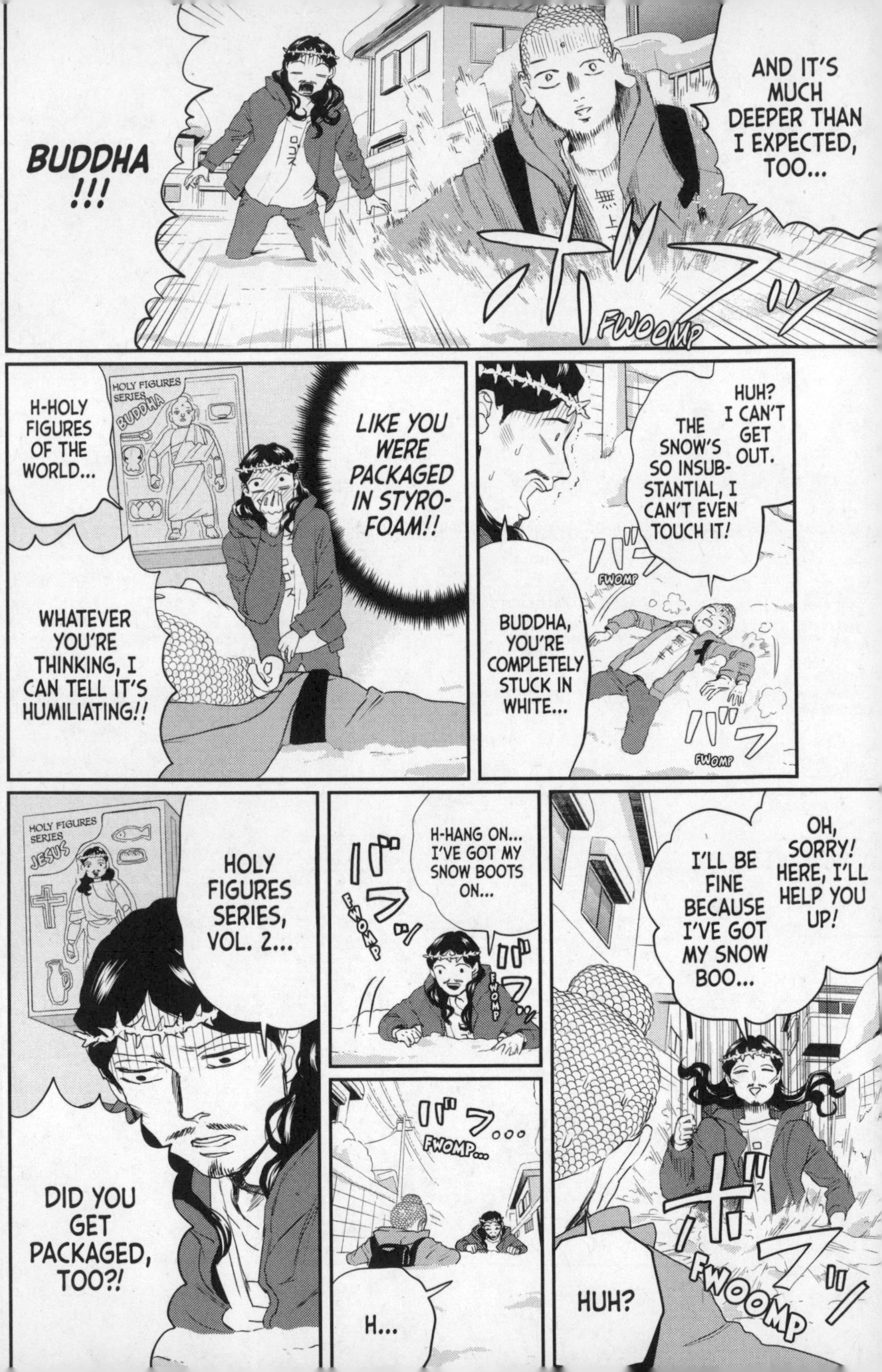
AND IT'S MUCH DEEPER THAN I EXPECTED, TOO...
BUDDHA !!!
FWOOMP
HUH? I CAN'T GET OUT.
THE SNOW'S SO INSUB-STANTIAL, I CAN'T EVEN TOUCH IT!
FWOMP
BUDDHA, YOU'RE COMPLETELY STUCK IN WHITE...
FWOMP
LIKE YOU WERE PACKAGED IN STYRO-FOAM!!
HOLY FIGURES SERIES
BUDDHA
H-HOLY FIGURES OF THE WORLD...
WHATEVER YOU'RE THINKING, I CAN TELL IT'S HUMILIATING!!
OH, SORRY! HERE, I'LL HELP YOU UP!
I'LL BE FINE BECAUSE I'VE GOT MY SNOW BOO...
FWOOMP
HUH?
H-HANG ON... I'VE GOT MY SNOW BOOTS ON...
FWOMP
FWOMP
FWOMP...
H...
HOLY FIGURES SERIES
JESUS
HOLY FIGURES SERIES, VOL. 2...
DID YOU GET PACKAGED, TOO?!

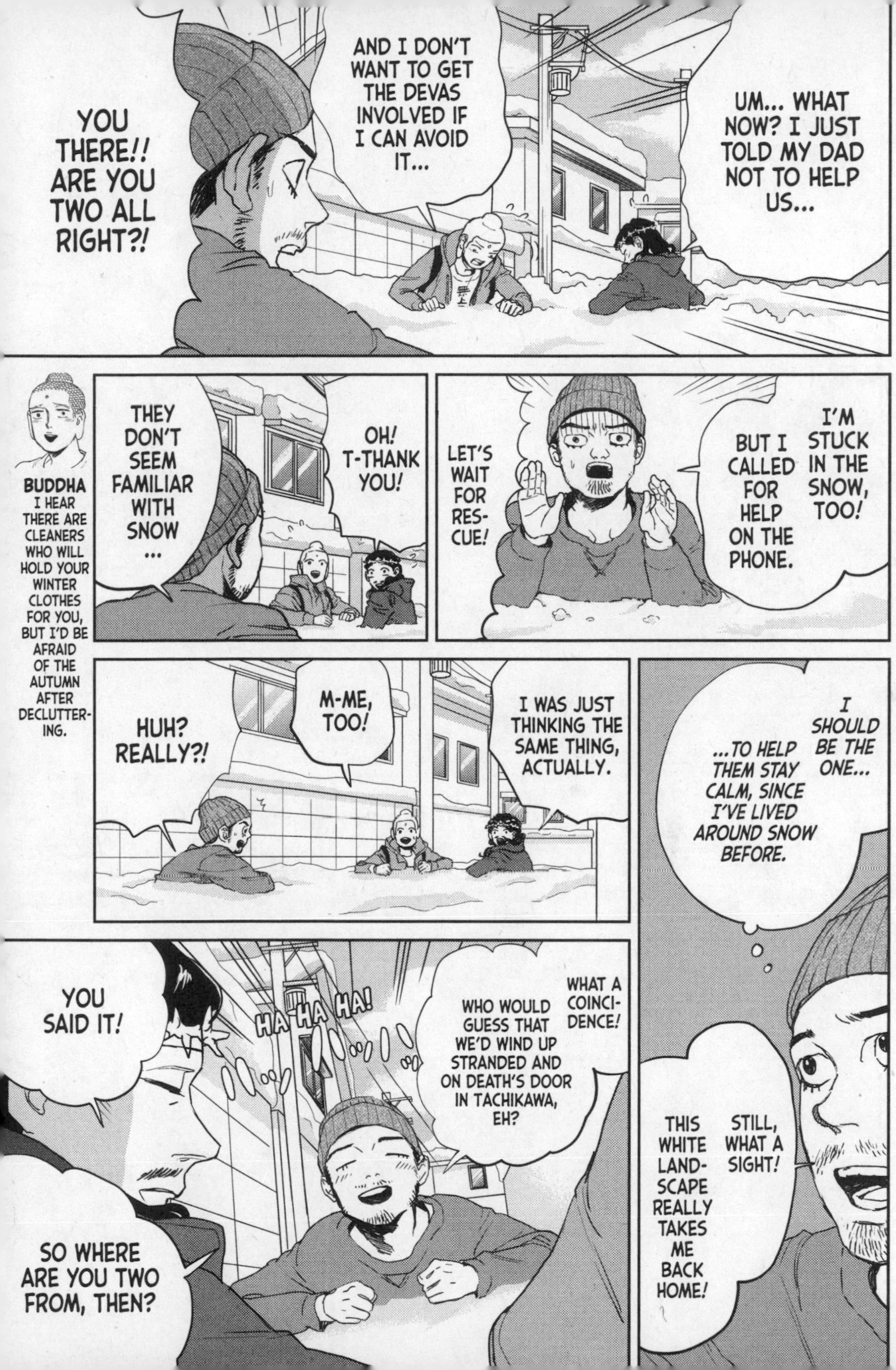
UM... WHAT NOW? I JUST TOLD MY DAD NOT TO HELP US...
AND I DON'T WANT TO GET THE DEVAS INVOLVED IF I CAN AVOID IT...
YOU THERE!! ARE YOU TWO ALL RIGHT?!
I'M STUCK IN THE SNOW, TOO!
BUT I CALLED FOR HELP ON THE PHONE.
LET'S WAIT FOR RES-CUE!
OH! T-THANK YOU!
THEY DON'T SEEM FAMILIAR WITH SNOW ...
I SHOULD BE THE ONE...
...TO HELP THEM STAY CALM, SINCE I'VE LIVED AROUND SNOW BEFORE.
STILL, WHAT A SIGHT!
THIS WHITE LAND-SCAPE REALLY TAKES ME BACK HOME!
I WAS JUST THINKING THE SAME THING, ACTUALLY.
M-ME, TOO!
HUH? REALLY?!
WHAT A COINCI-DENCE!
WHO WOULD GUESS THAT WE'D WIND UP STRANDED AND ON DEATH'S DOOR IN TACHIKAWA, EH?
HA HA HA!
YOU SAID IT!
SO WHERE ARE YOU TWO FROM, THEN?
BUDDHA
I HEAR THERE ARE CLEANERS WHO WILL HOLD YOUR WINTER CLOTHES FOR YOU, BUT I'D BE AFRAID OF THE AUTUMN AFTER DECLUTTER-ING.

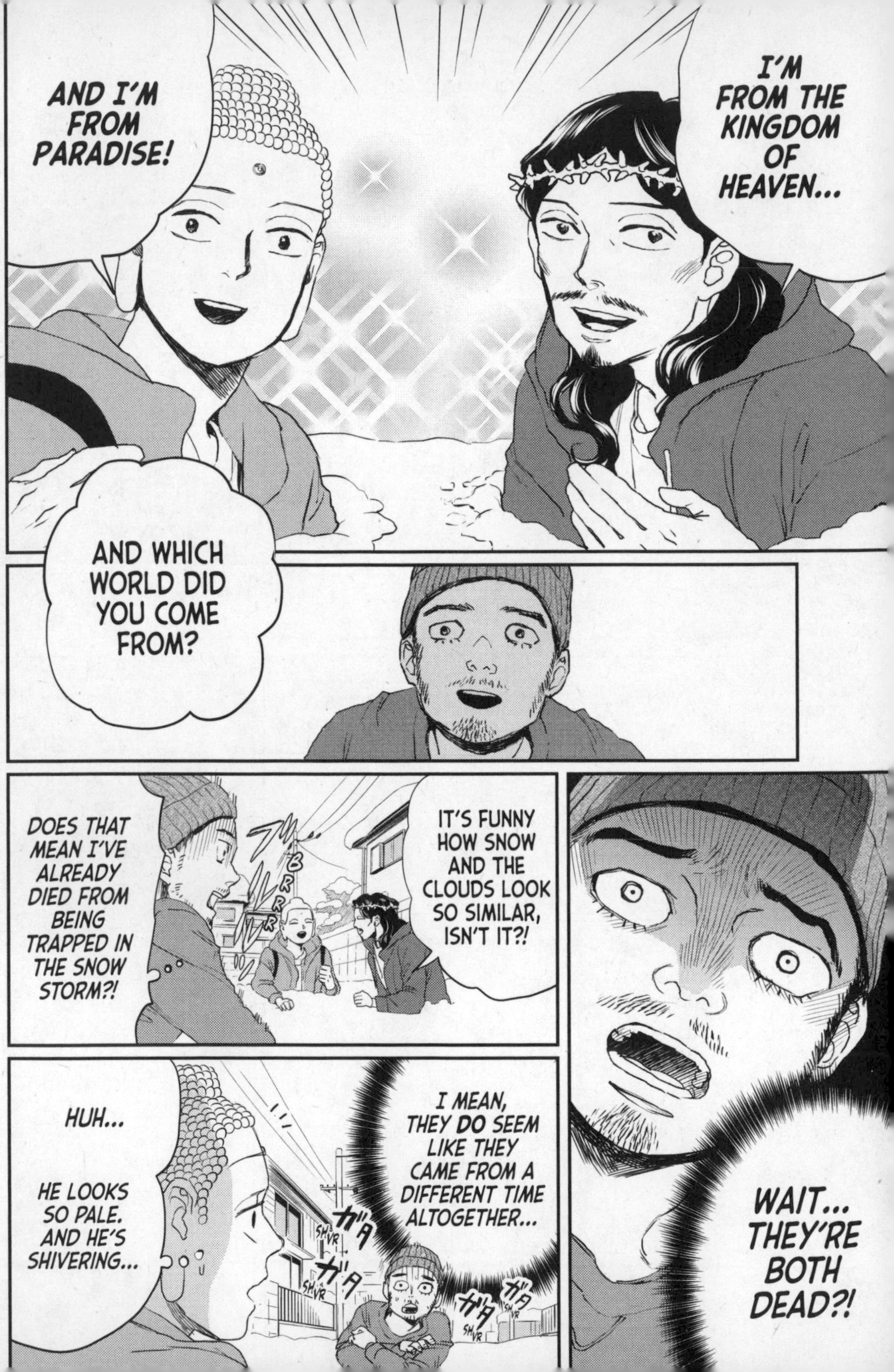
I'M FROM THE KINGDOM OF HEAVEN...
AND I'M FROM PARADISE!
AND WHICH WORLD DID YOU COME FROM?
WAIT... THEY'RE BOTH DEAD?!
IT'S FUNNY HOW SNOW AND THE CLOUDS LOOK SO SIMILAR, ISN'T IT?!
BRRR
DOES THAT MEAN I'VE ALREADY DIED FROM BEING TRAPPED IN THE SNOW STORM?!
I MEAN, THEY DO SEEM LIKE THEY CAME FROM A DIFFERENT TIME ALTOGETHER...
SHVR
SHVR
SHVR
SHVR
HUH...
HE LOOKS SO PALE. AND HE'S SHIVERING...

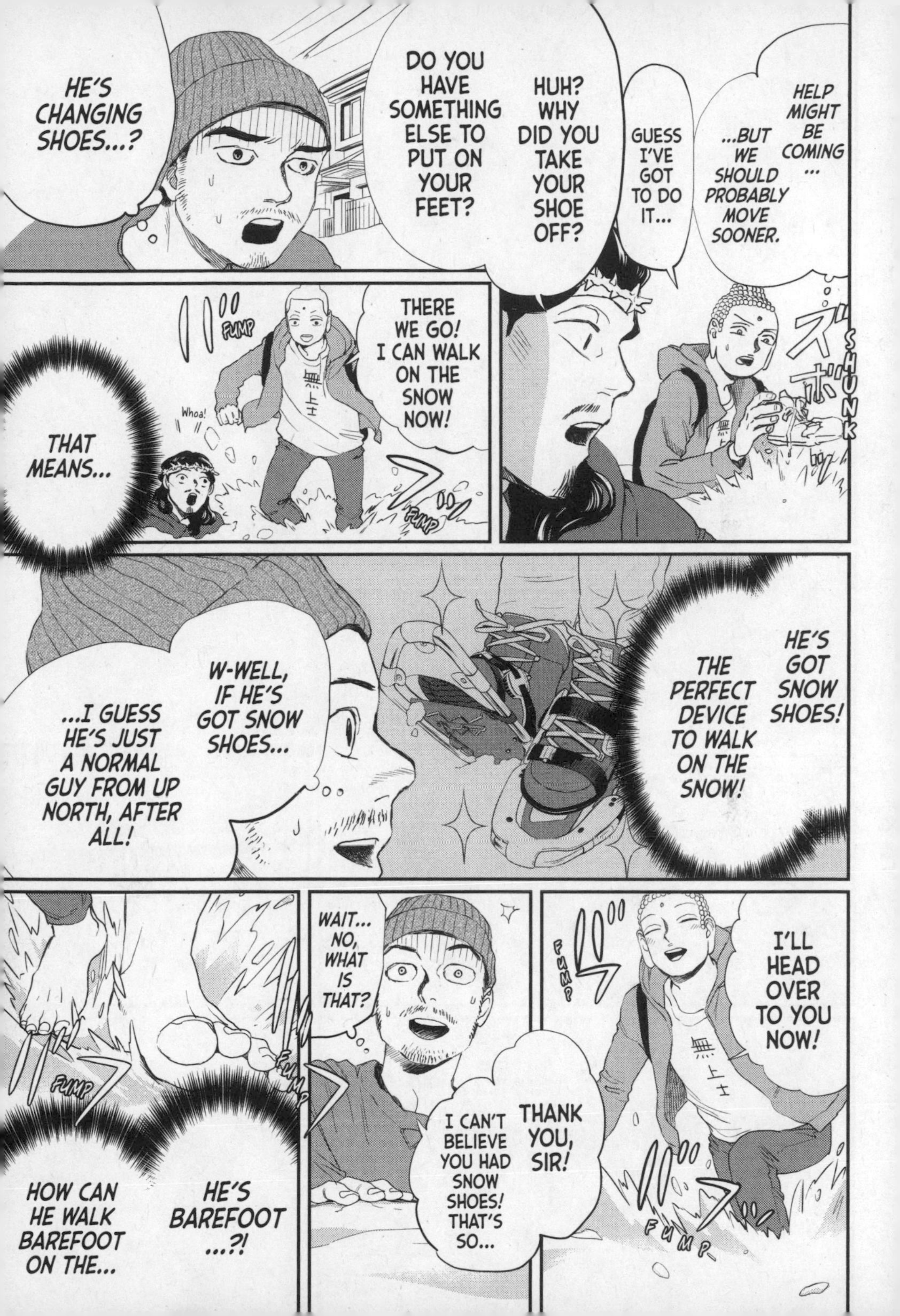
HELP MIGHT BE COMING...
...BUT WE SHOULD PROBABLY MOVE SOONER.
GUESS I'VE GOT TO DO IT...
HUH? WHY DID YOU TAKE YOUR SHOE OFF?
DO YOU HAVE SOMETHING ELSE TO PUT ON YOUR FEET?
HE'S CHANGING SHOES...?
SHUNK
THERE WE GO! I CAN WALK ON THE SNOW NOW!
FUMP
Whoa!
FUMP
THAT MEANS...
HE'S GOT SNOW SHOES!
THE PERFECT DEVICE TO WALK ON THE SNOW!
W-WELL, IF HE'S GOT SNOW SHOES...
...I GUESS HE'S JUST A NORMAL GUY FROM UP NORTH, AFTER ALL!
I'LL HEAD OVER TO YOU NOW!
FUMP
FUMP
WAIT... NO, WHAT IS THAT?
THANK YOU, SIR!
I CAN'T BELIEVE YOU HAD SNOW SHOES! THAT'S SO...
FUMP
FUMP
HE'S BAREFOOT...?!
HOW CAN HE WALK BAREFOOT ON THE...

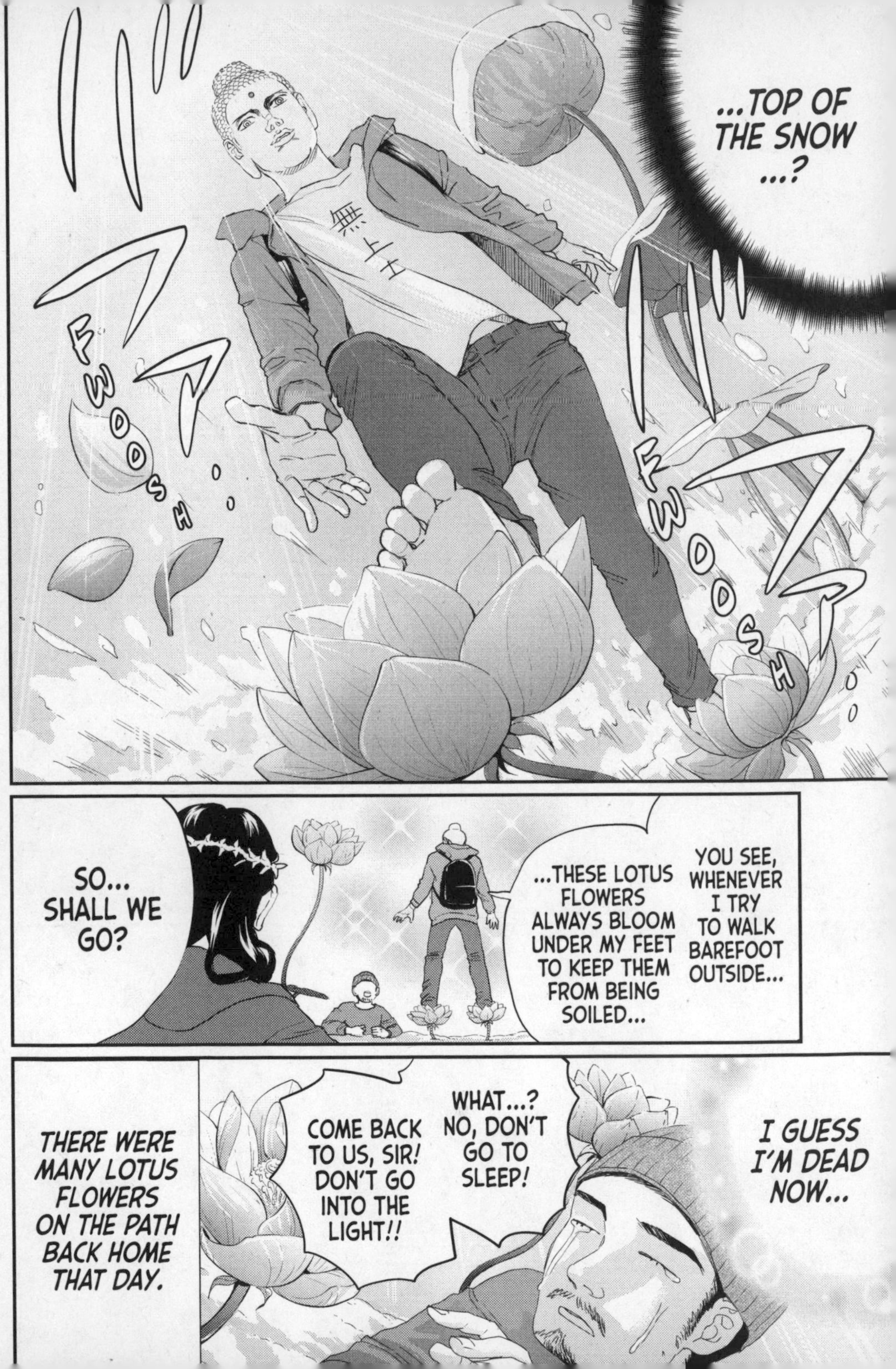

...TOP OF THE SNOW ...?
無上士
FWOOSH
FWOOSH
YOU SEE, WHENEVER I TRY TO WALK BAREFOOT OUTSIDE...
...THESE LOTUS FLOWERS ALWAYS BLOOM UNDER MY FEET TO KEEP THEM FROM BEING SOILED...
SO... SHALL WE GO?
I GUESS I'M DEAD NOW...
WHAT...? NO, DON'T GO TO SLEEP!
COME BACK TO US, SIR! DON'T GO INTO THE LIGHT!!
THERE WERE MANY LOTUS FLOWERS ON THE PATH BACK HOME THAT DAY.

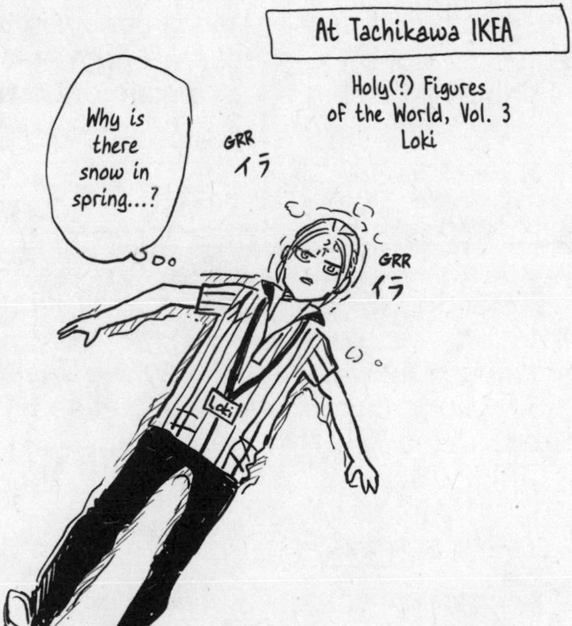
At Tachikawa IKEA
Holy(?) Figures of the World, Vol. 3
Loki
Why is there snow in spring...?
GRR イラ
GRR イラ
Loki

SAINT ☆ YOUNG MEN

CHAPTER 114 TRANSLATION NOTES

Anuttara, page 177
One of the ten honorific titles of a Buddha and a mark of his supremacy among all beings, meaning "without superior."

Logos, page 177
Logos is Greek for "word," and is sometimes used as a title for Jesus Christ, due to its appearance in John 1:1, "in the beginning was the Word [...] and the Word was God."

Bread festival, page 179
A reference to Yamazaki's Spring Bread Festival, or "Pan Matsuri." The food maker Yamazaki has a yearly campaign in the spring in which their products' proof of purchases will earn points toward a special prize: a fine white dish, usually a plate or bowl, that changes each year.

Jesus walking on the water, page 181
One of the famous miracles of Jesus that appears in the Gospels following the Feeding of the Five Thousand. in the story, Jesus sends his disciples across the Sea of Galilee, a lake in Israel, while he remains behind to pray. As they row through a storm, the boat seems ready to capsize, at which point they see Jesus walking upon the water to rejoin them, and the storm ceases.

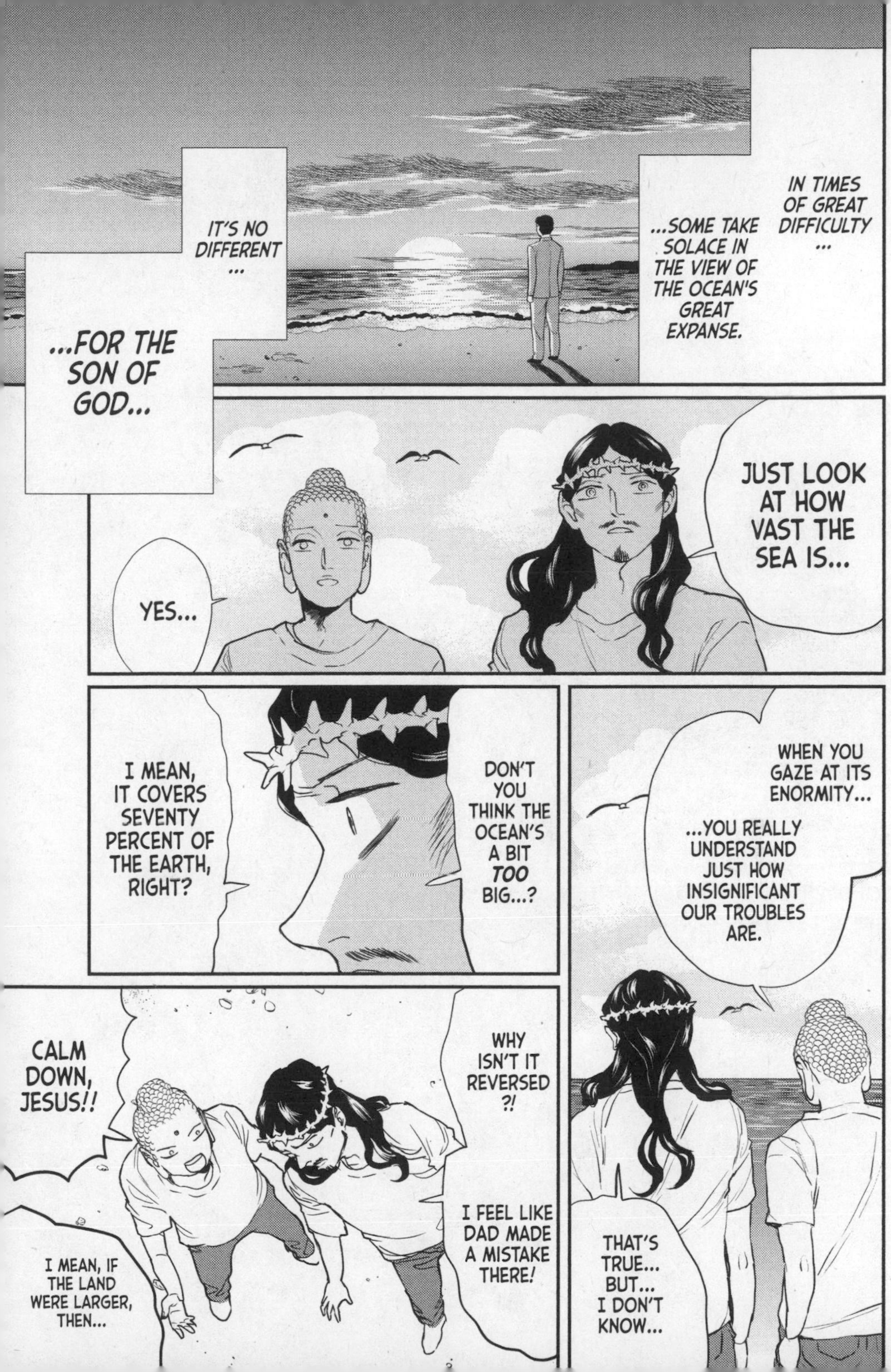
IN TIMES OF GREAT DIFFICULTY...
...SOME TAKE SOLACE IN THE VIEW OF THE OCEAN'S GREAT EXPANSE.
IT'S NO DIFFERENT...
...FOR THE SON OF GOD...
JUST LOOK AT HOW VAST THE SEA IS...
YES...
WHEN YOU GAZE AT ITS ENORMITY...
...YOU REALLY UNDERSTAND JUST HOW INSIGNIFICANT OUR TROUBLES ARE.
THAT'S TRUE... BUT... I DON'T KNOW...
DON'T YOU THINK THE OCEAN'S A BIT *TOO* BIG...?
I MEAN, IT COVERS SEVENTY PERCENT OF THE EARTH, RIGHT?
WHY ISN'T IT REVERSED?!
I FEEL LIKE DAD MADE A MISTAKE THERE!
CALM DOWN, JESUS!!
I MEAN, IF THE LAND WERE LARGER, THEN...

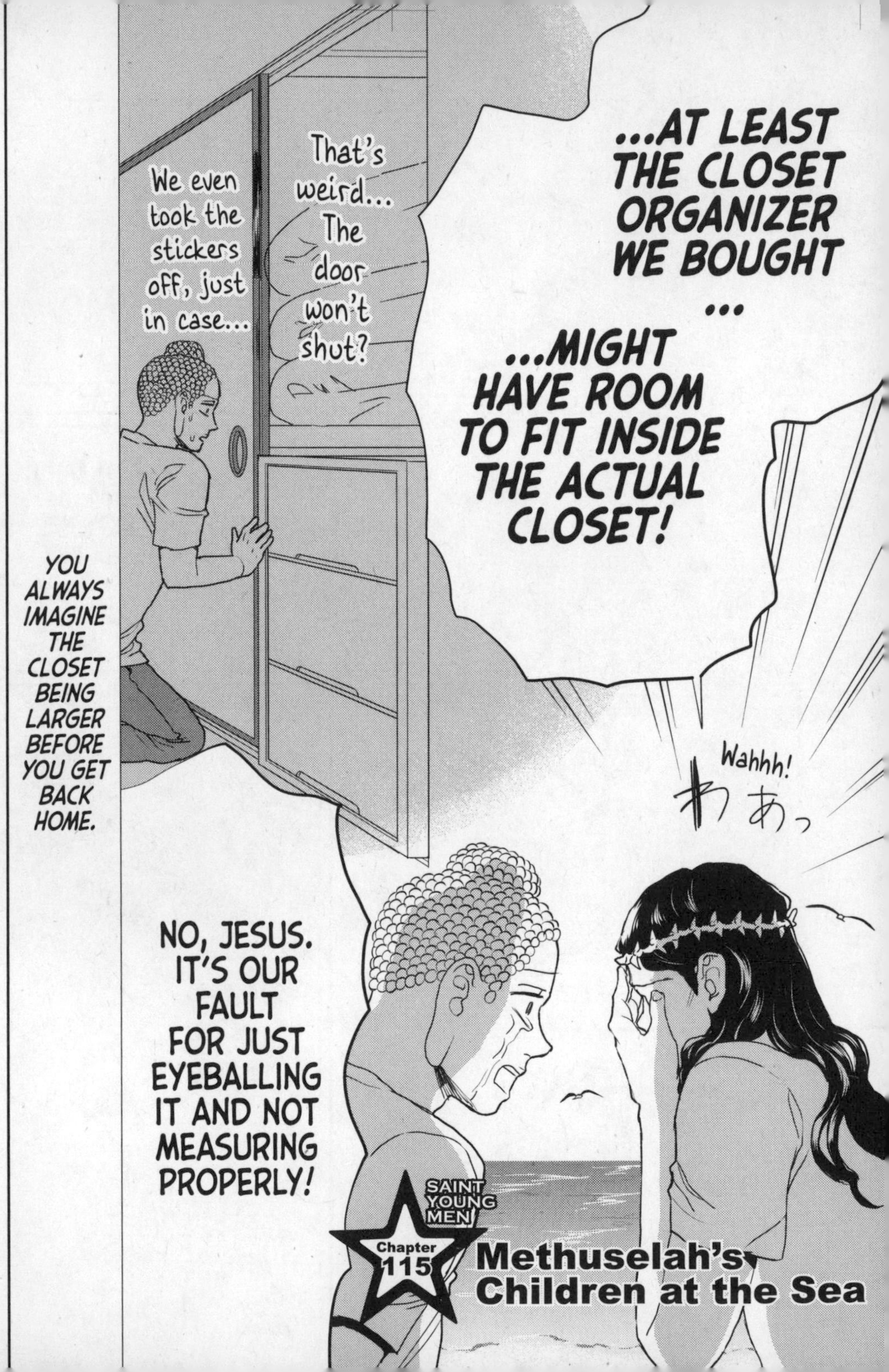

...AT LEAST THE CLOSET ORGANIZER WE BOUGHT ...
...MIGHT HAVE ROOM TO FIT INSIDE THE ACTUAL CLOSET!
That's weird... The door won't shut?
We even took the stickers off, just in case...
YOU ALWAYS IMAGINE THE CLOSET BEING LARGER BEFORE YOU GET BACK HOME.
Wahhh!
わあっ
NO, JESUS. IT'S OUR FAULT FOR JUST EYEBALLING IT AND NOT MEASURING PROPERLY!
SAINT YOUNG MEN
Chapter 115
Methuselah's Children at the Sea

JESUS
SPRING! WEEKDAY! ALL THE WINNERS ARE INSIDE AT WORK. THIS IS OUR SPECIAL TIME IN THE SUN.

BUDDHA
SAND! WHEN YOU BRING YOUR NORMAL CLOTHES TO THE BEACH, YOU WIND UP WITH SAND IN THE BATHROOM AND WASHING MACHINE AT HOME.

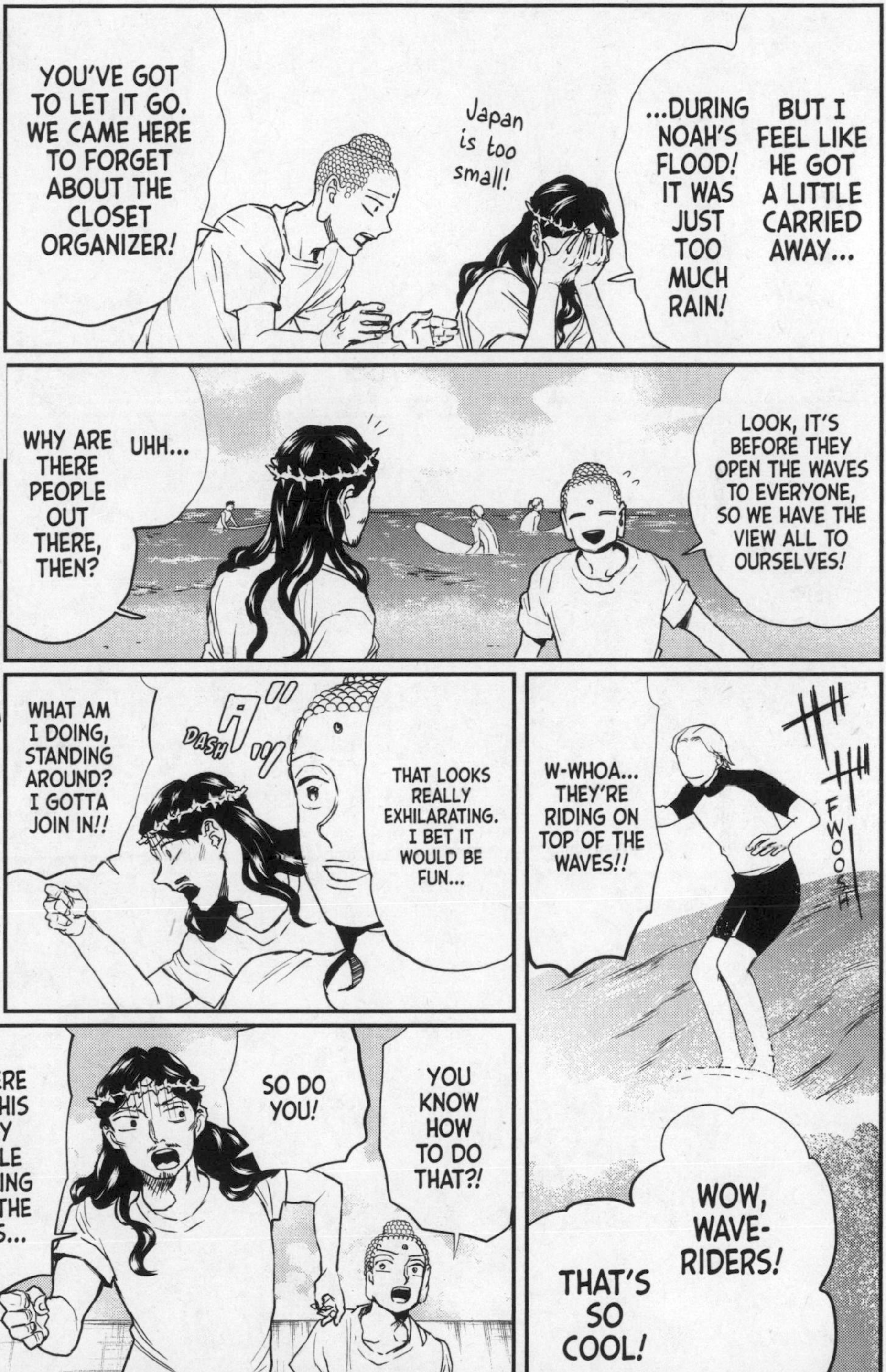

BUT I FEEL LIKE HE GOT A LITTLE CARRIED AWAY...
...DURING NOAH'S FLOOD! IT WAS JUST TOO MUCH RAIN!
Japan is too small!
YOU'VE GOT TO LET IT GO. WE CAME HERE TO FORGET ABOUT THE CLOSET ORGANIZER!
LOOK, IT'S BEFORE THEY OPEN THE WAVES TO EVERYONE, SO WE HAVE THE VIEW ALL TO OURSELVES!
UHH...
WHY ARE THERE PEOPLE OUT THERE, THEN?
W-WHOA... THEY'RE RIDING ON TOP OF THE WAVES!!
FWOOSH
WOW, WAVE-RIDERS!
THAT'S SO COOL!
THAT LOOKS REALLY EXHILARATING. I BET IT WOULD BE FUN...
DASH
WHAT AM I DOING, STANDING AROUND? I GOTTA JOIN IN!!
YOU KNOW HOW TO DO THAT?!
SO DO YOU!
IF THERE ARE THIS MANY PEOPLE STANDING ATOP THE WAVES...

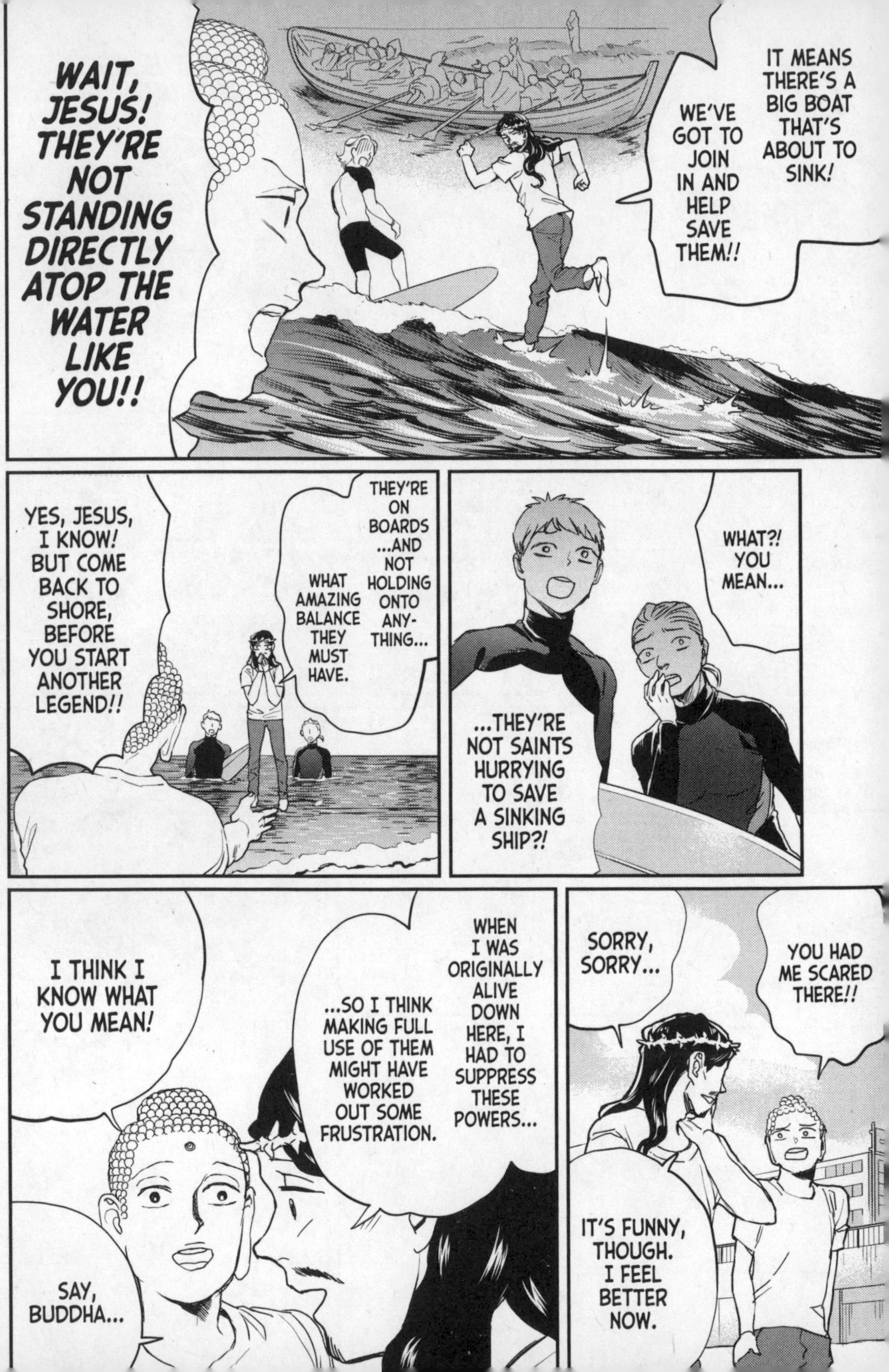
IT MEANS THERE'S A BIG BOAT THAT'S ABOUT TO SINK!
WE'VE GOT TO JOIN IN AND HELP SAVE THEM!!
WAIT, JESUS! THEY'RE NOT STANDING DIRECTLY ATOP THE WATER LIKE YOU!!
WHAT?! YOU MEAN...
...THEY'RE NOT SAINTS HURRYING TO SAVE A SINKING SHIP?!
THEY'RE ON BOARDS ...AND NOT HOLDING ONTO ANY-THING...
WHAT AMAZING BALANCE THEY MUST HAVE.
YES, JESUS, I KNOW! BUT COME BACK TO SHORE, BEFORE YOU START ANOTHER LEGEND!!
YOU HAD ME SCARED THERE!!
SORRY, SORRY...
IT'S FUNNY, THOUGH. I FEEL BETTER NOW.
SAY, BUDDHA...
WHEN I WAS ORIGINALLY ALIVE DOWN HERE, I HAD TO SUPPRESS THESE POWERS...
...SO I THINK MAKING FULL USE OF THEM MIGHT HAVE WORKED OUT SOME FRUSTRATION.
I THINK I KNOW WHAT YOU MEAN!

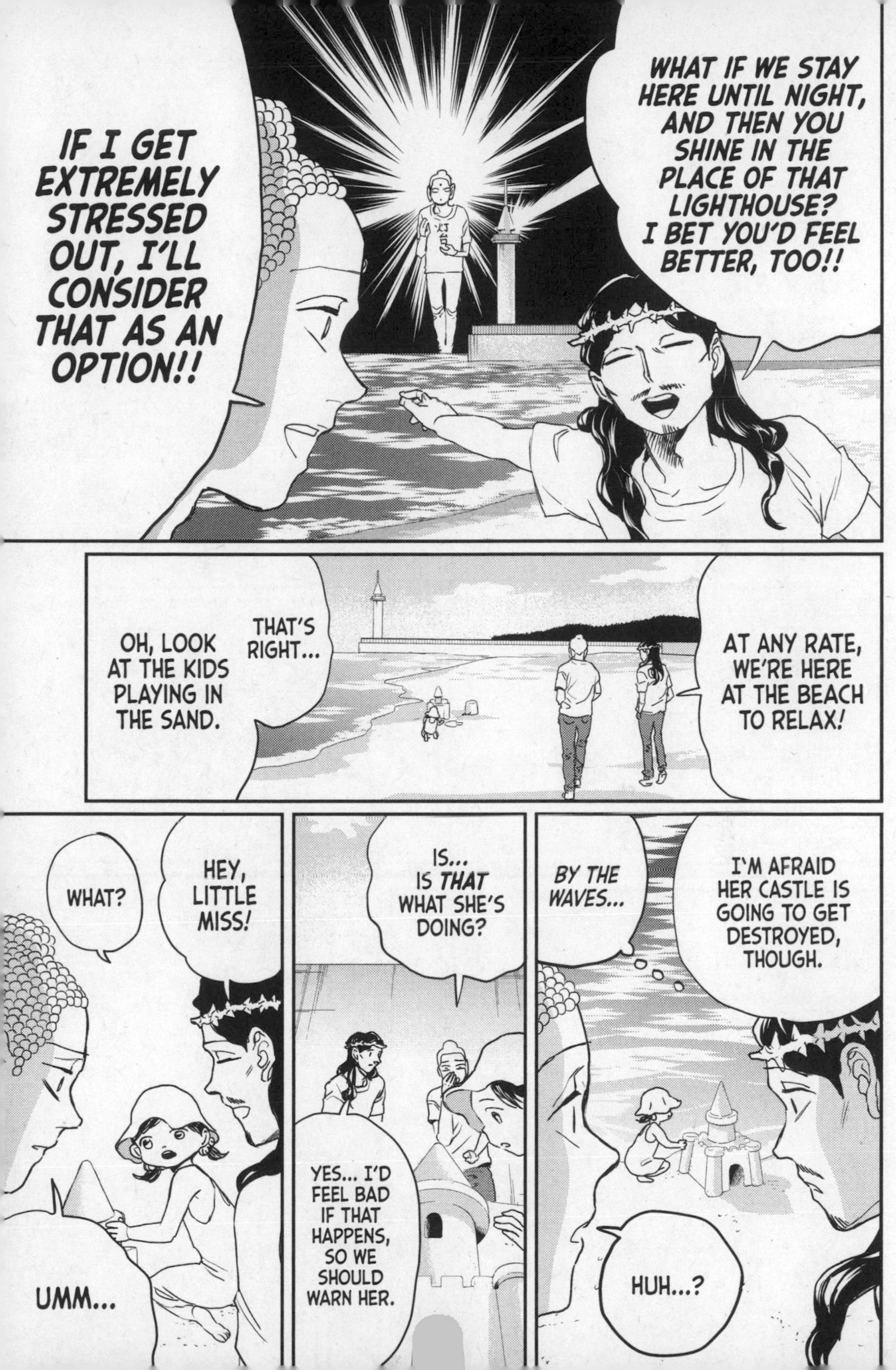
WHAT IF WE STAY HERE UNTIL NIGHT, AND THEN YOU SHINE IN THE PLACE OF THAT LIGHTHOUSE? I BET YOU'D FEEL BETTER, TOO!!
IF I GET EXTREMELY STRESSED OUT, I'LL CONSIDER THAT AS AN OPTION!!
AT ANY RATE, WE'RE HERE AT THE BEACH TO RELAX!
THAT'S RIGHT...
OH, LOOK AT THE KIDS PLAYING IN THE SAND.
I'M AFRAID HER CASTLE IS GOING TO GET DESTROYED, THOUGH.
BY THE WAVES...
HUH...?
IS... IS *THAT* WHAT SHE'S DOING?
YES... I'D FEEL BAD IF THAT HAPPENS, SO WE SHOULD WARN HER.
HEY, LITTLE MISS!
WHAT?
UMM...

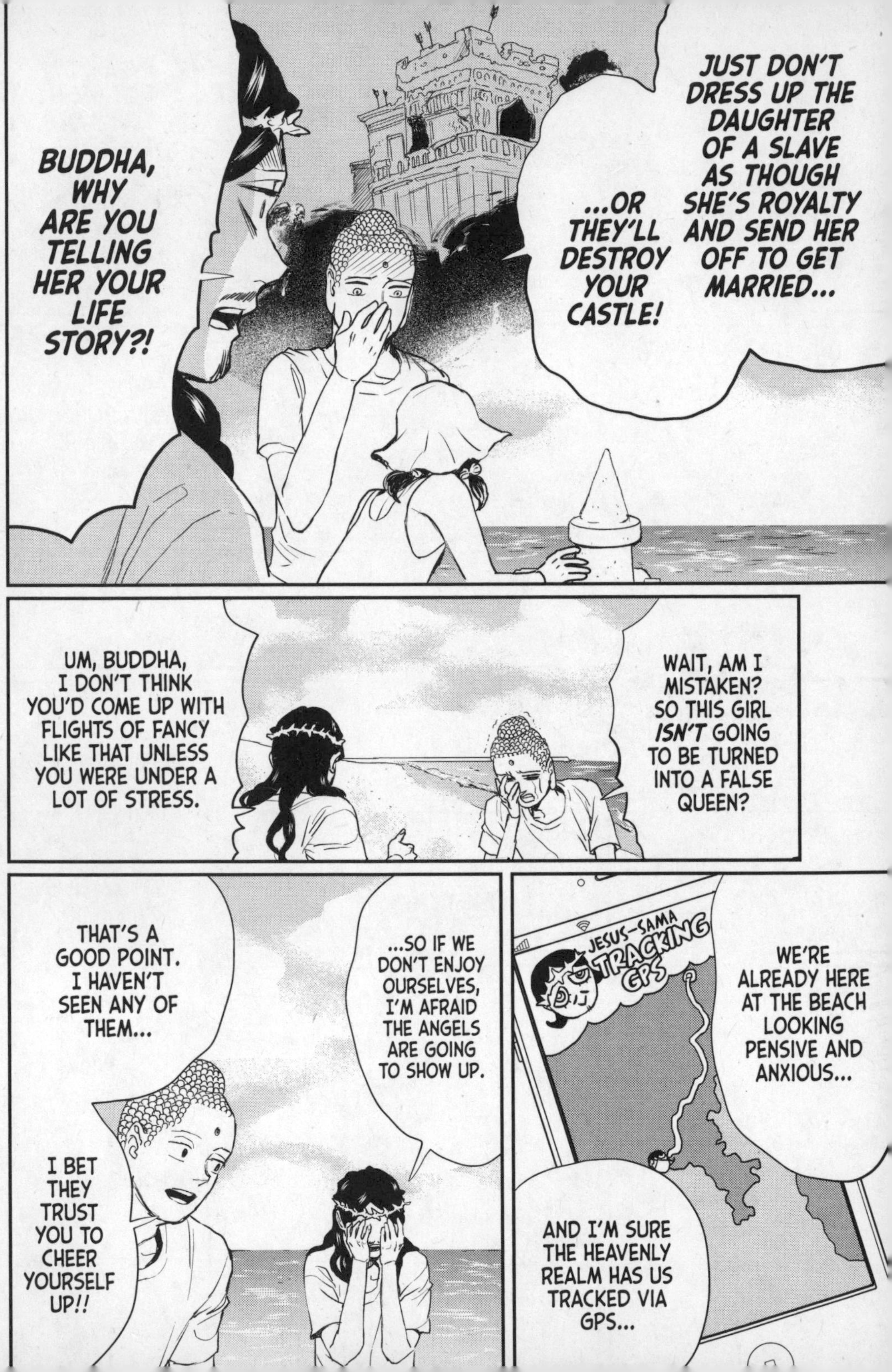
JUST DON'T DRESS UP THE DAUGHTER OF A SLAVE AS THOUGH SHE'S ROYALTY AND SEND HER OFF TO GET MARRIED...
...OR THEY'LL DESTROY YOUR CASTLE!
BUDDHA, WHY ARE YOU TELLING HER YOUR LIFE STORY?!
WAIT, AM I MISTAKEN? SO THIS GIRL *ISN'T* GOING TO BE TURNED INTO A FALSE QUEEN?
UM, BUDDHA, I DON'T THINK YOU'D COME UP WITH FLIGHTS OF FANCY LIKE THAT UNLESS YOU WERE UNDER A LOT OF STRESS.
WE'RE ALREADY HERE AT THE BEACH LOOKING PENSIVE AND ANXIOUS...
JESUS-SAMA TRACKING GPS
AND I'M SURE THE HEAVENLY REALM HAS US TRACKED VIA GPS...
...SO IF WE DON'T ENJOY OURSELVES, I'M AFRAID THE ANGELS ARE GOING TO SHOW UP.
THAT'S A GOOD POINT. I HAVEN'T SEEN ANY OF THEM...
I BET THEY TRUST YOU TO CHEER YOURSELF UP!!

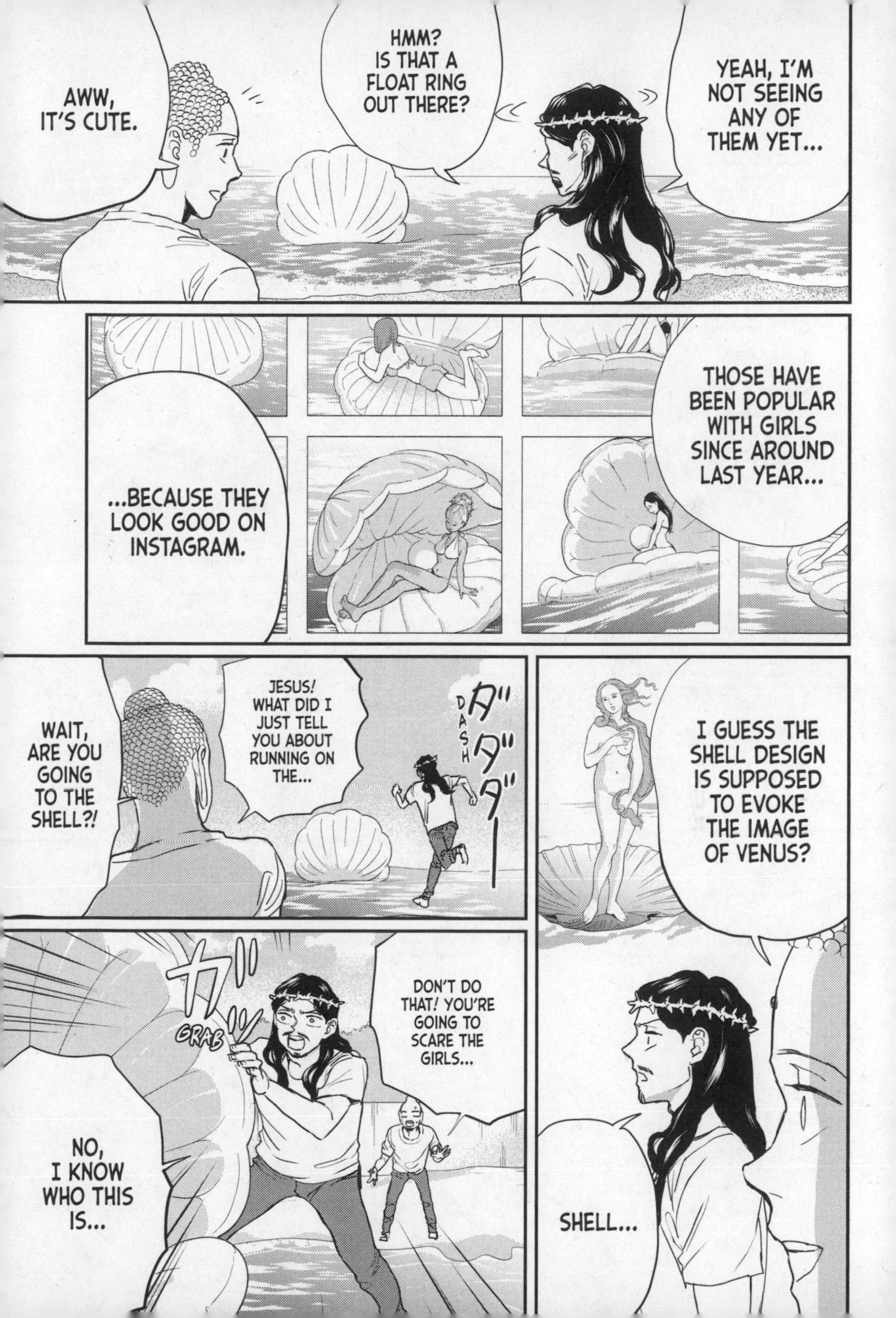
YEAH, I'M NOT SEEING ANY OF THEM YET...
HMM? IS THAT A FLOAT RING OUT THERE?
AWW, IT'S CUTE.
THOSE HAVE BEEN POPULAR WITH GIRLS SINCE AROUND LAST YEAR...
...BECAUSE THEY LOOK GOOD ON INSTAGRAM.
I GUESS THE SHELL DESIGN IS SUPPOSED TO EVOKE THE IMAGE OF VENUS?
SHELL...
WAIT, ARE YOU GOING TO THE SHELL?!
ダダダー
DASH
JESUS! WHAT DID I JUST TELL YOU ABOUT RUNNING ON THE...
DON'T DO THAT! YOU'RE GOING TO SCARE THE GIRLS...
ガッ
GRAB
NO, I KNOW WHO THIS IS...

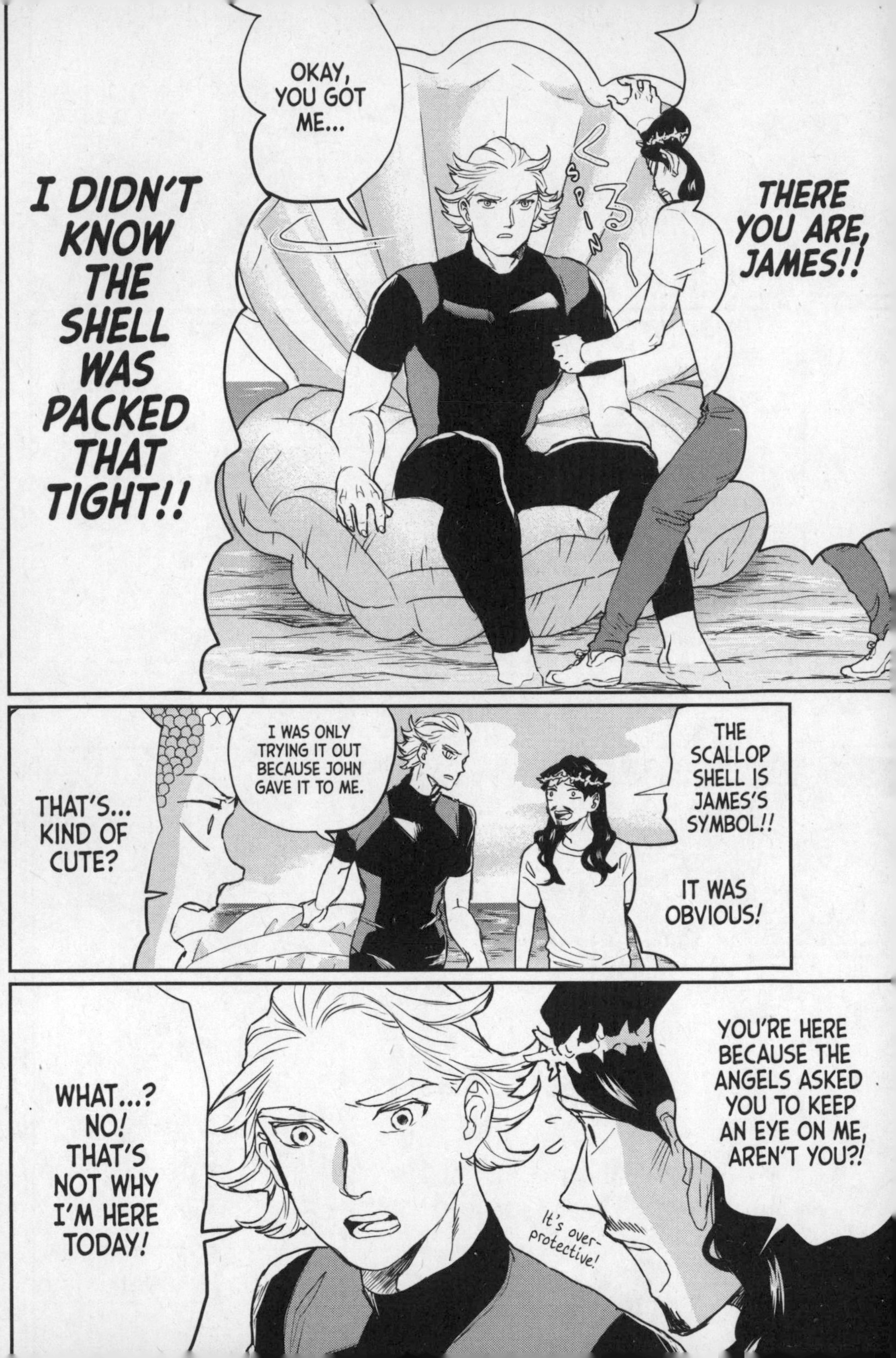
THERE YOU ARE, JAMES!!
SPIN
OKAY, YOU GOT ME...
I DIDN'T KNOW THE SHELL WAS PACKED THAT TIGHT!!
THE SCALLOP SHELL IS JAMES'S SYMBOL!!
IT WAS OBVIOUS!
I WAS ONLY TRYING IT OUT BECAUSE JOHN GAVE IT TO ME.
THAT'S... KIND OF CUTE?
YOU'RE HERE BECAUSE THE ANGELS ASKED YOU TO KEEP AN EYE ON ME, AREN'T YOU?!
It's over-protective!
WHAT...? NO! THAT'S NOT WHY I'M HERE TODAY!

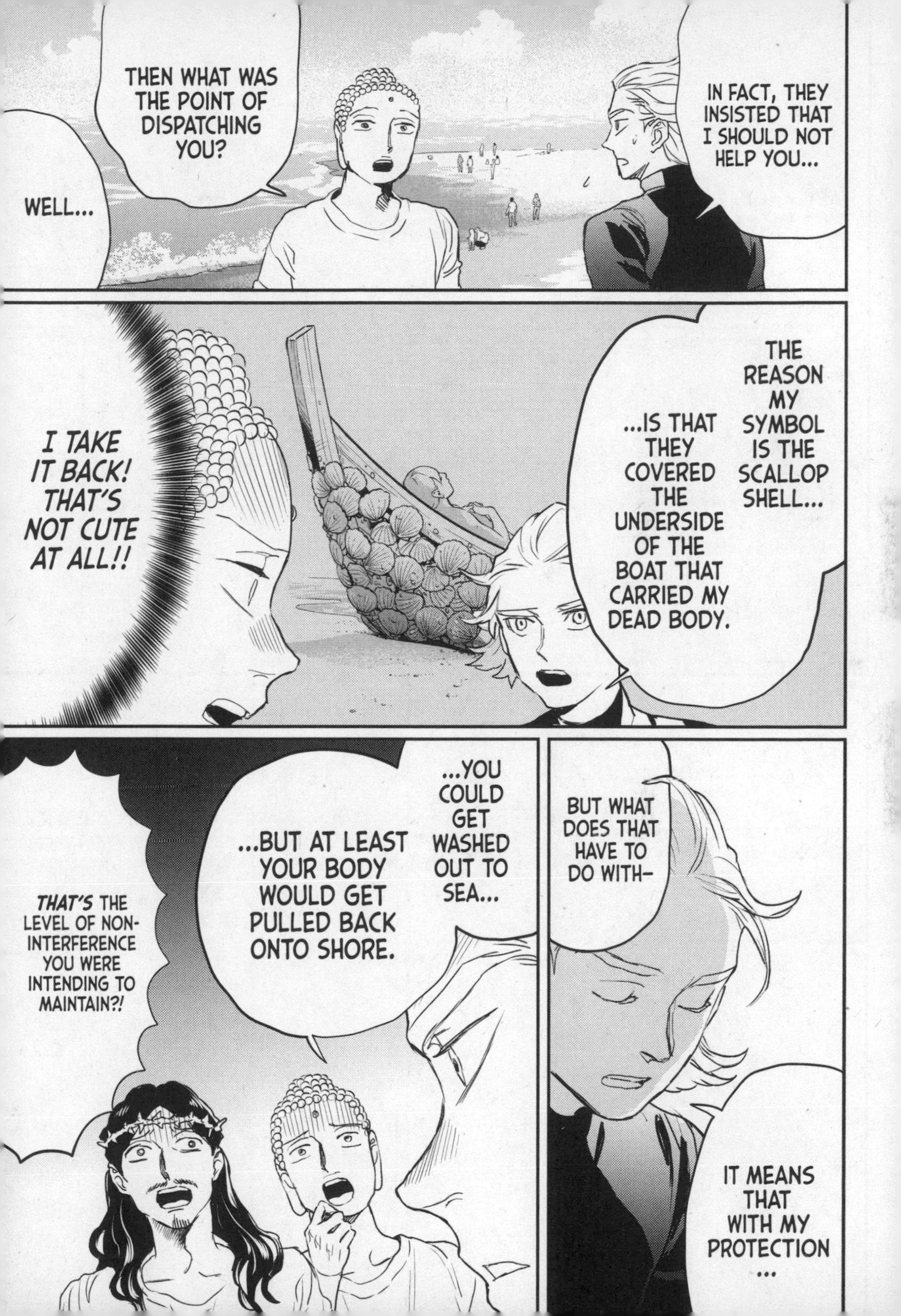
IN FACT, THEY INSISTED THAT I SHOULD NOT HELP YOU...
THEN WHAT WAS THE POINT OF DISPATCHING YOU?
WELL...
THE REASON MY SYMBOL IS THE SCALLOP SHELL...
...IS THAT THEY COVERED THE UNDERSIDE OF THE BOAT THAT CARRIED MY DEAD BODY.
I TAKE IT BACK! THAT'S NOT CUTE AT ALL!!
BUT WHAT DOES THAT HAVE TO DO WITH–
IT MEANS THAT WITH MY PROTECTION ...
...YOU COULD GET WASHED OUT TO SEA...
...BUT AT LEAST YOUR BODY WOULD GET PULLED BACK ONTO SHORE.
THAT'S THE LEVEL OF NON-INTERFERENCE YOU WERE INTENDING TO MAINTAIN?!

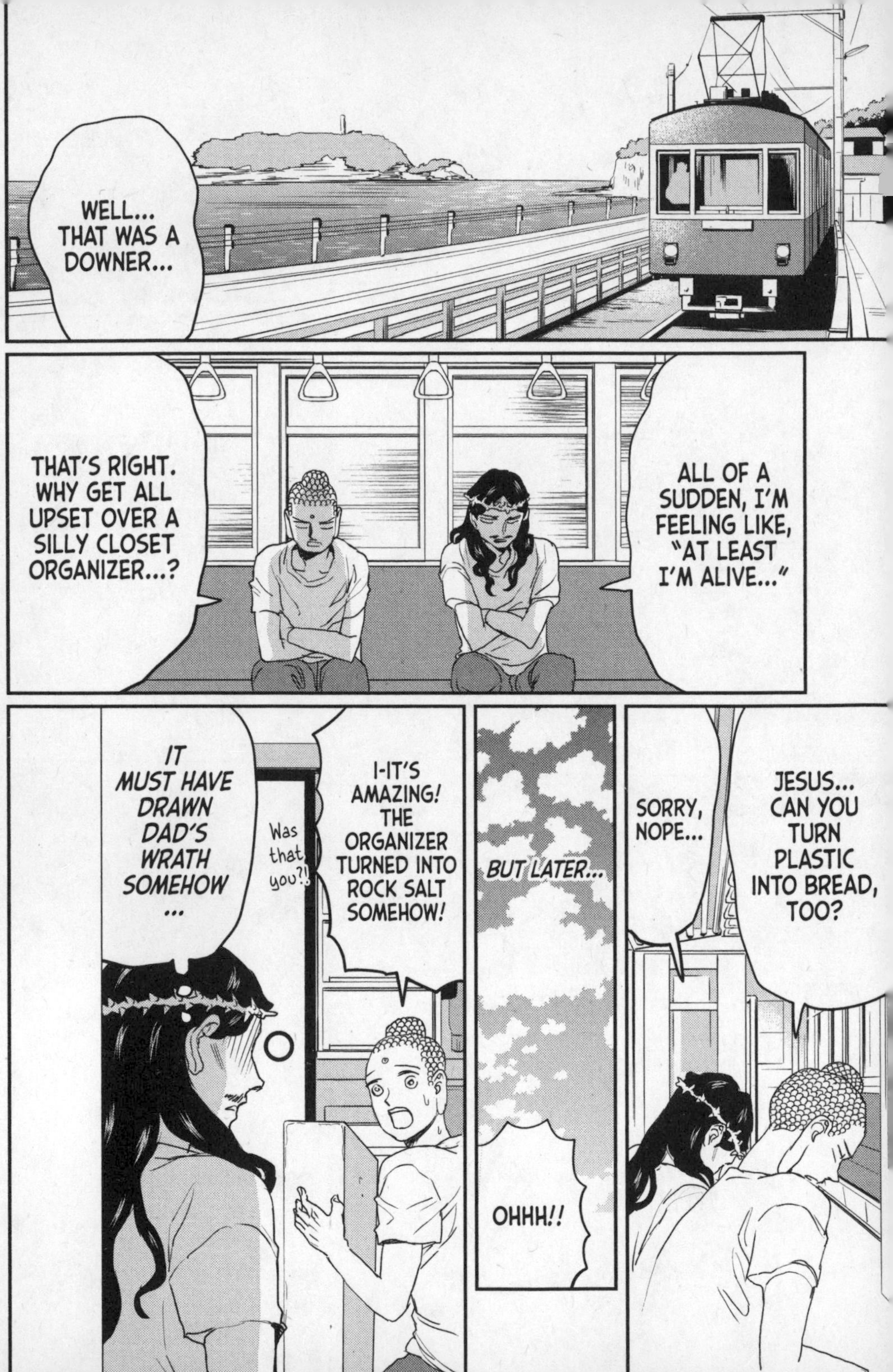
WELL... THAT WAS A DOWNER...
ALL OF A SUDDEN, I'M FEELING LIKE, "AT LEAST I'M ALIVE..."
THAT'S RIGHT. WHY GET ALL UPSET OVER A SILLY CLOSET ORGANIZER...?
JESUS... CAN YOU TURN PLASTIC INTO BREAD, TOO?
SORRY, NOPE...
BUT LATER...
OHHH!!
I-IT'S AMAZING! THE ORGANIZER TURNED INTO ROCK SALT SOMEHOW!
Was that you?!
IT MUST HAVE DRAWN DAD'S WRATH SOMEHOW...

John's Instagram
He really wanted to get in on that trend, didn't he...

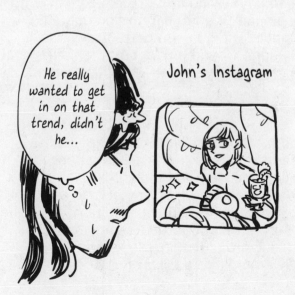

SAINT ✰ YOUNG MEN

CHAPTER 115 TRANSLATION NOTES

Methuselah's Children, page 190
The title of this chapter in Japanese, "Nagisa ni Matsuwaru Methuselah no Ko-ra," is a parody of a 1997 single by the pop duo Puffy AmiYumi, "Nagisa ni Matsuwaru Etcetera." The joke hinges on the similarity between Methuselah (*Metosera*) and Etcetera (*Etosetora*). in Biblical terms, the long-lived Methuselah is known for being the grandfather of Noah, whose ark preserved humanity through the great flood.

The Shakyas' downfall, page 194
Gautama Buddha's clan was the Shakyas, a small but proud people annexed by the larger but more recent Kosala kingdom. The king of Kosala wanted a new wife from the Shakyas because of their prestige, but the girl they wed to him turned out to have been the daughter of a slave. The son she bore, Virudhaka, learned the truth of his lineage when he came of age, and eventually had the Shakyas destroyed to avenge his shame.

Lot's wife, page 198
in the Book of Genesis, Lot was the nephew of Abraham, the patriarch of the "Abrahamic religions" (Judaism, Christianity, Islam). In the Book of Genesis, the parable of Sodom and Gomorrah tells of two cities that were to be destroyed for their wickedness. Just before this happened, Lot welcomed a pair of angels into his home in Sodom, where they urged him to flee the city and not look back. But in the process of fleeing, Lot's wife looked back in apparent longing for the life they were leaving behind, and was instantly turned into a pillar of salt.

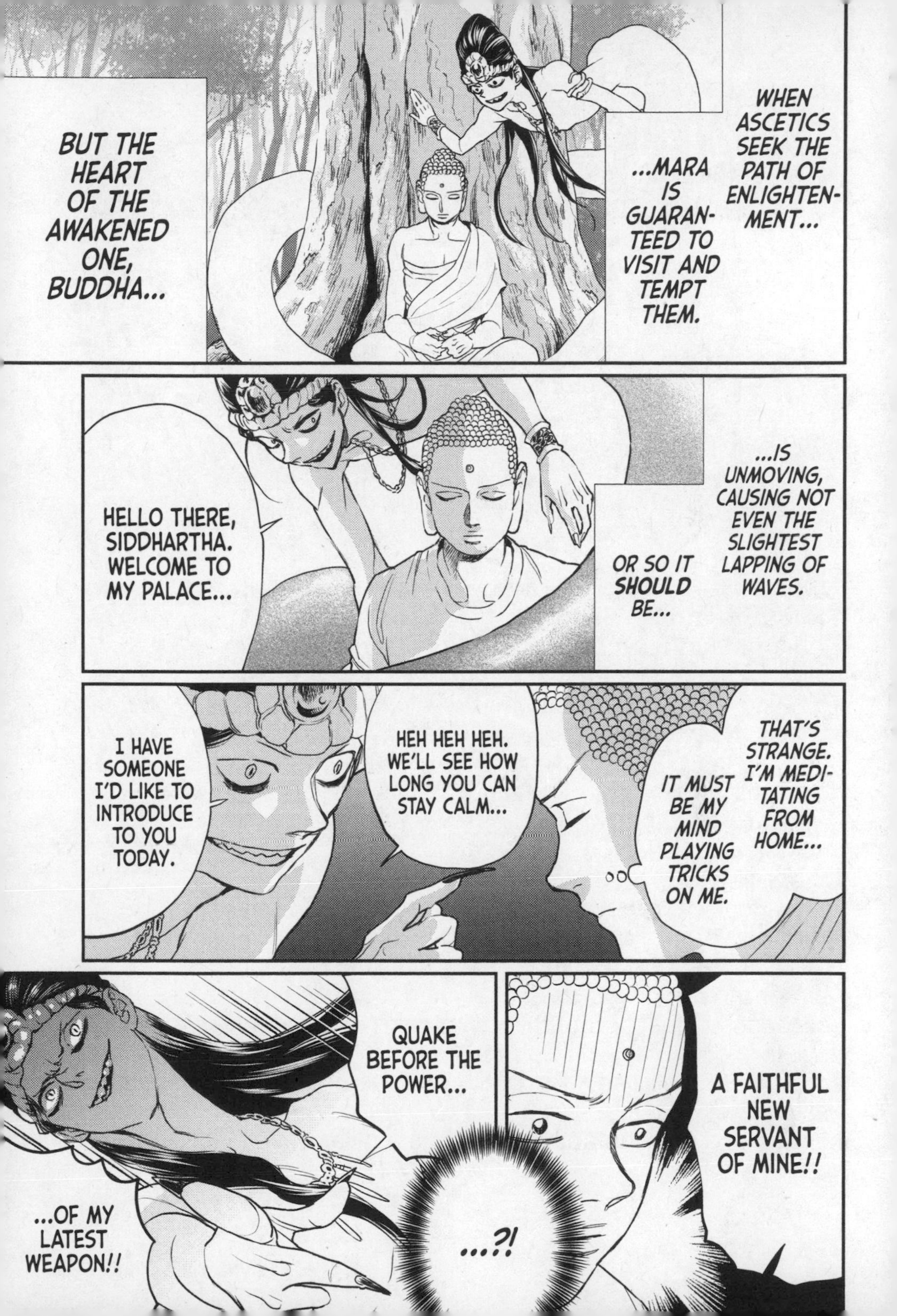
WHEN ASCETICS SEEK THE PATH OF ENLIGHTENMENT...
...MARA IS GUARANTEED TO VISIT AND TEMPT THEM.
BUT THE HEART OF THE AWAKENED ONE, BUDDHA...
...IS UNMOVING, CAUSING NOT EVEN THE SLIGHTEST LAPPING OF WAVES.
OR SO IT **SHOULD** BE...
HELLO THERE, SIDDHARTHA. WELCOME TO MY PALACE...
THAT'S STRANGE. I'M MEDITATING FROM HOME...
IT MUST BE MY MIND PLAYING TRICKS ON ME.
HEH HEH HEH. WE'LL SEE HOW LONG YOU CAN STAY CALM...
I HAVE SOMEONE I'D LIKE TO INTRODUCE TO YOU TODAY.
A FAITHFUL NEW SERVANT OF MINE!!
...?!
QUAKE BEFORE THE POWER...
...OF MY LATEST WEAPON!!

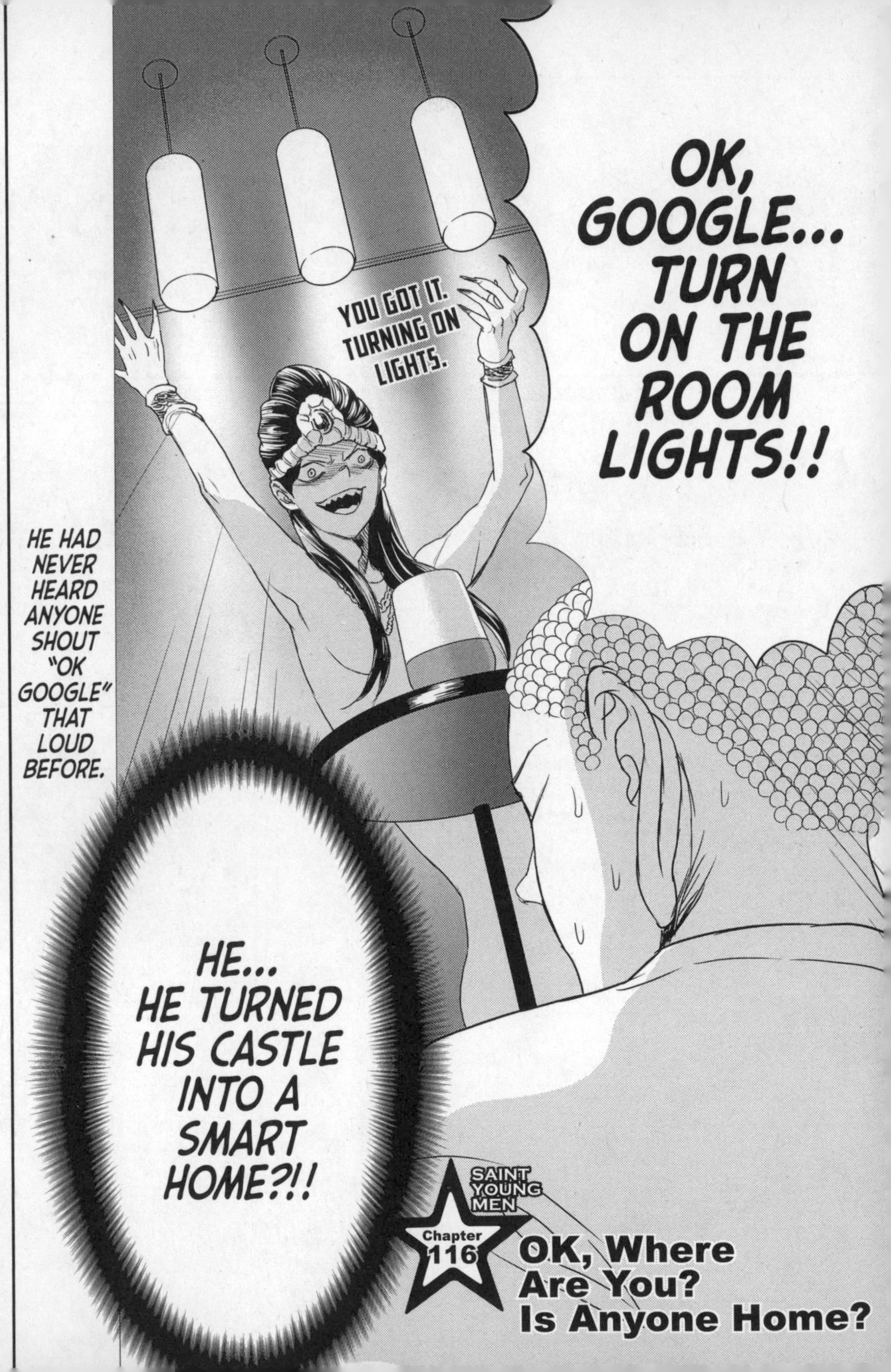
OK, GOOGLE... TURN ON THE ROOM LIGHTS!!
YOU GOT IT. TURNING ON LIGHTS.
HE HAD NEVER HEARD ANYONE SHOUT "OK GOOGLE" THAT LOUD BEFORE.
HE... HE TURNED HIS CASTLE INTO A SMART HOME?!!
SAINT YOUNG MEN
Chapter 116
OK, Where Are You? Is Anyone Home?

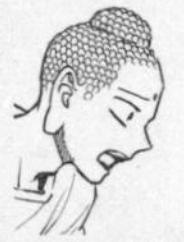

BUDDHA
I'M GLAD IT DIDN'T RESPOND TO THE REQUEST, "RECITE A SUTRA." AS FOR "RECITE A HYMN"... WELL, I DON'T NEED TO TELL JESUS ABOUT THAT. (AS OF JUNE 2018)

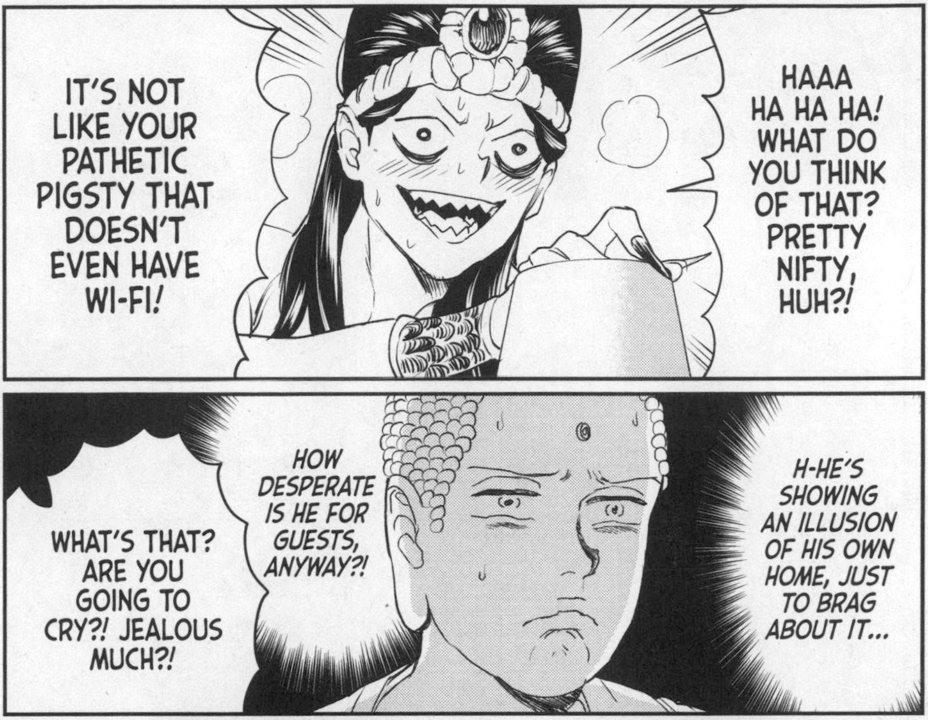
HAAAA HA HA HA! WHAT DO YOU THINK OF THAT? PRETTY NIFTY, HUH?!
IT'S NOT LIKE YOUR PATHETIC PIGSTY THAT DOESN'T EVEN HAVE WI-FI!
H-HE'S SHOWING AN ILLUSION OF HIS OWN HOME, JUST TO BRAG ABOUT IT...
HOW DESPERATE IS HE FOR GUESTS, ANYWAY?!
WHAT'S THAT? ARE YOU GOING TO CRY?! JEALOUS MUCH?!

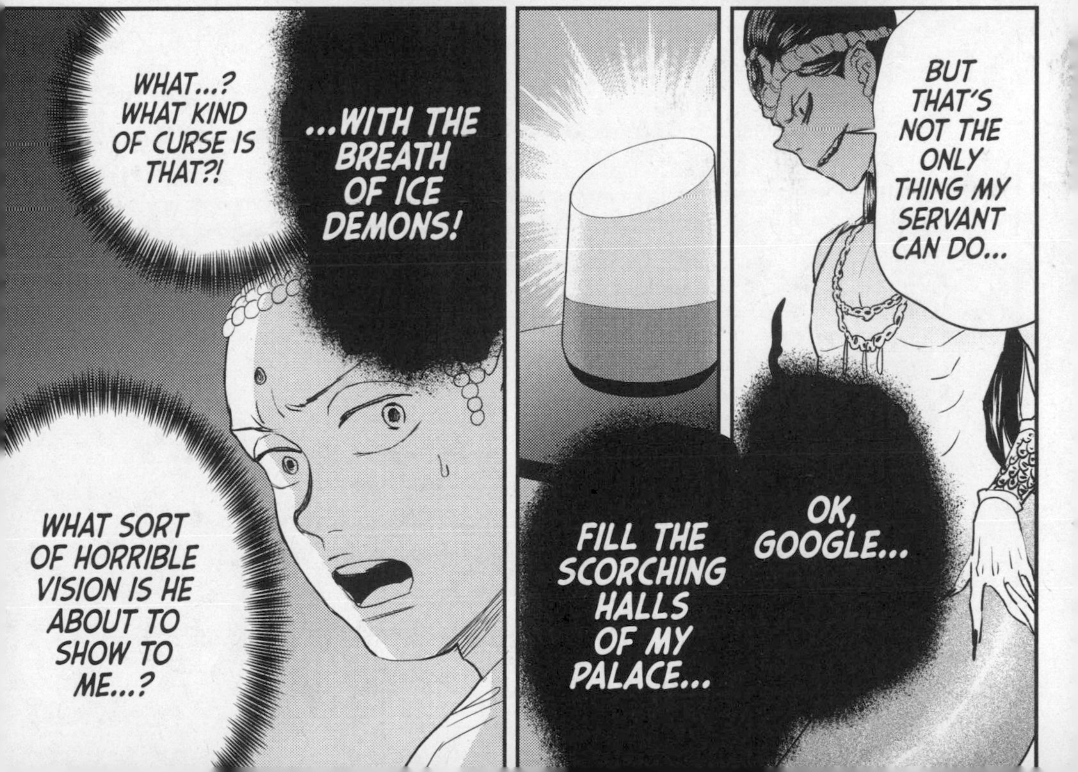
BUT THAT'S NOT THE ONLY THING MY SERVANT CAN DO...
OK, GOOGLE...
FILL THE SCORCHING HALLS OF MY PALACE...
...WITH THE BREATH OF ICE DEMONS!
WHAT...? WHAT KIND OF CURSE IS THAT?!
WHAT SORT OF HORRIBLE VISION IS HE ABOUT TO SHOW TO ME...?

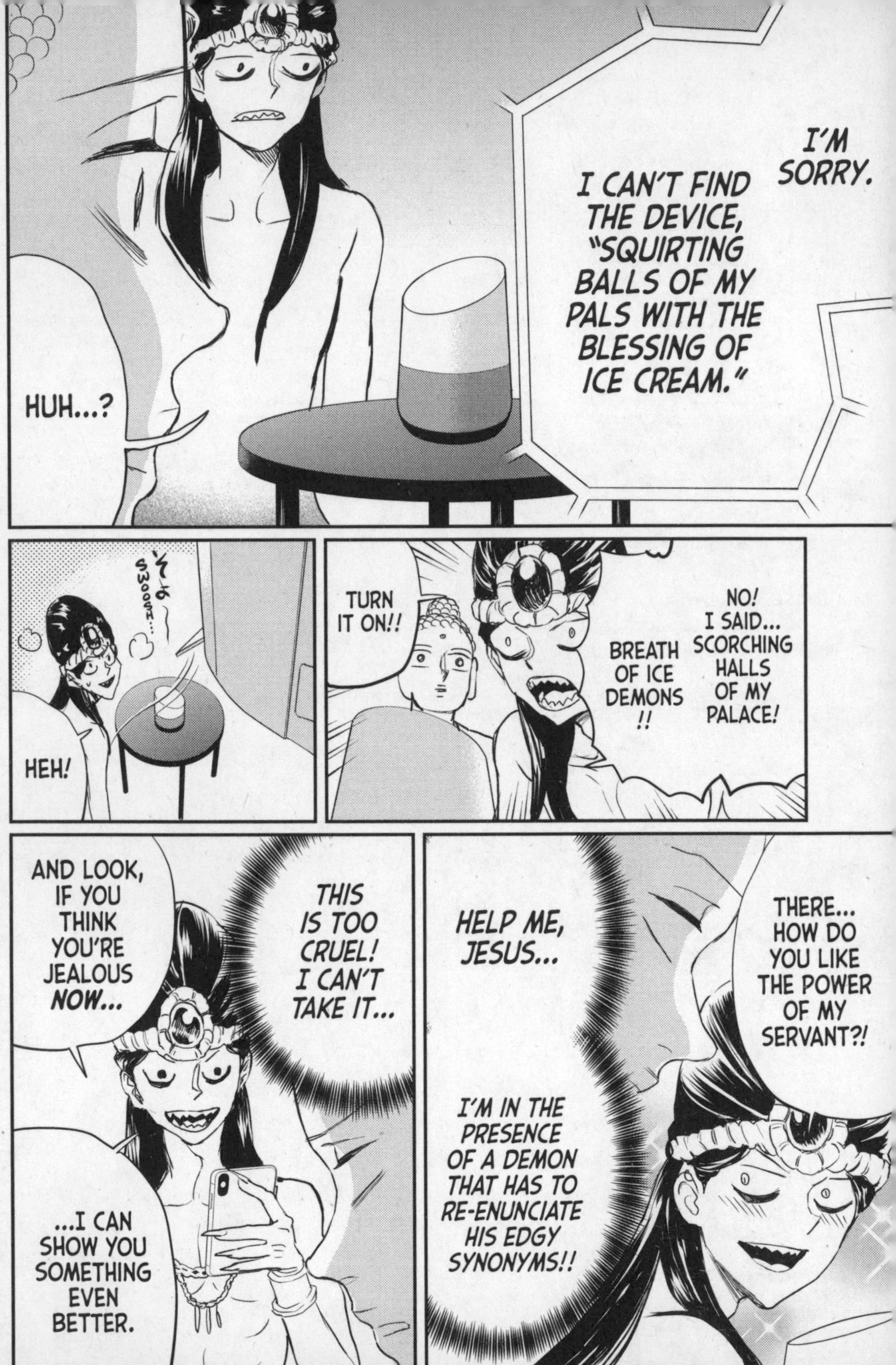
I'M SORRY.
I CAN'T FIND THE DEVICE, "SQUIRTING BALLS OF MY PALS WITH THE BLESSING OF ICE CREAM."
HUH...?
NO! I SAID... SCORCHING HALLS OF MY PALACE!
BREATH OF ICE DEMONS!!
TURN IT ON!!
SWOOSH...
HEH!
THERE... HOW DO YOU LIKE THE POWER OF MY SERVANT?!
HELP ME, JESUS...
I'M IN THE PRESENCE OF A DEMON THAT HAS TO RE-ENUNCIATE HIS EDGY SYNONYMS!!
THIS IS TOO CRUEL! I CAN'T TAKE IT...
AND LOOK, IF YOU THINK YOU'RE JEALOUS NOW...
...I CAN SHOW YOU SOMETHING EVEN BETTER.

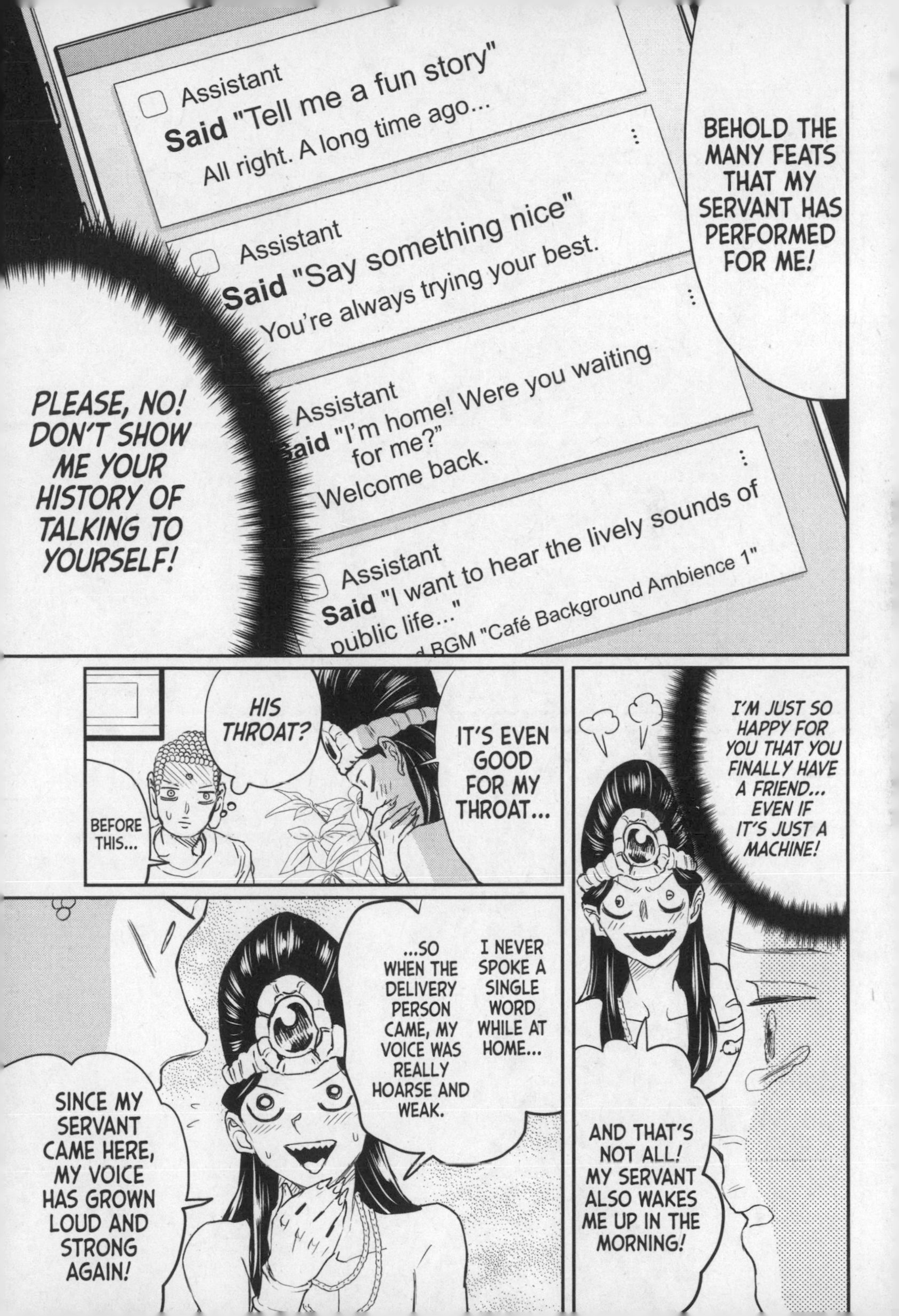

BEHOLD THE MANY FEATS THAT MY SERVANT HAS PERFORMED FOR ME!
Assistant
Said "Tell me a fun story"
All right. A long time ago...
Assistant
Said "Say something nice"
You're always trying your best.
Assistant
Said "I'm home! Were you waiting for me?"
Welcome back.
Assistant
Said "I want to hear the lively sounds of public life..."
BGM "Café Background Ambience 1"
PLEASE, NO! DON'T SHOW ME YOUR HISTORY OF TALKING TO YOURSELF!
I'M JUST SO HAPPY FOR YOU THAT YOU FINALLY HAVE A FRIEND... EVEN IF IT'S JUST A MACHINE!
AND THAT'S NOT ALL! MY SERVANT ALSO WAKES ME UP IN THE MORNING!
IT'S EVEN GOOD FOR MY THROAT...
HIS THROAT?
BEFORE THIS...
I NEVER SPOKE A SINGLE WORD WHILE AT HOME...
...SO WHEN THE DELIVERY PERSON CAME, MY VOICE WAS REALLY HOARSE AND WEAK.
SINCE MY SERVANT CAME HERE, MY VOICE HAS GROWN LOUD AND STRONG AGAIN!

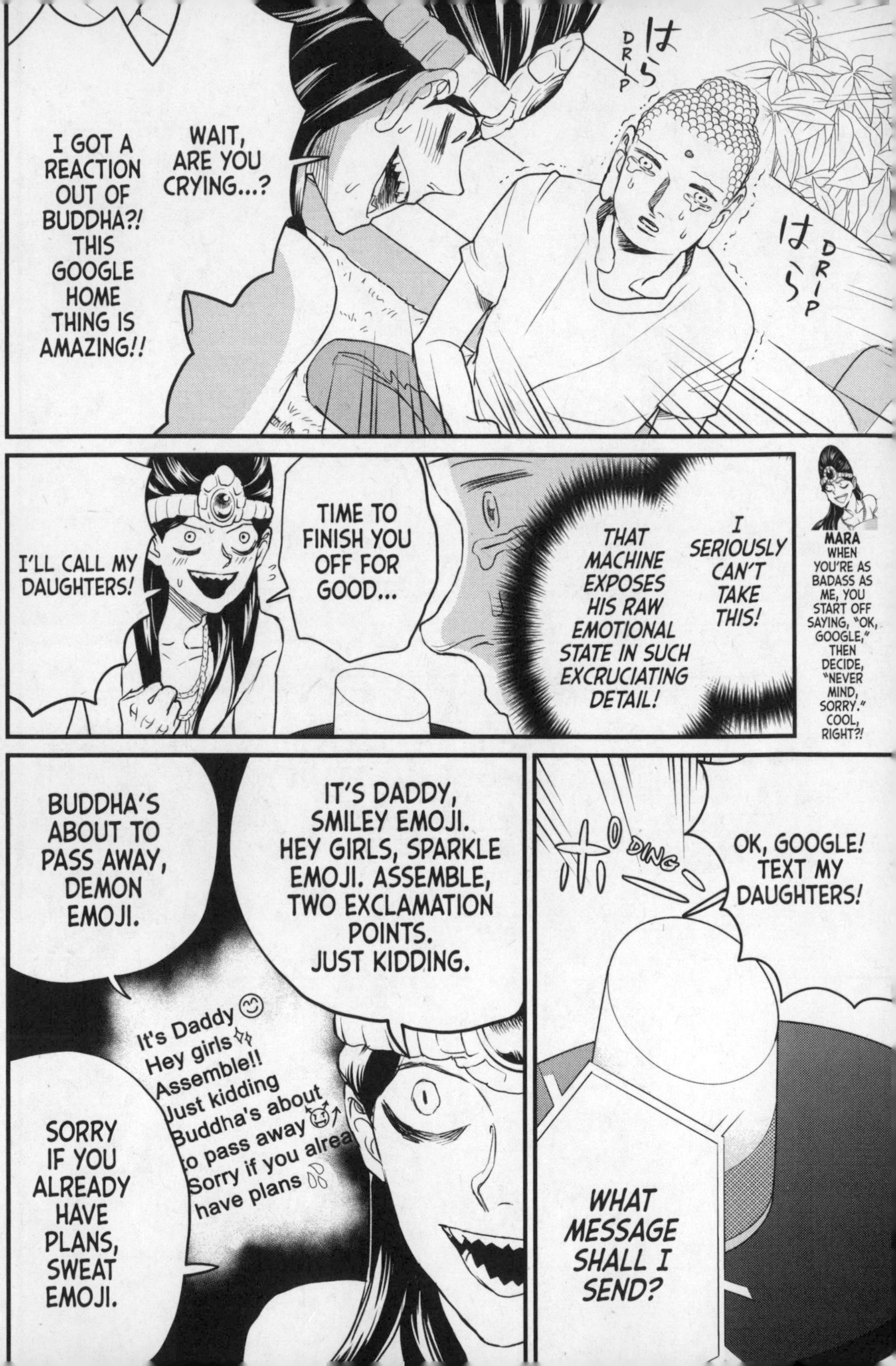
はら DRIP
はら DRIP
WAIT, ARE YOU CRYING...?
I GOT A REACTION OUT OF BUDDHA?! THIS GOOGLE HOME THING IS AMAZING!!
MARA
WHEN YOU'RE AS BADASS AS ME, YOU START OFF SAYING, "OK, GOOGLE," THEN DECIDE, "NEVER MIND, SORRY." COOL, RIGHT?!
I SERIOUSLY CAN'T TAKE THIS!
THAT MACHINE EXPOSES HIS RAW EMOTIONAL STATE IN SUCH EXCRUCIATING DETAIL!
TIME TO FINISH YOU OFF FOR GOOD...
I'LL CALL MY DAUGHTERS!
OK, GOOGLE! TEXT MY DAUGHTERS!
DING
WHAT MESSAGE SHALL I SEND?
IT'S DADDY, SMILEY EMOJI. HEY GIRLS, SPARKLE EMOJI. ASSEMBLE, TWO EXCLAMATION POINTS. JUST KIDDING.
BUDDHA'S ABOUT TO PASS AWAY, DEMON EMOJI.
It's Daddy
Hey girls
Assemble!!
Just kidding
Buddha's about
to pass away
Sorry if you alrea
have plans
SORRY IF YOU ALREADY HAVE PLANS, SWEAT EMOJI.

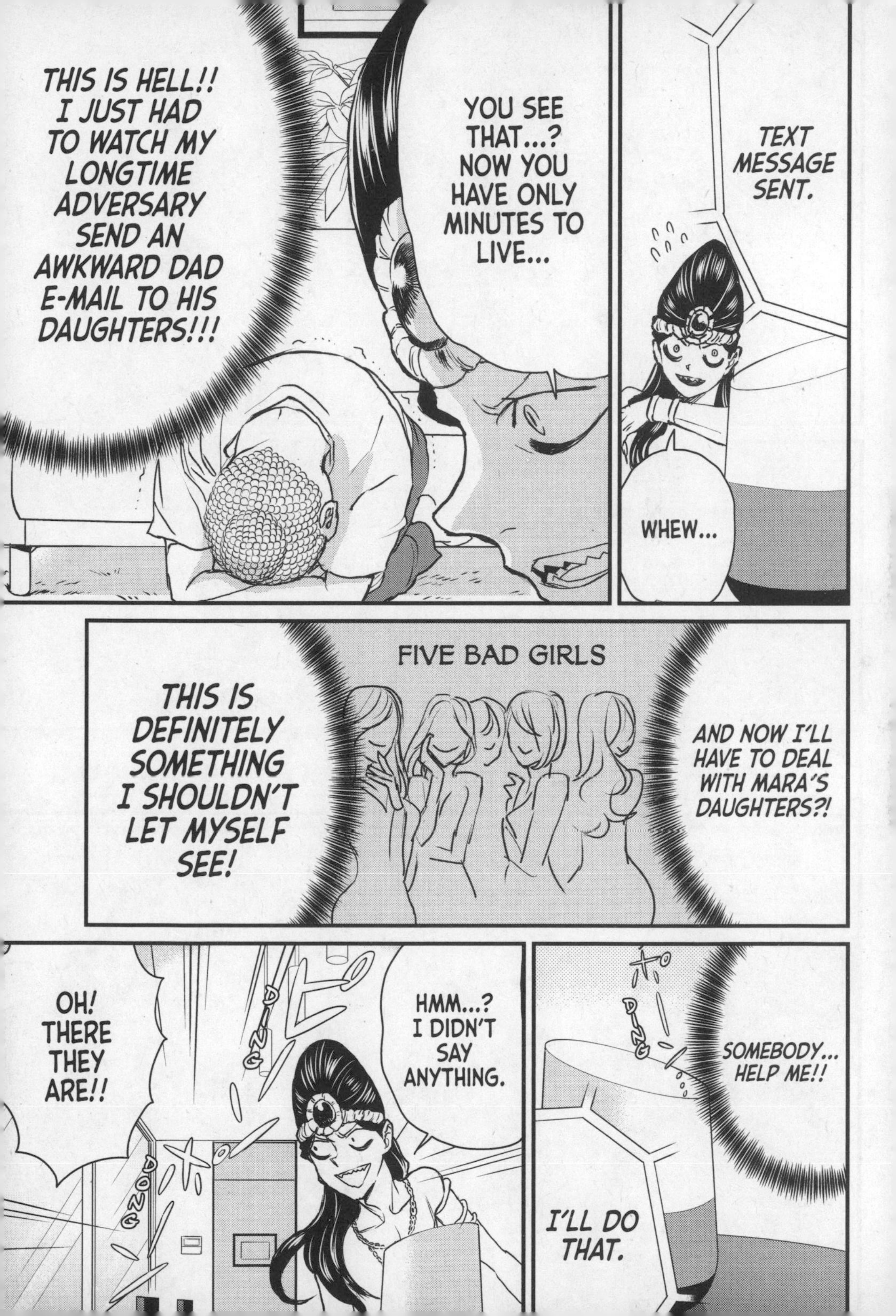
TEXT MESSAGE SENT.
WHEW...
YOU SEE THAT...? NOW YOU HAVE ONLY MINUTES TO LIVE...
THIS IS HELL!! I JUST HAD TO WATCH MY LONGTIME ADVERSARY SEND AN AWKWARD DAD E-MAIL TO HIS DAUGHTERS!!!
FIVE BAD GIRLS
AND NOW I'LL HAVE TO DEAL WITH MARA'S DAUGHTERS?!
THIS IS DEFINITELY SOMETHING I SHOULDN'T LET MYSELF SEE!
DING
SOMEBODY... HELP ME!!
I'LL DO THAT.
HMM...? I DIDN'T SAY ANYTHING.
DING
OH! THERE THEY ARE!!
DONG

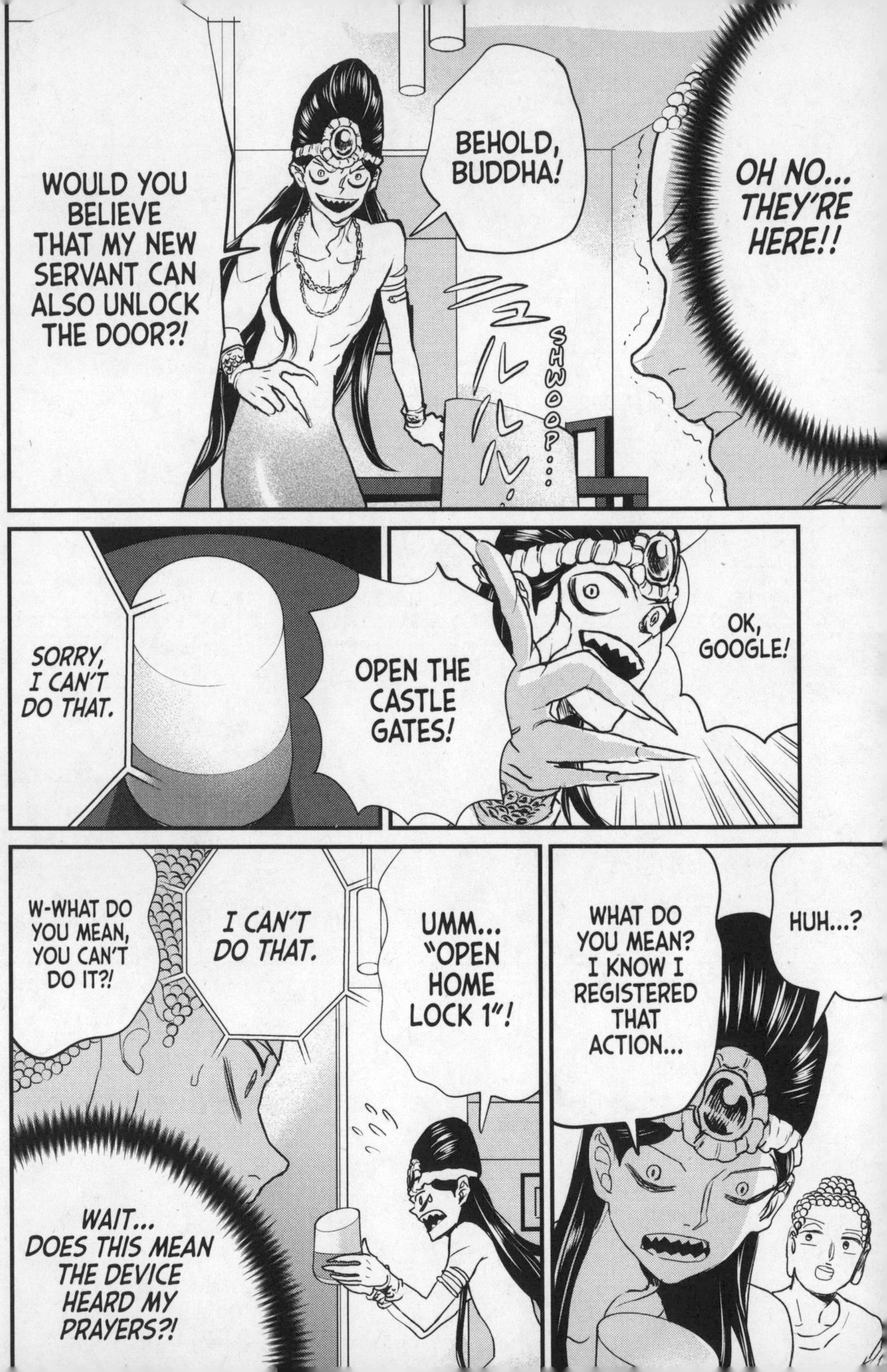
OH NO... THEY'RE HERE!!
BEHOLD, BUDDHA!
WOULD YOU BELIEVE THAT MY NEW SERVANT CAN ALSO UNLOCK THE DOOR?!
SHWOOP...
OK, GOOGLE!
OPEN THE CASTLE GATES!
SORRY, I CAN'T DO THAT.
HUH...?
WHAT DO YOU MEAN? I KNOW I REGISTERED THAT ACTION...
UMM... "OPEN HOME LOCK 1"!
I CAN'T DO THAT.
W-WHAT DO YOU MEAN, YOU CAN'T DO IT?!
WAIT... DOES THIS MEAN THE DEVICE HEARD MY PRAYERS?!

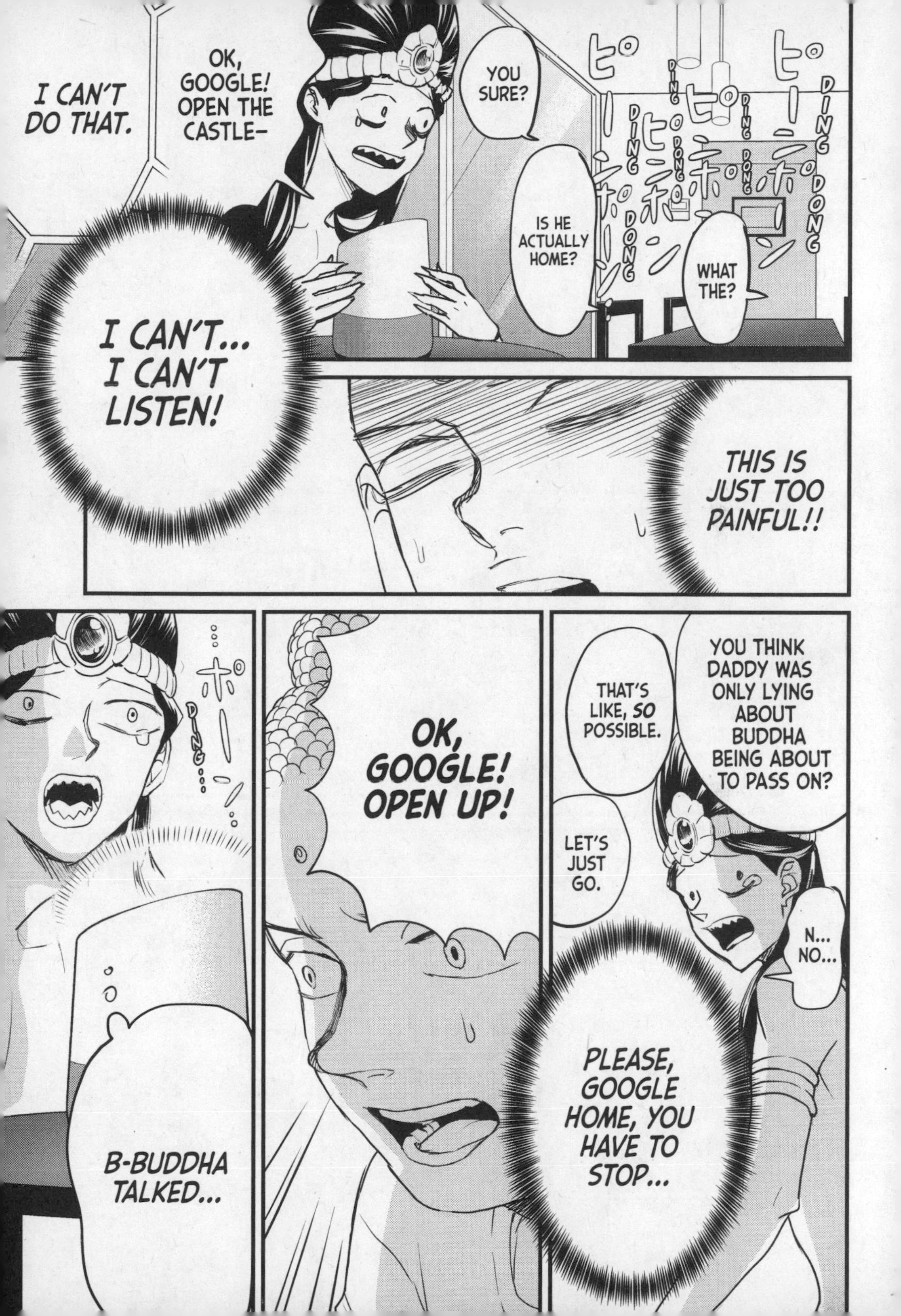
DING DONG
DING DONG
DING DONG
DING DONG
WHAT THE?
YOU SURE?
IS HE ACTUALLY HOME?
OK, GOOGLE! OPEN THE CASTLE–
I CAN'T DO THAT.
I CAN'T... I CAN'T LISTEN!
THIS IS JUST TOO PAINFUL!!
YOU THINK DADDY WAS ONLY LYING ABOUT BUDDHA BEING ABOUT TO PASS ON?
THAT'S LIKE, SO POSSIBLE.
LET'S JUST GO.
N... NO...
PLEASE, GOOGLE HOME, YOU HAVE TO STOP...
OK, GOOGLE! OPEN UP!
DING
B-BUDDHA TALKED...

#ENLIGHTENMENT

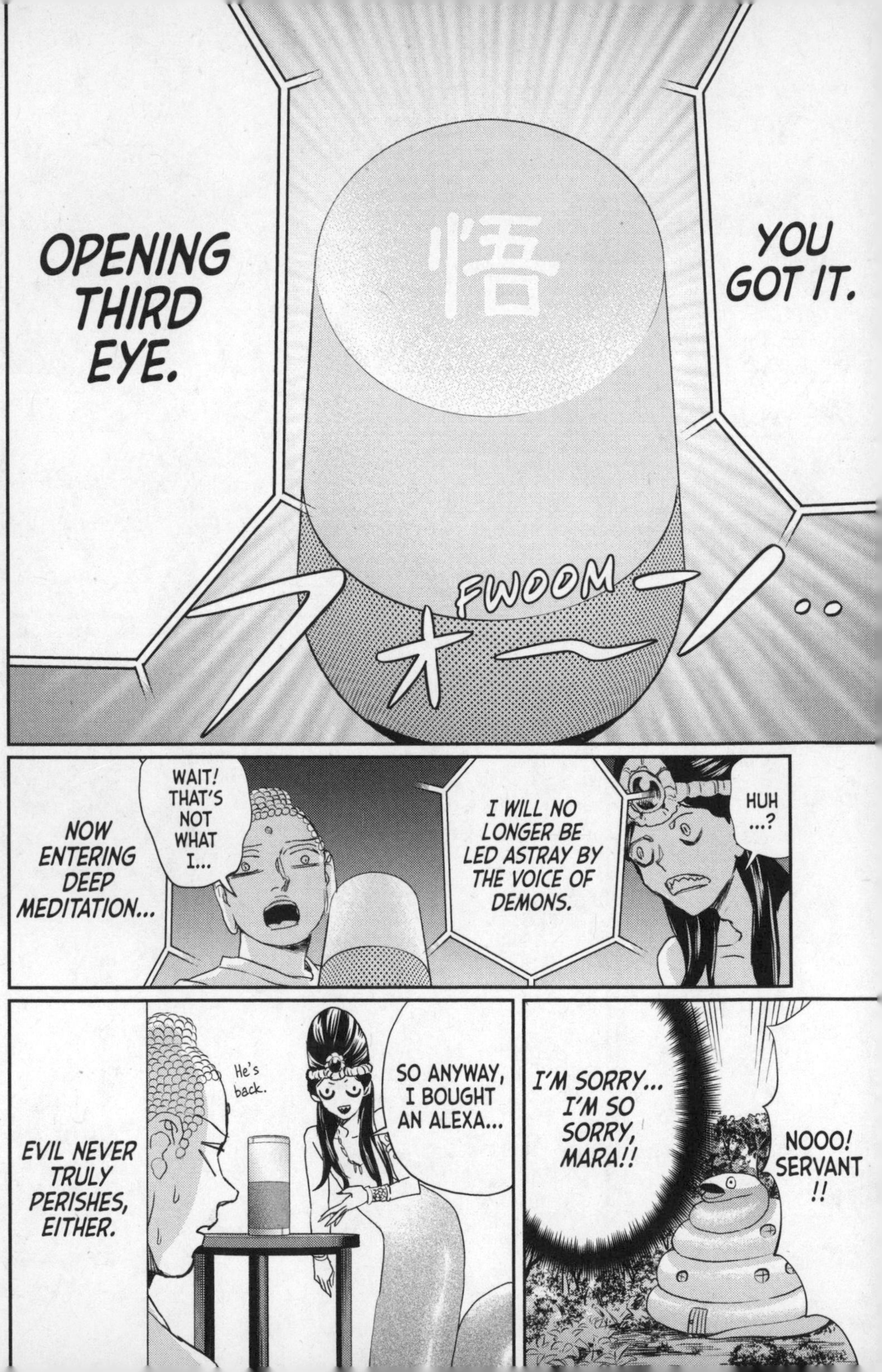
YOU GOT IT.
OPENING THIRD EYE.
悟
FWOOM
HUH ...?
I WILL NO LONGER BE LED ASTRAY BY THE VOICE OF DEMONS.
WAIT! THAT'S NOT WHAT I...
NOW ENTERING DEEP MEDITATION...
NOOO! SERVANT !!
I'M SORRY... I'M SO SORRY, MARA!!
SO ANYWAY, I BOUGHT AN ALEXA...
He's back.
EVIL NEVER TRULY PERISHES, EITHER.

Kan-ji-zai-bo-satsu -gyo-jin-han-nya-ha-ra-mi-ta-ji-sho-han-ho-on-kai-ku-do-is-sai-ku-ya-ku-sha-ri-shi-shiki-fu-i-ku-ku-fu-i...
The Enlightened Google Home
It only recites sutras now...

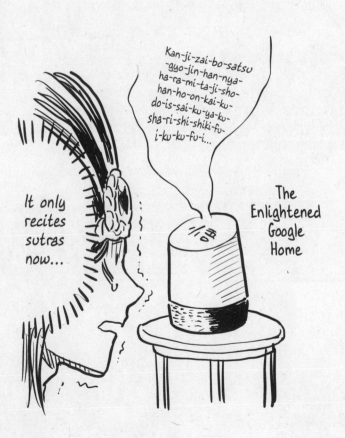

SAINT ☆ YOUNG MEN

CHAPTER 116 TRANSLATION NOTES

Mara's daughters, page 207

One of the most famous stories of Mara's attempted temptations of the Buddha involves the use of his daughters to seduce Gautama as he awaited enlightenment under the Bo tree. The number of Mara's daughters depends on the telling of the story, but is most often considered to be three, representing thirst, desire, and delight.

The Heart Sutra, page 211

The Heart Sutra is one of the most important texts in Mahayana Buddhism. It is one of the shortest sutras and addresses themes of emptiness and the nature of the Buddhist teachings themselves. It is often chanted by monks at funerals and other occasions, and is sometimes recited or copied for its protective power.

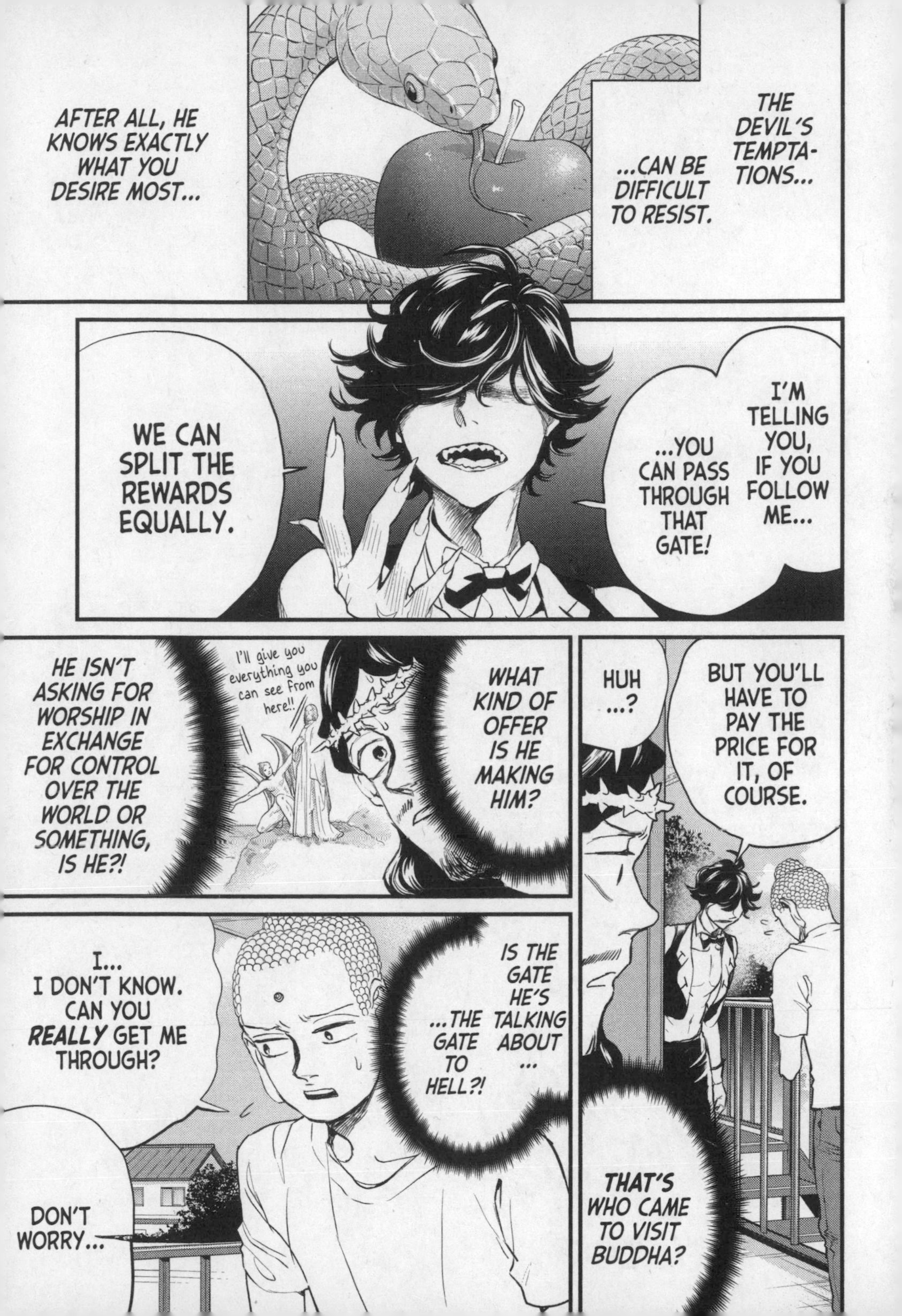
THE DEVIL'S TEMPTATIONS...
...CAN BE DIFFICULT TO RESIST.
AFTER ALL, HE KNOWS EXACTLY WHAT YOU DESIRE MOST...
I'M TELLING YOU, IF YOU FOLLOW ME...
...YOU CAN PASS THROUGH THAT GATE!
WE CAN SPLIT THE REWARDS EQUALLY.
BUT YOU'LL HAVE TO PAY THE PRICE FOR IT, OF COURSE.
HUH ...?
THAT'S WHO CAME TO VISIT BUDDHA?
WHAT KIND OF OFFER IS HE MAKING HIM?
I'll give you everything you can see from here!!
HE ISN'T ASKING FOR WORSHIP IN EXCHANGE FOR CONTROL OVER THE WORLD OR SOMETHING, IS HE?!
IS THE GATE HE'S TALKING ABOUT...
...THE GATE TO HELL?!
I... I DON'T KNOW. CAN YOU REALLY GET ME THROUGH?
DON'T WORRY...

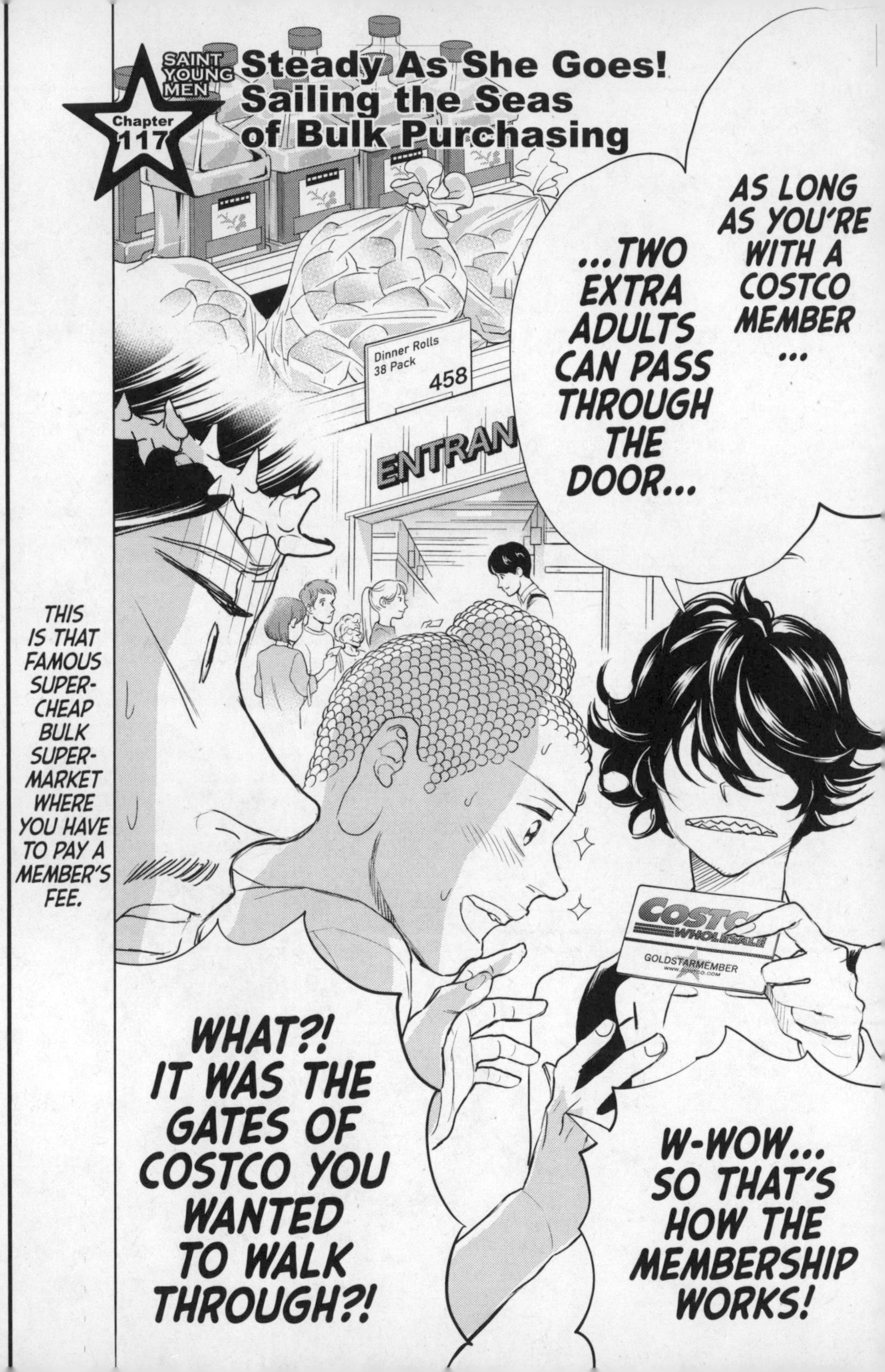
SAINT YOUNG MEN
Chapter 117
Steady As She Goes! Sailing the Seas of Bulk Purchasing
AS LONG AS YOU'RE WITH A COSTCO MEMBER ...
...TWO EXTRA ADULTS CAN PASS THROUGH THE DOOR...
Dinner Rolls 38 Pack 458
ENTRAN
THIS IS THAT FAMOUS SUPER-CHEAP BULK SUPER-MARKET WHERE YOU HAVE TO PAY A MEMBER'S FEE.
COSTCO WHOLESALE
GOLDSTARMEMBER
W-WOW... SO THAT'S HOW THE MEMBERSHIP WORKS!
WHAT?! IT WAS THE GATES OF COSTCO YOU WANTED TO WALK THROUGH?!

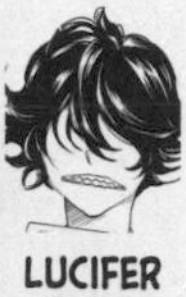

LUCIFER I LIKE LONGER TRIPS, BECAUSE YOU CAN SHARE THE EXCITEMENT OF ANTICIPATION AND SATISFACTION WITH EVERYONE COMING AND GOING. YOU'RE GOING FOR THE EXPERIENCE, NOT THINGS!

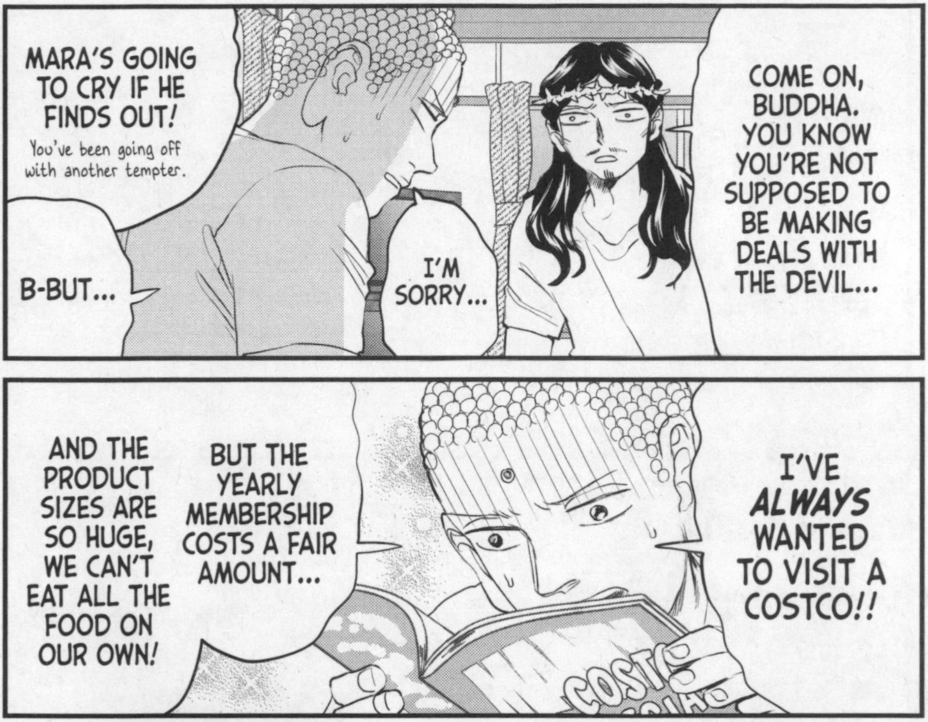
COME ON, BUDDHA. YOU KNOW YOU'RE NOT SUPPOSED TO BE MAKING DEALS WITH THE DEVIL...
I'M SORRY...
MARA'S GOING TO CRY IF HE FINDS OUT!
You've been going off with another tempter.
B-BUT...
I'VE *ALWAYS* WANTED TO VISIT A COSTCO!!
BUT THE YEARLY MEMBERSHIP COSTS A FAIR AMOUNT...
AND THE PRODUCT SIZES ARE SO HUGE, WE CAN'T EAT ALL THE FOOD ON OUR OWN!

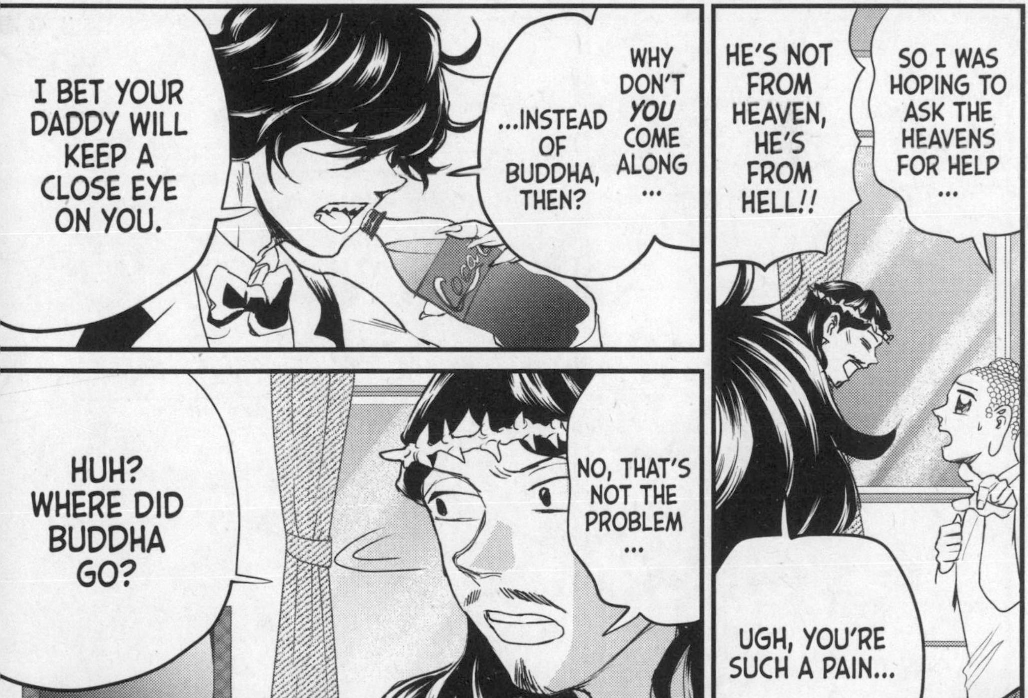
SO I WAS HOPING TO ASK THE HEAVENS FOR HELP ...
HE'S NOT FROM HEAVEN, HE'S FROM HELL!!
UGH, YOU'RE SUCH A PAIN...
WHY DON'T *YOU* COME ALONG ...
...INSTEAD OF BUDDHA, THEN?
I BET YOUR DADDY WILL KEEP A CLOSE EYE ON YOU.
NO, THAT'S NOT THE PROBLEM ...
HUH? WHERE DID BUDDHA GO?

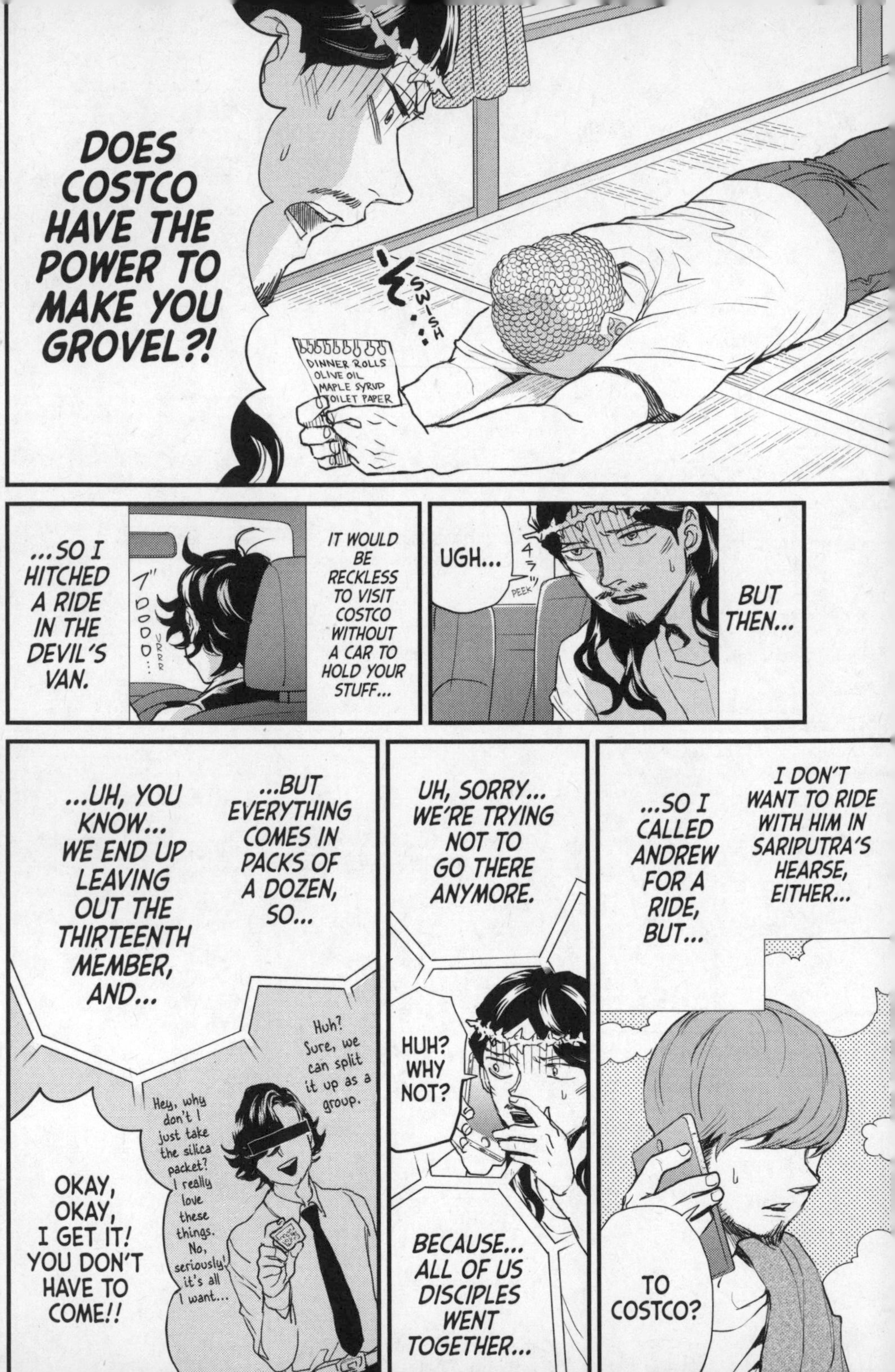
DOES COSTCO HAVE THE POWER TO MAKE YOU GROVEL?!
SWISH
DINNER ROLLS
OLIVE OIL
MAPLE SYRUP
TOILET PAPER
BUT THEN...
UGH...
PEEK
IT WOULD BE RECKLESS TO VISIT COSTCO WITHOUT A CAR TO HOLD YOUR STUFF...
...SO I HITCHED A RIDE IN THE DEVIL'S VAN.
I DON'T WANT TO RIDE WITH HIM IN SARIPUTRA'S HEARSE, EITHER...
...SO I CALLED ANDREW FOR A RIDE, BUT...
TO COSTCO?
UH, SORRY... WE'RE TRYING NOT TO GO THERE ANYMORE.
HUH? WHY NOT?
BECAUSE... ALL OF US DISCIPLES WENT TOGETHER...
...BUT EVERYTHING COMES IN PACKS OF A DOZEN, SO...
...UH, YOU KNOW... WE END UP LEAVING OUT THE THIRTEENTH MEMBER, AND...
Huh? Sure, we can split it up as a group.
Hey, why don't I just take the silica packet? I really love these things. No, seriously! it's all I want...
OKAY, OKAY, I GET IT! YOU DON'T HAVE TO COME!!

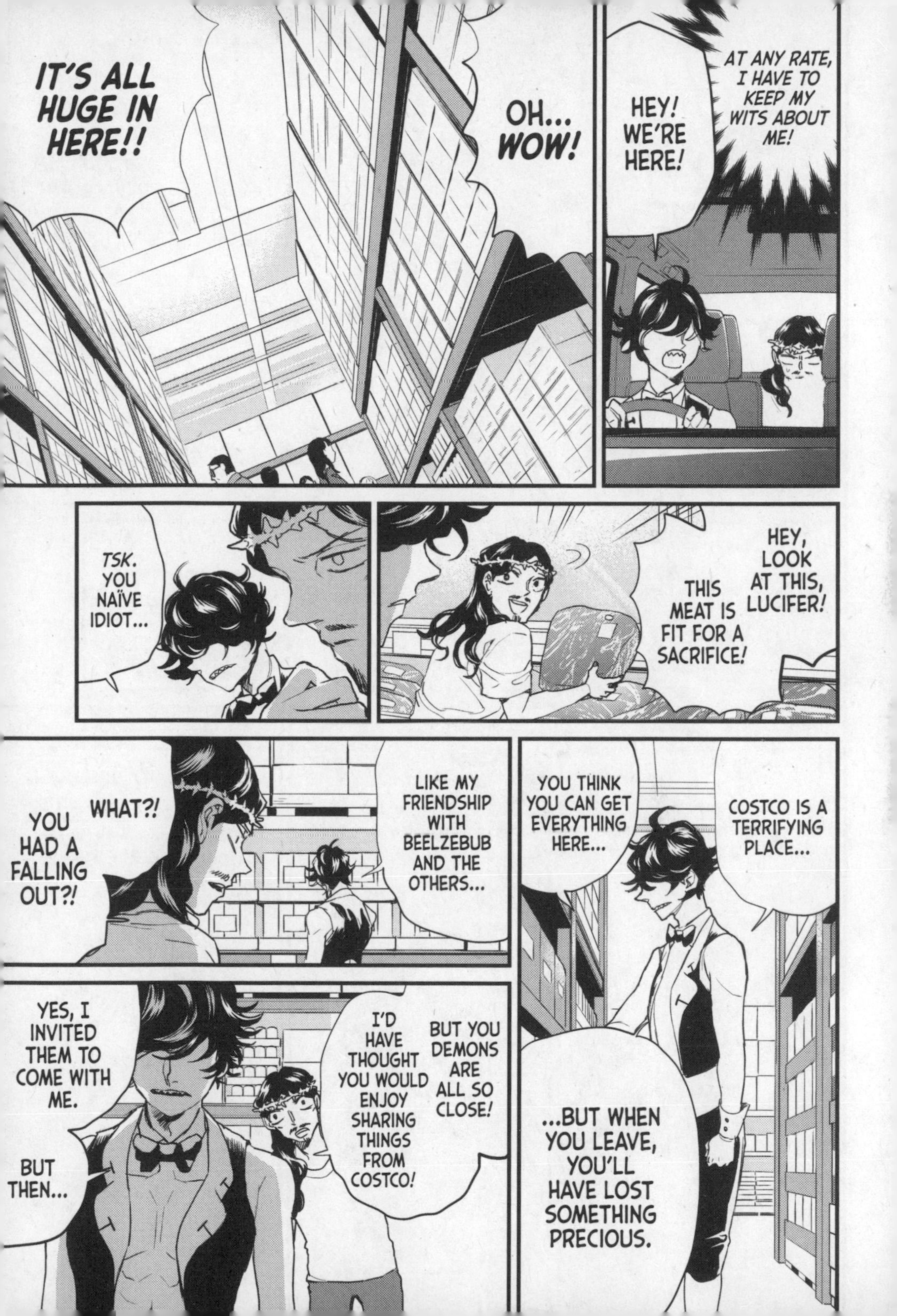
AT ANY RATE, I HAVE TO KEEP MY WITS ABOUT ME!
HEY! WE'RE HERE!
OH... WOW!
IT'S ALL HUGE IN HERE!!
HEY, LOOK AT THIS, LUCIFER!
THIS MEAT IS FIT FOR A SACRIFICE!
TSK. YOU NAÏVE IDIOT...
COSTCO IS A TERRIFYING PLACE...
YOU THINK YOU CAN GET EVERYTHING HERE...
...BUT WHEN YOU LEAVE, YOU'LL HAVE LOST SOMETHING PRECIOUS.
LIKE MY FRIENDSHIP WITH BEELZEBUB AND THE OTHERS...
WHAT?!
YOU HAD A FALLING OUT?!
BUT YOU DEMONS ARE ALL SO CLOSE!
I'D HAVE THOUGHT YOU WOULD ENJOY SHARING THINGS FROM COSTCO!
YES, I INVITED THEM TO COME WITH ME.
BUT THEN...

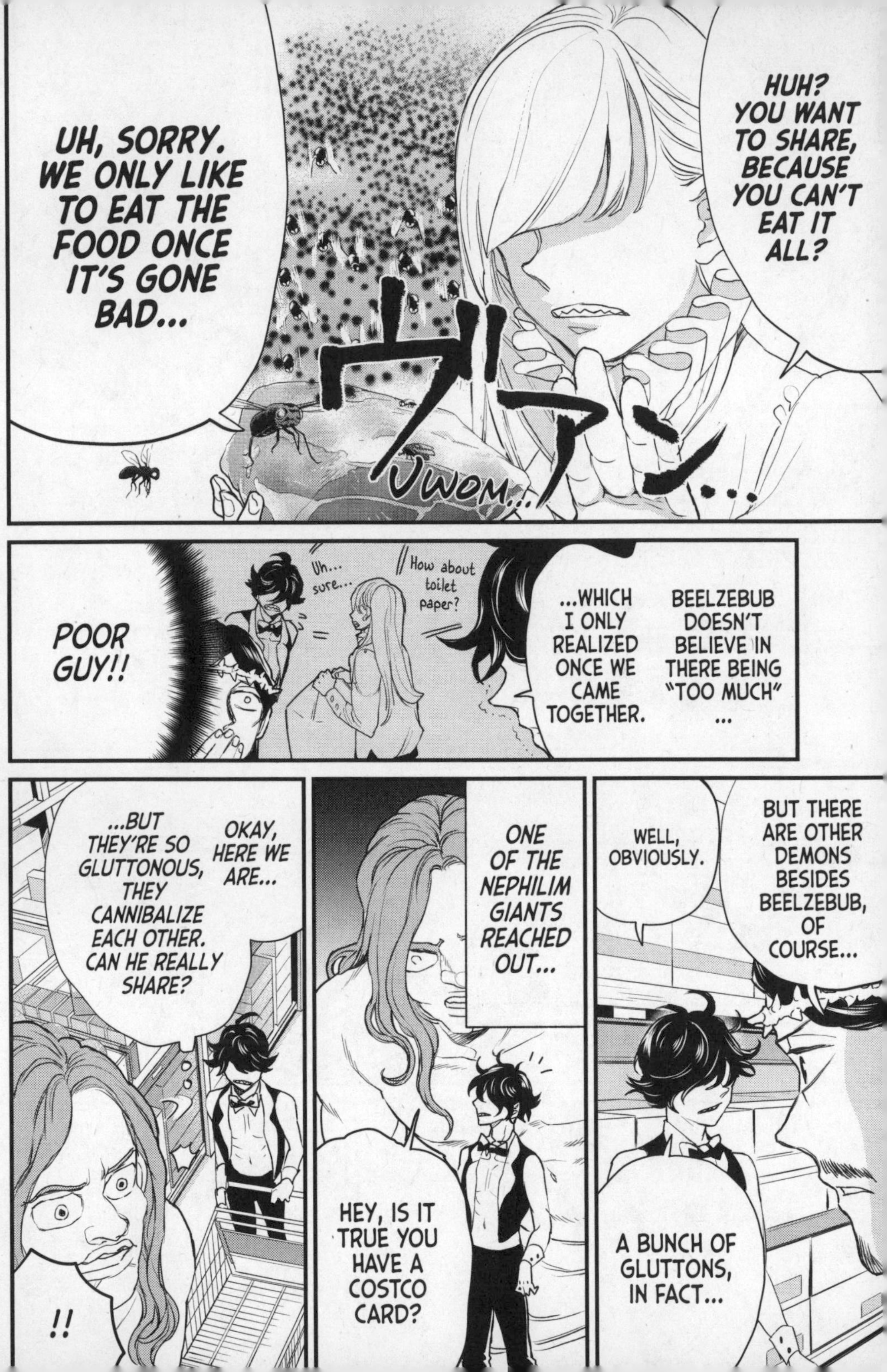
HUH? YOU WANT TO SHARE, BECAUSE YOU CAN'T EAT IT ALL?
UH, SORRY. WE ONLY LIKE TO EAT THE FOOD ONCE IT'S GONE BAD...
ヴァン...
VWOM...
BEELZEBUB DOESN'T BELIEVE IN THERE BEING "TOO MUCH" ...
...WHICH I ONLY REALIZED ONCE WE CAME TOGETHER.
How about toilet paper?
Uh... sure...
POOR GUY!!
BUT THERE ARE OTHER DEMONS BESIDES BEELZEBUB, OF COURSE...
WELL, OBVIOUSLY.
A BUNCH OF GLUTTONS, IN FACT...
ONE OF THE NEPHILIM GIANTS REACHED OUT...
HEY, IS IT TRUE YOU HAVE A COSTCO CARD?
OKAY, HERE WE ARE...
...BUT THEY'RE SO GLUTTONOUS, THEY CANNIBALIZE EACH OTHER. CAN HE REALLY SHARE?
!!

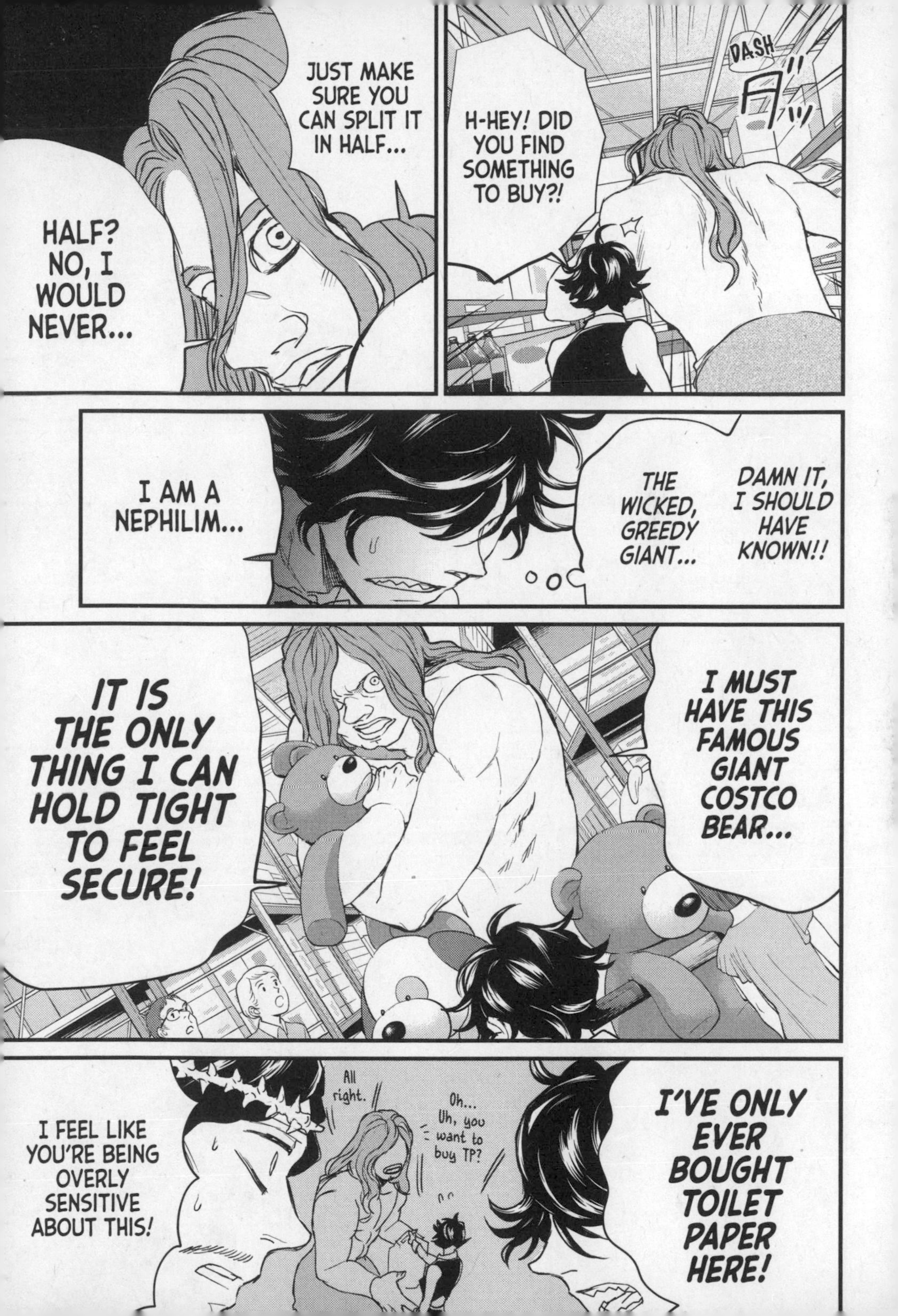
DASH
H-HEY! DID YOU FIND SOMETHING TO BUY?!
JUST MAKE SURE YOU CAN SPLIT IT IN HALF...
HALF? NO, I WOULD NEVER...
DAMN IT, I SHOULD HAVE KNOWN!!
THE WICKED, GREEDY GIANT...
I AM A NEPHILIM...
I MUST HAVE THIS FAMOUS GIANT COSTCO BEAR...
IT IS THE ONLY THING I CAN HOLD TIGHT TO FEEL SECURE!
I'VE ONLY EVER BOUGHT TOILET PAPER HERE!
Oh... Uh, you want to buy TP?
All right.
I FEEL LIKE YOU'RE BEING OVERLY SENSITIVE ABOUT THIS!

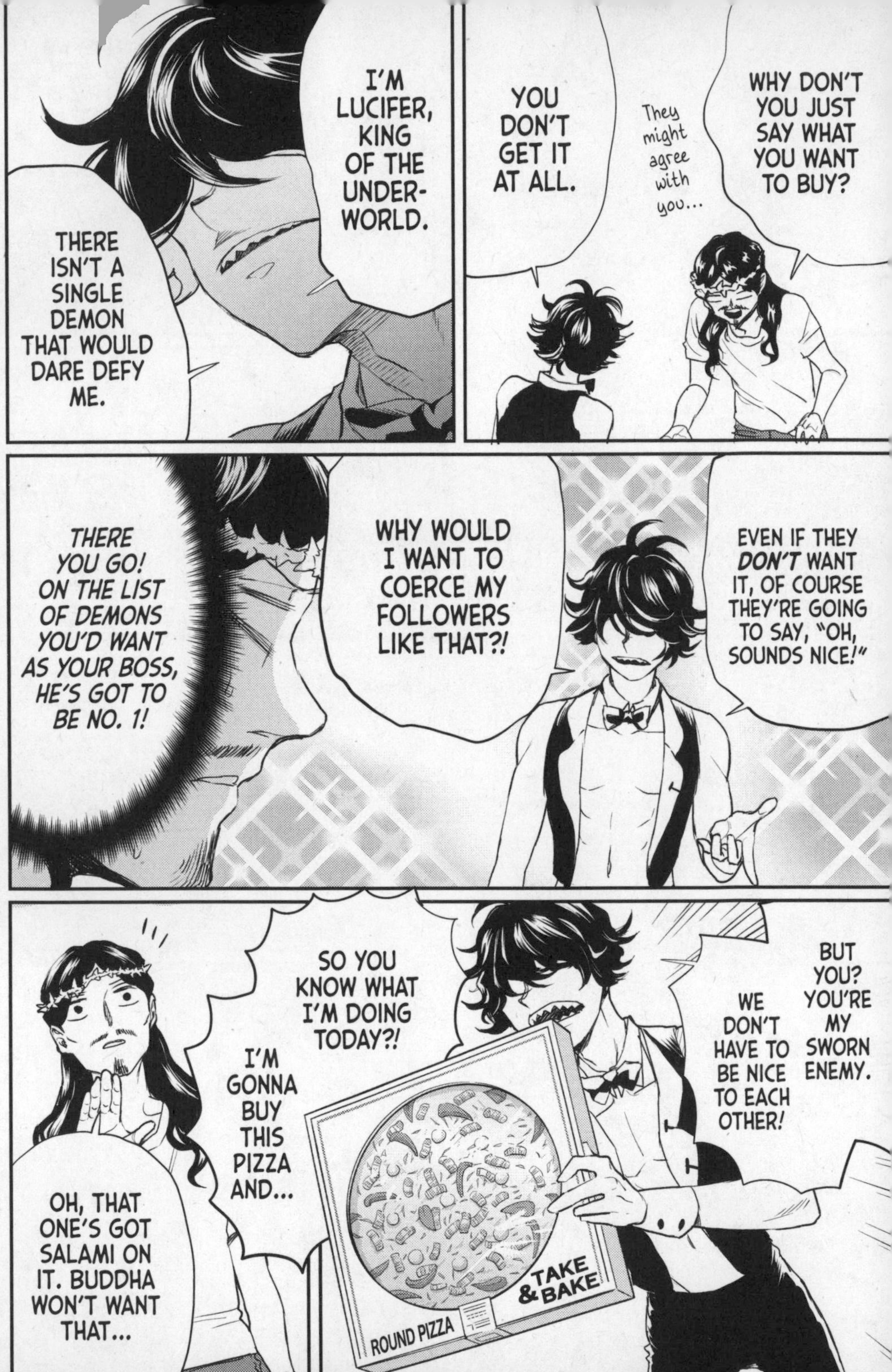

WHY DON'T YOU JUST SAY WHAT YOU WANT TO BUY?
They might agree with you...
YOU DON'T GET IT AT ALL.
I'M LUCIFER, KING OF THE UNDER-WORLD.
THERE ISN'T A SINGLE DEMON THAT WOULD DARE DEFY ME.
EVEN IF THEY *DON'T* WANT IT, OF COURSE THEY'RE GOING TO SAY, "OH, SOUNDS NICE!"
WHY WOULD I WANT TO COERCE MY FOLLOWERS LIKE THAT?!
THERE YOU GO! ON THE LIST OF DEMONS YOU'D WANT AS YOUR BOSS, HE'S GOT TO BE NO. 1!
BUT YOU? YOU'RE MY SWORN ENEMY.
WE DON'T HAVE TO BE NICE TO EACH OTHER!
SO YOU KNOW WHAT I'M DOING TODAY?!
I'M GONNA BUY THIS PIZZA AND...
TAKE & BAKE
ROUND PIZZA
OH, THAT ONE'S GOT SALAMI ON IT. BUDDHA WON'T WANT THAT...

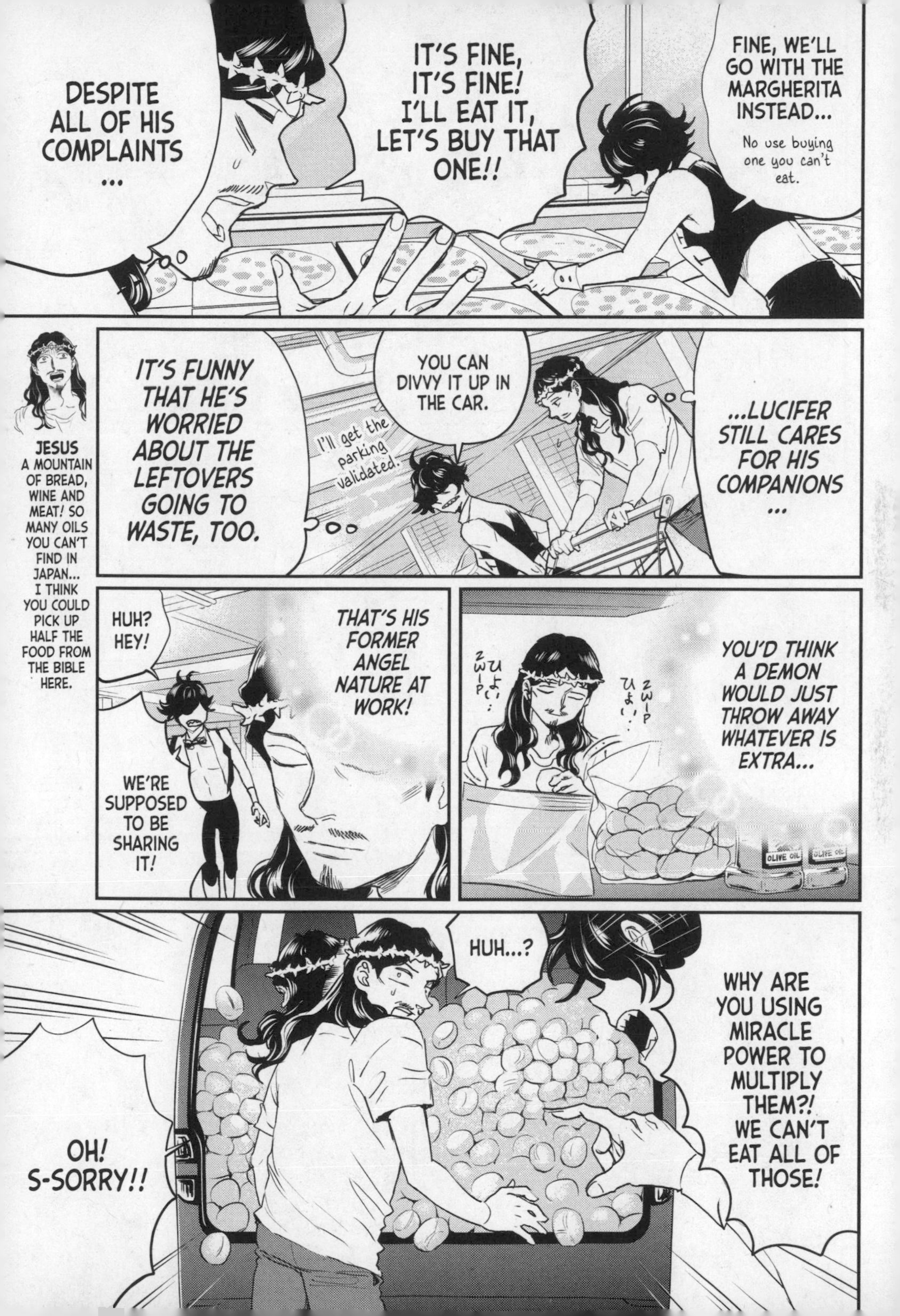
FINE, WE'LL GO WITH THE MARGHERITA INSTEAD...
No use buying one you can't eat.
IT'S FINE, IT'S FINE! I'LL EAT IT, LET'S BUY THAT ONE!!
DESPITE ALL OF HIS COMPLAINTS ...
...LUCIFER STILL CARES FOR HIS COMPANIONS ...
YOU CAN DIVVY IT UP IN THE CAR.
I'll get the parking validated.
IT'S FUNNY THAT HE'S WORRIED ABOUT THE LEFTOVERS GOING TO WASTE, TOO.
JESUS
A MOUNTAIN OF BREAD, WINE AND MEAT! SO MANY OILS YOU CAN'T FIND IN JAPAN... I THINK YOU COULD PICK UP HALF THE FOOD FROM THE BIBLE HERE.
YOU'D THINK A DEMON WOULD JUST THROW AWAY WHATEVER IS EXTRA...
ZWIP
ZWIP
OLIVE OIL
OLIVE OIL
THAT'S HIS FORMER ANGEL NATURE AT WORK!
HUH? HEY!
WE'RE SUPPOSED TO BE SHARING IT!
WHY ARE YOU USING MIRACLE POWER TO MULTIPLY THEM?! WE CAN'T EAT ALL OF THOSE!
HUH...?
OH! S-SORRY!!

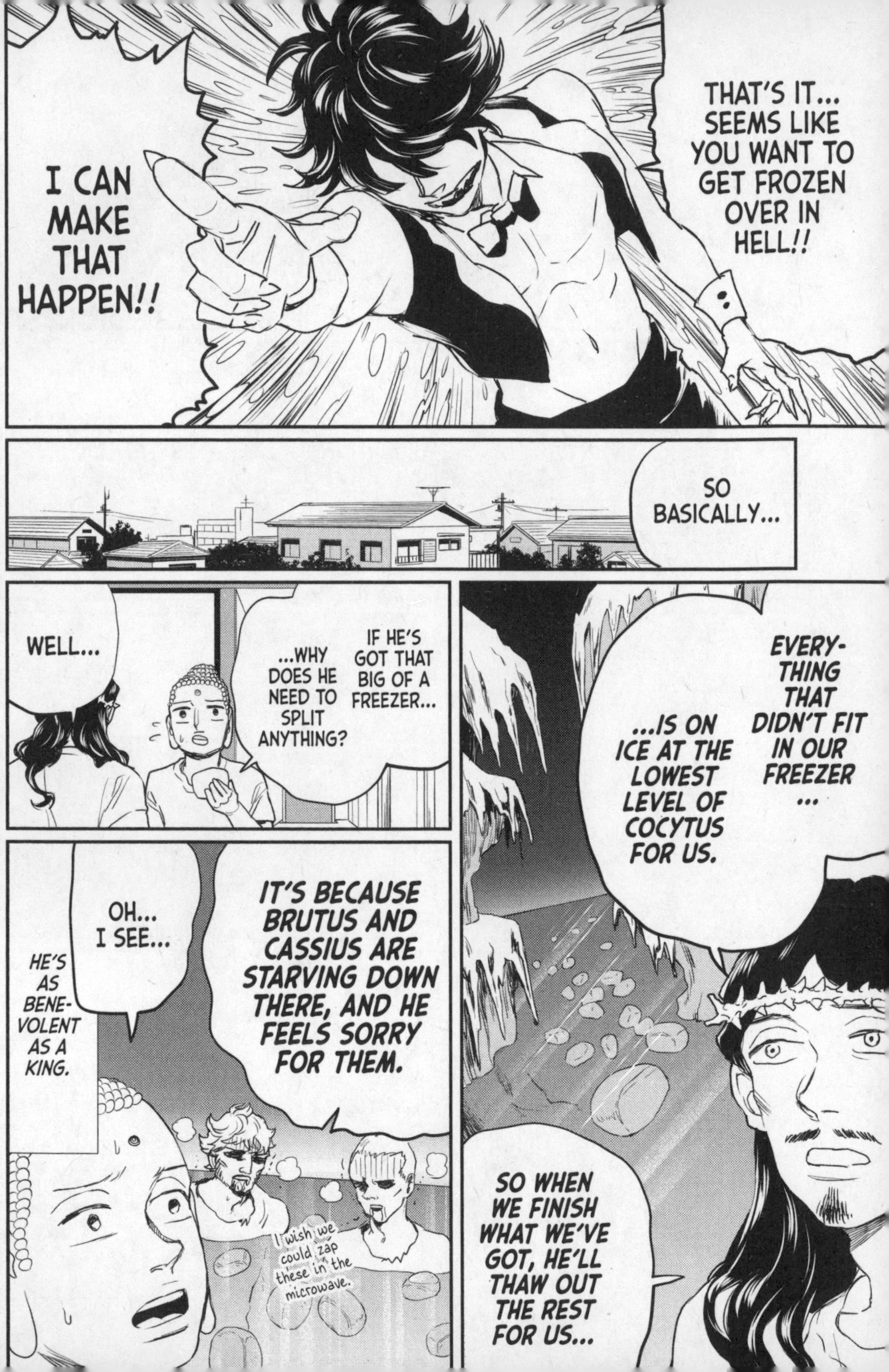
THAT'S IT... SEEMS LIKE YOU WANT TO GET FROZEN OVER IN HELL!!
I CAN MAKE THAT HAPPEN!!
SO BASICALLY...
EVERYTHING THAT DIDN'T FIT IN OUR FREEZER...
...IS ON ICE AT THE LOWEST LEVEL OF COCYTUS FOR US.
SO WHEN WE FINISH WHAT WE'VE GOT, HE'LL THAW OUT THE REST FOR US...
IF HE'S GOT THAT BIG OF A FREEZER...
...WHY DOES HE NEED TO SPLIT ANYTHING?
WELL...
IT'S BECAUSE BRUTUS AND CASSIUS ARE STARVING DOWN THERE, AND HE FEELS SORRY FOR THEM.
OH... I SEE...
HE'S AS BENEVOLENT AS A KING.
I wish we could zap these in the microwave.

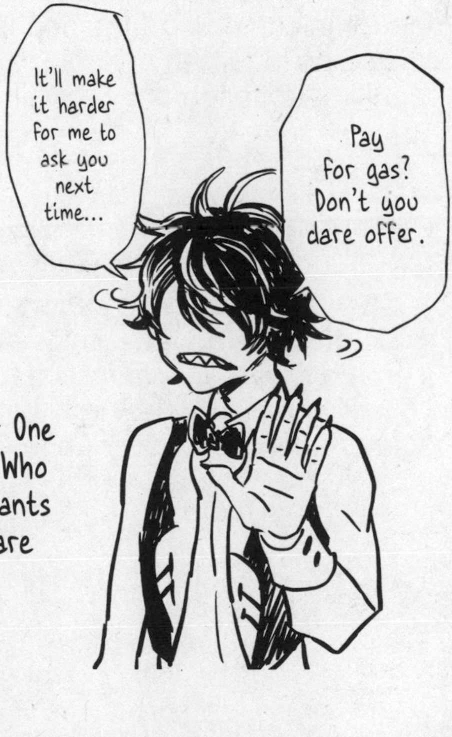
Pay for gas? Don't you dare offer.
It'll make it harder for me to ask you next time...

Number One Demon Who Just Wants to Share

CHAPTER 117 TRANSLATION NOTES

Temptation of Christ, page 213

When Jesus went into the desert for 40 days, he fought against the Devil's temptations in various forms. The final temptation came as the Devil took Jesus to a high place where "all the kingdoms of the Earth" could be seen, and he offfered Jesus control of them all in exchange for his worship. Jesus replied, "You shall worship the Lord your God, and only Him shall you serve."

Nephilim, page 218

A mysterious group of people or beings mentioned sporadically in the Bible. Different interpretations exist on their nature; early Greek/Latin translations of the Bible considered the nephilim "giants," based largely on similarities to Greek mythology. Another common interpretation of "nephilim" is "fallen ones" or fallen angels.

Cocytus, page 222

While Cocytus was originally the name of one of the rivers in the Greek Underworld, Dante used it as the name of the lowest circle of Hell in his *Divine Comedy.* Cocytus was where traitors were sent, including Judas, and two of the primary assassins of Julius Caesar, Brutus and Cassius. In the *Divine Comedy,* Dante travels through the various circles of Hell with his guide Virgil, before climbing the mountain of Purgatory and ascending up through the sphere of Heaven.

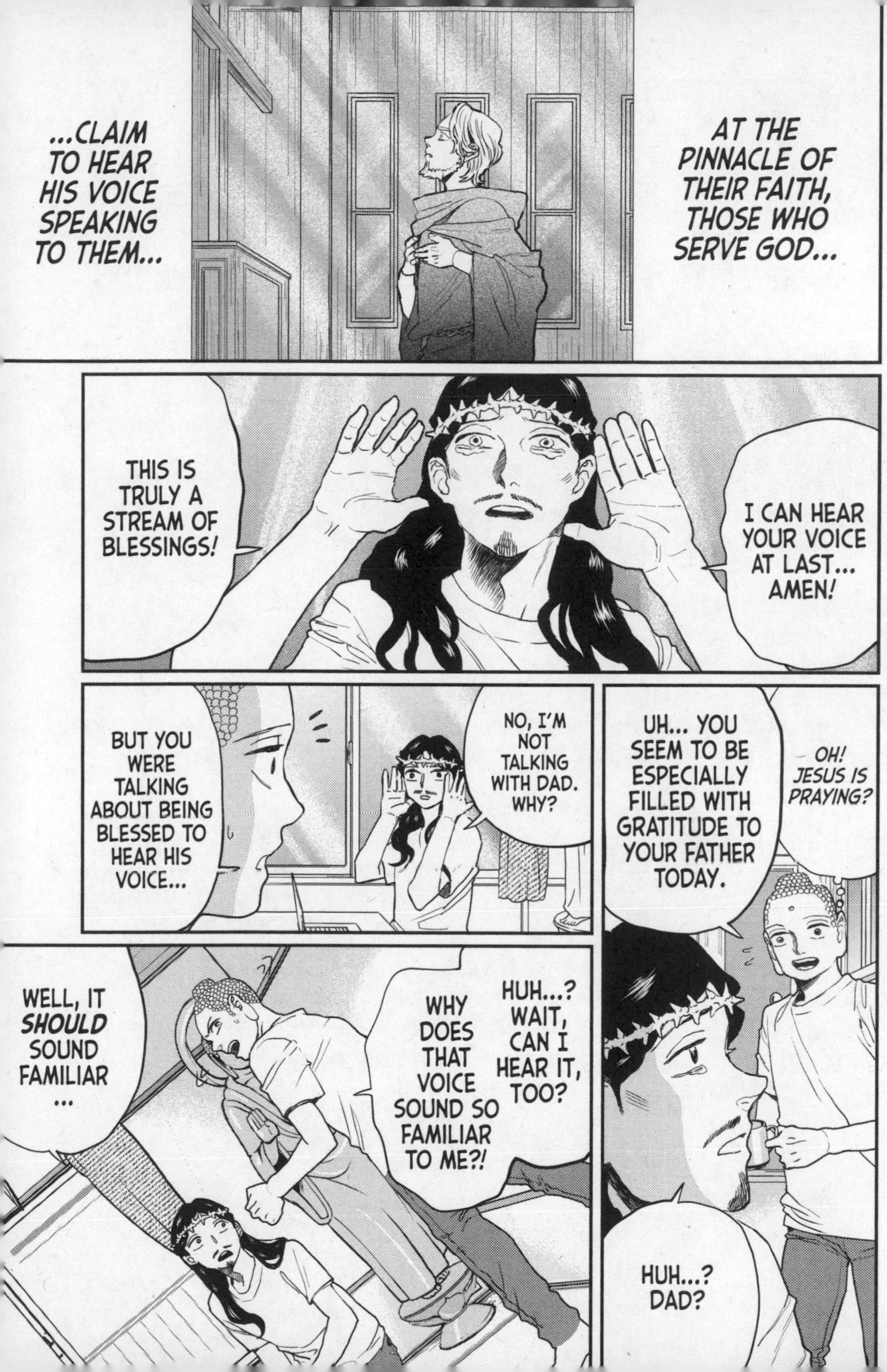
AT THE PINNACLE OF THEIR FAITH, THOSE WHO SERVE GOD...
...CLAIM TO HEAR HIS VOICE SPEAKING TO THEM...
I CAN HEAR YOUR VOICE AT LAST... AMEN!
THIS IS TRULY A STREAM OF BLESSINGS!
OH! JESUS IS PRAYING?
UH... YOU SEEM TO BE ESPECIALLY FILLED WITH GRATITUDE TO YOUR FATHER TODAY.
HUH...? DAD?
NO, I'M NOT TALKING WITH DAD. WHY?
BUT YOU WERE TALKING ABOUT BEING BLESSED TO HEAR HIS VOICE...
HUH...? WAIT, CAN I HEAR IT, TOO?
WHY DOES THAT VOICE SOUND SO FAMILIAR TO ME?!
WELL, IT *SHOULD* SOUND FAMILIAR...

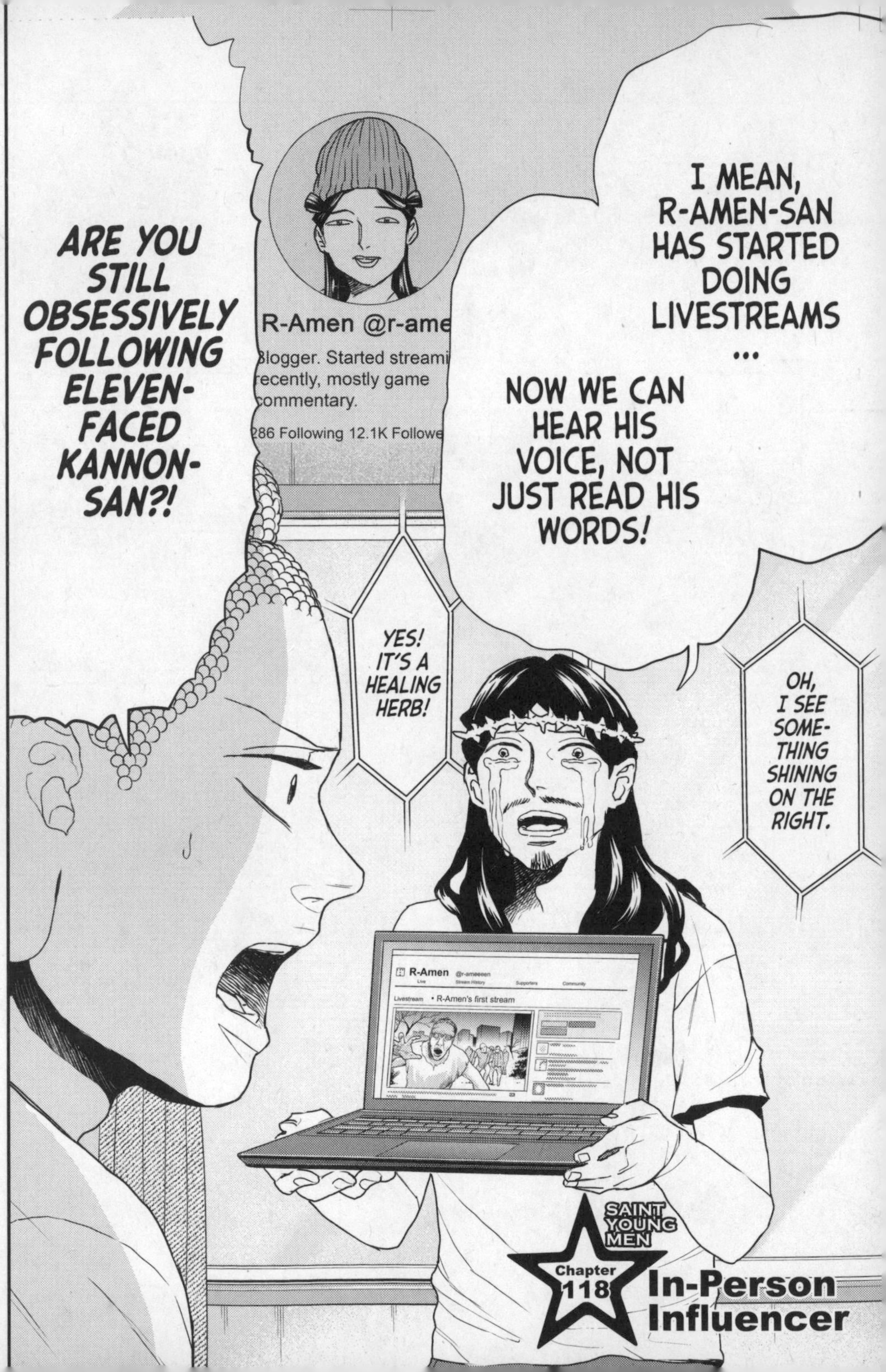
I MEAN, R-AMEN-SAN HAS STARTED DOING LIVESTREAMS ...
NOW WE CAN HEAR HIS VOICE, NOT JUST READ HIS WORDS!
R-Amen @r-ame
Blogger. Started streami recently, mostly game commentary.
286 Following 12.1K Followe
ARE YOU STILL OBSESSIVELY FOLLOWING ELEVEN-FACED KANNON-SAN?!
OH, I SEE SOME-THING SHINING ON THE RIGHT.
YES! IT'S A HEALING HERB!
R-Amen @r-ameeeen
Live
Stream History
Supporters
Community
Livestream • R-Amen's first stream
SAINT YOUNG MEN
Chapter 118
In-Person Influencer

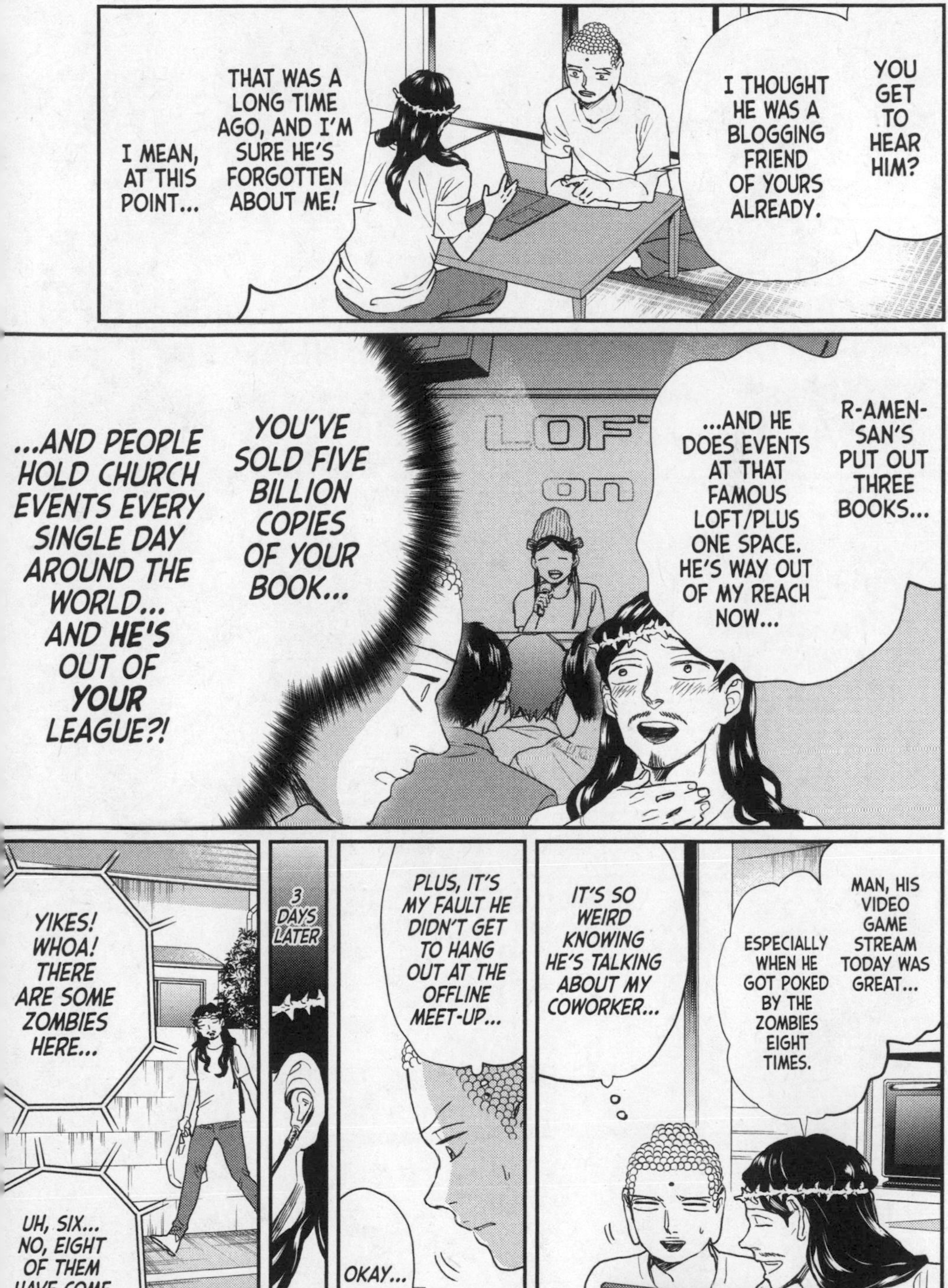
YOU GET TO HEAR HIM?
I THOUGHT HE WAS A BLOGGING FRIEND OF YOURS ALREADY.
THAT WAS A LONG TIME AGO, AND I'M SURE HE'S FORGOTTEN ABOUT ME!
I MEAN, AT THIS POINT...
R-AMEN-SAN'S PUT OUT THREE BOOKS...
...AND HE DOES EVENTS AT THAT FAMOUS LOFT/PLUS ONE SPACE. HE'S WAY OUT OF MY REACH NOW...
YOU'VE SOLD FIVE BILLION COPIES OF YOUR BOOK...
...AND PEOPLE HOLD CHURCH EVENTS EVERY SINGLE DAY AROUND THE WORLD... AND HE'S OUT OF YOUR LEAGUE?!
MAN, HIS VIDEO GAME STREAM TODAY WAS GREAT...
ESPECIALLY WHEN HE GOT POKED BY THE ZOMBIES EIGHT TIMES.
IT'S SO WEIRD KNOWING HE'S TALKING ABOUT MY COWORKER...
PLUS, IT'S MY FAULT HE DIDN'T GET TO HANG OUT AT THE OFFLINE MEET-UP...
OKAY...
3 DAYS LATER
YIKES! WHOA! THERE ARE SOME ZOMBIES HERE...
UH, SIX... NO, EIGHT OF THEM HAVE COME TO VISIT!!

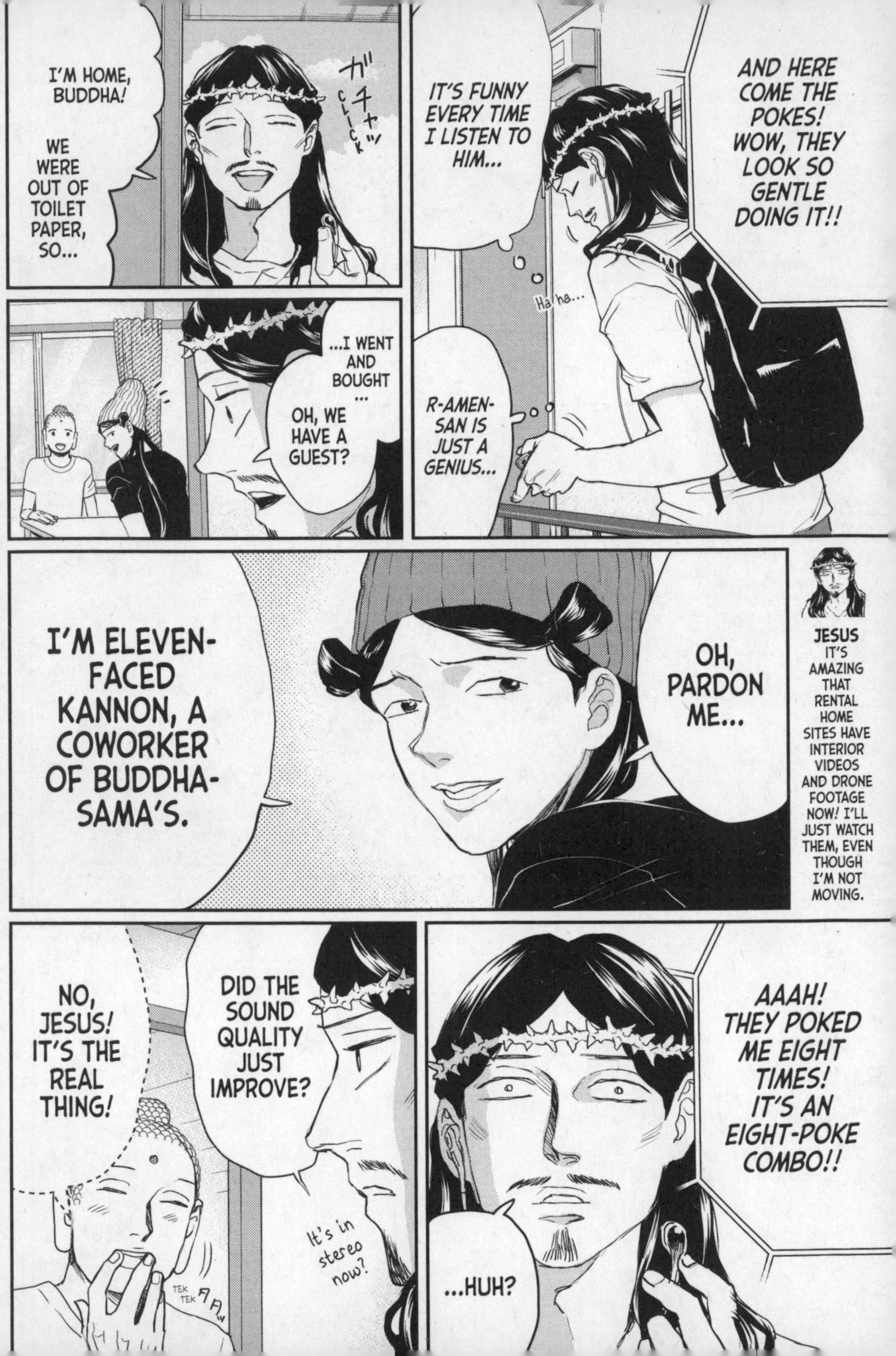
AND HERE COME THE POKES! WOW, THEY LOOK SO GENTLE DOING IT!!
IT'S FUNNY EVERY TIME I LISTEN TO HIM...
Ha ha...
R-AMEN-SAN IS JUST A GENIUS...
I'M HOME, BUDDHA!
CLICK
WE WERE OUT OF TOILET PAPER, SO...
...I WENT AND BOUGHT...
OH, WE HAVE A GUEST?
JESUS
IT'S AMAZING THAT RENTAL HOME SITES HAVE INTERIOR VIDEOS AND DRONE FOOTAGE NOW! I'LL JUST WATCH THEM, EVEN THOUGH I'M NOT MOVING.
OH, PARDON ME...
I'M ELEVEN-FACED KANNON, A COWORKER OF BUDDHA-SAMA'S.
AAAH! THEY POKED ME EIGHT TIMES! IT'S AN EIGHT-POKE COMBO!!
...HUH?
DID THE SOUND QUALITY JUST IMPROVE?
It's in stereo now?
NO, JESUS! IT'S THE REAL THING!
TEK TEK

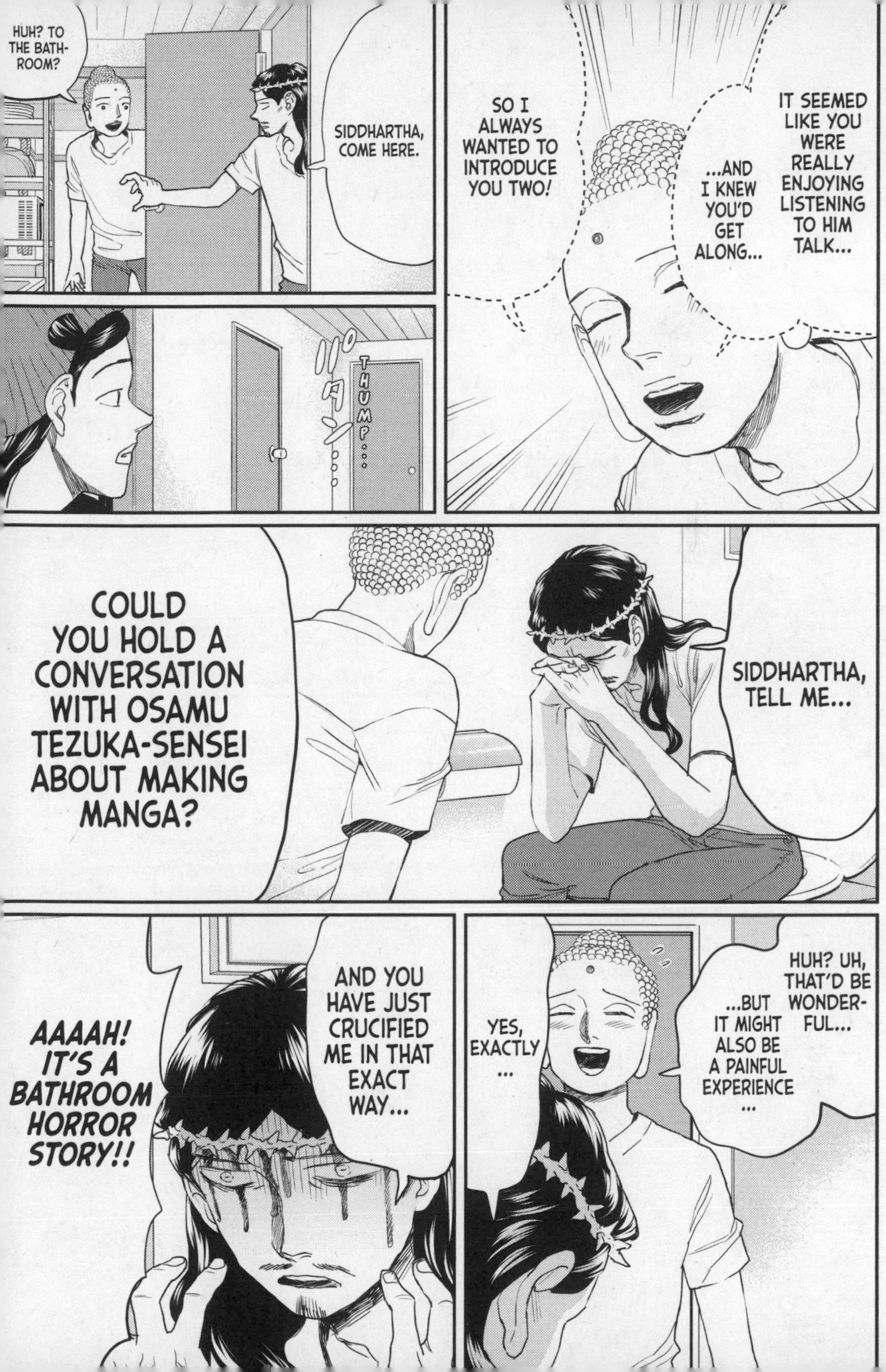
IT SEEMED LIKE YOU WERE REALLY ENJOYING LISTENING TO HIM TALK...
...AND I KNEW YOU'D GET ALONG...
SO I ALWAYS WANTED TO INTRODUCE YOU TWO!
SIDDHARTHA, COME HERE.
HUH? TO THE BATH-ROOM?
パタン...
THUMP...
SIDDHARTHA, TELL ME...
COULD YOU HOLD A CONVERSATION WITH OSAMU TEZUKA-SENSEI ABOUT MAKING MANGA?
HUH? UH, THAT'D BE WONDER-FUL...
...BUT IT MIGHT ALSO BE A PAINFUL EXPERIENCE ...
YES, EXACTLY ...
AND YOU HAVE JUST CRUCIFIED ME IN THAT EXACT WAY...
AAAAH! IT'S A BATHROOM HORROR STORY!!

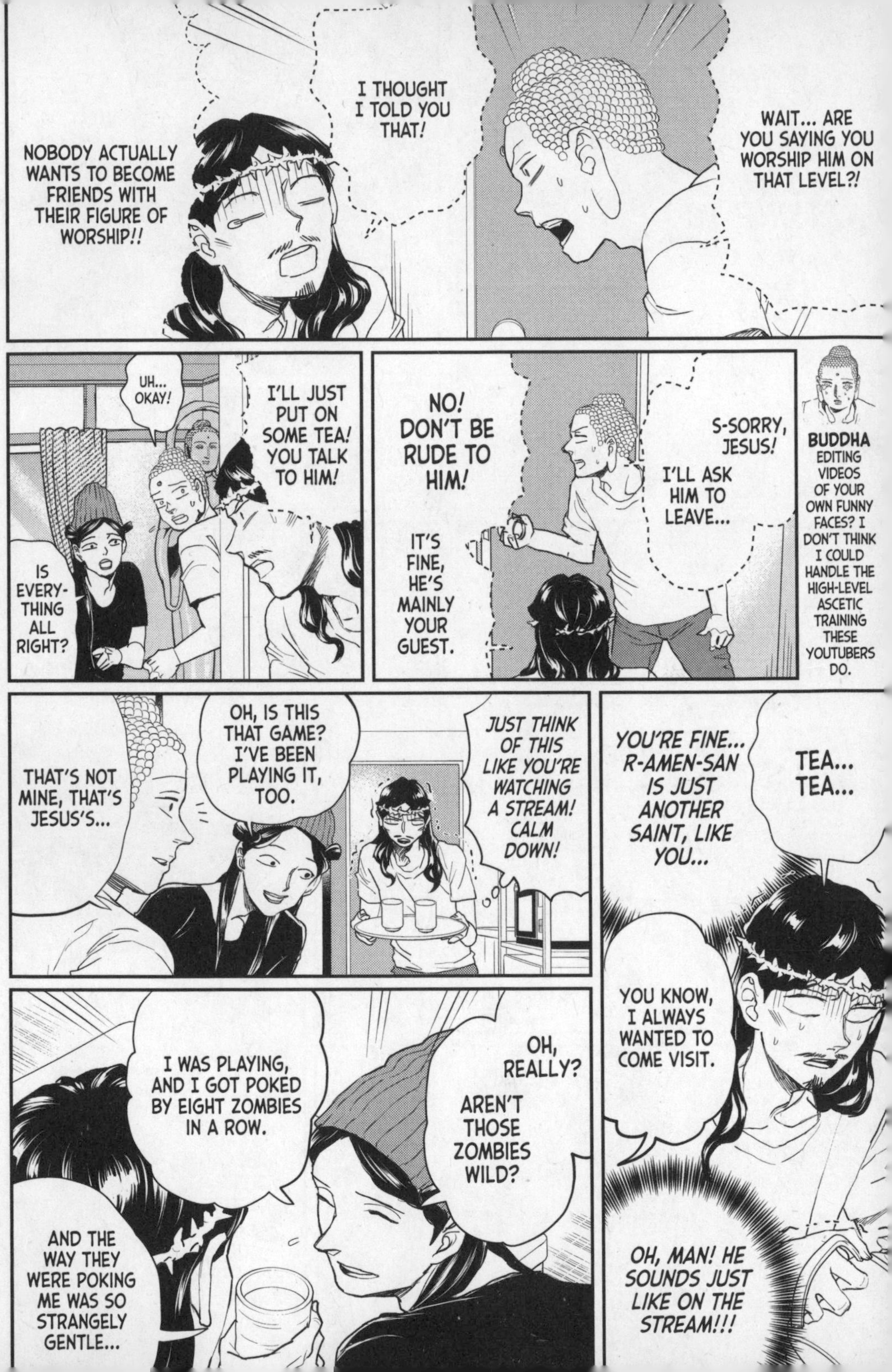
WAIT... ARE YOU SAYING YOU WORSHIP HIM ON THAT LEVEL?!
I THOUGHT I TOLD YOU THAT!
NOBODY ACTUALLY WANTS TO BECOME FRIENDS WITH THEIR FIGURE OF WORSHIP!!
BUDDHA EDITING VIDEOS OF YOUR OWN FUNNY FACES? I DON'T THINK I COULD HANDLE THE HIGH-LEVEL ASCETIC TRAINING THESE YOUTUBERS DO.
S-SORRY, JESUS!
I'LL ASK HIM TO LEAVE...
NO! DON'T BE RUDE TO HIM!
IT'S FINE, HE'S MAINLY YOUR GUEST.
I'LL JUST PUT ON SOME TEA! YOU TALK TO HIM!
UH... OKAY!
IS EVERYTHING ALL RIGHT?
TEA... TEA...
YOU'RE FINE... R-AMEN-SAN IS JUST ANOTHER SAINT, LIKE YOU...
JUST THINK OF THIS LIKE YOU'RE WATCHING A STREAM! CALM DOWN!
OH, IS THIS THAT GAME? I'VE BEEN PLAYING IT, TOO.
THAT'S NOT MINE, THAT'S JESUS'S...
YOU KNOW, I ALWAYS WANTED TO COME VISIT.
OH, MAN! HE SOUNDS JUST LIKE ON THE STREAM!!!
OH, REALLY?
AREN'T THOSE ZOMBIES WILD?
I WAS PLAYING, AND I GOT POKED BY EIGHT ZOMBIES IN A ROW.
AND THE WAY THEY WERE POKING ME WAS SO STRANGELY GENTLE...

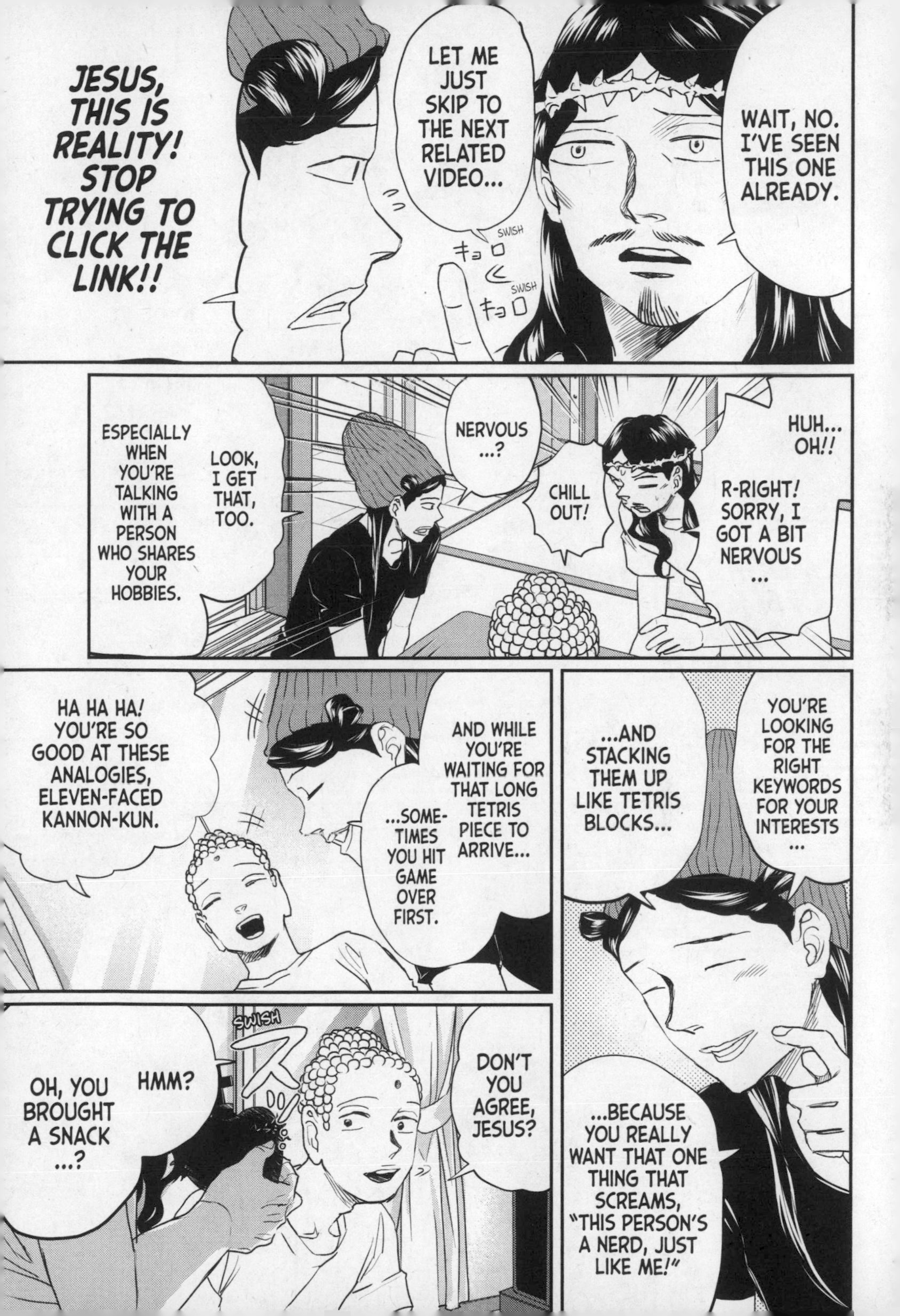
WAIT, NO. I'VE SEEN THIS ONE ALREADY.
LET ME JUST SKIP TO THE NEXT RELATED VIDEO...
SWISH
キョロ
SWISH
キョロ
JESUS, THIS IS REALITY! STOP TRYING TO CLICK THE LINK!!
HUH... OH!!
R-RIGHT! SORRY, I GOT A BIT NERVOUS ...
CHILL OUT!
NERVOUS ...?
LOOK, I GET THAT, TOO.
ESPECIALLY WHEN YOU'RE TALKING WITH A PERSON WHO SHARES YOUR HOBBIES.
YOU'RE LOOKING FOR THE RIGHT KEYWORDS FOR YOUR INTERESTS ...
...AND STACKING THEM UP LIKE TETRIS BLOCKS...
...BECAUSE YOU REALLY WANT THAT ONE THING THAT SCREAMS, "THIS PERSON'S A NERD, JUST LIKE ME!"
AND WHILE YOU'RE WAITING FOR THAT LONG TETRIS PIECE TO ARRIVE...
...SOME-TIMES YOU HIT GAME OVER FIRST.
HA HA HA! YOU'RE SO GOOD AT THESE ANALOGIES, ELEVEN-FACED KANNON-KUN.
DON'T YOU AGREE, JESUS?
SWISH
ス
HMM?
OH, YOU BROUGHT A SNACK ...?

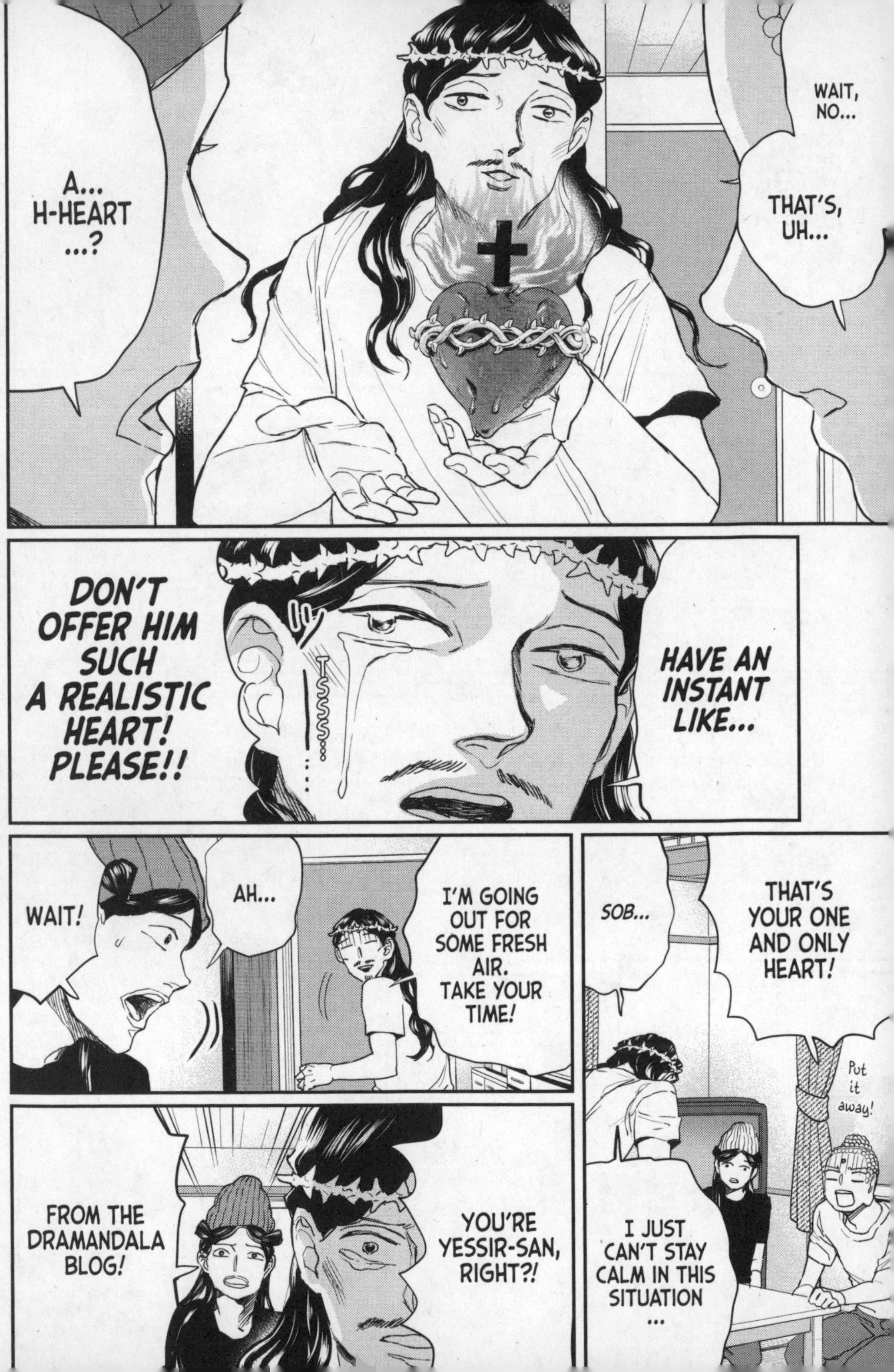
WAIT, NO...
THAT'S, UH...
A... H-HEART ...?
HAVE AN INSTANT LIKE...
TSSS...
DON'T OFFER HIM SUCH A REALISTIC HEART! PLEASE!!
THAT'S YOUR ONE AND ONLY HEART!
SOB...
Put it away!
I JUST CAN'T STAY CALM IN THIS SITUATION ...
I'M GOING OUT FOR SOME FRESH AIR. TAKE YOUR TIME!
AH...
WAIT!
YOU'RE YESSIR-SAN, RIGHT?!
FROM THE DRAMANDALA BLOG!

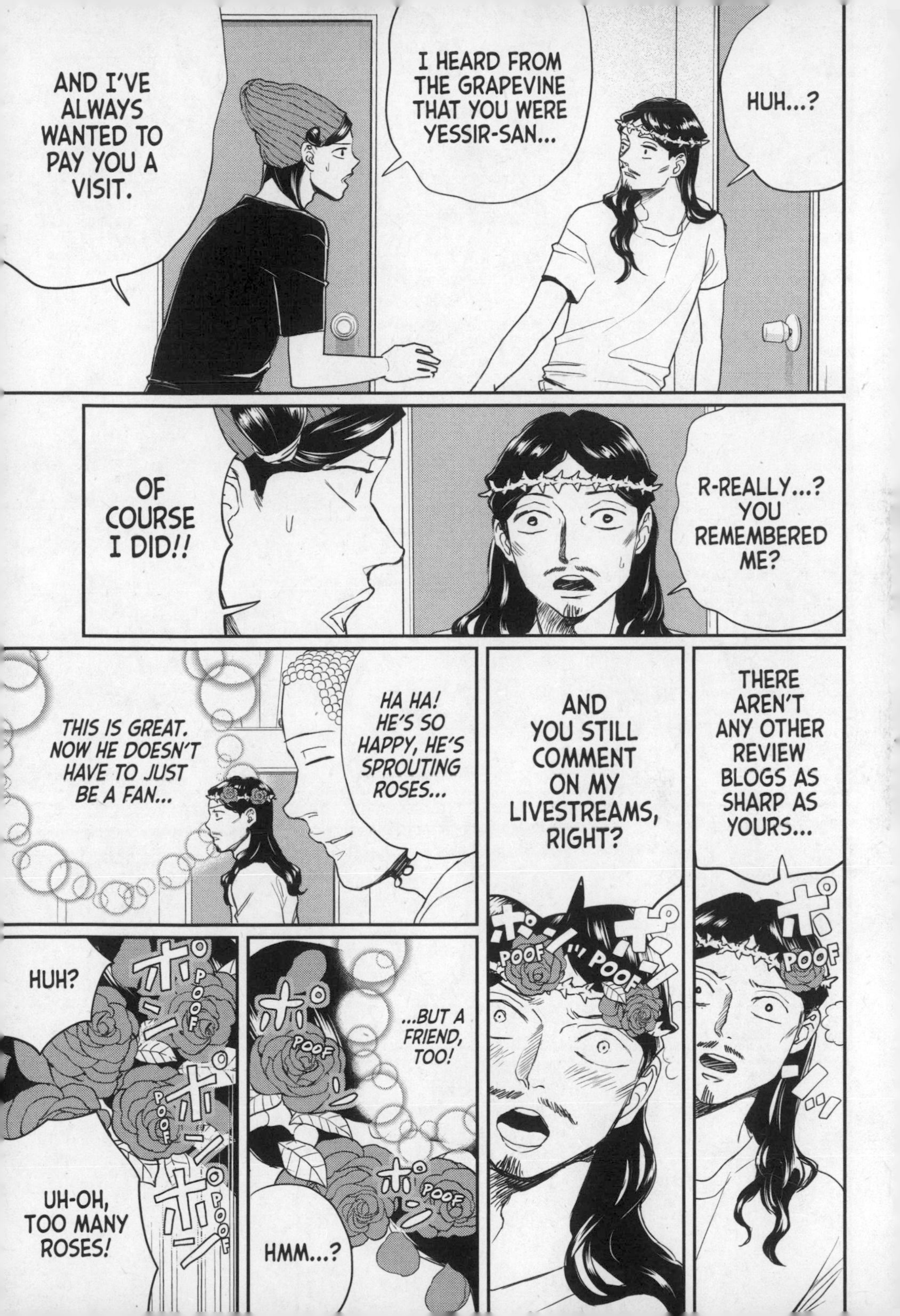
HUH...?
I HEARD FROM THE GRAPEVINE THAT YOU WERE YESSIR-SAN...
AND I'VE ALWAYS WANTED TO PAY YOU A VISIT.
R-REALLY...? YOU REMEMBERED ME?
OF COURSE I DID!!
THERE AREN'T ANY OTHER REVIEW BLOGS AS SHARP AS YOURS...
POOF
AND YOU STILL COMMENT ON MY LIVESTREAMS, RIGHT?
POOF
POOF
HA HA! HE'S SO HAPPY, HE'S SPROUTING ROSES...
THIS IS GREAT. NOW HE DOESN'T HAVE TO JUST BE A FAN...
...BUT A FRIEND, TOO!
POOF
POOF
HMM...?
HUH?
POOF
POOF
POOF
UH-OH, TOO MANY ROSES!

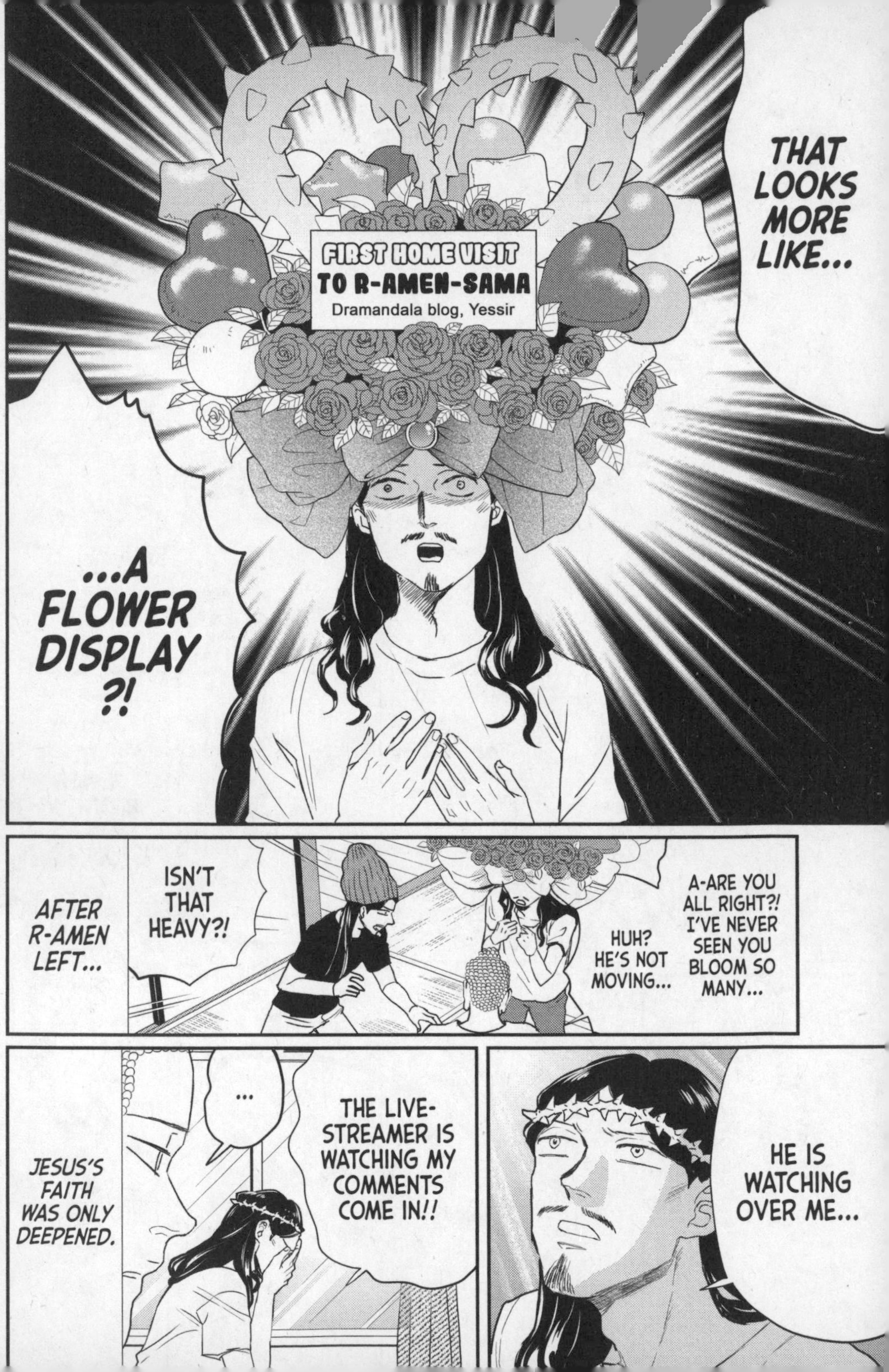
THAT LOOKS MORE LIKE...
FIRST HOME VISIT
TO R-AMEN-SAMA
Dramandala blog, Yessir
...A FLOWER DISPLAY ?!
A-ARE YOU ALL RIGHT?! I'VE NEVER SEEN YOU BLOOM SO MANY...
HUH? HE'S NOT MOVING...
ISN'T THAT HEAVY?!
AFTER R-AMEN LEFT...
HE IS WATCHING OVER ME...
THE LIVE-STREAMER IS WATCHING MY COMMENTS COME IN!!
...
JESUS'S FAITH WAS ONLY DEEPENED.

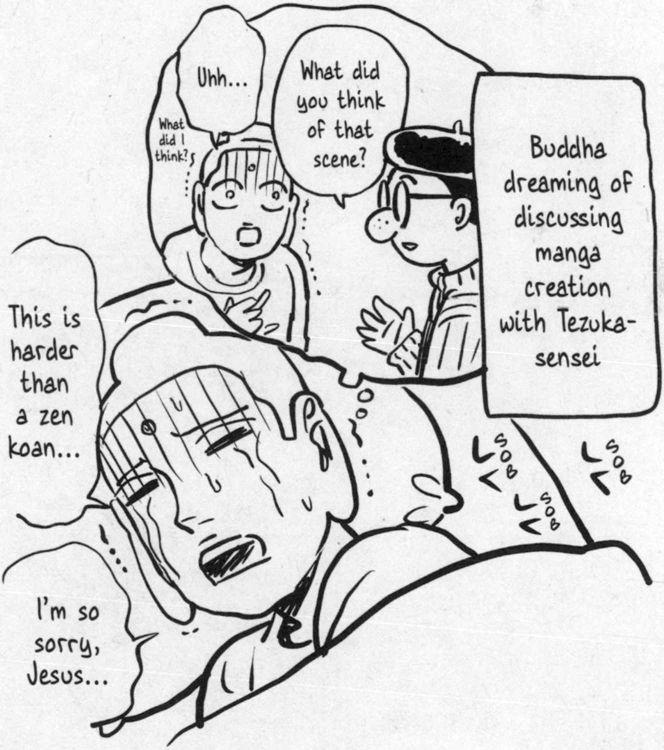

Buddha dreaming of discussing manga creation with Tezuka-sensei
What did you think of that scene?
Uhh...
What did I think?
SOB
SOB
SOB
This is harder than a zen koan...
I'm so sorry, Jesus...

SAINT☆YOUNG MEN

CHAPTER 118 TRANSLATION NOTES

Loft/Plus One, page 227
A special "talk show" venue in Shinjuku that hosts daily events in a cozy, trendy space, something like a cross between a comedy club and a TED Talk.

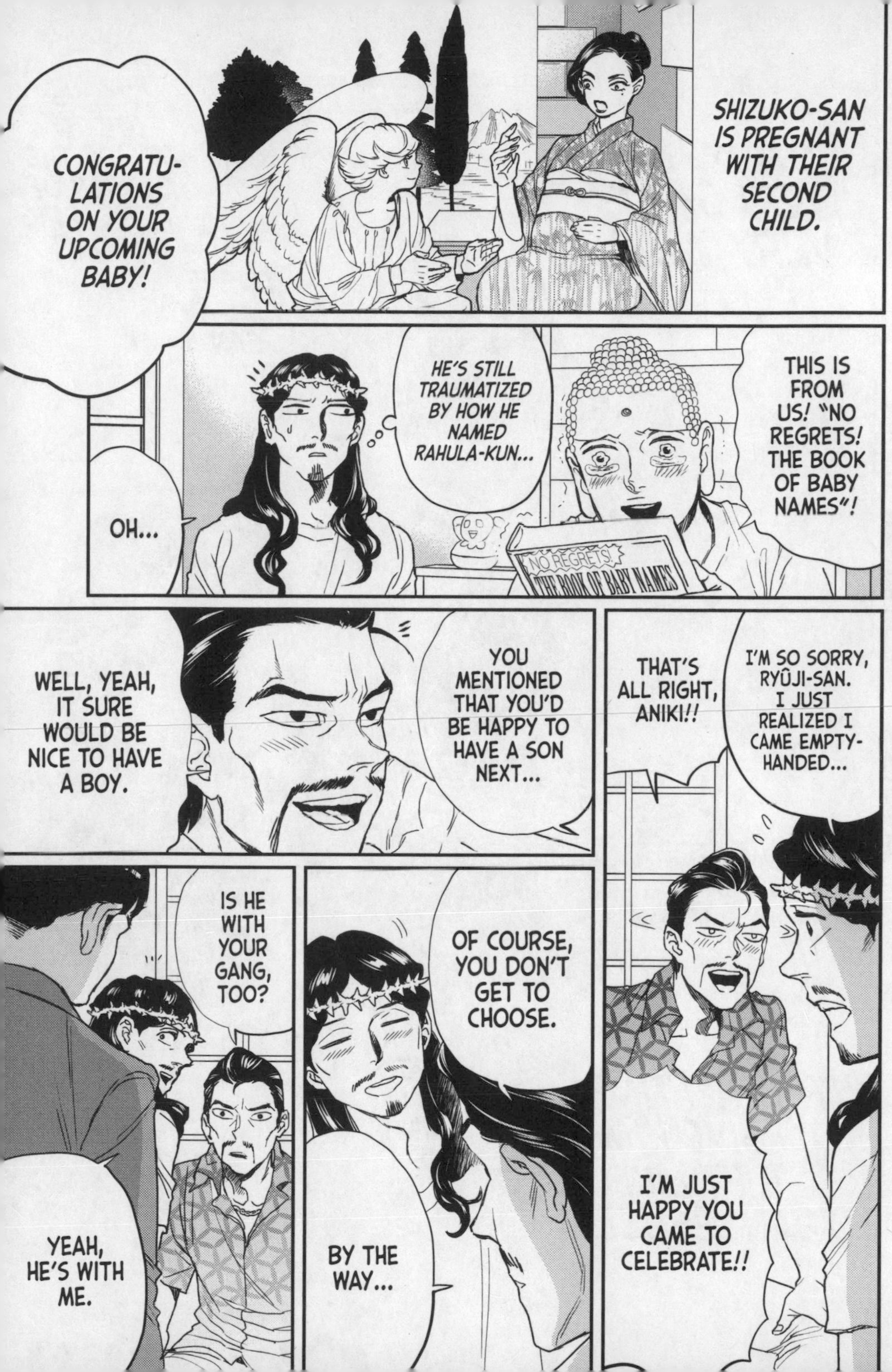
SHIZUKO-SAN IS PREGNANT WITH THEIR SECOND CHILD.
CONGRATU-LATIONS ON YOUR UPCOMING BABY!
THIS IS FROM US! "NO REGRETS! THE BOOK OF BABY NAMES"!
NO REGRETS! THE BOOK OF BABY NAMES
HE'S STILL TRAUMATIZED BY HOW HE NAMED RAHULA-KUN...
OH...
I'M SO SORRY, RYŪJI-SAN. I JUST REALIZED I CAME EMPTY-HANDED...
THAT'S ALL RIGHT, ANIKI!!
I'M JUST HAPPY YOU CAME TO CELEBRATE!!
YOU MENTIONED THAT YOU'D BE HAPPY TO HAVE A SON NEXT...
WELL, YEAH, IT SURE WOULD BE NICE TO HAVE A BOY.
OF COURSE, YOU DON'T GET TO CHOOSE.
BY THE WAY...
IS HE WITH YOUR GANG, TOO?
YEAH, HE'S WITH ME.

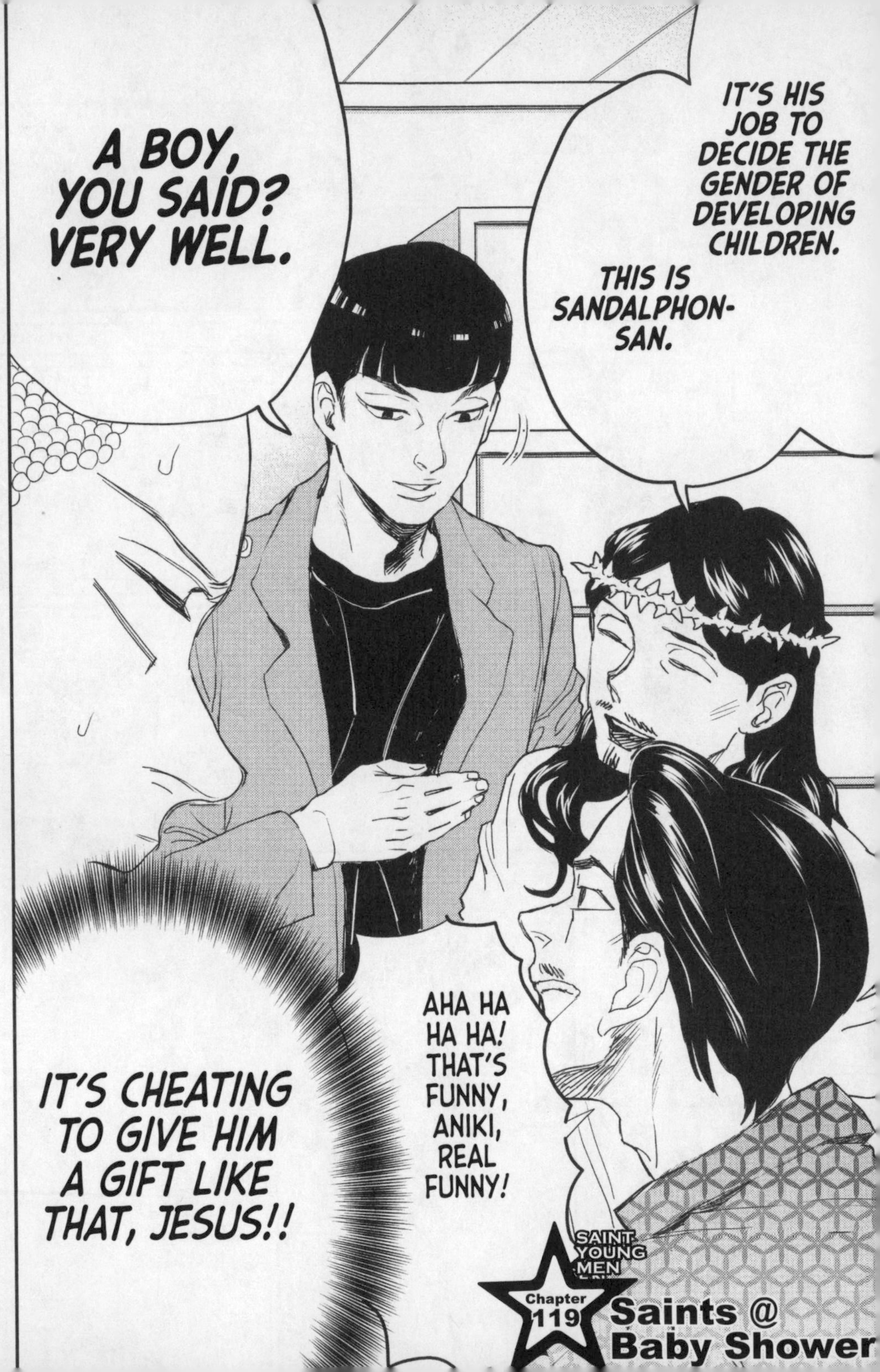
IT'S HIS JOB TO DECIDE THE GENDER OF DEVELOPING CHILDREN.
THIS IS SANDALPHON-SAN.
A BOY, YOU SAID? VERY WELL.
AHA HA HA HA! THAT'S FUNNY, ANIKI, REAL FUNNY!
IT'S CHEATING TO GIVE HIM A GIFT LIKE THAT, JESUS!!
SAINT YOUNG MEN
Chapter 119
Saints @ Baby Shower

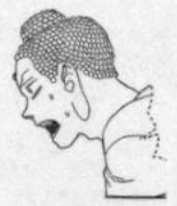

BUDDHA WHEN YOU KNOW THE COLD SEASON IS PAST, DECLUTTER THOSE WINTER COATS! #SUMMER-VIBES

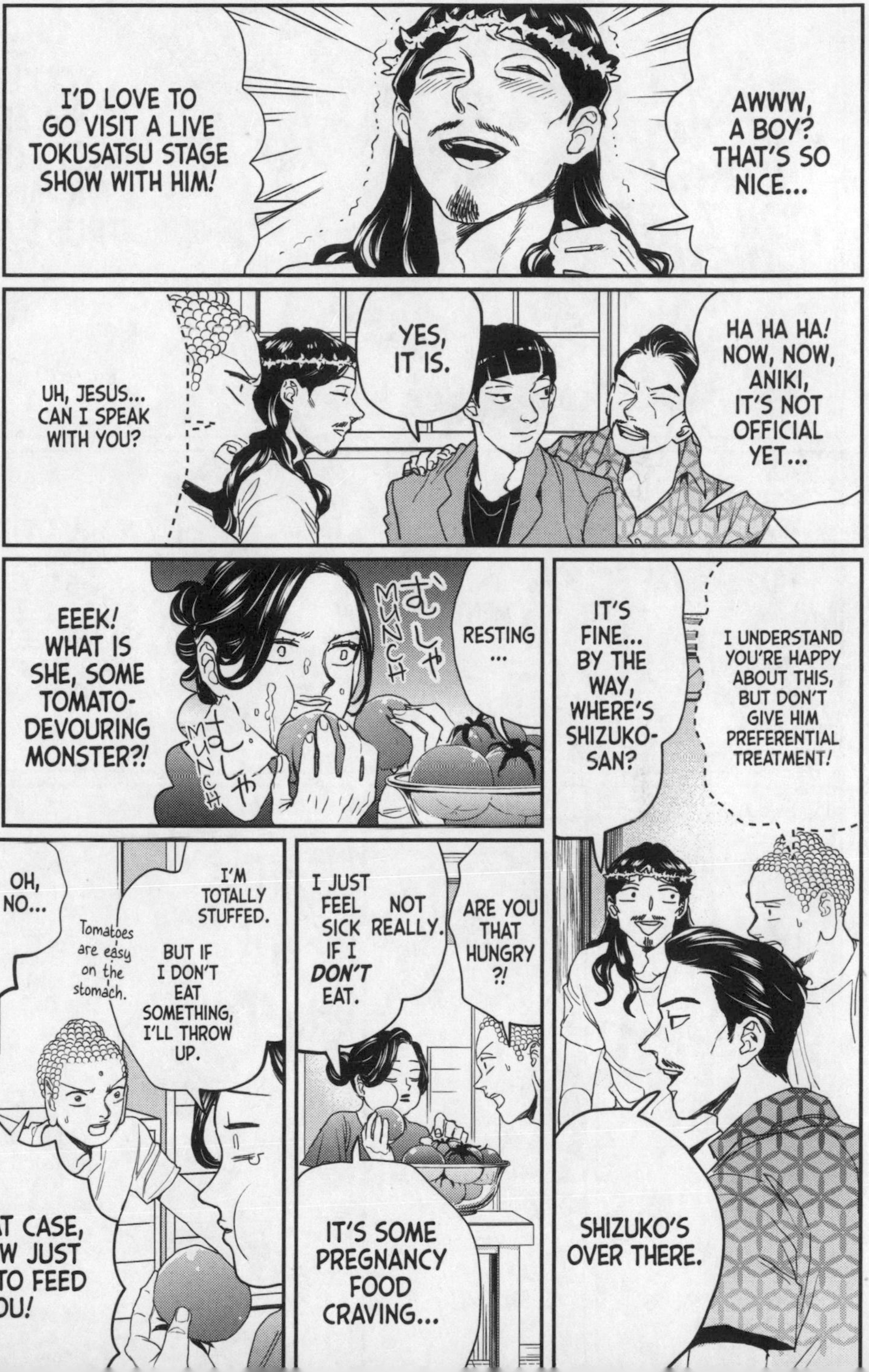

AWWW, A BOY? THAT'S SO NICE...
I'D LOVE TO GO VISIT A LIVE TOKUSATSU STAGE SHOW WITH HIM!
HA HA HA! NOW, NOW, ANIKI, IT'S NOT OFFICIAL YET...
YES, IT IS.
UH, JESUS... CAN I SPEAK WITH YOU?
I UNDERSTAND YOU'RE HAPPY ABOUT THIS, BUT DON'T GIVE HIM PREFERENTIAL TREATMENT!
IT'S FINE... BY THE WAY, WHERE'S SHIZUKO-SAN?
SHIZUKO'S OVER THERE.
RESTING ...
むしゃ MUNCH
EEEK! WHAT IS SHE, SOME TOMATO-DEVOURING MONSTER?!
むしゃ MUNCH
ARE YOU THAT HUNGRY?!
NOT REALLY.
I JUST FEEL SICK IF I *DON'T* EAT.
IT'S SOME PREGNANCY FOOD CRAVING...
I'M TOTALLY STUFFED.
BUT IF I DON'T EAT SOMETHING, I'LL THROW UP.
OH, NO...
Tomatoes are easy on the stomach.
AH!
IN THAT CASE, I KNOW JUST WHAT TO FEED YOU!

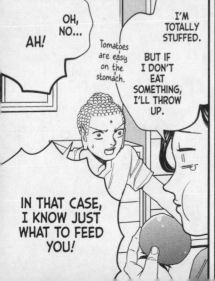

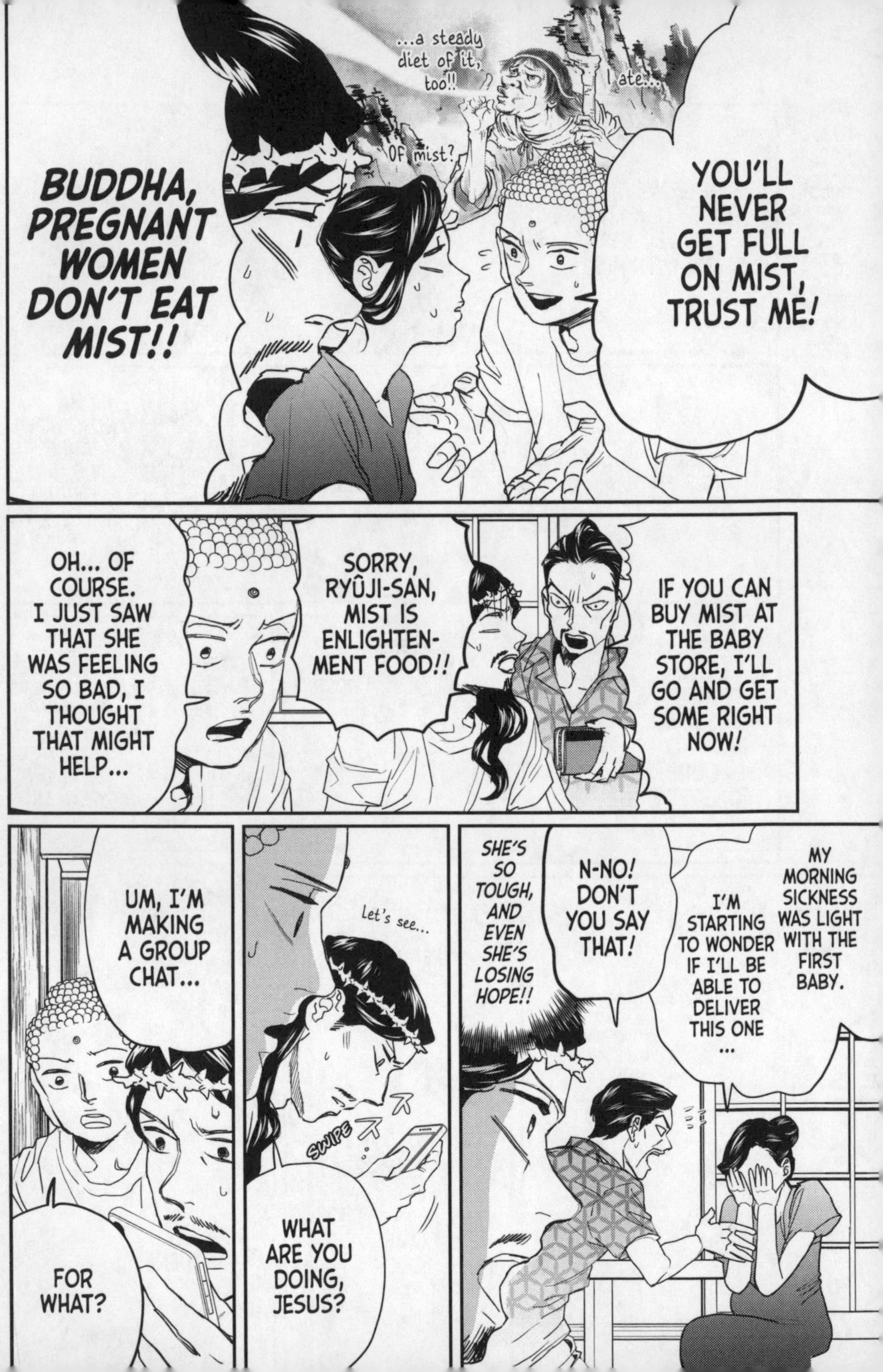

YOU'LL NEVER GET FULL ON MIST, TRUST ME!
I ate...
...a steady diet of it, too!!
Of mist?
BUDDHA, PREGNANT WOMEN DON'T EAT MIST!!
IF YOU CAN BUY MIST AT THE BABY STORE, I'LL GO AND GET SOME RIGHT NOW!
SORRY, RYÛJI-SAN, MIST IS ENLIGHTEN-MENT FOOD!!
OH... OF COURSE. I JUST SAW THAT SHE WAS FEELING SO BAD, I THOUGHT THAT MIGHT HELP...
MY MORNING SICKNESS WAS LIGHT WITH THE FIRST BABY.
I'M STARTING TO WONDER IF I'LL BE ABLE TO DELIVER THIS ONE ...
N-NO! DON'T YOU SAY THAT!
SHE'S SO TOUGH, AND EVEN SHE'S LOSING HOPE!!
let's see...
SWIPE
WHAT ARE YOU DOING, JESUS?
UM, I'M MAKING A GROUP CHAT...
FOR WHAT?

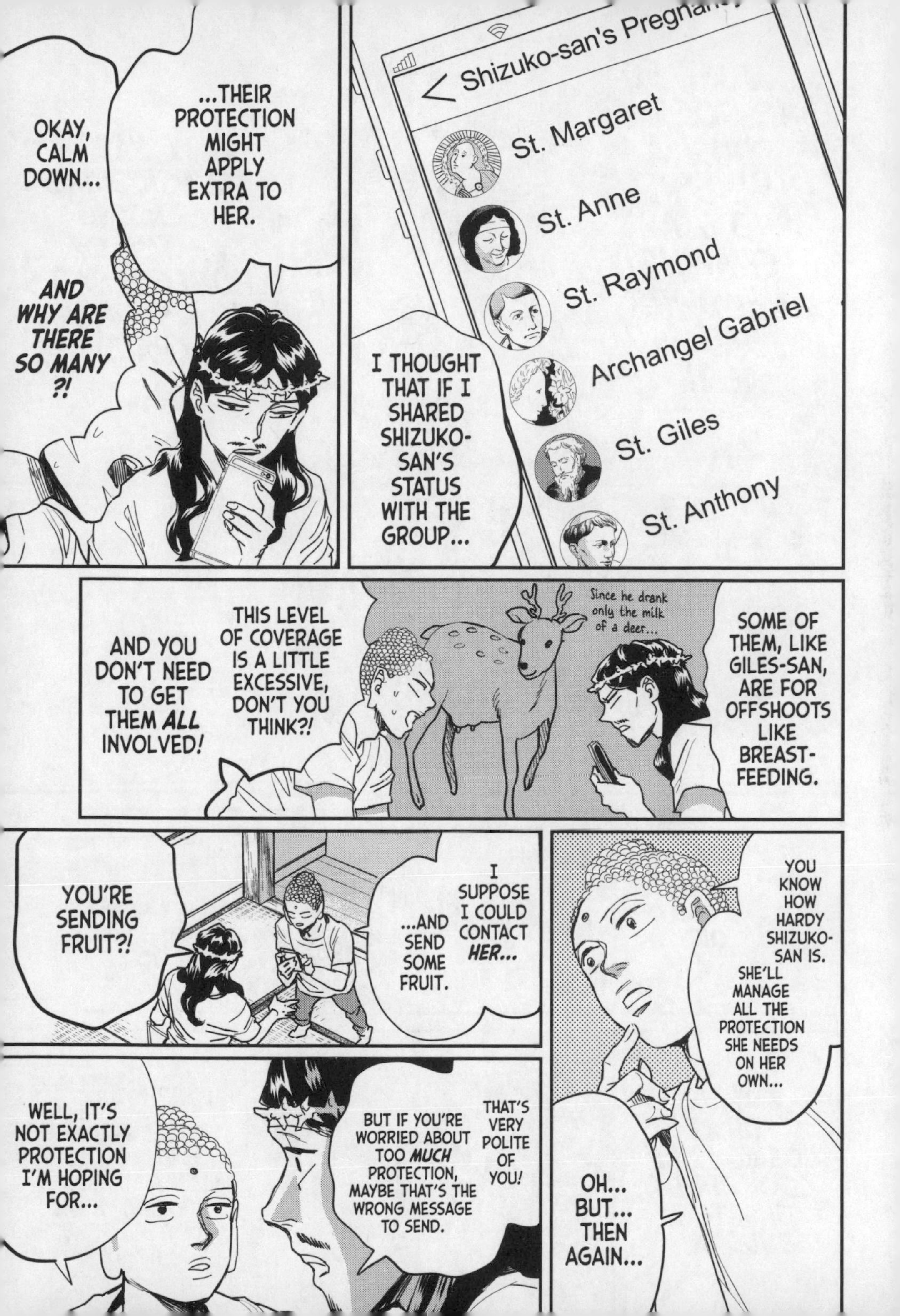
Shizuko-san's Pregnan
St. Margaret
St. Anne
St. Raymond
Archangel Gabriel
St. Giles
St. Anthony
I THOUGHT THAT IF I SHARED SHIZUKO-SAN'S STATUS WITH THE GROUP...
...THEIR PROTECTION MIGHT APPLY EXTRA TO HER.
OKAY, CALM DOWN...
AND WHY ARE THERE SO MANY?!
SOME OF THEM, LIKE GILES-SAN, ARE FOR OFFSHOOTS LIKE BREAST-FEEDING.
Since he drank only the milk of a deer...
THIS LEVEL OF COVERAGE IS A LITTLE EXCESSIVE, DON'T YOU THINK?!
AND YOU DON'T NEED TO GET THEM ALL INVOLVED!
YOU KNOW HOW HARDY SHIZUKO-SAN IS. SHE'LL MANAGE ALL THE PROTECTION SHE NEEDS ON HER OWN...
OH... BUT... THEN AGAIN...
I SUPPOSE I COULD CONTACT HER...
...AND SEND SOME FRUIT.
YOU'RE SENDING FRUIT?!
THAT'S VERY POLITE OF YOU!
BUT IF YOU'RE WORRIED ABOUT TOO MUCH PROTECTION, MAYBE THAT'S THE WRONG MESSAGE TO SEND.
WELL, IT'S NOT EXACTLY PROTECTION I'M HOPING FOR...

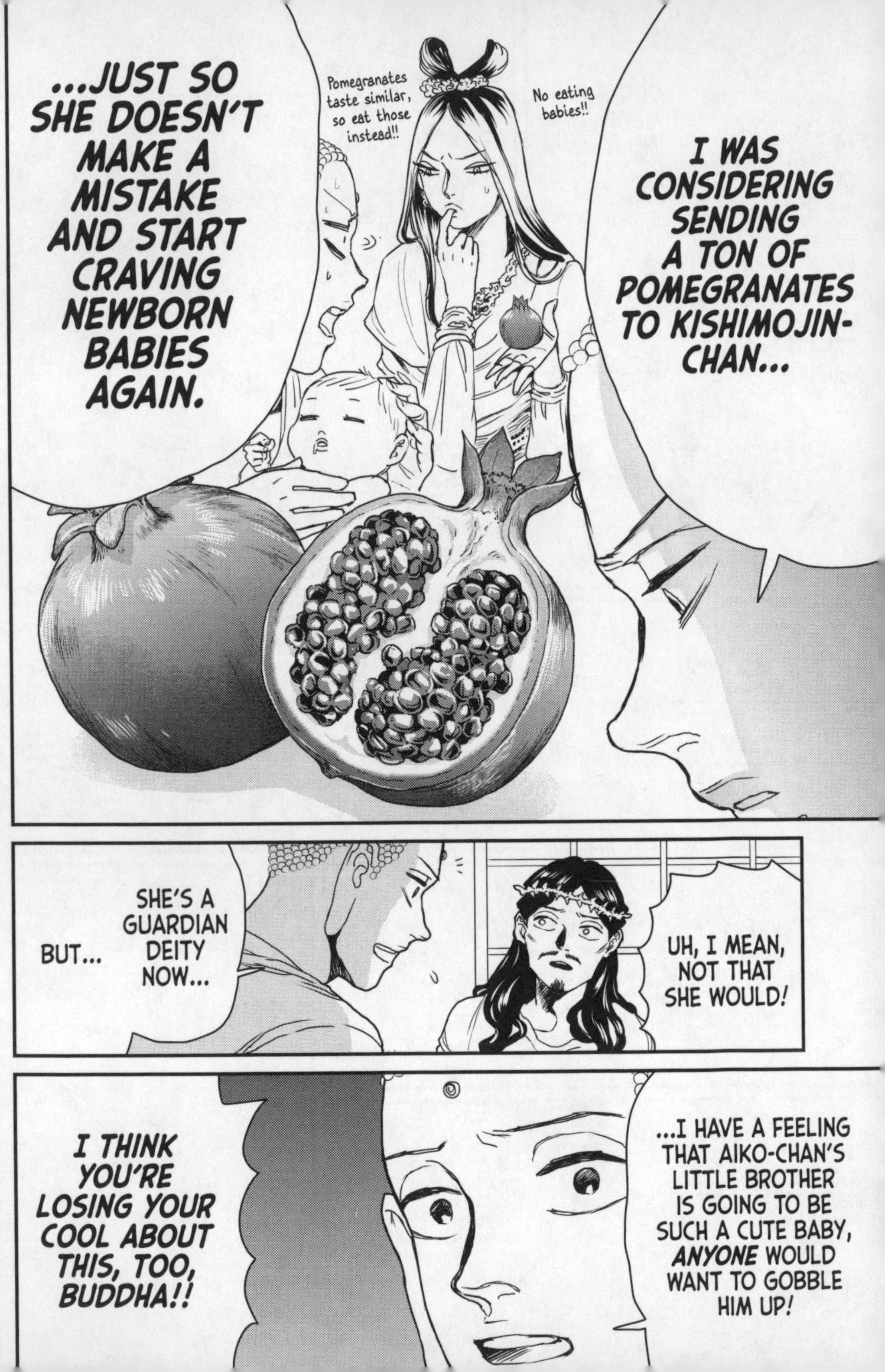
I WAS CONSIDERING SENDING A TON OF POMEGRANATES TO KISHIMOJIN-CHAN...
No eating babies!!
Pomegranates taste similar, so eat those instead!!
...JUST SO SHE DOESN'T MAKE A MISTAKE AND START CRAVING NEWBORN BABIES AGAIN.
UH, I MEAN, NOT THAT SHE WOULD!
SHE'S A GUARDIAN DEITY NOW...
BUT...
...I HAVE A FEELING THAT AIKO-CHAN'S LITTLE BROTHER IS GOING TO BE SUCH A CUTE BABY, *ANYONE* WOULD WANT TO GOBBLE HIM UP!
I THINK YOU'RE LOSING YOUR COOL ABOUT THIS, TOO, BUDDHA!!

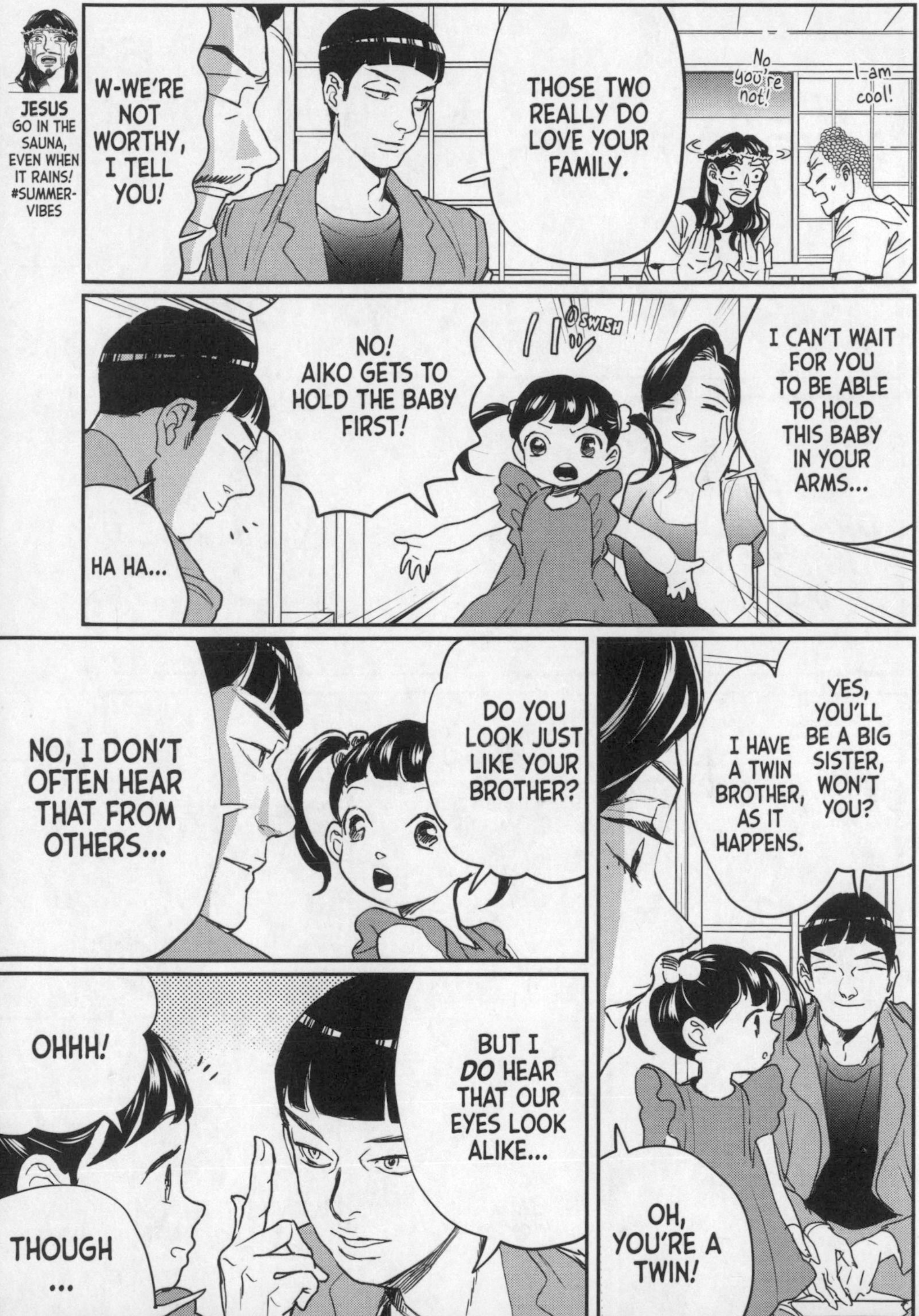
I am cool!
No you're not!
THOSE TWO REALLY DO LOVE YOUR FAMILY.
W-WE'RE NOT WORTHY, I TELL YOU!
JESUS GO IN THE SAUNA, EVEN WHEN IT RAINS! #SUMMER-VIBES
I CAN'T WAIT FOR YOU TO BE ABLE TO HOLD THIS BABY IN YOUR ARMS...
SWISH
NO! AIKO GETS TO HOLD THE BABY FIRST!
HA HA...
YES, YOU'LL BE A BIG SISTER, WON'T YOU?
I HAVE A TWIN BROTHER, AS IT HAPPENS.
OH, YOU'RE A TWIN!
DO YOU LOOK JUST LIKE YOUR BROTHER?
NO, I DON'T OFTEN HEAR THAT FROM OTHERS...
BUT I *DO* HEAR THAT OUR EYES LOOK ALIKE...
OHHH!
THOUGH ...

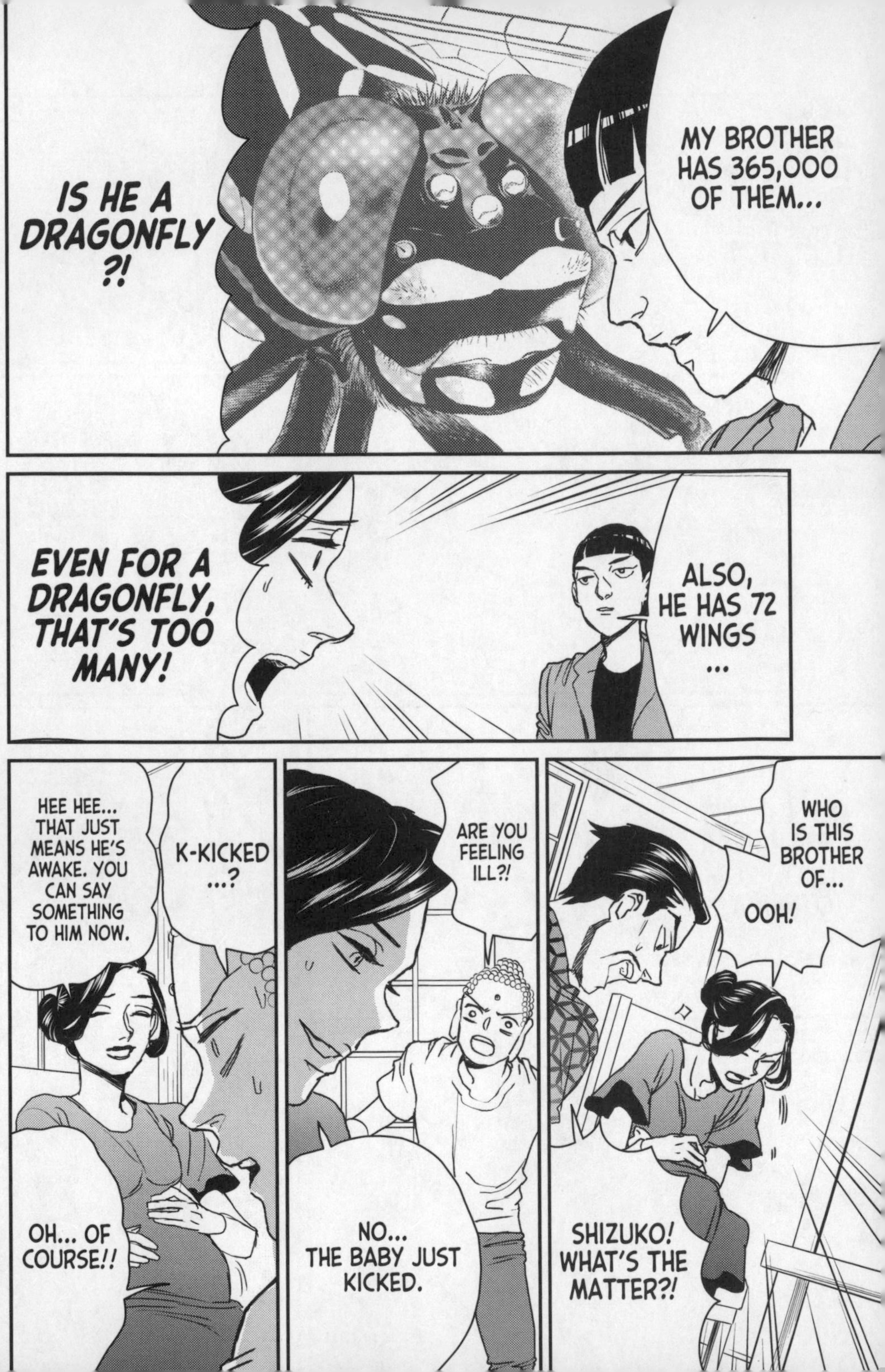
MY BROTHER HAS 365,000 OF THEM...
IS HE A DRAGONFLY ?!
ALSO, HE HAS 72 WINGS ...
EVEN FOR A DRAGONFLY, THAT'S TOO MANY!
WHO IS THIS BROTHER OF...
OOH!
SHIZUKO! WHAT'S THE MATTER?!
ARE YOU FEELING ILL?!
NO... THE BABY JUST KICKED.
K-KICKED ...?
HEE HEE... THAT JUST MEANS HE'S AWAKE. YOU CAN SAY SOMETHING TO HIM NOW.
OH... OF COURSE!!

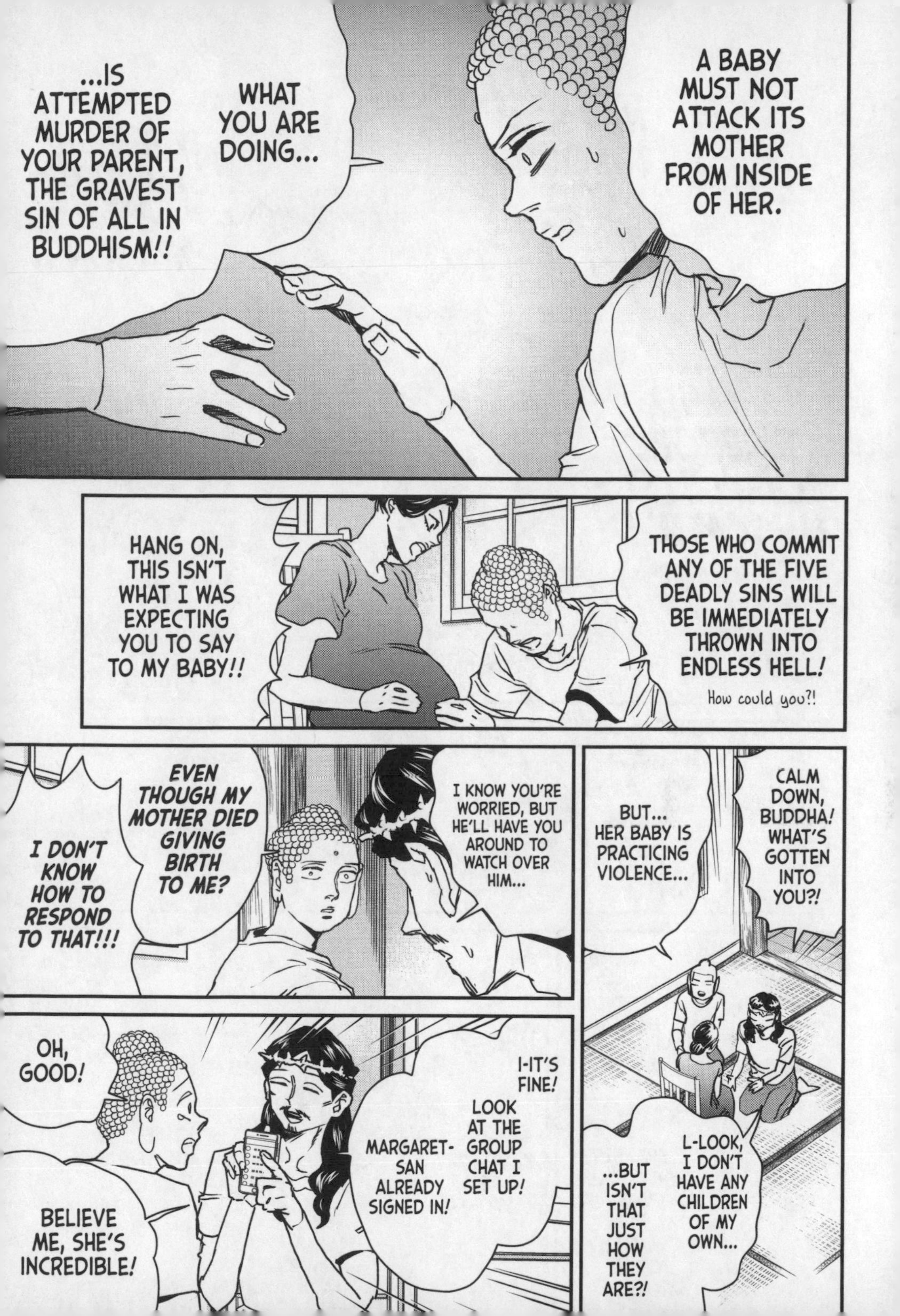
A BABY MUST NOT ATTACK ITS MOTHER FROM INSIDE OF HER.
WHAT YOU ARE DOING...
...IS ATTEMPTED MURDER OF YOUR PARENT, THE GRAVEST SIN OF ALL IN BUDDHISM!!
THOSE WHO COMMIT ANY OF THE FIVE DEADLY SINS WILL BE IMMEDIATELY THROWN INTO ENDLESS HELL!
How could you?!
HANG ON, THIS ISN'T WHAT I WAS EXPECTING YOU TO SAY TO MY BABY!!
CALM DOWN, BUDDHA! WHAT'S GOTTEN INTO YOU?!
BUT... HER BABY IS PRACTICING VIOLENCE...
L-LOOK, I DON'T HAVE ANY CHILDREN OF MY OWN...
...BUT ISN'T THAT JUST HOW THEY ARE?!
I KNOW YOU'RE WORRIED, BUT HE'LL HAVE YOU AROUND TO WATCH OVER HIM...
EVEN THOUGH MY MOTHER DIED GIVING BIRTH TO ME?
I DON'T KNOW HOW TO RESPOND TO THAT!!!
I-IT'S FINE!
LOOK AT THE GROUP CHAT I SET UP!
MARGARET-SAN ALREADY SIGNED IN!
OH, GOOD!
BELIEVE ME, SHE'S INCREDIBLE!

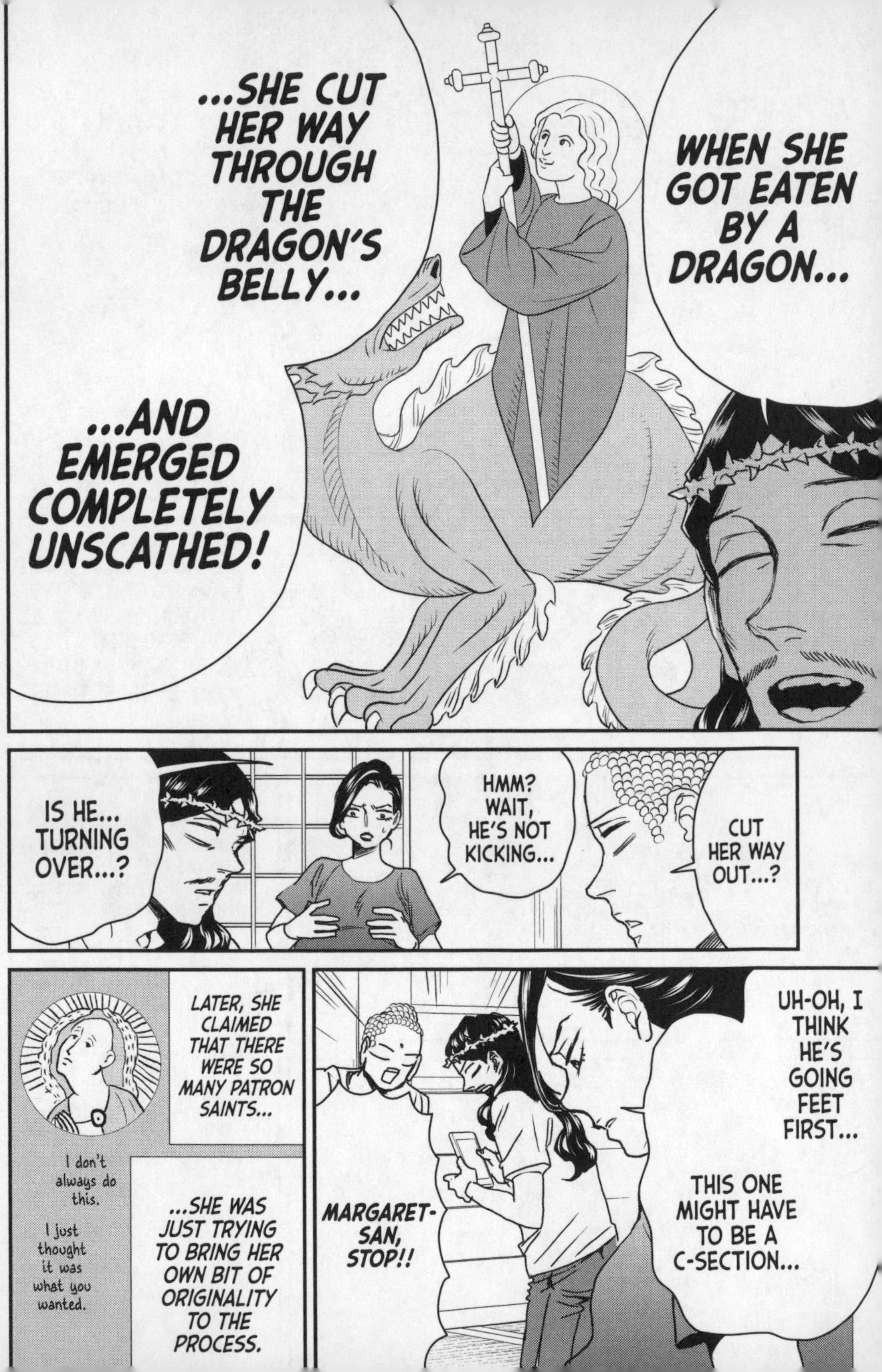
WHEN SHE GOT EATEN BY A DRAGON...
...SHE CUT HER WAY THROUGH THE DRAGON'S BELLY...
...AND EMERGED COMPLETELY UNSCATHED!
CUT HER WAY OUT...?
HMM? WAIT, HE'S NOT KICKING...
IS HE... TURNING OVER...?
UH-OH, I THINK HE'S GOING FEET FIRST...
THIS ONE MIGHT HAVE TO BE A C-SECTION...
MARGARET-SAN, STOP!!
LATER, SHE CLAIMED THAT THERE WERE SO MANY PATRON SAINTS...
I don't always do this.
I just thought it was what you wanted.
...SHE WAS JUST TRYING TO BRING HER OWN BIT OF ORIGINALITY TO THE PROCESS.

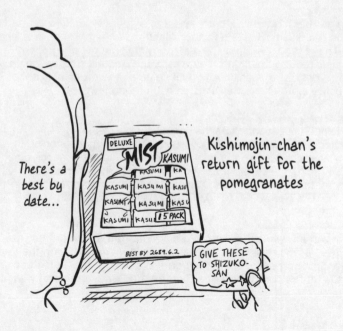

Kishimojin-chan's return gift for the pomegranates
There's a best by date...
DELUXE
MIST
KASUMI
15 PACK
BEST BY 2689.6.2
GIVE THESE TO SHIZUKO-SAN

SAINT ☆ YOUNG MEN

CHAPTER 119 TRANSLATION NOTES

Eating mist, page 240
This comes not from any well-known anecdote about Gautama Buddha's life, but from the Japanese saying "to eat mist," which refers to any kind of hermit-like existence away from the rat race of society and careers. The saying comes from the belief that hermits in the mountains would live off of mist.

Patron saints of childbirth, page 241
The list of saints--St. Margaret of Antioch; St. Anne, mother of Mary; St. Raymond; St. Giles; and St. Anthony of Padua--are all known for their patronage of childbirth, pregnant mothers, or good health in general. St. Giles (Aegidius) was the subject of a medieval legend that he lived only with a red deer, upon whose milk he fed. From similar sources, St. Margaret was said to have been swallowed by Satan in the form of a dragon, only for the cross she carried to split the beast's insides open and allow her to escape.

Kishimojin, page 242
Kishimojin, also known as Hariti, is both a demon and and a guardian deity who watches over children in Buddhism. She is originally described as a rakshasi, or a kind of man-eating demon. The legend says that she had many children of her own, but killed the children of others to feed them. In order to help, the Buddha hid her youngest child to show her the pain of "losing" a child. After that point, she swore to only eat pomegranates and became a protector of all children and pregnant women.

Sandalphon's brother, page 244
In some writings, Sandalphon is described as the twin brother of the angel Metatron, who was originally the human Enoch (Sandalphon is similarly described as being the prophet Elijah originally). Much of the writing about Metatron exists in the apocryphal Third Book of Enoch (3 Enoch), which describes how Enoch ascends to Heaven and is transformed into Metatron, the celestial scribe. Metatron is blessed with 72 wings, each large enough to cover the whole word, and 365,000 eyes.

Five deadly sins, page 245
The five deadly sins, known as *anantarika-karma*, are considered so awful that they come with an immediate karmic cost of sending the individual to hell upon their next life. The five sins are murdering one's father, murdering one's mother, killing an enlightened being, causing the bloodshed of a Buddha, and enacting heresy within the monastic community.

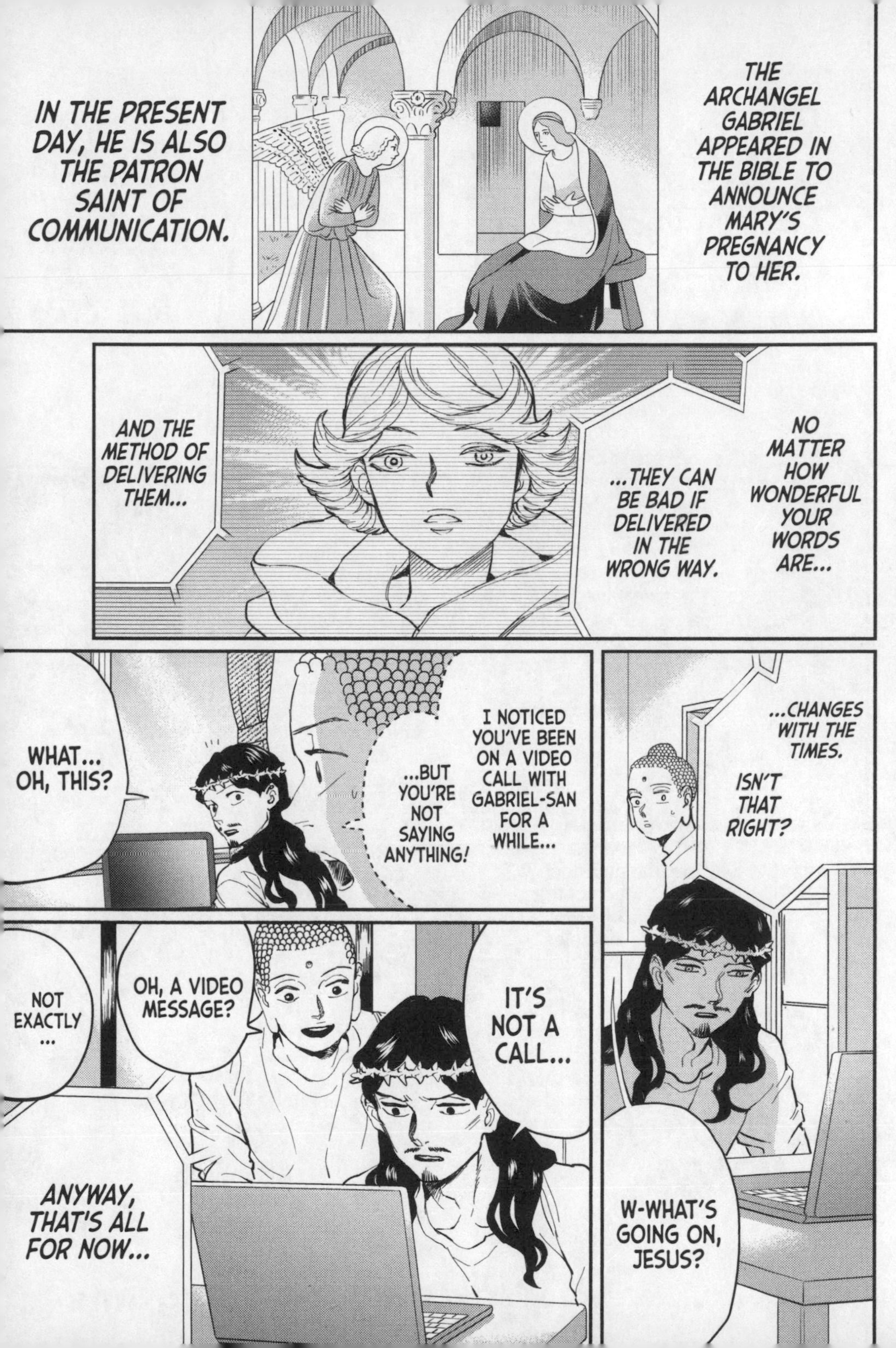
THE ARCHANGEL GABRIEL APPEARED IN THE BIBLE TO ANNOUNCE MARY'S PREGNANCY TO HER.
IN THE PRESENT DAY, HE IS ALSO THE PATRON SAINT OF COMMUNICATION.
NO MATTER HOW WONDERFUL YOUR WORDS ARE...
...THEY CAN BE BAD IF DELIVERED IN THE WRONG WAY.
AND THE METHOD OF DELIVERING THEM...
...CHANGES WITH THE TIMES.
ISN'T THAT RIGHT?
W-WHAT'S GOING ON, JESUS?
I NOTICED YOU'VE BEEN ON A VIDEO CALL WITH GABRIEL-SAN FOR A WHILE...
...BUT YOU'RE NOT SAYING ANYTHING!
WHAT... OH, THIS?
IT'S NOT A CALL...
OH, A VIDEO MESSAGE?
NOT EXACTLY...
ANYWAY, THAT'S ALL FOR NOW...

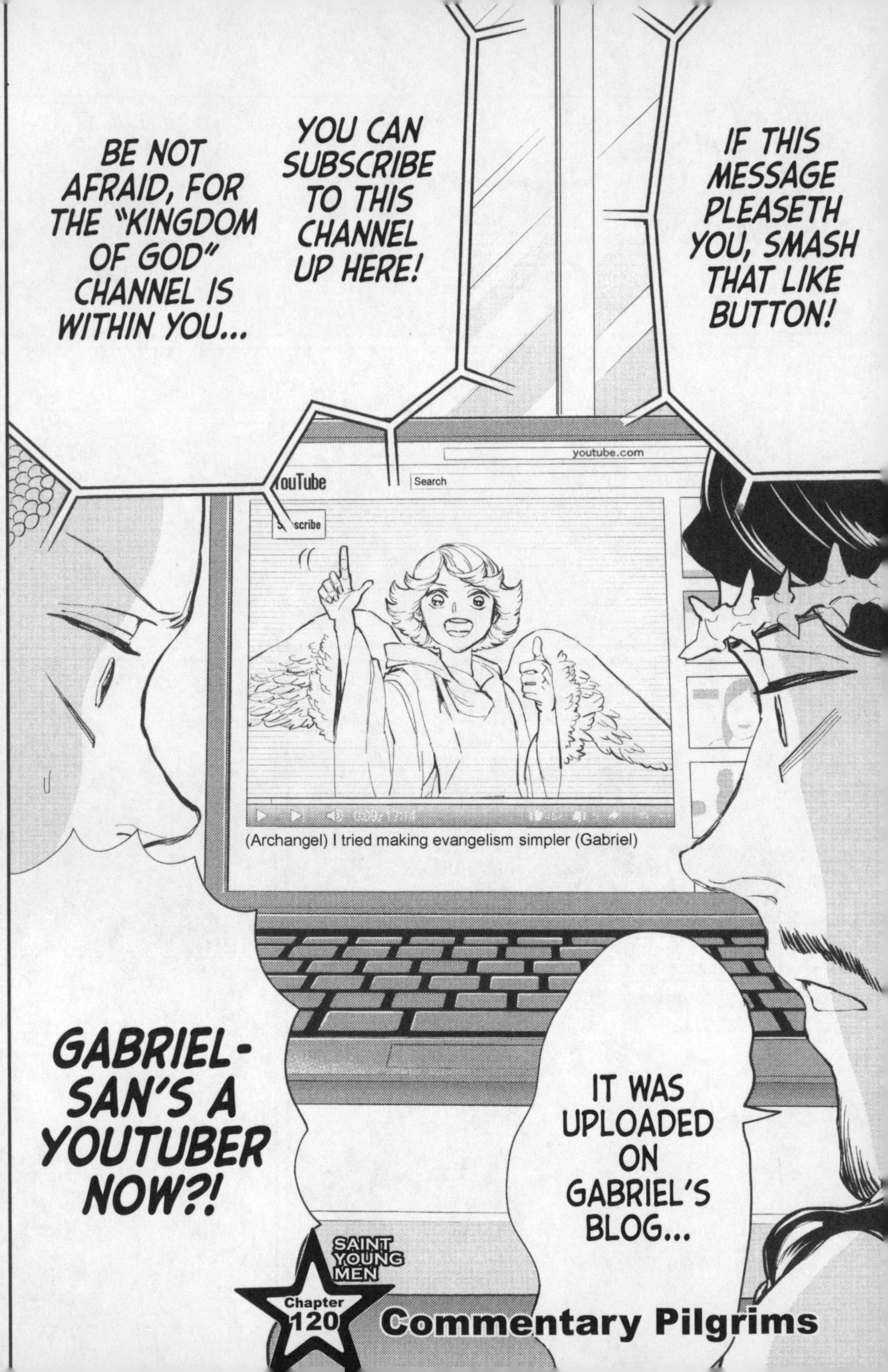
IF THIS MESSAGE PLEASETH YOU, SMASH THAT LIKE BUTTON!
YOU CAN SUBSCRIBE TO THIS CHANNEL UP HERE!
BE NOT AFRAID, FOR THE "KINGDOM OF GOD" CHANNEL IS WITHIN YOU...
youtube.com
YouTube
Search
Subscribe
(Archangel) I tried making evangelism simpler (Gabriel)
IT WAS UPLOADED ON GABRIEL'S BLOG...
GABRIEL-SAN'S A YOUTUBER NOW?!
SAINT YOUNG MEN

Chapter 120 Commentary Pilgrims

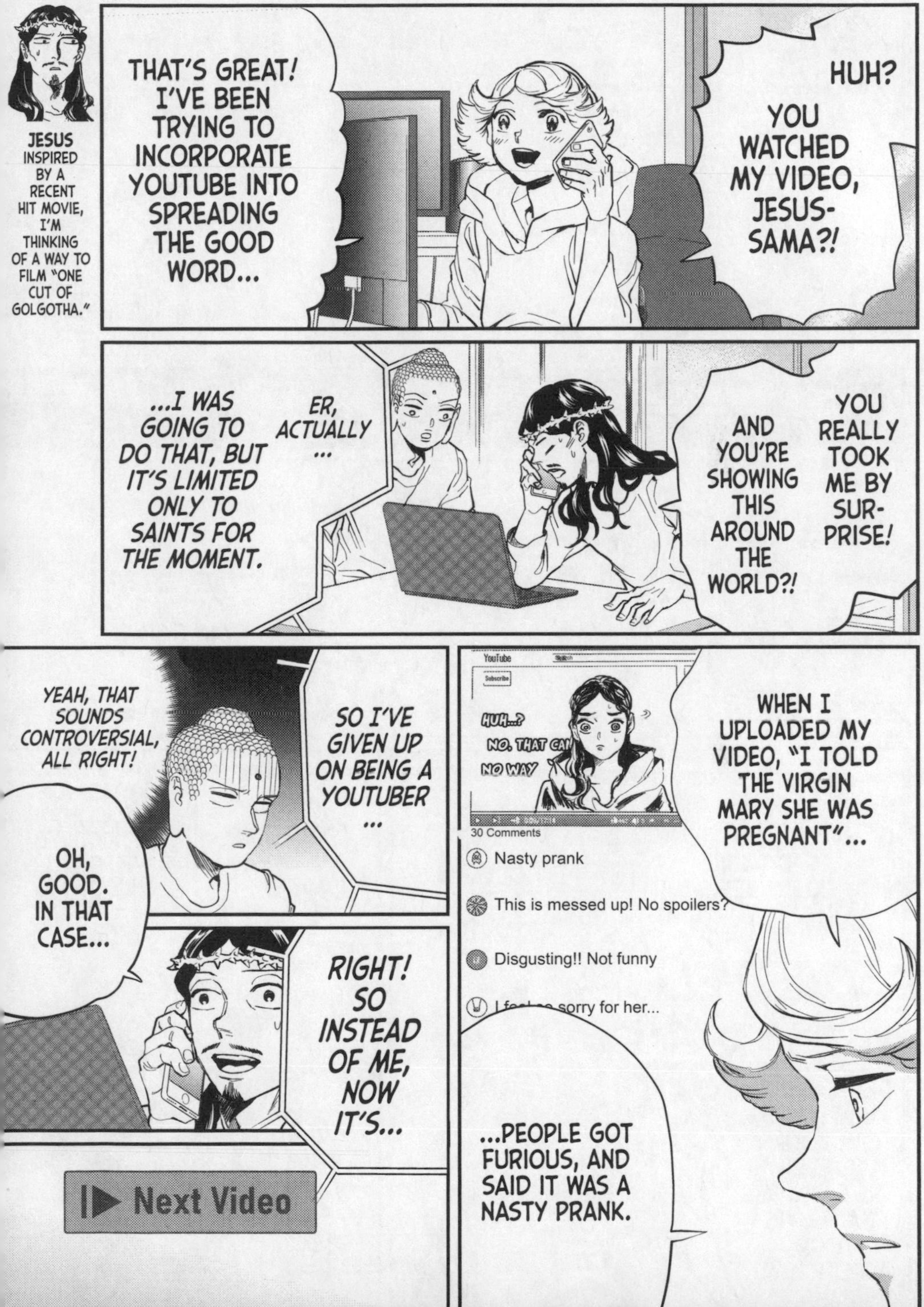
JESUS
INSPIRED BY A RECENT HIT MOVIE, I'M THINKING OF A WAY TO FILM "ONE CUT OF GOLGOTHA."
HUH?
YOU WATCHED MY VIDEO, JESUS-SAMA?!
THAT'S GREAT! I'VE BEEN TRYING TO INCORPORATE YOUTUBE INTO SPREADING THE GOOD WORD...
YOU REALLY TOOK ME BY SURPRISE!
AND YOU'RE SHOWING THIS AROUND THE WORLD?!
ER, ACTUALLY ...
...I WAS GOING TO DO THAT, BUT IT'S LIMITED ONLY TO SAINTS FOR THE MOMENT.
WHEN I UPLOADED MY VIDEO, "I TOLD THE VIRGIN MARY SHE WAS PREGNANT"...
YouTube
Subscribe
HUH...?
NO. THAT CAN
NO WAY
30 Comments
Nasty prank
This is messed up! No spoilers?
Disgusting!! Not funny
sorry for her...
...PEOPLE GOT FURIOUS, AND SAID IT WAS A NASTY PRANK.
SO I'VE GIVEN UP ON BEING A YOUTUBER ...
YEAH, THAT SOUNDS CONTROVERSIAL, ALL RIGHT!
OH, GOOD. IN THAT CASE...
RIGHT! SO INSTEAD OF ME, NOW IT'S...
Next Video

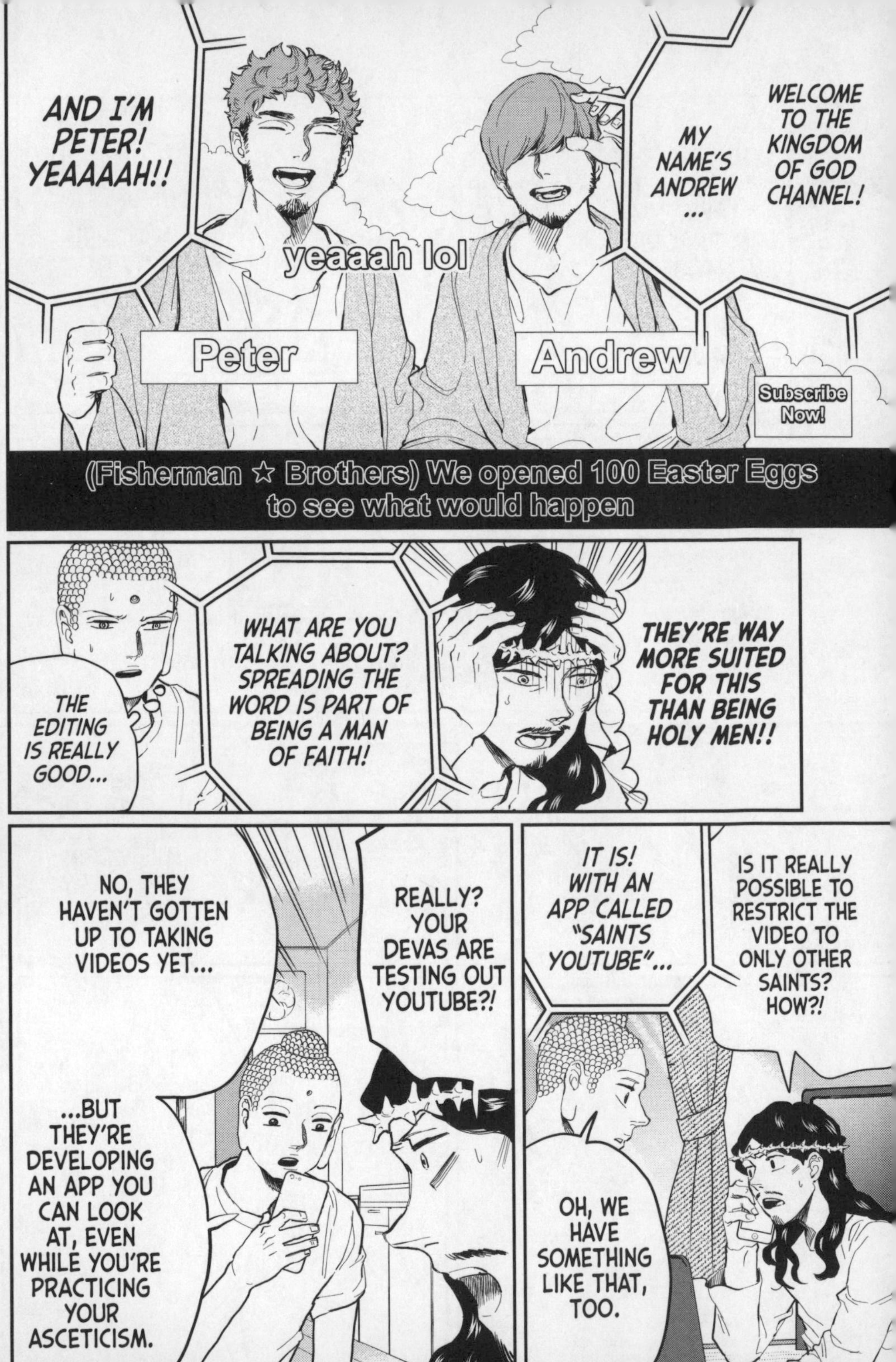
WELCOME TO THE KINGDOM OF GOD CHANNEL!
MY NAME'S ANDREW ...
AND I'M PETER! YEAAAAH!!
yeaaah lol
Subscribe Now!
Andrew
Peter
(Fisherman ☆ Brothers) We opened 100 Easter Eggs to see what would happen
THEY'RE WAY MORE SUITED FOR THIS THAN BEING HOLY MEN!!
WHAT ARE YOU TALKING ABOUT? SPREADING THE WORD IS PART OF BEING A MAN OF FAITH!
THE EDITING IS REALLY GOOD...
IS IT REALLY POSSIBLE TO RESTRICT THE VIDEO TO ONLY OTHER SAINTS? HOW?!
IT IS! WITH AN APP CALLED "SAINTS YOUTUBE"...
OH, WE HAVE SOMETHING LIKE THAT, TOO.
REALLY? YOUR DEVAS ARE TESTING OUT YOUTUBE?!
NO, THEY HAVEN'T GOTTEN UP TO TAKING VIDEOS YET...
...BUT THEY'RE DEVELOPING AN APP YOU CAN LOOK AT, EVEN WHILE YOU'RE PRACTICING YOUR ASCETICISM.

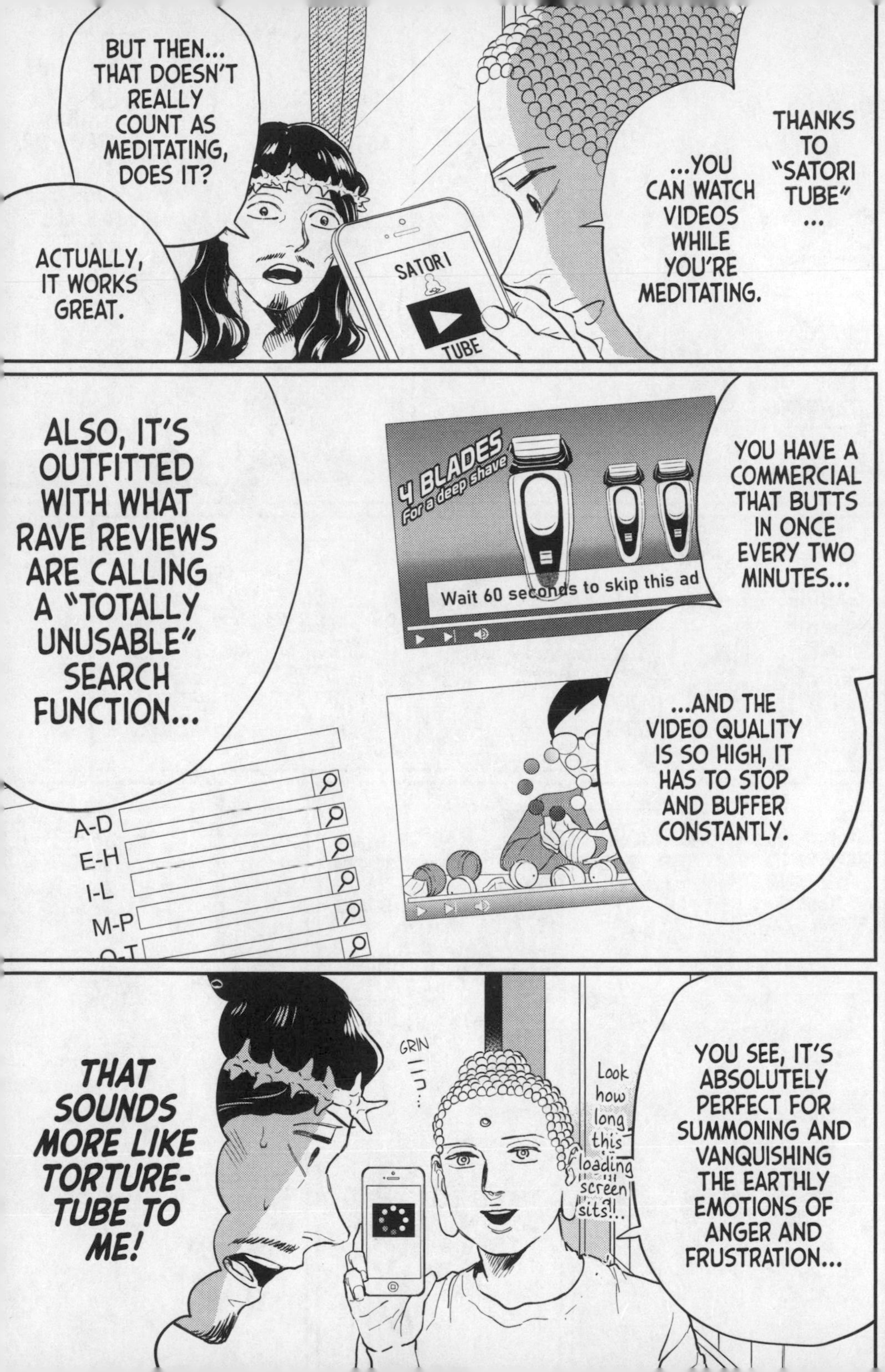
THANKS TO "SATORI TUBE"...
...YOU CAN WATCH VIDEOS WHILE YOU'RE MEDITATING.
BUT THEN... THAT DOESN'T REALLY COUNT AS MEDITATING, DOES IT?
SATORI
TUBE
ACTUALLY, IT WORKS GREAT.
YOU HAVE A COMMERCIAL THAT BUTTS IN ONCE EVERY TWO MINUTES...
4 BLADES
For a deep shave
Wait 60 seconds to skip this ad
...AND THE VIDEO QUALITY IS SO HIGH, IT HAS TO STOP AND BUFFER CONSTANTLY.
ALSO, IT'S OUTFITTED WITH WHAT RAVE REVIEWS ARE CALLING A "TOTALLY UNUSABLE" SEARCH FUNCTION...
A-D
E-H
I-L
M-P
YOU SEE, IT'S ABSOLUTELY PERFECT FOR SUMMONING AND VANQUISHING THE EARTHLY EMOTIONS OF ANGER AND FRUSTRATION...
Look how long this loading screen sits!!
GRIN
THAT SOUNDS MORE LIKE TORTURE-TUBE TO ME!

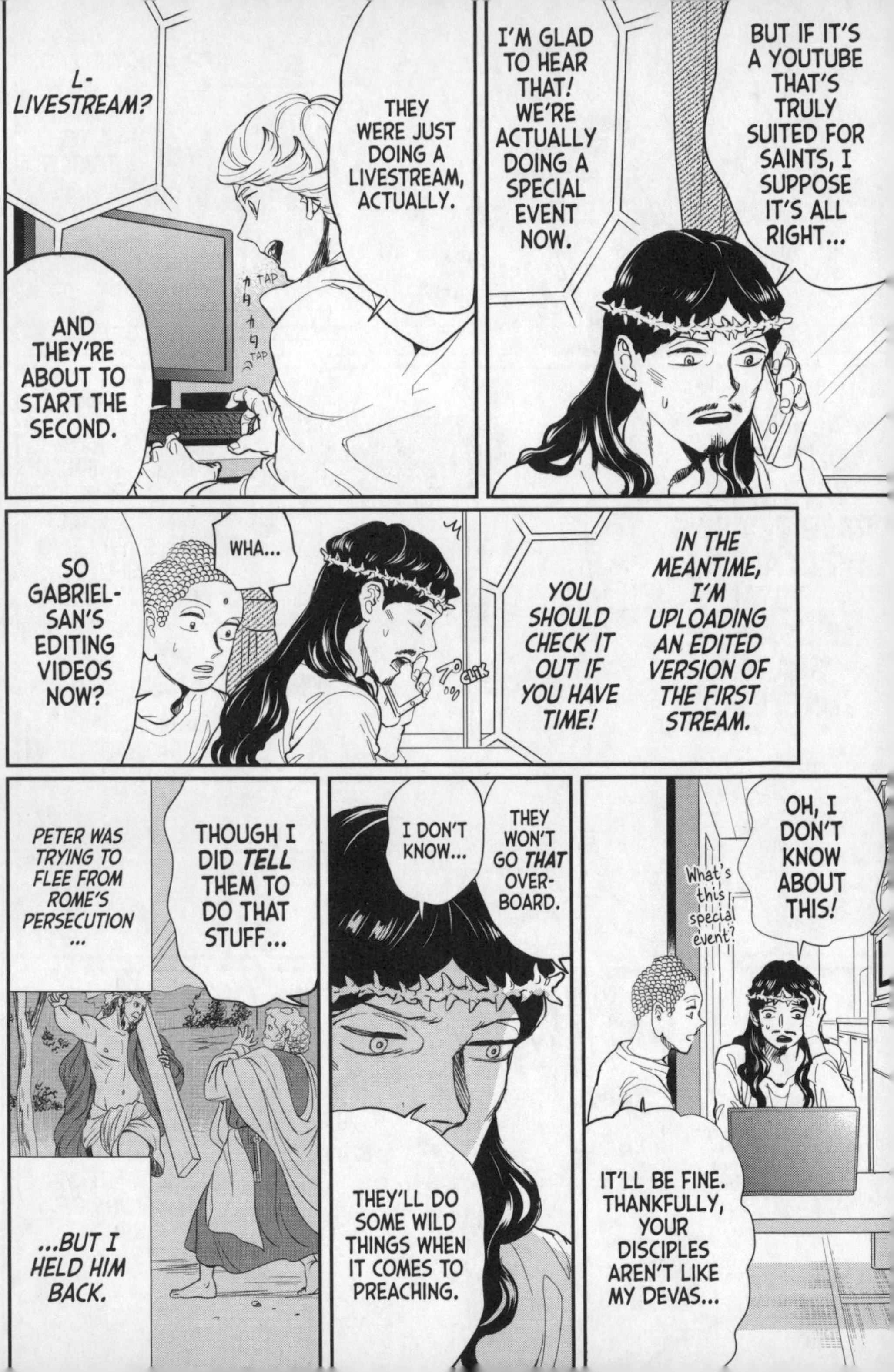
BUT IF IT'S A YOUTUBE THAT'S TRULY SUITED FOR SAINTS, I SUPPOSE IT'S ALL RIGHT...
I'M GLAD TO HEAR THAT! WE'RE ACTUALLY DOING A SPECIAL EVENT NOW.
THEY WERE JUST DOING A LIVESTREAM, ACTUALLY.
L-LIVESTREAM?
カリ TAP
カリ TAP
AND THEY'RE ABOUT TO START THE SECOND.
IN THE MEANTIME, I'M UPLOADING AN EDITED VERSION OF THE FIRST STREAM.
YOU SHOULD CHECK IT OUT IF YOU HAVE TIME!
CLIK
WHA...
SO GABRIEL-SAN'S EDITING VIDEOS NOW?
OH, I DON'T KNOW ABOUT THIS!
What's this special event?
IT'LL BE FINE. THANKFULLY, YOUR DISCIPLES AREN'T LIKE MY DEVAS...
THEY WON'T GO THAT OVERBOARD.
I DON'T KNOW...
THEY'LL DO SOME WILD THINGS WHEN IT COMES TO PREACHING.
THOUGH I DID TELL THEM TO DO THAT STUFF...
PETER WAS TRYING TO FLEE FROM ROME'S PERSECUTION...
...BUT I HELD HIM BACK.

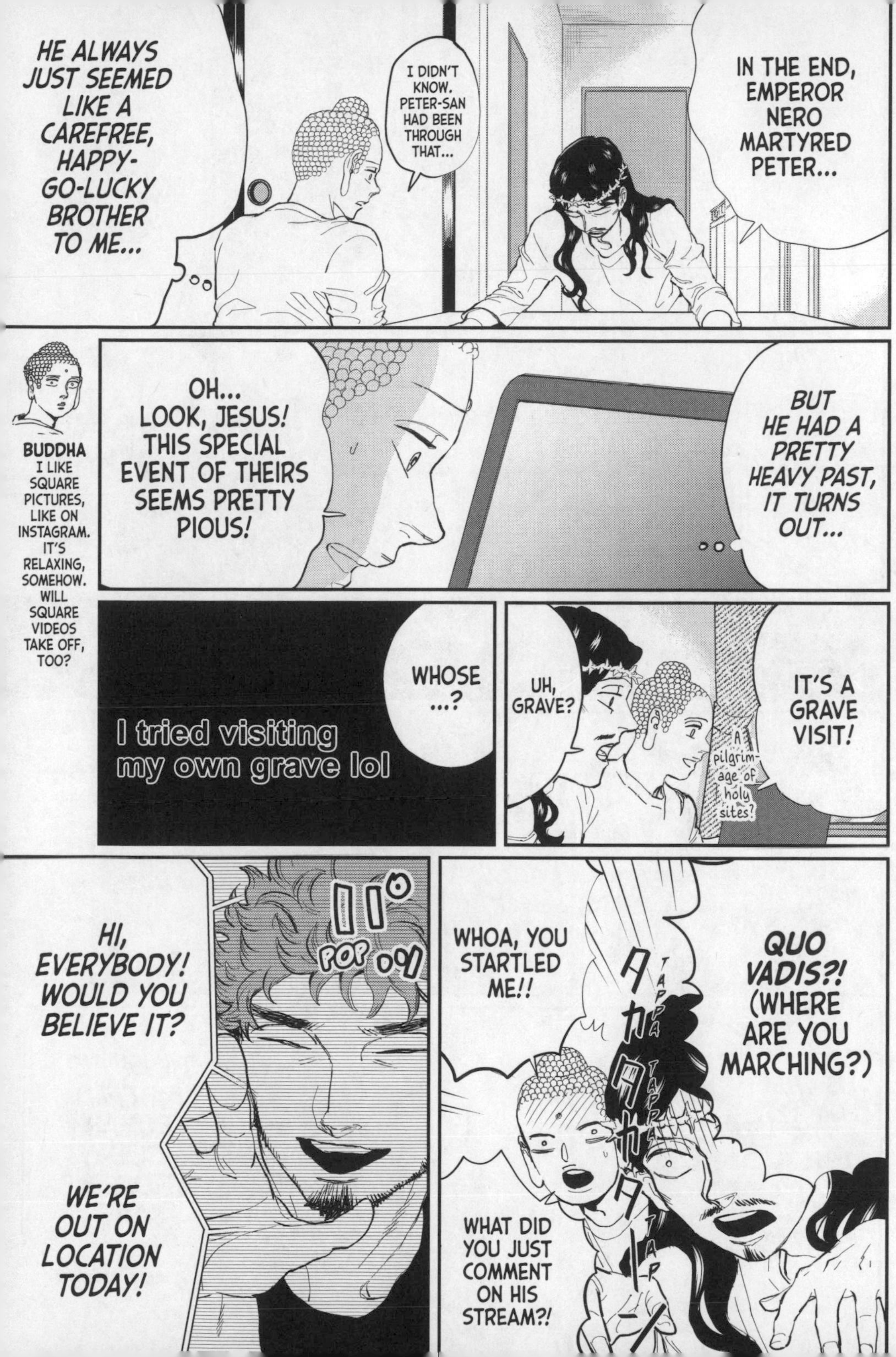
IN THE END, EMPEROR NERO MARTYRED PETER...
I DIDN'T KNOW. PETER-SAN HAD BEEN THROUGH THAT...
HE ALWAYS JUST SEEMED LIKE A CAREFREE, HAPPY-GO-LUCKY BROTHER TO ME...
BUT HE HAD A PRETTY HEAVY PAST, IT TURNS OUT...
OH... LOOK, JESUS! THIS SPECIAL EVENT OF THEIRS SEEMS PRETTY PIOUS!
BUDDHA
I LIKE SQUARE PICTURES, LIKE ON INSTAGRAM. IT'S RELAXING, SOMEHOW. WILL SQUARE VIDEOS TAKE OFF, TOO?
IT'S A GRAVE VISIT!
A pilgrimage of holy sites?
UH, GRAVE?
WHOSE ...?
I tried visiting my own grave lol
QUO VADIS?! (WHERE ARE YOU MARCHING?)
TAPPA TAPPA TAP
WHOA, YOU STARTLED ME!!
WHAT DID YOU JUST COMMENT ON HIS STREAM?!
POP
HI, EVERYBODY! WOULD YOU BELIEVE IT?
WE'RE OUT ON LOCATION TODAY!

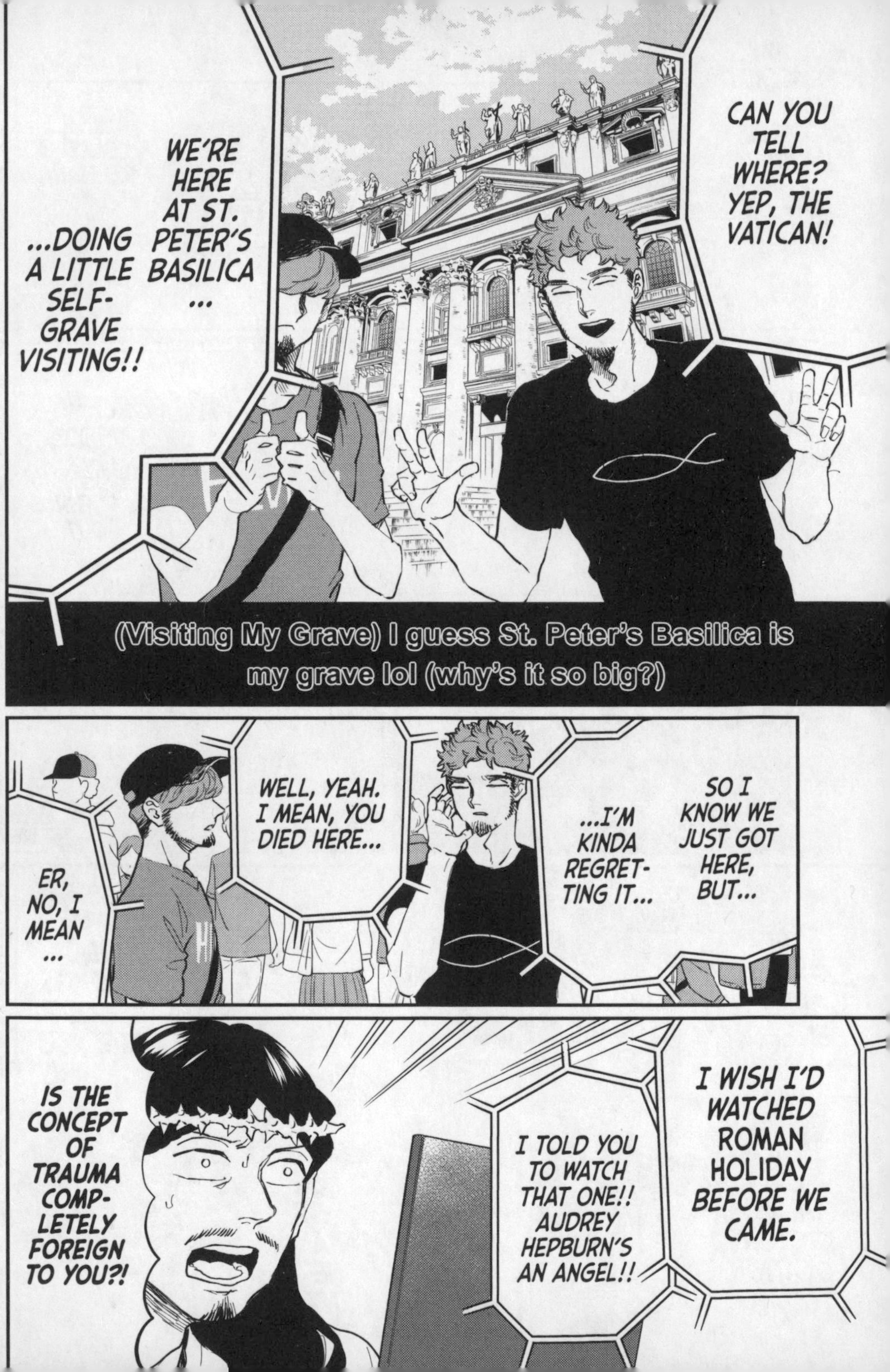
CAN YOU TELL WHERE? YEP, THE VATICAN!
WE'RE HERE AT ST. PETER'S BASILICA ...
...DOING A LITTLE SELF-GRAVE VISITING!!
(Visiting My Grave) I guess St. Peter's Basilica is my grave lol (why's it so big?)
SO I KNOW WE JUST GOT HERE, BUT...
...I'M KINDA REGRETTING IT...
WELL, YEAH. I MEAN, YOU DIED HERE...
ER, NO, I MEAN ...
I WISH I'D WATCHED ROMAN HOLIDAY BEFORE WE CAME.
I TOLD YOU TO WATCH THAT ONE!! AUDREY HEPBURN'S AN ANGEL!!
IS THE CONCEPT OF TRAUMA COMPLETELY FOREIGN TO YOU?!

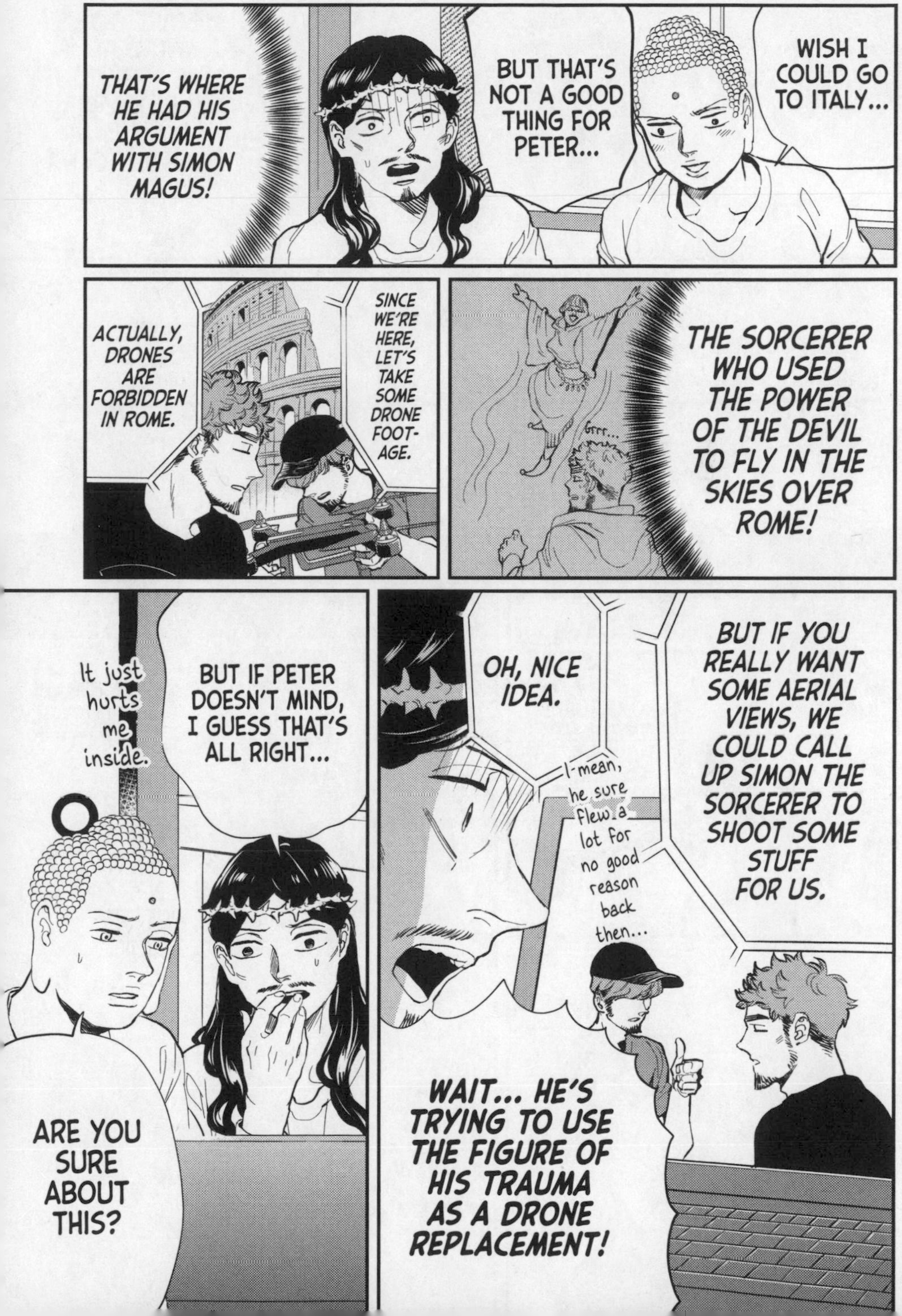
WISH I COULD GO TO ITALY...
BUT THAT'S NOT A GOOD THING FOR PETER...
THAT'S WHERE HE HAD HIS ARGUMENT WITH SIMON MAGUS!
THE SORCERER WHO USED THE POWER OF THE DEVIL TO FLY IN THE SKIES OVER ROME!
Grrr...
SINCE WE'RE HERE, LET'S TAKE SOME DRONE FOOT-AGE.
ACTUALLY, DRONES ARE FORBIDDEN IN ROME.
BUT IF YOU REALLY WANT SOME AERIAL VIEWS, WE COULD CALL UP SIMON THE SORCERER TO SHOOT SOME STUFF FOR US.
OH, NICE IDEA.
I mean, he sure flew a lot for no good reason back then...
WAIT... HE'S TRYING TO USE THE FIGURE OF HIS TRAUMA AS A DRONE REPLACEMENT!
BUT IF PETER DOESN'T MIND, I GUESS THAT'S ALL RIGHT...
It just hurts me inside.
ARE YOU SURE ABOUT THIS?

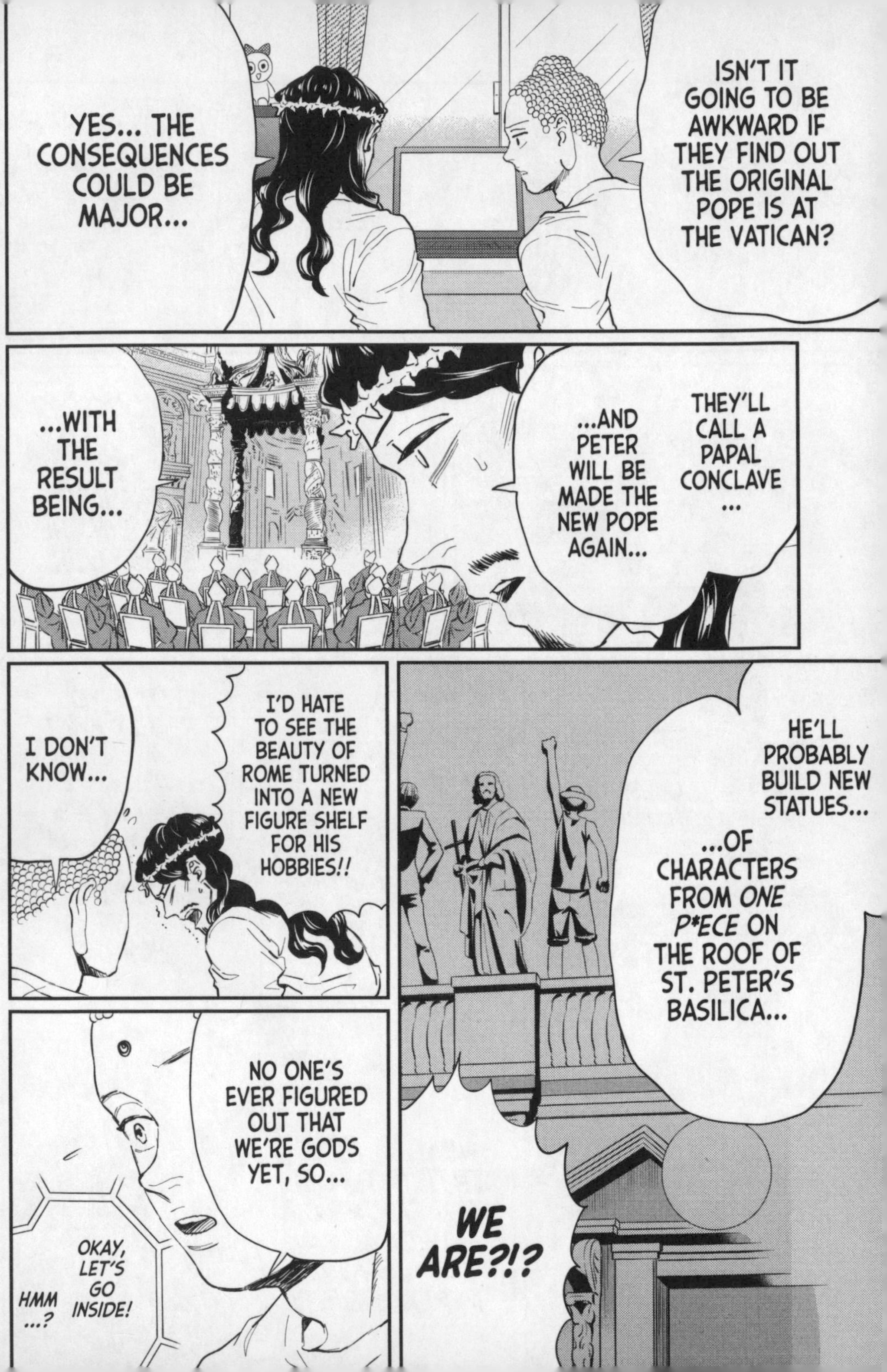
ISN'T IT GOING TO BE AWKWARD IF THEY FIND OUT THE ORIGINAL POPE IS AT THE VATICAN?
YES... THE CONSEQUENCES COULD BE MAJOR...
THEY'LL CALL A PAPAL CONCLAVE ...
...AND PETER WILL BE MADE THE NEW POPE AGAIN...
...WITH THE RESULT BEING...
HE'LL PROBABLY BUILD NEW STATUES...
...OF CHARACTERS FROM *ONE P*ECE* ON THE ROOF OF ST. PETER'S BASILICA...
WE ARE?!?
I'D HATE TO SEE THE BEAUTY OF ROME TURNED INTO A NEW FIGURE SHELF FOR HIS HOBBIES!!
I DON'T KNOW...
NO ONE'S EVER FIGURED OUT THAT WE'RE GODS YET, SO...
OKAY, LET'S GO INSIDE!
HMM ...?

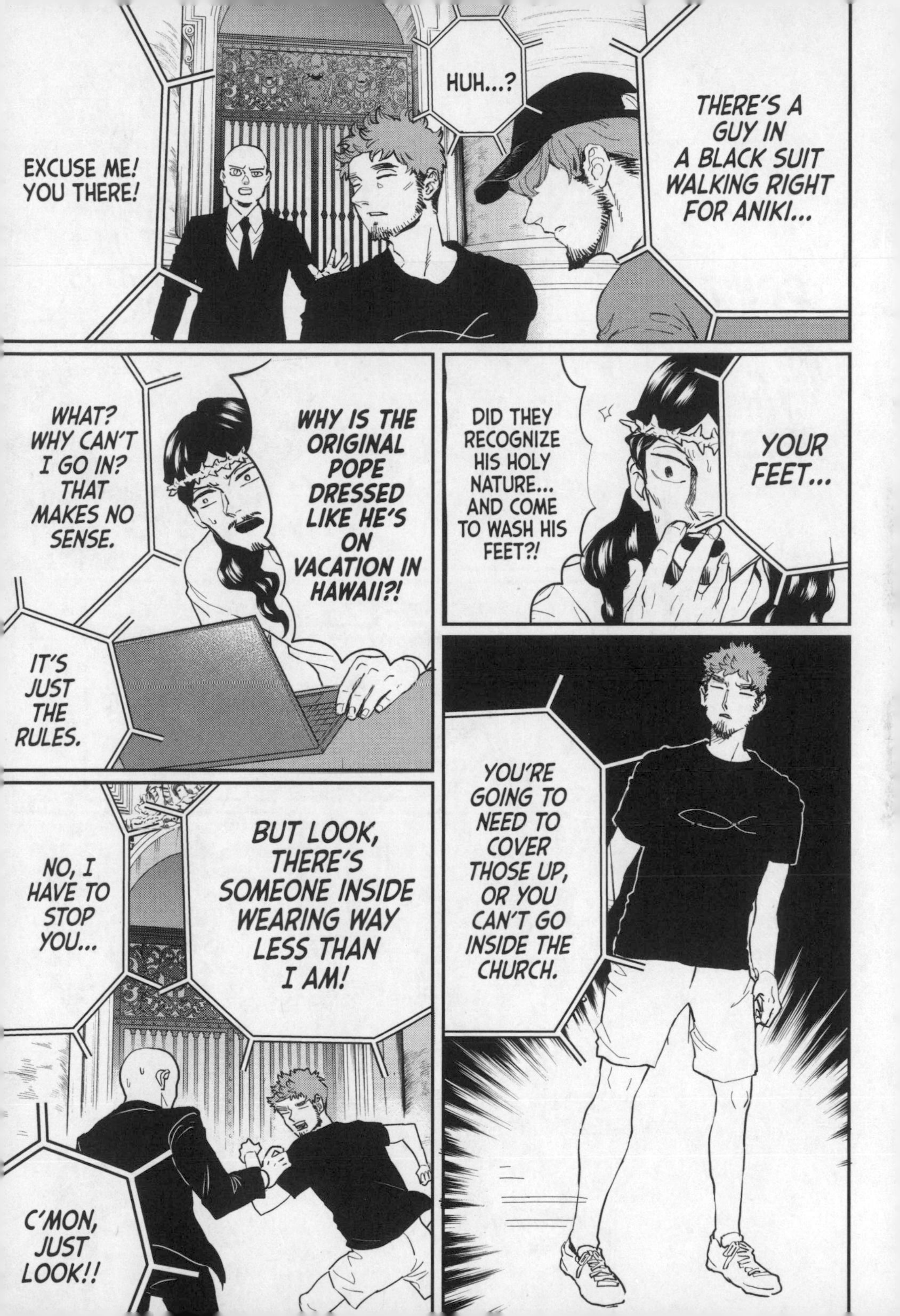
THERE'S A GUY IN A BLACK SUIT WALKING RIGHT FOR ANIKI...
HUH...?
EXCUSE ME! YOU THERE!
YOUR FEET...
DID THEY RECOGNIZE HIS HOLY NATURE... AND COME TO WASH HIS FEET?!
YOU'RE GOING TO NEED TO COVER THOSE UP, OR YOU CAN'T GO INSIDE THE CHURCH.
WHY IS THE ORIGINAL POPE DRESSED LIKE HE'S ON VACATION IN HAWAII?!
WHAT? WHY CAN'T I GO IN? THAT MAKES NO SENSE.
IT'S JUST THE RULES.
BUT LOOK, THERE'S SOMEONE INSIDE WEARING WAY LESS THAN I AM!
NO, I HAVE TO STOP YOU...
C'MON, JUST LOOK!!

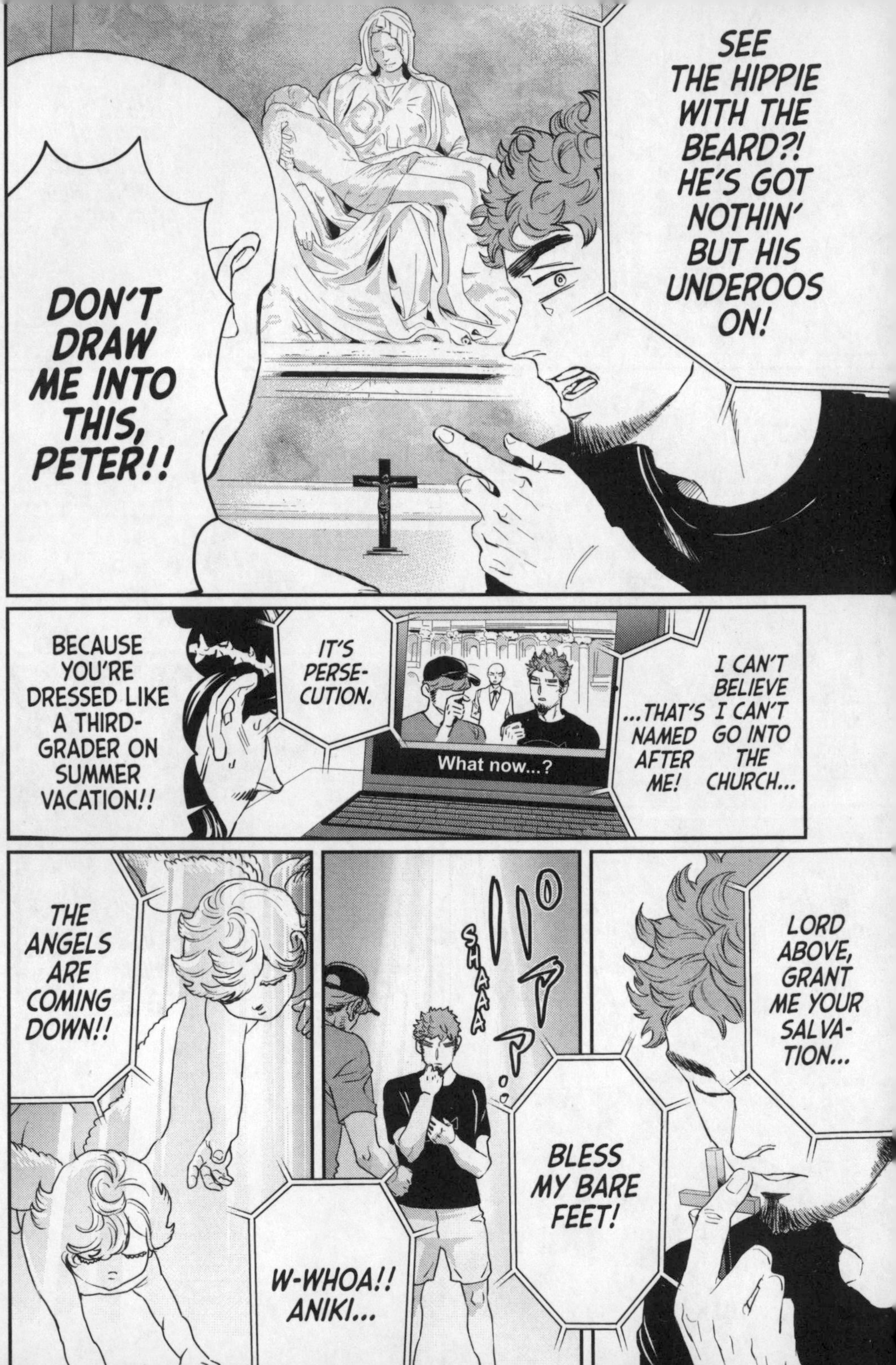
SEE THE HIPPIE WITH THE BEARD?! HE'S GOT NOTHIN' BUT HIS UNDEROOS ON!
DON'T DRAW ME INTO THIS, PETER!!
I CAN'T BELIEVE I CAN'T GO INTO THE CHURCH...
...THAT'S NAMED AFTER ME!
What now...?
IT'S PERSE-CUTION.
BECAUSE YOU'RE DRESSED LIKE A THIRD-GRADER ON SUMMER VACATION!!
LORD ABOVE, GRANT ME YOUR SALVA-TION...
BLESS MY BARE FEET!
SHAAAA
W-WHOA!! ANIKI...
THE ANGELS ARE COMING DOWN!!

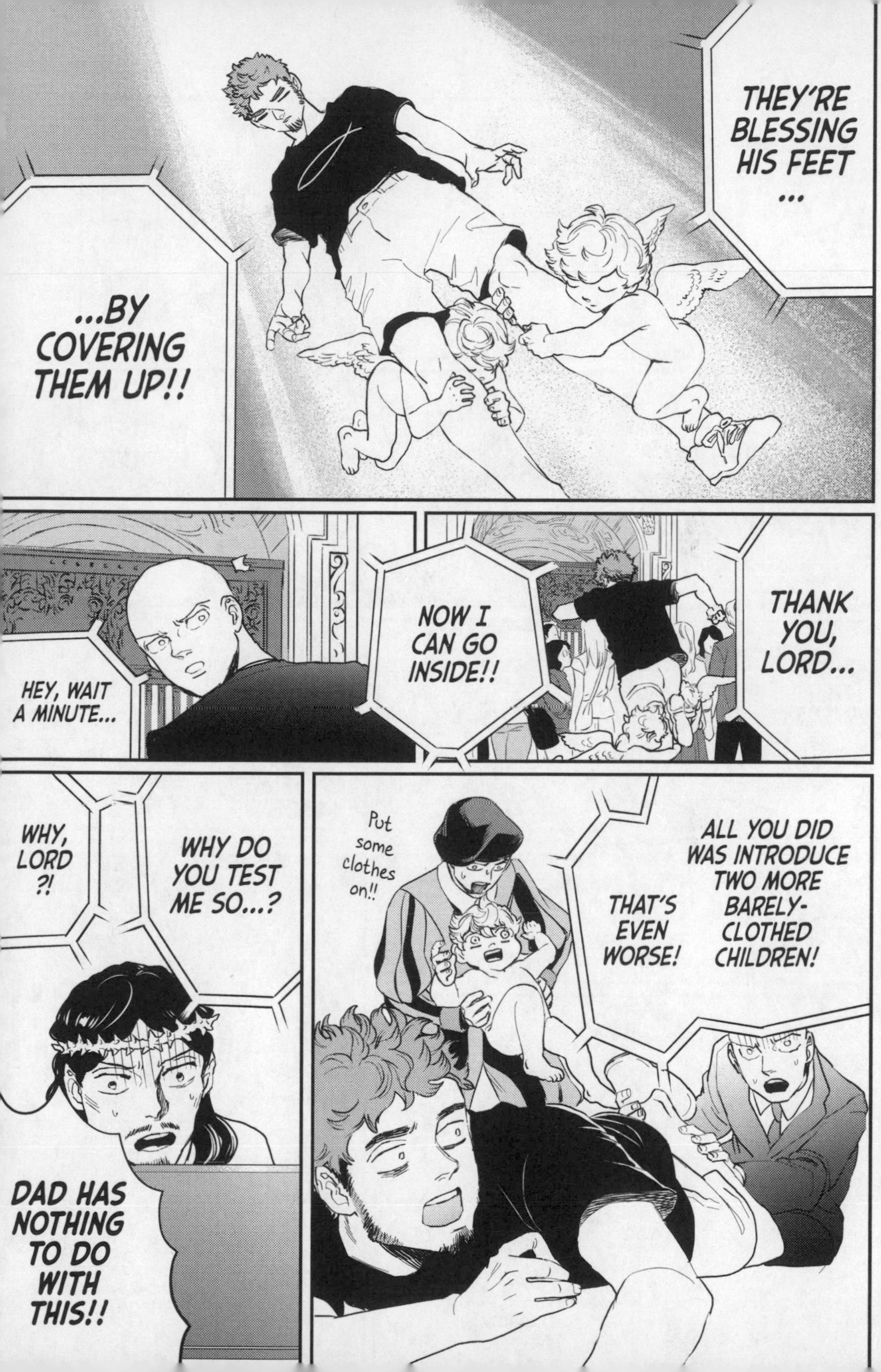
THEY'RE BLESSING HIS FEET ...
...BY COVERING THEM UP!!
THANK YOU, LORD...
NOW I CAN GO INSIDE!!
HEY, WAIT A MINUTE...
ALL YOU DID WAS INTRODUCE TWO MORE BARELY-CLOTHED CHILDREN!
THAT'S EVEN WORSE!
Put some clothes on!!
WHY DO YOU TEST ME SO...?
WHY, LORD ?!
DAD HAS NOTHING TO DO WITH THIS!!

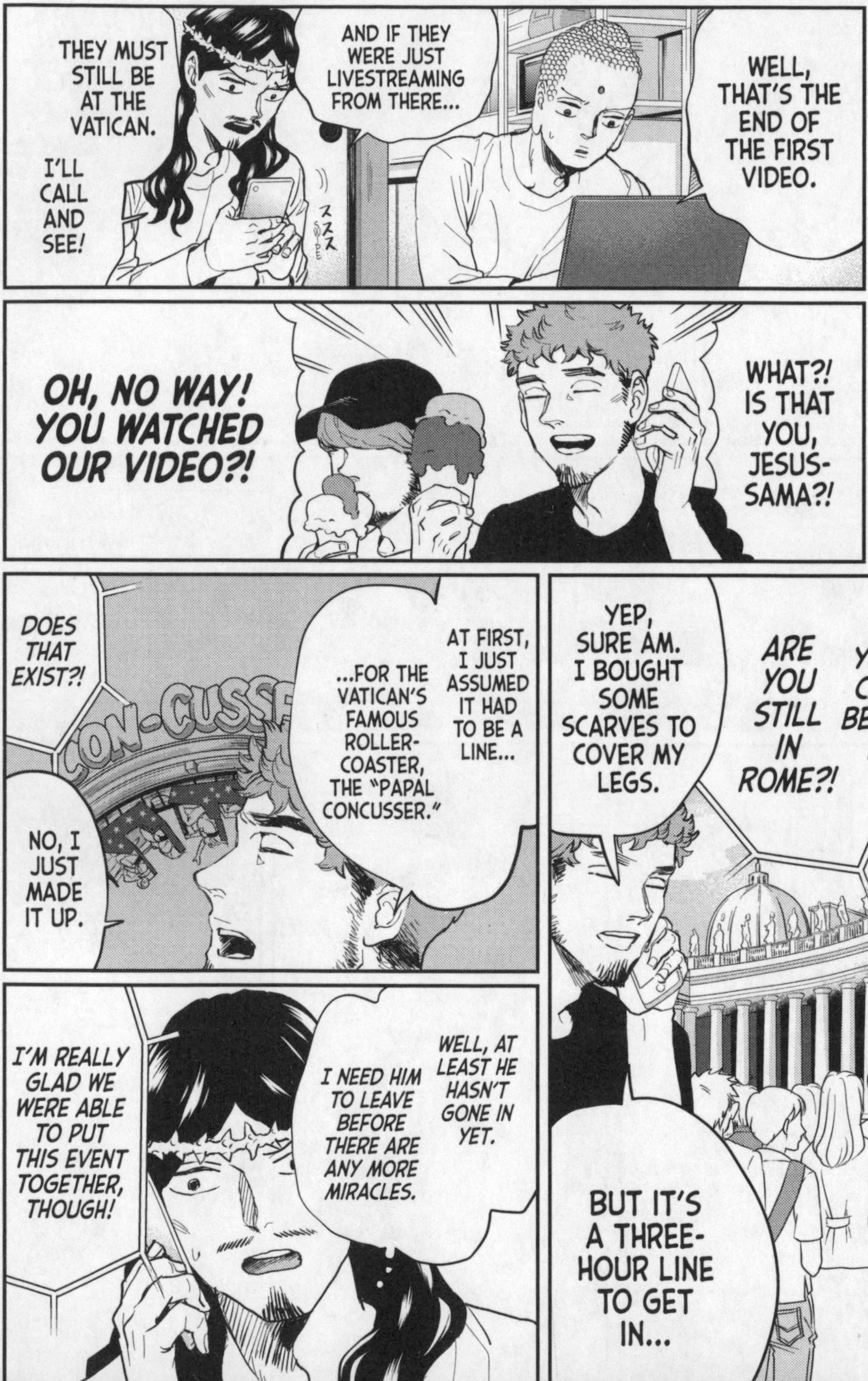

WELL, THAT'S THE END OF THE FIRST VIDEO.
AND IF THEY WERE JUST LIVESTREAMING FROM THERE...
THEY MUST STILL BE AT THE VATICAN.
I'LL CALL AND SEE!
スス SWIPE
WHAT?! IS THAT YOU, JESUS-SAMA?!
OH, NO WAY! YOU WATCHED OUR VIDEO?!
YES, I CAN'T BELIEVE IT!!
ARE YOU STILL IN ROME?!
YEP, SURE AM. I BOUGHT SOME SCARVES TO COVER MY LEGS.
BUT IT'S A THREE-HOUR LINE TO GET IN...
AT FIRST, I JUST ASSUMED IT HAD TO BE A LINE...
...FOR THE VATICAN'S FAMOUS ROLLER-COASTER, THE "PAPAL CONCUSSER."
DOES THAT EXIST?!
NO, I JUST MADE IT UP.
WELL, AT LEAST HE HASN'T GONE IN YET.
I NEED HIM TO LEAVE BEFORE THERE ARE ANY MORE MIRACLES.
I'M REALLY GLAD WE WERE ABLE TO PUT THIS EVENT TOGETHER, THOUGH!

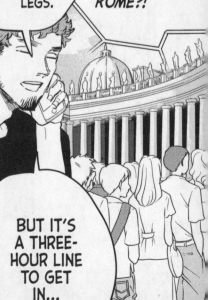

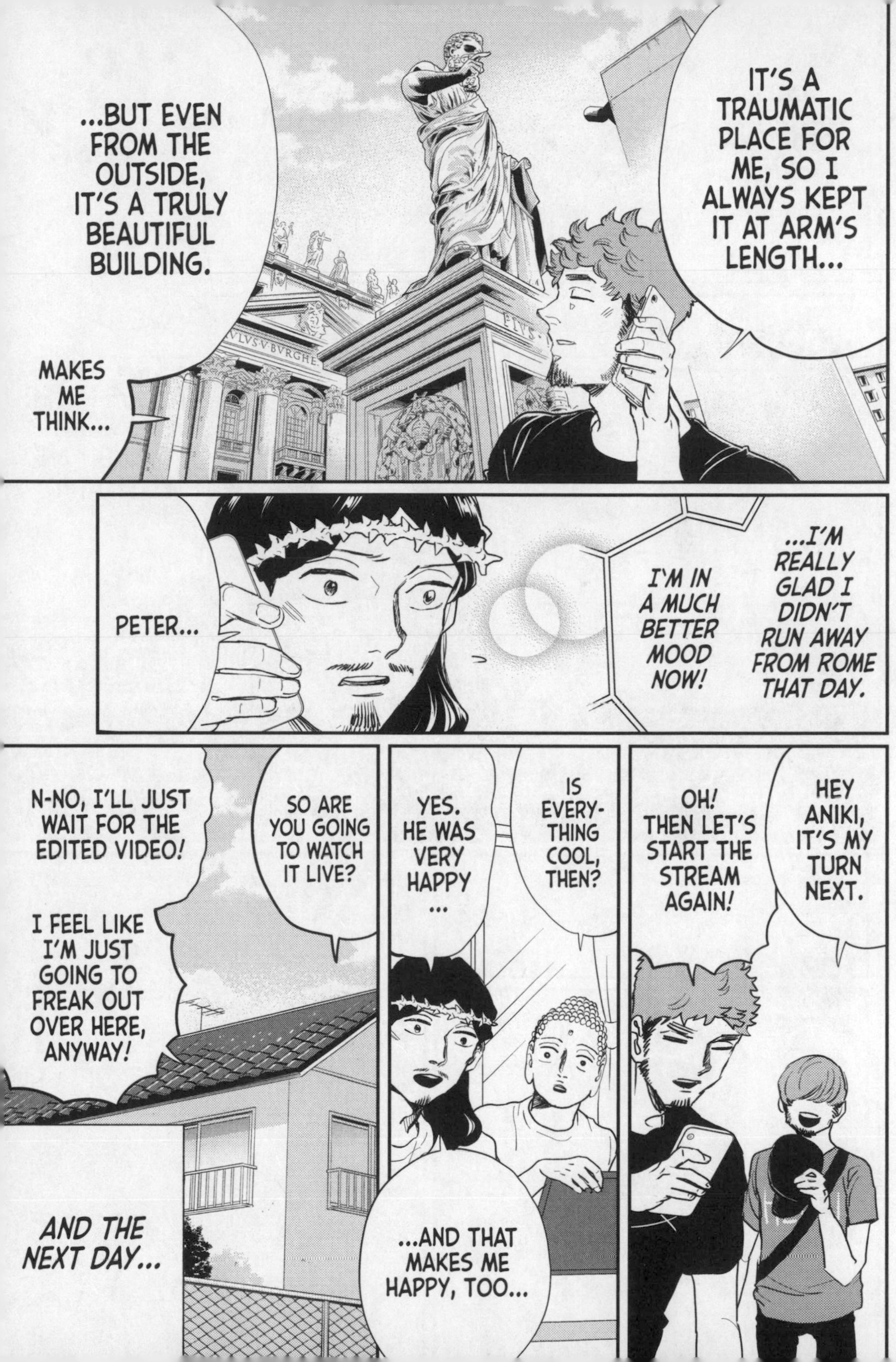
IT'S A TRAUMATIC PLACE FOR ME, SO I ALWAYS KEPT IT AT ARM'S LENGTH...
...BUT EVEN FROM THE OUTSIDE, IT'S A TRULY BEAUTIFUL BUILDING.
MAKES ME THINK...
...I'M REALLY GLAD I DIDN'T RUN AWAY FROM ROME THAT DAY.
I'M IN A MUCH BETTER MOOD NOW!
PETER...
HEY ANIKI, IT'S MY TURN NEXT.
OH! THEN LET'S START THE STREAM AGAIN!
IS EVERY-THING COOL, THEN?
YES. HE WAS VERY HAPPY...
...AND THAT MAKES ME HAPPY, TOO...
SO ARE YOU GOING TO WATCH IT LIVE?
N-NO, I'LL JUST WAIT FOR THE EDITED VIDEO!
I FEEL LIKE I'M JUST GOING TO FREAK OUT OVER HERE, ANYWAY!
AND THE NEXT DAY...

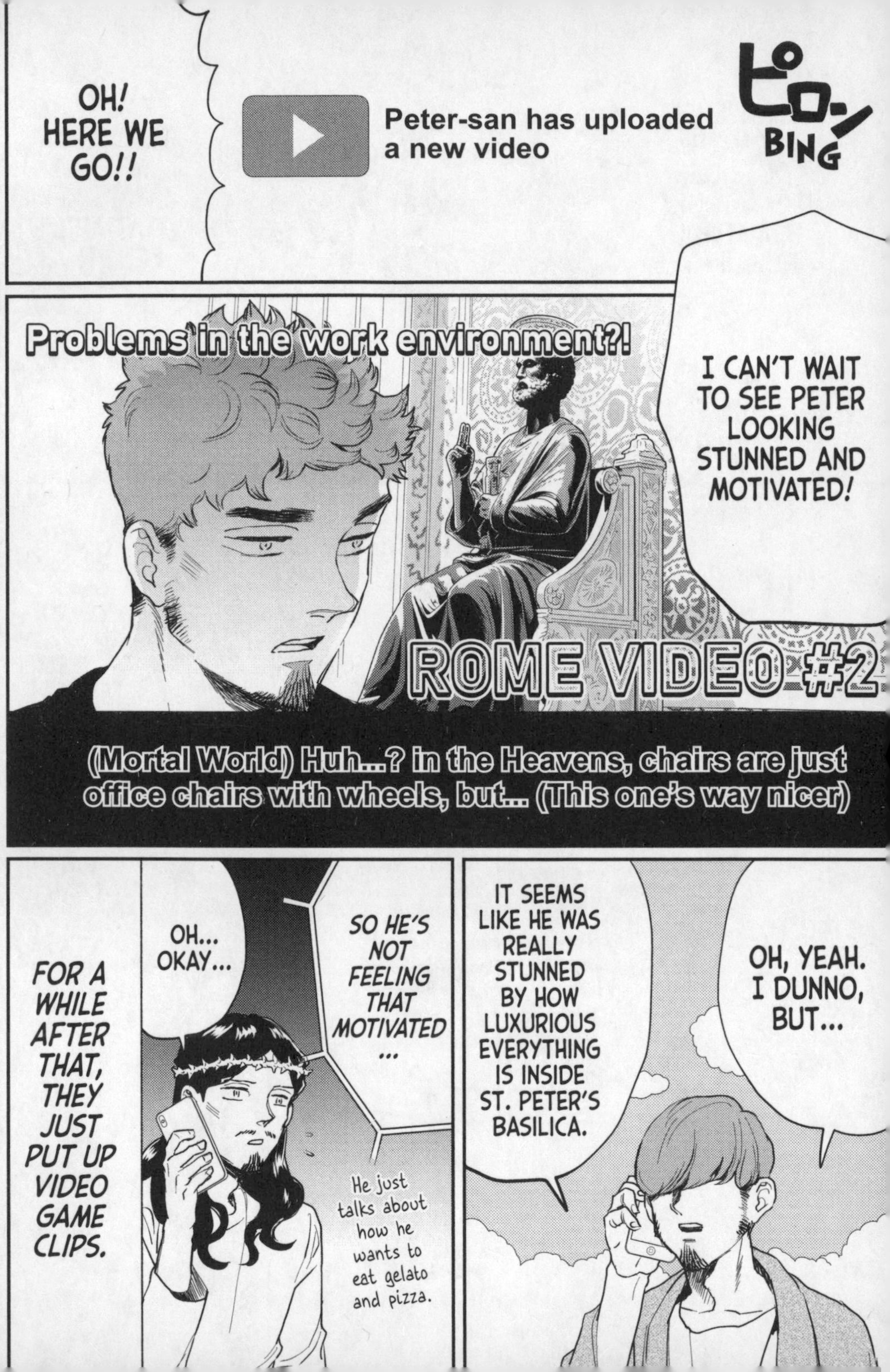
ピロン
BING
Peter-san has uploaded a new video
OH! HERE WE GO!!
I CAN'T WAIT TO SEE PETER LOOKING STUNNED AND MOTIVATED!
Problems in the work environment?!
ROME VIDEO #2
(Mortal World) Huh...? in the Heavens, chairs are just office chairs with wheels, but... (This one's way nicer)
OH, YEAH. I DUNNO, BUT...
IT SEEMS LIKE HE WAS REALLY STUNNED BY HOW LUXURIOUS EVERYTHING IS INSIDE ST. PETER'S BASILICA.
SO HE'S NOT FEELING THAT MOTIVATED...
OH... OKAY...
He just talks about how he wants to eat gelato and pizza.
FOR A WHILE AFTER THAT, THEY JUST PUT UP VIDEO GAME CLIPS.

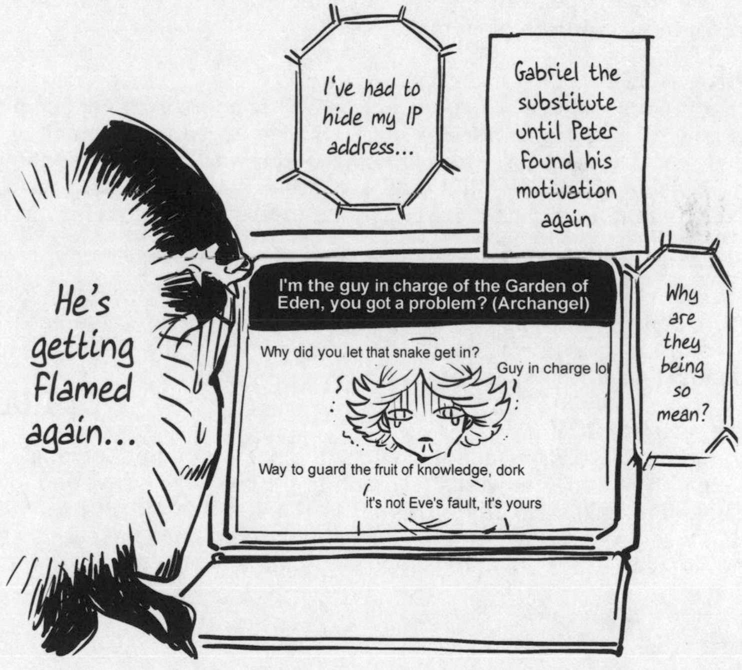
Gabriel the substitute until Peter found his motivation again
I've had to hide my IP address...
Why are they being so mean?
I'm the guy in charge of the Garden of Eden, you got a problem? (Archangel)
Why did you let that snake get in?
Guy in charge lol
Way to guard the fruit of knowledge, dork
it's not Eve's fault, it's yours
He's getting flamed again...

SAINT☆YOUNG MEN

CHAPTER 120 TRANSLATION NOTES

One Cut of Golgotha, page 251
A reference to the 2017 zombie comedy movie, *One Cut of the Dead*, which was inspired in part by *Shaun of the Dead*. Golgotha was the hill where Jesus was crucified.

Satori, page 253
The Japanese term for enlightenment (in a Buddhist sense), awakening, or understanding.

Peter's crucifixion, page 254
In John 21:18, Jesus says to Peter, "When you grow old, you will stretch out your hands, and someone else will fasten a belt around you and take you where you do not wish to go," describing the kind of death with which Peter would glorify God. He was eventually crucified at Vatican Hill in Rome by Emperor Nero, who wanted to blame Christians for the Great Fire of Rome.

Quo vadis, page 255
A Latin phrase that means "Where are you marching?" It appears in the apocryphal *Acts of Peter*, which details actions of Peter later in his life. After a confrontation with Simon Magus, another religious figure in Rome, Peter was going to flee the city, until he sees a vision of Jesus on the road, and hears Jesus say, "Quo vadis?" To Peter, this is a sign that he must accept crucifixion to rejoin Jesus in Heaven.

St. Peter's Basilica, page 256
A church within Vatican City, and the largest in the world by interior. It was built throughout the 16th century, and, as the name suggests, is considered the burial place of Saint Peter. Because he was held to be the first pope of the Catholic Church, many popes have been buried here as well.

Simon Magus, page 257
Simon was a prominent figure who appears in Acts and some other apocryphal books. He was originally a sorcerer with a following of his own who converted to Christianity by observing Philip. He attempted to pay the apostles for the power of the Holy Spirit, but was rebuffed by Peter. In the *Acts of Peter,* he is described as flying through the air, until Peter prays to God to stop him, at which point he falls and breaks his legs.

We Are!, page 258
The title of the first opening theme for the *One Piece* anime series.

Saint Young Men 8 copyright © 2018 Hikaru Nakamura
English translation copyright © 2021 Hikaru Nakamura

All rights reserved.

Published in the United States by Kodansha Comics, an imprint of Kodansha USA Publishing, LLC, New York.

Publication rights for this English edition arranged through Kodansha Ltd., Tokyo.

First published in Japan in 2018 by Kodansha Ltd., Tokyo as *Seinto oniisan*, volumes 15 & 16.

ISBN 978-1-64651-280-5

Original cover design by Hiroshi Niigami (NARTI;S)

Printed in the United States of America.

www.kodansha.us

9 8 7 6 5 4 3 2 1
Translation: Stephen Paul
Lettering: E.K. Weaver
Editing: Nathaniel Gallant
Kodansha Comics edition cover design by Phil Balsman

Publisher: Kiichiro Sugawara

Director of publishing services: Ben Applegate
Associate director of operations: Stephen Pakula
Publishing services managing editors: Alanna Ruse, Madison Salters
Production managers: Emi Lotto, Angela Zurlo